Without a doubt Michael Vl… :ology *of the Kingdom of God* presen… dom of God. The more I got into the book, the more I liked its straightforward exegesis and close theological reasoning. It is a real joy to be able to commend this work to others, for it will certainly represent one of the high-water marks on this sorely needed topic in our day. This will surely raise the discussion of the kingdom of God to a whole new level and it probably will become a classic in our times. I enthusiastically commend it to all who love God's word and who look forward to his soon appearance.

Walter C. Kaiser, Jr., Ph.D.
President Emeritus
Gordon-Conwell Theological Seminary

This is much welcomed treatment of the Bible's teaching on the kingdom of God. I have always appreciated the careful scholarship of Michael Vlach. This book is no exception. This will be a standard to which pastors and teachers should turn for years to come.

Mark L. Bailey, Ph.D.
President, Dallas Theological Seminary

Seldom in recent years has a book been written on the Kingdom of God that was at once both an academic book but also a book for the church. Michael Vlach of Master's Seminary has written the most perceptive book on the Kingdom of God that I have seen in years. The outline is clear and natural, and every pastor, as well as every scholar, will profit from the reading of this superb book. May God bless this book to make a difference in the life of your church. Vlach understands as few do God's overall plan for the Kingdom of God involving both Israel and the church.

Paige Patterson, Ph.D.
President
Southwestern Baptist Theological Seminary
Fort Worth, Texas

I first met Mike Vlach about 25 years ago when he was a pastoral intern at a church in Lincoln, Nebraska. We spent a few hours talking about the kingdom of God and whether there was a spiritual form during the present church age or was it totally future, except for God's sovereign rule. I agree with Dr. Vlach that the kingdom John the Baptist came preaching and Jesus spoke of is totally future. Matthew 13 teaches that it is postponed until after the second coming of Christ. In a day when so many wrongly think the current church age is a spiritual form of the kingdom, Dr. Vlach brings a sober reality to the issue by surveying the entire Bible on the matter and argues that kingdom is the best organizing theme of Scripture. Anyone interested in the Bible should be interested in this excellent work.

Thomas D. Ice, Ph.D.
Executive Director
Pre-Trib Research Center

Dr. Vlach has done all of us a big favor. He wades through a daunting number of interpretive problems and textual details, but does it with clarity, brevity, and simplicity. He shows great courtesy to the scholars with whom he disagrees, and interacts with their best arguments. Dispensationalists must embrace this work. All others must not ignore it.

Michael G. Vanlaningham, Ph.D.
Professor of Biblical Studies
Moody Bible Institute

In his book, *He Will Reign Forever: A Biblical Theology of the Kingdom of God*, Michael Vlach offers a biblical theology of the kingdom of God, explaining key Bible passages concerning the timing and nature God's kingdom. This includes an explanation of texts from Genesis 1 through Revelation 22. This is a readable yet thorough treatment of God's kingdom program that takes into account progressive revelation and how God's kingdom plan unfolds throughout history.

Mitch Glaser, Ph.D.
President, Chosen People Ministries

Michael Vlach's *He Will Reign Forever* may be one of the most refreshing books I have reviewed in a while. Closely reasoned, well-written, clearly understandable, and comprehensive in scope, this work will please those who have been longing for a biblical theology of kingdom that does not follow the assumptions of the "conventional wisdom" of evangelicalism that requires belief in the presence of the Messianic, Davidic Kingdom in this Church Age. While not everyone will accept the interpretation of all the various passages, the detailed analysis that Vlach gives will provide the basis for ongoing discussions of a biblical view of the kingdom of God in fresh ways for the next generation.

Mike Stallard, Ph.D.
Director of International Ministries
Friends of Israel Gospel Ministry

Michael Vlach has done a great service to God's people by writing *He Will Reign: A Biblical Theology of the Kingdom of God.* The subject is timely, important, and handled with skillful reverence for the authority of Scripture. Sadly, many contemporary notions regarding the Kingdom of God are not biblically grounded and quite often reflect ideas read into, rather than out of, the biblical text. Dr. Vlach's work is a welcome remedy for this problem! The Kingdom is rescued from clichés and restored to its biblically defined, God-centered glory. Praise God for this wonderful work of biblical theology!

David M. Doran, D.Min.
President, Detroit Baptist Theological Seminary
DMin, Trinity Evangelical Divinity School

This book is dedicated to Trevor Craigen,
my mentor and friend.

CONTENTS

FOREWORD
By John MacArthur

Daniel 2 records an episode where Nebuchadnezzar, king of Babylon, was troubled by a dream that provoked so much panic in his heart that "his sleep left him" (v. 1). He was afflicted with both insomnia and amnesia. Only a misty memory of the dream remained in his consciousness, but it nevertheless made such an impression on him that he was desperate to recover a clear memory of it, and he longed to know its meaning. So he called in his sorcerers and soothsayers "to tell the king his dreams" (v. 2). For obvious reasons, the king's wise men were unable to describe, much less interpret, a dream the king himself couldn't clearly remember. Nebuchadnezzar was so frustrated by this that he threatened to kill all the wise men in Babylon (his top advisors)—and even issued an order for their mass execution (vv. 12-13).

At that point Daniel intervened and offered to try to interpret the dream. God showed Daniel both the dream and its interpretation "in a vision of the night" (v. 19). It was an image—a massive, imposing Colossus representing a succession of world empires. The figure had a head made of gold. Its arms and chest were silver. The midriff and thighs were bronze. The legs were made of iron, and the feet were a blend of iron and clay. Those sections (each made of distinctive materials that diminished in value, beauty, and quality from top to bottom) represented a succession of world empires.

As Daniel explained the meaning to Nebuchadnezzar, he said, "You are the head of gold. Another kingdom inferior to you shall arise after you, and yet a third kingdom of bronze, which shall rule over all the earth. And there shall be a fourth kingdom, strong as iron, because iron breaks to pieces and shatters all things. And like iron that crushes, it shall break and crush all these. And as you saw the feet and toes, partly of potter's clay and partly of iron, it shall be a divided kingdom, but some of the firmness of iron shall be in it, just as you saw iron mixed with the soft clay" (vv. 38-41).

In other words, Daniel's prophecy laid out the flow of world history precisely as it later unfolded. Four successive empires dominated the world in the long era that spans the remainder of Old and New Testament history, starting with the Babylonians under Nebuchadnezzar (the golden head). Babylon fell to Medo-Persia (the silver torso). That empire was conquered by Greece (the abdomen and legs of bronze). And the glory of Greece was eclipsed by the Roman empire (the legs of iron). The stamp of Roman rule is still evident in the ordering of nations today, and the feet of iron and clay represent a final attempt to unite the whole world in one great empire—perilously fragile but with an appearance of strength. The best evidence suggests that this is a yet-future coalition of nations, and it will most likely be a revived form of the Roman Empire.

But the most important detail in Nebuchadnezzar's dream is what happens at the end of it. All the world's empires are finally and permanently shattered by a giant stone, hurled into this graphic picture of world history by the hand of God Himself. "A stone was cut from a mountain by no human hand, and ... it broke in pieces the iron, the bronze, the clay, the silver, and the gold" (v. 45). Daniel is emphatic about the importance and the certainty of this prophecy: "God has made known to the king what shall be after this. The dream is certain, and its interpretation sure."

What does the stone signify? Its meaning is clear: "The God of heaven will set up *a kingdom that shall never be destroyed,* nor shall the kingdom be left to another people. It shall break in pieces all these kingdoms and bring them to an end, and it shall stand forever."

Thus a prophecy given to an ancient pagan king perfectly foretells the climax of Scripture's entire story line. Every other yet-to-be-fulfilled prophecy in Scripture ultimately points to that very same truth. It was the theme of John the Baptist's preaching: "The kingdom of heaven is at hand" (Matt 3:2). Jesus Himself echoed the same message from the time He began to preach publicly: "Repent, for the kingdom of heaven is at hand" (Matt 4:17). It's what our Lord instructed the Twelve to preach: "Proclaim as you go, saying, 'The kingdom of heaven is at hand'" (Matt 10:7). He described the Christian message as "this gospel of the kingdom" (Matthew 24:14; see also 4:23; 9:35). Acts 19:8 describes the apostle Paul's standard approach to ministry as he went from city to city: "He entered the synagogue and continued speaking out boldly for three months, reasoning and persuading them *about the kingdom of God.*"

Christians too easily forget or ignore the glaring fact that the kingdom of God was so prominent in Jesus' own mind and message. The kingdom is what we are commanded to "seek first" (Matt 6:33). If that's not a priority, our values are skewed. We ought to be thinking about and longing for the kingdom of God daily. After all, the very first petition in the Lord's prayer is, "Your kingdom come" (Luke 11:2).

We don't hear enough, think enough, or talk enough about the kingdom. But it is coming—and the general spirit of apathy that surrounds the subject is to the detriment of our spiritual health and sanctification.

As Dr. Michael Vlach so clearly shows in this book, a very powerful argument can be made that the kingdom of God is the central and unifying theme of Scripture, and it is the climactic fulfillment of the story of redemption. In his words, the kingdom of God is both "the grand theme of Scripture and the solution for all that's wrong."

If you are a believer, there is a true and important sense in which "the kingdom of God has [already] come near to you" (Luke 10:9). Indeed, "the kingdom of God is in your midst" (Luke 17:21). "To you has been given the mystery of the kingdom of God" (Mark 4:11). The kingdom of heaven belongs to people who exhibit true, childlike, saving faith (Matthew 5:3; Mark 10:14). That includes every genuine believer.

But the greatest fulfillment of the kingdom promise is yet to come, and it will be unspeakably glorious. "There will be no end to the increase of His government or of peace, on the throne of David and over his kingdom, to establish it and to uphold it with justice and righteousness from then on and forevermore" (Isaiah 9:7).

Sadly, the average Christian today has no clear concept of the kingdom—what it is, why it is important, or why Christ wanted us to pray that the Lord would hasten its coming. As Dr. Vlach demonstrates, most Christians' concepts of the kingdom are overspiritualized, too abstract, and lacking in biblical substance.

This book is a wonderful remedy for that flaw. In fact, I've never seen a finer treatment of the subject. It is a careful, thorough, superbly documented survey of what Scripture teaches about the kingdom, tracing the unfolding of this great theme through biblical history and into eternity future. The work is well researched, thoroughly biblical, compellingly logical, and eminently readable. From the first page of the introduction, it is clear that this is no dry academic treatise. Dr. Vlach writes from the heart, yet with profound scholarly insight, in a way that I believe will fill *your* heart with excitement and expectation. It will also inform your mind with clear understanding. It will energize your prayers with urgency and passion. It will inundate your soul with earnest anticipation. And it will give you a healthy, holy longing for the kingdom to come on earth as it is in heaven.

PREFACE

The kingdom of God is not just an interesting academic pursuit for me. It is intensely personal and practical. It is the basis of my hope and the solution to everything wrong in the world. Every frustration, fear, and doubt can be answered by the kingdom of God.

My heart longs for the kingdom. I think about its coming daily. If statistics are correct, I am well into the latter half of my lifespan. Both of my parents have passed away. One of my sisters recently succumbed to a cruel fatal disease. It seems as if every month I hear of someone diagnosed with cancer or some life-threatening situation. My experiences certainly are not unique. The world my children are inheriting seems to worsen daily. Increasingly, good is called evil and evil is considered good. Traditional values are mocked. Even a creation ordinance like marriage has been redefined.

Yet in spite of these sober and disappointing realities, I love life. I love relationships—my wife, my children, friends, co-workers, and students. I am more enthralled than ever with the color and beauty of God's creation—the mountains, forests, and beaches. I love the four seasons, especially the fall with its spectacular colors of leaves and visits to favorite pumpkin patches. I never tire of college football with its colors, bands, rivalries, and traditions. I also love Thanksgiving meals with family and am a sap for the same old Christmas traditions and songs every year. I love fishing and reading comic books with my sons and hearing my daughters sing. I enjoy listening to music and watching a great movie. I could go on and on.

Life is full of excitement, color and activity. The thought of not being able to participate in life with all its beauty and relationships is depressing if I take my eyes off Jesus for a moment. I think of the haunting words of the atheist Christopher Hitchens who hopelessly said before he died, "It will happen to all of us that at some point you'll be tapped on the shoulder and told, not just that the party is over, but slightly worse: the party's going on but you have to leave."

I, too, do not want the party to end. I want life. But I also don't want this fallen and tragedy-soaked world to continue forever either. So I find myself conflicted. I love being alive and in God's creation. Yet I am grieved and frustrated by this fallen and dangerous world. I think this is the reality of being a "son of the kingdom" in this age before the kingdom actually arrives. If you know Jesus, your desires are probably similar. You love life. You love God's creation and the many good things He has given you, yet you are frustrated because of this broken world. You, too, have a heart for God's kingdom, even if you have not thought of it in those terms. That is why Christians need to understand God's kingdom plans. When you study the kingdom you are examining the grand theme of Scripture and the solution for all that's wrong.

Yet many Christians live without understanding God's kingdom purposes. They know they are saved and headed for a better place someday, but their understanding of the kingdom is foggy and often clouded with unbiblical conceptions. The kingdom has been over-spiritualized for so long and made so abstract that many Christians wonder why they don't long for it. Bad theology has taught us the kingdom of God is simply an inner heart experience or some wispy spiritual experience in the sky after you die. You know the scene, the cultural depictions—sitting on a cloud forever. Perhaps there is some shuffleboard for recreation. Or perhaps sitting in a church pew forever. A well-known *Far Side* commercial once showed a man with wings on a cloud in heaven with a halo on his head. Looking incredibly bored, he said, "Wish I'd brought a magazine." Sadly, many think this is what the future holds. But your heart does not long for this, and it shouldn't. This is not the kingdom God offers.

We need a proper understanding of the kingdom. In the following pages we will discuss how the Bible presents the kingdom of God. From Genesis through Revelation the kingdom involves a beautiful and fantastic restoration of all things. It involves God's reign over every aspect of creation. It includes people, animals, and all creatures in the universe. It involves food, music, celebration, laughing, and rejoicing. Most importantly, the kingdom brings a thriving relationship with God and our Savior, Jesus Christ, who is at the center of God's kingdom program. It also involves real interactions and activity with other people who know God. The kingdom also includes nations doing real cultural activities (see Rev 21:24, 26). In other words, the kingdom is life and life abundantly (see John 10:10).

The kingdom also makes everything we do and every trial we face worth it. "Through many tribulations we must enter the kingdom of God" (Acts 14:22). And, "If we endure, we will also reign with Him" (2 Tim 2:12). A tangible kingdom awaits all who devote their lives to King Jesus. No matter how bad things get, a wonderful kingdom awaits.

Before we embark on our study, I would like to thank Dr. Trevor Craigen, my professor and then colleague and most importantly, friend. He encouraged me during my early seminary days to keep studying and writing about the kingdom.

INTRODUCING THE KINGDOM

The kingdom of God is a major theme of Scripture. The goal of this book is to present a comprehensive biblical theology of the kingdom of God from a new creationist perspective. Let me define what I mean by this.

First, this is a *biblical theology* of the kingdom. It examines a wide variety of kingdom passages from both the Old Testament (OT) and New Testament (NT). This work traces the kingdom theme from Genesis 1 through Revelation 22 with many stops along the way. The goal is to be comprehensive, examining and harmonizing most kingdom passages, particularly those that address the kingdom's *nature* and *timing*. Also, when the kingdom interacts with other important themes such as covenants, promise, seed, salvation, people of God, and others, this work addresses those as they relate to the kingdom.

There are two reasons for adopting a biblical theology approach. First, it is helpful to look at the kingdom theme from the perspective of unfolding progressive revelation. The doctrine of the kingdom unfolds throughout the canon of Scripture over many centuries. Second, this approach satisfies my desire to address a wide variety of kingdom passages, including many that are often overlooked. In short, this book will survey many kingdom passages in order to grapple with the full array of evidence.

In addition, this book offers a *new creationist perspective* on the kingdom. What is a new creationist perspective? It is a holistic understanding of the kingdom that gives justice to the multi-faceted dimensions of God's kingdom program. A new creationist approach affirms that God's kingdom program involves both spiritual and material elements. It also acknowledges the importance of individuals, the nation Israel, Gentile peoples, and the church. Also, this perspective understands that Jesus the Messiah is the center of the kingdom program and the One who restores all things (Col 1:15–20) through His two comings to earth. All of these play a role in the kingdom.

The title "new creationist" is based on a model of God's purposes known as the "new creation model."[1] This model emphasizes the physical, social, political, and geographical aspects of God's kingdom. This includes a coming new earth, activities on the new earth, and bodily resurrection.[2] As Craig Blaising states, "The new creation model expects that the ontological order and scope of eternal life is essentially continuous with that of present earthly life except for the absence of sin and death."[3] Thus, eternal life is embodied life on earth. This approach "does not reject physicality or materiality, but affirms them as essential both to a holistic anthropology and to the biblical idea of a redeemed creation."[4] It affirms the tangible nature of the kingdom as taught in passages such as Isaiah 2; 11; 25; 65, 66; Romans 8; and Revelation 21.

This model is contrary to over-spiritualized views of the kingdom associated with a "spiritual vision model" perspective that downplays the importance of physical and national matters in God's kingdom. A spiritual vision approach often makes the kingdom primarily a spiritual entity, denying the importance of material and tangible parts in God's purposes. It also tends to ignore or reinterpret the significance of national Israel and land promises in Scripture.

---

1 See Craig A. Blaising, "Premillennialism" in *Three Views on the Millennium and Beyond*, ed. Darrell L. Bock (Grand Rapids: Zondervan, 1999), 160–81. Blaising explicitly uses this designation and gives a detailed explanation of what a new creation model is. For more discussion on the new creation model see also Steven L. James, "New Creation Eschatology and the Land," Ph.D. diss., Southwestern Baptist Theological Seminary, 2015. J. Richard Middleton, *A New Heaven and a New Earth: Reclaiming Biblical Eschatology* (Grand Rapids: Baker, 2014), 304. Not everyone who identifies with a new creation model will agree on all details of Bible prophecy, but they do emphasize literal fulfillment of physical promises and refute the spiritualization of physical promises.

2 Blaising, "Premillennialism," 162.

3 Ibid.

4 Ibid.

A new creation model approach, on the other hand, emphasizes the future relevance of matters such as nations, kings, economics, agriculture, the animal kingdom, and social-political issues. Life in the future kingdom of God will be largely similar to God's purposes for the creation before the fall of Adam, which certainly involved more than just a spiritual element. God did not create Adam to sit on a cloud forever. Adam was tasked to rule from and over the earth for God's glory. He failed. But Jesus, who is the Last Adam (1 Cor 15:45), and those who identify with Him, will have a successful reign from and over the earth in fulfillment of God's purposes for humanity (Matt 19:28; Rev 5:10). The kingdom of God is dynamic and active, not static.

The final heaven or new earth is not an ethereal spiritual presence in the sky. As Moore points out, "The point of the gospel is not that we would go to heaven when we die. Instead, it is that heaven will come down, transforming and renewing the earth and the entire universe."[5] Far from being only a spiritual entity, the eternal destiny of the redeemed includes a holistic renewal of human existence and our environment:

> The picture then is not of an eschatological flight from creation but the restoration and redemption of creation with all that entails: table fellowship, community, culture, economics, agriculture and animal husbandry, art, architecture, worship—in short, *life* and that abundantly.[6]

The new creation model was the primary approach of the church of the late first and early second centuries A.D. It was found in apocalyptic and rabbinic Judaism, and in second century Christian writers such as Irenaeus of Lyons.[7] The new creationist perspective, as presented in this work, is a form of dispensationalism and consistent with ideas presented in both revised and progressive dispensationalism. A new creationist thinking approach can be summarized in the following points:

5 Russell D. Moore, "Personal and Cosmic Eschatology," in *A Theology for the Church*, ed. Daniel L. Akin (Nashville: B&H, 2007), 912.

6 Ibid. 859. Emphasis in original.

7 Blaising, "Premillennialism," 164.

1. **A new creationist approach affirms the importance of the material realm in God's purposes.** God's creation includes both material and immaterial elements (Col 1:16). Both are important. The original kingdom of Genesis 1–2 was physical and so too will the coming kingdom. God does not abandon His creation—He will restore it. A new creationist approach rejects over-spiritualized Platonist tendencies to view physical matters negatively. God will complete His purposes for this earth to be ruled over successfully.

2. **A new creationist approach affirms that physical promises in the Bible will be fulfilled just as the Bible writers expected.** The Bible includes many physical promises (i.e. land, material prosperity, etc.). Just as spiritual promises like forgiveness of sins, a new heart, and the indwelling Holy Spirit have been fulfilled, so too must land and physical blessings promised in Scripture. A new creationist perspective affirms spiritual realities but denies that the Bible spiritualizes, transcends, or reinterprets physical promises. Both spiritual and physical promises will be fulfilled just as God promised.

3. **A new creationist approach affirms that the coming new earth will be this present earth purged and restored.** This earth that God created "very good" (Gen 1:31) is not headed for annihilation but restoration. The creation was subjected to futility because of man's sin but it has "hope" since the glorification of God's people involves creation being freed from its current corruption (Rom 8:20). Jesus refers to cosmic renewal as the "regeneration" (Matt 19:28) and Peter calls it the "restoration of all things" (Acts 3:21). The new earth will be "new" in that it will be purified, refreshed, and restored; yet it is still this "earth." God will succeed in making His creation everything He intended for it to be. Satan does not get the final victory over this earth.

4. **A new creationist approach affirms the importance of individuals, Israel, and nations in God's plans.** God works with various groups. First, He saves individuals (Matt 11:28–29). Second, God sovereignly chooses and uses the nation Israel as a vehicle

for His plans (Gen 12:2; Rom 11:26). Third, God will bless all people groups and nations (Gen 12:3; 22:18; Rev 5:9). Isaiah 19:16–25 promises that in the coming kingdom the nations of Egypt, Assyria, and Israel will be present as geo-political entities. Revelation 21:24, 26 tells of multiple nations and kings bringing their glory into the New Jerusalem. The gospel is going to all nations in this present age, but a future era is coming when national entities will serve the Lord. The Bible teaches the importance of individuals, Israel, and the nations. It also affirms the importance of the church, which in this age, is God's instrument for kingdom proclamation before Jesus returns to set up His kingdom.

5. **A new creationist approach affirms the importance of particular and universal entities.** When it comes to realities such as Israel and the nations of the world, both work together in harmony. Isaiah 27:6 states, "In the days to come Jacob will take root, Israel will blossom and sprout, and they will fill the whole world with fruit." As God blesses Israel, He will bless other nations (Amos 9:11–15). Likewise, when God fulfills His land promises with Israel (Gen 15:18–21) He will bless other nations in their lands as well (Isa 19). Universal blessings to the nations do not negate particular promises to the nation Israel. Nor do God's plans to bless the nations mean Israel is no longer significant in God's purposes. In fact, fulfillment concerning the *particular* (Israel) leads to the fulfillment of the *universal* (the world). Both are important and promises to both will be fulfilled because of Jesus. Since Israel and Israel's land are microcosms of what God will do for all people groups, the narrower particular elements concerning Israel do not need to be denied or universalized.

6. **A new creationist approach affirms God's kingdom will involve social, political, geographical, agricultural, architectural, artistic, technological, and animal elements.** With Genesis 1:26–28, God tasked man with a kingdom/cultural mandate—to rule and subdue the earth. The kingdom of God is not a static, colorless existence in the sky but a vibrant and multi-dimensional

experience on the new earth. Man was created to interact with his environment, including culture. He will continue to do so in the kingdom of God in a holistic manner. This involves international harmony, tranquility in the animal kingdom, planting of vineyards, and the building of houses (see Isa 2:2–4; 11; 65:17–25). This will occur because of the Last Adam, Jesus the Messiah (1 Cor 15:24–28, 45), who will succeed from and over the realm (earth) where the first Adam failed.

A new creationist perspective also asserts that the kingdom program includes many features that are complementary, not mutually exclusive. Some treatments of the kingdom of God exclude important facets. The following are examples of statements that are too narrow or incomplete:

- "The kingdom is not physical; it is spiritual."
- "The kingdom is no longer about nations; it is about individuals."
- "The kingdom is no longer about Israel; it is about Jesus."
- "The kingdom is no longer national; it is international."

These contrasts are not biblical. They create false dichotomies and "either/or" scenarios when "both/and" fits better. Sometimes remnants of Platonism arise when spiritual aspects of the kingdom only are emphasized or the kingdom is declared to be "spiritual" not "earthly." This book's approach, however, often sees "both/and" instead of "either/or" scenarios.

Another important issue is how the NT and OT relate to each other. Some claim the NT *transforms* or *transcends* the storyline begun in the OT.[8] But this work asserts that the NT *continues* the storyline of the OT prophets in a literal and straightforward manner. No transforming or transcending of the Bible's storyline is necessary. God does not reinterpret His previous inspired revelation. Nor is there a reality shift from OT expectation to

8 For example, Beale states, "Thus, the NT storyline will be a *transformation* of the OT one in the light of how the NT is seen to be an unfolding of the OT." G. K. Beale, *A New Testament Biblical Theology: The Unfolding of the Old Testament in the New* (Grand Rapids: Baker Academic, 2011), 6. Stephen Wellum says that with the coming of Jesus, "many of the themes that were basic to the Old Testament have now been *transposed and transformed*." Peter J. Gentry and Stephen J. Wellum, *Kingdom through Covenant: A Biblical-Theological Understanding of the Covenants* (Wheaton, IL: Crossway, 2012), 598. Emphases in the above quotations are mine.

NT fulfillment. NT fulfillment is consistent with the original message and intent of the OT writers. Great continuity exists between OT expectation and NT fulfillment.[9] This includes matters such as the fulfillment of promises concerning the nation Israel, Jerusalem, and the temple. Literal fulfillment of OT realities will be fulfilled over the course of Jesus' two comings. Unfulfilled promises at Jesus' first coming do not need to be spiritualized. They look forward to literal fulfillment at His return (see Acts 3:18, 21).

Yet another key feature of this book is the attention given to contingency or conditions concerning the timing of the kingdom. As part of His sovereign plan God has determined that the kingdom's arrival on earth is based on certain factors and responses. As William Barrick states, "Part of the reason God's kingdom has not yet come stems from fallen mankind's consistent antagonism to God's sovereign purpose for His own earthly kingdom."[10] God has determined that His kingdom is linked with Israel's acceptance of the Messiah. Passages such as Leviticus 26:40–45; Matthew 23:37–39; Luke 19:41–44; and Acts 3:19–21 show this to be the case. God is sovereign over all things, yet human responses affect the timing of some eschatological events (see Jer 18:1–10).

This work also views ethnic and national Israel as a key component in the Bible's storyline. This work rejects replacement or fulfillment theology. Israel and Israel's land are not shadows and types that become nonsignificant once Jesus arrives. Instead, Israel and Israel's land, under the leadership of the reigning Messiah, are microcosms of what God will do for all people groups in the kingdom. What is true for the particular (Israel and Israel's land) will also be true for the universal (other nations and their lands). Thus, we affirm both national Israel's significance and what God will do for all nations (Rom 11:12, 15).

Finally, this book is not primarily about the various millennial views,[11] but it does strongly affirm what is called premillennialism. There will be an

9 By NT fulfillment we refer to literal fulfillment of the OT expectations through two comings of Jesus the Messiah. We are not saying all aspects of the OT prophetic message have occurred yet, but they will be in the future.

10 William D. Barrick, "The Kingdom of God in the Old Testament," in *The Master's Seminary Journal* 23 (Fall 2012): 174.

11 While this book addresses opposing views of the kingdom at times, it is focused mostly on a positive presentation of the kingdom. It does not address every objection made against the view presented here.

earthly kingdom of Jesus after this present age but before the eternal state. The Bible's story line demands a future earthly reign of the Last Adam and Messiah (Jesus) upon the earth. Jesus and those who belong to Him must successfully reign *from* and *over* the realm (earth) where the first Adam was tasked to rule but failed (see Gen 1:26–28). This kingdom of the Messiah must occur before the eternal state begins when Jesus hands His successful mediatorial kingdom reign to God the Father (see 1 Cor 15:24, 28). Thus, a future, earthly kingdom before the eternal state is an important part of the Bible's narrative.

I hope this treatment of the kingdom is more than an academic pursuit. The kingdom is a fantastic hope for the believer and all people who believe in Jesus. My hope is that this study can help provide a proper understanding of the kingdom and draw people devotionally to a closer relationship with the King. As Paul joyfully declared:

> Now to the King eternal, immortal, invisible, the only God, be honor and glory forever and ever. Amen (1 Tim 1:17).

PART

1

INTRODUCTION TO THE KINGDOM PROGRAM

CHAPTER

1 THE IMPORTANCE OF THE KINGDOM

There are many great themes in the Bible—"covenant," "promise," "glory of God," "the holiness of God," "salvation," "law," "people of God," etc. But is it possible to identify a central theme of Scripture that functions like a hub or center in which other important themes are connected? Scholars continue to debate this issue, and some even think the search for one such central theme is misguided. James Hamilton aptly observes, "Some conclude that the very fact that so many 'centers' have been proposed proves that there is no center."[1]

All of the themes mentioned above are important and deserving of serious study, and there is no reason to pit one theme against another. Yet, this book asserts that the kingdom of God is the grand central theme of Scripture that encompasses all other biblical themes. As Graeme Goldsworthy notes, "In focusing on the kingdom of God we are really looking at a key element that gives biblical theology its coherence."[2]

1 James M. Hamilton, Jr., *God's Glory in Salvation through Judgment: A Biblical Theology* (Wheaton, IL: Crossway, 2010), 52. Hamilton argues "salvation through judgment" is the center of the Bible's storyline.

2 Graeme Goldsworthy, "The Kingdom of God as Hermeneutic Grid," in *Southern Baptist Journal of Theology* 12 (Spring 2008) 4. See also, Alva J. McClain, *The Greatness of the Kingdom: An Inductive Study of the Kingdom of God* (Winona Lake, IN: BMH Books, 1959), 4–5. John Bright is also right when he notes, "The concept of the Kingdom of God involves, in a real sense, the total message of the Bible." John Bright, *The Kingdom of God* (New York: Abingdon-Cokesbury Press, 1953), 7. Pentecost notes, "The great theme of God's kingdom program can be found throughout the Bible, from Genesis to Revelation. It is a theme that unifies all of Scripture." J. Dwight Pentecost, *Thy Kingdom Come: Tracing God's Kingdom Program and Covenant Promises Throughout History* (Wheaton, IL: Victor Books, 1990), 11.

There are several reasons why the kingdom of God is the central and unifying theme of Scripture. First, the kingdom is a thread that runs from the first chapter of the Bible through the last.[3] Genesis 1 begins with God as Creator/King of the universe and man as God's image-bearer who is created to "rule" and "subdue" the earth for God's purposes and glory (see Gen 1:26–28). Then the last chapter of the Bible (Rev 22) shows God and the Lamb on the throne and God's people ruling on the new earth:

> There will no longer be any curse; and *the throne of God and of the Lamb* will be in it, and His bond-servants will serve Him... . and *they will reign forever and ever* (Rev 22:3, 5).[4]

As the Bible begins, man is in God's presence with a kingdom to reign over (see Gen 3:8). At the end of the Bible, redeemed mankind is again in God's direct presence as God's people reign over the earth forever and ever.[5]

So kingdom language is found at the beginning and end. The story begins with God as King and man's right to rule under Him. It then culminates with God on the throne and man reigning under Him over a new earth. What takes place between these sections is the fall of man, the promise plan of salvation, and the arrival of King Jesus and the redemption He brings. After the period between Jesus' two comings there will be the restoration of all things by which God reverses the curse and establishes His kingdom upon the earth. In sum, God's kingdom program involves five major parts or developments:

1. Creation
2. Fall
3. Promise

3 Richard Mayhue notes, "With the exceptions of Leviticus, Ruth, and Joel, the OT explicitly includes various mentions in 36 of its 39 books. Except for Philippians, Titus, Philemon, 1, 2, and 3 John, the NT directly mentions the subject in 21 of its 27 books. All in all, 57 of the 66 biblical books (86 percent) include the kingdom theme." Richard L. Mayhue, "The Kingdom of God: An Introduction," in *The Master's Seminary Journal* 23 (Fall 2012): 168.

4 Emphases mine.

5 Thus there is a close connection between man's kingdom reign and reigning in the immediate presence of God for His glory.

4. Redemption
5. Restoration

The relationships of these five parts to the kingdom program can be seen in the following:

KINGDOM PROGRAM → → → → → → →

1. Creation	**2. Fall**	**3. Promise**	**4. Redemption**	**5. Restoration**
(Gen 1–2)	(Gen 3)	(Gen 3:15–Mal)	(Gospels–Epistles)	(Revelation)

The kingdom theme in the five parts of the Bible's storyline can be summarized:

1. First, the kingdom is present with *creation* as God the King of creation tasks His image-bearer, man, to rule and subdue His creation.

2. Second, the *fall* marks man's failure to rule God's creation; both God's image-bearers (humans) and the creation come under the devastating effects of the fall.

3. Third, the *promise* plan guarantees the seed of the woman will eventually succeed over the power behind the serpent (Satan); the fall will be reversed and man will effectively rule over creation.

4. Fourth, Jesus the King brings *redemption* through His atonement, and His death is the basis for the kingdom and reconciliation of all things.

5. Fifth, with the *restoration* of all things God's kingdom plan is fulfilled as Jesus successfully reigns over the earth; this kingdom merges into the perfect kingdom of the Father.

The Bible's storyline shows how the *kingdom created* goes to the *kingdom fallen*, which then leads to the *kingdom restored*. This storyline is centered and anchored in Jesus the Messiah.

Second, the kingdom permeates OT history and prophecy. In addition to the kingdom mandate of Genesis 1:26–28, God assembled His chosen people Israel to become a kingdom (see Exod 19:5–6). With the

Abrahamic Covenant Israel was chosen to be the means of bringing blessings to the families of earth (see Gen 12:2–3).[6]

Samuel–Kings describes the rise and fall of the kingdom in Israel. The prophets, who take center stage while Israel was in decline, prophesied about future days when the kingdom would be restored to Israel with blessings to the nations (see Amos 9:11–15). Daniel 2 and 7 reveal that God's kingdom will be established suddenly and dramatically after four successive Gentile empires.[7]

Much of the OT describes the establishment of God's kingdom on earth with the nation Israel. Yet even with Israel's decline and fall, the prophets predict a future kingdom where God will restore the kingdom upon the earth. At the heart of the coming kingdom will be a special King, One in whom the kingdom program finds fulfillment (see Isa 9:6–7). This King is Jesus the Messiah (see Luke 1:32–33) who is the centerpiece and focal point of this glorious kingdom.

Third, the kingdom of God was central in the ministries of John the Baptist and Jesus:

> Now in those days John the Baptist came, preaching in the wilderness of Judea, saying, "Repent, for the kingdom of heaven is at hand" (Matt 3:1–2).
>
> From that time Jesus began to preach and say, "Repent, for the kingdom of heaven is at hand" (Matt 4:17).

---

6 Sailhamer points out, "One of the central issues in the message of the Pentateuch is the coming king and his eternal kingdom." John H. Sailhamer, *The Meaning of the Pentateuch: Revelation, Composition, and Interpretation* (Downers Grove, IL: InterVarsity, 2009), 37.

7 Stephen Dempster states, "Significantly, a key concept in the last narrative section of the Tanakh that begins with Daniel and ends with Chronicles is the term 'kingdom' (of God)." Stephen G. Dempster, *Dominion and Dynasty: A Theology of the Hebrew Bible*, New Studies in Biblical Theology, ed. D. A. Carson (Downers Grove, IL: InterVarsity, 2003), 48–49.

Both the forerunner of Jesus and Jesus himself made the kingdom the focus of their ministries.[8] The kingdom was also the message of the twelve apostles who received their commission from Jesus:

> These twelve Jesus sent out after instructing them: "Do not go in the way of the Gentiles, and do not enter any city of the Samaritans; but rather go to the lost sheep of the house of Israel. And as you go, preach, saying, 'The kingdom of heaven is at hand'" (Matt 10:5–7).

Put together, Jesus, John the Baptist, and the apostles were consumed with proclaiming the kingdom.[9] Belief in Jesus the Messiah qualified one for entrance into this kingdom (see John 3:3).

Jesus urged His hearers to seek the kingdom and its righteousness (Matt 6:33) and to pray for its coming (Matt 6:10). The parables of Matthew 13 reveal "mysteries" concerning the kingdom of heaven. On the night before His death Jesus mentions the kingdom of God five times (see Luke 22). The resurrected Jesus spent forty days instructing His disciples concerning the kingdom of God (see Acts 1:3). The last question asked of Jesus before He ascended into heaven was, "Lord, is it at this time you are restoring the kingdom to Israel?" (Acts 1:6). Acts closes with Paul proclaiming the kingdom of God to Jewish leadership (Acts 28:17–31).

Fourth, the focus of NT eschatology is on the second coming of Jesus and His kingdom reign. Jesus declared that end times events were signs the kingdom of God was near (Luke 21:31). Jesus said placement on His throne accompanies His second coming in the company of His angels (Matt 25:31). Jesus' return in Revelation 19 is followed by a thousand-year reign mentioned in Revelation 20:1–6, followed by the final form of the kingdom in the eternal state (see Rev 21–22:5). One could argue the entire book of Revelation describes how the kingdom of God dramatically replaces the

8 Herman Ridderbos stated, "The central theme of Jesus' message ... is the coming of the kingdom of God." Herman Ridderbos, *The Coming of the Kingdom* (Philadelphia, PA: Presbyterian and Reformed, 1962), xi. Schreiner states, "The kingdom of God is a central theme in Jesus' ministry." Thomas R. Schreiner, *New Testament Theology: Magnifying God in Christ* (Grand Rapids: Baker, 2008), 79.

9 Ibid. "It may be rightly said that the whole of the preaching of Jesus Christ and his apostles is concerned with the kingdom of God."

kingdom of Satan. Thus, the claim that "kingdom" is the primary theme of Scripture is well supported.

RELATIONSHIP TO OTHER KEY THEMES

The kingdom theme connects harmoniously with other major themes of the Bible. For instance, "covenant" is a major theme of Scripture, and the covenants are the instruments through which the kingdom program unfolds.[10] The Noahic Covenant promises stability of nature as the platform for God carrying out His kingdom purposes. The Abrahamic Covenant reveals that Abraham will be the father of a great nation, Israel, who will serve as the platform for bringing blessings to all nations. The Davidic Covenant shows that the ultimate King will be a descendant of David who will rule and bless the entire world from Israel. The New Covenant explains how God will change the hearts of His people and grant His Holy Spirit so they will always obey Him. Each of these covenants works together in harmony to guarantee that God's kingdom purposes will be fulfilled. Dwight Pentecost is right that "God's kingdom program" is "the outworking of His eternal and unconditional covenants."[11]

Next, Walter Kaiser has rightly emphasized the importance of the "promise" theme in Scripture.[12] The promise plan begins after the fall with the promise of a "seed" of the woman who would one day crush the power behind the serpent (Satan) and reverse the curse (see Gen 3:15). This promise plan narrowed and became more specific through the lines of Noah, Shem, Abraham, Isaac, Jacob, Judah, and David. Finally, it finds specific fulfillment in the ultimate "seed," Jesus Christ (see Gal 3:16). "Promise" is such a major part of God's purposes that I have included it in my five-point paradigm of history: Creation, Fall, *Promise*, Redemption, and Restoration. Some paradigms omit "promise," and jump from "fall" to "redemption." Yet "promise" should be included since a major part of the Bible's story is

10 For example, Goldsworthy shows how "covenant" fits within the kingdom concept: "Some would prefer covenant as a central theme rather than that of kingdom. But the covenant is the formalizing of a relationship which conveys membership in the kingdom." Goldsworthy, "The Kingdom of God as Hermeneutic Grid," 11.

11 Pentecost, *Thy Kingdom Come*, 9.

12 See Walter C. Kaiser, Jr., *Toward an Old Testament Theology* (Grand Rapids: Zondervan, 1978).

centuries of expectation of the Messiah. Yet this promise plan also comes under the umbrella of the kingdom since it is through the promised "Seed" (Jesus) that God saves His creation.

Likewise, salvation and the redemption of God's image bearers is an important theme. Jesus came to save sinners and His atoning ministry is a major emphasis (see Mark 10:45). Yet as important as human salvation is, it is not the primary theme of Scripture. God's kingdom program encompasses not only human salvation but also all things. Humans are the high point of creation since they are made in God's image. Yet Colossians 1:15–20 discusses the reconciliation of all things material and immaterial in the cosmos because of the cross of Christ.[13]

The cross is the basis for reconciling both people and creation. Acts 3:19–21 confirms that salvation of people is related to the "restoration of all things." Peter told the leaders of Israel in this section that if they "repent and return" they would be forgiven of their sins and then participate in the "times of refreshing" (the kingdom) and the restoration of all things. In other words, salvation leads to kingdom. Thus, the kingdom program is broader than salvation of people since it involves all things. John 3:3 indicates that unless one is born again he cannot enter the kingdom of God. Salvation is the requirement for entering God's kingdom. When people believe they join the right side of God's kingdom program and are qualified to enter the kingdom when it comes.

Then there is the glory of God, which some see as the theme of Scripture. There can be, however, a distinction between a *theme* of Scripture and the *purpose* for which God does what He does. God works all things for His glory and the kingdom program is the way and means through which God brings glory to Himself. God is the majestic sovereign of the universe who manifests His glory through His kingdom program.

Not everyone agrees that "kingdom" is the main theme of Scripture, and there are good Christians who passionately posit another theme. The goal here is not to pit one theme against others since they all fit together perfectly. Nor is agreement on this issue necessary for one to benefit from this book. Even if one believes another theme is more central, all should agree

13 Universal reconciliation is not the same as universal salvation. All things will be reconciled to Christ, which includes the judgment and destiny of nonbelievers.

the kingdom is a crucial part of God's plans and a thorough study of it is beneficial. The major themes of Scripture work together in a symphonic-like harmony. Yet "kingdom" is a key theme of the Bible. As one tracks the kingdom theme through Scripture he or she is tracking the storyline of the Bible.[14] Dempster rightly notes that the "many stories" in Scripture "constitute a single Story. And this Story is about the reclamation of a lost human dominion over the world through a Davidic dynasty."[15] When the story reaches God's intended goal the saints of God will be ruling the new earth in a never-ending perfect kingdom in the direct presence of God (Rev 22:3, 5).

WHAT IS A KINGDOM?

We now define the term "kingdom." The word is *malkuth* in Hebrew and *basileia* in Greek.[16] There are other terms relevant to the kingdom concept. But like any term, the meaning of "kingdom" and similar terms is not found primarily in the etymology or origin of the word but in its usage. Usage determines meaning.

Malkuth and *basileia* often are translated as "royalty," "royal power," "reign," and "kingdom." The concept of "kingdom" includes at least three essential elements:

1. *Ruler*—a kingdom involves a ruler with rightful and adequate authority and power.
2. *Realm*—a kingdom involves a realm of subjects to be ruled.
3. *Rulership*—a kingdom involves the exercise of ruling.[17]

---

14 Pentecost says he discovered that as he traced the kingdom theme from Genesis through Revelation: "That theme provided a unifying structure that bound all the Bible together into a unit, and by which all the history recorded there could be understood and related." Pentecost, *Thy Kingdom Come*, 9. I agree with his assessment.

15 Dempster, *Dominion and Dynasty*, 231.

16 *Malkuth* is found 91 times in the Hebrew Bible. The term *mamlakah* is translated "kingdom; sovereignty; dominion; reign" and occurs about 115 times in the OT.

17 McClain, *The Greatness of the Kingdom*, 17. Barrick mentions four elements: "first, a *right to rule*; second, a *ruler*; third, a *realm* to be ruled; and, fourth, the exercise of the function of *rulership*. These defining elements help to maintain an understanding of biblical teaching beyond a mere reference to the right of kingship or limiting it to the person of the King himself." Barrick, "The Kingdom of God in the Old Testament," 176.

All three elements are needed for a kingdom, including active ruling. As Pentecost points out, "Essential to the word *kingdom* is the actual exercise of authority in a realm over which one has the sovereign right to rule. If the exercise of authority is not in view, the concept of kingdom is not present."[18] Thus, "there can be no kingdom in the truest sense without the ruler, the realm, and the reigning function."[19]

At times, one of these three elements can be singled out and designated as "kingdom." For example, in Revelation 1:6 believers are referred to as a kingdom: "and He has made us to be a kingdom." Yet Revelation 5:10 places the actual kingdom reign in the future: "You have made them to be a kingdom... and they will reign upon the earth." So in Revelation 1:6 the subjects are referred to as a kingdom. They are the nucleus of the kingdom. But the function of ruling does not occur until the reign on earth begins.

Also, in Luke 19, the nobleman who represents Jesus is said to go "to a distant country to receive a kingdom for himself, and then return" (Luke 19:12). Here "kingdom" refers to receiving kingdom authority. Kingdom authority was granted in a distant country, but the actual kingdom reign occurs when the nobleman returns to his realm of authority to reward his servants and punish his enemies (see Luke 19:11–27).

Some have offered a more general understanding of kingdom claiming that it is primarily the authority to rule and does not necessarily include a territory, domain or subjects.[20] Yet the idea of a kingdom without a realm is difficult to maintain. A realm seems necessary for a kingdom to exist. Goldsworthy rightly argues against an abstract understanding of kingdom, saying a kingdom must include both a realm and the function of ruling:

> Some have sought to distinguish between a realm and the dynamic of God ruling and to opt for one or the other as the

18 Pentecost, *Thy Kingdom Come*, 14.

19 McClain, *The Greatness of the Kingdom*, 17.

20 See George Eldon Ladd, Crucial *Questions about the Kingdom of God* (Grand Rapids: Eerdmans, 1952), 79. Also, Yarbrough writes, "to the extent that Jesus' view of the kingdom is informed by the Old Testament, he is less apt to be speaking about a geographically bordered region and more apt to be speaking about a 'reign' or 'supreme authority' that exists without any particular physical or political boundaries." Robert W. Yarbrough, "The Kingdom of God in the New Testament: Matthew and Revelation," in *The Kingdom of God*, ed. Christopher W. Morgan and Robert A. Peterson (Wheaton, IL: Crossway, 2012), 107.

> meaning of the kingdom. I find this distinction unconvincing. The Bible does not leave the kingdom in the abstract. If God rules, he rules somewhere, even if somewhere is everywhere. There is no abstract rule without a realm.[21]

Thus, it is best to define the kingdom of God as "the rule of God over His creation."[22]

21 Goldsworthy, "The Kingdom of God as Hermeneutic Grid," 7.

22 McClain, *The Greatness of the Kingdom*, 19.

CHAPTER 2

PROPER STARTING POINTS FOR UNDERSTANDING THE KINGDOM

Before examining specific passages about the kingdom, we now highlight some challenges for studying the kingdom along with listing some beliefs that affect our understanding of it. This is connected with hermeneutics, which is the art and science of interpretation. Hermeneutics deals with principles by which we understand language and the Bible. Looking at interpretive beliefs is important since one's position on the kingdom is influenced by other beliefs and assumptions.[1]

CHALLENGES FOR UNDERSTANDING THE KINGDOM

One reason there are so many views on the kingdom is because of differing interpretive beliefs toward this topic and passages related to it. Kenneth Barker rightly notes, "Interpreters will continue to arrive at different conclusions on such passages [related to the kingdom] until they can fully agree at the hermeneutical and presuppositional levels."[2] For example,

1 Kim Riddlebarger points out the necessity of evaluating the presuppositions of an interpreter: "Everyone has presuppositions which color how they read the Scriptures. The assumption that any one of these millennial views is the result of a straightforward, unbiased reading of Scripture is overly simplistic. To understand why Christians reach such diverse opinions, we must identify and carefully evaluate the presuppositions they hold before they come to the biblical texts. It is vital to know what these presuppositions are and determine how they affect our reading of prophetic sections of the Bible." Kim Riddlebarger, *A Case for Amillennialism: Understanding the End Times* (Grand Rapids: Baker, 2003), 33.

2 Kenneth L. Barker, "Evidence from Daniel," in *A Case for Premillennialism: A New Consensus*, eds. Donald K. Campbell and Jeffrey L. Townsend (Chicago: Moody, 1992), 136. Barker was specifically referring to several kingdom passages in the book of Daniel.

why do some Christians study Revelation 20 and see a future thousand-year reign of Christ on the earth after Jesus' second coming (premillennialism), while others see a spiritual reign of Jesus taking place in this present age (amillennialism)? Both grapple with the same text of Scripture. The answer is that they operate from differing interpretive assumptions that influence their understandings.

Since Christians are still sharply divided on foundational areas of interpretation, strong disagreements on the kingdom will continue. One should be transparent about his or her interpretation principles in addition to simply stating what his or her views are.

Also, there are various positions on the kingdom, and even those who share a particular kingdom view can differ on some details. Such variance can be confusing and disheartening to those who simply want to know what the Bible has to say about this topic. Why is this the case?

One reason is there are many kingdom passages to interpret and harmonize. The more information there is on a topic, the more data one must grapple with and harmonize. This leads to more opportunities for disagreement. Also, whenever one feels strongly about a particular view it is easy to emphasize certain passages that appear to support one's position while ignoring others that are more challenging. By nature we gravitate toward information that supports our position while overlooking or downplaying evidence to the contrary. So we need to be comprehensive. We should address all relevant passages on the subject, including those that seem to be problematic for our view. Not doing so skews our understanding and causes us to commit the fallacy of appealing to selective evidence.

In approaching the kingdom one also must also grapple with the relationship between the two testaments, which could be the single greatest factor determining a kingdom view. How does the OT relate to the NT and how does the NT use the OT? Does the NT rely on the literal and contextual meanings of the OT prophets, or does the NT transcend, reinterpret or spiritualize the OT expectations of the kingdom? Are matters such as nations, Israel, land, and temple in the OT shadows and types that lose their significance once Jesus arrives? Or do these matters still have relevance in God's plans? How one answers these questions will largely determine one's kingdom view.

In light of these considerations, we now present beliefs that influence our understanding of the kingdom. These operate more as statements of what we believe rather than comprehensive defenses of these beliefs. A full defense would involve its own book-length treatment, so these are offered more as propositional statements that affect the views in this book.

STARTING POINTS

First, all kingdom passages in the Bible harmonize and complement each other. Because there is a divine author behind the Bible, all passages of Scripture harmonize, including those addressing the kingdom. No passage contradicts another passage. We may not always understand how these passages harmonize, but any perceived problems or contradictions are from the perspective of finite humans. They are not true contradictions.

Second, the proper approach to understanding the kingdom is through a consistent use of grammatical-historical-literary interpretation. The goal of the grammatical-historical-literary method is to sufficiently discover the authorial intent of a Bible writer as found in his written text.[3] This approach seeks to understand what a Bible author meant by what he wrote, knowing that under inspiration his intent is God's intent. This is sought through understanding the vocabulary, grammar, historical background, and genre of the books of the Bible. Thus, we search for a passage's meaning by examining the passage itself, seeking the author's intention in his written text via grammatical, historical, and literary means.[4] We do not believe there are hidden meanings in texts. The divinely inspired intent of the Bible authors is God's intent with no gap between the two.

We believe this approach should be used throughout all of God's inspired Scripture, including prophetic passages in the OT. Doing so will

3 As Bruce states in regard to the books of the Bible, "A basic requirement for the understanding of these documents is their grammatico-historical interpretation or exegesis—bringing out of the text the meaning the writers intended to convey and which their readers were expected to gather from it." F. F. Bruce, "Interpretation of the Bible," in *Evangelical Dictionary of Theology*, ed. Walter A. Elwell (Grand Rapids: Baker, 1984), 565.

4 Not all scholars view grammatical-historical-literary hermeneutics as sufficient for every passage. Some argue for a fuller divine or *sensus plenior* meaning embedded in some passages of the OT. Others hold to a canonical approach in which earlier revelation is shaped and informed by later revelation or the canon as a whole. This is not the place for a full discussion of these various views. Our approach, though, is that later revelation builds upon the literal and contextual meaning of older revelation and that meaning is centered in the authorial intent of the passage at hand and not in later revelation that harmonizes with but does not change or alter the meaning of previous revelation.

lead to the conclusion that a future earthly kingdom of the Messiah is coming. Although an opponent of the view that there will be an earthly kingdom of Jesus after His return, Floyd Hamilton observed, "Now we must frankly admit that a literal interpretation of the Old Testament prophecies gives us just such a picture of an earthly reign of the Messiah as the Premillennialist pictures."[5]

Third, symbols in kingdom passages have a literal meaning that can be understood through grammatical-historical-literary interpretation. God sometimes uses symbols and vivid imagery to convey truths. In studying kingdom passages we will encounter dragons, horns, statues, and frightening beasts. This often happens in Ezekiel, Daniel, Zechariah and Revelation. The symbols in these books were given to be understood and point to literal meanings. Some are explained and others are not, and some are harder to decipher than others. Nevertheless, behind each symbol is a specific meaning. We should not approach most of the Bible in a contextual manner, but then shift to "symbolic interpretation" or some other approach when we address symbols or prophetic sections. A difference exists between how God reveals a particular revelation and how readers should interpret that revelation. The use of symbols does not sanction symbolic hermeneutics. A grammatical-historical-literary approach accounts for the meaning of symbols. We should apply sound interpretation principles to all Bible passages including those with symbols.

We can learn from the first example of prophetic symbolism in the Bible. In Genesis 37:9–11 symbols were used in a prophetic context concerning a dream of Joseph:

> Now he had still another dream, and related it to his brothers, and said, "Lo, I have had still another dream; and behold, the sun and the moon and eleven stars were bowing down to me." He related it to his father and to his brothers; and his father rebuked him and said to him, "What is this dream that you have had? Shall I and your mother and your brothers actually come to bow ourselves down before you to the ground?"

5 Floyd Hamilton, *The Basis of Millennial Faith* (Grand Rapids: Eerdmans, 1942), 38.

The symbols of "sun," "moon," and "stars" are used. Yet the interpretation of these symbols is not difficult. Joseph's brothers and father understood the symbols to mean Joseph would be elevated above them. The "sun" is Jacob. The "moon" is Rachel, Joseph's mother. The "eleven stars" are Joseph's brothers. Grammatical-historical interpretation accounts for the meaning of these symbols. So this first example of prophetic symbolism shows symbols can be understood with normal interpretive principles.

Another example of prophetic symbolism exists in Daniel 2 with Nebuchadnezzar's statue dream. Nebuchadnezzar's statue involved a head of gold—"The head of that statue was made of fine gold" (Dan 2:32a). Then in 2:38, Daniel tells the king, "You are the head of gold." The head of gold represents Nebuchadnezzar and his kingdom. Nebuchadnezzar's statue also involved the symbols of breasts and arms of silver, a belly and thighs of bronze, legs of iron, and feet partly of iron and clay (see Dan 2:32b–33). We are not told explicitly what these other images represented. But a precedent was established with the head of gold representing a literal kingdom, Babylon. So the other images represent literal kingdoms as well. The remaining kingdoms most likely are Medo-Persia, Greece, Rome, and a latter form of the Roman Empire respectively. Thus, the symbolism in this statue can be known.

Likewise, in the book of Revelation "seven stars" represent "the angels of the seven churches," and "seven lampstands" represent "seven churches" (Rev 1:20). These symbols are explicitly explained. Yet other symbols are not explained. Certainly, the unexplained symbols offer challenges, but they too can be understood. There is no need to look for cryptic or spiritualized meanings or despair of meaning altogether. About half of the symbols in Revelation are explained, which can help in understanding those that are not.

Concerning the use of symbols in Revelation, Robert L. Thomas offers a helpful point: "To justify a spiritualizing approach on the basis of the book's many symbols misses a significant distinction between the way God gave the revelation to John and the way readers should interpret that revelation."[6]

6 Robert L. Thomas, "A Classical Dispensational View of Revelation," in *Four Views on the Book of Revelation*, ed. C. Marvin Pate (Grand Rapids: Zondervan, 1998), 181.

Fourth, the NT builds upon the contextual meanings of the OT kingdom passages and themes. Much information about the kingdom is found in the OT books. Also, the OT is the informing theology of the NT. This is evidenced by the approximately three hundred quotations of the OT in the NT. So a proper study of the kingdom should not ignore the OT and simply jump to the NT. The NT is building upon and relying upon the previous revelation of OT kingdom passages.

Scholars do not always agree on how literally the NT writers relied upon the OT expectations. While discussions on this issue can be varied and complicated, there are two main approaches concerning how the NT writers viewed the OT expectations. The first is to see Jesus and the NT writers as *affirming and expecting the literal fulfillment of the OT promises* as understood by the original OT authors and audiences. This includes the literal fulfillment of national and physical blessings for ethnic Israel along with blessings for Gentiles. Those who adopt this approach believe some expectations of the OT were literally fulfilled with the first coming of Jesus, while others await literal fulfillment at His second coming. The promises that will be fulfilled at the second coming of Jesus include many of the national and physical promises to Israel, along with creation's restoration (see Isa 11; 65:17–25).

The second main view *is to see non-literal fulfillment of OT promises.* Jesus fulfills the OT in that He absorbs, transcends, or alters the trajectory of the OT expectations. But there is no literal fulfillment of these promises. Some believe the OT promises are fulfilled in Jesus and/or the church. Also, OT promises are often viewed as temporary types and shadows that give way to greater spiritual realities. The differences between these two approaches can be seen in the following chart:

OT Expectation

Salvation and restoration of the nation Israel in an earthly kingdom of God under the Messiah with land and physical blessings for Israel as the basis for bringing blessings to the nations.

NT Reinterpretation/Transcending Fulfillment (Option 2)

- With coming of Jesus the expectation of the OT is transcended.
- Jesus and the church are the true Israel and national, physical, and land promises are fulfilled spiritually in Jesus and/or the church, not the nation Israel.
- National and physical elements of OT promises and covenants are viewed as types, shadows, and figures that are transcended by greater NT realities.

NT Literal Fulfillment (Option 1)

- With the coming of Jesus the expectation of the OT is literally maintained.
- The coming of Jesus means the literal fulfillment of the OT expectation. Since there are two comings of Jesus, certain OT promises are fulfilled with Jesus' first coming (appearing of the Messiah; New Covenant salvation; and indwelling Holy Spirit to believing Jews and Gentiles) while others await the second coming (physical and national promises to Israel, restoration of nations and nature).

We affirm the first option. The NT does not reinterpret or transcend the OT expectations. Instead, the NT continues the OT storyline and affirms literal fulfillment of the OT promises and covenants in all their dimensions through two comings of Jesus. Below are some statements from those who believe the NT reinterprets or transcends the OT and why we disagree with this approach.

Few theologians of the twentieth century have been as influential as George Eldon Ladd in their kingdom beliefs.[7] Ladd's kingdom views were based on his belief that the NT sometimes reinterprets the OT and that the NT often uses the OT prophetic passages non-contextually. For example, Ladd declared, "The fact is that the New Testament frequently interprets Old Testament prophecies in a way *not suggested by the Old Testament context.*"[8]

For Ladd the NT discovers deeper meaning from the OT passages: "Old Testament prophecies must be interpreted in the light of the New Testament to find their deeper meaning"[9] Also, Ladd argued the NT at times transcends the physical blessings of the OT for Israel into spiritual blessings for the church. Physical promises to Israel are now "reinterpreted":

> The Old Testament must be interpreted by the New Testament. In principle it is quite possible that the prophecies addressed originally to literal Israel describing physical blessings have their fulfillment exclusively in the spiritual blessings enjoyed by the church. It is also possible that the Old Testament expectation of a kingdom on earth could be reinterpreted by the New Testament altogether of blessings in the spiritual realm.[10]

Ladd even appealed to the concept of "radical reinterpretation" when it comes to how the NT uses the OT. For example, concerning Peter's understanding of Jesus' ascension in Acts 2, Ladd said:

---

7 George Ladd is well known for his promotion of Historic Premillennialism.

8 George Eldon Ladd, "Historic Premillennialism," in *The Meaning of the Millennium: Four Views*, ed. Robert G. Clouse (Downers Grover, IL: InterVarsity, 1977), 20. Emphasis in original.

9 Ibid., 23.

10 George E. Ladd, "Revelation 20 and the Millennium," *Review and Expositor* 57 (1960): 167. Emphases mine.

> This involves a rather *radical reinterpretation of the Old Testament prophecies,* but no more so than the entire reinterpretation of God's redemptive plan by the early church.[11]

In discussing Hebrews 8:13 and the New Covenant Ladd said: "Here again we have a *radical reinterpretation* of the Old Testament prophets."[12] As these examples show, Ladd made a stark disconnect between the meaning in the OT and that in the NT.

Ladd certainly is not alone in his reinterpretation and spiritualization of the OT. More recently, in his defense of an amillennial view of the kingdom, Kim Riddlebarger asserted belief in reinterpretation of OT eschatology:

> But eschatological themes are *reinterpreted* in the New Testament, where we are told these Old Testament images are types and shadows of the glorious realities that are fulfilled in Jesus Christ.[13]

Riddlebarger believes this priority of the NT over the OT means that at times the NT *spiritualizes* the OT prophecies:

> If the New Testament writers *spiritualize* Old Testament prophecies by *applying them in a nonliteral sense,* then the Old Testament passage must be seen in light of that New Testament interpretation, not vice versa.[14]

These quotes above reveal a close connection between belief in reinterpretation of the OT and spiritualizing of the OT. While referencing the kingdom, Louis Berkhof stated that Jesus "enlarged and *transformed* and *spiritualized*

11 George Eldon Ladd, *A Theology of the New Testament* (Grand Rapids: Eerdmans, 1974, Revised edition, 1994), 373. Emphases mine.

12 George Eldon Ladd, *The Last Things: An Eschatology for Laymen,* (Grand Rapids: Eerdmans, 1978), 27. Emphasis mine.

13 Riddlebarger, *A Case for Amillennialism,* 37. Emphases mine. For him, OT themes such as the nation of Israel, the temple, and the Davidic throne, are reinterpreted by the NT.

14 Ibid. Emphases mine.

it."[15] In a similar manner, Gary Burge argues that land promises of the OT have been "reinterpreted" in regard to Christ's kingdom:

> For as we shall see (and as commentators regularly show) while the land itself had a concrete application for most in Judaism, Jesus and his followers *reinterpreted* the promises that came to those in his kingdom.[16]

N. T. Wright uses "redefining" in regard to Jesus and His kingdom:

> Jesus spent His whole ministry *redefining* what the kingdom meant. He refused to give up the symbolic language of the kingdom, but filled it with such a new content that, as we have seen, he powerfully subverted Jewish expectations.[17]

As these quotations show, some assert the kingdom message of the OT authors is reinterpreted, redefined, and spiritualized by Jesus and the NT writers. *That is not our view. We reject the concept of reinterpretation.* Later revelation from God builds upon, harmonizes with, and complements earlier revelation; it does not reinterpret earlier revelation. God does not reinterpret what He stated previously. Instead, the contextual meaning of the OT is the informing theology for the NT, and OT prophetic themes are understood quite literally by the NT writers. Blaising is correct when he notes, "The New Testament carries forward the OT eschatological hope and adds to it the revelation that the Messiah of the eschatological kingdom is Jesus of Nazareth."[18] The following chart shows the NT writers and persons rely literally and contextually upon OT themes:

15 Louis Berkhof, *The Kingdom of God* (Grand Rapids: Eerdmans, 1951), 13. Emphases mine.

16 Gary M. Burge, *Jesus and the Land: The New Testament Challenge to "Holy Land" Theology* (Grand Rapids: Baker, 2010), 35. Emphasis mine.

17 N. T. Wright, *Jesus and the Victory of God*, (Minneapolis: Augsburg Fortress Press, 1997), 471. Emphasis mine.

18 Craig A. Blaising, "Premillennialism," 195.

OT	NT
Restoration of Israel	Matt 19:28/Acts 1:6
Salvation of Israel	Luke 1:68–69/Rom 11:26
Consolation of Israel	Luke 1:25
Descendant of David will rule over Israel	Luke 1:32–33
Fulfillment of Abrahamic Covenant with Israel	Luke 1:54–55
Physical deliverance from Israel's enemies	Luke 1:70–74
Salvation for both Gentiles and Israel	Luke 2:32
Rescue of Jerusalem from Gentiles	Luke 21:24/Rev 11:1–2
Salvation for people of Jerusalem	Matt 23:37–39
Importance of Israel's temple	Matt 24:15/Rom 9:4/ 2 Thess 2:4/Rev 11:1–2
Significance of land of Israel	Matt 24:16 / Luke 21:20–24
Abomination of Desolation and Israel	Matt 24:15/2 Thess 2:3–4
Personal Antichrist	2 Thess 2:3–4/1 John 2:18/ Rev 13:1–7
Tribulation for Israel	Matt 24:9–21
Worldwide Tribulation/Judgment/Wrath	Rev 3:10
Day of the Lord	1 Thess 5:1–4/2 Thess 2/ 2 Pet 3:10–12
Restoration of the creation	Matt 19:28/Rom 8:19–22
Cosmic signs in connection with Tribulation	Matt 24:29
Judgment of Nations	Matt 25:31–46
New Covenant fulfilled with Israel	Rom 11:27
Kingdom of God after worldwide Tribulation	Luke 21:31
OT covenants, promises, temple service for Israel	Rom 9:4

How does this issue of NT use of the OT relate to the kingdom program? Our view is the NT writers are not transforming and reinterpreting the kingdom message of the OT. The kingdom promised in the OT is the kingdom the NT reveals. Certainly as progressive revelation unfolds, new information will be given, including the news that Jesus is the Messiah and there will be two comings of Jesus. But new revelation is not contradictory revelation, nor does it reinterpret earlier revelation. It is in harmony with previous revelation.

This issue of properly understanding the OT directly relates to how God wants us to understand His purposes as they play out in history. To use an example, in American football there are misdirection plays where the offense tries to make the defense think the play is going one way only to shift and take the football in another direction. The play may seem to be going right but then the runner shifts direction and actually runs to the left. The desire is for the defense to run one way only to find that the ball carrier is going the other way. But God is not running misdirection plays with His revealed purposes. He is not leading us to think He is going one way only to go another. God does not direct us to think Israel, land, and physical promises are important and part of His kingdom purposes only to shift direction and say later that these matters are no longer significant or are transcended. In Galatians 3:15 Paul said that once a covenant is ratified "no one sets it aside or adds conditions to it." When God commits himself to a promise or covenant He does not alter what He promised.

Fifth, the primary meaning of a specific passage, whether from the OT or NT, is found in that passage and not in other passages. God inspired all passages of Scripture for a purpose and all sections have a meaning God intended through the human authors. The OT is inspired just like the NT. When we read an OT passage we should expect to find the primary meaning of that section there. Later revelation in the NT may offer inspired commentary. Or it may draw significance or application from an earlier passage, but the NT does not change or reinterpret the meaning of former passages. What the original writers and audiences understood matters. If not, then in what sense was the original revelation a revelation to the original writers and audiences?

Sixth, fulfillment of God's prophetic and kingdom purposes occurs with the two comings of Jesus. Jesus is the center of God's kingdom program, and all God's promises, including kingdom promises, are "Yes" in Jesus (see 2 Cor 1:20). However, not all kingdom promises were fulfilled with Jesus' first coming. Since there are two comings of the Messiah, fulfillments of prophecy occur with both His comings.[19]

19 "Old Testament prophets often anticipated the work of the Messiah as a whole, not distinguishing the accomplishments of the two Advents separated by millennia." Gordon R. Lewis and Bruce A. Demarest, *Integrative Theology: Historical, Biblical, Systematic, Apologetic, Practical* (Grand Rapids: Zondervan, 1994), 3:407.

For example, with His first coming Jesus fulfilled the promise of a coming Son of David (Matt 1:1) who established the New Covenant with His death (Luke 22:20). Yet in Matthew 19:28 Jesus predicted three matters to be fulfilled with His second coming—the renewal of the cosmos ("regeneration"), the assumption of His glorious Davidic throne, and the twelve apostles ruling over the twelve tribes of Israel. Those await future fulfillment. In his speech before the people of Israel in Acts 3, Peter declared both present and future fulfillments of OT prophecies in connection with Jesus. Compare:

> *Acts 3:18 (Present Fulfillment)*: "But the things which God announced beforehand by the mouth of all the prophets, that His Christ would suffer, He has thus fulfilled."

> *Acts 3:20–21 (Future Fulfillment)*: "and that He may send Jesus, the Christ appointed for you, whom heaven must receive until the period of restoration of all things about which God spoke by the mouth of His holy prophets from ancient time."

Peter states that prophecies concerning Jesus' suffering have already been fulfilled, but when it comes to the "restoration of all things" the prophets predicted, that awaits future fulfillment. We must discern the difference between first and second coming fulfillments, not making fulfillment fit only into one of Christ's two comings.[20] With His first coming Jesus established the basis for His kingdom reign upon the earth with His death. According to Revelation 5:9–10 Jesus is worthy to reign on the earth because of His atoning death for His people. With His second coming Jesus will reign over the earth (Matt 19:28; 25:31).

If an OT promise was not fulfilled with Jesus' first coming, we do not have to spiritualize it. It will come to fruition in the future. For example,

20 For example, Bandy and Merkle state, "All of God's promises given in the Old Testament are primarily fulfilled in Jesus' first coming." They then favorably quote Graeme Goldsworthy who wrote, "I want to assert that ALL prophecy was fulfilled in the gospel event at the first coming of Jesus." Alan S. Bandy and Benjamin L. Merkle, *Understanding Prophecy: A Biblical-Theological Approach* (Grand Rapids: Kregel, 2015), 82. Such statements indicate the heavy emphasis some place on the first coming of Jesus. On the other side, some early dispensationalists of the nineteenth century erred on the other side by placing very little fulfillment of OT promises with Jesus' first coming. The better approach is to see significant fulfillment with both the first and second comings of Jesus.

Zechariah 9:9 was fulfilled when Jesus came to Israel lowly on a donkey (Matt 21:5), but fulfillment of Zechariah 9:10 awaits the second coming since it describes the Messiah's universal reign over the earth. Jesus does not physically rule on this earth from sea to sea. But He will when He returns again. In sum, if a prophecy has not been fulfilled yet, it will be in the future.

Another point must be addressed. Not all theologians mean the same thing when they refer to "fulfillment" in Jesus. When we speak of "fulfillment" of kingdom promises in Jesus we assert that Jesus literally brings to fulfillment *all* that was predicted in the OT. Some erroneously hold fulfillment in Jesus means OT promises are absorbed into Jesus in such a way that literal fulfillment of OT promises and covenants is no longer necessary. But this is not the right approach. In Matthew 5:18 Jesus stated, "For truly I say to you, until heaven and earth pass away, not the smallest letter or stroke shall pass from the Law until all is accomplished." Since Jesus is referring to all stated in the Law and the Prophets (Matt 5:17), this means everything predicted in the OT must happen. The universe cannot pass away until everything transpires just as predicted.

Understanding this is important since many believe "fulfillment" in Jesus means the details of national, land, and physical promises in the OT will not be fulfilled literally because they supposedly are absorbed into or transcended by Jesus, or typologically fulfilled in Jesus. But this is not accurate. Jesus himself does not use this approach. In Matthew 24–25 Jesus declared that the details of many OT prophetic texts still needed to be fulfilled after His first coming. He said to look for future fulfillment of the abomination of desolation event predicted by the prophet Daniel (see Dan 9:27) and what this means for the people of Israel (Matt 24:15–22). He predicted fulfillment of the cosmic signs Isaiah referred to (Matt 24:29 with Isa 13:10). Jesus foretold the judgment of Gentile nations in fulfillment of what Joel 3 predicted (Matt 25:31–46). So Jesus expected literal fulfillment of several OT prophecies in connection with His second coming. He did not say these were absorbed into His person or that they were transcended in a spiritual manner. It is not the case that the details of OT prophecies are filtered through Jesus in such a way that non-literal fulfillment is now the expectation. What the OT predicted concerning the Messiah (Jesus) and Messiah's realm will all occur just as stated.

Seventh, the kingdom involves a holistic restoration of all things. We affirm the goodness of God's original creation. So God's plans for the cosmos are both *spiritual* and *physical* as well as *personal* and *national* and *international.* Just as God's creation included material and immaterial realms, so too will the new creation. The coming kingdom will have physical/material elements alongside spiritual aspects. This perspective rejects any approach that elevates spiritual matters and downplays the importance of physical and national matters in God's plans.[21] Both are important. We disagree with one author who states that he has "serious questions" about attempts to equate the kingdom with matters such as "a restoration of national Israel or a spatial, physical kingdom that manifests itself on this earth in a geopolitical manner."[22] Instead, the better view is that physical and national matters also are important to God's kingdom purposes.

When it comes to spiritual and physical issues this is a "both/and" situation and not an "either/or." When God created the universe He deemed everything as "very good" (Gen 1:31). Colossians 1:16 reveals Jesus created all things—both material and immaterial: "For by Him all things were created, both in the heavens and on earth, visible and invisible, whether thrones or dominions or rulers or authorities—all things have been created through Him and for Him." Colossians 1:20 also states Christ has "reconcile[d] all things to Himself" and this was done "through the blood of His cross." Thus, Christ is interested in reconciling all things, which includes the entire cosmos.

The Abrahamic, Davidic, and New Covenants include both spiritual and physical promises. Deuteronomy 30:1–10 promises both regeneration (spiritual) and prosperity in the land of promise (physical). The New Covenant passages of Jeremiah 31–33 and Ezekiel 36–37 predict a new heart, the indwelling Spirit, and forgiveness of sins. But these spiritual promises are in harmony with land and physical prosperity promises. The spiritual blessings serve as the basis for receiving the physical promises, but the physical promises are also significant. Both exist alongside each other.

21 For more on the New Creation Model and Spiritual Vision Model see Blaising, "Premillennialism," 160–81.

22 Riddlebarger, *A Case for Amillennialism*, 110.

A person and nation must be rightly related to God to receive them, but physical blessings are a real and tangible reward for trusting in God.

The kingdom can have spiritual requirements and characteristics (see Rom 14:17) and yet be physical in nature including social, political, economic, and agricultural elements (see Isa 65:17–25). The idea of a 'spiritual' kingdom only smacks of Platonism and its elevation of the spiritual over the physical. For instance, I disagree with one author's assertion that "in the NT, in contrast to the expectation of Judaism, the kingdom's character is 'heavenly' and 'spiritual,' not 'earthly' and 'political.'"[23] This is a false dichotomy and is closer to forms of Platonism than the Bible. The kingdom of God has spiritual requirements and characteristics, yet it also is physical and national with a relationship to the earth.

We also recognize the importance of land in God's purposes. More will be said on this issue later, but land is not something transcended or relegated to the realm of type or shadow. It is part of God's creation purposes from the beginning. Land is the realm where the first Adam was to "rule" and "subdue" (see Gen 1:26–28). And it is the realm where the Last Adam, Jesus, will reign over as well (see Matt 19:28; Rev 5:10). As Walter Kaiser has observed, "It is not as if God decided that His promise of the land was somehow no longer valid or that He was now tiring of that promise and had therefore decided to scrap it."[24]

Also, it is not the case that "land" only applies to Israel. What God is doing with Israel is a microcosm of what He will do for other nations. When the kingdom is fully operative, all people groups will experience land and physical blessings (Isa 27:6).[25] The blessings of Jesus' reign will extend over the entire planet and He will rule over every square inch of God's creation.

Eighth, lack of repetition of an OT promise in the NT does not mean the OT promise has been dropped or fulfilled non-literally. There are many promises concerning the kingdom and Israel in the OT, but not all of them are restated

23 Bruce K. Waltke, "Kingdom Promises as Spiritual," in *Continuity and Discontinuity: Perspectives on the Relationship Between the Old and New Testaments*, ed. John S. Feinberg (Wheaton, IL: Crossway, 1988), 270.

24 Walter C. Kaiser, Jr., "Evidence from Jeremiah," in *A Case for Premillennialism: A New Consensus*, ed. Donald K. Campbell and Jeffrey L. Townsend (Chicago: Moody, 1992), 104.

25 For a fine defense of the literal nature of the OT land promises and their implications for the new earth see Antonine DeGuglielmo, "The Fertility of the Land in the Messianic Prophecies," *Catholic Biblical Quarterly* (1957): 306–11.

in the NT. So how should promises not repeated in the NT be understood? Will they be fulfilled in the future? Or does lack of restatement in the NT mean the promises are no longer in effect or that the church spiritually fulfills the promises? For example, the details of a restored Jerusalem in connection with the New Covenant are explained in passages like Jeremiah 31:38–40, but these details are not restated in the NT.[26]

Our view is that NT silence on an OT text should not be understood to mean an OT promise has been dropped or transformed. What God has revealed once is sufficient. It is precarious to hold that unless God repeats what He said earlier we should not believe it is still in effect. Shouldn't the opposite be the case? As S. Lewis Johnson put it:

> There is no need to repeat what is copiously spread over the pages of the Scriptures. There seems to be lurking behind the demand a false principle, namely, that we should not give heed to the OT unless its content is repeated in the New. The correct principle, however, is that we should not consider invalid and worthy of discard any of the OT unless we are specifically told to do so in the New, as in the case of the law of Moses (the cultus particularly).[27]

Lack of restatement does not mean an OT promise is revoked. If an OT promise is not fulfilled at the time of Jesus' first coming, then it will be fulfilled at His second advent.

---

26 Although Luke 21:24 implies a restored Jerusalem.

27 S. Lewis Johnson, Jr., "Evidence from Romans 9–11," in *A Case For Premillennialism*, 223. Kaiser, too, disagrees that the NT must reassert a future restoration of Israel to its land in order for this doctrine to be true. Applying this standard to other areas would lead to absurd conclusions: "When it is asked what Christ and the apostles taught about a Jewish return to the land, the answer that is triumphantly given by our objectors is 'Nothing!' There is no return to the land, no restoration, no repossession of Jerusalem, no rebuilding of the temple! So the New Testament principle of interpretation must take precedence over any alleged Old Testament abiding promise. But it could just as well be asked: Where do Christ and the apostles teach anything about a prohibition on marrying one's own sister, aunt, or the like? Or where do they say a word against abortion? The answer, of course, is 'Nowhere!' But very few would then contend that there is no teaching that is relevant for the Christian believer on these and other similar points!" Walter C. Kaiser, Jr., "The Land of Israel and the Future Return (Zechariah 10:6–12)," in *Israel, the Land and the People: An Evangelical Affirmation of God's Purposes*, ed. H. Wayne House (Grand Rapids: Kregel, 1988), 221–22.

Ninth, God's plans involve both individuals and nations. I once read a statement in a theology book that God dealt with nations in the OT but now His focus is on individuals in the NT. This, however, is a false dichotomy. While individuals and individual salvation certainly are important in the NT, God's plans still include nations. Both must be grasped to understand God's kingdom program. It is not the case that with Christ's first coming God's plans for Israel and other nations were entirely transcended by individual spiritual salvation.[28] As Kaiser notes, "God's activities do include political and geographical elements."[29] We should avoid "nation bias," which is a negative view of God working with a nation or nations.

Passages like Isaiah 2:2–4; 19:24–25; Amos 9:11–15, and Zechariah 14 show God's design for both Israel and other nations. God's plans for Israel also are affirmed in the NT. The message of the kingdom was first directed to "the lost sheep of the house of Israel" (Matt 10:6). God's future plans for Israel are discussed in Matthew 19:28; Acts 1:6; and Romans 11:26. Nations and kings are even mentioned as part of God's plan for the coming kingdom of Messiah (Rev 2:26–27) and eternal state (see Rev 21:24, 26).

As with the physical/spiritual dynamic, this is a "both/and" not an "either/or" scenario. Ethnicity and national distinctions are not erased. Revelation 5:9 says Jesus' blood purchased "men from every tribe and tongue and people and nation." Randy Alcorn rightly notes that the verse does *not* say these people "were *formerly* of every tribe, language, people, and nation. Their distinctions aren't obliterated but continue into the intermediate Heaven and then into the eternal Heaven."[30]

Spiritual unity in Christ exists alongside ethnic and national diversity (see Eph 2:11–3:6). Just as God is both unity (one God) and diversity (three persons), God's people evidence both unity and diversity. The kingdom of God involves diversity of nations, including Israel. The truth, as Blaising states, is "Blessing on Israel and all nations, blessing on the land of Israel

---

28 We disagree with George Ladd when he states that the "nationalistic elements in the Jewish concept of the kingdom" are done away with "to lay stress on the spiritual elements." George E. Ladd, *The Presence of the Future* (Grand Rapids: Eerdmans, 1974), 110–11. These concepts are not mutually exclusive.

29 Kaiser, "Evidence from Jeremiah," 104. He also says, "If we Westerners persist in excluding these elements from our view of history, we shall be vulnerable to the charge of dualism, docetism, and spiritualism."

30 Randy Alcorn, *Heaven* (Carol Stream, IL: Tyndale House, 2004), 376. Emphasis in original.

and on all the earth, come together in the holistic scope of the promised eschatological kingdom."[31]

There are three levels of how God is dealing with mankind. First, He works with *individuals*. Second, there is a *national* level where God uses Israel as an instrument of universal blessing. Israel functions as a microcosm of what God will do for other nations. Third, there is the *international* level, in which God brings the restoration of nations alongside Israel (Isa 19:24–25). All three are important and complementary. Avoid assumptions that God's plans are individual but not national,[32] or that God's plans are international, not national. These are false dichotomies. Or put another way,

It is not:

God's plans are individual not national

or

God's plans are international not national

Instead, it is:

God's plans are *individual* and *national* (Israel)
and *international* (the nations).

Tenth, both particular and universal promises are important and will be fulfilled. The Bible reveals particular promises God made to the nation Israel, including land and physical blessings. There are also universal promises to all people groups who believe in God. However, it has become increasingly popular to claim particular promises to Israel are universalized in such a way that one should not expect fulfillment of particular promises to Israel. Allegedly passages such as Matthew 5:5 and Romans 4:13 indicate Israel's land promises have been universalized and the specific land dimensions for Israel have disappeared in this process. But this approach, as Blaising

31 Blaising, "Premillennialism," 195.

32 Contra George Ladd who stated, "Our Lord's offer of the Kingdom of God was not the offer of a political kingdom, nor did it involve national and material blessings.... Jesus addressed Himself to the individual; and the terms of the new relationship were exclusively those of personal decision and faith." George Eldon Ladd, *The Gospel of the Kingdom: Popular Expositions on the Kingdom of God* (Grand Rapids: Eerdmans, reprint 1981), 109. Our view is that the offer of the kingdom contained both individual and national implications. It is a false dichotomy to see only one element.

has pointed out, is a "false hermeneutical dichotomy."[33] The inclusion of the nations in God's covenants and promises does not mean the forfeiture of Israel's specific promises. Both can exist because both are important to God. Plus, if one realizes that what God is doing for Israel is a microcosm of what He will do for all nations in the kingdom, why would the particular cease to be important? To compare:

> It is not:
> The universal promises transcend the particular promises.

> Instead, it is:
> The particular and universal promises work together and both will be fulfilled.

Blaising is correct that "The part *must* be present and remain for a whole to be complete."[34] Also, "The universal does not replace the particular in the story of the Bible. Rather the story of the Bible encompasses an interaction among the parts, individuals and nations, until a whole with all its constitutive parts is completed."[35]

Eleventh, by God's sovereign design human responses can influence the timing of fulfillment of some prophecies. This point is often overlooked but it is important to the Bible's storyline. God's purposes are sure because of His sovereignty. Yet the fulfillments of some prophecies are influenced by human responses. *When* a specific prophecy is fulfilled can be contingent on how a person or group responds to God. Contingency is explicitly taught in Jeremiah 18:7–10 where God says:

> At one moment I might speak concerning a nation or concerning a kingdom to uproot, to pull down, or to destroy it; if that nation against which I have spoken turns from its evil, I will relent concerning the calamity I planned to bring on it. Or at another moment I might speak concerning a nation or concerning a kingdom to build up or to plant it; if it does evil in My

33 Craig A. Blaising, "Israel and Hermeneutics," in *The People, the Land, and the Future of Israel: Israel and the Jewish People in the Plan of God*, ed. Darrell L. Bock and Mitch Glaser (Grand Rapids: Kregel, 2014), 164.

34 Ibid. Emphasis in original.

35 Ibid.

> sight by not obeying My voice, then I will think better of the good with which I had promised to bless it.

This shows predictions about nations can be altered based on responses to God. As Toussaint observes in regard to Jeremiah 18, "Here the response of a nation to God's prophecy may affect its future."[36]

Contingency also occurred in 1 Kings 11:38 when Ahijah the prophet promised Jeroboam his house would be as enduring as David's if he obeyed God. Jeroboam's disobedience, though, disqualified him from experiencing this promise. Yet, this promise from God was still genuine. Likewise, Jonah prophesied Nineveh would be destroyed in forty days, but national repentance delayed God's judgment (Jonah 3). In addition, Isaiah told Hezekiah he would die soon (2 Kings 20:1) but Hezekiah prayed and was granted fifteen more years of life. With Acts 3:19–21 Peter says Israel's salvation is linked with the return of Jesus and the restoration of all things.

So then, contingency must be considered when it comes to the timing of the kingdom's establishment. This helps explain why Jesus can declare the kingdom as being "near" in the early part of His earthly ministry (Matt 4:17), but then days before His death declare the kingdom as only being "near" with His second coming (Luke 21:31). It also may explain why Jesus told the people of Israel they could have had "peace," if they believed in Him, but instead national destruction was soon coming because of unbelief (see Luke 19:41–44). The response of a nation or people can affect the timing of a prophecy's fulfillment. Of course, this is part of God's design and does not surprise Him, but from the human perspective a change in the timing of fulfillment may occur.

36 Stanley Toussaint, "The Contingency of the Coming of the Kingdom," in *Integrity of Heart, Skillfulness of Hands: Biblical and Leadership Studies in Honor of Donald K. Campbell*, ed. Charles H. Dyer and Roy B. Zuck (Grand Rapids: Baker, 1994), 225.

CHAPTER

3 GOD'S SOVEREIGN UNIVERSAL KINGDOM

The kingdom program starts with God's *universal kingdom*, which is God's absolute sovereignty and control over all creation from heaven at all times.[1] No area of the universe is exempt from God's control. Nor has there ever been a time when God's dominion over His creation has been compromised or lost. Several passages discuss God's eternal and sovereign reign over all things at all times. For example, Psalm 145:13 states the eternal nature of God's reign:

> Your kingdom is an everlasting kingdom,
> And Your dominion endures throughout all generations.

Psalm 103:19 declares the extent of God's universal kingdom over all things:

> The LORD has established His throne in the heavens,
> And His sovereignty rules over all.

Not only is God's kingdom eternal and unending, it extends to everything. David affirmed God's universal kingdom with his prayer in 1 Chronicles 29:11–12:

> Yours, O LORD, is the greatness and the power and the glory and the victory and the majesty, indeed everything that is in the

1 See McClain, *The Greatness of the Kingdom*, 22–36. "By God's universal kingdom is meant the activity of God... in exercising his sovereignty over all things." See also, Bruce K. Waltke, "The Kingdom of God in the Old Testament," in *The Kingdom of God*, ed. Christopher W. Morgan and Robert A. Peterson (Wheaton, IL: Crossway, 2012), 49.

> heavens and the earth; Yours is the dominion, O LORD, and You exalt Yourself as head over all. Both riches and honor come from You, and You rule over all, and in Your hand is power and might; and it lies in Your hand to make great and to strengthen everyone.

God's "greatness," "power" and "glory" extend to "everything" in both the "heavens and the earth." This exertion of God's kingdom control occurs through both miracles and providence. Even the powerful pagan king of Babylon, Nebuchadnezzar, eventually affirmed that God is sovereign and does what He wishes over His creation:

> "But at the end of that period, I, Nebuchadnezzar, raised my eyes toward heaven and my reason returned to me, and I blessed the Most High and praised and honored Him who lives forever; For His dominion is an everlasting dominion,
> And His kingdom endures from generation to generation.
> "All the inhabitants of the earth are accounted as nothing,
> But He does according to His will in the host of heaven
> And among the inhabitants of earth;
> And no one can ward off His hand
> Or say to Him, 'What have You done?'" (Dan 4:34–35).

This is significant coming from the king whom Daniel earlier referred to as the "head of gold" (Dan 2:38). Daniel also told him, "You, O king, are the king of kings, to whom the God of heaven has given the kingdom, the power, the strength and the glory" (Dan 2:37). Even as Nebuchadnezzar was acknowledged as "king of kings" on the earth, Daniel says that the "God of heaven" gave Nebuchadnezzar his "kingdom." As the book of Daniel unfolds we learn later that Nebuchadnezzar was a prideful man. So God humbled him and he was made to eat grass like cattle (see Dan 4). But when God allowed him to come to his senses, the powerful king acknowledged God as Sovereign King.

Thus, God's reign over the universe is eternal and extends to all things, even Gentile earthly kingdoms. But how does this truth harmonize with passages that teach God's kingdom is future? Jesus told His disciples to pray, "Your kingdom come" (Matt 6:10), indicating they were to pray for a kingdom still to come. This is where McClain's distinction between

God's "universal kingdom" and His "mediatorial Kingdom" is helpful.[2] God's universal kingdom over all things already exists. The center of God's kingdom and throne is in heaven where He exercises His will.[3] Yet the "mediatorial kingdom" has special reference to God's reign upon the earth through mediators or representatives. God is King of creation, but He has determined that man, as His image bearer, should "rule" and "subdue" the creation on His behalf (see Gen 1:26–28). Man's sin introduced a negative element into God's mediatorial kingdom. So the kingdom program from Genesis 3 onward will involve God's plan to bring this rebellious planet back into perfect conformity with His will. The ultimate man, Jesus, will accomplish this. Yet even as God's mediatorial kingdom evidences sin and the curse, God's universal reign over all assures us that God is still in absolute control. To compare:

> **Universal Kingdom**: God's eternal rule over all creation.
>
> **Mediatorial Kingdom**: God's rule on the earth through man who acts as God's representative.

One section that addresses both the universal kingdom and mediatorial kingdom in the same context is Revelation 4–5. Revelation 4 reveals God the Father exalted and worshipped from His universal kingdom throne in heaven. Then Revelation 5 introduces Jesus as the One who is worthy to take the scroll from the Father's right hand. This scroll is the title deed to the earth with judgments that unleash the wrath of God that will culminate in Jesus' kingdom on earth. Then those who were purchased by Jesus with His blood (Rev 5:9) will participate in His kingdom reign—"You have made them to be a kingdom and priests to our God; and *they will reign upon the earth*" (Rev 5:10). So Revelation 4 introduces a heavenly throne room scene

2 See McClain, *The Greatness of the Kingdom*, 34–36. Barrick adds, "Referring to the overall kingdom program as the universal kingdom and to the outworking of that kingdom through history as the mediatorial kingdom helps in the discussion and development of theological thought." Barrick, "The Kingdom of God in the Old Testament," 173. Waltke argues for two forms when he says, "The Bible bears witness to two forms of God's kingdom: a universal kingdom and a particular kingdom." Waltke, "The Kingdom of God in the Old Testament," 49. He then says, "The kingdom of God is sometimes called the mediatorial kingdom of God because it mediates the will of God on earth." (57).

3 See Psalm 2:4 where we are told that God "sits in the heavens."

(God's universal kingdom) that culminates in a mediatorial kingdom reign of Jesus and His saints on the earth.

While most kingdom passages focus on God's mediatorial kingdom on the earth (Dan 2:44; Matt 6:10; Acts 1:6), God's universal kingdom is always in operation. He is always in control and He always prevails. For a time men may resist God' mediatorial kingdom plans, yet they never escape God's universal rule. As McClain states, "It is not for men to choose whether or not they will be under the rule of the Universal Kingdom. Whether they like it or not, they are already under it (Ps. 75:4–7)."[4] The goal is for this planet to be brought into perfect conformity with God's will. When the ultimate Mediator, Jesus, successfully reigns over the earth, the mediatorial kingdom will be brought into conformity with God's Universal Kingdom (see 1 Cor 15:24, 28). And God's will on earth will be done as it is in heaven (see Matt 6:10).

4 Ibid., 31.

PART

2

THE KINGDOM PROGRAM IN THE OLD TESTAMENT

CHAPTER 4 THE KINGDOM AND CREATION (GENESIS 1–11)

Here we begin our through-the-Bible examination of the kingdom of God. Just as classic stories sometimes begin with "Long long ago" or "Once upon a time," so too God's kingdom program takes us way back to an age long ago, to the days of creation as recorded in the opening chapters of Genesis.[1] As God's book opens we are told, "In the beginning God...." Let the story begin.

THE KINGDOM CREATED (GENESIS 1)

Genesis 1 reveals the glories of God's creation: "In the beginning God created the heavens and the earth" (Gen 1:1). In six days God created a spectacular universe full of wonder and mystery—the sun and planets, animals, birds, fish, vegetation, land, and sea. This will be the realm for God's mediatorial kingdom.

Yet the new world needed a ruler. Yes, God was King and could directly rule over this new kingdom himself, but this was not His plan. So He created man. "Then God said, 'Let Us make man in Our image, according to Our likeness'" (Gen 1:26a). The details of man's origin are described in more detail in Genesis 2 but two points are important here. First, the creation of man is according to the counsel of the plural Godhead—"Let us make man..." This one God can speak as "us" because within the unity of

1 "God began His kingdom program at creation, long before the establishment of an earthly messianic kingdom." Barrick, "The Kingdom of God in the Old Testament," 174.

God there is also plurality. Later revelation will reveal this plurality consists of three persons—Father, Son, and Holy Spirit. The unity and diversity of God is mirrored in man who himself is both unity and diversity. There is man or humanity (unity) but this man is comprised of male and female (diversity) (Gen 1:27).

Second, man is created in the "image" of God according to His "likeness." These concepts of "image" and "likeness" belong only to man. No definitions are given but their meanings can be understood. "Image" carries the idea of "representation." God is spirit but God "wants to have his representatives in physical form."[2] Just as an ancient king would place an image of himself in an area of his realm to show his sovereignty, God makes man in His image to represent Him in the newly created world. Thus, "image" has kingship implications. Yet in this case these representations of God are living, breathing human beings, not lifeless statues. While God is the King, He created man as a king, a vice-regent and mediator over the creation.

The term "likeness" indicates man is in relationship with God; he is a son of God. Because man is a son of God, he is able to represent God. So sonship is closely connected to rulership.[3] As Peter Gentry points out, "The term 'likeness' indicates that *ādām* has a special relationship to God like that of a father and son."[4] This is supported by Genesis 5:3, which states that Seth was a son in the "likeness" of Adam.

As "image" and "likeness" of God, man is created as king and son. He is placed into relationship with God. Man is now positioned and equipped to rule and subdue the earth on God's behalf. Genesis 1:26–28 states:

> Then God said, "Let Us make man in Our image, according to Our likeness; and let them rule over the fish of the sea and over the birds of the sky and over the cattle and over all the earth, and over every creeping thing that creeps on the earth." God created

2 Sung Wook Chung, "Toward the Reformed and Covenantal Theology of Premillennialism," in *A Case for Historic Premillennialism: An Alternative to "Left Behind" Eschatology*, ed. Craig L. Blomberg and Sung Wook Chung (Grand Rapids: Baker, 2009), 136.

3 Gentry explains that "in the culture and language of the ancient Near East.... The king is the image of god because he has a relationship to the deity as the son of god and a relationship to the world as ruler for the god." Gentry and Wellum, *Kingdom through Covenant*, 192.

4 Ibid., 195.

> man in His own image, in the image of God He created him; male and female He created them. God blessed them; and God said to them, "Be fruitful and multiply, and fill the earth, and subdue it; and rule over the fish of the sea and over the birds of the sky and over every living thing that moves on the earth."

Man has a task to complete. First, he is to "multiply" and "fill the earth." God's plan for mankind involves more than just Adam and Eve. It involves their offspring. Adam and Eve were made to produce other image bearers who too would share their God-given responsibilities.

Second, God instructs man to "rule" and "subdue" the creation. The Hebrew term for "rule," which is used twice in Genesis 1:26–28, is *rādāh* and means "have dominion," "rule," or "dominate."[5] It is used later of the Messiah's future reign in Psalm 110:2: "The Lord will stretch forth Your strong scepter from Zion, saying, 'Rule [*rādāh*] in the midst of Your enemies.'"

The word for "subdue" is *kābaš*, which means "dominate" or "bring into bondage."[6] The term "especially speaks of the work of a king (e.g., 2 Sam. 8:11)."[7] Both verbs "rule" and "subdue" are linked to dominion and show, as Merrill observes, that "man is created to reign in a manner that demonstrates his lordship, his domination (by force if necessary) over all creation."[8] This is evident in man's naming of the animals, which was a demonstration of dominion (see Gen 2:19–20). Thus, there is a royal and kingly aspect to the language of Genesis 1:26–28. McClain observes, "the very first of the divine injunctions laid upon him [man] was regal in character."[9]

This relationship between the image of God and ruling over the creation is so close that some have concluded that the image of God is the function of ruling. But the function of ruling is probably a *consequence* of

5 See Francis Brown, S. R. Driver, and Charles A. Briggs, *A Hebrew and English Lexicon of the Old Testament* (Oxford: Clarendon, 1962), 921.

6 The term is used for subduing the land of Canaan so it could provide for the people of Israel. See Numbers 32:22, 29 and Joshua 18:1.

7 Gentry and Wellum, *Kingdom through Covenant*, 196.

8 Eugene H. Merrill, "A Theology of the Pentateuch," in *A Biblical Theology of the Old Testament*, ed. Roy B. Zuck (Chicago: Moody Press, 1991), 15.

9 McClain, *The Greatness of the Kingdom*, 42.

man being in the image of God. The main point is that man is God's image bearer created to rule the earth on God's behalf. Man is a *mediator* for God. This task to rule appears to be both a blessing and a command.

The relationship between God and man was that of "a sovereign-vassal nature."[10] This is why God's kingdom program begins in the first chapter of the Bible.[11] God makes a wonderful creation and tells man to rule over it for His glory. As Sung Wook Chung rightly observes, "God, as the King of kings, creates his viceroys, his subject kings."[12]

The Realm of the Kingdom

The *realm* of this kingdom rule for man is earth, not heaven. As Psalm 115:16 declares, "The heavens are the LORD's, but the earth He has given to the human race." So the kingdom is an earthly kingdom, with Adam established as its king. He is to rule *from* and *over* the earth with "an earthly vocation."[13] In addition to his spiritual relationship with God, Adam possessed physical and social/political authority. This was to manifest itself in every area—agriculture, architecture, domestication of animals, harnessing of energy and natural resources, and other areas.[14] As Middleton notes, "the human creature is made to worship God in a distinctive way: by interacting with the earth, using our God-given power to transform our earthly environment into a complex world (a sociocultural world) that glorifies our creator."[15] This truth has important implications for the kingdom of the Last Adam, Jesus, who, like the first Adam, must exercise His kingdom reign from and over the earth.

---

10 Merrill, "A Theology of the Pentateuch," 18.

11 As Goldsworthy notes, "we may propose that the first expression of the kingdom is in the Garden of Eden." Graeme Goldsworthy, "The Kingdom of God as Hermeneutic Grid," in *Southern Baptist Journal of Theology* 12 (Spring 2008): 11.

12 Chung, "Toward the Reformed and Covenantal Theology of Premillennialism," 136.

13 Middleton, *A New Heaven and a New Earth*, 39.

14 See Wayne Grudem, *Politics According to the Bible: A Comprehensive Resource for Understanding Modern Political Issues in Light of Scripture* (Grand Rapids: Zondervan, 2010), 325. Grudem says, "God expected Adam and Eve and their descendants to explore and develop the earth's resources in such a way that they would bring benefit to themselves and other human beings."

15 Middleton, *A New Heaven and a New Earth*, 41.

Man's Authority after Adam

Authority to rule over creation was not intended to be the sole possession of Adam. The command for Adam and Eve to fill the earth with other image bearers indicated this. Also, the members of the Godhead say, "Let them rule." The plural "them" could refer specifically to Adam and Eve, but such a limitation is not likely. Since Scripture presents Adam as the head of the human race (see Rom 5:12–21), "them" probably refers to all mankind from Adam and Eve as they multiply and fill the earth. Mankind's right to rule creation is reaffirmed in Psalm 8:4–8. This psalm explains the truth of Genesis 1:26–28 that man has a kingly function in regard to the earth.[16] Notice the kingly language of the psalm:

> "And You crown him with glory and majesty."
> "You make him to rule over the works of Your hands."
> "You have put all things under his feet" (Ps 8:5b–6).

This wording regarding subjection is later used of kings in the Bible and then Jesus the Messiah (see 1 Cor 15:27).

In relation to the creation, man is both a king and a mediator. So even from the beginning, God's kingdom program included this earth and man ruling over it. Goldsworthy is correct that "the first expression of the kingdom is creation with its climax in the Edenic fellowship between God and the human pair" who were "assigned dominion over the rest of creation."[17]

The significance of Genesis 1:26–28 cannot be overemphasized. Merrill deems this section "the great kingdom principle" that "is able to integrate the multifaceted materials of universal, patriarchal, and Mosaic revelation in an eminently satisfying manner."[18] The storyline after the fall of man in Genesis 3 will be the process by which God restores man to the kingdom mandate of Genesis 1:26–28. If there is to be a successful earthly

16 "The objects of the dominion are exactly the same (though in different order) as those of the Genesis mandate: flocks and herds, beasts of the field, birds of the air, and fish of the sea (Ps. 8:7)." Merrill, "A Theology of the Pentateuch," 16.

17 Goldsworthy, "The Kingdom of God as Hermeneutic Grid," 9. "God is reigning Lord. Yet, he delegates to humans the role of dominion over the rest of creation. Thus, God rules through his human viceregents." (8). See also, Paul R. Williamson, *Sealed with an Oath: Covenant in God's unfolding purpose* (Downers Grove, IL: InterVarsity, 2007), 46.

18 Merrill, "Theology of the Pentateuch," 86.

kingdom, God's image bearers must be saved and restored. This will all be tied to the ultimate man and king—Jesus the Last Adam and Messiah.

The "Very Good" Creation

Six times God pronounced His creation "good" (Gen 1:4, 10, 12, 18, 21, 25). Then in 1:31 He said it was "very good" (1:31). This includes the earth and all its physical aspects. There are religions and philosophies based on the belief that the physical world is illusion (Hinduism) or that the physical world is really just perception but not reality (Idealism). The philosopher Plato (427–347 B.C.) elevated spiritual matters over the physical. Two thousand years of church history show that the fog of Platonism has often clouded Christians. Many think God's ultimate purposes involve escape from the "carnal" physical world to a glorious spiritual existence in the sky. A strong contrast is made between earth and heaven, so much that the ultimate goal is to escape earthly existence.

But anti-material views are wrong. Physical things are not bad. In fact, the material and immaterial aspects of God's creation are in harmony with each other. The creation account in Genesis knows of no such dichotomy. Man was created as a complex unity of material (body) and immaterial (soul). Genesis 2:7 declares that "the LORD God formed man of dust from the ground, and breathed into his nostrils the breath of life; and man became a living being." Man came into being when the physical matter from the ground was joined with the breath of life from God.

God placed man in a physical environment suitable for beings with physical bodies. There was a real place called "Eden." God also made sensual delights for Adam, including food: "Out of the ground the LORD God caused to grow every tree that is pleasing to the sight and good for food" (Gen 2:9). Adam was also given physical work to do. He was to "cultivate" and "keep" the Garden of Eden God entrusted to Him (Gen 2:15). Then God made a real flesh and blood mate for Adam—a woman, Eve, who would be Adam's equal, yet also different from Adam (see Gen 2:18–25). From this point onward, man's service to God would also include his treatment of other human beings.

So from the beginning the kingdom mandate from God was holistic. It included matters both spiritual and physical. It involved relationships with other human beings. Understanding this helps us avoid any misconceptions that God's kingdom purposes are only spiritual. Or that when Jesus arrives on the scene, the kingdom He offers is just "spiritual" in nature.

THE KINGDOM CONSTITUTION (GENESIS 2:15–17)

With Genesis 2:15–17 God offered conditions for Adam and Eve's continued privileges. God put Adam into the garden "to cultivate it and keep it" (2:15). Earlier, man was tasked with ruling and subduing the earth; now a particular manifestation of this involved Adam's active involvement in the Garden of Eden.

The couple is allowed to eat from any tree in the garden, but they were to avoid eating from the tree of the knowledge of good and evil. To eat from it meant death. Chung calls this command "the constitution of the kingdom in Eden" in which "the core values of the Edenic kingdom are to be freedom within the context of obedience."[19] This command did not function as a call for Adam and Eve to merit or work for their salvation. Adam was created as a son and king in fellowship with God. Instead, this was an opportunity for these volitional beings to willingly express obedience to their Creator with their hearts. Avoiding the "tree of the knowledge of good and evil" was to be an expression of worship.

The command also established God-imposed limitations for Adam. Adam had many privileges, but he must obey God and operate within His framework. He must do so as a faithful steward of the task given to him by God. He needed to understand and show that his kingship was to operate under the recognition of the ultimate King—God.

KINGDOM MISSION FAILED: THE FALL (GENESIS 3)

The fall of man was a horrible failure. The kingdom program and man's role in it took a dramatic turn for the worse. Adam and Eve sinned and declared their independence from God by acting autonomously and eating of the forbidden tree. This was no small indiscretion. While eating fruit from a tree does not seem like much, the context of this act meant everything. It was a statement of autonomy and a declaration of independence

19 Chung, "Toward the Reformed and Covenantal Theology of Premillennialism," 138.

from the Creator. Adam and Eve doubted God's truthfulness and goodness and focused instead on their own desires.

The one who instigated this rebellious event was Satan, the power behind the serpent in the garden. While God was advancing his kingdom program, Satan was pursuing what William Barrick has called, "the anti-kingdom program."[20] Satan sought to foil God's kingdom program by bringing down God's image-bearers. From this point on, the great cosmic battle between God's kingdom and Satan's kingdom will dominate history.

In declaring his independence from God man experienced suffering and death. Spiritual separation from God appeared immediately and physical death would follow. The ground was cursed. Consequently, man's mission to rule and subdue the earth on God's behalf was a failure, at least for now.

God created man in His image with all the gifts, capacities, and talents to rule His wonderful creation, but man decided to serve himself and plunge the world into disaster. Man still possessed the image of God and the mandate to rule and subdue the earth remained (see Ps 8), but the task now was doomed. Instead of the creation working for man, it would now work against him. God told Adam:

> "Cursed is the ground because of you;
> In toil you will eat of it
> All the days of your life.
> Both thorns and thistles it shall grow for you;
> And you will eat the plants of the field" (Gen 3:17b–18).

The cursed ground would now frustrate man in the very realm where he was tasked to rule.

Sin is a spiritual issue, but its results are not only spiritual. It affects the creation as a whole. As Middleton points out, "Sin, evil, and death in all their forms—is fundamentally anti-creational."[21]

Understanding the impact of sin on creation gives insight to the often-asked question, "Why do evil and suffering happen if God exists?" The answer is found in man's failure to obey God and fulfill the kingdom

20 Barrick, "The Kingdom of God in the Old Testament," 178.

21 Middleton, *A New Heaven and a New Earth*, 79.

mandate of Genesis 1:26–28. A successful reign of man would mean a world that functions as it should with beauty, order, and righteousness. No moral or natural evil would exist. Every incident of moral evil and nature run amok can be traced back to man's failure to successfully rule the creation. The unintended consequences of the fall would go far beyond anything Adam could envision, but such are the costs of disobeying God. Also, since God made man to mediate His rule on earth, God is not obligated to immediately fix whatever evil or calamity that befalls man. Mankind is reaping the results of Adam's sin. Thus, the blame for all moral and natural evil lies with man, not God. With Genesis 3:15, God will implement a plan to fix the fallen world, but the blame for a world gone wrong belongs exclusively with man.

The Effect of the Fall on Relationships

God is relational. Man by nature is a relational being. God created man for three relationships: (1) God; (2) other humans; and (3) the creation. All three relationships suffered because of man's sin. First, man became spiritually separated from God and under God's death sentence. Eventually, man would also physically die. Second, tension and turmoil now existed between human beings. God told Eve,

> "In pain you will bring forth children;
> Yet your desire will be for your husband,
> And he will rule over you" (Gen 3:16b).

In a fallen world child-bearing will be painful for the woman. Eve is also told her "desire" would be for her husband. Some understand this as sexual desire. Despite childbearing being painful, women will still desire physical relations with their husbands. Others think "desire" refers to relational tension between the woman and her husband. With this view, the woman, who should be in submission to her husband, will attempt to usurp his authority, but her husband "will rule over" her. If correct, this foretells the struggles within the marriage relationship. We lean toward this latter view.

Third, the creation was now set to work against Adam. "Cursed is the ground because of you" (Gen 3:17b). "Both thorns and thistles it shall grow for you" (3:18a). With the fall, man's work will be much harder. He will find frustration in the very area he is called to master—the creation.

Thus, all three relationships man was placed into are severely damaged by the fall—with God, human beings, and creation. Fortunately, though, hope sprouted at this time of man's darkest hour.

Hope for a Coming Savior-King (Genesis 3:15)

Man could not save and repair himself. His only hope was for divine intervention. Fortunately, God offered hope. In Genesis 3:15 God declared a coming seed of the woman would one day deliver a fatal blow to the power behind the deceiving serpent—Satan:

> "And I will put enmity
> Between you [Satan] and the woman [Eve],
> And between your seed and her seed;
> He shall bruise you on the head,
> And you shall bruise him on the heel."

God declares "enmity" between two rival camps—Satan and his people and the people of God represented by the woman.

The concept of "seed" has both a many and a single element to it. Not only will there be "enmity" between the serpent (Satan) and the woman, this battle will continue through their descendants ("between your seed and her seed"). This has been an ongoing war throughout human history. Yet this battle will come to a climax when an individual from the seed of the woman, a "He," brings victory. This "He" (Jesus, Gal 3:16) will bruise the head of the serpent, who is Satan. While Satan will inflict harm on this coming deliverer ("you shall bruise him on the heel"), the victorious seed of the woman will deliver a mortal wound to Satan. The victory will ultimately come to the righteous seed from the woman, yet not without cost.

The restoration of creation must involve the defeat of Satan and this defeat must come from man. As Mark Saucy notes, "this Evil One is destined to be finally subdued by human beings."[22] A specific seed of the woman will need to accomplish this. This will happen through Jesus, the Last Adam, Serpent-slayer, and Curse-remover who will rule over the earth. As Chung points out:

> Since the devil's work is not only spiritual in character but also physical and institutional in its effects, we should interpret Genesis 3:15 as God's promise to restore not only Adam's spiritual rule but also his physical rule on earth and in time before the advent of the new heavens and earth, which will be eternal. Clearly, this dominion will be exercised not by the first Adam but by the second/last Adam as the representative of a new kind of humanity.[23]

The coming deliverer must rule from the same realm as Adam. This will relate to the coming Last Adam (1 Cor 15:45) and His successful kingdom reign over the earth.

When will this deliverer arrive? Eve may have thought her first child, Cain, was this deliverer. A possible translation of Genesis 4:1 is: "I [Eve] have gotten a man, even the Lord."[24] A literal translation may indicate she believed her offspring, Cain, was the promised deliverer of Genesis 3:15. Later, Lamech thought his son, Noah, could be the one to bring deliverance from the curse:

> Lamech lived one hundred and eighty-two years, and became the father of a son. Now he called his name Noah, saying, "This one will give us rest from our work and from the toil of our

22 Mark R. Saucy, "Israel as a Necessary Theme in Biblical Theology," in *The People, the Land, and the Future of Israel: Israel and the Jewish People in the Plan of God*, ed. Darrell L. Bock and Mitch Glaser (Grand Rapids: Kregel, 2014), 171. Saucy also observes, "Evil must be overcome *within* history and it must be overcome by means of a restored human vice regency (Heb. 2:8–9; Ps. 8)" (172).

23 Chung, "Toward the Reformed and Covenantal Theology of Premillennialism," 140–41.

24 This is my own literal translation of Gen 4:1. Kaiser, who adopts this understanding, states: "If this suggestion is correct, then Eve understood that the promised male descendant of human descent would be, in some divine way, 'the LORD.' If so, then Eve's instincts about the coming Messiah were correct, but her timing was way off." Walter C. Kaiser, Jr., *The Messiah in the Old Testament* (Grand Rapids: Zondervan, 1995), 42.

> hands arising from the ground which the Lord has cursed" (Gen 5:28–29).

What is striking is Noah's father, Lamech, believed Noah could be the one to remove the curse.[25] There are three main things to note here. First, Lamech was aware of the curse in Genesis 3. Second, Lamech was awaiting an individual who would take away the curse. Third, there was an expectation Noah could be this savior from the curse. With hindsight we know Noah was not the savior and curse remover that Genesis 3:15 predicted, yet this expectation existed.

These two passages involving Cain and Noah probably show a specific hope of a coming deliverer—someone who would restore mankind and remove the curse. Plus, this expectation was passed down from generation to generation. The expectation of Eve was also the expectation of Lamech. This hope was probably passed down to successive generations. So in the earliest times there was an expectation of a coming deliverer. A specific expectation remained that God would restore the creation through a special man.

THE KINGDOM AND THE UNIVERSAL FLOOD (GENESIS 6–9)

Man continued to act wickedly and God expressed His regret for putting man on the earth (see Gen 6:5–6). God would now use the creation as an instrument of His wrath. Such would be the results of the coming global deluge.

Williamson observes the coming flood was "a reversal of creation."[26] The separation and distinction that was part of creation in Genesis 1 was being "eradicated" in Genesis 6–7.[27] The distinction between the expanse of heaven, the subterranean waters, and the surface of the earth was obliterated

25 Chase explains, "Lamech's words in Gen 5:29 suggest his knowledge of both the judgment and the deliverance God promised in the garden." This includes the idea Noah may be involved with "reversing the curse under which humanity lived." Mitchell L. Chase, "The Genesis of Resurrection Hope: Exploring its Early Presence and Deep Roots," in *Journal of the Evangelical Theological Society* 57 (September, 2014): 476. Walton states, "It may have been Lamech's hope that Noah would somehow bring about the reversal of the curse." John H. Walton, *Genesis*, in NIVAC (Grand Rapids: Zondervan, 2001), 281.

26 Paul R. Williamson, *Sealed with an Oath: Covenant in God's Unfolding Purpose* (Downers Grove, IL: InterVarsity, 2007), 60.

27 Ibid.

as "on the same day all the fountains of the great deep burst open, and the floodgates of the sky were opened" (Gen 7:11b). So with the flood, "the creative process (bringing order out of a watery chaos) is thus reversed."[28] The flood is a stage in the "cosmic disintegration" that began in the Garden of Eden.[29]

The Kingdom and the Noahic Covenant

With the global flood it might seem God's plans for man and creation failed. But God promised that a coming seed of the woman would defeat the power behind the serpent and reverse the curse. So the destruction of the human race could not be total. Noah found favor with God (see Gen 6:8). He would be preserved through the flood and be an instrument through which God's kingdom plan would play out. The baton of the kingdom mandate was handed to Noah who in some ways functioned as a "Second Adam."[30]

After the flood, Noah functioned much like Adam in that Noah was the new representative of humanity through whom God's purposes would proceed. In a way similar to Adam, God tells Noah to "be fruitful and multiply" and "populate the earth abundantly" (Gen 9:7). Also, God told Noah, "I will establish my covenant with you" (Gen 6:18). This covenant involved the human race along with the birds and animals (6:18–20). In Genesis 9:8–10 God again says He will "establish" His "covenant" with Noah, Noah's descendants, and "every living creature." God would never again destroy the earth with water (9:11).

The language of this "covenant" is similar to Genesis 1:26–28 and shows this covenant with Noah is connected with what occurred with Adam. Thus, "Noah was to be the beginner of a new undertaking of covenant commitment, a new vice-regent through whom the sovereign purposes of God

28 Ibid.

29 Ibid.

30 Merrill refers to "Noah as a 'Second Adam.'" Merrill, "A Theology of the Pentateuch," 23. Gentry says, "Noah is presented in the narrative as a new Adam.... Noah is recommissioned with all of the ordinances given at creation to Adam and Eve and their family." Wellum and Gentry, *Kingdom through Covenant*, 163.

could find fruition."[31] Paul Williamson has rightly noted that "the Noahic covenant is not marginal, but rather foundational for salvation history."[32]

The Noahic covenant of Genesis 8:20–9:17 starts with a declaration from God concerning nature:

> "I will never again curse the ground on account of man, for the intent of man's heart is evil from his youth; and I will never again destroy every living thing, as I have done" (Gen 8:21).

> "While the earth remains,
> Seedtime and harvest,
> And cold and heat,
> And summer and winter,
> And day and night
> Shall not cease" (Gen 8:22).

God declares He will never destroy the earth again with a flood. And He guarantees to preserve the stability of nature. This promise must have been assuring since it guaranteed the uniformity of nature and opportunity for man to function without threat of global catastrophe. As long as "the earth remains" humans can rely on the cycle of seasons. Not only is this promise a blessing to all of creation, it will allow for God's kingdom and salvation plans to unfold in history. *Thus, the Noahic Covenant functions as the platform for God's plans to play out.*[33] It is also the basis for the other biblical covenants that will follow.[34] God's

31 Merrill, "A Theology of the Pentateuch," 23. Pentecost notes, "Thus, God reestablished His kingdom on earth after the pattern of His original creation in Eden. The kingdom program of God received a new beginning, and Noah and his family constituted the subjects of that kingdom." Pentecost, *Thy Kingdom Come*, 45.

32 Williamson, *Sealed with an Oath*, 60.

33 "Thus the covenant made with Noah creates a firm stage of history where God can work out his plan for rescuing his fallen world." Gentry and Wellum, *Kingdom through Covenant*, 169.

34 Irvin Busenitz explains, "The certainty of other covenants is, at times, anchored in the order of nature promised in this first covenant. In Jer 33:20–21, God employs the unfailing regularity of the natural order as a guarantee of the covenant with David (2 Samuel 7) and the covenant with Levi (Numbers 17; 25:10–13). Even God's covenant of unfailing kindness and peace toward Israel is hereby assured (Isa 54:9–10)." Irvin A. Busenitz, "Introduction to the Biblical Covenants: The Noahic Covenant and the Priestly Covenant," *The Master's Seminary Journal* 10 (Fall 1999): 186.

concern for creation also points toward the future restoration of all things when the totality of the curse will be removed.[35]

The Noahic Covenant promised stability of nature, but it also promised tension between humans and the animal kingdom. As Genesis 9:2 states:

> "The fear of you and the terror of you will be on every beast of the earth and on every bird of the sky; with everything that creeps on the ground, and all the fish of the sea, into your hand they are given."

This indicates "a further breakdown in human relations with the animal kingdom."[36] Such fear was not in the pre-fall creation nor will it exist in Messiah's kingdom. When the kingdom of God is established harmony will exist between humans and animals (see Isa 11).

God also instituted capital punishment for those guilty of murdering God's image bearers: "Whoever sheds man's blood, by man his blood shall be shed, for in the image of God He made man" (Gen 9:6). Thus, Genesis 9:6 inaugurates human government. McClain believes Genesis 9:6 is "one of the most important landmarks in all of human history, for here God not only decrees the beginning of human government in a sinful world but also lays down the moral and social foundation of all such government."[37]

Other events in Noah's life also parallel those of Adam. Like Adam, Noah was a gardener tending to farming and a vineyard (Gen 9:20). And like Adam, Noah was involved with a shameful incident that coincided with nakedness (see Gen 9:21–23). The bizarre incident of Noah's drunkenness and nakedness may reveal that Noah, like Adam, "is a disobedient *son* whose sin results in shameful nakedness."[38] Noah would be important in God's plans, but he was not the curse-remover to come.

35 "In this covenant, God pledges to preserve the stability of nature. Such stability is necessary if He is going to enter history to save His people. Moreover, since all living things will never again be destroyed completely by God in a flood, we see that the whole earth is the beneficiary of this covenant. This demonstrates God's love for all of His creatures and gives us a hint that one day all things will be renewed." see "Noahic Covenant," http://www.ligonier.org/learn/devotionals/noahic-covenant/. Accessed June 28, 2013.

36 Williamson, *Sealed with an Oath*, 63.

37 McClain, *The Greatness of the Kingdom*, 47.

38 Wellum and Gentry, *Kingdom through Covenant*, 170. Emphasis in original.

The Noahic Covenant sets the scene for the Abrahamic Covenant. As Merrill explains, the last verses of Genesis 9 and the genealogies of Genesis 10–11 "disclose the ever-narrowing focus of covenant development that finally finds its center in Abraham and his descendants."[39] Like Adam, Noah had three sons. The third son, Shem, would be "the heir of the covenant promise."[40] His line eventually would bring forth Abraham. We see an intersection between the themes of kingdom and seed. Pentecost notes "the legacy of theocratic administration would pass from Noah to Shem and to Shem's descendants."[41]

NATIONS IN THE KINGDOM PROGRAM (GENESIS 10–11)

Genesis 10–11 with its lists of people groups may not seem very interesting at first glance,[42] yet the information here is very significant. *These chapters highlight the importance of nations in God's plans and set the scene for the coming nation, Israel (Gen 12:2), and her role to the nations.* Chapters 10 and 11 reveal nations matter to God and His plans to restore all things include all people groups.

The Components of a Nation

Genesis 10 lists the nations as they descended from the sons of Noah. Verse 5 gives information concerning what constitutes a nation:

> From these coastlands of the nations were separated into their lands, every one according to his language, according to their families, into their nations.

Here "nations" (*goyim*) are mentioned twice and are linked with three concepts: "land," "language," and "families." The term for "land" is *eretz*,

39 Merrill, "A Theology of the Pentateuch," 24.

40 Ibid.

41 Pentecost, *Thy Kingdom Come*, 48.

42 "Most contemporary scholars, whatever their field, tend to view the Table of Nations in Genesis 10 as an archaic enigma." J. Daniel Hays, *From Every People and Nation: A Biblical Theology of Race* (Downers Grove, IL: Inter-Varsity, 2003), 192.

a word found in Genesis 1:1 concerning God creating the heavens and the "earth" (*eretz*). Soon, man was commanded to "fill the earth (*eretz*)" (Gen 1:28) and this command is repeated after the flood (Gen 9:1). Thus, a strong link exists between the creation in Genesis 1, the conditions after the flood (Gen 9:1), and the nations in Genesis 10–11. In addition, Andrew Kim observes that these elements of nation, land, family, and language, "are echoed in the Abrahamic Covenant of Genesis 12 where Abraham is commanded to leave his country (*eres*) to become a great nation (*goy*) to bless all the families (*misphaha*) of the earth."[43] This truth establishes a strong connecting link between the nations of Genesis 10–11 and what God will do through Abraham and Israel starting in Genesis 12.

A nation is more than just a family, tribe, clan, or group in close proximity. The concept of a nation, as Köstenberger points out, includes "ethnicity, language, territory, religion, kingship and history."[44] This is supported by Genesis 12. When God appeared to Abram, Abram already had a family. He had "relatives" (12:1) including a father, wife (Sarah), and nephew (Lot). But God planned to "make" Abram "a great nation" (12:2). There also is a political structure to a nation. As Gerhard Von Rad has pointed out, the "Table of Nations [of Gen 10] is not according to race or language, but politically and historically structured as distinct from one another."[45] Therefore, land and political structure are at the heart of nationhood. Such political structure for nationhood is present even on the new earth. Revelation 21:24, 26 mentions nations and their kings contributing to the New Jerusalem. A proper view of the kingdom of God, therefore, must include a proper understanding of how nations fit into the kingdom program.

Babel and the Spread of Nations (Genesis 11:1–9)

The Babel incident of Genesis 11:1-9 is important for two main reasons. First, it explains how the nations came to exist. Second, it reveals man's

43 Andrew Kim, "A Biblical Theology of Nations: A Preliminary Investigation," unpublished paper presented at the Evangelical Theological Society Annual Meeting, 2013, 4.

44 Andreas J. Köstenberger, "Nations," in *New Dictionary of Biblical Theology*, ed. T. Desmond Alexander and Brian S. Rosner (Downers Grove, IL: InterVarsity, 2000), 676.

45 Gerhard Von Rad, *Genesis* (Philadelphia, PA: Westminster, 1972), 140. See Kim, "A Biblical Theology of Nations," 5.

continual defiance to God and His commands, specifically rebellion to God's specific command for man to spread over the earth. This second point will be discussed first.

Why was the Babel incident so rebellious? God told the first humans to "multiply and fill the earth" (Gen 1:28). So God's plans from the beginning were global. Man was not to congregate in Eden but instead was to go and rule over the whole earth. After the flood, when Noah was the main representative of man on earth, God told him, "Be fruitful and multiply, and fill the earth" (Gen 9:1). God also said, "Populate the earth abundantly and multiply in it" (Gen 9:7b). So again, man was not to settle in one spot. Yet staying in one area is exactly what he attempted to do. Genesis 11:4 explains:

> They said, "Come, let us build for ourselves a city, and a tower whose top will reach into heaven, and let us make for ourselves a name, otherwise we will be scattered abroad over the face of the whole earth."

The people did not want to be "scattered abroad over the face of the whole earth." Sinful pride and disobedience is evident in the personal pronouns "us" (twice), "ourselves" (twice), and "we." Second, the people also wanted self-glorification—"let us make a name for ourselves." They desired to make a name for themselves. Clearly, they were not interested in God's desires or God's glory. When God calls Abraham, He promises the patriarch, "[I] will make your name great" (Gen 12:2). So God was not opposed to exalting people, but it must be done His way. It is for people of faith, like Abraham, and not for sinful and prideful men like those at Babel.

Third, the people wanted access to heaven—"a tower whose top will reach into heaven." They desired this because they did not want to be "scattered abroad" over the earth. This was direct disobedience to the Adamic and Noahic commands to multiply, fill, and populate the earth. Again, man is a covenant breaker. He will not submit to God's kingdom purposes. Merrill notes the kingdom implications here:

> Man, charged as the image of God to be His vice-regent on the earth, was dissatisfied with that high and holy calling and

> rebelled against his sovereign with the end in view of supplanting His lordship and assuming it for himself.[46]

William Barrick also points out how sin relates to the kingdom program: "Part of the reason God's kingdom has not yet come stems from fallen mankind's consistent antagonism to God's sovereign purpose for His own earthly kingdom."[47]

This rebellion is located in Babylon, which became the center of opposition to God's plans. The man, "Nimrod (Gen 10:8–10), provided leadership in a movement to sidetrack the kingdom program of the Lord in favor of one of human creation."[48] Later in the book of Revelation, Babylon will represent the capital city of Satan's kingdom (see Rev 17–18).

Parallels between the Fall and Babel

The rebellion against God's plans at Babel has similarities with the sin of Adam in Eden. With both, the members of the Godhead convene to address a sinful situation and take drastic action. In Eden, God said, "Behold, the man has become like one of Us, knowing good and evil" (Gen 3:22a). This use of "Us" in the Godhead parallels Genesis 11:7a: "Come, let Us go down and there confuse their language." So the plural members of the Godhead address a rebellion of man in both the Garden and at Babel.

The next similarity is judgment alongside a blessing. Adam and Eve were expelled from the Garden of Eden as a judgment for sin (see Gen 3:23). Yet this was also a blessing because it prevented an even worse situation from occurring. Genesis 3:22b states that if man remained in the Garden he would "stretch out his hand, and take also from the tree of life, and eat, and live forever." If Adam and Eve remained in Eden and participated in the tree of life they may have been forever confirmed in their sinful state. So their expulsion was not only a judgment, it contributed to their own good. Likewise, with the Babel event, God judges prideful mankind by confusing his language, which leads to scattering. Thus, this is a judgment.

46 Merrill, "A Theology of the Pentateuch," 25.

47 Barrick, "The Kingdom of God in the Old Testament," 175.

48 Ibid. 174–75. See also Eugene Merrill, *Everlasting Dominion: A Theology of the Old Testament* (Nashville, TN: B&H Publishing Group, 2006), 223–24.

But it is also a blessing since God causes man to scatter throughout the earth in line with His original plan for man to fill the earth. In sum, the parallel between Genesis 3 and 11 is this: *the members of the Godhead convene to address a rebellion by man concerning a specific command by God. God responds with both judgment and blessing so the kingdom program and the restoration of all things may someday occur.*

	Genesis 3 (Eden)	Genesis 11 (Babel)
Situation	Rebellion of man to a specific command (not eat of tree)	Rebellion of man to a specific command (spread over the earth)
Response of God	Members of Godhead convene to address rebellion ("Us")	Members of Godhead convene to address rebellion ("Us")
Judgment	Expulsion from the Garden of Eden	Confusion of languages; people scattered
Blessing/Protection	Man shielded from being confirmed in sinful state	Man caused to spread over the earth in line with God's original command

Table of Nations (Genesis 10)

The list of nations in Genesis 10 precedes the Babel event of Genesis 11, even though Genesis 11:1–9 explains how nations began. This non-chronological order may indicate that the presence of nations is a positive development and not just the result of sin. When one encounters the nations of Genesis 10, there is no indication these nations are a bad thing. Genesis 11:1–9 reveals the sinful Babel event led to the development of nations. So the placing of the Table of Nations in chapter 10 before the Tower of Babel event in chapter 11 may reveal that nations have a positive function in God's purposes. Their existence is linked with the command for man to spread over the earth in fulfillment of Genesis 1:28 and 9:1. As Clines notes:

> If the material of Ch.10 had followed the Babel story, the whole Table of Nations would have had to read under the sign of judgment; but where it stands it functions as the fulfillment of the

> divine command of Gen 9:1...which looks back in its turn to Gen 1:28.[49]

Nations, therefore, are an important part of God's kingdom purposes. What occurs at Babel is not just "a failure and punishment, but of God's intended will for the diversity of nations from creation."[50] That nations are a part of God's plans is stated in Acts 17:26: "and He made from one man every nation of mankind to live on all the face of the earth, having determined their appointed times and the boundaries of their habitation." Plus, Revelation 21:24, 26, and Revelation 22:3 mention "nations" and "kings" on the new earth. Nations have a positive role in the eternal state.

With the events of Genesis 12, the focus shifts to Abraham and the great nation of Israel. Israel will dominate the storyline after this chapter. Yet grasping a proper connection between Genesis 10–11 and Genesis 12 is important. The Table of Nations is the context from which Abraham and the nation Israel will occur. Genesis 10–11 provides the context for Israel to be the platform for universal blessings. God's purposes for the nation Israel are not simply for the benefit of Israel alone. God's uses Israel as a vessel to bless all people groups.

SUMMARY OF KINGDOM PROGRAM IN GENESIS 1–11

Genesis 1–11 contains important information concerning the kingdom program. The following summarizes the key points:

1. God, as Creator, is the King over the universe, which is His kingdom.
2. The entire kingdom of creation, including material and immaterial elements, is deemed "very good."
3. God made man in His image as a son and king to rule over God's creation; man's main task is to rule from and over the earth for God's glory.

49 D. J. A. Clines, *The Theme of the Pentateuch*, 2nd ed. (Sheffield: JSOT Press; Sheffield Academic Press, 1997), 74.

50 Bernhard W. Anderson, *From Creation to New Creation: Old Testament Perspectives*, Overtures to Biblical Theology (Minneapolis: Fortress, 1994), 167–76.

4. Man failed his kingdom task by acting autonomously and sinning against his Creator.
5. As a result of the fall, the creation became subject to the curse and death; man's ability to rule over the creation was damaged.
6. God promised a coming seed of the woman who would reverse the curse and defeat the power behind the serpent (Satan).
7. The people of God expected a coming redeemer who would reverse the curse.
8. God judged sinful mankind with a universal flood.
9. The Noahic Covenant, which offers stability of nature, functions as the platform for God's kingdom purposes to play out in history.
10. Noah functioned like a second Adam over creation yet he too was sinful.
11. God's kingdom program includes nations as evidenced with the Babel incident and the Table of Nations.
12. The presence of nations sets the scene for God's plans to use a specific nation, Israel, to bring blessings to all people groups.

CHAPTER 5

THE KINGDOM AND THE ABRAHAMIC COVENANT (GENESIS 12–50)

Genesis 1–11 focused on broad global issues. God the King created a wonderful world where man was tasked as God's son and king to subdue and rule it. But man failed in his responsibility and God introduced a curse upon the realm he was supposed to rule over. Later, God used another event—the worldwide flood—to punish mankind and start over with another representative of mankind—Noah, who also was given the mandate to multiply and populate the earth. Noah, though, was also sinful and mankind again showed its rebellion against the King by conspiring to stay in one place and give glory to himself. By confusing his language at the Tower of Babel incident God forced man to spread out over the earth. This was a judgment but also part of God's plan for man to locate to different geographical areas. As Genesis 1–11 comes to a close, man's sin is a major obstacle to the kingdom program, but hope for restoration and salvation continues.

In Genesis 12, the kingdom mandate given to Adam and then Noah is now given to Abraham and his descendants. The Abrahamic Covenant will be built upon the revelation made previously with Adam and Noah, yet with more specificity. From Genesis 3:15 there was expectation of a "seed" who would reverse the curse. The "seed" line went through Noah and Shem. Then God's plan for deliverance narrowed as Abraham became the vehicle for God's kingdom purposes. But as God's kingdom program narrows it is not for making the kingdom relevant only to Israel. Through Abraham, Isaac, and Jacob blessings will flow to the world. National election, therefore, will be a means for international blessings. Abraham and his physical descendants are not an end in themselves but they are means to universal blessings.

THE GIVING OF THE ABRAHAMIC COVENANT (GENESIS 12:1–3)

God's kingdom program involves the Abrahamic Covenant. As Keith Essex rightly notes, "The Abrahamic Covenant undergirds the totality of the biblical revelation. Specifically elucidated in Genesis, its promises govern the pattern of all that follows in Exodus to Revelation."[1] Details of this covenant are revealed progressively through the rest of the book of Genesis, but the foundation of the covenant is found in Genesis 12:1–3:

> Now the LORD said to Abram,
> "Go forth from your country,
> And from your relatives
> And from your father's house,
> To the land which I will show you;
> And I will make you a great nation,
> And I will bless you,
> And make your name great;
> And so you shall be a blessing;
> And I will bless those who bless you,
> And the one who curses you I will curse.
> And in you all the families of the earth will be blessed."

God told Abraham (then Abram) to leave his homeland of Ur and go to a land He would show him. When Abraham does this, God makes Abraham a covenant partner.[2] Three parties will benefit from this covenant:

1. Abraham
2. The great nation to come from Abraham (Israel)
3. The families/nations of the earth (Gentile groups)

1 Keith Essex, "The Abrahamic Covenant," in *The Master's Seminary Journal* 10 (1999): 212.

2 See Eugene H. Merrill, "A Theology of the Pentateuch," 26. This passage shows the Abrahamic Covenant contained a conditional element in that Abraham needed to leave his homeland to participate in this covenant. But there is also an unconditional element for when Abraham does this, God unilaterally commits to fulfill all that He promises. Thus, it is correct to call this covenant an unconditional royal grant covenant made by God with Abraham.

First, God promises Abraham personal blessings—"And I will bless you, and make your name great." There is also the promise that "a great nation" would come from Abraham. This "great nation" is Israel.

God does not stop with blessing just Abraham and Israel. His purposes are broader. The purpose of Abraham and the nation Israel is found in verse 3—"And in you all the families of the earth will be blessed." Dumbrell says the Hebrew grammar here indicates the intended purpose of Abraham and the great nation to come from him is universal blessing:

> The Heb. syntax indicates this, and the clause is most probably to be taken as a result clause indicating what will be the consummation of the promises that the preceding verses have announced. That is to say, the personal promises given to Abram have final world blessing as their aim.[3]

Thus, Genesis 12:2–3 indicates the purpose of Abraham and the great nation to come from him (Israel) is worldwide blessing. Christopher Wright points out: "Beyond doubt, then, there was a universal purpose in God's election of Abraham, and therefore also a universal dimension to the very existence of Israel. Israel as a people was called into existence because of God's mission to bless the nations and restore his creation."[4] Thus, Abraham and the nation Israel are not and end in themselves but channels for blessings. As Robert Martin-Achard declared, "The choice of Israel... belongs to the realm of means not ends."[5] Israel's mission is linked with the world. This is repeated several times in Genesis:

> since Abraham will surely become a great and mighty nation, and in him all the nations of the earth will be blessed? (Gen 18:18).

> "In your seed all the nations of the earth shall be blessed, because you have obeyed My voice" (Gen 22:18).

3 William J. Dumbrell, *Covenant and Creation: A Theology of OT Covenants* (Nashville: Thomas Nelson, 1984), 65.

4 Christopher J. H. Wright, *The Mission of God: Unlocking the Bible's Grand Narrative* (Downers Grove, IL: InterVarsity), 251.

5 Robert Martin-Achard, *A Light to the Nations* (Edinburgh: Oliver and Boyd, 1962), 40–41.

> "I will multiply your descendants as the stars of heaven, and will give your descendants all these lands; and by your descendants all the nations of the earth shall be blessed" (Gen 26:4).
>
> "Your descendants will also be like the dust of the earth, and you will spread out to the west and to the east and to the north and to the south; and in you and in your descendants shall all the families of the earth be blessed" (28:14).[6]

Grasping this truth of universal blessings through Israel helps with avoiding two errors. The first is thinking the promises of the Abrahamic Covenant are only for Israel. The second error is assuming later Gentile participation in the covenant means Gentiles will be incorporated into Israel. Both Israel and Gentiles will be related to the Abrahamic Covenant yet each will retain their ethnic identities (see Isa 19:24–25; Eph 3:6).

ISRAEL AS A MICROCOSM

What God is accomplishing with Abraham is connected with His dealings with Adam and Noah. As Merrill states, the covenant with Abraham "is built squarely on them in all its essential elements."[7] For example, that Abraham's offspring would become a great nation (Gen 12:2; 15:5; 17:4–5) corresponds to the "be fruitful and multiply" command (Gen 1:28).[8] The themes of the Abrahamic Covenant "affirm in every respect the covenant mandate of Genesis 1:26–28, with the special proviso that Abraham and his descendants were to serve as models of, as witnesses to, the implementation on the earth."[9] What God is accomplishing with Abraham and Israel will function as "a microcosm of the kingdom of God and would function in that capacity as an agency by which God would reconcile the whole creation to Himself."[10]

6 Emphases are mine.

7 Merrill, "A Theology of the Pentateuch," 26.

8 Ibid., 27.

9 Ibid.

10 Ibid.

Merrill's mention of Israel as "microcosm" rightly presents Israel as a model or template of what God will do for all nations. This is more accurate than the common view that the nation Israel is an inferior type that is transcended by the church. Since God's plans include nations, the nation Israel will have a role to play in regard to the nations. And just as God offers spiritual and physical blessings to Israel, so too will He give spiritual and physical blessings to other people groups. To put another way:

> It is not: Israel and the land are types and shadows transcended by the church.
>
> Instead, it is: Israel and the land are microcosms of what God will do for all nations in the kingdom.

There is another key element concerning Israel's role in God's kingdom program. As God unfolds His plan to establish His global kingdom and restore all things, the nation Israel will function as a beachhead to establish God's kingdom purposes. As Mark Saucy states, "The constitution of Israel *as a nation* marks a new beachhead for salvation against the *gods of the nations*."[11]

THE KINGDOM AND THE LAND

Land is an important part of God's kingdom purposes,[12] and "is essential to any meaningful definition of dominion and nationhood."[13] The significance of man and land is seen in the names given to each. The man is *adam* and the ground is *adama*. In reference to these terms, T.D. Alexander notes, "At harmony with God, each is dependent on the other."[14] Man was tasked with ruling over the earth in general and the land of the Garden of Eden in particular. When man fell, the ground worked against him

11 Saucy, "Israel as a Necessary Theme in Biblical Theology," 173. Emphases in original.

12 Sailhamer says "land" and "blessing" are "Two primary themes that dominate the Creation account." See John H. Sailhamer, "Genesis," in *The Expositor's Bible Commentary*, ed. Frank E. Gaebelein, vol. 2 (Grand Rapids: Zondervan, 1990), 19.

13 Merrill, "A Theology of the Pentateuch," 28.

14 T.D. Alexander, *From Paradise to Promised Land: An Introduction to the Pentateuch* (Grand Rapids: Baker Academic, 2002), 129.

and he was expelled from the first geographical area he was called to work over—the garden.

As Genesis 12 begins, Abraham was told to "go to the land" God would show him (Gen 12:1). Abraham left his homeland in faith and ventured to the land of Canaan (Gen 12:4–5). This obedient response led to God presenting land to him:

> Abram passed through the land as far as the site of Shechem, to the oak of Moreh. Now the Canaanite was then in the land. The LORD appeared to Abram and said, "To your descendants I will give this land" (Gen 12:6–7a).

Abraham then "settled in the land of Canaan" (see Gen 13:12) where God again made a promise:

> The LORD said to Abram, after Lot had separated from him, "Now lift up your eyes and look from the place where you are, northward and southward and eastward and westward; for all the land which you see, I will give it to you and to your descendants forever.... Arise, walk about the land through its length and breadth; for I will give it to you" (Gen 13:14–17).

The dimensions of the land are from the river of Egypt to the river Euphrates (15:18). These are specific boundaries. Reaffirmations of the land promise would be offered during days of peril for Israel (see Jer 16:15). This shows the perpetuity of the land promise and that Israel's disobedience does not forever nullify the promise.

The mention of the Hebrew word *eretz* in Genesis 12 and 13 again emphasizes the importance of land. The term that was first found in Genesis 1:1–2a. "In the beginning God created the heavens and the earth [*eretz*]. The earth [*eretz*] was formless and void... ." The term *eretz* can be translated "earth" or "land." So "land" is significant. As Merrill notes, "The very creation of the heavens and the earth, in fact, was to provide a locus in which the reigning purposes of God for mankind would be carried out."[15] The Garden of Eden, for instance, "became the microcosmic expression of kingdom territory" and the place where God dwelt and "had fellowship with

15 Merrill, "A Theology of the Pentateuch," 28.

His image, His vice-regent."[16] The fall of Adam did not extinguish man's responsibility to the earth/land nor did it remove the necessity of a geographical locale as the foundation for man's functioning. As God's plans for universal restoration and blessing narrow on Abraham and Israel, land will be of great importance. The land of Canaan will become "the focus of God's redemptive and reigning activity on the earth."[17]

Israel's connection to the land of promise is deep. In fact, inseparable is a better word. As Merrill puts it, "The biblical witness is that Israel is inconceivable without land, whether in historical or eschatological times."[18] When the Bible affirms Israel's place in the plan of God Israel's land is part of the package. A nation in the truest sense involves land as a base of operation. Thus, Israel's role involves land.

THE KING-PRIEST (GENESIS 14:17–24)

A brief encounter with kingdom implications takes place in Genesis 14 when Abraham encountered Melchizedek who is identified as "king of Salem" and "priest of God most high." Melchizedek was a king-priest. The writer of Hebrews will make a typological connection between Melchizedek and the superior King-Priest, Jesus (Heb 7). Psalm 110, a messianic psalm that finds fulfillment with Jesus, predicts both the reign of God's King (Ps 110:2) and His priestly function (Ps 110:4). When Jesus comes He will successfully unite the offices of King and Priest. Thus, Melchizedek corresponds to Jesus, the ultimate King-Priest.

Abraham himself manifests the traits of a king. The king of Gerar (see Gen 20:2) establishes a friendship treaty with Abraham suggesting that the local king, Abimelech, perceives Abraham as his equal. Also, the sons of Heth said to Abraham, "Hear us, my lord, you are a mighty prince among us" (Gen 23:5–6). T. Desmond Alexander observes, "While Abraham is never called a king, these... suggest he is one in all but name."[19]

---

16 Ibid.

17 Ibid., 29.

18 Ibid.

19 T. Desmond Alexander, *From Eden to the New Jerusalem: An Introduction to Biblical Theology* (Grand Rapids: Kregel, 2008), 82–83.

THE KINGDOM AND THE TRIBE OF JUDAH (GENESIS 17:6 AND 49:8–10)

Another connection between God's kingdom program and Abraham involves God's promise that "kings will come forth from you" (Gen 17:6). The promise of coming kings was also given to Jacob in Genesis 35:11: "God also said to him [Jacob], 'I am God Almighty; Be fruitful and multiply; A nation and a company of nations shall come from you, and kings shall come forth from you.'" While it may be tempting to think ahead to the kings of Israel with this statement, the first kings from Abraham were Edomite kings from the line of Esau. Genesis 36:31–43 lists these "kings who reigned in the land of Edom before any king reigned over the sons of Israel" (v. 31). So even before the kings of Israel existed, kings from the line of Esau are mentioned. Of course this is not the complete fulfillment of the "kings" promise and is only a foretaste of what is to come. Gordon Johnston observes that with Genesis 37–50, the reader "is poised to learn how God would begin to initially fulfill his promise to establish a dynasty of kings for Israel as well."[20] The "climax" of Genesis 37–50 is found "in Jacob's oracle of a coming ruler from the tribe of Judah in 49:8–12."[21]

Genesis 49:1 reveals that the elderly Jacob gathered his twelve sons concerning what would "befall" them "in the days to come." Jacob prophesied concerning the destiny of "the twelve tribes of Israel" (49:28). What Jacob says to Judah in 49:8–12 has great significance concerning the kingdom. Regarding Judah, Jacob said, "Your hand shall be on the neck of your enemies" (49:8), indicating the subjection of Judah's opponents to Judah. Having one's foot on the neck of an enemy meant complete victory over the opponent. The verse also says, "your brothers shall praise you," and "Your father's sons shall bow down to you." This refers to Judah's leadership role among the tribes of Israel, which was true both historically, and

20 Herbert W. Bateman IV, Darrell L. Bock, and Gordon H. Johnston, *Jesus the Messiah: Tracing the Promises, Expectations, and Coming of Israel's King* (Grand Rapids: Kregel, 2012), 40.

21 Ibid.

eschatologically.[22] Then with verse 9, the imagery of a lion is used three times concerning Judah:

- "Judah is a lion's whelp."
- "He couches, he lies down as a lion."
- "And as a lion who dares rouse him up?"

This "lion" language indicates royalty. Later, Jesus is referred to as "the Lion that is from the tribe of Judah" (Rev 5:5).

With Genesis 49:10, Jacob predicted a kingly rule would come with Judah and Judah's descendants:

> "The scepter shall not depart from Judah,
> Nor the ruler's staff from between his feet,
> Until Shiloh comes,
> And to him shall be the obedience of the peoples."

The focus here is on the individual, "Shiloh." Two symbols of authority are mentioned. The term translated "scepter" can range in meaning from "rod" to "club" to "staff" to "scepter." These concepts are not mutually exclusive. In this context there may be both warrior and kingly connotations. The word "staff" also implies a warrior's club or a staff as an emblem of authority. Since victory in battle is closely tied with a reigning monarch, a close connection exists between a warrior and a king. Perhaps the picture is of a warrior/king winning the battle with a club that is also a symbol of his authority.

Shiloh

Jacob's prophecy tells of a kingly line from Judah that culminates in one called, "Shiloh." There is debate as to whether the proper translation is "Shiloh" (as in the NASB or NKJV) or "until he comes to whom it belongs" (as in the NIV and HCSB). Various translations of the Bible differ on this, but the latter is probably correct. If so, the context tells of "an unidentified figure

22 Ibid. 43–44. Johnston points out several ways Judah was a leader historically: (1) Judah was the largest tribe in the wilderness (Num 23:3–4; 10:4) and he led the Israelite march; (2) Moses blessed Judah with power for the conquest (Deut 33:7–11); (3) Judah was the first tribe allotted land by Joshua (Josh 15:1); (4) Judah was the designated leader for the conquest of Canaan (Judg 1:2–4); (5) Judah exercised hegemony over the tribes of Israel at David's enthronement over all Israel (2 Sam 5:1–5).

arising upon the scene of history to whom the weapons of military victory and the emblems of royal authority belong."[23] This will culminate in Jesus the Messiah.

The reference to "the obedience of the peoples" is strategic since it indicates the realm of this coming one extends beyond the tribe of Judah and the twelve tribes of Israel. *The realm of this rule will include Gentiles.* A ruler will come from the tribe of Judah whose reign will extend over the earth. His rule will not just extend over the tribes of Israel—His reign will also be global. So in the first book of the Bible, we see God's kingdom will be mediated through Israel but also will extend to the whole world.

Exuberant Prosperity

The kingdom program includes blessings in the physical realm. Genesis 49:11-12 describes an "exuberant, intoxicating abundance"[24] of Shiloh's reign:

> "He ties his foal to the vine,
> And his donkey's colt to the choice vine;
> He washes his garments in wine,
> And his robes in the blood of grapes.
> His eyes are dull from wine,
> And his teeth white from milk."

These material blessings are similar to Edenic conditions before the fall. Normally, one would not tie a donkey to a vine since a valuable vine could be eaten or trampled. But when the special ruler reigns, vines will be so common they could be used as hitching posts for donkeys. No concern exists that donkeys will eat or trample the vines because even if they did it would not matter since vines are so abundant. In addition, wine will be so prevalent that clothes could be washed in them. Also, eyes will be affected by an abundance of wine, and teeth will be whiter because of all the milk consumed (49:12).

23 Ibid., 46-47.

24 Derek Kidner, *Genesis: An Introduction & Commentary*, in Tyndale Old Testament Commentaries, ed. D. J. Wiseman (Downers Grove, IL: InterVarsity, 1967), 219.

All these images, which in ancient times described great prosperity, indicate the kingdom will include lavish physical prosperity, like a restoration of Eden. Johnston is correct that "Here is the place where kingship and restoration of what was lost in Eden come together."[25] So physical prosperity is linked with the Messiah's reign. There is no dichotomy or dualism between the spiritual and physical. Imagery from Genesis 49:8–12 is found in Zechariah 9:9–10, which predicts a coming "king" who comes on a "donkey" who will have a "dominion" "from sea to sea" and "to the ends of the earth."

SUMMARY OF THE KINGDOM PROGRAM IN GENESIS 12–50

The kingdom program in Genesis 12–50 can be summarized as follows:

1. God's kingdom program narrows through Abraham and the great nation (Israel) that will come from him.
2. Abraham and the great nation will function as vehicles for the blessings of the families/nations of the earth.
3. Both Israel and Israel's land will function as microcosms of what God will do for all people groups.
4. The kingly line will come through Jacob's son, Judah, and his descendants, and will culminate in "one to whom it belongs."
5. The coming descendant of Judah will rule over the Gentiles and bring material prosperity.

25 Johnston, *Jesus the Messiah*, 43.

CHAPTER

6 THE KINGDOM AT THE TIME OF MOSES

Genesis ends with favorable conditions for the multiplying Hebrew people in Egypt. But Exodus opens with a new leader of Egypt feeling threatened by them. Pharaoh enslaved the Hebrews and brought great hardship to God's people. This was no surprise. Earlier God told Abraham that his descendants would be enslaved and oppressed in a land [Egypt] that was not theirs for four hundred years (Gen 15:13), but God would then judge their enemy and bring deliverance along with many possessions (Gen 15:14). Exodus picks up with the Hebrews being enslaved in Egypt and details God's punishment of Egypt and the deliverance of the developing people of Israel.

The books of Moses (Exodus, Leviticus, Numbers, and Deuteronomy) continue the storyline. God's kingdom plan involves the establishment of a "nation" that would be the means through which universal blessings would occur. But this nation needed to be set apart unto God for service. It must be different from the other nations. Israel needed to worship God and live righteously so other nations would be drawn to God. Before all this could happen they needed deliverance. Israel's role in the Abrahamic Covenant could never happen if the people remain enslaved in Egypt. The nation must be free to pursue its destiny.

Refusing warnings from Moses, Pharaoh would not let God's people go. So God executed His judgments against the gods of Egypt via the ten plagues and in doing so established His superiority over Egypt's gods. These demonstrations were signs of kingdom power from the sovereign God.

Moses led the people of Israel from slavery in Egypt to Mount Sinai where they received their covenant from God. Moses is not called a "king" but he functions in many ways like one. As the one to whom God spoke and gave His law on behalf of the people of Israel, Moses functioned as a mediatorial leader.

ISRAEL TO BE A KINGDOM OF PRIESTS (EXODUS 19:5–6)

God's encounter with Moses and the Hebrew people at Mount Sinai was a strategic moment in the kingdom program. Here God gives the Mosaic Covenant, which contained detailed laws to govern God's relationship with His people. This covenant was not a means for salvation. It was a gracious covenant given to a redeemed nation at this time.[1] Earlier God told Moses "when you have brought the people out of Egypt, you shall worship God at this mountain" (Exod 3:12b). That they were to worship God indicates the people were already in relationship with God. They had obeyed God by properly applying the Passover sacrifice to their doorposts, showing they had trusted in God and believed in His provision for deliverance, and through faith they crossed the Red Sea to escape the oncoming Egyptians. Before the first commandment was given God says, "I am the Lord your God" (Exod 20:2), showing a relationship between God and the people. The keeping of the law was to be a heartfelt act of worship, a required means of sanctification.[2] As Schreiner explains, "Such obedience is not legalistic but instead represents a grateful response to Yahweh's love and grace."[3]

At Sinai, Israel became a nation and a kingdom. Israel received its national constitution (the Mosaic Covenant) and was *en route* to possessing a land. Free from the tyranny of Egypt, Israel was to be the realm over

1 Block notes, "Obedience to the Decalogue... has never been intended as the way of salvation but as the appropriate response to salvation already received." Daniel I. Block, "Law, Ten Commandments, Torah," in *Holman Illustrated Bible Dictionary*, ed. Chad Brand, Charles Draper, and Archie England (Nashville, TN: Holman Bible Publishers, 2003), 1016.

2 See John S. Feinberg, "Salvation in the Old Testament," in *Tradition and Testament: Essays in Honor of Charles Lee Feinberg* (Chicago: Moody Press, 1981), 39–77.

3 Thomas R. Schreiner, *The King in His Beauty: A Biblical Theology of the Old and New Testaments* (Grand Rapids: Baker, 2013), 100.

which God's reign would function and the base from which God's kingdom purposes were to expand. It would be several centuries until Israel officially had a "king" like the rest of the nations, but Israel would now function as a kingdom. Moses was to be their leader. The kingdom concept is explicitly brought up in Exodus 19:5–6 where God says:

> "'Now then, if you will indeed obey My voice and keep My covenant, then you shall be My own possession among all the peoples, for all the earth is Mine; and you shall be to Me a kingdom of priests and a holy nation.' These are the words that you shall speak to the sons of Israel."

The purpose of this gracious covenant was so Israel could be God's "own possession," and fulfill an important role to "all the peoples." Israel should be "a kingdom of priests" and "a holy nation." This is the first time the term "kingdom" is explicitly used in regard to the rule of God and shows that what God is doing with Israel is part of His mediatorial kingdom program on earth.

A "priest" represents others before God. Israel was to carry a priestly role to other nations. As J. Dwight Pentecost observed, Israel was to be a kingdom of priests "that mediated the truth of God to the other nations of the earth."[4] In reference to Exodus 19:6 McClain points out, "it is not only that God will reign over one nation... but that through the nation thus ruled there will be mediated the blessings of God to all other nations."[5] Again, Israel is not a kingdom simply for its own sake. Israel has a place of privilege but this privilege was to result in blessing the world (see Rom 11:15). Deuteronomy 4:6–8 affirms this truth:

> So keep and do them [God's commandments], for that is your wisdom and your understanding *in the sight of the peoples* who will hear all these statutes and say, 'Surely this great nation is a wise and understanding people.' For what great nation is there that has a god so near to it as is the LORD our God whenever we call on Him? Or what great nation is there that has statutes

4 Pentecost, *Thy Kingdom Come*, 91.

5 McClain, *The Greatness of the Kingdom*, 62.

> and judgments as righteous as this whole law which I am setting before you today?[6]

As the nations looked upon Israel, they were to be drawn to Israel's God. This put great responsibility upon Israel. In sum, Exodus 19:5–6 proves that God's commandments via the Mosaic Covenant were not only for Israel's good but also for others. Failure to obey God's commandments would have an impact beyond Israel. If Israel failed to obey God not only will she harm herself, she will extinguish God's witness among the nations. The people accept this call willingly. According to Exodus 19:8 the people responded together: "All that the LORD has spoken we will do!"

MOSAIC LAW AND THE KINGDOM

So how does the Mosaic Covenant relate to the kingdom program? God's kingdom program includes several other covenants including the Noahic Covenant, the Abrahamic Covenant, the Davidic Covenant, and the New Covenant. These eternal and unconditional covenants are the means through which God's kingdom program is manifested. They are the *means* or *vehicles* through which the kingdom program is fulfilled.

The Mosaic Covenant is not an eternal and unconditional covenant, but it is connected with the Abrahamic Covenant that preceded it. *Obedience to the Mosaic Covenant was the means through which the people of Israel could remain connected to the blessings of the Abrahamic Covenant.* If Israel wanted to experience the blessings of the Abrahamic Covenant the people needed to heed the commands of the Mosaic Covenant.[7] If not, they would be judged and removed from its blessings. So the Mosaic Covenant was the opportunity for Israel to show obedience and righteousness. Unlike the Abrahamic Covenant, the Mosaic Covenant was a conditional covenant. That is why the Mosaic Covenant has "if... then" statements within it. "If" Israel obeys

6 Deuteronomy 26:19 declared, "He shall set you [Israel] high above all nations which He has made, for praise, fame, and honor."

7 Barrick rightly states, "In order to receive the promised blessings contained in the Abrahamic Covenant, Israel would have to obey the stipulations of the Mosaic Covenant. In other words, obedience to the Mosaic Covenant would be the means by which the Israelites would manifest their faith in the Abrahamic Covenant (cf. Jas 2:14–26)." William D. Barrick, "The Mosaic Covenant," *The Master's Seminary Journal* 10 (Fall 1999): 225.

"then" blessings will occur. But "if" the people do not obey, "then" curses and even dispersion to hostile gentile nations will occur. This is explained in Deuteronomy 28–29.

But Israel did not keep the Mosaic Covenant. So Israel experienced curses and dispersion. The Law of Moses was holy and good and a revealer of sin, yet it did not enable anyone to keep its commands. So there is the need of another covenant to enable the people to obey God. This is where the New Covenant enters. According to Jeremiah 31:31–34 God will make a New Covenant with Israel. It is distinct from the Mosaic Covenant—"'not like the covenant which I made with their fathers in the day I took them by the hand to bring them out of the land of Egypt, My covenant which they broke, although I was a husband to them,' declares the LORD" (Jer 31:32). Unlike the Mosaic Covenant, the New Covenant will enable Israel to obey God. It will enable them because God grants a new heart and His indwelling Holy Spirit.

Another reason exists for the Mosaic Covenant. In addition to being a revealer of sin and the temporary means by which Israel could remain related to the Abrahamic Covenant, it functioned as a temporary guardian for Israel until Jesus arrived (see Gal 3:23–25). The Mosaic Covenant period is pictured as an era of childhood while the era of Jesus and the New Covenant is viewed as the era of maturity.

CONTINGENCY AND THE KINGDOM (LEVITICUS 26)

Leviticus 26 discusses the relationship of the Abrahamic and Mosaic Covenants and predicts consequences to Israel for both obedience and disobedience. This chapter also reveals how Israel can once again experience the blessings of the Abrahamic Covenant after judgment and dispersion.

Verses 1–13 lay out the promise of blessings for obedience. If Israel walks in God's statutes and obeys His commandments, the people will be blessed in every way. They will experience national prosperity including abundant rain and harvests. The people will not fear wild animals or hostile people groups. They will also enjoy God's special presence—"I will also walk among you and be your God, and you shall be My people" (26:12). In short, obedience to the Mosaic Law will lead to remaining in the promises of the Abrahamic Covenant.

Yet Leviticus 26 also spells out devastating curses for disobedience (26:14–39). These include a reversal of all the blessings described in Leviticus 26:1–13. This also involves removal from the land of promise and dispersion to the nations:

> "But you will perish among the nations, and your enemies' land will consume you. So those of you who may be left will rot away because of their iniquity in the lands of your enemies...." (Lev 26:38–39).

In short, disobedience to the law means removal from the blessings of the Abrahamic Covenant. There will be removal from the land and captivity to other nations. Becoming landless was a shocking promise. After all, the people were dramatically rescued from captivity in Egypt. Would captivity really happen again? Yes. Israel would not be exempt from punishment for disobedience. They could find themselves in a similar position with a need for another wake up call. As Barrick rightly notes, "The nation's apathy toward Yahweh and His covenants would result in God making them landless again. In order to cure their selective amnesia, Yahweh would return them to the bondage from which He had delivered them."[8]

But Israel's date with captivity will not be permanent. Divine retribution has the goal of repentance. Verses 40–45 discuss a conditional element that, when satisfied, leads to a reversal of Israel's banishment to the nations. This section assumes a coming dispersion of Israel to the nations. But God declares that "if" the people repent and come to Him in faith then He will restore Israel and place them again in the blessings of the Abrahamic Covenant:

> "If they confess their iniquity and the iniquity of their forefathers, in their unfaithfulness which they committed against Me, and also in their acting with hostility against Me—I also was acting with hostility against them, to bring them into the land of their enemies—or if their uncircumcised heart becomes

8 William D. Barrick, "The Eschatological Significance of Leviticus 26," *The Master's Seminary Journal* 16 (2005): 99. Brueggemann states, "It is hard enough for landed people to believe land will be lost. It is harder to imagine Yahweh will do it." Walter Brueggemann, *The Land: Place as Gift, Promise, and Challenge in Biblical Faith* (Philadelphia: Fortress, 1977), 113.

> humbled so that they then make amends for their iniquity, then I will remember My covenant with Jacob, and I will remember also My covenant with Isaac, and My covenant with Abraham as well, and I will remember the land" (Lev 26:40–42).

The return to blessing does not happen automatically. Israel must come to her senses with a humble and contrite heart. There needs to be national repentance and acknowledgement that not only has the current generation sinned, but those before sinned too. If Israel does this God will remember His covenant with Abraham. This return to Abrahamic Covenant blessings includes "the land" which God remembers to give Israel (v. 43). Just as the consequences of Israel's disobedience involve dispersion to other lands, repentance will lead to restoration in the land of promise. To compare (→ = "results in"):

Israel's disobedience → Israel being taken captive
in the land of their enemies

Followed by:

Israel's repentance → Israel returning to the land of promise

The reason there must be a restoration of Israel to the Promised Land is because God is faithful to His promises:

> "Yet in spite of this, when they are in the land of their enemies, I will not reject them, nor will I so abhor them as to destroy them, breaking My covenant with them; for I am the LORD their God. But I will remember for them the covenant with their ancestors, whom I brought out of the land of Egypt in the sight of the nations, that I might be their God. I am the LORD" (Lev 26:44–45).

If God were to leave Israel in permanent dispersion, He would break His unconditional covenant with Abraham. But that cannot happen. Instead, God will "remember" His covenant with Israel's ancestors and bring Israel back to their Promised Land. That God connects this promise with what He did for Israel is also important. As Barrick points out, "The

Land-Giver and Exodus-Causer will always be loyal to His covenants and to His covenant people."[9]

Paul will reaffirm God's covenant faithfulness to Israel in Romans 11. After declaring a day is coming when "all Israel will be saved" (Rom 11:26), he ties this with God's faithfulness: "but from the standpoint of God's choice they [Israel] are beloved for the sake of the fathers; for the gifts and the calling of God are irrevocable" (11:28b–29).

This leads to an important question. Is Israel's repentance a pre-condition for the establishment of the Messianic Kingdom? The answer is, Yes. "The restoration of Israel from worldwide dispersion will depend upon repentance (cf. Jer 3:11–18; Hos 5:13–6:3; Zech 12:1–10)."[10] Arnold Fruchtenbaum notes that "confession of Israel's national sin" is "a major precondition that must be met before Christ will return to establish the Messianic Kingdom."[11] This truth will relate to Jesus' declaration, "Repent for the kingdom of heaven is at hand" (Matt 4:17). Jesus will call for national repentance, which is necessary for the arrival of the kingdom.

A COMING KING FROM ISRAEL (NUMBERS 24:3–9, 17–19)

Numbers 24 foretells a coming kingdom involving Israel. The message comes from a Gentile prophet, Balaam, recruited by Balak, king of Moab, to curse the Israelites moving through his land. Concerning Israel Balaam declared: "And his king shall be higher than Agag, and his kingdom shall be exalted" (24:7). Balaam predicts a "king" and "kingdom" for Israel. He foretells the domination of this king of Israel: "He will devour the nations who are his adversaries, and will crush their bones in pieces, and shatter them with his arrows" (24:8). Balaam then uses "lion" language for Israel:

---

9 Barrick, "The Eschatological Significance of Leviticus 26," 97.

10 Ibid., 124.

11 Arnold G. Fruchtenbaum, *Israelology: The Missing Link in Systematic Theology* (Tustin, CA: Ariel Ministries Press, 1989), 784, 781. Saucy writes, "This restoration is conditioned on the confession and humbling of the hearts of the people, but the final outcome is assured." Robert L. Saucy, *The Case for Progressive Dispensationalism: The Interface between Dispensational & Non-Dispensational Theology* (Grand Rapids: Zondervan, 1993), 222.

"He couches, he lies down as a lion, and as a lion, who dares rouse him?" (24:9). The connection with Jacob's declaration in Genesis 49:9 is evident:

> Judah is a lion's whelp;
> From the prey, my son, you have gone up.
> He couches, he lies down as a lion,
> And as a lion, who dares rouse him up? (Gen 49:9).

As Balaam foresees the power of the kingdom of Israel, he tells Balak what this means for his people "in the days to come" (24:14):

> I see him, but not now;
> I behold him, but not near;
> A star shall come forth from Jacob,
> A scepter shall rise from Israel,
> And shall crush through the forehead of Moab,
> And tear down all the sons of Sheth (Num 24:17).

Balaam prophesied of a future king from Israel. With insight from God Balaam could "see him" and "behold him" even if his manifestation was "not now" or "not near." This coming king is described by royal terms—a "star" and "scepter." Numbers 24:19 also states, "One from Jacob shall have dominion."

God used this pagan prophet to reaffirm an earlier truth from Genesis 49:10—a king will arise from Israel who will have victory and dominion over Israel's enemies. These predictions of Israel's kingdom concerning Moabites, Edomites, and Canaanites would be related to early Israelite kings, particularly David who would lead Israel in victory. But although Israel would experience victory at times over these groups and other Gentile enemies, complete victory was not accomplished, hinting that complete fulfillment was still pending. The full fulfillment of the Numbers 24 prophecies points forward to the ultimate Son of David, the eschatological Messiah—Jesus. He is the "Lion" (Rev 5:5) and the "Star" (Rev 22:16) who brings these prophecies to ultimate fulfillment.

INSTRUCTIONS FOR WHEN ISRAEL HAS A KING (DEUTERONOMY 17:14–20)

God gave Israel instructions for the coming time when a monarch would rule in Israel (see Deut 17:14–20). There was a coming day when Israel would "enter the land" and live in it (17:14). God planned for Israel to have a king. But there were criteria for this king:

- He must be chosen by the Lord (15).
- He must be an Israelite and not a foreigner (15).
- He was not to multiply horses to avoid trusting in military might and not the Lord (16).
- He was not to multiply wives lest they turn his heart away from the Lord (17).
- He was not to multiply silver and gold. He was to diligently obey the words of the law (18–19).
- Doing these things meant longevity for him and his sons (20).

These commands would be relevant in Samuel–Kings when the monarchy in Israel was inaugurated. Solomon's reign would show why it was important for these commands to be obeyed. Solomon would violate these regulations and sow seeds for the decline of Israel's kingdom.

ISRAEL'S SCATTERING AND RESTORATION

Israel was to be a means of blessing the nations, and the Mosaic Covenant was the means through which Israel could remain linked to the blessings of the Abrahamic Covenant. Yet Deuteronomy contains prophetic sections that foretell Israel's failure. This includes Israel's expulsion from their land for covenant disobedience. But what does this mean for the kingdom program? Does Israel's failure and expulsion from the land mean the kingdom program will fail? Not at all. Two sections in Deuteronomy offer a broad panorama of what will happen to Israel. This includes scattering to the nations followed by restoration.

Deuteronomy 4:25–31

With Deuteronomy 4:25–31 God predicted the distant future for Israel. After several generations and after Israel "remained long in the land," God said Israel would "act corruptly" and "do that which is evil in the sight of the Lord" (4:25). This would lead to God scattering the people among the nations (4:27). From there Israel would serve the gods of the nations (4:28). But this is not the end for Israel. God states that in "the latter days," while Israel is in distress, the people will "return to the Lord your God" (4:30). Then God, with compassion, will remember the "covenant" He made with Israel's "fathers" (4:31).

This shows Israel's place in God's plans is not to be nullified through disobedience. Even though Israel will be dispersed to the nations and worship other gods, they will in "the latter days" (4:30) return to the Lord and God will honor the Abrahamic Covenant. This is a specific prediction that must be fulfilled with the nation Israel. God will never permanently reject Israel although He may punish the people for a time. The people to whom the kingdom promises are being mediated will fall on hard times because of wickedness, but God's faithfulness will lead to restoration.

Deuteronomy 30:1–10

Deuteronomy 30:1–10 contains a 'big picture' prophecy concerning God's future plans for Israel and mirrors the prophetic truths of Deuteronomy 4:25–31, yet with more details. Its themes of *dispersion, gathering, and restoration* also are emphasized in later revelation (see Ezekiel 36). As such, it is one of the most important prophetic sections in Scripture.

Deuteronomy 30 describes what will happen to Israel after Israel has been blessed and then later dispersed to the nations because of disobedience. This is striking since at the time of this revelation the Israelites had not even started the conquest of the Promised Land. They were not even in the land yet and God tells them what will happen in the distant future after they are dispersed from their land.

Deuteronomy 28 and 29 tell of blessings and curses that await Israel for both covenant obedience and disobedience. Then with Deuteronomy 30:1 God predicts Israel will be "banished" "in all nations." This predicts not only banishment to one nation but a widespread dispersion. Certainly, this occurred collectively with the Assyrian and Babylonian captivities along with dispersions that occurred in A.D. 70 and 135.

Verse 2 then says the people of Israel will "return" to the Lord "and obey Him with all your heart and soul." The same Israel that will be dispersed will evidence heart-felt repentance and return to God. This leads to restoration—"then the LORD your God will restore you from captivity" (30:3). The concept of "restoration" refers to a reversal of fortunes. The tragic condition of banishment will give way to restoration. This restoration of Israel is a major theme of later prophets:

> **Jer 16:15**: but, "As the LORD lives, who brought up the sons of Israel from the land of the north and from all the countries where He had banished them. For I will *restore them to their own land* which I gave to their fathers."

> **Jer 30:3**: "For behold, days are coming," declares the LORD, "when I will *restore the fortunes of My people Israel and Judah.*" The LORD says, "I will also bring them back to the *land* that I gave to their forefathers and they shall possess it."

> **Ezek 38:8**: After many days you will be summoned; in the latter years you will come into the *land that is restored* from the sword.

> **Amos 9:14**: "Also I will *restore* the captivity of My *people Israel*, And they will *rebuild the ruined cities* and live in them."

> **Acts 3:21**: "whom heaven must receive until the period of *restoration of all things* about which God spoke by the mouth of His holy prophets from ancient time."

Deuteronomy 30:3b also states that God will "gather you again from all the peoples where the Lord your God has scattered you." This is explained more in v. 4 as God says He will "gather" His people from "the ends of the earth." The concept of the gathering of Israel from the nations is an important theme weaved throughout the rest of Scripture:

> **Isa 11:12**: And He will lift up a standard for the nations and assemble the banished ones of Israel, and will gather the dispersed of Judah from the four corners of the earth.

> **Jer 29:14**: "I will be found by you," declares the LORD, "and I will restore your fortunes and will gather you from all the nations and from all the places where I have driven you," declares the LORD, "and I will bring you back to the place from where I sent you into exile."
>
> **Jer 31:10**: Hear the word of the LORD, O nations, and declare in the coastlands afar off, And say, "He who scattered Israel will gather him."
>
> **Ezek 11:17**: Therefore say, "Thus says the Lord GOD, 'I will gather you from the peoples and assemble you out of the countries among which you have been scattered, and I will give you the land of Israel.'"
>
> **Ezek 20:34**: "I will bring you out from the peoples and gather you from the lands where you are scattered, with a mighty hand and with an outstretched arm and with wrath poured out."
>
> **Ezek 36:24**: "For I will take you from the nations, gather you from all the lands and bring you into your own land."
>
> **Matt 24:31**: "And He will send forth His angels with a great trumpet and they will gather together His elect from the four winds, from one end of the sky to the other."

Deuteronomy 30:5 then discuss Israel's physical restoration back to its land with physical prosperity:

> "The LORD your God will bring you into the land which your fathers possessed, and you shall possess it; and He will prosper you and multiply you more than your fathers."

Israel and her land are inseparable. *A dispersion from the land must be reversed by a restoration to the land.* If one happens, so too must the other. God links the return of Israel to the land with the land of the "fathers." The "fathers" are the patriarchs of Israel. Thus, the land promise of the Abrahamic Covenant must be fulfilled. But the regathering and restoration of Israel to the land of promise can only occur with spiritual salvation and a new heart:

"Moreover the Lord your God will circumcise your heart and the heart of your descendants, to love the Lord your God with all your heart and with all your soul, so that you may live" (Deut 30:6).

Deuteronomy 30:6 is the first reference to the New Covenant in the Bible although it is not named such here (see Jer 31:31–34). Israel's problem has always been a heart issue. Israel did not obey the Mosaic Covenant because hearts were sinful. Yet a day is coming when God will remedy the heart problem by circumcising hearts.[12] When He does this, the people will truly love Him with their hearts and obey Him willingly.

In sum, Deuteronomy 30 displays two main truths. First, Israel's disobedience and dispersion to the nations does not mean the end of the nation's significance. This refutes the idea that God will permanently reject Israel because of Israel's disobedience. The nation that was judged is the same nation that will be regathered from dispersion and restored.

Second, both physical blessings and spiritual salvation are promised to Israel. Israel will again possess the land of promise and prosper there. Israel also will experience circumcision of the heart that involves regeneration and salvation. This heart circumcision anticipates the promise of Jeremiah 31:31–34 and the New Covenant blessing of a new heart. Israel will be saved spiritually and restored back to its land with physical blessings. This is a both/and situation. In verse 9 God promises to bless the work of their hands, the offspring of their bodies, the offspring of their cattle, and the produce of the ground. Spiritual salvation is at the root of these physical blessings but these physical blessings are real and there is no reason to deny their literal fulfillment.

SUMMARY OF THE KINGDOM PROGRAM IN THE ERA OF MOSES

The era of Moses is about the exodus from Egypt and the establishment of Israel as a kingdom of priests. Israel also received the Mosaic Covenant. Important prophecies were given concerning Israel's future disobedience and scattering. Israel's regathering and restoration will follow these. As

12 Heart circumcision is related to the concept of regeneration in which God causes a person or group to become alive spiritually.

Moses passes off the scene the leadership torch will be passed to Joshua who will lead the people into the Promised Land. The kingdom program in the era of Moses can be summarized as follows:

1. God's plan to develop a great nation occurs as the Hebrew people grow in number.
2. God delivers His people from Egypt so they can be a nation and a kingdom before Him not only for their benefit but also for the nations.
3. God calls Israel to be a kingdom of priests to represent God before the nations.
4. God graciously gives Israel the Mosaic Covenant so the people can express their devotion to God and be distinct and separate from the other nations.
5. Israel is promised blessings for obedience and curses for disobedience to the Mosaic Covenant.
6. God promises Israel that after she is dispersed to the nations for disobedience she will be saved and restored in the latter times; dispersion is followed by restoration.
7. God gives instructions for when Israel will have a king.

CHAPTER 7

THE KINGDOM FROM ISRAEL'S CONQUEST THROUGH CAPTIVITY

The era of Moses experienced the development of Israel as a great nation. Israel received the Mosaic Covenant and the promise of many descendants was being fulfilled. With Moses' death the emphasis shifts to fulfillment of Israel's land promises. This occurs under Joshua as Israel occupies the land. Israel goes through a period of ups and downs under the judges and then the monarchy begins under Saul. Saul, though, acts wickedly and God uses David for His kingdom purposes. Through David, the Davidic Covenant promises an eternal kingdom for Israel in the line of David and blessings to mankind. Under the third king, Solomon, Israel begins to fulfill the promise of blessing the nations. But disobedience by Solomon and Israel alters Israel's trajectory and leads to a divided kingdom and withdrawal of God's blessings. Israel and Judah are both headed to captivity. Yet God is faithful to His promises although His people are not always faithful to Him.

JOSHUA

The end of Deuteronomy witnessed a transition in the mediatorial kingdom plan of God. The leadership torch is passed from Moses to Joshua. Deuteronomy 34:9 notes this: "Now Joshua the son of Nun was filled with the spirit of wisdom, for Moses had laid his hands on him; and the sons of Israel listened to him and did as the Lord had commanded Moses." As J.

Dwight Pentecost observes, "This verse identifies Joshua as Moses' successor in the line of theocratic leadership."[1]

The book of Joshua affirms God's plans to fulfill the land promises of the Abrahamic Covenant. The term for "land" (*eretz*) occurs 102 times in Joshua. Schreiner notes, "The importance of land in Joshua can scarcely be overestimated."[2] Thus, Joshua is a book "consumed with the place where Yahweh rules over his people."[3]

Under Joshua, Israel possessed the Promised Land. The people removed their enemies and experienced the fulfillment of God's promises. In addition to Joshua's leadership in the conquest, dividing the land was also his role. "Dividing the land among the conquering tribes was a sign of his theocratic leadership."[4]

The events of Joshua reveal God is the ultimate King. Israel's success occurs because God is a divine warrior who fights for Israel. For example, the tactics of the battle of Jericho (see Josh 6), where the people walked around the walls of Jericho for seven days and then blew trumpets to make the walls fall, testify that victory is not based on Israel's genius or power. Such a tactic seems absurd from a human perspective. But God uses this to show victory belongs to Him.

However, Israel fell short by not removing the Canaanites fully as the Lord commanded. Thus, the conquest was successful but incomplete. God kept His promises, yet the people did not always keep theirs. This failure to obey would later haunt Israel and contribute to the idolatry and downfall of the kingdom.

The land was an essential aspect of the Abrahamic Covenant and Israel was to possess it just as God said. Since God promised that Israel's occupation of the land would be followed by dispersion and then restoration to the land at a later time (Deut 30), the initial conquest of the land in Joshua was not the final fulfillment of the Abrahamic Covenant.

---

1 Pentecost, *Thy Kingdom Come*, 124.

2 Schreiner, *The King in His Beauty*, 107. He is also correct that "the land is no abstraction" (108).

3 Ibid. 108.

4 Pentecost, *Thy Kingdom Come*, 125.

The prophets continue to emphasize the prominence of the land for Israel because of the patriarchs (see Jer 16:15).

JUDGES

Judges details the ups and downs (mostly downs) of Israel's experiences in the land under the leadership of the judges (see Judg 2:16). In spite of warnings that disobedience would lead to judgment, the people continued to sin, and the scourge of God's judgment would occur. Yet during times of peril for Israel the people would cry out for deliverance and a judge was raised up for this purpose. God himself is the ultimate Judge (see Gen 18:25), and the judges, while imperfect in character, would reflect important characteristics of this role, particularly that of *deliverer*. Each deliverance by a judge was a reminder of God's faithfulness to the Abrahamic Covenant. While God's people would be judged for disobedience, judgment could not lead to irreversible destruction.[5]

The judges possessed authority since the Lord was with them (Judg 2:18). They served as mediators of God's plans and leaders of Israel until the establishment of the monarchy. On multiple occasions the Spirit of God controlled the judges. In regard to Othniel, Judges 3:10 states, "The Spirit of the LORD came upon him, and he judged Israel."[6] Yet these judges did not possess dynastic rights. On one occasion the people asked for a dynasty from Gideon: "Then the men of Israel said to Gideon, 'Rule over us, both you and your son, also your son's son, for you have delivered us from the hand of Midian.'" (Judg 8:22). Yet Gideon rightly refused: "But Gideon said to them, 'I will not rule over you, nor shall my son rule over you; the Lord shall rule over you'" (Judg 8:23). As Pentecost observes, "Gideon rightly refused to become a king, but he did not refuse to be a judge. Gideon obviously knew that the right to rule did not come from the people, but rather from his appointment by God."[7]

5 "If the Abrahamic Covenant could be canceled because of disobedience, God would never have raised up a judge. He would, instead, have let Israel be destroyed and accomplish His purpose through other means." Pentecost, *Thy Kingdom Come*, 127.

6 See also Judges 6:34; 11:29; 13:25; 14:6, 19; 15:14.

7 Ibid. 131.

The judges played an important part in God's kingdom program. They were deliverers who restored the people when they repented. Yet it is significant that "there was no king in Israel" (17:6; 18:1; 19:1; 21:25). This was a hint "the judges were not a permanent solution for Israel's problem."[8] They functioned as a bridge to a coming new form of theocratic rule in Israel—the monarchy administered by kings.[9]

RUTH

In the Septuagint and English Bible, Ruth is sandwiched between Judges and 1–2 Samuel. Judges revealed the poor state of Israel without a king while 1–2 Samuel introduced the monarchy to Israel. Ruth offers a transition between the two. Through a set of events that reveal the sovereign hand of God, Ruth, a Moabite woman, experiences God's grace and marries Boaz. Through this union Ruth gave birth to Obed, the grandfather of David, the man after God's own heart with whom the Davidic Covenant would be made. The book of Ruth, therefore, contributes to the kingdom program. The woman, Ruth, is an ancestor of David. Second, Ruth becomes an example of God's grace to those outside of Israel. From Ruth "a future son of David would bring many more Ruths, many more Gentiles into the fold of God's people, and fulfill the promise of universal blessing made to Abraham."[10]

1 AND 2 SAMUEL

Sinful Israel floundered in the period of the judges when there was no king. The book of Ruth offered hope by showing how Ruth and Boaz were ancestors of the coming king David. With the books of Samuel a transition occurs from the judges to the monarchy in Israel. Thus, 1 and 2 Samuel concern the early stages of the kingdom in Israel, focusing on the significance of David and the Davidic Covenant. They reveal that God's presence and kingdom program will be mediated through kings.

---

8 Schreiner, *The King in His Beauty*, 127.

9 See Pentecost, *Thy Kingdom Come*, 131.

10 Pentecost, *Thy Kingdom Come*, 135.

Key kingdom truths are found at both the beginning and the end. Two songs, one by Hannah at the beginning (see 1 Sam 2:1–10) and one by David at the conclusion (see 2 Sam 22), are bookend summations of the kingdom in Israel. Also significant are David's final words in 23:1–7. These sections "function as an inclusio that brackets the entire work."[11]

The song of Hannah has personal, national, and universal implications. Hannah extols God's goodness to her (2:1). She then tells of how God vindicates the righteous and humbles the wicked (2:3–9). With verse 10 she predicts two things: (1) coming global judgment and (2) the exaltation of God's anointed king[12]:

> "Those who contend with the Lord will be shattered;
> Against them He will thunder in the heavens,
> The Lord will judge the ends of the earth;
> And He will give strength to His king,
> And will exalt the horn of His anointed" (1 Sam 2:10).

Hannah's expectation of an anointed king shows it was God's plan for Israel to have a king. The books of Samuel are not anti-monarchial. Deuteronomy 17 predicted Israel would someday have a king, and that was realized in Saul. The people desired to have a king like the rest of the nations (1 Sam 8:1–9), and God allowed Saul to become Israel's first king. God viewed this request as a rejection of himself—"they have rejected Me from being king over them" (8:7). But as David Howard has pointed out, "The problem with this request was not that God was against kingship *per se*.... The problem with the request for kingship in 1 Samuel 8 was the motivations behind it. The people wanted a king to rule over them 'like all the nations.'"[13] Their hope was in a human king, not the Lord.

Saul's reign is the subject of 1 Samuel 10–31. Saul was anointed as king "and the Spirit of God came upon him mightily" (1 Sam 10:10). His reign over Israel is significant historically. For the first time since Joshua,

11 Schreiner, *The King in His Beauty*, 137.

12 Kaiser, *The Messiah in the Old Testament*, 72.

13 David M. Howard, *An Introduction to the Old Testament Historical Books* (Chicago: Moody, 1993), 158–59.

Israel had a permanent national military leader.[14] His reign "was an important step in the transition from the system of judges to the establishment of the monarchy."[15]

Yet Saul was not a godly king.[16] After waiting seven days for Samuel to arrive and offer sacrifices before a battle with the Philistines, Saul assumed the priestly office and offered sacrifices himself. He wrongly assumed the duties of the priesthood. Samuel strongly rebuked Saul and told him, "The Lord would have established your kingdom over Israel forever. But now your kingdom shall not endure" (13:13–14a). This statement is striking since God revealed in Genesis 49:10 that the kingdom line would run through Judah. Saul, however, was from the tribe of Benjamin. This appears to be a case of contingency in which God offers a legitimate blessing, but the promised blessing is withdrawn because of sin. Saul could have experienced an eternal dynasty but his actions disqualified him from it. This took place under God's sovereignty, but Saul's disobedience disqualified him from a blessing that was genuinely offered.

With 1 Samuel 16:1–13 the Lord sent Samuel to Bethlehem to anoint the next king. David, the eighth and youngest son of Jesse, was chosen. Unlike Saul, David was a man after God's own heart. And unlike Saul, David was from the tribe of Judah and was qualified for the kingship via the line of Judah (see Gen 49:10). When Samuel anointed David, "the Spirit of the Lord came mightily upon David from that day forward" (16:13). And consequently, "the Spirit of the Lord departed from Saul" (16:14).

David was anointed as king before he actually reigned as king. Of course, there is a strong connection between the concepts of anointing and reigning, but in David's case, there is a time gap between his anointing and his reign as king over Israel. For a time, Saul still remained king over Israel although the Spirit of God had been removed from him. David himself still recognized Saul's position as king while Saul was alive. This may

14 Phil Logan and E. Ray Clendenen, "King, Kingship," in *Holman Illustrated Bible Dictionary*, ed. Chad Brand, Charles Draper, and Archie England (Nashville, TN: Holman Reference, 2003), 986.

15 Ibid.

16 Schreiner argues that Saul "was like Adam and like Israel." *The King in His Beauty*, 149. He also states that the Saul vs. David drama "reflects the conflict between the offspring of the serpent (Saul) and the offspring of the woman (David), showing the triumph of the latter even through persecution" (148).

have implications for the greater David, Jesus Christ, who will be exalted as Messiah with His ascension (see Acts 2) while His messianic reign awaits a future time at His second coming (see Matt 25:31).

The transition from Saul to David represents another stage in the development of the monarchy in Israel. Unlike Saul, David fused the loose twelve tribes of Israel into a nation. He unified the northern and southern tribes and established a court and a standing army.[17] David captured Jerusalem and made it the religious and political capital of Israel. Logan and Clendenen observe that when David eventually passes the power of the kingdom to his son, Solomon, "the transition from the system of the judges to that of the monarchy was complete."[18] From here on the position of king was both hereditary and for life.

THE DAVIDIC COVENANT (2 SAMUEL 7)

Second Samuel details David's reign over Judah and then all Israel. Chapter 7 is one of the most significant passages concerning the kingdom of God in the Bible. With the Davidic Covenant, God promises David a dynasty and kingdom that will never end. Earlier, Genesis 17:6 and 35:11 promised kings would come from Abraham's descendants. Genesis 49:10 declared the "scepter" would come through Judah's line. Balaam promised a "star" and "scepter" would come from Israel (Num 24). These texts pointed toward the Davidic Covenant.

The heart of the Davidic Covenant is found in 2 Samuel 7:12–16, yet what precedes and follows are important as well. With 7:9, God told David, "I will make you a great name." This parallels the promise to Abraham that God would make his name great (see Gen 12:2). God then pronounced coming prosperity and security for Israel in verse 10: "I will also appoint a place for My people Israel and will plant them, that they may live in their own place and not be disturbed again, nor will the wicked afflict them any more as formerly." Peace and protection for the nation Israel is strategic to the covenant. This promise, too, shows a connection with the Abrahamic Covenant. Israel will be planted in her own land and will never be removed

17 Logan and Clendenen, "King, Kingship," 986.

18 Ibid..

or disturbed again. The Davidic Covenant also will have implications beyond Israel for the Gentiles (see 7:19), yet the nation Israel is promised both prosperity and security.

With 2 Samuel 7:12–16 God tells David:

> "When your days are complete and you lie down with your fathers, I will raise up your descendant after you, who will come forth from you, and I will establish his kingdom. He shall build a house for My name, and I will establish the throne of his kingdom forever. I will be a father to him and he will be a son to Me; when he commits iniquity, I will correct him with the rod of men and the strokes of the sons of men, but My lovingkindness shall not depart from him, as I took it away from Saul, whom I removed from before you. Your house and your kingdom shall endure before Me forever; your throne shall be established forever."

Johnston observes "three central promises" here: "(1) God would secure the throne of David and his son (Solomon) in a context of peace; (2) God would provide David an heir (Solomon) who would build the temple; and (3) God would provide a perpetual dynasty for David."[19]

David is the focal point of this covenant but it also extends beyond David's earthly life since God mentions David's death and coming son. Plus, 7:19 says these words include "the distant future." David's immediate descendant is Solomon who would build the temple. Solomon also committed acts worthy of correction.

The "forever" language of this covenant demands that this passage looks beyond Solomon to an even greater Son of David. God promised David that his "house and kingdom shall endure before Me forever" and his "throne shall be established forever." The "house" is a reference to a dynasty, and a dynasty looks beyond first and second generations. The kingdom will remain within the line of David. Since both David and Solomon and other descendants of David have died, the ultimate fulfillment of this covenant must be met in One who is eternal. Did David consciously understand this? Much debate exists on this issue but the best answer is that he

19 Johnston, *Jesus the Messiah*, 69.

did. In Acts 2, Peter explicitly stated that David "looked ahead" as a prophet and "spoke of" Jesus Christ as the fulfillment of the covenant:

> "Brethren, I may confidently say to you regarding the patriarch David that he both died and was buried, and his tomb is with us to this day. And so, because he was a prophet and knew that GOD HAD SWORN TO HIM WITH AN OATH TO SEAT one OF HIS DESCENDANTS ON HIS THRONE, he looked ahead and spoke of the resurrection of the Christ..." (Acts 2:29–31).

According to Peter, David was a prophet who understood a future son would sit on his throne. David possessed prophetic knowledge of Jesus' resurrection. That Jesus is the one to whom the Davidic Covenant pointed is explicitly stated in Luke 1:32–33. Here the angel Gabriel told Mary:

> He [Jesus] will be great and will be called the Son of the Most High; and the Lord God will give Him the throne of His father David; and He will reign over the house of Jacob forever, and His kingdom will have no end."

Gentiles to Be Blessed

The Davidic Covenant includes promises for David, Solomon, and Israel as a nation. But they are not the only ones to benefit from it. In his prayer, David stated: "What You have done so far was a little thing to You, Lord GOD, for You have also spoken about Your servant's house in the distant future. And this is a revelation for mankind, Lord GOD" (v. 19) (HCSB). This "revelation for mankind" or "charter for mankind"[20] reveals that the Davidic Covenant has universal implications beyond Israel. Gentiles, too, will be blessed by it.

David marveled at the greatness of God's promise and its universal implications for mankind. The Davidic Covenant parallels the Abrahamic Covenant in bringing blessings for both Israel and all mankind. As Kaiser

20 Paul Williamson translates this as "this is the instruction of/for humanity" and "relates to David's exalted status in the larger scheme of things." Paul R. Williamson, *Sealed with an Oath: Covenant in God's Unfolding Purpose* (Downers Grove, IL: InterVarsity, 2007), 129.

notes, "Just as God has promised Abraham and his line that all mortals would be blessed through his seed (Gen 12:3; 18:18; 22:17–18; 26:3–4; 28:13–14), even so God had announced to David that the 'multitude of nations' who would believe in the Seed that came from his line would be part of the 'charter for all humanity.'"[21] Later, Amos predicted the rebuilt Davidic dynasty would mean the inclusion of Gentiles into the people of God alongside Israel (see Amos 9:11–12). So then, *the Davidic Covenant was given to David and the nation Israel. But this covenant would not be only for Israel. Mankind as a whole would benefit from this Davidic Covenant.* As Robert Saucy explains:

> ... the Davidic promise has universal dimensions. It was not limited to a narrow nationalism that concerned only the kingdom of Israel. Rather, the blessing of the righteous rule of the promised Davidic seed was to extend to all nations.[22]

Truths concerning the Davidic Covenant are also found in the Royal Psalms of 2, 45, 72, 89, 110, and 132. Second Samuel ends with a psalm of David (ch. 22) and David's final words (23:1–7). David reaffirms God's goodness and the everlasting covenant God made with him. Schreiner summarizes well the purpose of 1–2 Samuel in God's plan to fulfill the Abrahamic Covenant promise of universal blessings:

> What 1–2 Samuel has made clear is that this universal blessing will stream to the world through a king from David's line. The covenant with David (2 Sam 7), which promises that a son from his line will rule, will be the means by which the covenant with Abraham becomes a reality.[23]

21 Walter C. Kaiser, Jr., "Single Meaning, Unified Referents," in *Three Views on the New Testament Use of the Old Testament*, ed. Kenneth Berding and Jonathan Lunde (Grand Rapids: Zondervan, 2007), 71–72. Williamson writes that "the dynastic promise has ramifications beyond Israel's borders; it is tied in somehow with God's universal purpose in creation and the prospect of international blessing promised through Abraham (Gen 12:3) and his royal seed (Gen 22:18)." Williamson, *Sealed with an Oath*, 129.

22 Robert L. Saucy, *The Case for Progressive Dispensationalism*, 62.

23 Schreiner, *The King in His Beauty*, 164.

1 AND 2 KINGS

With 1 Chronicles 28:1, an aged David assembled the officials of Israel at Jerusalem to instruct them concerning Solomon's role in the kingdom. David said, "Of all my sons (for the Lord has given me many sons), He has chosen my son Solomon to sit on the throne of the kingdom of the Lord over Israel" (28:5). David used the words, "kingdom of the Lord" to show the kingdom stemming from the Davidic Covenant was God's kingdom. Martin J. Selman says two features are "noteworthy" from this verse. First, the phrase "throne of the kingdom" shows "that the term 'throne' is a fixed symbol of a kingdom."[24] Second, "God's kingdom is 'over Israel.'" This means "the human kingdom of Israel currently ruled by the ailing warrior David and the inexperienced youth Solomon was in some mysterious way closely bound up with the kingdom of God."[25] First Chronicles 29:23 states, "Then Solomon sat on the throne of the Lord as king," again showing the throne in Jerusalem was God's throne.

Later, in 2 Chronicles 13:8, Solomon's grandson Abijah, king of Judah, told the northern kingdom of Israel, "So now you intend to resist the kingdom of the Lord through the sons of David." While Abijah was not a godly king (see 1 Kgs 15:3), this still shows the connection between the kings in the line of David and Solomon and the kingdom of God.[26]

Solomon and the Kingdom High Point (1 Kings 1–10)

With David's impending death, God guided and protected Solomon as David's successor to the throne. The early Solomon "loved the LORD, walking in the statutes of his father David" (1 Kgs 3:3). God was pleased with Solomon and his request for wisdom and understanding to judge God's people. He granted Solomon the greatest wisdom on the earth (see 1 Kgs 3).

At this time Israel was at its greatest both materially and militarily. The conditions in 1 Kings 4–10 are significant. These were glorious days, almost Eden-like times for Israel. The three main provisions of the Abrahamic Covenant—land, seed, and universal blessing—appeared on

24 Martin J. Selman, "The Kingdom of God in the Old Testament," *Tyndale Bulletin* 40 (1989): 163.

25 Ibid.

26 Ibid, 163–64.

track for fulfillment. First, Israel was in the land of promise. According to 1 Kings 4:21, "Solomon ruled over all the kingdoms from the River to the land of the Philistines and to the border of Egypt." Although not quite at the dimensions promised in Genesis 15 the land promise was being fulfilled splendidly. Second, the seed promise was developing: "Judah and Israel were as numerous as the sand that is on the seashore in abundance; they were eating and drinking and rejoicing" (1 Kgs 4:20). And third, the universal blessing aspect of the Abrahamic Covenant was starting to unfold in ways beyond David's reign. This is evident with 1 Kings 10. Israel's leader, Solomon, became wiser than all: "So King Solomon became greater than all the kings of the earth in riches and in wisdom" (1 Kgs 10:23). With Israel blessed and in position to be a blessing to others, the nations began to seek Israel for blessing. As 1 Kings 10:24–25 reveals:

> All the earth was seeking the presence of Solomon, to hear his wisdom which God had put in his heart. They brought every man his gift, articles of silver and gold, garments, weapons, spices, horses, and mules, so much year by year.

The promise that Israel would bring blessings to the nations of the earth was happening (see Gen 12:2–3). Nations were seeking the wisdom of Israel through Solomon. A great example of this was the Queen of Sheba who came to Jerusalem to speak with him "about all that was in her heart" (v. 3). The queen was stunned by what Solomon had to offer. Not only did Solomon answer all her questions, she was astounded by how Israel's king functioned:

> When the queen of Sheba perceived all the wisdom of Solomon, the house that he had built, the food of his table, the seating of his servants, the attendance of his waiters and their attire, his cupbearers, and his stairway by which he went up to the house of the LORD, there was no more spirit in her (1 Kgs 10:4–5).

The queen praised both Solomon and the God of Israel (v. 9). She then gave Solomon gold, spices, and precious stones (v. 10). On at least three occasions we are told Gentile powers sought and brought wealth to Israel (see 1 Kgs 10:24–25; 10:10, 24). This testifies to what would continue if Israel obeyed God and looks forward to the eternal state when the nations and kings of the earth will once again bring their wealth into the New Jerusalem (see Rev 21:24, 26).

The similarities of the promises of the Abrahamic Covenant with initial (not final) fulfillment in 1 Kings 4 are evident:

Land:
On that day the LORD made a covenant with Abram, saying, "To your descendants I have given this *land*, From the river of *Egypt* as far as the great river, the river Euphrates..." (Gen 15:18a).

Now Solomon ruled over all the kingdoms from the River to the *land* of the Philistines and to the *border of Egypt* (1 Kgs 4:21a).

Seed:
"I will greatly *multiply your seed* as the stars of the heavens and *as the sand which is on the seashore*" (Gen 22:17a).

Judah and Israel were as numerous as the sand that is on the seashore in abundance (1 Kgs 4:20a).

Universal Blessing:
"*And in you all the families of the earth will be blessed*" (Gen 12:3c).

Men came from all peoples to hear the wisdom of Solomon, from all the kings of the earth who had heard of his wisdom (1 Kgs 4:34).

Kings:
"*Kings will come forth from you*" (Gen 17:6c).

King Solomon was king over all Israel (1 Kgs 4:1).

Prosperity:
For You said, "I will surely *prosper* you" (Gen 32:12a).

they [Judah and Israel] were *eating and drinking and rejoicing* (1 Kgs 4:20b).

> So Judah and Israel *lived in safety, every man under his vine and his fig tree*, from Dan even to Beersheba, all the days of Solomon (1 Kgs 4:25).

These comparisons show progress toward completion of the Abrahamic promises. Only one thing could halt it—disobedience. Unfortunately, that is exactly what happens and is the sad legacy starting with 1 Kings 11.

The Kingdom Downfall (1 Kings 11–2 Kings)

The kingdom in the OT reached its high point under Solomon. Yet as McClain noted, "In the very period of the historical kingdom's greatest success, there were already present the seeds of political catastrophe."[27] Solomon violated the commands given by God for kings in Deuteronomy 17:14–17, including not multiplying wives for himself. Sadly, Solomon loved many foreign women and had "seven hundred wives, princesses, and three hundred concubines" who "turned his heart away" from God (1 Kgs 11:3). First Kings 11:4–8 details the result of Solomon's growing corruption including idolatrous worship:

> For when Solomon was old, his wives turned his heart away after other gods; and his heart was not wholly devoted to the Lord his God, as the heart of David his father had been. For Solomon went after Ashtoreth the goddess of the Sidonians and after Milcom the detestable idol of the Ammonites. Solomon did what was evil in the sight of the Lord, and did not follow the Lord fully, as David his father had done. Then Solomon built a high place for Chemosh the detestable idol of Moab, on the mountain which is east of Jerusalem, and for Molech the detestable idol of the sons of Ammon. Thus also he did for all his foreign wives, who burned incense and sacrificed to their gods.

With tragic irony, the king who imparted wisdom to Gentile powers was now forsaking the God of Israel to worship foreign gods. Foreign women influenced his heart. Israel's progress was put in reverse. The nation's witness came to a halt as Israel stopped being a light to the nations and instead

27 McClain, *The Greatness of the Kingdom*, 104.

became like them in their idolatry. The seeds of destruction were sewn. First Kings 8–10 was a high point for Israel but chapter 11 begins the slide toward captivity.

Solomon died after a forty-year reign and his son, Rehoboam, followed him as king over Israel. Rarely in history has someone like Solomon started with such promise and potential but ended with such disappointment. The kingdom rapidly deteriorated and even the selection of kings changed. "After Solomon, the kings are no longer chosen *directly* by Jehovah, but they take the throne either by inheritance or force."[28] The kingdom was divided in 931 B.C. between the ten northern tribes of Israel and the two southern tribes of Judah.

The northern tribes of Israel experienced nineteen consecutive bad kings which culminated in the Assyrian captivity of 722 B.C. Israel violated the Mosaic Covenant with idolatry, disobedience, child sacrifices, star-worship, and involvement in the occult. Judah faired a little better for a time. God evaluated only eight of the following twenty kings of Judah as "good." Four kings led Judah in religious reforms. Yet while Judah's decline developed more slowly, the decay of Judah led eventually to the Babylonian captivity.

When one compares the Eden-like situation for Israel in the early chapters of 1 Kings with the captivity conditions at the end of 2 Kings, the question must be asked, "What happened?" How did Israel go from such hope and promise to such dismal conditions? The answer is that Israel and her kings did evil and forsook the commands of God. Now both Israel and Judah were bound in captivity because of covenant disobedience. Yet as bleak as matters were, there was still hope. Second Kings ends with Jehoiachin's release from prison and dining at the table of the king of Babylon (2 Kgs 25:27–30). A hint of hope remains. Thus, 1 and 2 Kings explain how Israel went from a high point to captivity to hope for the future. Schreiner explains, "Even though the story of 1–2 Kings is the account of paradise lost, there is still hope for a paradise regained."[29]

---

28 McClain, *The Greatness of the Kingdom*, 115.

29 Schreiner, *The King in His Beauty*, 166.

The period after Solomon was "characterized in general by a more indirect rule of God."[30] Instead of the kings, the prophets became the "immediate spokesmen for God" conveying the will of God to the kings and people.[31] The disheartening failure of the kings of Israel is eclipsed by the powerful message of God's prophets. As the kingdoms of Israel and Judah decayed and then collapsed into captivity, the prophets arose as conveyors of God's messages. They explained Israel's failure to obey the Mosaic Covenant and foretold the devastating consequences for disobedience. Yet the prophets also offered hope. Because of God's covenant faithfulness to Abraham and the patriarchs, darkness and judgment would be followed by light and restoration. The same nation that fell because of disobedience would rise again because of God's grace and faithfulness.

In sum, the nation chosen by God to be a kingdom of priests, a holy nation, and a chosen people, failed its mission. Israel was supposed to be a holy witness to the nations but instead became just like the nations, even serving their gods. As a result, dispersion to the nations occurred just as God predicted (Deut 30). Yet this dispersion to the nations would not be permanent. With the decline of the monarchy, the prophets became prominent as they preached repentance and a future restoration of Israel. The kingdom program remains alive.

SUMMARY OF KINGDOM PROGRAM IN THE CONQUEST-CAPTIVITY ERA

1. God's plans to establish Israel as a great nation and kingdom developed under Joshua as Israel possessed the land of Canaan.

2. Israel's incomplete removal of the Canaanites was viewed as disobedience and would later contribute to problems for Israel's kingdom.

30 McClain, *The Greatness of the Kingdom*, 115.

31 Ibid..

3. Israel had its first king in Saul, yet Israel's insistence to have a king like the rest of the nations was viewed by God as a rejection of Him.

4. God rejected Saul and chose David to be king over Israel. David, a descendant of Judah, was a man after God's own heart and the recipient of the Davidic Covenant—a covenant that promised an eternal dynasty in the line of David and blessings to both Israel and the nations.

5. The kingdom in Israel reached a high point under David's son, Solomon, who was the last king to rule over a united Israel. Solomon, though, sowed seeds of destruction for the nation as he turned from God.

6. The kingdom of Israel became divided between the ten tribes of Israel and the two tribes of Judah.

7. While Judah experienced a few good kings, both Israel and Judah were characterized by disobedience and experienced captivity—Israel by Assyria, and Judah by Babylon.

8. Even in captivity there is a glimmer of hope for Israel as Jehoiachin is released from prison.

CHAPTER

8 THE KINGDOM IN THE ROYAL PSALMS

The psalms contribute to God's kingdom program, particularly those known as the "Royal Psalms"–2, 72, 89, 110, and 132.[1] These discuss God's king and his rule. The informing theology for them is the Davidic Covenant of 2 Samuel 7 which promised the following:

1. When David died God would establish a kingdom from a descendant of David (2 Sam 7:12).
2. David's descendant would have a "house" and a "throne" that would be established forever (v. 13).
3. Israel would be safe and secure in their land (v. 10).
4. Gentiles would participate in this covenant–"charter for mankind" (v. 19).
5. This covenant concerns the present time of David and Solomon and also "the distant future" (v. 19).

The Royal Psalms are linked with the kings of Israel and offer comfort to the people of Israel and warning to Israel's enemies. God's enemies may resist and revolt, but their efforts are futile. God will establish His king from

1 Because of its significance, we will also address Psalm 8. Although this psalm is a hymn of praise and not a royal psalm it contributes greatly to the kingdom program and is referenced several times in the NT with kingdom implications.

Jerusalem and he will rule over Israel and the nations with righteousness and justice.

Debate exists concerning the primary subjects of these psalms. Are they directed primarily to David? Solomon? Other kings in David's line? Or do they refer to the ultimate David–Jesus the Messiah? Or, are all of these in view?

Scholars have differed on these questions. Based on the authority of the NT, we know the Royal Psalms find ultimate fulfillment in Jesus the Messiah. Yet the connection of these psalms with Jesus can be accomplished in various ways. First, David and events in David's life can correspond with Jesus and events in His life. For example, David's enemies prefigured Jesus' enemies (see John 13:18).

Second, at times the writer of a psalm thinks specifically of the coming Messiah. This occurs in Psalm 110 where David is privy to a conversation between God and His Messiah–"The Lord says to My Lord..." (110:1a). Here there are three parties–(1) David the psalmist, (2) God (*Yahweh*) and (3) the Messiah (*Adonai*). Peter affirms that David specifically anticipated the Messiah in Acts 2 when Peter says David "was a prophet ... who looked ahead and spoke of the resurrection of the Christ" (2:30–31). In the context of Acts 2, Peter declares that David understood his own words in Psalm 16; 132; and 110 to be explicit predictions about Jesus (see Acts 2:25–36). David knew the Messiah needed to be resurrected so He could sit at the right hand of the Father and one day rule from the throne of David. So with Psalm 110, David was not referring to himself but the Messiah (Acts 2:29). Thus, there are messianic psalms where the psalmist looks ahead to the Messiah.

In sum, there are statements in the psalms concerning David and kings in the line of David that correspond to Jesus and events in His life. And there are times when a psalmist directly refers to the coming Messiah.

THE KINGDOM REIGN OVER NATIONS (PSALM 2)

Psalm 2 is a royal or coronation psalm that speaks of the establishment of God's son and king on Mount Zion. There are differing opinions concerning whom this psalm is referring. Is this psalm only about David, Solomon, or another king in the line of David?[2] Or is it a direct messianic prophecy fulfilled with Jesus the Messiah? Or does the psalm originally refer to a historical Davidic king who typologically anticipates Jesus the Messiah? Johnston states that "Psalm 2 initially functioned as an oracle of legitimization... of the historical Davidic king. Yet interpreted in its most literal sense, the prophetic features are only fulfilled in the reign of the Messiah in the future eschatological kingdom."[3]

Our view is that Psalm 2 is messianic. It pictures the coming rule of the Messiah over the nations that is fulfilled with Jesus the Messiah. The NT applies this psalm to Jesus (see Acts 4:25–28). Plus, several Jewish sources understood this psalm to be messianic.

The author of Psalm 2 is not stated, but Acts 4:25–26 reveals it was written by David ("through the mouth of our father David"). The three main characters of the psalm are: (1) the kings of the earth, (2) the Lord, and the (3) Lord's anointed one. It begins with "the nations in an uproar" (v. 1). The "kings of the earth" and the "rulers" are taking a stand against "the Lord" (Yahweh) and against "His Anointed" (v. 2).

Wicked people want to free themselves from the authority of God and His King (v. 3). But this opposition is futile:

> He who sits in the heavens laughs,
> The Lord scoffs at them.
> Then He will speak to them in His anger
> And terrify them in His fury, saying,
> "But as for Me, I have installed My King
> Upon Zion, My holy mountain" (Ps 2:4–6).

God is in the heavens mocking His opponents. Their opposition to Him leads to "anger" and "fury." Then God declares He will install His King in Jerusalem—"Upon Zion, My holy mountain." God deals with His enemies by installing His King on the earth, in the same sphere where the opposition occurs.

2 Johnston, *Jesus the Messiah*, 75.

3 Ibid., 76.

Psalm 2:7 then states: "I will surely tell of the decree of the LORD: He said to Me, 'You are My Son, Today I have begotten You.'" Here the LORD announces that the "king" is also His "Son." This "son" language parallels 2 Samuel 7:14 in regard to a coming descendant of David: "I will be a father to him and he will be a son to Me." The immediate referent of 2 Samuel 7:14 was Solomon but since the Davidic Covenant is an eternal covenant that involves "the distant future" (7:19) the ultimate referent is the Messiah.

God tells His King/Son, "Ask of Me, and I will surely give the nations as Your inheritance, and the very ends of the earth as Your possession" (v. 8). God intends for His Davidic King to rule over the nations of the earth. While both David and Solomon had geographical reigns, the reign depicted here anticipates Messiah's reign over all nations.

This then leads to a devastating rule, "You shall break them with a rod of iron" (9a). God's King reigns over the nations with an iron-like rule. The psalm ends with the exhortation to the nations to "show discernment" (10) and "do homage to the Son" because "His wrath may soon be kindled" (12a). But those who "take refuge in Him" will be "blessed" (12b). The nations need to repent and worship the Son, because He will rule the earth and they need to be ready.

Psalm 2 teaches that the nations of the earth are in rebellion against God. While they rebel the Lord scoffs at them and then places His King, who is also His Son, in Jerusalem to rule the world. Thus, the reign of God will occur in the same place where opposition to Him is presently occurring. Since this day is coming the nations should worship the Son because His wrath will soon come. The NT reveals that the "Son" of Psalm 2:7 is fulfilled in Jesus the Messiah (see Acts 13:33; Heb 1:5; 5:5). Revelation 2:26–27 declares that Jesus the Messiah will delegate His reign over the nations to His followers who are faithful during this present age. While the identity of this King and Son is now revealed in Jesus the Messiah, the complete fulfillment of the psalm awaits Jesus' second coming when He assumes the Davidic throne and reigns upon the earth (see Matt 25:31; Rev 19:11ff.).

MAN'S RIGHT TO RULE (PSALM 8)

Psalm 8 is not a royal psalm. It is a hymn of praise. Yet, because of its importance to God's kingdom program and its use in the NT, it is necessary to address it. The psalm functions much like a commentary on Genesis 1:26–28 and reaffirms man's right to rule over the creation.[4]

The first and last verse of Psalm 8 offer a declaration of praise—"O LORD, our Lord, How majestic is Your name in all the earth!" (8:1a, 9). Thus, attention is given to the greatness of God. God's glory is evident by His wondrous creation: "Who have displayed Your splendor above the heavens!" (8:1b). Focus is also drawn to God's "heavens" and "the moon and the stars." When David says these are "the work of your fingers" (8:3), this shows the direct involvement of God with His creation. God's greatness is seen in His wondrous universe. Then in verses 4–8, David points out the high point of God's creation—man, and the dignity he possesses:

> What is man that You take thought of him,
> And the son of man that You care for him?
> Yet You have made him a little lower than God,
> And You crown him with glory and majesty!
> You make him to rule over the works of Your hands;
> You have put all things under his feet,
> All sheep and oxen,
> And also the beasts of the field,
> The birds of the heavens and the fish of the sea,
> Whatever passes through the paths of the seas.

God made man "a little lower than God" and crowned him "with glory and majesty." Man has the right "to rule over the works of Your hands." This language is kingly and reaffirms man's role as a vice-regent over God's creation.

The connection with Genesis 1:26–28 in Psalm 8:4–8 is clear. In Genesis 1 Adam was created in God's image so he could serve God by ruling and subduing the creation on God's behalf for God's glory. Psalm 8 shows that man still possesses the right to rule the creation. David is writing

4 Goldingay observes, "... vv. 5–8 parallel the Gen. 1 story of God's making men and women godlike and giving them power over the rest of the animate world." John Goldingay, *Psalms: Volume 1: Psalms 1–41*, in Baker Commentary on the Old Testament Wisdom and Psalms (Grand Rapids: Baker, 2006), 159.

thousands of years later in a fallen world, yet the fall and the curse have not removed this right. Although he is fallen, man is still royalty. As John Goldingay states, "Like Gen. 1–2, the psalm reckons that human beings in general are kings, which puts kings in their place."[5]

The truths of Psalm 8 will be picked up by Paul in 1 Corinthians 15:25–28 and the writer of Hebrews in Hebrews 2:5–8. The fulfillment of Psalm 8 will occur in a world to come in connection with the ultimate Man, Jesus, the Last Adam, who will succeed in the realm where the first Adam failed.

A COMING UNIVERSAL AND RIGHTEOUS REIGN (PSALM 72)

Psalm 72 "describes the blessings that flow from the righteousness of God's theocratic ruler."[6] Yet there is debate concerning the author and to whom the psalm is addressed. Was it written by David or Solomon? The psalm is attributed to Solomon. If accurate, then either Solomon is writing about himself, which seems unlikely, or more probably, he is writing about the coming Ruler, the Messiah, whose reign will transcend even his own glorious reign.[7] In taking this latter view Kaiser writes, "This psalm is a direct messianic prediction because it uses the future tense throughout and because not even Solomon in all his glory could have fulfilled what is said here."[8] The conditions described go far beyond the historical situation of either man and they point forward to Jesus the Messiah.

According to Psalm 72, God is called to bestow the "king" with two characteristics—righteousness and justice (v. 2). The king is also one who will defend the weak and the poor: "May he vindicate the afflicted of the people, save the children of the needy, and crush the oppressor" (v. 4). He will also have a universal reign: "May he also rule from sea to sea and from the River to the ends of the earth" (v. 8). "All nations" will "serve him" (v. 11). This

5 Goldingay, *Psalms*, 159.

6 Allen P. Ross, "Psalms," in *Bible Knowledge Commentary: An Exposition of the Scriptures: Old Testament*, ed. John F. Walvoord and Roy B. Zuck (Victor, 1985), 846.

7 If the author of Psalm 72 is David, then David is writing about his son, Solomon, the coming Messiah, or both. Since the descriptions here about a righteous king are so grand and go beyond any mere human king, including Solomon, the ultimate referent is Jesus.

8 Kaiser, *The Messiah in the Old Testament*, 133.

shows again that the Davidic Covenant goes beyond Israel to the nations. As Saucy puts it, "the Davidic promise... was not limited to a narrow nationalism that concerned only the kingdom of Israel. Rather, the blessing of the righteous rule of the promised Davidic seed was to extend to all nations."[9] Thus, Gentiles are included in the rule of the Messiah, not just Israel.

> Then His protection of the needy is also emphasized:
> For he will deliver the needy when he cries for help,
> The afflicted also, and him who has no helper.
> He will have compassion on the poor and needy,
> And the lives of the needy he will save.
> He will rescue their life from oppression and violence,
> And their blood will be precious in his sight (12–14).

These verses mention "the poor and the needy" who need rescue. The presence of poor and needy people points to an intermediate kingdom because the conditions described do not harmonize with our present world or the final eternal state. As Grudem states, "All of this speaks of an age far different from the present age but short of the eternal state in which there is no more sin or suffering."[10] This age, therefore, appears consistent with a millennial reign as described in Revelation 20:1–6.

The reign of the king also means material prosperity: "May there be abundance of grain in the earth or on top of the mountains. Its fruit will wave like the cedars of Lebanon; and may those from the city flourish like vegetation of the earth" (v. 16). A foretaste of these conditions was experienced in the glorious reign of Solomon (see 1 Kgs 8), yet the ultimate fulfillment awaits the kingdom of Jesus the Messiah. As Michael Grisanti states:

> Although this psalm may have been written at the beginning of Solomon's reign, it envisions ideals never fully realized in Israel's history. Only during the millennial reign of Christ will the peace and prosperity depicted by this psalm find fulfillment.[11]

9 Robert L. Saucy, *The Case for Progressive Dispensationalism*, 62.

10 Wayne Grudem, *Systematic Theology: An Introduction to Biblical Theology* (Grand Rapids: Zondervan, 1994), 1129.

11 Michael A. Grisanti, "The Davidic Covenant," in *The Master's Seminary Journal* 10 (1999): 244.

THE DAVIDIC COVENANT AND THE COMING RIGHTEOUS RULER (PSALM 89)

Psalm 89 was composed by Ethan the Ezrahite a Levite and musician who is mentioned as a wise man in 1 Kings 4:31. The psalm offers two key contributions to the kingdom program. First, it reveals Ethan's attempt to harmonize his belief in God's oath to David with judgment for covenant breaking in his day. With verses 19–37 he offers information concerning God's covenant with David given in 2 Samuel 7. While 2 Samuel 7 does not use the actual word "covenant," Psalm 89:28 does: "My lovingkindness I will keep for him [David] forever, and My covenant shall be confirmed to him."

God promises to "establish his [David's] descendants forever, and his throne as the days of heaven" (v. 29). The eternal nature of this covenant with David and his descendants is affirmed in verses 34–37:

> "My covenant I will not violate,
> Nor will I alter the utterance of My lips.
> "Once I have sworn by My holiness;
> I will not lie to David.
> "His descendants shall endure forever
> And his throne as the sun before Me.
> "It shall be established forever like the moon,
> And the witness in the sky is faithful."

Thus, Psalm 89 affirms the Davidic Covenant and its promise of a perpetual kingdom for David's descendants. The certainty of this covenant being fulfilled is also linked with the sun, moon, and sky.

Second, Ethan's frustration reveals the necessity of a coming righteous Ruler. As Ethan extols these glorious truths he is frustrated by the conditions of his day. The Lord gave victory to the king's enemies (40–44) and leads him to ask, "How long, O' Lord? Will you hide yourself forever?" (46). And, "Where are Your former lovingkindnesses, O Lord, which You swore to David in Your faithfulness?" (49). So then, his frustration reveals two key truths. First, as Grisanti observes, "at this point in Israel's history, the ideal of a just king who would bring the nation lasting peace and prosperity was still an unfulfilled ideal." And second, "the inability of Davidic rulers to live and rule in accordance with God's demands causes the reader to look forward for a Davidic figure who would one day perfectly satisfy those divine expectations."[12] Even Solomon, who presided over the high point of Israel's kingdom, was not the one to bring complete fulfillment of the glories of the Davidic Covenant. Psalm 89 ends with a somber realization of the need for someone else who could.

THE KING/PRIEST (PSALM 110)

Psalm 110 is one of the most significant passages in the Bible. While consisting of only seven verses, it is not only the most quoted psalm in the NT, it is the most quoted OT passage in the NT.[13] The topic here is God's king, i.e. David's Lord, who is both king and priest.[14] This king-priest, as Elliott Johnson observes, "will totally defeat and subjugate his earthly adversaries after a session at Yahweh's right hand."[15]

Since the NT contains so many references to Psalm 110, a proper understanding of this psalm is necessary for understanding God's kingdom purposes. Later, in our chapter on the kingdom in Hebrews, we will explain how the NT writers used this psalm. But our focus now will be on the meaning of Psalm 110 in its own context.

Author and Subject of Psalm 110

Some debate surrounds this psalm's authorship.[16] Is it David himself as the superscription states—"A Psalm of David." Or is it Solomon or some other king? The best understanding is that it is David. The superscription appears reliable. Plus, the traditional Jewish and Christian understanding

---

12 Grisanti, "The Davidic Covenant," 245.

13 Hay says there are approximately thirty-three quotations and allusions to Psalm 110 in the NT. David M. Hay, *Glory at the Right Hand* (Nashville: Abingdon Press, 1973), 163-65.

14 Elliott E. Johnson notes, "Interpreters of Psalm 110 are generally agreed that the subject of this psalm is an Israelite king-priest." "Hermeneutical Principles and the Interpretation of Psalm 110," *Bibliotheca Sacra* (1992): 429.

15 Johnson, "Hermeneutical Principles," 430.

16 Ibid. Johnson notes "No less than 10 historic occasions are proposed for the setting (the *Sitz im Leben*) of this short psalm....".

is that David is the author. Jesus explicitly attributes the psalm to David in Matthew 22:43, which should solve the issue.[17]

Who is the king-priest of Psalm 110? The traditional Jewish and Christian understanding is that David intentionally wrote of the coming Messiah. Some assert David is referring to himself or to Solomon. But these latter two options are not likely. Neither David nor Solomon fit the magnificent description given here. The mention of "My Lord" indicates someone superior to David. Also, neither David nor Solomon fit the picture of the king-priest described in Psalm 110. The Mosaic era did not allow for a person to hold both offices.[18] Priests came from the tribe of Levi while kings were to be from the tribe of Judah. Yet God's man in this psalm is both king and priest. Also, Jesus interpreted Psalm 110 as referring to himself in Matthew 22:41–45.[19] Delitzsch is right that David in this psalm "looks forth into the future of his seed and has the Messiah definitely before his mind."[20]

Interpreting Psalm 110

As the psalm opens David overhears words spoken by the Lord (*Yahweh*) to David's Lord (*Adonai*). Verse 1 states, "The Lord said to my Lord." The word "said" is not the best translation. The HCSB is more accurate by interpreting this as a "declaration." This is a solemn oracle from Yahweh to David's Lord. What Yahweh tells David's Lord is this: "Sit at My right hand until I make Your enemies a footstool for Your feet" (v. 2).

While the psalm does not explicitly mention a "throne" of God, a throne is in view since God's man is sitting at the "right hand" of Yahweh. David's Lord is positioned at the throne of God. The "right hand" of the Lord is the place of highest honor, power, privilege, and closeness to

17 "Then how does David in the Spirit call him, 'Lord,' saying..." (Matt 22:43). The Pharisees did not challenge Jesus' claim that David wrote this psalm.

18 King Saul assumed the priestly office and offered burnt offerings (see 1 Sam 13:9) with disastrous consequences. He was strongly rebuked by Samuel and had the potential for an eternal dynasty over Israel removed (1 Sam 13:13–14). According to 1 Chronicles 21:28, David offered sacrifices but doing such was far from the norm for him (see also 2 Sam 6:17–18).

19 If the religious leaders understood Psalm 110 to be a reference to David or Solomon they probably would have challenged Jesus' argument but they did not.

20 F. Delitzsch, "Psalms," in *Commentary on the Old Testament*, C. F. Keil and F. Delitzsch, trans. J. Martin (Grand Rapids: Eerdmans, 1980), 1:66.

Yahweh. This place of prominence is unique, and is not true of any historic Davidic king. This individual at Yahweh's right hand is a man, but a very unique man. He shares a throne with God indicating that the one sharing God's throne is deity as well.

The Location of Psalm 110:1

Where is this scene in Psalm 110:1 taking place? Is this throne of Yahweh a distinctively heavenly throne, or is Yahweh's throne David's throne on earth? The evidence points to a heavenly throne. Psalm 2, which parallels Psalm 110 states that the Lord "sits in the heavens" and "laughs" and "scoffs" at His earthly enemies (Ps 2:4). Since both testaments present Yahweh as enthroned in heaven,[21] Yahweh's throne in Psalm 110:1 is probably heaven. While the Bible presents God as actively involved in the affairs of earth and His universal kingdom extends over all, God the Father is pictured as reigning from heaven (see Rev 4–5). Since David's Lord is pictured as being at the right hand of Yahweh then His presence at this point in verse 1 must be in heaven as well. Yahweh is seated on His heavenly throne while David's Lord, the Messiah, is right beside Him.

Several NT passages affirm that the throne of Yahweh and the position of being at His right hand are in heaven. Acts 2:33 states that after His ascension to heaven (Acts 1:9–11) Jesus was "exalted to the right hand of God," which must be heaven since Jesus ascended from earth to heaven. Hebrews 10:12 says, "but He, having offered one sacrifice for sins for all time, SAT DOWN AT THE RIGHT HAND OF GOD." Before his martyrdom, Stephen saw the heavens open and Jesus standing at the right hand of God (see Acts 7:55, 56). Both the OT and NT present the Father's throne and the position of the right hand of God as in heaven.

The Meaning of Psalm 110

According to Psalm 110, Messiah's session at the right hand of God in heaven is only for a period of time—"until I make Your enemies a footstool

21 First Chronicles 29:23 does state that "Solomon took the throne of the LORD in place of his father, David." This does not show that Yahweh's throne is the earthly throne of David but that the earthly Davidic throne's source is Yahweh.

for your feet" (v. 1). The preposition "until" (*ad*) indicates a time element and shows a transition from one state of events to another. As Johnson states, it "distinguishes present opposition from a future conquest over the enemies."[22]

God's exalted man enjoys a position of honor and privilege in the midst of opposition from enemies ("sit at my right hand"), but this leads to an active subjugation of these opponents ("until I make Your enemies a footstool for your feet"). The language of making one's enemies a "footstool" refers to total dominance and subjugation of one's opponents. In the ancient Near East a victorious king would sometimes place his foot on the neck of his conquered foe to show utter dominance over this enemy.

Verse 2 discusses the ruling that will occur: "The Lord will stretch forth Your strong scepter from Zion, saying, 'Rule in the midst of Your enemies.'" The "scepter" (or "rod") can refer to a shepherd's instrument. The context here, though, is kingly. This reference to "scepter" certainly has connections with Genesis 49:10 and the promise that "The scepter shall not depart from Judah... until Shiloh comes." Thus, a strong kingly rule occurs at this time.

Unlike the heavenly context for the events of 1:1a, the locale for this kingly rule of God's king in verse 2 is "from Zion" which is Jerusalem. Thus, the heavenly session at the "right hand" of Yahweh" occurs "until" the time comes for David's Lord to rule from Jerusalem. God's king, i.e. David's Lord, transfers his presence from the Lord's throne in heaven to a kingly reign on earth from Jerusalem. Michael Rydelnik notes this transition: "Although the King initially awaits victory in God's heavenly throne room, vv. 2–3 indicate a descent from heaven to earth."[23] This reveals a tangible kingly rule from Jerusalem *after* a session in heaven.

This transition from heaven to earth for a kingdom rule is found in other texts. Zechariah 14 says the Lord will come from heaven to earth to defeat a siege against Jerusalem (Zech 14:4–5). The result is "the Lord will be king over all the earth" (14:9). Also, when discussing His second coming Jesus stated, "But when the Son of Man comes in His glory, and all the

22 Johnson, "Hermeneutical Principles," 433.

23 Michael Rydelnik, *The Messianic Hope: Is the Hebrew Bible Really Messianic?* (Nashville, TN: B&H, 2010), 173.

angels with Him, then He will sit on His glorious throne" (Matt 25:31). This "glorious throne" is the earthly Davidic throne Jesus will assume. This is followed by a judgment and kingdom (Matt 25:32–46). To summarize, with Psalm 110:1–2 David's Lord enjoys a session of honor and privilege from God's right hand in heaven until the time comes for Him to reign over His enemies from Jerusalem. While closely connected, there is a distinction between sitting at the right hand of Yahweh in verse 1a and ruling over God's enemies with a strong scepter from Zion in 1b–2. The former takes place in heaven while the latter is from the sphere of Zion (i.e. Jerusalem).

Psalm 110:3a discusses the willingness of some to follow the king: "Your people will volunteer freely in the day of Your power." The earthly reign of the Messiah coincides with the willing reign His followers (see Rev 2:26–27). When God's man reigns on the earth, those who love and follow Him will do so as well.

Then verse 4 explicitly introduces the priestly element of the psalm: "The Lord has sworn and will not change His mind, 'You are a priest forever according to the order of Melchizedek.'" Here is the startling statement that the King is also a Priest. With rare exceptions this unification did not occur in the OT. Kings of Israel were kings, and priests were priests. But this man of God is a King-Priest. He is not a Levitical priest but a priest "according to the order of Melchizedek." The primacy of the Levitical priesthood was an essential aspect of the Mosaic Covenant, but not so with the New Covenant. Hebrews states explicitly that Jesus' perpetual priesthood is linked with Melchizedek, not Levi (see Heb 7). The change in priesthood is part of the transition from the Old Covenant to the New Covenant (see Heb 8:13).

Psalm 110:5b–6 then offers a vivid depiction of what God's king will do, and it is violent:

> He will shatter kings in the day of His wrath.
> He will judge among the nations,
> He will fill them with corpses,
> He will shatter the chief men over a broad country.

The Messiah crushes the enemies of God. As God's King-Priest comes and rules from Jerusalem He destroys His enemies. This is followed by a scene in which the king drinks from a "brook" and lifts up his head (v. 7). This pictures refreshment in the midst of triumph over His enemies.

Psalm 110 is a direct messianic psalm written by David about the coming Messiah. David reveals that the Messiah, who is both a King and a Priest, will have a session at the right hand of God the Father for a period of time that will be followed by a kingdom reign on earth from Jerusalem. Later, in his defense of the resurrected and ascended Jesus, Peter said Jesus the Messiah was the one "whom heaven must receive until the period of restoration of all things about which God spoke by the mouth of His holy prophets from ancient time" (Acts 3:21). Peter said Jesus "must" have a session in heaven. Based on Psalm 110, which Peter quotes in Acts 2, Peter knew Jesus must be received into heaven for a time before the restoration of all things occurs. Psalm 110:1–2 may hint at the necessity of two comings of the Messiah.

THE FOREVER DAVIDIC COVENANT (PSALM 132)

Psalm 132 affirms the forever nature of the Davidic Covenant. It is a prayer offered on behalf of David in regard to some crisis. The writer petitions the Lord to protect the dynasty of David and the city of Jerusalem. "For the sake of David Your servant, do not turn away the face of Your anointed" (v. 10). The covenant God made with David is unbreakable and must come to pass: "The Lord has sworn to David a truth from which He will not turn back: 'Of the fruit of your body I will set upon your throne'" (v. 11).

This unbreakable covenant with David did not mean a sinful generation of Israel would not face punishment and temporary displacement from the throne of David. Verse 12 states, "If your sons will keep My covenant and My testimony which I will teach them, their sons also shall sit upon your throne forever." An unbroken succession of kings on the throne of David is dependent on obedience. If there is obedience unbroken succession would occur. But if not, then a temporary break could happen. As Johnston puts it, "Obedience by David's successors would be rewarded with an enduring dynasty, but disobedience would place the royal house in temporary jeopardy."[24]

Historically, this proved to be the case. Through disobedience and failure to heed the warning of the prophets, the royal household of David and the people of Judah were captured and sent into exile in Babylon along with a destruction of Jerusalem and the temple. Yet the captivities did not mean the total absolution of the Davidic Covenant. Verse 11 shows God will fulfill His covenant with David. There will be a future restoration of the Davidic dynasty. But it will be done through the ultimate David, Jesus the Messiah. As the angel Gabriel would later tell Mary concerning Jesus, "He will be great and will be called the Son of the Most High; and the Lord God will give Him the throne of His father David; and He will reign over the house of Jacob forever, and His kingdom will have no end" (Luke 1:32–33).

While a descendant of David was on the throne there was the threat of removal for disobedience. But once the removal took place there was the hope of restoration, a hope that one day will be realized through Jesus. This affirms in vivid language that the fulfillment of the Davidic Covenant is tied to one who bodily comes from the line of David. Verse 13 tells us "the Lord has chosen Zion; He has desired it for His habitation." This reaffirms the importance of Jerusalem in God's kingdom program. This is where God will rest forever (14). God will bless His people and not allow His enemies to triumph (15–18).

SUMMARY OF THE KINGDOM PROGRAM IN THE ROYAL PSALMS

The kingdom program in the Royal Psalms can be summarized as follows:

1. Kingdom theology in the psalms is reliant on the original Davidic Covenant promises of 2 Samuel 7.

2. God will fulfill His covenant with David and David's descendants.

24 Johnston, *Jesus the Messiah*, 102.

3. God will fulfill His covenant with David through One who is a descendant of David.
4. The fulfillment of the Davidic Covenant involves restoration and peace for Israel and protection from Israel's enemies.
5. The Gentile nations foolishly resist God's kingdom program.
6. God mocks the nations who devise vain things knowing He will establish His King from Jerusalem.
7. God's Man, who is King, Priest, and Son, will be exalted to God's right hand in heaven.
8. This exaltation of God's Man at God's right hand is for a period of time and will lead to God's King being installed as King in Jerusalem where He will exercise His rule over the nations.

A NOTE ON THE KINGDOM IN WISDOM LITERATURE

This work does not have a specific chapter on the kingdom in the wisdom literature. Yet this does not mean there is no relationship between the kingdom and books such as Job, Proverbs, Song of Songs, and Ecclesiastes. Schreiner rightly notes that while many do not believe the kingdom of God is that significant to the wisdom books, "every wisdom book emphasizes the fear of the Lord, and fearing the Lord is what it means to live under Yahweh's lordship."[25]

The book of Job, for instance, details a cosmic struggle between God and Satan with the man, Job, as the battleground for this conflict (see Job 1–2). While the book relates to many areas, one of them is the continuing conflict between God and Satan that goes back to Genesis 3:15. The book of Job reveals that "God reigns over Satan.... Human beings are no match for Satan, but God is."[26] Also, Job 1:3 says Job was "the greatest of all the men of the east." Job used kingly language of himself. Concerning his

25 Schreiner, *The King in His Beauty*, 233.

26 Ibid., 249.

position before his calamity, Job said he "sat as chief, and dwelt as a king among the troops" (Job 29:25).

The Song of Songs tells of the incredible beauty and joy of the marriage relationship between a man and a woman. In doing so it pictures the relationship between Jesus and His people (see Eph 5:31–32). Proverbs emphasizes the fear of the Lord as the beginning of wisdom. Much of the wisdom literature also emphasizes Solomon as a kind of model of what a wise king is and in so doing corresponds to what Jesus, the ultimate King, will represent.[27] The wisdom literature books, therefore, contribute to the kingdom program.

27 See G. K. Beale, *A New Testament Biblical Theology: The Unfolding of the Old Testament in the New* (Grand Rapids: Baker Academic, 2011), 73. Beale says Proverbs may be a "court" document "that addresses the Israelite kings and the members of his royal court, especially highlighting that the king and other courtly leaders were to be the models of Torah life and the ideal representatives of Yahweh to the people. This fits well with my contention about Solomon being portrayed in Proverbs as an ideal wise and kingly figure," 74.

CHAPTER

9 THE KINGDOM IN ISAIAH

MESSAGE OF THE MAJOR PROPHETS

The demise and fall of the kingdom in Israel did not mean an end to God's kingdom program. In the midst of disobedience and apostasy God affirms His plans to restore Israel. This is not because Israel deserves it but because God is faithful to the patriarchs with whom He made unconditional and eternal promises. With the tribes of Israel and Judah nearing captivity the prophets proclaim a glorious restoration of the kingdom to Israel with blessings to the Gentiles. The overall message of the major prophets of Isaiah, Jeremiah, and Ezekiel is this—*Israel was being judged and dispersed to the nations for covenant disobedience, but in the latter days Israel would be regathered and restored to her land and experience New Covenant blessings, both material and spiritual, under the leadership of the ultimate Son of David. As a result, the nations, who will be judged for a time, will also benefit from the reign of the Messiah and the restoration of Israel and become the people of God alongside Israel in an earthly kingdom.*

ISAIAH

The book of Isaiah (c. 740–680 B.C.) gives detailed information concerning the kingdom during a time of judgment. Isaiah warned Judah concerning covenant disobedience. The people broke the Mosaic Covenant and national consequences were on the brink. God will purify Israel through judgment, but this will be followed by restoration and renewal of covenant relationship. Israel will be restored and Jerusalem will function as the capital city of God's worldwide kingdom. Formerly hostile nations will become

God's people alongside Israel.[1] This will be accomplished through the ultimate Servant of the Lord who represents and restores the nation Israel and brings blessings to the nations of the earth (see Isa 49:3–6). The center of Isaiah's message is the Davidic Covenant of 2 Samuel 7, which he refers to often.[2] For Isaiah, "there was to be a future time of peace and prosperity for Israel and the nations when God would fulfill His promises to David."[3] While Assyria and then Babylon were the immediate threats facing Israel, Isaiah tells of coming universal judgment and the establishment of Messiah's kingdom over the earth.

NATIONS STREAMING TO JERUSALEM (ISAIAH 2:1–4)

Isaiah 2 addresses the coming kingdom and the roles of Israel and the nations in it. It predicts international harmony among nations as a result of Messiah's reign from Jerusalem. The sons of Israel that God raised up "revolted" against Him (Isa 1:2). They were a "sinful nation" and "people weighed down with iniquity" (1:4). The once "faithful city" became a "harlot" and justice was not found in it (1:21). But a reversal of fortune will occur as "Zion will be redeemed with justice" (1:27). This is explained in Isaiah 2:1–4 where a glorious kingdom exists and nations stream to Jerusalem to worship God.[4]

Isaiah 2 begins, "The word which Isaiah the son of Amoz saw concerning Judah and Jerusalem" (2:1). The Israelite connection here is important. This text concerns the geographical areas of "Judah and Jerusalem." Yet some do not grasp this truth. Alexander is not correct when he states, "the Prophet sees the church, at some distant period, exalted and conspicuous, and the nations resorting to it for instruction in the true religion...."[5] This

---

1 See Robert B. Chisholm, Jr., "A Theology of Isaiah," in *A Biblical Theology of the Old Testament*, ed. Roy B. Zuck (Chicago: Moody, 1991), 305.

2 John H. Sailhamer, "Evidence from Isaiah 2," in *A Case for Premillennialism: A New Consensus*, ed. Donald K. Campbell and Jeffrey L. Townsend (Chicago: Moody, 1992), 79.

3 Ibid..

4 The language here closely parallels Micah 4:1–3, highlighting the significance of this message.

5 Joseph A. Alexander, *Commentary on Isaiah* (Grand Rapids: Kregel, 1992), 96.

does not do justice to what Isaiah is saying and introduces a spiritualizing element that is not warranted. Isaiah is addressing international harmony among nations in the kingdom with Jerusalem at its center, not the church. Isaiah 2:2–4 reads:

> Now it will come about that
> In the last days
> The mountain of the house of the Lord
> Will be established as the chief of the mountains,
> And will be raised above the hills;
> And all the nations will stream to it.
> And many peoples will come and say,
> "Come, let us go up to the mountain of the Lord,
> To the house of the God of Jacob;
> That He may teach us concerning His ways
> And that we may walk in His paths."
> For the law will go forth from Zion
> And the word of the Lord from Jerusalem.
> And He will judge between the nations,
> And will render decisions for many peoples;
> And they will hammer their swords into plowshares and their spears into pruning hooks.
> Nation will not lift up sword against nation,
> And never again will they learn war.

This section highlights four key elements:

1. The preeminence of Mount Zion.
2. Gentile pilgrimage to Mount Zion.
3. The Lord judging the nations.
4. The removal of weapons of warfare.[6]

All of this occurs in "the last days," which, in the OT prophets, refers to the days of Messiah and Israel's restoration. In the NT "last days" has significance

6 See Sailhamer, "Evidence from Isaiah 2," 85.

for both the first and second comings of Jesus the Messiah.[7] Since what is described in Isaiah 2 has not occurred yet concerning "Judah and Jerusalem" the fulfillment of this text awaits the second coming of Jesus.

The term "mountain" refers to Mount Zion in Jerusalem, the mountain on which God's temple sits. The "house of the Lord" is the temple. Mount Zion in Jerusalem will be exalted and elevated above the mountains and hills around it. In Isaiah's day, Mount Zion did not tower above other mountains but in the "last days" it will. But is this a reference to changes in Mount Zion's physical elevation, or is this a figurative elevation to prominence? We see no reason why both cannot be true. A physical entity can also convey a figurative meaning. Thus, Mount Zion can be elevated physically and in prominence. Zechariah 14:4–8 indicates that when Jesus returns to earth there will be massive geographic changes that affect the Mount of Olives, Jerusalem, and the land of Israel.

As Isaiah continues, this kingdom is centered in Israel, but it is not only for Israel. There is a *universal* element since "all the nations will stream to it" (2:2d) and "many peoples will come and say, 'Come, let us go up to the mountain of the Lord'" (2:3a). The rest of verse 3 indicates that Gentile nations desire to go to the temple in Jerusalem to learn how to walk in God's paths and follow His law. Such positive statements concerning Gentile nations are striking since the nations of Assyria and Babylon are imminent threats to the nation Israel and Israel is not thinking fondly of the Gentile nations at this point. Nations are often the enemies of Israel. In fact, the era of the "times of the Gentiles" continues until this very day (see Luke 21:24). But during this kingdom era, the nations, as Grogan puts it, "come, not for plunder, but in peace, not to rob, but to learn."[8]

Diligent Jews would make pilgrimages to the holy city as part of their worship. But in the last days, "what had been Israel's experience in the

7 Hebrews 1:2 indicates that "in these last days" God "has spoken to us in His Son." Yet the NT also speaks of many eschatological events that have not been fulfilled with the first coming of Jesus and await future fulfillment (see 1 Thess 4–5; 2 Thess 1–2; 2 Pet 3, etc.). The interpreter will need skill in deciphering which aspects of OT eschatology apply to Jesus' first coming and which apply to His second coming.

8 G. W. Grogan, "Isaiah," in *The Expositor's Bible Commentary*, ed. Frank E. Gaebelein, vol. 6 (Grand Rapids: Zondervan, 1986), 35.

past would one day be that of all the nations."[9] There are also implications concerning the exodus and Mount Sinai here. At the time of the exodus the Hebrews went to Mount Sinai to receive God's law, but during this messianic era the nations are streaming to Mount Zion to learn God's law.[10]

Verse 4 details the Lord's reign at this time. He will "judge between the nations" and "render decisions for many peoples." Several things are worthy of note here. First, literal geo-political nations exist in the days of the kingdom. And these nations are doing real activity. Second, the Lord is making political judgments and decisions for these nations. The word "judge" (*shaphat*) means to "govern, vindicate, or punish." According to Brown-Driver-Briggs the term in Isaiah 2:4 concerns "decid[ing] controversy" in regard to "civil, political, domestic, and religious questions."[11] Thus, the Lord will make executive and judicial decisions concerning the nations in need of righteous decisions. These nations, which appear to disagree at times or have conflicts of interest, will accept His announcements peacefully.

The need for settling disputes among nations points to an intermediate kingdom in the future since these conditions do not fit either this present age or the coming eternal state. As Saucy writes, "That sin is present during the Messiah's reign is evident in his settling disputes among the nations (cf. Isa 2:4)...."[12] This is not occurring today. But it will be in the latter days. This combination of conditions also is found in Zechariah 14 where the Lord who is present on earth after His coming (see Zech 14:9) will bring "punishment" on nations that do not act as they should (Zech 14:18–19).

According to v. 4 universal peace will exist. The money and materials usually poured into military weapons will be devoted to peaceful pursuits. Swords will be hammered into plowshares and spears into pruning hooks,

9 Sailhamer, "Evidence from Isaiah 2," 90.

10 Ibid., 91. I agree with Sailhamer that the nations will not be under the Mosaic Law but the New Covenant law predicted for the latter days in Jeremiah 31 and Ezekiel 36. He says, "The translation 'law' in Isaiah 2:3 in the NASB rather than 'Law,' then, accurately reflects the emphasis of this passage away from the Sinai Law per se. The 'law' as used here in Isaiah is the internalized law of passages such as Jeremiah 31:33 and Ezekiel 36:27."

11 F. Brown, S. Driver, and C. Briggs, "שָׁפַט," *The Brown-Driver-Briggs Hebrew and English Lexicon* (Hendrickson, 2000), 1047.

12 This is Saucy's view, Robert L. Saucy, *The Case for Progressive Dispensationalism*, 234.

showing there is no longer a need for weapons of warfare. Whether there will be a literal transformation of swords and spears is a secondary issue. The main point is that weapons for warfare are no longer needed at this time. When one considers how much money is poured into military purposes by countries today, it is staggering to think of the good that can be accomplished when valuable resources are no longer used for warfare. Such will be the case when the Lord is reigning upon the earth. Also, human ingenuity will no longer be used for weapons of destruction. As Bultema notes, "All military science, which today has reached such terrifying proportions, will then belong to a dark past."[13]

Poetic Language and Literal Meaning

In the attempt to understand Isaiah 2 figuratively for the church, some have appealed to the poetic nature of Isaiah 2:2–4. Supposedly, if a poetic element exists then one should not expect a literal fulfillment of what is described, and this text can be applied nonliterally to the church. Yet, this perspective fails on two accounts. First, while a poetic element may exist there is also a narrative aspect. Sailhamer observes that this passage "within its context in Isaiah is intended to be taken more as narrative than as poetry."[14]

Second, Isaiah 2:2–4 parallels Micah 4:1–3 very closely. This is significant because in addition to poetic expressions of Jerusalem's restoration in Micah, Micah also offers poetic descriptions of Jerusalem's *destruction*. In 3:12, Micah states, "Zion will be plowed as a field, Jerusalem will become a heap of ruins, and the mountain of the temple will become high places of a forest." The implication is this: "If the prophecy regarding the destruction of Jerusalem was understood literally, even though it was poetic in form, it is natural to take the vision of its restoration literally as well."[15] Or to state another way, if Jerusalem's destruction can be both poetic and literal, so too can the city's restoration.

In sum, Isaiah 2:2–4 teaches God's kingdom will be on earth, centered in Jerusalem. Gentile nations will flock to Jerusalem to worship God

13 Harry Bultema, *Commentary on Isaiah* (Grand Rapids: Kregel, 1981), 56.

14 Sailhamer, "Evidence from Isaiah 2," 96.

15 Ibid.

and learn His ways. There is global peace among nations. This shows a harmony between Israel and the nations. For the first time in history a Ruler, the Lord, will offer perfect judgments on behalf of the nations. These nations will no longer prepare for war but will use their resources for peaceful purposes. This speaks of more than spiritual salvation in the church today. It describes ideal conditions on the earth among nations under the Messiah. These conditions have not happened yet in human history but they will transpire when Messiah's kingdom is established.

Does Isaiah 2:2–4 Speak of the Church?

At this point we will address in more detail the view that Isaiah 2 is fulfilled in the church today. John Calvin asserted that the "prophecy" of Isaiah 2 was "concerning the restoration of the Church."[16] He also said, "The fulfillment of this prophecy, therefore, in its full extent, must not be looked for on earth."[17] More recently, Kenneth Gentry argues that "Judah and Jerusalem" here "represent the whole of the people of God, just as 'Israel and Judah' do in Jeremiah 31:31...."[18] In reference to 2:2-4 Gentry declares, "Isaiah says that Christ's church will be established."[19] And, "'All nations' will stream (Isa 2:2) into the church."[20] Strimple says the Isaiah 2:2-4 prophecy "is being fulfilled *now* as men and women of every tribe on the face of the earth call upon the name of Zion's King and become citizens of 'the Jerusalem that is above.'"[21] Kim Riddlebarger claims a present fulfillment of Isaiah 2:2-4 and Micah 4:1-5 based on his understanding of Hebrews 12:18-24:

16 John Calvin, *Commentary on Isaiah–Volume 1*. Christian Classics Ethereal Library (Grand Rapids: Christian Classics Ethereal Library, n.d.), 66.

17 Calvin, *Commentary on Isaiah*, 66.

18 Kenneth Gentry, "Postmillennialism," in *Three Views on the Millennium and Beyond*, ed. Darrell L. Bock (Grand Rapids: Zondervan, 1999), 36. This denies the Jewish element to this prophecy in an unwarranted fashion. While the people of God certainly expands to include Gentiles, specific prophecies concerning Judah, Jerusalem, and Israel can still expect literal fulfillment. It does not follow that since later salvation history will include Gentiles as the people of God that this passage must have its Jewish elements transcended to something else.

19 Ibid., 37.

20 Ibid.

21 Robert B. Strimple, "Amillennialism," in *Three Views on the Millennium and Beyond*, ed. Darrell L. Bock (Grand Rapids: Zondervan, 1999), 93. Emphasis is in the original.

> The author of the Epistle to the Hebrews could not be more clear about how he understand this prophecy [Micah 4:1–5/Isa 2:2–4]. Though Old Testament prophets spoke of the earthly city of Jerusalem, the New Testament writers did not say these prophecies would be fulfilled in a future earthly Jerusalem. On the contrary, the author of Hebrews said the prophecy was already fulfilled in the person and work of Christ.[22]

After quoting Hebrews 12:18–24 for support he goes on to say, "In Jesus Christ, the heavenly Jerusalem has already come, even now."[23]

But this understanding is not correct for several reasons. First, 2:1 says the message concerns Judah and Jerusalem. Any view that divorces the Jewish geographical element from the prophecy is violating the context of the passage. Judah and Jerusalem are not the "church." In reference to John Calvin's view, Bultema rightly warns against such an understanding based on the wording of 2:1:

> This indication ["Judah and Jerusalem"] should have been sufficient for all exegetes to keep them from applying it to the Church or heaven, as has been done most of the time. Calvin says, 'This concerns a scene of the restoration of God's Church–a matter of utmost significance.' This entirely contradicts the opening words *concerning Judah and Jerusalem*.[24]

Second, Isaiah 2 predicts more than salvation. It describes *global international peace*. While personal salvation is important, God's kingdom involves more than salvation, it also includes a holistic restoration of all things including international harmony among nations. To claim Isaiah 2 is about salvation into the church strips the Isaiah passage of its primary meaning. There is no international peace today. One amillennial theologian rightly rejected this spiritualization of Isaiah 2. Anthony Hoekema criticized fellow amillennialists on this issue:

---

22 Kim Riddlebarger, *A Case for Amillennialism*, 73–74.

23 Ibid.

24 Bultema, *Commentary on Isaiah*, 51.

> All too often, unfortunately, amillennial exegetes fail to keep biblical teaching on the new earth in mind when interpreting Old Testament prophecy. It is an impoverishment of the meaning of these passages to make them apply only to the church or to heaven.[25]

While I disagree with Hoekema when he places the fulfillment of Isaiah 2 only in the coming eternal state and not in an intermediate kingdom, his understanding of the passage is a vast improvement over the 'church-fulfillment' view. Hoekema rightly states that the 'church-fulfillment' perspective is "an impoverishment of the meaning." The message of Isaiah 2:1–4 cannot be fulfilled with the church today: "Only on the new earth will this part of Isaiah's prophecy be completely fulfilled."[26] Thus, Isaiah 2:2–4 must be fulfilled in the future.

Third, Hebrews 12:18–24 does not prove Isaiah 2:2–4 is fulfilled in the church. The writer of Hebrews declares that Christians today are related to a city still to come (see Heb 13:14). That Christians are positionally related to the coming New Jerusalem does not prove Isaiah 2:2–4 is fulfilled today.

Fourth, the fulfillment in the church view presents an imbalanced and even unfair understanding of the blessing/curse motif in regard to the nation Israel. It distributes curses to Israel but not the blessings of restoration. Jamieson, Fausset, and Brown rightly argue that the promised blessings of Isaiah 2 must not be spiritualized:

> If the curse foretold against Israel has been literally fulfilled, so shall the promised blessing be literal. We Gentiles must not, while giving them the curse, deny them their peculiar blessing by spiritualizing it.[27]

Since the conditions of Isaiah 2:2–4 have not occurred yet, fulfillment awaits a future time. The fulfillment will take place after Jesus' return. It will take place in connection with the Davidic reign of the ultimate Son

25 Anthony A. Hoekema, *The Bible and the Future* (Grand Rapids: Eerdmans, 1979), 205–06.

26 Ibid., 205.

27 Robert Jamieson, Andrew Robert Fausset, and David Brown, *A Commentary: Critical, Practical and Explanatory, on the Old and New Testaments* (J. B. Names & Co., 1883), 100.

of David, Jesus. The view that Isaiah 2:2–4 is taking place in the church today spiritualizes the text. It spiritualizes Judah and Jerusalem along with literal nations coming to Jerusalem.

Hoekema's futuristic understanding of Isaiah 2 is a positive development since the contents of Isaiah 2 have not been fulfilled yet. Yet placing the fulfillment of Isaiah 2:2–4 only in the eternal state and not in an intermediate kingdom (or millennium) has two major flaws. First, the kingdom of Isaiah is directly related to the Davidic reign of the Son of David (see Isa 9:6–7). One key aspect of amillennial theology is that the Davidic kingdom reign of the Messiah is being fulfilled in this age between the two comings of Jesus. But if Isaiah 2 is fulfilled in the eternal state, this puts the kingdom of Isaiah 2 outside the direct Davidic reign of Jesus. According to 1 Corinthians 15:24–28 Jesus delivers His kingdom over to God the Father after Jesus has successfully reigned over His enemies. Those who hold to the "eternal state" view of Isaiah 2 separate the fulfillment of Isaiah 2 from the millennium and Davidic reign of Jesus.

Second, the kingdom promises of Isaiah 2 and other texts (Isa 9; 11) involve the restoration of national Israel with a role to other nations. If one wants to be literal with the international conditions of Isaiah 2, one must also be literal with the role national Israel plays with these conditions. We find it difficult to hold that Isaiah 2 is describing a period of global international peace, yet national Israel's role during this time is not theologically significant.

THE CHILD WHO WILL RULE (ISAIAH 9:6–7)

Isaiah 9:6–7 is a familiar passage for Christians who rightly identify this section with Jesus Christ. Jesus is the "son" who is "given to us." This section also has important implications in regard to the kingdom of God:

> For a child will be born to us, a son will be given to us;
> And the government will rest on His shoulders;
> And His name will be called Wonderful Counselor, Mighty God,
> Eternal Father, Prince of Peace.
> There will be no end to the increase of His government or of peace,
> On the throne of David and over his kingdom,
> To establish it and to uphold it with justice and righteousness
> From then on and forevermore.

> The zeal of the Lord of hosts will accomplish this.

Like other kingdom prophecies of Isaiah this prediction is rooted in the Davidic Covenant where God promised that the throne of David's kingdom would be established forever (2 Sam 7:12–16). This individual who will rule comes as "a child" and "a son." This finds fulfillment in the nativity accounts of Jesus in the early chapters of Matthew and Luke.

The declaration that "the government will rest on His shoulders" shows there is a social-political dimension to this leader's rule. While some believe that Messiah's kingdom means an end to all politics and government this is not the picture Isaiah paints. The concept of government is not bad. It only seems that way in a fallen world where governmental structures are tainted by corruption and wrongdoing. But government is needed whenever people are gathered in proximity to each other. Isaiah 9 reveals that government will exist, but for the first time in history it will be a righteous government under a righteous King with righteous results.

THE SUFFERING SERVANT

A coming child will be king. But later Isaiah also speaks of a coming "servant." This "servant," introduced in Isaiah 41, is identified with Israel. Information about the servant is also found in Isaiah 42; 49; 52–53. Much debate has occurred over the identity of the servant in these chapters, whether he represents the nation Israel or is a person within Israel. That he is a personal representative of Israel is preferred simply because he does things that Israel as a nation could not do. In Isaiah 50:10 the people of Israel are asked, "Who is among you that fears the Lord, that obeys the voice of His servant?" This question makes no sense if the "servant" is the people of Israel for Israel would not ask itself this question. But it does make sense if the servant is a person who represents Israel. Also, this servant must be a specific person because He is the only one who can restore disobedient Israel. Isaiah 49:6 says of the servant:

> He [God] says, "It is too small a thing that You should be My Servant To raise up the tribes of Jacob and to restore the preserved ones of Israel."

Israel is sinful and disobedient and cannot restore herself. Like a person lost at sea with no raft needs an outside force to pull him out, Israel needs a Savior since she cannot save herself. But God's "Servant" is one who "raise(s) up" and "restore(s)" the people of Israel. The purpose of the Servant is to restore Israel, not make the nation Israel insignificant. When the NT writers later identify Jesus with Israel (see Matt 2:15) they identify Jesus with Israel and show He is qualified to restore the people.

But the clearest evidence for a unique person is found in Isaiah 52–53 where the Servant atones for the sins of His people, Israel:

> But the LORD has caused the iniquity of us all
> To fall on Him (53:6b).
> And as for His generation, who considered
> That He was cut off out of the land of the living
> For the transgression of my people, to whom the stroke was due?
> (53:8b).

Israel certainly suffered in history, but the nation is not able to atone for its own sins. But a righteous Suffering Servant of Israel can do this.

This Suffering Servant intersects with the kingdom program in two ways. First, the coming King and Servant is the same person. As Schreiner rightly states, "If we tie the servant to the Davidic promises earlier in Isaiah, it is clear that the servant is a royal figure."[28] The NT makes this evident. This coming man of God will have two primary functions. He will be both a Servant who makes an atoning sacrifice, and a King who brings a kingdom reign. NT revelation reveals Jesus is the One who fulfills both roles. His role as Suffering Servant was fulfilled with His first coming, while His reign as Davidic King will occur at His second coming (see Acts 3:18, 20–21).

Second, Isaiah's depiction of the Suffering Servant also shows that the objective basis for the kingdom of God is atonement for sin. There is no kingdom or participation in the kingdom without atonement. No kingdom without the cross (Col 1:20).

28 Schreiner, *The King in His Beauty*, 344.

THE KING WHO WILL TRANSFORM NATURE (ISAIAH 11)

Isaiah 11 contains detailed information concerning the nature of the coming kingdom of God. Four things are emphasized here: (1) the King from Jesse; (2) restored harmony for the animal kingdom; (3) blessings to the nations; and (4) the restoration of Israel.

The King from Jesse

First, Isaiah 11:1 emphasizes the righteous character of the coming King. Verse 1 states:

> Then a shoot will spring from the stem of Jesse,
> And a branch from his roots will bear fruit.

Isaiah draws upon the Davidic Covenant and God's promise that David's kingdom would last forever through his descendants and culminate in an ultimate Son of David (see 2 Sam 7:12–16). David himself was the son of Jesse so the coming Davidic King will be a descendant of Jesse as well.

The Spirit of the Lord will rest on Him (v. 2). This indicates that the Messiah and His deeds will be connected with the work of the Holy Spirit, something the NT affirms. In Matthew 12:28 Jesus declared, "But if I cast out demons by the Spirit of God, then the kingdom of God has come upon you." Then with verse 4 we are given insights into the Messiah's reign, a reign consistent with a coming intermediate kingdom before the eternal state since it involves coercive and punitive elements. As Waymeyer puts it:

> Isaiah 11 also indicates that certain aspects of this kingdom rule will be coercive, and even punitive. According to verse 4, as the Messiah reigns over this coming kingdom, He will judge the poor with righteousness (v. 4a), defend the afflicted with fairness (v. 4b), strike the earth with the rod of His mouth (v. 4c), and slay the wicked with the breath of His lips (v. 4d). This need for the Messiah to defend the poor and afflicted and to bring punitive judgment upon the wicked "indicates the presence of

> rebellious activity not in keeping with the eternal kingdom order in which sin is absent."[29]

Not only are the conditions of verse 4 not consistent with the coming eternal kingdom, they do not match current conditions of this present age in which there is much unfairness and mistreatment of the poor and helpless. They also cannot be relegated to just the second coming event, since what is described in v. 4 includes conditions of a sustained reign (i.e. helping the poor and afflicted).

Restored Harmony for the Animal Kingdom

Many wonder about the presence of animals in the future. Isaiah 11:6–9 reveals that Messiah's reign extends to the creation, including animals. Before looking at this section, though, it is helpful to draw some conclusions about animals from the creation account.

Genesis reveals the importance of the animal kingdom in God's creation. While man is the apex of creation animals are also significant. Similar to man, God "formed" every "beast" and "bird" "out of the ground" (Gen 2:19). Also, every beast and bird is said to have "the breath of life" (Gen 7:14–15). The animals were also an integral part of the creation that man was called to subdue and rule over (see Gen 1:26–28). Some animals were also saved from the global flood of Noah's day. God stated that He wanted "to keep them alive" (Gen 6:20). Significantly, the covenant God made with Noah was also a covenant with the animal world:

- "Now behold, I Myself do establish My covenant with you... and with every living creature... the birds, the cattle, and every beast of the earth" (Gen 6:9–10).
- "I establish My covenant with you; and all flesh shall never again be cut off by the water of the flood" (Gen 6:11).

29 Matthew Waymeyer, "Additional Old Testament Passage," unpublished Th.D. paper, The Master's Seminary (March 2014), 2. The quotation at the end of the quote is from Craig Blaising, "The Kingdom that Comes with Jesus," in *The Return of Christ: A Premillennial Perspective* (Nashville, TN: B&H Academic, 2011), 144.

- "This is the sign of the covenant which I am making between Me and you and every living creature" (Gen 6:12).

Thus, the deliverance of the animal kingdom from the flood and the perpetuity of the animal world are important to God. So it is not surprising that animals are included in the restored kingdom. Animals, too, will experience the reversal of the fall. Isaiah 11:6–9 describes how Messiah's kingdom will bring harmony to the animal kingdom:

- "the wolf will dwell with the lamb" (6a)
- "the leopard will lie down with the young goat" (6b)
- the calf and the young lion will live in harmony (6c)
- the cow and bear will graze together as will their offspring (7a, b)
- "and the lion will eat straw like the ox" (7c)
- children can play with poisonous snakes and not be harmed (8)
- No harm will be done on God's kingdom throughout the whole world (9)

There are several implications for animals and the kingdom. First, animals are in harmony with other animals. This is "animal-animal harmony." The examples are striking and go against our present experience: Wolves and lambs getting along? Leopards and goats? A calf and a lion? A cow and bear? Widespread harmony among traditional enemies in the animal kingdom is not experienced in this age. But this will be the norm in the coming kingdom.

Second, there is "animal-human" harmony. Isaiah 11:8 states: "The nursing child will play by the hole of the cobra, and the weaned child will put his hand on the viper's den." In our age, what could be more horrifying for a parent than to spot his or her precious child coming upon the hole of a cobra? Or a child putting his hand on a viper's den? Yet in Messiah's kingdom this situation is not cause for fear. No danger exists. The description also looks back to man's dominion right over animals as mentioned in Genesis 1:26–28.

Third, Isaiah says, "the lion will eat straw like the ox" (11:7c). The nature and diet of carnivorous animals might be altered to fit the new kingdom conditions. Perhaps the conditions for animals will resemble those before the fall.

Other passages also refer to a restoration of animals. Isaiah 65:25 declares that "the wolf and the lamb will graze together, and the lion will eat straw like the ox." And "dust will be the serpent's food." Some spiritualize the literal meaning of these verses but there is no good reason to do this. Nature and the animal kingdom were casualties of the fall of man. So why wouldn't the restoration of all things (Acts 3:21) include a restoration of nature and animals? Psalm 8:6–8 reveals that man's mandate to rule over the creatures of the earth has not been revoked:

> You make him to rule over the works of Your hands; You have put all things under his feet, All sheep and oxen, And also the beasts of the field, The birds of the heavens and the fish of the sea, Whatever passes through the paths of the seas.

Isaiah 11:6–9 shows that Messiah's kingdom is not just a spiritual kingdom; it is a kingdom that transforms every aspect of creation—including the animal realm. In Eden man and animals lived in harmony, so too will it be in Messiah's kingdom.

Blessings to the Nations

Messiah's kingdom also means blessings to Gentile nations according to 11:10:

> Then in that day
> The nations will resort to the root of Jesse,
> Who will stand as a signal for the peoples;
> And His resting place will be glorious.

This truth of Gentiles being blessed by Israel's Messiah goes back to Genesis 12:2–3 which states that blessings to the families of the earth would be mediated through Abraham and the great nation coming from him. It is also something God's ultimate Servant will do according to Isaiah 49:3–6.

The Gentile nations will be drawn to the "root of Jesse" which has ultimate reference to Jesus the Messiah. Thus, an essential aspect of Messiah's kingdom is the presence of nations who benefit from the King of Israel.

The Restoration of Israel

Messiah's kingdom also involves a restoration of the nation Israel in what can be referred to as a second exodus. This happens as God regathers His people a second time from among the nations where they were scattered. Isaiah 11:11 declares:

> Then it will happen on that day that the Lord
> Will again recover the second time with His hand
> The remnant of His people, who will remain,
> From Assyria, Egypt, Pathros, Cush, Elam, Shinar, Hamath,
> And from the islands of the sea.

This assembling of the "banished ones of Israel" occurs "from the four corners of the earth" (11:12). Both the northern and southern tribes will live in harmony as "Ephraim will not be jealous of Judah, and Judah will not harass Ephraim" (11:13). This return of Israel will be like a second exodus from Egypt (11:16).

Isaiah 11 presents a wonderful depiction of Messiah's kingdom. This kingdom will evidence reversals of the curse as the animal kingdom and nature once again work in harmony with man. The nations of the earth will serve the King and Israel will be restored.

GENTILES TO BECOME THE PEOPLE OF GOD (ISAIAH 19)

Isaiah 13–23 foretells the fate of Gentile nations at the time of the ominous Assyrian threat. The prophet speaks of conditions for both the immediate situation and the future. Here our focus is on Isaiah 19, which addresses the future of Egypt and how Egypt will be related to God's kingdom plans.

God's kingdom purposes involve more than Israel. They also include Gentile nations. The pattern presented in Isaiah 19 is judgment first and then blessing. God judges Egypt but then saves and blesses the nation as part of Yahweh's rule upon the earth. In a coming day believing Gentile nations will be included in the people of God alongside Israel. Isaiah 19, thus, connects the people of God with the kingdom of God.

The immediate historical situation of Isaiah 19 is the soon-coming Assyrian march through the region. Isaiah 19:1–15 reveals that some wanted to reach out to Egypt for help against the Assyrian threat. But this hope is futile since Egypt will be consumed by God's judgment. God will cause civil strife within Egypt (2) and demoralize the Egyptians by confounding their plans. They will seek occult help but it will be futile (3). Egypt will be given over to a cruel leader (4). Even the trusted Nile River will fail them (7). Pharaoh's trusted advisors will be worthless (11–14).

However, an important transition occurs in verse 16, which starts the second main section of the chapter. On five occasions Isaiah refers to a period called "in that day" (16, 18, 19, 21, 23). While there may be some connections with historical fulfillment at that time, the descriptions of "that day" go far beyond anything that has occurred yet in history.[30] Egypt will have a healthy fear of Judah who is the dominant power in the region (16–17). The people of Egypt will learn Hebrew (18). There will even be a national monument to the God of Israel in the land of Egypt:

> In that day there will be an altar to the LORD in the midst of the land of Egypt, and a pillar to the LORD near its border. It will become a sign and a witness to the LORD of hosts in the land of Egypt (Isa 19:19–20a).

This "altar to the LORD" emphasizes a national recognition of God. Nations today often have monuments and memorials, but a prominent one to the Lord will be placed in Egypt. Also, Egypt will be saved at the hand of Israel's Messiah: "for they will cry to the LORD because of oppressors, and He will send them a Savior and a Champion, and He will deliver them" (20b). This shows the Savior of Israel will also be the Savior of other nations. And this coincides with a national salvation of Egypt. Verse 21 declares, "Thus the Lord will make Himself known to Egypt, and the Egyptians will know the Lord in that day." Egypt "will return to the LORD," and God "will respond to them and heal them" (22).

International harmony will be present at this time (see Isa 2:2–4). Egypt and Assyria will worship God together (23). This context sets the

30 Charles Spurgeon notes, "Attempts have been made to explain it [Isa 19:18–25], as if it were already fulfilled. I believe all such attempts to be utter failures. This promise stands on record to be, fulfilled at some future day." Charles H. Spurgeon, "Fruits of Grace," sermon http://www.spurgeon.org/sermons/3515.htm. Accessed Oct 25, 2013.

scene for the startling declaration concerning Egypt, Assyria, and Israel in 19:24–25:

> In that day Israel will be the third party with Egypt and Assyria, a blessing in the midst of the earth, whom the Lord of hosts has blessed, saying, "Blessed is Egypt My people, and Assyria the work of My hands, and Israel My inheritance."

Alexander rightly notes that with this text "we have one of the clearest and most striking predictions of the calling of the Gentiles that the word of God contains."[31]

Note the following. First, in a coming day ("in that day") three traditional political enemies—Egypt, Assyria, and Israel—will all be the people of God and worship the God of Israel. This has never occurred in history, so the circumstances presented must await the future. Zechariah 14 affirms this when it mentions Egypt and other nations going up to Jerusalem to worship the Lord who is then reigning over the earth (see Zech 14:16–19, 9). Second, Egypt and Assyria are said to be "a blessing in the midst of the earth," which shows that earth is the realm for this kingdom. Third, these events take place when Israel exists and is a dominant power in the region. Egypt has a healthy respect for Israel during this time (16–17).[32] So there is a future role for Israel as a political entity. Fourth, titles once used only of Israel in the OT are expanded to include Gentiles. Egypt is called "my people," and Assyria is designated "the work of My hands." Those designations were once only used of Israel. This shows that the people of God expands to include Gentiles.

Next, there are two theological implications from Isaiah 19. *First, nations will be part of the kingdom of God.* What is described is more than the gospel message spreading to various people in the world, as we see in this present age. Isaiah speaks of a time when nations as national entities are

31 Alexander, *Commentary on Isaiah*, 364.

32 "19:23–25 looks forward to the day when Israel will be a world power equal to Egypt and Assyria." Margaret Barker, "Isaiah," in *Eerdmans Commentary on the Bible*, ed. James D. G. Dunn and John W. Rogerson (Grand Rapids: Eerdmans, 2003), 514.

serving the Lord. Egypt, Assyria, and Israel are there. Other nations will be in this kingdom period too.

Second, the people of God concept expands to include Gentiles alongside Israel who also exists as the people of God. Some think passages that speak of Gentiles being blessed alongside Israel means that believing Gentiles are incorporated into Israel. But this is not the case. The text does not say Egypt and Assyria become "Israel." Instead, these nations become the people of God *alongside* Israel. "Israel" does not expand to include Gentiles. Instead, the people of God expands to include Gentiles alongside Israel. Or put another way:

It is not:

> Egypt and Assyria are morphed into a redefined Israel.

Instead, it is:

> Egypt and Assyria (and other believing Gentiles) become the people of God alongside believing Israel.

Becoming the people of God does not mean loss of ethnicity or national affiliation. Nor does it mean Gentiles become Israel. Jews and Gentiles participate together in the people of God but they do not morph into each other.[33] The concept of "Israel" does not expand but the concept of the people of God does. Thus, the kingdom of God includes Gentiles as God's people.

WORLDWIDE JUDGMENT FOLLOWED BY WORLDWIDE KINGDOM (ISAIAH 24–27)

Isaiah 24–27 is one of the most detailed prophetic sections in the Bible. Its similarities with the book of Revelation have been noted. It has been deemed "Isaiah's Little Apocalypse" since it is a microcosm of the contents in Revelation. Isaiah 24 predicts a coming worldwide judgment of God on unbelievers while chapters 25–27 describe kingdom blessings following

33 This is Paul's point in Ephesians 3:6 when he states that believing Gentiles in the church are "fellow heirs," "fellow members of the body," and "fellow partakers of the promise." The use of several *syn-* compounds in Ephesians 2:11–3:6 shows that Gentiles participate with believing Jews in the people of God but they do not become Israel.

tribulation. That chapter 24 is referring to universal global judgment is clear from the language of the chapter itself, and from the fact that chapters 13–23 detail God's messages for the nations.

Isaiah 24:1 sets the tone for the rest of the chapter: "Behold, the Lord lays the earth waste, devastates it, distorts its surface and scatters its inhabitants." This involves the earth being "completely laid waste and completely despoiled" (24:3). No persons, whatever their social status, can escape (24:2). Earth's inhabitants have "transgressed laws, violated statutes, broke the everlasting covenant" (24:5). Because men violated the Creator/ creature relationship a curse envelops the earth and a future burning with fire awaits (24:5). Verses 19–20 indicate the earth itself "is shaken violently" and "reels to and fro like a drunkard." Isaiah 24:21 states that "in that day" God "will punish the host of heaven on high, and the kings of the earth on earth." In a coming tribulation period both angelic and earthly rebels will be punished. Yet this judgment of heavenly and earthly transgressors appears to have two phases:

> They will be gathered together
> Like prisoners in the dungeon,
> And will be confined in prison;
> And after many days they will be punished (Isa 24:22).

There is a gathering of wicked beings who are confined in prison. Then "after many days" their punishment occurs. A significant gap of time exists between the initial incarceration of these heavenly and earthly rebels and their final punishment. This supports the concept of an intermediate kingdom (or millennium) in which the return of the Lord means a cessation of activities for the wicked although the final sentencing does not occur for many days. In Revelation, Satan will be bound and sentenced to the "abyss" with a complete cessation of his activities immediately after the return of Jesus (Rev 20:1–3). Yet a thousand years later Satan is released for a short time only to meet his fiery doom in God's judgment (Rev 20:7–10). Likewise, the enemies of the Lord Jesus are dealt with at His return (Rev 19:11–21) yet final sentencing to the lake of fire awaits the Great White Throne Judgment after the completion of the thousand-year reign of Christ (see Rev 20:11–15).

Isaiah 25 transitions to kingdom conditions and blessings that will occur after the earth's frightful judgment. The kingdom is a great banquet God gives His people. "The Lord of hosts will prepare a lavish banquet for all peoples on this mountain" (25:6a). It is a banquet with "aged wine" and "choice pieces with marrow" (25:6b). This is a literal banquet and celebration with great food and wine. Jesus used banquet imagery in Matthew 8:11 when He stated, "I say to you that many will come from east and west, and recline at the table with Abraham, Isaac and Jacob in the kingdom of heaven." On the night before His death Jesus promised He would both eat and drink with His disciples again in the kingdom of God (Luke 22:16, 18). Just as the Passover meal with His disciples was a literal meal, so too will the kingdom banquet. That the kingdom of God includes banquets and celebrations with food and drink is not surprising. God created Adam to enjoy the pleasures of Eden, including food and drink. Why wouldn't the kingdom not include banquets, celebrations and wholesome participation in such delights?

Chapter 26 is a song of trust for God's protection that will be sung by God's people when the kingdom is established. Thanks and confidence permeate this song. The Lord has "increased the nation" of Israel and has "extended all the borders of the land" (26:15). Perhaps at this time the nation Israel possesses the full dimensions of the land promised in Genesis 15:18–21. Physical resurrection from the grave is promised in 26:19: "Your dead will live; their corpses will rise." This affirms the truth of resurrection of the body.

Isaiah 27 also addresses kingdom conditions. Verse 1 says the Lord "will punish Leviathan the fleeing serpent" and "will kill the dragon who lives in the sea." This appears to be a reference to the Lord's defeat of Satan who in Scripture is identified as both a "serpent" and a "dragon" (see Rev 12:9; 20:2). Thus, kingdom conditions will involve the removal of the great enemy of mankind—Satan. Brevard Childs notes that Isaiah 27:1 announces that "God will destroy the reality of evil in all its ontological dimensions." This includes a "strike against its cosmic source once and for all."[34] The fulfillment of this is described in Revelation 20:1–3 when Satan is bound

34 Brevard S. Childs, *Isaiah* (Louisville, KY: Westminster John Knox Press, 2001), 196.

at the time of the second coming of Jesus to earth. The kingdom involves the defeat of Satan.

Isaiah 27:6 declares that the blessing of Israel brings benefits to the entire world: "In the days to come Jacob will take root, Israel will blossom and sprout, and they will fill the whole world with fruit." This again affirms that Israel operates as the platform for God's plans to bless the nations of the earth. Israel is a microcosm of universal blessings. As God blesses Israel, He blesses the world. Paul mentions this truth in Romans 11:

> Now if their [Israel's] transgression is riches for the world and their failure is riches for the Gentiles, how much more will their fulfillment be! (Rom 11:12).

> For if their [Israel's] rejection is the reconciliation of the world, what will their acceptance be but life from the dead? (Rom 11:15).

In sum, Isaiah's Little Apocalypse shows that a global kingdom follows global tribulation. This pattern also will occur in other prophetic books.

KINGDOM CONDITIONS FOLLOWING GLOBAL JUDGMENT (ISAIAH 34–35)

Isaiah 34–35 describes global judgment followed by kingdom blessings. The prophet, Isaiah, calls on the nations to listen carefully because "the Lord's indignation is against all the nations, and His wrath against all their armies" (34:2). Edom, as representative of nations hostile to Israel, is singled out (34:5). Its devastation will be great and is orchestrated by God's Spirit (34:16b).

Isaiah 35 then describes kingdom conditions after judgment. This passage was used by Jesus to assure John the Baptist that Jesus truly was the Messiah who had the authority to bring in the kingdom (see Matt 11:2–5).

When the kingdom arrives nature will benefit: "The wilderness and the desert will be glad," and "the Arabah will rejoice and blossom" (35:1). Once dry areas will become lush: "waters will break forth in the wilderness" (6). Also, "The scorched land will become a pool and the thirsty ground springs of water" (7). The creation subjected to futility by man's fall will be restored and resemble Edenic conditions. And just as nature is restored, the kingdom will also bring a reversal of the effects of the curse:

> Then the eyes of the blind will be opened
> And the ears of the deaf will be unstopped.
> Then the lame will leap like a deer,
> And the tongue of the mute will shout for joy (Isa 35:5–6a).

The descriptions here are literal. This is supported by Jesus' use of this passage in Matthew 11:2–5 when John the Baptist sent his disciples to ask Jesus the question, "Are You the Expected One, or shall we look for someone else?" (vv. 2–3). Jesus appealed to Isaiah 35:5–6 to assure John that He (Jesus) truly was the Messiah:

> Jesus answered and said to them, "Go and report to John what you hear and see: the BLIND RECEIVE SIGHT and the lame walk, the lepers are cleansed and the deaf hear, the dead are raised up, and the POOR HAVE THE GOSPEL PREACHED TO THEM" (Matt 11:4–5).

Jesus was performing physical miracles. These miracles were tangible demonstrations of kingdom power. The One standing before Israel was the One who could bring the kingdom conditions of Isaiah 35. He was proving this by performing miracles of healing. John the Baptist could know Jesus truly was the Expected One, the Messiah. He proved it by His kingdom miracles.

The main point of Isaiah 35 is that kingdom conditions will come after a period of judgment. These conditions were presented to Israel at the time of Jesus' first coming, but as Luke 19:41–44 indicates, Israel missed its time of "visitation" and in doing so missed "the things which make for peace." The fulfillment of Isaiah 35 now awaits Jesus' second coming.

THE SERVANT, ISRAEL, THE LAND, AND THE NATIONS (ISAIAH 49)

While the word "kingdom" is absent from Isaiah 49 this chapter makes a significant contribution to the kingdom program. Several key elements of the kingdom are present—the Servant who represents Israel, the nation

Israel, Gentiles who are blessed by the Servant, and Israel's return from captivity to her land and blessings of the kingdom.

The Servant

With Isaiah 49 the Servant addresses the islands that represent the far reaches of the earth. With v. 3 this Servant reveals that God called Him: "He said to Me, 'You are My Servant, Israel, In Whom I will show My glory.'" Thus, the "Servant" is called Israel. Yet because of what this Servant does He cannot only be equated with the nation Israel, the remnant of Israel, or Isaiah. He is a single Israelite who represents the nation Israel, a corporate representative on behalf of the nation. This must be the case since in verses 5–6 He is going to do something that the nation or believing remnant could not accomplish for itself—restore Israel.

The Nation Israel

Verse 5 states that the Servant will "bring Jacob back to Him, so that Israel might be gathered to Him." The "gathered" language is used often in the OT and is found in Deuteronomy 30:3: "[God] will *gather* you again from all the peoples where the LORD your God has scattered you." Then in 49:6a there is another statement that the Servant will "raise up" and "restore" Israel:

> He says, "It is too small a thing that You should be My Servant, to raise up the tribes of Jacob and to restore the preserved ones of Israel."

This again picks up on the restoration passage of Deuteronomy 30 which states, "then the LORD your God will restore you from captivity" (30a).

Thus, Isaiah 49:5–6 reveals that *the Servant of Israel will restore the nation Israel. His task is not to make the nation irrelevant or to redefine Israel into a purely spiritual community*. As Robert Saucy states:

> This use of "Israel" for the coming Messiah, however, cannot be made the basis of teaching that all who finally are "in Christ" are therefore equal to Israel. Isaiah is applying the honorific title of "Israel" to the Messiah because he is the true servant who will finally accomplish the task of Israel. But this does not indicate

a change in the meaning of Israel or the rejection of the nation as the servant.[35]

Gentiles

The restoration of Israel is not the Servant's only work. Only restoring Israel is not big enough for God. God says "It is too small a thing" to stop with only the restoration of Israel (49:6a). This Servant will also bring salvation to the nations:

> "I will also make You a light of the nations
> So that My salvation may reach to the end of the earth" (49:6b).

The Servant's mission is both particular and universal. It involves both Israel (particular) and the nations (universal). As Blaising observes, "Isaiah 49 shows that the servant 'Israel' will bring national Israel back to God and also extend Yahweh's salvation to the ends of the earth (49:5–6)."[36] The nations will not be morphed or absorbed into Israel. They will be saved alongside the nation Israel. And this salvation of the nations, like Israel's salvation, will be based on the suffering and atoning work of the Servant who "will sprinkle many nations" (Isa 52:15).

Land and Restoration

The Lord says the Servant will be "a covenant of the people" and will "restore the land" and make the people "inherit the desolation heritages" (v. 8). God, through His Servant, will keep His covenant promises to Israel, including restoration to the "land" after a period of desolation. The nations that once tormented Israel will help the Jewish people return (see 49:22). The return to the land will be so complete that the people will wonder if the land can contain all the people (49:20). The importance of land for

35 Robert L. Saucy, "Israel and the Church: A Case for Discontinuity," in *Continuity and Discontinuity: Perspectives on the Relationship Between the Old and New Testaments*, ed. John S. Feinberg (Wheaton, IL: Crossway, 1988), 242. Saucy also makes the valid point that Israel is viewed as "a corporate personality" in which the head ministers to the body so the body may accomplish its mission.

36 Craig A. Blaising, "A Premillennial Response," in *Three Views on the Millennium and Beyond*, ed. Darrell L. Bock (Grand Rapids: Zondervan, 1999), 146.

Israel was first brought up in Genesis 12. Hundreds of years later it is still important and will continue to be relevant.

Worldwide Recognition of the Servant and Israel

The Lord says His Servant will be "despised" and "abhorred" but then vindicated by those who once despised Him. "Kings will arise, Princes will also bow down" (49:7). Such global recognition of the Servant by Gentile leaders did not occur with Jesus' first coming but it will happen with His second coming.[37] And not only will the leaders of the nations bow before the Servant, they will escort the people of Israel back to their land (49:22–23). This too awaits future fulfillment.

THE COMING NEW EARTH (ISAIAH 60–66)

Isaiah 60–66 describes great blessings to come upon Israel and the nations with the kingdom and a new earth. Essential to these kingdom conditions is the sacrificial death of the Servant of the Lord discussed in Isaiah 52 and 53. Atonement for sin must precede the kingdom.

Isaiah 59 is a transitional chapter in that Israel's national sin is recognized (59:1–8) and a confession of sin is offered (59:9ff.). Then, significantly, "A Redeemer will come to Zion, and to those who turn from transgression in Jacob" (20). This speaks of the return of the Messiah. Then we are told about the blessings of the New Covenant for Israel:

> "As for Me, this is My covenant with them," says the Lord: "My Spirit which is upon you, and My words which I have put in your mouth shall not depart from your mouth, nor from the mouth of your offspring, nor from the mouth of your offspring's offspring," says the Lord, "from now and forever" (Isa 59:21).

Paul draws upon Isaiah 59:20–21 in his declaration that national Israel will be saved and participate in the New Covenant (Rom 11:26–27).

In sum, national sin leads to national recognition and repentance, which then leads to the Messiah's return and Israel's participation in the

37 A glimpse of such Gentile worship was found with the magi who came to worship Jesus according to Matthew 2:1–12.

New Covenant. Isaiah 60:1–3 then sets the tone for the incredible kingdom conditions that are further described in Isaiah 60–66:

> "Arise, shine; for your light has come,
> And the glory of the Lord has risen upon you.
> For behold, darkness will cover the earth
> And deep darkness the peoples;
> But the Lord will rise upon you
> And His glory will appear upon you.
> Nations will come to your light,
> And kings to the brightness of your rising."

Darkness is upon the earth but God's glory shines upon Israel and consequently nations come to this light. This could correspond to the creation account in Genesis 1 when darkness was replaced with God's light. Blessings for Israel according to Isaiah 60–61 include:

- The nations and their kings will come to Israel (60:5, 11).
- Israel will prosper materially (60:6–9, 17).
- Violence will be removed from the land (60:18).
- Israel will rely on the light of the Lord, not on the sun and the moon (60:19–20).
- All the people will be righteous (60:21a).
- The people will "possess the land forever" (60:21b).
- The land will produce double (61:7).
- The ruins of Israel's cities will be restored (61:4).
- Israel will receive an "everlasting covenant" (61:8).

Isaiah 62 then reveals God cannot keep quiet about His plans to save and bless Israel. The nations will see Israel's restoration. Isaiah 63 shows that God's plans to save Israel involve a violent encounter between the Deliverer of Israel and hostile nations:

"I have trodden the wine trough alone,
And from the peoples there was no man with Me.
I also trod them in My anger
And trampled them in My wrath;
And their lifeblood is sprinkled on My garments,
And I stained all My raiment.
"For the day of vengeance was in My heart,
And My year of redemption has come.
"I looked, and there was no one to help,
And I was astonished and there was no one to uphold;
So My own arm brought salvation to Me,
And My wrath upheld Me.
"I trod down the peoples in My anger
And made them drunk in My wrath,
And I poured out their lifeblood on the earth" (Isa 63:3–6).

The nations that descend upon Israel for her destruction will face Israel's Messiah who intervenes dramatically on her behalf. His garments are stained with blood as He defends Israel unilaterally. As Rydelnik and Spencer state, "God has acted alone because no one else was willing to take up the cause of beleaguered Israel (Isa 63:4–5). The destruction of the nations will come through the singular activity of the Son of God."[38]

Isaiah 65:17–25

Isaiah 65:17–25 is the first explicit reference to a "new earth": "For behold, I create new heavens and a new earth" (65:17). The amazing conditions described in this passage include:

- Jerusalem will be a source of joy (19a).
- There will be no more weeping and crying (19b).
- No infants will die (20a).
- Older people will live out their lives and not die early (20b).

38 Michael Rydelnik and James Spencer, "Isaiah," in *The Moody Bible Commentary: A One-Volume Commentary on the Whole Bible by the Faculty of Moody Bible Institute*, ed. Michael Rydelnik and Michael Vanlaningham (Chicago: Moody, 2014), 1098.

- One who dies at age 100 will be considered cursed (20c).
- People will live in the houses they build (21a).
- Those who plant vineyards will eat the fruit of their labor (21b).
- People will live long lives and enjoy what they worked for (22).
- The animal kingdom will exist in harmony (25).

The conditions described here are far better than what is experienced in this fallen world.

God says He will "create Jerusalem for rejoicing" and its "people" will experience "gladness" (v. 18). No "weeping" or "crying" will exist in it (v. 19). So again the significance of transformed conditions in Jerusalem is emphasized. Verse 20 tells of longevity of life:

> No longer will there be in it an infant who lives but a few days,
> Or an old man who does not live out his days;
> For the youth will die at the age of one hundred
> And the one who does not reach the age of one hundred
> Will be thought accursed.

During this period infant mortality is nonexistent and no "old man" will die prematurely. Thus, living expectations for both young and old are dramatically better than they are in this present age. Yet this is not a period with no death whatsoever. There will be some cases of death. For example, "the youth will die at the age of one hundred," and a person who dies at the age of one hundred will be considered "accursed." Since long life is the norm during this era news that a person died at age 100 will be surprising. Something wrong must have happened or death would not have occurred at such an early age.

This naturally leads to the issue of *when* such conditions will occur. During this present era the human lifespan is in the 70–80 year range (see Ps 90:10), so death at age 100 is not considered premature. If someone dies around 100 today we don't exclaim, "What happened? What went wrong?"[39]

39 Westermann notes, "If a person happens not to attain to a hundred years, there must be some exceptional reason for this." Claus Westermann, *Isaiah 40–66: A Commentary* (Philadelphia: Westminster Press, 1969), 409.

Yet in the coming eternal state, as described in Revelation 21:4, "there will be no more death." Death no longer exists. So when do the conditions of Isaiah 65:20 occur? The best view is that the conditions of Isaiah 65:20 occur in an *intermediate kingdom* that comes between our present era and the eternal state. This coincides with the millennium of Revelation 20. Compare:

Present Age (Ps 90:10)	**Intermediate Kingdom (Isa 65:20; Rev 20:1–6)**	**Eternal State (Rev 21:4)**
Lifespan is around 70 to 80 years	Increased lifespan but death still occurs	No death

Verse 21 reveals the presence of dwelling places, agriculture and enjoyment of produce: "They will build houses and inhabit them; they will also plant vineyards and eat their fruit." This shows continuity with experiences in this age. Just as people today live in dwelling places and plant vineyards and eat its fruit, so too these will happen on the "new earth." Those activities are not unspiritual. Adam was to cultivate the Garden of Eden and he was allowed to eat the fruit of all the trees (except the tree of the knowledge of good and evil). Why wouldn't the new earth also include these kinds of activities?

Isaiah 65:22 details the fairness of these times: "They will not build and another inhabit, they will not plant and another eat." Hard workers will not have the results of their labor unfairly taken from them. Those who plant will enjoy the fruit of their work. Unfairness and corruption often characterize life in this fallen world, but not so on the "new earth." The experiences of building and planting still continue on the new earth. What is missing, though, is corruption and mistreatment.

Isaiah 65:25a discusses changes in the animal world: "The wolf and the lamb will graze together, and the lion will eat straw like the ox; and dust will be the serpent's food." Animals that don't normally get along will do so. Plus, the nature of animals may be altered to fit the new harmonious conditions of this era, even if it means meat-eating lions will eat straw. Like Isaiah 11, this verse indicates restoration of the created order, including animals.

Also, similarity exists between what people do now and what they will do in the coming kingdom. This is no "church service in the sky" experience but a real and tangible existence for human beings on a restored earth. People still have emotions, live in cities, plant vineyards, live in houses, and work. Animals are also present.

Isaiah 65:17–25 also has relevance to an intermediate kingdom. Christians of the second century viewed this passage as support for a coming millennial kingdom on earth. Martin Erdmann claims Isaiah 65:20–25 formed "the scriptural basis, besides Rev. 20:1–10, on which Asiatic millennialism built its chiliastic [millennial] doctrine."[40] This was true for Justin Martyr. In reference to Isaiah 65 Justin said, "For Isaiah spoke thus concerning this period of a thousand years."[41] Erdmann also observes that Justin's reference to OT prophets "indicates his reliance on the Old Testament as the primary source of his chiliasm. He did not shy away from utilizing different passages from the Hebrew Bible to strengthen his argument in favor of a literal millennium."[42]

Did Isaiah Use "Ideal Present" Language?

Isaiah 65:17–25 predicts an era with childbirth and rare cases of death. Some believe such descriptions should not be taken literally. Allegedly, Isaiah was describing conditions his original readers would not be able to grasp. So when the conditions of Isaiah 65 are fulfilled there will be no childbirth or death. Sam Storms, for example, believes Isaiah 65 is an example of exaggerated language in terms of "ideal present" language:

> The best and most intelligible way that the original author of this prophecy could communicate the *realistic future* glory of the new heaven and new earth, to people who were necessarily limited by the progress of revelation to that point in time, was to portray it in the hyperbolic or exaggerated terms of an ideal present.[43]

40 Martin Erdmann, *The Millennial Controversy in the Early Church* (Eugene, OR: Wipf and Stock, 2005), 118.

41 Justin Martyr, *Dialogue with Trypho, The Ante-Nicene Fathers* 80, 1:239.

42 Erdmann, *The Millennial* Controversy, 138.

43 Sam Storms, *Kingdom Come: The Amillennial Alternative* (Mentor, 2013), 35.

Thus, for Storms, "His [Isaiah's] point isn't to assert that people will actually die or that women will continue to give birth. Rather, he has taken two very concrete and painful experiences from the common life of people in his own day to illustrate what to them, then, was an almost unimaginable and inexpressible glory yet to come."[44]

There are problems with this view. In addition to denying what the text appears to be saying, this perspective underestimates what Isaiah's audience was capable of grasping. If Isaiah had declared, "There is no childbirth or death at all on the coming new earth," would his audience not be able to understand this language? Would stating this confuse them or be so far beyond their thinking? Probably not. We need to give the original audience more credit concerning what they could understand. After all, Isaiah 25:8 predicts the removal of death. Storms even acknowledges that Isaiah 25 explicitly states a day is coming when no death exists.[45] So there is no issue with Isaiah or Isaiah's audience being able to grasp the concept of no death. When Isaiah predicts a future day where there is childbirth in the kingdom and examples of premature death, he most probably means what he says. And his audience could grasp this. This seems to be a simpler and better way to understand Isaiah's words. The theory of "ideal present" language in Isaiah 65 does not seem justified.

CONCLUSION

Isaiah contains many great truths about the kingdom program. The prophet relies heavily upon the promises given to David in the Davidic Covenant. There is a coming day when the nations of the earth will stream to Jerusalem to worship and learn about Israel's God. The Lord will make executive decisions on behalf of the nations, and the weapons of warfare will give way to tools of peace (see Isa 2:2–4). The coming kingdom is centered in the Messiah who comes as a child, and on Him the government of the kingdom will rest. He will sit on the throne of His father David, and there will be no end to His kingdom, which will be characterized by justice and righteousness (Isa 9:6–7). Edenic conditions will be restored as evidenced by peace

44 Storms, *Kingdom Come*, 35–36.

45 Ibid., 167.

in the animal kingdom (see Isa 6:6–9). The road to the kingdom is *via* the Suffering Servant who atones for sin (Isa 52–53). There will also be a time of global tribulation for the nations of the earth, who are judged for being covenant breakers. But after this judgment the kingdom will be established (see Isa 24–27). At this time the nations of the earth will become the people of God alongside Israel who still remains God's people (see Isa 19). Glorious conditions will occur on the earth.

CHAPTER

10 THE KINGDOM IN JEREMIAH

Jeremiah's ministry covered the final fifty years of Judah's kingdom leading up to the Babylonian captivity. The prophet declared Judah's violations of the Mosaic Covenant and the devastating consequences to come. Yet during bleak times the Lord offered words of hope anchored in the glories of a coming kingdom. This included the promise of a New Covenant and its blessings of salvation and restoration. Jeremiah makes a major contribution by detailing how the New Covenant relates to the kingdom program.

BLESSINGS FOR A UNITED ISRAEL (JEREMIAH 3:12–18)

Jeremiah 3:12–18 foretells a united Israel that will experience kingdom blessings as a result of turning to the Lord. God sent Jeremiah with a message to the northern kingdom of Israel that was taken captive by the Assyrians: "'Return, faithless Israel,' declares the LORD; 'I will not look upon you in anger. For I am gracious'" (3:12). The term "return" (*shub*) carries the meaning of repentance. Thus, the condition for forgiveness was repentance. Israel needed to acknowledge its iniquities, and admit it "transgressed against the LORD" (3:13).[1] If Israel does this the LORD will take them from cities where

1 "While God offers to allow Israel to return (vv. 12, 14), the offer does carry conditions (v. 13). Guilt and covenant disobedience need to be acknowledged, and Israel's return needs to be with 'her whole heart.'" John Martin Bracke, *Jeremiah 1–29*, Westminster Bible Companion (Louisville, KY: John Knox, 2000), 39.

they have been scattered and "bring you to Zion" (3:14). Kingdom conditions for Israel are contingent on turning back to the Lord.

Then, not only will the LORD bring Israel back to its homeland, He said, "I will give you shepherds after My own heart, who will feed you on knowledge and understanding" (3:15). For so long the northern tribes of Israel listened to false prophets and teachers, but one day God will give them shepherds aligned with God's heart.

That Jeremiah is discussing future times is evident by the words "in those days" (3:16) and "at that time" (3:17). Verse 16 promises two things for Israel. First, Israel will be "multiplied and increased in the land." Second, there will be no need for the Ark of the Covenant—"They shall say no more, 'The ark of the covenant of the Lord.' And it shall not come to mind, nor shall they remember it, nor shall they miss it, nor shall it be made again" (3:16). The ark represented the presence of God in the Mosaic Covenant era, yet in the future the presence of God will be with His people even more directly. Also, this shows a transition in the last days away from the Mosaic Covenant to the New Covenant (see Jer 31:31–34). Since the New Covenant replaces the Mosaic Covenant, there is no longer any need for the ark which represented the Old Covenant.[2]

The regal nature of this period is clear since Jerusalem will be called "The Throne of the Lord" (3:17). But this kingdom is not just for Israel since Jeremiah says, "all the nations will be gathered to it" (3:17). Again this shows Israel's kingdom is not just for Israel but also for all nations that walk by the ways of the Lord. Israel is a means for blessing the nations and is not an end in itself. This kingdom period will be characterized by heart obedience since the people will no longer walk by their stubborn hearts (3:17).

Harmony in Israel characterizes this period as "the house of Judah will walk with the house of Israel, and they will come together from the land of the north to the land that I gave your fathers as an inheritance" (3:18). For the first time since Solomon's reign, Israel will be united and the tribes of Israel will be at peace with each other. This unification will be in the "land" God promised to Israel's fathers. Even after division and dispersion of the tribes of Israel the expectation of a literal land is still part of Israel's

2 Kaiser says, "The Ark of the Covenant, traditionally the throne of God, would now be replaced by Jerusalem, the new throne of God." Kaiser, "Evidence from Jeremiah," 107.

hope. After captivity the prophets still speak of a future land for Israel. This connection of a coming land for Israel with what God promised the fathers shows the original land promised to Abraham's descendants is not a type or shadow that is superseded or replaced. God's purposes include many facets including a literal land where a restored Israel resides.

In sum, this passage shows that temporary judgment for disobedience does not mean God is done with the nation Israel. Blessings will come to Israel, yet these blessings are contingent on Israel's repentance. Jeremiah 3:12–18 is a backdrop for the coming declaration of Jesus—"Repent for the kingdom of heaven is at hand" (Matt 4:17).

ISRAEL'S REPENTANCE TO BLESS NATIONS (JEREMIAH 4:1–2)

Contingency resurfaces again in Jeremiah 4:1–2. Whereas, Jeremiah 3:12–18 emphasized kingdom blessings for Israel if national repentance transpired, Jeremiah 4 reveals that Israel's repentance will lead to blessings for the nations:

> "*If* you will return, O Israel," declares the LORD... *then* the nations will bless themselves in Him, and in Him they will glory.

This reaffirms the truth of Genesis 12:2–3 and 22:18 that God's plans include the nation Israel and Gentile nations. Israel needs to know that their obedience or disobedience affects others as well as themselves. Israel's repentance can lead to the salvation of Gentiles.

RESTORATION OF ISRAEL TO THE LAND (JEREMIAH 16:14–15)

Jeremiah 16 explicitly predicts the coming restoration of Israel to the land. Discussing events to come the LORD declares, "days are coming" (16:14a). He then states the exodus from Egypt will no longer be what people think about (16:14b). Why? God will accomplish an even more amazing act by restoring the tribes of Israel from their dispersion. This is what people will talk about. God is going to bring the sons of Israel from the north and from the countries where they had been banished (16:15a). The result—"For I will restore them to their own land which I gave to their fathers" (16:15b). This again shows that the restoration of Israel is a major theme of the prophets and that land promises to Israel will be fulfilled because of God's faithfulness to the patriarchs of Israel. Just as Israel's first exodus was a real deliverance for the people of Israel, so too will this future restoration.

CONTINGENCY AND NATIONS (JEREMIAH 18:1–11)

Jeremiah 18 is foundational for understanding contingency in God's dealing with nations, and it has important ramifications for Israel's relationship to the kingdom of God. Here we find conditions for blessings. This chapter reveals how God responds to nations and emphasizes both God's sovereignty and His varied responses to nations based on their actions. The context of Jeremiah 18 is God's use of the potter and clay analogy:

> The word which came to Jeremiah from the LORD saying, "Arise and go down to the potter's house, and there I will announce My words to you." Then I went down to the potter's house, and there he was, making something on the wheel. But the vessel that he was making of clay was spoiled in the hand of the potter; so he remade it into another vessel, as it pleased the potter to make (Jer 18:1–4).

The potter and clay analogy emphasizes God's sovereignty and the Creator's superiority and control over His creatures. This analogy is part of Paul's argument in Romans 9 where Paul explains God's sovereignty with His saving purposes (Rom 9:20–23). Then the potter and clay analogy is related to Israel:

> Then the word of the Lord came to me saying, "Can I not, O house of Israel, deal with you as this potter does?" declares the Lord. "Behold, like the clay in the potter's hand, so are you in My hand, O house of Israel. At one moment I might speak concerning a nation or concerning a kingdom to uproot, to pull down, or to destroy it; if that nation against which I have spoken turns from its evil, I will relent concerning the calamity I planned to bring on it. Or at another moment I might speak concerning a nation or concerning a kingdom to build up or to plant it; if it does evil in My sight by not obeying My voice, then I will think better of the good with which I had promised to bless it. So now

> then, speak to the men of Judah and against the inhabitants of Jerusalem saying, 'Thus says the Lord, "Behold, I am fashioning calamity against you and devising a plan against you. Oh turn back, each of you from his evil way, and reform your ways and your deeds'" (Jer 18:5–11).

Particularly important is the statement that God might declare calamity upon a nation, yet if that nation repents of its evil then God will "relent concerning the calamity" He predicted (vv. 7–8). In other words, if a nation repents, God will not bring judgment upon the nation. Likewise, God might speak of blessing for a nation, yet if that nation does evil in God's sight, then God will not bring blessing. So then, *by God's sovereign design the responses of a nation can influence God's dealings with that nation.* As Toussaint observes concerning Jeremiah 18, "Here the response of a nation to God's prophecy may affect its future."[3]

One example of this principle is Jonah. Jonah prophesied Nineveh would be destroyed in forty days—"Yet forty days and Nineveh will be overthrown" (Jonah 3:4). But the people of Nineveh and their king "believed in God" and repented (Jonah 3:5–9). As a result, God relented concerning his judgment upon them: "When God saw their deeds, that they turned from their wicked way, then God relented concerning the calamity which He had declared He would bring upon them. And He did not do it" (Jonah 3:10). Judgment was predicted for Nineveh in forty days, yet Nineveh repented and justice was delayed. Ninevah's repentance delayed judgment.

Compare the principle in Jeremiah 18 with what occurs in Jonah 3:

> **Jeremiah 18:8**: "if that nation against which I have spoken turns from its evil, *I will relent concerning the calamity I planned to bring on it.*"

> **Jonah 3:10**: "When God saw their deeds, that they turned from their wicked way, *then God relented concerning the calamity which He had declared He would bring upon them.* And He did not do it" (Jonah 3:10).

3 Toussaint, "The Contingency of the Coming of the Kingdom," 225.

THE RIGHTEOUS REIGN OF DAVID (JEREMIAH 23:1–8)

In regard to Jeremiah 23:1–8, Walter Kaiser says "the announcement of the final king in the line of David lies at the heart of this great messianic text."[4] This section starts with a woe to false shepherds who destroyed and scattered God's people, Israel (23:1). The Lord, though, will gather the remnant of His flock from the countries where they were driven. They will be brought back to the land where they will prosper—Israel "will be fruitful and multiply" (23:3). This is a real restoration. As Charles Feinberg stated, "Just as the scattering of the people was literal, so will the regathering be."[5]

The Lord promises He will "raise up shepherds over them" who will take care of His people (23:4). The heart of the promise is then found in verses 5 and 6:

> "Behold, the days are coming," declares the Lord,
> "When I will raise up for David a righteous Branch;
> And He will reign as king and act wisely
> And do justice and righteousness in the land.
> In His days Judah will be saved,
> And Israel will dwell securely;
> And this is His name by which He will be called,
> 'The LORD our righteousness.'"

That these events will happen in the future is evident by the words "days are coming." What is coming is a restoration of the Davidic kingdom through a coming of David who is a "righteous Branch." He will reign wisely in the land of Israel. He will lead Judah to salvation and Israel will dwell securely under His reign. Israel experienced the Davidic reign coming to an end. But an ultimate David will restore the kingdom to Israel and the nation will be blessed again under its King.

A connection exists between spiritual and physical blessings here. "Judah will be saved" has spiritual implications. Yet "Israel will dwell securely" which refers to physical protection from enemies. The "land" is mentioned twice. Verse five says the "righteous Branch" will "do justice and

---

4 Kaiser, "Evidence from Jeremiah," 108.

5 Charles L. Feinberg, "Jeremiah," in *Expositor's Bible Commentary*, vol. 6, ed. Frank E. Gaebelein (Grand Rapids: Zondervan, 1986), 517.

righteousness in the land." Then verse 8 declares, "Then they will live in their own land." The passage also likens Israel's future restoration to the exodus when the Lord "brought the Israelites out of Egypt." When this future restoration occurs the talk will no longer be about the first exodus but about the time when the Lord "brought the descendants of Israel up out of the land of the north and out of all the countries where he had banished them" (23:8) (NIV). This comparison with the first exodus is significant. Just as the first exodus was a literal rescue of the people of Israel, so too will this coming second exodus be a restoration of national Israel from the nations. Feinberg rightly observes that "the messianic hope is the national restoration of Israel (cf. 16:14–15)."[6]

NEW COVENANT CONDITIONS (JEREMIAH 30–33)

The most detailed information concerning the kingdom of God in Jeremiah is found in chapters 30–33, a section called "the Book of Consolation." Much attention in Jeremiah before this has focused on the judgment of Judah. Yet Jeremiah 30–33 offers great hope after judgment.

According to Jeremiah 32:1, Jerusalem was in the final stage of an eighteen-month siege by the Babylonians.[7] Other cities of Judah had already fallen. The situation appeared hopeless. Yet in the midst of turmoil, including Jeremiah's imprisonment, are hopeful prophecies about the salvation and restoration of all Israel. Feinberg summarizes the message of hope for Israel in Jeremiah:

- The permanence of the nation Israel
- The Gentiles coming to the truth
- The New Covenant given to all Israel
- The rule of the Davidic King over Zion[8]

6 Feinberg, "Jeremiah," 519.

7 Ibid., Chapters 32–33 were given in the tenth year of Zedediah just when "the final blow was about to fall."

8 Ibid., 558.

Promise of Restoration (Jeremiah 30)

Jeremiah 30 begins with the promise of restoration for Israel:

> "For behold, days are coming," declares the LORD, "when I will restore the fortunes of My people Israel and Judah." The LORD says, "I will also bring them back to the land that I gave to their forefathers and they shall possess it" (30:3).

The time markers at the beginning and end of this chapter show the period of this restoration is future. Verse 3 states, "days are coming," and verse 24 declares "in the latter days." The conditions described in chapters 30–33 have not been fulfilled at any point in history; they look forward to future fulfillment.

Israel will be restored to "the land" in connection with the promise given to Israel's "forefathers." Thus, New Covenant conditions in this section are linked with the Abrahamic Covenant and its promise of a land forever. What God promised to Abraham, Isaac, and Jacob must come to fruition just as He predicted. There is no indication land is no longer important or that land is merely a shadow or type of something else.

This restoration of Israel to the land will be preceded by a great "day" or what other Bible writers refer to as "the Day of the Lord." This Day of the Lord is also a "time of Jacob's distress" (30:7) in which Israel faces terrible calamity. But in the end, "he [Israel] will be saved from it" (30:7). The day will be very difficult but it results in salvation for the nation. What Jeremiah reveals is consistent with the message of other prophetic books—the salvation and restoration of Israel will occur, but this is preceded by tribulation and distress (see Isa 24–25; Dan 12:1–3; Matt 24; Rev 6–19). Or in other words, tribulation precedes kingdom. Jeremiah 30 reveals coming kingdom conditions:

- the offspring of Israel will return from captivity (10)
- nations that oppressed Israel will be punished (11)
- Israel's health will be restored and wounds will be cured (17)
- the city will be rebuilt (18)
- the palace will stand on its rightful place (18)
- Israel will be the people of God (22)

The Promise of the New Covenant (Jeremiah 31)

Promises of restoration for Israel abound in Jeremiah 31. A unified Israel will be the people of God (1). Israel will be rebuilt (4). The nation will be filled with joy (4–6). Israel will be regathered from remote parts of the earth (8). Agriculture and livestock will prosper (12). The young and old in Israel will be joyful (13). Sorrow over negative things will cease (16).

Until this point, the emphasis has been on the physical blessings associated with Israel's restoration. But with Jeremiah 31:31–34, the New Covenant discusses the promise of a new heart that will be at the center of Israel's restoration and relationship with God. This "new covenant" will be made "with the house of Israel and the house of Judah" (31). Thus, a united Israel is the vehicle through which this covenant comes. This New Covenant is not the Mosaic Covenant which Israel broke (32). The New Covenant involves the promise from God, "I will put My law within them and on their heart I will write it; and I will be their God, and they shall be My people" (33). The Mosaic Covenant was good and holy but it did not enable Israel to obey God. But God will provide the enablement to obey by putting His law within the hearts of His people.

God then links His covenant faithfulness to Israel with the fixed order of the sun, moon, and stars. He also links it with the heavens and the foundations of the earth (35–37). *This shows the perpetuity of Israel's existence as a nation in the plan of God.* As long as people can view the cosmic bodies in the heavens, they can know God has not removed the nation Israel from His plans. The city will also be rebuilt from the Tower of Hananel to the Corner Gate (38). This shows the importance of Jerusalem in God's purposes. Complete fulfillment of the New Covenant involves the restoration of the city of Jerusalem (see Luke 21:24).

Physical and Spiritual Blessings of the Kingdom (Jeremiah 32:36–44)

Jeremiah 32:36–44 encapsulates the restoration of Israel spiritually and physically in the kingdom under the New Covenant. It concerns the "city" of Jerusalem captured by Babylon (36). The Lord will reverse these circumstances by gathering the people of Israel "out of all the lands" where they had been scattered. God "will bring them back to this place [Jerusalem] and make them dwell in safety" (37).

The scope of this regathering is beyond Babylon. The reference to "lands" indicates something on a global scale. The people will live in safety and God will be their God (38). Then again, the Lord refers to a heart transformation for Israel by saying, "I will give them one heart and one way, that they may fear Me always" (39a). This will benefit not only those who see these things come to pass but "the good of their children after them" (39b).

The New Covenant of Jeremiah 31:31 is also called "an everlasting covenant" (40). God then reaffirms His plan to "plant them in this land" (41). All the disasters brought upon the people will be replaced with "all the good that I am promising them" (42). "Men will buy fields for money" and "sign and seal deeds" (44a). This will occur all throughout the land, as God "will restore their fortunes" (44b).

God's New Covenant blessings involve a mixture of spiritual and physical blessings. The people will have a new heart and a right relationship with God, yet this translates into physical prosperity—dwelling in the Promised Land and perpetual peace. There is no dualism between physical and spiritual blessings as if the former are not important or give way to spiritual blessings only.

The Five Unconditional Covenants (Jeremiah 33)

As the Book of Consolation ends, we see another affirmation of the restoration of Israel after judgment. Uniquely, Jeremiah 33 explicitly refers to all five unconditional covenants—Noahic, Abrahamic, Priestly, Davidic, and New Covenants. All five together convey the absolute seriousness of God's intent to restore the nation Israel. To use a modern saying—God brings in all the big guns to show how serious He is about restoring Israel.

Jeremiah 33 begins with a solemn declaration from the creator God who made the earth (33:2). Then God reveals His plans to restore Israel: "I will restore the fortunes of Judah and the fortunes of Israel and will rebuild them as they were at first" (33:7). The five unconditional covenants are then brought in to establish this.

First, the *New Covenant* was explicitly mentioned in Jeremiah 31, especially 31:31–34. In 31:34b God said concerning Israel: "I will forgive their iniquity, and their sin I will remember no more." In Jeremiah 33:8 the forgiveness aspect of the New Covenant is again mentioned: "I will cleanse them from all their iniquity by which they have sinned against Me, and I will pardon all their iniquities by which they have sinned against Me and by which they have transgressed against Me." Thus, the restoration of Israel is linked with the New Covenant and its promise of forgiveness.

Second, Jeremiah brings up the *Davidic Covenant.* He says, "days are coming" when the Lord will fulfill His promises with Israel and Judah (33:14). This includes the springing forth of "a righteous Branch of David" who will "execute justice and righteousness on the earth" (33:15). There will be a salvation of Judah and protection of Jerusalem (33:16). With the Davidic Covenant in mind, God declares, "David shall never lack a man to sit on the throne of the house of Israel" (33:17). Thus, New Covenant kingdom conditions will take place under a coming David, the ultimate Son of David—Jesus the Messiah.

Third, Jeremiah mentions the *Priestly Covenant* in verse 18: "and the Levitical priests shall never lack a man before Me to offer burnt offerings, to burn grain offerings and to prepare sacrifices continually.'" While not as well known as the other unconditional covenants of Scripture, the Priestly covenant God made with Phineas is also important.[9] The background for this covenant is found in Numbers 25. At a time when many in Israel joined themselves to Baal of Peor, Phineas took a spear and pierced a man of Israel and a Midianite woman who entered a tent for immoral purposes before all the congregation of Israel. The Lord honored Phineas with a covenant of peace that involved a perpetual priesthood for him and his descendants:

> Then the LORD spoke to Moses, saying, "Phinehas the son of Eleazar, the son of Aaron the priest, has turned away My wrath from the sons of Israel in that he was jealous with My jealousy among them, so that I did not destroy the sons of Israel in My jealousy. Therefore say, 'Behold, I give him My covenant of peace; and it shall be for him and his descendants after him, a

9 Busenitz notes, "The perpetual nature of the Priestly Covenant suggests that it should stand as a separate covenant" and "the terminology employed is similar to the covenants made with Noah, Abraham, David, and the New Covenant." Irvin A. Busenitz, "Introduction to the Biblical Covenants: The Noahic Covenant and the Priestly Covenant," *The Master's Seminary Journal* 10 (1999): 188.

> covenant of a perpetual priesthood, because he was jealous for his God and made atonement for the sons of Israel'" (25:10–13).

Next, not only are these kingdom promises sure because of the irrevocable nature of the New Covenant, the Davidic Covenant, and the Priestly covenant, they are sure because of the *Noahic Covenant*. In Genesis 8:22b, God's covenant with Noah included the following promise:

> "And day and night
> Shall not cease."

In Jeremiah 33:19–22, the Noahic Covenant,[10] couched in "day" and "night" language, is linked with the Davidic and Priestly Covenants:

> The word of the LORD came to Jeremiah, saying, "Thus says the LORD, 'If you can break My covenant for the day and My covenant for the night, so that day and night will not be at their appointed time, then My covenant may also be broken with David My servant so that he will not have a son to reign on his throne, and with the Levitical priests, My ministers. As the host of heaven cannot be counted and the sand of the sea cannot be measured, so I will multiply the descendants of David My servant and the Levites who minister to Me.'"

The restoration of national Israel is again linked to the Noahic Covenant in 33:25–26:

> Thus says the LORD, "If My covenant for day and night stand not, and the fixed patterns of heaven and earth I have not established, then I would reject the descendants of Jacob and David My servant, not taking from his descendants rulers over the descendants of Abraham, Isaac and Jacob. But I will restore their fortunes and will have mercy on them."

10 There is some debate as to whether the language refers to the Noahic Covenant or an earlier creation covenant. Paul Williamson states that Jeremiah 33:20–26 "is most likely a reference to the Noahic covenant, as is the further elaboration in Jeremiah 33:25. Clearly, the covenant in question is considered permanent and unbreakable, and the assurance given here resonates with the strong affirmative language used in the context of the Noahic covenant (cf. Gen. 8:21–22)." Paul R. Williamson, *Sealed with an Oath: Covenant in God's Unfolding Purposes* (Downers Grove, IL: InterVarsity Academic, 2007), 66.

The message is simple—if the normal patterns of nature are still in effect then one can know God's plans to restore Israel are still in effect. The Noahic Covenant continues to operate as the platform through which God's kingdom purposes are played out in history.

Lastly, the *Abrahamic Covenant* appears to be alluded to in Jeremiah 30:22:

> As the host of heaven cannot be counted and the *sand of the sea* cannot be measured, so I will *multiply the descendants* of David My servant and the Levites who minister to Me.

This compares with the Abrahamic Covenant promise of Genesis 22:17:

> Indeed I will greatly bless you, and I will greatly *multiply your seed* as the stars of the heavens and as the *sand which is on the seashore.*[11]

Summary of the Kingdom Program in Jeremiah

The kingdom program is significant in Jeremiah. Because of covenant disobedience, Judah will experience judgment and captivity by Babylon. Yet because of God's faithfulness to the Abrahamic Covenant, the people of Israel will be regathered from the nations and restored to their own land where they will forever live in prosperity and peace. The coming New Covenant guarantees the people of Israel will be saved and have a new heart as the basis for their obedience to the Lord. All of this will take place under the fulfillment of the Davidic Covenant in which the ultimate descendant ("branch") of David will rule over a restored Israel. Thus, in the midst of catastrophic judgment, there is a message of hope based on the faithfulness of God to His name and His covenant promises. Both Israel and the nations will see this and give glory to God who made heaven and earth.

11 The italics in both Scripture references are mine.

CHAPTER

11 THE KINGDOM IN EZEKIEL

Ezekiel was a priest and prophet at the time of the Babylonian Exile. He prophesied between 592 and 570 B.C. and was transported to Babylon in the second deportation of 598. The destruction of the temple occurred in 586.

Two themes permeate the book—judgment and restoration for Israel. Judgment through exile will happen because of Israel's covenant unfaithfulness. Israel continually broke the Mosaic Covenant and was subject to curses and dispersion. This resulted in the dramatic removal of God's presence among His people. In vivid language, Ezekiel prosecuted the case against Israel's leaders for their idolatry and failure to be shepherds over Israel. Yet because God is faithful to His name and His covenant promises, Israel will be restored as the basis for God's restoration of His entire creation.

The book of Ezekiel can be divided into three major sections:

1. God's judgment on Judah (chs. 1–24)
2. God's judgment on Gentile Nations (chs. 25–32)
3. God's blessings on restored Israel (chs. 33–48)

The first two sections (1–24 and 25–32) emphasize judgment, first for Judah, and then for the nations. The last section (33–48) speaks of restoration for a united Israel and directly relates to the establishment of God's kingdom. This includes the return of God's presence to Israel.

Ezekiel's message is consistent with what Deuteronomy 28–30 predicted. Israel failed its calling to be a holy and set apart nation that would be a light to the nations of the world. Because Israel did not keep the Mosaic

Covenant the people were judged and scattered to the nations. Yet these nations that torment God's people will also be judged. Since God is the God of both Israel and the nations, He will show Israel and the nations who He is. For Israel this means regathering from the nations and restoration in the land of promise. Also, the coming New Covenant with its promise of a new heart and indwelling Holy Spirit will be the basis for Israel's spiritual salvation and restoration to the land (Ezek 36–37). The New Covenant will enable Israel to obey God and avoid idolatry. The nations will know the Lord because of these things.

Thus, the message of Ezekiel is a message that God's kingdom plan for both Israel and the nations is still on track, even with such devastating circumstances upon Israel at the time. As Merrill states:

> Above all, Ezekiel was concerned to demonstrate that Yahweh is not only the God of Israel (or Judah) but also of all the earth and that His faithfulness to His covenant pledges to His own people will attest to His sovereignty over all creation in the day when He vindicates them.[1]

Now we turn to specific passages that reveal information about the kingdom program in Ezekiel. Most of the discussion here will be on the restoration chapters of 33–48, yet other sections will be addressed as well.

THE DEPARTURE OF GOD'S GLORY (EZEKIEL 8–11)

With chapters 8–11 Ezekiel is taken in the Spirit to see abominable actions in the temple in Jerusalem. He also views the departure of the glory of the Lord. God's glory had been with Israel since the exodus from Egypt and coincided with the kingdom in Israel. From the Garden of Eden onward it has been God's desire for His people to rule over the earth in His direct presence. But the departure of God's glory from the temple was a catastrophic event. This represented the removal of the kingdom from Israel. The departure of the glory appears in stages, emphasizing the sad and tragic nature of what was happening:

1 Eugene Merrill, "A Theology of Ezekiel and Daniel," in *A Biblical Theology of the Old Testament*, ed. Roy B. Zuck (Chicago: Moody, 1991), 367.

- 9:3: The glory is between the cherubim above the mercy seat.
- 9:3: The glory moves to the temple threshold, the front door.
- 10:1: The glory moves back temporarily.
- 10:4: The glory moves again to the threshold.
- 10:18–19: The glory moves to the east gate by the outer wall.
- 11:22–25: The glory of God leaves the temple and hovers over the Mount of Olives and departs.

McClain comments on this reluctant departure of God's glory:

> We cannot fail to be impressed with the gracious circumstances of the Lord's withdrawal: not suddenly, but slowly and gradually by stages, with seeming tender reluctance; as if He were actually yearning to remain in the place He had chosen for His dwelling place.[2]

The Lord would still speak through His prophets, but His special presence in the temple was no more—at least for the time. The removal of God's glory from the temple was a terrible moment in Israel's history as it marked a temporary end of the mediatorial kingdom. As Pentecost explains, "The departure of the glory of God from its dwelling place between the cherubim marked the temporary end of this form of theocratic administration."[3]

Yet in the midst of this awful event comes a great declaration of hope. Even though Israel is scattered among the countries (11:16), the people are told, "Therefore say, 'Thus says the Lord GOD, I will gather you from the peoples and assemble you out of the countries among which you have been scattered, and I will give you the land of Israel'" (11:17). God promises Israel restoration to the land. Then comes the incredible promise of the New Covenant concerning a new spirit and a new heart:

> "And I will give them one heart, and put a new spirit within them. And I will take the heart of stone out of their flesh and

2 McClain, *The Greatness of the Kingdom*, 124.

3 Pentecost, *Thy Kingdom Come*, 162. McClain states, "We have here one of the most important milestones in all of human history. From the initial coming of the Glory at Sinai to its departure from Jerusalem, the Mediatorial Kingdom had endured for approximately eight centuries." *The Greatness of the Kingdom*, 125.

> give them a heart of flesh, that they may walk in My statutes and keep My ordinances and do them. Then they will be My people, and I shall be their God" (11:19–20).

The removal of God's presence from Israel was only temporary. Just as Ezekiel saw the glory of the Lord depart the temple in Jerusalem, the prophet will see the glory of the Lord return to the temple. This is the message of Ezekiel 43:1–7:

> He led me to the gate, the one that faces east, and I saw the glory of the God of Israel coming from the east.... The glory of the Lord entered the temple by way of the gate that faced east. Then the Spirit lifted me up and brought me to the inner court, and the glory of the Lord filled the temple. While the man was standing beside me, I heard someone speaking to me from the temple. He said to me: "Son of man, this is the place of My throne and the place for the soles of My feet, where I will dwell among the Israelites forever. The house of Israel and their kings will no longer defile My holy name by their religious prostitution and by the corpses of their kings at their high places" (HCSB).

When Jesus returns a second time He will come to the Mount of Olives on the East side (see Acts 1:9–12). Zechariah 14:2–3 states a day is coming when the Lord will fight the nations in battle and then "On that day His feet will stand on the Mount of Olives" (HCSB). The Lord will then "be king over all the earth" (Zech 14:9). The return of the glory of the Lord to Jerusalem in the person of Jesus Christ means the return of God's glory to Israel and the reign of the Lord as King over all the earth.

THE COMING SPRIG (EZEKIEL 17:22–24)

Kingdom implications exist in Ezekiel 17:22–24 where a horticulture expression is used of a messianic figure who will restore the Davidic kingdom.[4] The Lord will take a sprig from a regal cedar and plant it on a high mountain. As Merrill observes, "The diminutive shoot will itself become a giant tree, so

4 Other horticulture expressions with messianic implications in the OT include "shoot," "sprout," and "branch."

impressive that all other trees will marvel at the God who can make so much out of so little."[5] This "sprig" will be planted on Israel's high mountain and become a majestic cedar (17:23). The point is God's kingdom will have small and humble beginnings that give way to a glorious manifestation seen by all. The "sprig" here ultimately finds fulfillment with the coming King, Jesus the Messiah. The kingdom truths of Ezekiel 17:22–24 could be part of the informing theology of Jesus' mustard seed parable in Matthew 13:31–32 in which the kingdom has small beginnings but then grows into a large tree.

ISRAEL'S COMING RESTORATION (EZEKIEL 20:33–44)

The restoration of Israel for the glory of God's name is the focus of Ezekiel 20. Israel was dispersed because of disobedience to the Lord. But God will restore the nation. He will establish His rule over Israel: "'As I live,' declares the Lord GOD, 'surely with a mighty hand and with an outstretched arm and with wrath poured out, I shall be king over you'" (20:33). This will be accomplished as God brings His people back from the lands where they were scattered (20:34). He will bring Israel into "the wilderness of the people" and from there He will "enter into judgment" with them "face to face" (20:35). Israel will "pass under the rod" of judgment (20:37).

Two things will be accomplished. First, the Lord will bring Israel "into the bond of the covenant" (20:37). Second, He will remove the rebels so they do not experience the blessings of the land (20:38). From God's holy mountain "the whole house of Israel... will serve Me in the land" (20:40). God states that He will bring Israel into the land because He "swore" to the "forefathers" that He would do so. God is a covenant-keeping God. What He promised to Israel's patriarchs He will accomplish. This He does for His own glory, not because Israel is worthy. "'Then you will know that I am the Lord when I have dealt with you for My name's sake, not according to your evil ways or according to your corrupt deeds, O house of Israel, declares the Lord GOD'" (20:44). The events described in this section will occur in connection with the return of Jesus at His second coming.

5 Merrill, "A Theology of Ezekiel and Daniel," 381.

ISRAEL, THE LAND, AND THE KINGDOM (EZEKIEL 33–39)

The judgment sections that precede Ezekiel 33 may lead one to think God's covenant promises to Israel are lost. But that is not the case. Ezekiel 33–39 speaks to the gathering, salvation, restoration, and unification of Israel under the Davidic King and the New Covenant. Neither Israel's past disobedience nor persecution of the nation will stop God from fulfilling His promises to the patriarchs of Israel.

The setting for the message of kingdom restoration in Ezekiel 33–39 is dramatic. The date was December 586 B.C. and Jerusalem was in ruins. Word of the tragedy was just reaching the Jews in Babylon. What worse news could there be than that Jerusalem, the city of the great King, had been destroyed? What about the land promised to Abraham, Isaac, and Jacob? Were the promises forever gone? As news is about to reach Ezekiel and the exiles, Ezekiel receives a series of night oracles. These oracles, as Ralph Alexander puts it, were "to encourage the exiles that ultimately God would remove these invaders and restore the land to Israel. Then He will enter into a covenant of peace with Israel."[6]

From False Shepherds to the True Shepherd (Ezekiel 34)

Using the analogy of sheep and shepherd, the Lord indicts the false shepherds of Israel who failed to guide the people. Instead of caring for the people, they only cared for themselves and brought ruin to God's people (Ezek 34:1–10). But the sheep of Israel who are "scattered" to the nations will be gathered by the Lord and placed back in their "land" (Ezek 34:11–13a). The Lord "will feed them on the mountains of Israel, by the streams, and in all the inhabited places of the land" (34:13b). The false shepherds will be judged and replaced with a true Shepherd, one from the line of David who will restore the people:

> "Then I will set over them one shepherd, My servant David, and he will feed them; he will feed them himself and be their shepherd. And I, the Lord, will be their God, and My servant

6 Ralph Alexander, *Ezekiel* (Chicago: Moody, 1976), 118.

> David will be prince among them; I the LORD have spoken" (Ezek 34:23–24).

This gathering of the sheep of Israel under the Davidic Shepherd also involves a "covenant of peace" (v. 25a) which is another reference to the "New Covenant." This covenant brings physical prosperity and peace. It involves the elimination of "harmful beasts from the land," a reference to hostile predators so the people can live securely with no threats in their land (v. 25b). Rain will come in its proper seasons (v. 26). Trees will yield their fruit (v. 27). Famine will not occur again (v. 29a). No longer will Israel "endure the insults of the nations" (v. 29b). The Lord will restore Israel to the kingdom with all its spiritual and physical blessings. Israel's restoration will occur as a result of the Davidic Messiah.

The Restoration of Israel, the New Covenant, and the Land (Ezekiel 35–37)

Ezekiel 35–37 predicts Israel's coming restoration. These chapters expand on the prophecy of Deuteronomy 30 that Israel's scattering to the nations would be followed by regathering. This will occur in the context of New Covenant blessings of a new heart and God's indwelling Spirit, along with physical blessings and restoration to the land. In sum, God will save and restore Israel from the nations and grant Israel both spiritual and physical blessings associated with the New Covenant. This message of hope would be comforting for a people experiencing the full brunt of the Babylonian Captivity.

Ezekiel 35:1–36:15 tells of coming judgment for those who possessed Israel. Edom is singled out as a nation that continually desired evil for Israel. She will be judged by the standard she judged Israel. Chapter 36 begins with a prophecy for the "mountains of Israel" that Israel would not always endure the "insults" of the nations that take her captive (see Ezek 36:6). The mountains of Israel will soon see the return of the people of Israel and the cities will be inhabited (36:10).

Ezekiel 36:16 through chapter 37 describes the restoration of Israel to the land. This restoration occurs because of God's desire for His own glory and not because Israel is worthy: "It is not for your sake, O house of Israel, that I am about to act, but for My holy name..." (36:22). The nations who mocked God by their insults of Israel will then know that the Lord is God when He proves himself holy among the people of Israel in the sight of the nations (36:23).

These verses reveal important truths. First, the banishment of Israel to the nations because of disobedience is temporary and will be reversed by restoration. Second, God's commitment to restore Israel is not because of Israel's inherent goodness but because of God's holy name and His covenant promises. And third, the restoration of Israel is a strong message to the nations that the Lord is God. Verses 24–38 detail what the restoration of Israel involves:

- Israel will be gathered from the nations and placed in their own land (v. 24).
- Israel will be cleansed from filthiness and idolatry (v. 25).
- Israel will receive a new heart that replaces its old hardened heart (v. 26a).
- Israel will receive the indwelling Holy Spirit that enables Israel to obey God (v. 27).
- Israel will live in the land God gave to Israel's forefathers (v. 28a).
- Israel will be God's people, and God will be Israel's God (v. 28b).
- Israel will experience agricultural prosperity ("grain," "fruit of tree") along with no more "famine" (v. 29–30).
- Israel will experience salvation from sin (v. 33a).
- Israel will see its cities inhabited (v. 33b).
- Israel's land will be cultivated (v. 34).
- Israel will see an increase in population (vv. 37–38).

These points can be summarized: *After a period of banishment to the nations Israel will experience spiritual salvation and restoration to the land of promise within the context of the New Covenant that brings both spiritual and physical blessings. As God accomplishes these things the nations will know He is God. God's plans for Israel are spiritual, physical, and national. All three elements are connected with the coming New Covenant.*

There is no indication the physical and national aspects of the covenant are being redefined or are only typological of greater realities to come. The spiritual blessings of regeneration, a new heart, and indwelling Spirit will exist alongside the physical blessing of land. The desolate land becomes like the Garden of Eden (v. 35) which shows that kingdom conditions involve a reversal of the curse and a restoration to Edenic conditions before the fall.

Ezekiel 37:1–14 continues the restoration message of chapter 36 but adds a dramatic vision that pictures this restoration. Israel is likened to dry bones in a valley that are miraculously resurrected to life. This chapter also links the New Covenant ministry of the Holy Spirit with Israel's restoration and placement in the land—"I will put My Spirit within you and you will come to life, and I will place you on your own land" (37:14). Israel's restoration as a nation to its land is miraculous, like dry bones coming to life with new sinews, skin, etc.

The United Kingdom of Israel and Judah (Ezekiel 37:15–28)

Ezekiel describes the coming unification of Israel in 37:15–23. After Solomon, the kingdom of Israel was divided into two kingdoms—the ten tribes of Israel in the north and the two tribes of Judah in the south. Such division reflected the decaying kingdom of Israel. But when the gathering and restoration of Israel takes place, Israel will be a united kingdom: "and I will make them one nation in the land, on the mountains of Israel; and one king will be king for all of them; and they will no longer be two nations and no longer be divided into two kingdoms" (37:22). The kingdom that split in two after Solomon and then went into captivity under Assyria and Babylon will be restored to one united glorious kingdom.

This will take place under the coming "David"—"My servant David will be king over them" (37:24a). Again, there is the promise of living in the "land" of Israel's forefathers (37:25a). They and the generations thereafter will live in this land "forever" and "David... will be their prince forever" (25b). Twice the New Covenant is referred to in this section. It is called a "covenant of peace" and an "everlasting covenant" (26). God's presence will be "in their midst forever" (28).

The Final Failed Attempt to Conquer Israel (Ezekiel 38–39)

The dominant message of Ezekiel 33–39 is the restoration of Israel to her land under the New Covenant and the Davidic King. Yet there is one final message. It concerns an attempt by Israel's enemies to devour the nation, an attempt that will be squelched immediately. Ezekiel 38 and 39 describe an attack on Israel by Gog and Magog along with its allies at a time when Israel is dwelling securely in the land.

Ezekiel 38 and 39 contain several difficult issues, including the identity of Gog and Magog and the timing of this invasion. It is not our intent to fully investigate these issues, but when Israel experiences peace and security under the Messiah and New Covenant blessings, Gentile powers will attempt a massive invasion against her. But God will consume Israel's enemies with fire and supernaturally protect Israel, who is dwelling securely without need of military weapons for defense. When God's covenant of peace with Israel is tested during kingdom conditions, God shows His faithfulness by decisively defending Israel. Revelation 20:7–10 explicitly mentions the Gog and Magog invasion at the end of Jesus' thousand-year kingdom. This fits well with what Ezekiel presents concerning an invasion of Israel during a time when Israel is experiencing peace and protection under her Messiah. What occurs with the Gog and Magog invasion is a swift and decisive execution of rebels. Both Ezekiel and Revelation picture a dramatic fiery end for the opponents of Israel.

Ezekiel 38–39 reveals Israel will never again come under the domination of Gentile powers. What a message of comfort this must have been to the exiles who just received bleak news concerning Jerusalem's destruction. Things looked very difficult at the moment but God had not forgotten His covenant promises to Abraham, Isaac, and Jacob. Israel will permanently be restored and the blessings of the kingdom will never end. Judgment is not the final word for Israel.

THE RETURN OF GOD'S GLORY (EZEKIEL 40–48)

Ezekiel 40–48 contributes to the kingdom program by detailing the return of the glory of the Lord to a new temple in Jerusalem. Chapters 8–11 explained the sad and tragic removal of the glory of the Lord from Israel because of disobedience. But with chapters 40–48 a reversal occurs with the return of the glory of the Lord. To compare:

> **Ezek 8–11**: God's glory departs Israel for Mosaic Covenant violations
>
> **Ezek 40–48**: God's glory returns to Israel in connection with New Covenant blessings

Ezekiel's vision in 40–48 focuses on a coming temple and land for Israel. There are four main divisions: (1) the description of the coming kingdom temple (40:5–42:20); (2) the glory of the Lord returns to the temple (43:1–9); temple regulations (43:10–46:24); and (4) the land of Israel in the kingdom (47:1–48:35).[7]

Bible students have debated just about everything in these nine chapters. Most of the debate centers on Ezekiel's vision of a coming temple and the mention of "atonement." How does this relate to the coming of Jesus and His atonement? There are three major interpretations of this passage. The first is that Ezekiel's temple found historical fulfillment with the returns from exile and rebuilding of the temple before Christ.

A second is the figurative or spiritual approach that views Ezekiel 40–48 as spiritually fulfilled in Jesus and the church. With this view no future fulfillment of these chapters is necessary since the temple concept is fulfilled in Jesus and those identified with Jesus (i.e. the church).

A third view is Ezekiel 40–48 refers to a coming literal temple. This view posits a future literal temple Jesus will inhabit at His return to earth.

We adopt the third view. What Ezekiel described certainly was not fulfilled in the previous temple rebuilding. The dimensions of Ezekiel's temple go far beyond what has occurred. The glory of the Lord did not return to the temple nor has Israel experienced the peace and prosperity associated with this temple. Ezekiel 40–48 lists great architectural details for this temple and it is difficult to spiritualize these details. What is described in chapters 40–48 simply has not happened yet.

Next, while the temple concept is applied to both Jesus and the church in the NT, this does not rule out a literal Ezekiel's temple in the future.

7 The language of these points is similar to that of Ralph Alexander, *Ezekiel*.

While the Mosaic Covenant and its elements are superseded by Jesus and New Covenant realities (Heb. 8:5; 9:23–24; 10:1), the NT never says the New Covenant temple of Ezekiel 40–48 is revoked or transcended. Also, NT writers were well aware of the significance of Jesus and the church but still predicted the significance of Jerusalem temples in God's plans (see 2 Thess 2:4[8]; Rev 11:1–2). In Romans 9:4 Paul says "temple service" is still the present possession of Israel even though Israel is in a state of unbelief. Since the NT affirms many of the details of OT eschatology as still needing to be fulfilled, including the restoration of Israel, it is legitimate to expect a literal fulfillment of Ezekiel's temple as well. Jesus can be the ultimate temple (see John 2:19–21) while other temples serve a purpose in God's plans. This does not have to be an either/or situation. The concept of "temple" is multi-dimensional in Scripture.

In his study of prophecies of the ancient world Richard Hess has observed that "specific events and matters" mentioned in prophetic texts "were intended to have a literal fulfillment."[9] The people who penned the original prophecies and the people who heard them "expected a kind of literal fulfillment, where the prophecies touched upon known events in the real world in which they lived."[10] This means "the prophecies in the Old Testament are best interpreted in a manner that would agree with a one-to-one historical correspondence."[11] Concerning Ezekiel's temple, Hess concludes that a real physical temple was intended:

> All of this demonstrates that wherever it can be checked—among Samaritans and Second Temple mainstream Jews and in the separatist Jewish community of Qumran—the vision of Ezekiel was

---

8 I am not claiming the temple of 2 Thessalonians 2 is Ezekiel's temple. It appears to be a temple in the coming tribulation period that the man of lawlessness enters in connection with the abomination of desolation spoken of by Daniel (see Dan 9:27). The point is there can be multiple senses of temple. Jesus is a temple. The church is a temple. The Christian's body is a temple. And there can be future temples in Jerusalem in the plan of God.

9 Richard Hess, "The Future Written in the Past," in *A Case for Historic Premillennialism*, ed. Craig L. Blomberg and Sung Wook Chung (Grand Rapids: Baker, 2009), 30.

10 Ibid..

11 Ibid..

understood as intending a real, physical temple in the centuries after the prophet wrote.[12]

The case for a literal fulfillment of Ezekiel's temple is also bolstered by the structure and message of the book of Ezekiel. The two main themes of the book are judgment and restoration for Israel. Covenant disobedience brought judgment and dispersion for Israel. In Ezekiel 8–11, Ezekiel saw real events in a real temple. He saw false worship and abominations, which led to the departure of the glory of the Lord from Solomon's temple. Ezekiel saw a literal temple, with literal idolatry, and a literal removal of the glory of God from the temple. When Ezekiel moves on to discuss the restoration of Israel, he again sees a literal temple not defiled with false worship, and he views the coming of the glory of the Lord to this glorious temple. Thus, if what Ezekiel saw in chapters 8–11 concerned a tangible temple, so too, the temple of Ezekiel 40–48 must be real. The two sections mirror each other, the first in regard to disobedience and judgment, the second in regard to obedience and restoration:

Ezek 8–11: Ezekiel sees the glory of the Lord depart from God's temple in Jerusalem.

Ezek 40–48: Ezekiel sees the glory of the return to God's temple in Jerusalem.

When Israel is restored there will be a restored temple in Jerusalem. As God deals with Israel during this time, this temple will be a center of Israel's expression of worship to the Lord. Overall, Israel failed in its worship of God under the Mosaic Covenant. Yet under the Messiah and New Covenant conditions, the people will express their worship of God. The expression of worship is not necessary for salvation since the nation is already saved at this point (see Zech 12:10; Rom 11:26–27). Yet this will be a way for Israel to express worship of the Lord in view of Christ's ultimate sacrifice. Just as sacrifices under the Mosaic Covenant were *typological*, pointing forward to Christ's ultimate sacrifice, the sacrifices described with Ezekiel's temple could be *retrospective*, drawing attention to Christ's completed sacrifice. The

12 Ibid., 32–33.

blood of bulls and goats could never take away sin (see Heb 10:4); instead, they point to Christ's perfect sacrifice.

Since Revelation 21 says there will be no temple in the eternal state, this kingdom temple must be fulfilled in the coming millennium (see Rev 20:1–6). So not only will Jerusalem be restored and function as the capital of Messiah's kingdom, there will also be a temple in the city that functions as the headquarters of the Messiah.

CONCLUSION

Ezekiel offers much detailed information concerning the coming kingdom of God. The prophet gives hope to Israel that judgment and exile will give way to restoration and kingdom. This is centered in the New Covenant blessings under a righteous Davidic King.

CHAPTER

12 THE KINGDOM IN DANIEL

The prophet Daniel ministered during Judah's Babylonian captivity. More than any other book in the OT, Daniel revealed the connection between God's universal kingdom and the mediatorial earthly kingdom, and the course of Gentile kingdoms in history before God's kingdom is established on earth. Passages like Genesis 1:26–28 and Psalm 8 reveal God's plan for man to rule over the earth. This right to rule was never forfeited and continues after the fall. Human government is the primary means this rule is carried out. Yet because man and human governments are fallen and sinful they are antagonistic to God's will and do not successfully carry out the dominion mandate. As these governments function they are still under God's sovereignty. Yet the time will come when God's kingdom will replace rebellious human governments and God's kingdom will be established on the earth. Thus, the kingdom of God, which replaces rebellious human kingdoms, is the central theme of Daniel. As Merrill explains:

> The central theological theme of Daniel—that the arrogant, God-denying sovereignty of man will be overturned so that God might reign—finds unequivocal fulfillment in the eternal dominion of his saints who, despite all apparent evidence to the contrary, will eventually prevail.[1]

1 Eugene H. Merrill, "A Theology of Ezekiel and Daniel," 395.

NEBUCHADNEZZAR'S STATUE DREAM (DANIEL 2)

Daniel 2 tells of a coming kingdom of God that will suddenly and decisively crush and replace the reigning Gentile kingdoms. Not long after King Nebuchadnezzar of Babylon ascended to the throne, he had a recurring dream that disturbed him greatly (2:1). Sensing the magnitude of his dream, Nebuchadnezzar summoned his wise men with an incredible demand. They were to relate the king's dream without being told of its contents and then interpret its meaning. Failure meant execution. They pleaded their case to the king, decrying the unfairness of such a request, but to no avail. On the verge of execution, Daniel, who was also under the sentence of death, asked for time to beseech the Lord for the dream and its contents (2:18). Then, "The mystery was revealed to Daniel in a night vision" (2:19), and after giving thanks to God, Daniel gained access to the king to relate the dream and interpret its contents.

Daniel told Nebuchadnezzar that his dream concerned "what will take place in the latter days" (2:28) and "what would take place in the future" (2:29). In the king's dream he saw "a single great statue... which was large and of extraordinary splendor" (2:31). This single statue was made of various parts:

- Head of fine gold (2:32)
- Breast and arms of silver (2:32)
- Belly and thighs of bronze (2:32)
- Legs of iron (2:33)
- Feet partly of iron and partly of clay (2:33)

The king also saw a "stone" that "was cut out without hands" that struck the statue on its feet (2:34). The entire statue including the head of gold, the breast and arms of silver, the belly and thighs of bronze, the legs of iron and the feet of iron and clay "were crushed all at the same time" and became like "chaff" that was swept to the winds "so that not a trace of them was found" (2:35). The "stone" that struck the statue, however, "became a great mountain and filled the whole earth" (2:35).

Daniel then offered the interpretation of the great statue and the stone that destroyed it and how the stone grew into a great mountain. Concerning the head of gold Daniel told Nebuchadnezzar, "You are the head of gold" (2:38). Thus, the golden head represented Nebuchadnezzar and the kingdom of Babylon. Daniel does not explicitly say what the remaining three kingdoms represent, but the breast and arms of silver most likely represent the kingdom of Medo-Persia, which followed the Babylonian kingdom. The belly and thighs of bronze represent the kingdom of Greece. The legs of iron refer to the kingdom of Rome (2:39–40).[2] Rome was the most powerful kingdom of ancient times and is well described by iron. Then the feet of iron and clay indicate a kingdom related to the fourth iron kingdom of Rome, but this form of the kingdom is not as stable since it has the element of "clay" associated with it. Daniel says this kingdom is "divided," and yet while strong, also has a "brittle" element to it (2:41–42). Thus, this fourth kingdom begins as a very strong iron kingdom but then is weaker.

The "stone" that "was cut out without hands" is God's kingdom. It does not have a human origin. It strikes the feet of the statue and becomes "a great mountain that fills the whole earth." "Mountain" in this context is a symbol of a kingdom. Verses 44–45 state what this kingdom will do to the previous kingdoms:

> In the days of those kings the God of heaven will set up a kingdom which will never be destroyed, and that kingdom will not be left for another people; it will crush and put an end to all these kingdoms, but it will itself endure forever. Inasmuch as you saw that a stone was cut out of the mountain without hands and that it crushed the iron, the bronze, the clay, the silver and the gold, the great God has made known to the king what will take place in the future; so the dream is true and its interpretation is trustworthy.

"In the days of those kings" is probably a reference to the ten "toes" of the feet mentioned in verse 42. Thus, during the days of the final form of the fourth kingdom (Rome), the kingdom of God will "crush and put an end to all these kingdoms" and "will itself endure forever."

2 According to Pfandl, "The Church Fathers generally identified the four kingdoms of Dan 2 as Babylon, Medo-Persia, Greece, and Rome." Gerhard Pfandl, "Interpretations of the Kingdom of God in Daniel 2:44," in *Andrews University Seminary Studies*, vol. 34, No.2, n.d. 268. He also notes, "the Christian interpreters during the first few centuries, understood the four kingdoms in Dan 2 to be Babylon, Medo-Persia, Greece, and Rome" (250).

Daniel 2, therefore, teaches five kingdoms with the fifth and final kingdom crushing the others:

1. Babylon (head of Gold)
2. Medo-Persia (breast and arms of silver)
3. Greece (belly and thighs of bronze)
4. Rome (legs of iron) and later form of Roman empire (feet mixed with iron and clay)
5. God's kingdom (a stone cut out without hands that becomes a great mountain)

The main point of Daniel 2 is that after Babylon four major Gentile powers will rule over the world and Israel, but a day is coming when God's kingdom will suddenly crush these kingdoms and will be established as a geo-political entity over the earth forever.

God's kingdom dramatically and decisively destroys and replaces the existing Gentile powers that preceded it. As McClain states, "Now it is deeply significant that in these visions the heavenly Kingdom comes down and destroys and supplants *existing* political powers."[3] A stone from heaven shatters the Gentile kingdoms leading to the establishment of God's kingdom on earth. There is no gradual development. It comes suddenly.

Debate has occurred concerning whether this kingdom from God is spiritual or earthly. The kingdom has a spiritual dynamic since it comes from heaven. But when this kingdom comes it invades earth and reigns in the realm in which the other four kingdoms ruled. Thus, it is an *earthly* kingdom since it presides and functions on the earth. The kingdom of God will be spiritual in origin but earthly in regard to its sphere of existence and domain.

This earthly aspect of the kingdom is a connecting point between the fourth kingdom (Rome) and the fifth kingdom (God's kingdom). The fourth kingdom "shatters all things" and "breaks in pieces" its enemies (2:40). Likewise, the fifth kingdom, God's kingdom, "will crush and put an end to all these kingdoms" (2:44). There is a parallel here–just as the fourth kingdom of Rome crushed all rival political kingdoms on earth, so too the kingdom of God will crush the earthly political kingdoms when it comes. The kingdom's coming is not progressive over time but sudden.

3 McClain, *The Greatness of the Kingdom*, 153.

This is a stone that violently brings an end to the kingdoms that preceded it. The kingdoms that use to exist are like "chaff" that are swept away by strong winds.

So then, just as the previous four kingdoms are literal kingdoms, so too, God's coming kingdom is a real geographical and political kingdom that will exist on the earth. In reference to Daniel 2, Blaising states, "This kingdom is not simply a higher order of spiritual reality that coexists with the present course of affairs, but it is a complete *replacement* of present conditions on earth with a new worldwide and multinational world order."[4] From our perspective in history, this event is linked with the second coming of Jesus the Messiah when He returns to put an end to rival earthly kingdoms and establishes His kingdom upon the earth (see Zech 14:9; Rev 19:15).

Some have argued that God's kingdom is the church but this understanding is unlikely. According to Daniel 2:44–45, when God's kingdom is established it crushes and puts an end to the prevailing Gentile powers of the day who are swept away like chaff with no remnants remaining. This did not happen when the church began. The Roman Empire continued for centuries after the church started and its demise was not because of the church. The kingdom of Daniel 2 replaces the fourth kingdom when it comes; it does not exist alongside it in a spiritual sense. Plus, just as the four previous kingdoms were tangible geo-political entities, so too will God's kingdom be a geo-political entity. While the church has a mission to the nations, it is not a geo-political group like Babylon, Medo-Persia, Greece, or Rome. The Christian church simply is not the fifth kingdom.

God created man to rule and subdue the earth (Gen 1:26–28). He established a kingdom on earth with Israel (see 1 and 2 Samuel), but Israel failed its mission and was dispersed to the Gentile nations. God granted authority to Babylon and then to Medo-Persia, Greece, Rome, and then a weaker but revived Roman Empire. But after this period of Gentile domination or what Jesus called "the times of the Gentiles" (Luke 21:24) God's kingdom will be established over the entire earth. King Nebuchadnezzar's dream involved the broad panorama of human history from his day through the kingdom of Israel's Messiah.

4 Blaising, "Premillennialism," 193.

THE FOUR GREAT BEASTS (DANIEL 7)

Daniel 7 parallels Daniel 2 by addressing a series of Gentile kingdoms that will rule before God's earthly kingdom is established. In 553 B.C. Daniel received "a dream and visions" while he was in his bed (7:1). He saw "the great sea" stirred by "the four winds of heaven" (7:2). Then he witnessed four great beasts coming up from the sea (7:3):

1. The first beast was like a lion with wings like an eagle. Its wings were plucked and it was made to stand on two feet like a man and a human mind was given to it (7:4).

2. The second beast was like a bear that was raised up on one side and had three ribs in its mouth. It was told to "devour much meat" (7:5).

3. The third beast was like a leopard with four wings of a bird and it had four heads. Dominion was given to it (7:6).

4. The fourth beast was "dreadful," "terrifying," and "extremely strong." It had large iron teeth and crushed everything in its path. This beast was different from the other beasts that preceded it and it had ten horns (7:7). From among the ten horns a "little horn" came up and uprooted three of the previous horns. This "little horn" had eyes like a man and spoke great boasts (7:8).

These four kingdoms parallel the four parts of the statue that Nebuchadnezzar saw in his dream, showing the strong connection between the two sections:

1. Head of gold (Dan 2) and beast like a lion (Dan 7) = Babylon

2. Arms and breast of silver (2) and second beast like a bear (7) = Medo-Persia

3. Belly and thighs of bronze (2) and third beast like a leopard (7) = Greece

4. Legs of iron (2) and terrifying fourth beast (7) = Rome

Daniel then described a heavenly throne room scene with 7:9–10 in which the "Ancient of Days," a reference to God the Father, takes His seat upon His throne. This scene includes "burning fire" and many who are attending to God on His throne. Daniel observes that the horn keeps speaking "boastful words." He then saw the fourth beast killed and given to burning fire (7:11). Verses 7:13–14 then introduce the "Son of Man" figure:

> "I kept looking in the night visions,
> And behold, with the clouds of heaven
> One like a Son of Man was coming,
> And He came up to the Ancient of Days
> And was presented before Him.
> And to Him was given dominion,
> Glory and a kingdom,
> That all the peoples, nations and men of every language
> Might serve Him.
> His dominion is an everlasting dominion
> Which will not pass away;
> And His kingdom is one
> Which will not be destroyed."

As Jesus and the NT writers make clear, Jesus is the "Son of Man" figure of Daniel.[5] Thus, this section presents the Son of Man (Jesus) coming before God the Father to receive "dominion, glory and a kingdom." The result is that all peoples and nations will serve Him and His dominion will last forever.

Here a heavenly scene results in an earthly kingdom over the nations. Some have concluded that since the Son of Man comes to the Ancient of Days in heaven, the Son of Man's kingdom occurs in heaven and not on earth. Allegedly, Jesus' kingdom reign occurs from heaven in this age between His two comings. But this is not accurate. Yes, Daniel 7:13–14 is a heavenly scene, but it is a heavenly scene that leads to a coming earthly reign, one in which the saints will receive the kingdom and replace the authority of the nations opposed to God on earth (see Dan 7:24–27).

The Son of Man's authority for His kingdom comes from heaven—from the Ancient of Days. But receiving authority in a heavenly context

5 Some assert the "son of man" figure in Daniel 7:13–14 only refers to the saints who possess the kingdom at the end of Daniel 7. But like Daniel 9:24–27, Daniel 7 refers to both the Messiah and the people of the Messiah. Daniel 7:13–14 points to a specific Messiah figure.

does not mean His kingdom is only in heaven. The heavenly scene leads to an earthly kingdom. A similar situation is found in Revelation 4–5, a section closely connected to what is described in Daniel 7:13–14.[6] Here, a heavenly scene reveals Jesus the Messiah before the Father. Jesus receives the title deed to the earth by taking a scroll with divine judgments from the right hand of the Father (Rev 5:4–8). Yet this occurs so a kingdom reign on earth can occur. Revelation 5:10 predicts a "reign upon the earth."

This truth of a heavenly scene followed by an earthly kingdom also is taught in Psalm 110:1–2 where a session of the Messiah at the right hand of God leads to an earthly kingdom. It is also explained in Luke 19:11–27 where Jesus refers to himself as a nobleman who goes to a distant country (heaven) to receive a kingdom, and then comes back to rule.

Also, the "clouds" imagery of Daniel 7:13 is used of Jesus' second coming in the NT. Jesus links His coming in glory on the clouds of heaven in fulfillment of Daniel 7:13 with His second coming to earth:

> And then the sign of the Son of Man will appear in the sky, and then all the tribes of the earth will mourn, and they will see the SON OF MAN COMING ON THE CLOUDS OF THE SKY with power and great glory. And He will send forth His angels with A GREAT TRUMPET and THEY WILL GATHER TOGETHER His elect from the four winds, from one end of the sky to the other (Matt 24:30–31).

In addition, the apostle John saw the fulfillment of Daniel 7:13 in connection with Jesus' second coming: "BEHOLD, HE IS COMING WITH THE CLOUDS, and every eye will see Him" (Rev 1:7a).

As Daniel 7 progresses Daniel is distressed and asks someone standing by what this all means. Most probably an angel answers him stating that Daniel will be told the interpretation of the dream (7:15–16). He is told that the four great beasts are four kings that will arise from the earth (7:17). Verse 18 then declares: "But the saints of the Highest One will receive the kingdom and possess the kingdom forever, for all ages to come." We see the connection between the kingdom of the Son of Man and what this means

6 For more on the striking parallels between Daniel 7:13–14 and Revelation 4–5 see G. K. Beale and Sean M. McDonough, "Revelation," in *Commentary on the New Testament Use of the Old Testament*, ed. G. K. Beale and D. A. Carson (Grand Rapids: Baker, 2007), 1098.

for the saints of God. When the kingdom of the Son of Man arrives, those who are His saints will participate in this reign.[7]

Daniel then inquired for more information about the fourth beast, the ten horns, and the little horn that was making great boasts (7:19–20). Daniel saw that the "horn was waging war with the saints and overpowering them." But this ended when the Ancient of Days passed judgment in favor of the saints. Then "the saints took possession of the kingdom" (7:21–22). Significant here is that the kingdom of the Son of Man and the possession of His kingdom by the saints of God occurs *after* the persecution of the little horn. Persecution occurs and then the kingdom comes, which results in a dramatic reversal of fortune for God's people. There is no indication that the saints of God are participating or reigning in God's kingdom before the career of the evil little horn runs its course. This appears consistent with the reign of the beast in the book of Revelation who persecutes the saints but then is defeated by the returning Jesus Christ (see Rev 19). Verses 25–27 give more information on these events:

> He [little horn] will speak out against the Most High and wear down the saints of the Highest One, and he will intend to make alterations in times and in law; and they will be given into his hand for a time, times, and half a time.
>
> But the court will sit for judgment, and his dominion will be taken away, annihilated and destroyed forever.
>
> Then the sovereignty, the dominion and the greatness of all the kingdoms under the whole heaven will be given to the people of the saints of the Highest One; His kingdom will be an everlasting kingdom, and all the dominions will serve and obey Him.

The picture here is of withering persecution against the saints of God. The little horn both blasphemes God and pours his wrath out on the followers of God. He even tries to usurp God's authority by altering "times" and "law," areas of reality that belong to God. This occurs for "a time, times, and half a time," which is 3.5 years. But there is a courtroom scene where the little horn's dominion is "taken away" and the saints possess God's kingdom

7 See Martin J. Selman, "The Kingdom of God in the Old Testament," *Tyndale Bulletin* 40 (1989): 172.

forever. This shows that God's kingdom includes vindication of the saints. When the kingdom comes, God's people are vindicated and rewarded.

In sum, Daniel 7 teaches the following truths concerning the kingdom of God:

- There will be four successive Gentile kingdoms that rule over the earth.
- During the reign of the fourth kingdom there will arise ten kings.
- From among these ten kings an individual will sprout who will subdue three of the previous ten kings; this individual will be an enemy of God who persecutes God's people, Israel.
- The Son of Man receives universal authority from the Ancient of Days, which leads to the defeat of the individual waging war against God's people.
- When this happens God's kingdom will be established and His people will possess this kingdom forever.

In sum, Daniel 2 and 7 teach that four earthly kingdoms, including a final form of the fourth kingdom (Rome), will exist, but God's kingdom will come dramatically and replace these earthly kingdoms. This kingdom will be an everlasting kingdom.

MESSIAH TO BE CUT OFF (DANIEL 9:24–27)

Daniel 9:24–27 describes a 490-year period concerning Daniel's people, Israel, and Jerusalem. It is not our purpose here to go into a full explanation of this passage or discuss all its controversial points but to show how this section intersects with the kingdom program. Particularly significant is a statement predicting the time of Messiah's death and what the result of His death means.

Daniel 9:24 tells of a period of "seventy weeks." The word for "weeks" can also be translated "sevens." Thus, there is a period of "seventy sevens." A period of seventy sevens (70 x 7) equals 490. But 490 what? The 490 most probably refers to years. Thus, God's plans for Daniel's people and the holy city involve a 490-year period. As a result of this period six things will be accomplished:

–"to finish the transgression"
–"to make an end to sin"
–"to make atonement for iniquity"
–"to bring in everlasting righteousness"
–"to seal up vision and prophecy"
–"to anoint the most holy place"

Kenneth Barker observes the likelihood that "the kingdom is inherent in the terms used in 9:24, particularly in the second part of the verse."[8] He also points out that "in the context, all six of these goals are earthly"[9] since they are specifically related to Daniel's people (Israel) and the holy city of Jerusalem (9:24). Certainly, these things will have broader application to others outside of Israel, but here they directly relate to Israel. The first three relate to Messiah's atonement and dealing with sin in regard to Israel's transgression against God. The last three relate to Messiah's kingdom when it is established. While the basis for these matters is found in Jesus' death at His first coming, the full realization of these predictions awaits the coming of His kingdom.

Daniel 9:26 indicates that after the first sixty-nine weeks (or 483 years), "the Messiah will be cut off and have nothing." This statement is shocking. Many OT passages speak of the glories of Messiah's kingdom. Yet Daniel is telling us the Messiah is "cut off" which refers to His death. The result is that He "has nothing." Incredibly, Messiah comes to His people, Israel, and is met with death and no kingdom. This occurred with the crucifixion of Jesus the Messiah.

Then after this cutting off Daniel states: "and the people of the prince who is to come will destroy the city and the sanctuary. And its end will come with a flood; even to the end there will be war; desolations are determined" (Dan 9:26b). This destruction of the "city" and "sanctuary" was fulfilled when the Romans destroyed Jerusalem and the temple in A.D. 70,

8 Kenneth L. Barker, "Evidence from Daniel," in *A Case for Premillennialism: A New Consensus*, eds. Donald K. Campbell and Jeffrey L. Townsend (Chicago: Moody, 1992), 143.

9 Ibid., 144.

just a few decades after Jesus' death. So instead of kingdom blessings from the Messiah, the Messiah is cut off with terrible consequences for the land and people of Israel. This corresponds to the "times of the Gentiles" Jesus referred to in Luke 21:24.

Daniel predicted that the Messiah would face rejection and death at His first coming. Thus, Daniel 9:24–27 offers evidence that Israel's Messiah would face opposition before His kingdom is established. Suffering precedes glory. And desolation for Israel precedes kingdom blessings.

TRIBULATION, RESURRECTION, AND THEN KINGDOM (DANIEL 12:1–3)

According to Daniel 12:1–3 there are three important precursors to the kingdom of God's arrival. The first is a unique and perilous time of "distress" for the people of Israel: "Now at that time Michael, the great prince who stands guard over the sons of your people, will arise. And there will be a time of distress such as never occurred since there was a nation until that time" (Dan 12:1a). Israel has experienced much tribulation in its history, but this period is exceptional, matchless in its intensity, and coincides with tribulation events described in Daniel 9:27 and 11:36–45. Such a period of tribulation for Israel is also found in Revelation 12. Here Michael the archangel is present (Rev 12:7) and Satan persecutes Israel (Rev 12:13–17).

Then we see a second precursor with Daniel 12:1b: "and at that time your people, everyone who is found written in the book, will be rescued." This unique period of distress for Israel leads to a rescue of Israel. Such a rescue of Israel during intense turmoil is also explained in Zechariah 14 and Matthew 24:29–31. With the former, Jerusalem is rescued in the midst of intense attack from the nations. In the latter, Jesus gathers repentant Israel from the areas they were scattered.

A third precursor is resurrection: "Many of those who sleep in the dust of the ground will awake, these to everlasting life, but the others to disgrace and everlasting contempt" (Dan 12:2). Put together, Daniel explains (1) a unique period of distress; (2) the rescue of Israel; and (3) resurrection from the dead. These three events then lead to the kingdom and blessings in God's kingdom: "Those who have insight will shine brightly like the brightness of the expanse of heaven, and those who lead the many to righteousness, like the stars forever and ever" (Dan 12:3). Tribulation gives way to kingdom.

Jesus quotes Daniel 12:3 when discussing coming judgment and kingdom in Matthew 13:41–43. When Jesus comes again He removes the wicked from His kingdom and "Then THE RIGHTEOUS WILL SHINE FORTH AS THE SUN in the kingdom of their Father" (Matt 13:43).

CONCLUSION

The book of Daniel has great implications for God's kingdom program. It highlights the progression of Gentile kingdoms that will exist before the establishment of God's kingdom upon the earth. It also reveals Israel's Messiah would be killed, and turmoil for Israel would exist before the kingdom is established.

CHAPTER

13 THE KINGDOM IN THE MINOR PROPHETS

The kingdom of God plays a major role in the theology of the Minor Prophets. These prophets launch an indictment against Israel for her unfaithfulness to the Lord in breaking the Mosaic Covenant. Judgment was necessary but will be followed by kingdom blessings, not because Israel was worthy, but because God is faithful to His promises. Israel will be saved and restored and other nations will be included in the people of God alongside Israel.

HOSEA

The book of Hosea details God's covenant faithfulness to Israel in spite of Israel's unfaithfulness to God. Hosea's marriage to the adulterous Gomer pictures God loves for Israel in spite of her spiritual adultery. Particularly significant to the kingdom program is Hosea 2–3. This section proclaims judgment upon Israel for covenant disobedience as earlier explained in Leviticus 26:14–39 and Deuteronomy 28:15–68. Yet this section also looks beyond a time of judgment to a period of restoration for Israel as predicted in Leviticus 26:40–45 and Deuteronomy 30:1–8. Much like Leviticus 26 and Deuteronomy 28 and 30, Hosea 2–3 offers a big-picture portrait of Israel's destiny.

With Hosea 2:1–13 God presents His case for punishing Israel with curses for covenant disobedience. The last verse (v. 13) summarizes what He will do: "I will punish her [Israel] for the days of the Baals when she used to offer sacrifices to them." Instead of loving and obeying God, the people forsook God to join in idolatrous Baal worship. The result would be curses upon the people and the land.

But the restoration of Israel is the subject of 2:14–3:1–5. The significance of this section is great since it discusses the nature and timing of the kingdom and also mentions the Messiah's relationship to it. Using intimate language, such as a man would say to a woman he loves, God says, "I will allure her" and "speak kindly to her" (2:14). God will give Israel "vineyards" (2:15a). Then Israel will sing a happy song just like she did when she came out of Egypt at the exodus (2:15b). Thus, restoration for Israel will involve material prosperity and rejoicing similar to what occurred when God delivered the nation from Egypt.

God also will institute a "covenant" that involves the animal kingdom and peace: "In that day I will also make a covenant for them with the beasts of the field, the birds of the sky and the creeping things of the ground. And I will abolish the bow, the sword and war from the land, and will make them lie down in safety" (2:18). The first part of this promise alludes to Genesis 1:26–28 and its reference to beasts, birds, and man's role in ruling the creation. Man's responsibility to creation has never been forfeited and kingdom conditions will include a restoration in this area. These promises are also consistent with what God said would happen for Israel if Israel obeyed His commandments (Deut 28:1–14). So this "covenant" involves a restoration of the animal kingdom and harmony between God's people and creation. God will also remove war and hostilities from the land so the people can rest securely.

The significance of Israel's land is highlighted in Hosea 2:21–23a:

> "It will come about in that day that I will respond," declares the Lord. "I will respond to the heavens, and they will respond to the earth, and the earth will respond to the grain, to the new wine and to the oil, and they will respond to Jezreel. I will sow her for Myself in the land."

This reaffirms that Israel's land remains significant in God's purposes and that the coming restoration of Israel will involve land and agricultural blessings. Food and wine will work in harmony with the earth, which will also function rightly with the heavens where rain comes. Also, the people who were separated from God will be His people once more (2:23). In sum, curses for covenant disobedience will be reversed when Israel repents.

Hosea 3:4–5 predicts Israel's future:

> For the sons of Israel will remain for many days without king or prince, without sacrifice or sacred pillar and without ephod or household idols. Afterward the sons of Israel will return and seek the Lord their God and David their king; and they will come trembling to the Lord and to His goodness in the last days.

Three timing statements are important here: (1) "many days" (2) "afterward" and (3) "in the last days." First, for "many days" the people of Israel will be without "king or prince," "sacrifice," "sacred pillar," "ephod or household idols." Together, these items indicate that Israel's sovereignty and self-determination as a nation will not exist for a long time. The reference to "king or prince" refers to Israel's governmental rulers. "Sacrifice" and "sacred pillar" refer to religious and temple activity. So for "many days" Israel will not function and worship independently as it desires.

So when does Israel go for "many days" without these matters? Does this begin with the exile in the OT or does it begin with the destruction of Jerusalem in A.D. 70? The latter is the better option since the Roman destruction of Jerusalem led to a complete cessation of all the things mentioned in Hosea 3:4. With the A.D. 70 destruction, the temple was destroyed and the people of Jerusalem were scattered. The impact of this event remains until our day. From our standpoint in history the "many days" covers nearly two thousand years. Yet that is not the end of the story for Israel.

The next timing term is "afterward." After the period of "many days" several things will happen. First, Israel will repent ("return"). This long period of exile for Israel will culminate in repentance. Second, Israel will seek God and "David their king." This reference to David could be to a resurrected David or the Messiah we now know as Jesus. The latter view is most likely. Jesus is the ultimate David, the One to whom the Davidic Covenant finds its aim. Third, with great respect Israel will come to God and experience blessings. Thus, Israel's belief leads to kingdom conditions. Concerning Hosea 2:14–23 Chisholm rightly states, "Israel's positive response would lead to covenant renewal and blessing."[1] This is consistent with the truth of Leviticus 26:40–45 that Israel's repentance will mean reinstatement to the blessings of the Abrahamic Covenant, including land.

Finally, these blessings are connected with "in the last days." This connects with Deuteronomy 4:30 which declared, "When you are in distress and all these things have come upon you, in the latter days you will return to the LORD your God and listen to His voice." This period of "in the last days" likely refers to the time of the second coming of Christ to earth. At that time Israel will be saved (cf. Zech 12:10; Rom 11:26–27). The trampling of Jerusalem will end (Luke 21:24) and the restoration of the tribes of Israel will occur (Matt 19:28).

The last chapter of Hosea ends with a promise of restoration for Israel. "I will heal their apostasy, I will love them freely, for My anger has turned away from them" (14:4). In sum, Hosea contributes to the kingdom program by revealing that God's faithful love for Israel will eventually overcome the nation's disobedience and faithlessness. Kingdom blessings will follow judgments. When the kingdom comes the people of Israel will dwell safely in their land with all threats from nature and human warfare removed. Agricultural blessings will abound. This all happens under the coming Davidic King.

JOEL

The book of Joel emphasizes the Day of the Lord with its coming blessings for Israel and judgment for nations that harmed Israel. With Joel 1, a plague of locusts and drought serve as the backdrop for a coming eschatological Day of Lord which is the focus of Joel 2:18–3:21.[2] The coming restoration of Israel is the focus of this section. As Irvin Busenitz points out, this restoration is threefold—material restoration (2:21–27), spiritual restoration (2:28–32), and national restoration (3:1–21).[3] Joel 2:18 "is the

1 Robert B. Chisholm, Jr., "Hosea," in *The Bible Knowledge Commentary: An Exposition of the Scriptures by Dallas Seminary Faculty, Old Testament* (Victor Books, 1985), 1385.

2 See Irvin A. Busenitz, *Joel & Obadiah* (Christian Focus: Geanies, Fearn, Ross-shire, Great Britain, 2003), 161.

3 Ibid.

thesis statement upon which the final section of the book hinges."[4] The verse reads: "Then the LORD will be zealous for His land and will have pity on His people."

With 2:21–27 there is material restoration. The land of Israel is personified and is told to "rejoice and be glad" (21). Blessings to the land by the Lord will include benefits for beasts, pastures, and trees (22). God will provide the early and latter rains which will lead to an abundance of grain, wine, and oil (23–24). The people will have plenty to eat (26). Eschatological blessings include material blessings.

Spiritual restoration is then emphasized in 2:28–32. Verse 28 begins with, "It will come about after this." The wording here has led some to hold that the spiritual restoration described in 2:28–32 chronologically follows the material blessings described in 2:21–27. Yet while the term translated "after this"—*aharaken*—often refers to sequence in time, there are occasions where chronological sequence is not in view.[5] Homer Heater asserts that "The time element of Joel 2:28–32... should not be considered step two in a process in which 2:21–27 is step one. These are concomitant events."[6] The material blessings occur at the time of the spiritual blessings.

Joel 2:28–32 notes that God will pour out His Spirit "on all mankind" so the children of Israel will prophesy and old men will dream dreams (28). This pouring out of God's Spirit will even extend to "male and female servants" (29). Joel then links this pouring out of the Spirit with cosmic signs associated with the Day of the Lord (30–31). Debate occurs whether "all mankind" refers only to Israel or mankind in general. The Hebrew term *basar* could refer to either. The context, however, seems to favor the former, thus emphasizing the spiritual restoration of Israel. This by no means is contrary to other passages that emphasize eschatological blessings including Gentiles (see Amos 9:11–12). But in this context the term probably refers to Israelites specifically.

---

4 Ibid., 162.

5 Possible cases where sequence is not in view include 2 Samuel 8:1; 10:1; 13:1; 15:1; 21:18; 2 Kings 6:24; 1 Chronicles 18:1; 19:1.

6 Homer Heater, Jr., "Evidence from Joel and Amos," in *A Case for Premillennialism: A New Consensus*, ed. Donald K. Campbell and Jeffrey L. Townsend (Chicago: Moody, 1992), 161. Heater also says, "I agree with [W.A.] VanGemeren that 2:28–32 explicates 2:26–27." See also W. A. VanGemeren, "The Spirit of Restoration," *Westminster Theological Journal* 50 (1988): 85–86.

Joel 3:1–2 predicts national restoration and the judgment of Israel's enemies. The prophet states that "in those days" when God will "restore the fortunes of Judah and Jerusalem" He will "gather all the nations" to the valley of Jehoshaphat to judge these nations. This judgment is "on behalf of My people and my inheritance, Israel." This is a judgment for the plundering and wickedness that the nations inflicted on Israel and Jerusalem. The Lord will establish His presence in Zion and Jerusalem will never be overrun by the nations again (3:17). Joel 3:18–21 describes kingdom conditions in Israel during this time. "The mountains will drip with sweet wine" and "the hills will flow with milk" (3:18). Judah will have perpetual peace as God avenges her enemies (3:21).

To summarize, the locust plague of Joel 1 is a harbinger of a future Day of the Lord when the Lord will restore Israel and bless the nation materially and spiritually. Joel, then, refers to a holistic restoration in which material, spiritual, and national components work together in harmony. The emphasis is on the blessings that will come to Israel yet other OT prophets reveal that kingdom blessings will also extend to Gentiles who will be included in the people of God. This is found in the next book—Amos.

AMOS

Amos was a Judean prophet who directed his message primarily to the northern kingdom of Israel. Most of his book concerns God's judgment of Israel for her sins and for breaking the Mosaic Covenant. Yet God will show mercy to Israel. As God says in 9:8: "Nevertheless, I will not totally destroy the house of Jacob." After nine and a half chapters of judgment language, Amos shifts to discussion of restoration for Israel and blessings to the nations who also will be included in the people of God. As 9:11–12 states:

> "In that day I will raise up the fallen booth of David,
> And wall up its breaches;
> I will also raise up its ruins
> And rebuild it as in the days of old;
> That they may possess the remnant of Edom
> And all the nations who are called by My name,"
> Declares the LORD who does this.

Amos' reference to "In that day" may involve the Day of the Lord concept mentioned earlier (2:16; 3:14; 5:18–20; 8:3). Or the phrase may simply refer to a time in the future. Either way it refers to future messianic days when blessings will come upon Israel with subsequent results for the nations.

The "booth" or "tent" of David involves the dynasty given to David via the Davidic Covenant of 2 Samuel 7:12–16. The mention of "its breaches" refers to the divided kingdom of Israel. Because of covenant disobedience, the united monarchy under David and his son, Solomon, eventually gave way to a divided and broken kingdom. The tribes of Israel and Judah separated after Solomon's reign. The Davidic kingdom that started with great promise was deteriorating and would cease for a time. But God promised to repair and "wall up" the kingdom by uniting it and restoring it. He will "rebuild it as in the days of old." Thus, the Davidic kingdom that was once united and strong will be restored to its former glory.

A translation and interpretation issue exists with the latter part of 9:11. God is going to raise up either "its ruins" or "his ruins" Most translations opt for the former, "its ruins," and in doing so understand the raising up to refer to the fallen booth or hut of David. Some translations interpret the raising up in regard to "his ruins," and in doing so emphasize not the "booth" but David, who in this context must be the coming Messiah. This understanding is more personal and focused on the person of the Messiah. Walter Kaiser adopts this latter understanding saying, "The masculine singular suffix on 'his ruins'. . . referred to David himself and not to the 'hut,' which is feminine."[7] The implications of this are messianic. "Thus, under a new, coming David (the Messiah himself), the destroyed house of that promised line of David would rise from the ashes."[8]

Yet God's future blessings do not end with the restoration of the kingdom to Israel under the Messiah. This rebuilt Davidic kingdom also will bless the nations. "Edom," a traditional enemy of Israel, will be possessed by Israel. While at first glance this may appear to be a harsh military conquest with negative implications for Edom, the immediate context is positive. For the next statement links Edom with "all the nations who are

7 Walter C. Kaiser, Jr., *The Promise-Plan of God: A Biblical Theology of the Old and New Testaments* (Grand Rapids: Zondervan, 2008), 166.

8 Ibid.

called by My name." Israel's possession of Edom leads to Edom's inclusion in the people of God. This shows that Israel's restoration involves blessings for other nations. This blessing of the nations through Israel connects with Genesis 12:2–3 where blessings to Gentiles would flow from Abraham and Israel. Thus, when the kingdom is restored to Israel, the Gentile nations will participate in this glorious event.

Amos 9:11–12 reveals that God's kingdom will involve both Israel and Gentile nations who become the people of God while retaining their ethnic status as Gentiles alongside Israel. Both Israel and the nations are the people of God ("called by My name") yet they still possess their distinct identities. In Acts 15:14–18, James will quote Amos 9:11–12 as evidence that the OT prophets predicted a time when Gentiles would be part of God's kingdom program without becoming Jews. This occurs because of the ultimate Davidic King—Jesus the Messiah.

Verses 13–15 then detail the wonderful kingdom blessings that will coincide with the restored kingdom to Israel. "The mountains will drip with sweet wine" (9:13). Cities will be rebuilt and vineyards will be planted (9:14). Israel will never again be removed from her land (9:15). As was the case with Joel 2:21–27, material blessings will become the experience of the nation Israel. Amos, thus, contributes to the kingdom plan by showing that the former kingdom of Israel will be restored and experience spiritual and material blessings. Gentile nations, too, will benefit from this kingdom and be included in the people of God alongside Israel.

MICAH

Micah of Moresheth was an eighth-century prophet who prophesied about the coming Assyrian and Babylonian captivities. Yet his predictions went beyond his day to the coming kingdom of God and what its conditions would be like. Of particular note is how God's coming kingdom will affect the nations of the earth.

Micah declared that the people of Israel disobeyed the Mosaic Covenant and judgment was pending. Yet Israel would be restored in a coming kingdom. Micah offers three messages found in chaps. 1–2; chaps. 3–5; and chaps. 6–7. Each section begins with a call to "hear" or "listen" to what God was declaring. The first section (chaps. 1–2) is a message of coming judgment. Yet at the close of this section, which is characterized by lamenting and a listing of the sins of Judah, is a ray of hope. As 2:12 states:

> "I will surely assemble all of you, Jacob,
> I will surely gather the remnant of Israel.
> I will put them together like sheep in the fold;
> Like a flock in the midst of its pasture
> They will be noisy with men."

After a period of judgment, God will restore Israel. The mention of "Jacob" and "Israel" indicates a reunited kingdom of Israel. God is like a Shepherd who will put His sheep, Israel, back into the fold and back into a state of protection and blessing. Verse 13b then states: "So their king goes on before them, and the LORD at their head." The Lord is the king who will lead His people Israel.

The second main section, chapters 3–5, shows that the judgment of Israel will be followed by kingdom blessings for Israel and the nations. Chapter 3 concerns judgment for Israel's leaders including its rulers and false prophets. Then chapters 4–5 give explicit details about the coming kingdom of God. Micah 4:1–2 declares:

> And it will come about in the last days
> That the mountain of the house of the Lord
> Will be established as the chief of the mountains.
> It will be raised above the hills,
> And the peoples will stream to it.
> Many nations will come and say,
> "Come and let us go up to the mountain of the Lord
> And to the house of the God of Jacob,
> That He may teach us about His ways
> And that we may walk in His paths."
> For from Zion will go forth the law,
> Even the word of the Lord from Jerusalem.

Micah's prophecy about "the last days" is similar to Isaiah 2:2–3. That both Isaiah and Micah gave this message shows its significance. The "last days" in the OT refers to a future time period when God restores the nation Israel. Jerusalem with its temple will be the capital city of this kingdom.

For both Isaiah and Micah, the exaltation of Mount Zion and its temple indicates a restoration of Jerusalem and Israel, yet this restoration is not just for Israel. According to Micah, the nations are blessed during this period. Together the "people" and the "nations" pour into Jerusalem to learn the "ways" of Israel's God. They want to learn about His "paths," and "law." Such conditions have never occurred in human history. Currently, we live in the "times of the Gentiles" in which Gentiles trample Jerusalem and the nations express hostility against Israel. But a time is coming when the times of the Gentiles will be fulfilled and Jerusalem will be restored and become a place for blessings to the nations (Luke 21:24).

Such a message rebuked Micah's audience. A day was coming when Gentile nations would stream to Jerusalem to learn God's ways and commandments, and yet the current generation of Israel, as stewards of God's law, was rebelling against the Lord. Micah 4:3 also indicates that the Lord will "judge between many peoples and render decisions for mighty, distant nations." Note the presence of literal geo-political nations during this time of the kingdom. There are "peoples" and "nations." The kingdom of God does not consist of a generic humanity in which there are no ethnicities or nations. Those matters are part of God's kingdom. Nations at this time still need guidance and the Lord makes wise executive decisions on their behalf.

Reminiscent of Isaiah 2, the nations of the earth will turn their weapons into peaceful instruments—"swords into plowshares" and "spears into pruning hooks" (4:3). The Lord ends warfare during this time so there will be no need for weapons of war. The resources once devoted to war will be converted to peaceful pursuits. Again, such conditions have never been experienced on earth, but they will be a reality when the Lord's kingdom is established. Verse 4 then states:

> Each of them will sit under his vine
> And under his fig tree,
> With no one to make them afraid,
> For the mouth of the LORD of hosts has spoken.

During this kingdom people will be secure. They rest peacefully on their property with no threat of crime or war. A person can enjoy the fruit of his labor with no threat of it being stolen or destroyed. Thus, the picture here is prosperity and security, the blessed results of a righteous King and kingdom that have removed warfare and crime from the earth.

Micah 4:6–8 states that Israel will be regathered from its scattering. These "outcasts" will be made "a strong nation" and God "will reign over them in Mount Zion" forever (4:7). The "former dominion will come" indicating a restoration of Israel's kingdom under the Lord her King (4:8). In sum, Micah 4 offers important information about God's kingdom:

1. After judgment and captivity God will restore a united Israel.
2. God's kingdom will be established on the earth with Jerusalem and its temple functioning as the capital of this kingdom.
3. The nations who previously oppressed Israel will come to Jerusalem to learn the ways of Israel's God.
4. The Lord will make executive decisions on behalf of the nations.
5. Warfare among nations will cease and resources previously devoted to military causes will be redirected to peaceful pursuits.
6. Peace and prosperity will be the norm, even extending to private property.

Following the description of kingdom conditions in Micah 4, the fifth chapter reveals where the King will come from. It is from "Bethlehem" that "One will go forth for Me to be ruler in Israel" (5:2). That this ruler is divine is evidenced by His eternality—"His goings forth are from long ago, from the days of eternity" (5:2). This is no mere human king, but a King who is God. The NT links the fulfillment of this verse with Jesus (see Matt 2:5–6). Micah 5:4–6 also discusses what this coming ruler will do. "He will arise and shepherd His flock" (v. 4). And He will shepherd His people Israel. Also, He will protect Israel from invaders (5–6).

Micah 7 promises a coming restoration of Israel. The prophet warns Israel's enemies not to rejoice over Israel's demise. Israel may currently be in darkness but the Lord is Israel's light (7:8). Israel has sinned but God will lead the nation into the light and experience His righteousness (7:9).

Israel's walls will be rebuilt and the nation's "boundary" will "be extended" (7:11). The mention of a land boundary" along with "Egypt" and "Euphrates" may allude back to Genesis 15:18 where Israel's yet to be fulfilled land boundaries are discussed. Also, people from the nations ("from sea to sea and mountain to mountain") will come to Jerusalem. Reminiscent of Isaiah 19:24–25, this includes the traditional enemies of Israel—Egypt and Assyria (7:12). Again, the global implications of Israel's King and kingdom are manifest. This King also functions as a Shepherd—"Shepherd Your people with Your scepter" (7:14). He will cause His "flock" to dwell securely and "dwell in the midst of a fruitful field" (7:14).

During this kingdom reign, Israel can expect the miraculous: "As in the days when you came out of the land of Egypt, I will show you miracles" (7:15). This verse explicitly links kingdom conditions with miracles. At His first coming, Jesus' kingdom presentation was filled with miracles, and so too will the kingdom be when Jesus returns a second time to earth. Forgiveness of sins is also part of the kingdom. God "pardons iniquity" and "passes over the rebellious act" of His people (7:18). The Lord is the one who will "cast all their sins into the depths of the sea" (7:19). This great chapter predicting a future salvation and restoration of Israel is based on God's covenantal love with the patriarchs including "Jacob" and "Abraham" (7:20). Thus, Micah gives one of the most detailed descriptions of God's kingdom in the Minor Prophets.

NAHUM AND HABAKKUK

Nahum predicted the coming destruction of Nineveh. Ironically, this instrument of God's judgment upon the northern tribes of Israel would itself be judged. The prophet also addressed comfort for Judah (1:12, 15; 2:2) who will benefit from Nineveh's calamity:

> For the Lord will restore the splendor of Jacob
> Like the splendor of Israel,
> Even though the devastators have devastated them
> And destroyed their vine branches (Nah 2:2).

The term "restore" refers to a positive reversal of fortune.[9] Nahum picks up the prevalent theme from Deuteronomy 30:3 that Israel will be restored after a period of captivity. "Splendor" means "majesty" or "excellence." Thus, destruction and wreckage from captivity will give way to restoration and return to glory. As Richard Patterson summarizes, "A repentant, redeemed Israel will be freed from exile and restored to its promised land to enjoy an era of peace and prosperity permeated by the glorious presence of her heavenly Redeemer."[10] Isaiah 49:6 declared that the Servant of the Lord will "raise up the tribes of Jacob and to restore the preserved ones of Israel." He will also "restore the land" to His people (49:8). This hope of the restoration of Israel was on the minds of the apostles when they asked Jesus, "Lord, is it at this time you are *restoring* the kingdom to Israel?" (Acts 1:6).[11]

Habakkuk ministered to Judah in pre-exilic times. He "informs his readers that the everlasting... God of glory (2:14; 3:3–4) is sovereign (2:20) over all individuals and nations (1:5, 14; 2:6–19; 3:3–15), guiding them according to His predetermined purpose to bring glory to Himself (2:14)."[12] This shows the sovereignty of God in bringing about His kingdom plans.

ZEPHANIAH

Little is known about Zephaniah the man. His ministry occurred during the reign of Josiah (640–609 B.C.). The theme of Zephaniah is God's judgment for disobedience. In particular, this judgment takes the form of the "Day of the Lord" which dominates Zephaniah more than any other OT book. This Day of the Lord has implications for Israel and the nations. It is a time of "wrath," "trouble," "distress," destruction," "desolation," "darkness," and "doom" (1:14). The Day of the Lord is a time of devastating judgment upon "all the inhabitants of the earth" (1:18). Yet while the main focus of the

9 The Hebrew term *shub* means "to return" or "turn back." Patterson notes that "'restore the splendor' carries with it the more usual thought of 'restore the fortune.'" Richard D. Patterson, *Nahum, Habakkuk, Zephaniah* in The Wycliffe Exegetical Commentary, ed. Kenneth Barker (Chicago: Moody, 1991), 57.

10 Ibid.

11 Emphases mine.

12 Ibid., 134.

Day of the Lord is judgment, it also involves restoration. This restoration includes the Gentile nations and Israel.

Zephaniah predicted that the Lord would "gather nations" and "assemble kingdoms" so He could pour out His "indignation" and "burning anger" (3:8). The Day of the Lord means fierce judgment and wrath from the Lord. But the judgment phase of the Day of the Lord gives way to a blessings phase, which includes the restoration of the nations:

> "For then I will give to the peoples purified lips,
> That all of them may call on the name of the LORD,
> To serve Him shoulder to shoulder.
> From beyond the rivers of Ethiopia
> My worshipers, My dispersed ones,
> Will bring My offerings" (3:9–10).

These "peoples" will receive "purified lips" from the Lord signifying that they have been restored. Nations that once blasphemed the Lord will use their words for true worship. This even includes those "beyond the rivers of Ethiopia"—the upper Nile area of southern Egypt, Sudan and northern Ethiopia. Thus, God's blessings to the nations reach distant lands. As with other OT passages (Isa 2:2–4; Amos 9:11–12), Zephaniah predicted Gentile nations would be included in the people of God alongside Israel. Not only is there a coming restoration of Israel, there will also be a restoration of Gentile nations.[13]

The restoration of Israel is the focus of Zephaniah 3:12–20. Israel itself will be punished, yet the Lord will leave a "remnant of Israel" that does what is right (3:13). This Day of the Lord ushers in a time of restoration for Israel. Israel will "Shout for joy" because the Lord will be in their midst and the judgments against the nation will be taken away (3:14–15). Israel will not fear her enemies anymore because the Lord protects her (3:17). He will save the lame and gather the outcasts (3:19). Zephaniah 3:20 repeats a theme that began in Deuteronomy 30:3 and has been repeated in other prophetic sections such as Jeremiah 29:14 and Ezekiel 38:8—gathering and restoration. God says, "At the time when I *gather* you together.... When I

13 Ibid., 370–71.

restore your fortunes before your eyes."[14] Thus, late in the OT, the promise of a gathering and restoration of Israel remains a prominent part of the nation's hope.

In sum, Zephaniah is a somber book of warning for both Israel and the nations. This is centered in the frightful Day of the Lord that is coming. Israel, too, will face God's judgments but these judgments give way to a kingdom in which both Israel and the nations will be restored as the people of God. Zephaniah, like the other OT prophets, predicts a restoration of Israel. But this restoration of Israel also results in the restoration of Gentile nations. As Charles L. Feinberg has pointed out, "Regathered and restored, the nation [Israel] will be a source of blessing to the world."[15] As a result, "Every day that the salvation of Israel draws nearer, that of the world's salvation draws nearer also."[16]

HAGGAI

After Obadiah, Haggai is the shortest book in the OT. Written around 520 B.C., Haggai offers significant data concerning the kingdom of God. Haggai 2:6–9 describes glorious conditions for Israel's temple after a time of judgment on the nations:

> For thus says the LORD of hosts, "Once more in a little while, I am going to shake the heavens and the earth, the sea also and the dry land. I will shake all the nations; and they will come with the wealth of all nations, and I will fill this house with glory," says the LORD of hosts. "The silver is Mine and the gold is Mine," declares the LORD of hosts. "The latter glory of this house will be greater than the former," says the LORD of hosts, "and in this place I will give peace," declares the LORD of hosts.

The Lord says that "in a little while" He is going to "shake the heavens and the earth" and "all the nations" (2:6–7). This "in a little while" language does not mean the predicted events must occur within a very

14 Emphasis is mine.

15 Charles L. Feinberg, *The Minor Prophets* (Chicago: Moody, 1990), 235.

16 Ibid., 236.

short time period, but it does mean they are imminent and can break forth on the scene unexpectedly at any time. As Eugene Merrill points out, the wording of Haggai here "was for the purpose of stressing the imminence of the event."[17] The fact that history shows these events did not happen soon after the prophecy was revealed does not remove the truth that they were impending to the original audience.

The temple in Jerusalem will be filled with God's glory in a way never seen before in history (2:9). Some have understood the shaking of the heavens and the earth metaphorically in reference to the first coming of Jesus and the upheaval His coming meant to the Jewish religious system. But this view is unlikely. First, what Haggai is discussing parallels what happened with the exodus from Egypt (v. 5), which was a literal shaking of the cosmos. Homer Kent is correct when he states, "The first shaking was physical and geographical at Sinai. There is no good reason to take this second shaking of the earth and heavens above it in any less literal sense."[18] Second, the writer of Hebrews refers to this section as a future event in Hebrews 12:26–27 when he discusses the receiving of a kingdom that cannot be shaken. In doing so, the writer of Hebrews further links Haggai 2:6–9 with the coming of God's kingdom. Thus, there are canonical reasons to view Haggai 2:6–9 as still future from our standpoint. Just as God literally shook the land around Mount Sinai in regard to His people at the giving of the law, a greater shaking is coming that will have universal implications for God's kingdom. As Kaiser says concerning Haggai 2:6–9: "In those previous shakings, God came to aid only his people in their time of deep need. But in the last day, in connection with his second coming, there will be a worldwide shake-up that will signal the final appearance of Christ as he comes to reign forever."[19]

Haggai 2:20–23 offers other kingdom implications:

> Then the word of the Lord came a second time to Haggai... "Speak to Zerubbabel governor of Judah, saying, 'I am going to shake the heavens and the earth. I will overthrow the thrones

17 Eugene H. Merrill, *Haggai, Zechariah, Malachi: An Exegetical Commentary* (n.p.: Biblical Studies Press, 2013), 42.

18 Homer A. Kent, Jr., *The Epistle to the Hebrews: A Commentary* (Winona Lake, IN: BMH Books, 1972), 275.

19 Kaiser, *The Messiah in the Old Testament*, 206.

> of kingdoms and destroy the power of the kingdoms of the nations; and I will overthrow the chariots and their riders, and the horses and their riders will go down, everyone by the sword of another.' 'On that day,' declares the LORD of hosts, 'I will take you, Zerubbabel, son of Shealtiel, My servant,' declares the LORD, 'and I will make you like a signet ring, for I have chosen you,'" declares the LORD of hosts.

Again, the Lord revealed to Haggai that He was going to shake the heavens and earth and overthrow the Gentile kingdoms of the earth. The reference to Zerubbabel being made like a signet ring has Davidic and kingdom implications. The signet ring on a king's hand is much like the presidential seal to an American president. It represents rights, privileges and authority to the office holder.[20] The fulfillment of this prediction will be at the time of upheaval of the heavens and earth and the overthrow of Gentile kingdoms. Again, this is a future event according to Hebrews 12:26–28.

Also, a "signet ring" was a sign of royal authority, so Zerubbabel is linked with the coming kingdom. Zerubbabel was of Davidic descent (see Matt 1:12), and thus, like David, typified the coming of the ultimate David—Jesus Christ. One objection to this idea may be that this promise was made to Zerubbabel himself and not a descendant of Zerubbabel. But the context of this passage seems to point to the indefinite future. It is "on that day," the day of cosmic upheaval and Gentile overthrow, that the promise will be fulfilled. Thus, to see Zerubbabel as being a type of Christ and the fulfillment of this passage being in the time of Christ seems reasonable. Also, since the coming of the kingdom involves the physical resurrection of the saints, a resurrected Zerubbabel will be present to experience the blessings of the kingdom.

ZECHARIAH

Some of the most detailed information concerning the timing and nature of the kingdom of God is found in Zechariah. Zechariah wrote his book between 520–518 B.C. This makes Zechariah a post-exilic prophet. This is

20 Ibid., 210.

significant since Zechariah writes much about future events concerning Israel such as land, tribulation, and kingdom. In doing so, this excludes the idea that the complete fulfillment of God's promises occurred with the historical returns from exile. These matters have future relevance to Israel.

Israel and Gentiles as God's People (Zechariah 2:10–13)

Zechariah 2 instructs Zion to be joyous because the Lord is "coming to dwell" among them (2:10). Yet this dwelling among Israel is not just a blessing for Israel. "Many nations will join themselves to the Lord on that day and become My people" (2:11). The Lord's kingdom is for both Israel and the Gentile nations. Both are the people of God. Isaiah 19:24–25 indicated that the nations will be God's people alongside Israel. The people of God concept includes elements of unity and diversity. There is unity among the nations and Israel. Both worship together and belong to the same God. Yet there is diversity in that the Gentiles are still Gentiles and Israel is still Israel. Gentiles are not incorporated into Israel although they become the people of God alongside believing Israel.

Verse 12 states that the Lord will possess Judah "in the holy land" and will choose Jerusalem. This again shows that the restoration of Israel includes a literal holy land for His people.

Playing in the Streets and Kingdom Implications (Zechariah 8:1–8)

Zechariah 8 offers beautiful descriptions of God's coming kingdom. It begins with God restoring Jerusalem. With "great wrath" and "jealousy" (8:2) the Lord returns to Zion and dwells in Jerusalem (8:3). The great city will have another name—"City of Truth" (8:3). This capital city of God's kingdom will be characterized by sweet peace and fellowship as the Lord himself says:

> Thus says the LORD of hosts, "Old men and old women will again sit in the streets of Jerusalem, each man with his staff in his hand because of age. And the streets of the city will be filled with boys and girls playing in its streets" (Zech 8:4–5).

When the Lord comes and reigns from Jerusalem both elderly and young people will be talking and playing in the streets. This shows that age and age discrepancies still exist in this form of God's kingdom. Also, normal human activity is occurring. People will be in the streets, probably talking and interacting with each other. Children are playing and laughing. Perhaps they are chasing each other in a game of tag or kicking a ball around. Whatever they are doing it includes running and laughing. The blessings of God's kingdom are certainly profound but they can also be blessedly real and simple. As Alva McClain states in regard to this passage, "This is no kingdom of asceticism where the normal impulses of humanity, implanted by divine creation, will be rigorously suppressed." This is a time of "glad release" and "joyous and safe recreation."[21]

This passage should not be "spiritualized." It is not "ideal language" that points to some greater spiritual reality. The kingdom of God means peace in the midst of wholesome fellowship and play. In this present age streets of major cities are often not safe, but they will be when the Messiah reigns. The elderly will safely be in the streets conversing with each other and watching children play with no threat of harm. No criminals exist. Children can play and laugh with no predators or bullies. Wild animals are no threat.

The Lord will bring His people from the East and West to live in Jerusalem (8:7–8). The physical blessings that will occur when God's people are in the land include agricultural prosperity and moisture from the sky (8:12). Many people and nations will seek the Lord in Jerusalem (8:22). The blessings of God's kingdom surely include physical blessings.

As Zechariah 8 reveals, age and age discrepancies still exist when the Lord's kingdom is established. Old men and women at this time need the aid of a staff "because of age." They possess some weakness because of advanced years. This suggests an intermediate kingdom (or millennium) era different from the present evil age but distinct also from the eternal state in which all negative aspects of aging and death are removed. There has never been a time when the conditions of Zechariah 8 have happened. On the other hand, there will be no elderly who are weak in the final eternal state for all remnants of the curse will have been removed (see Rev 21 and 22). What Zechariah describes, therefore, must take place in an initial phase of

21 McClain, *The Greatness of the Kingdom*, 228.

God's kingdom before the eternal state begins. Such an intermediate state between the present age and the eternal state is described in Revelation 20.

The King's Coming and Worldwide Reign (Zechariah 9:9–10)

Zechariah 9:9 predicted that Israel's King would arrive on a donkey. All four Gospel writers quote this passage. They see it as fulfilled by Jesus as He entered Jerusalem days before His death. Zechariah 9:10 then speaks of the King's power as He removes instruments of warfare and speaks peace to the nations. The universality of His reign is evident in that "His dominion will be from sea to sea" and to "the ends of the earth." Verse 10 has not been fulfilled yet since the King is not ruling over the entire planet yet. But this will occur when Jesus the Messiah returns at His second coming. Thus, Zechariah 9:9 has already been fulfilled but 9:10 awaits future fulfillment. This is one of the implications of there being two comings of Jesus. Certain messianic prophecies were fulfilled with Jesus' first coming, while others await fulfillment at His second coming. This is tied to the idea of "prophetic foreshortening" in which "events far removed in time and events in the near future are spoken of as if they were very close together."[22]

The Earthly Kingdom and Nations (Zechariah 14)

With Zechariah 14, we learn much about the earthly kingdom, both in *timing* and *nature*. While we will survey the chapter as a whole, we will start with v. 9:

> And the LORD will be king over all the earth; in that day the Lord will be the only one, and His name the only one.

This is an explicit declaration that the Lord will be king over the earth. At that time no nation will worship its own gods, unlike today, for the Lord will establish His rule and there will be no doubt who the true God is. Now we can survey how the rest of Zechariah 14 fits with this important truth.

A Kingdom after Tribulation (1–9)

Verses 1–8 show that the Lord's reign upon the earth is preceded by a time of calamity upon Jerusalem. Verse 1 says "a day is coming" which puts the

22 Anthony A. Hoekema, *The Bible and the Future* (Grand Rapids: Eerdmans, 1979), 148.

events of Zechariah 14 in the future. Verse 2 then predicts a time of turmoil that will befall Jerusalem:

> For I will gather all the nations against Jerusalem to battle, and the city will be captured, the houses plundered, the women ravished and half of the city exiled, but the rest of the people will not be cut off from the city.

God says "I will gather" which indicates that what is about to take place accords with His sovereign plans and initiative. We also see that "the nations" will be coming "against Jerusalem." Note that "nations" here is plural which means the attack involves several nations, not just one.

The city being attacked is "Jerusalem." Again, Jerusalem has important significance to God. The consequences of this attack upon Jerusalem initially are awful—the city is captured; houses are plundered; women are taken advantage of; and half the city is exiled. But according to v. 3, "the Lord will go forth and fight against those nations." The calamity upon Jerusalem is temporary. Jerusalem is attacked and wounded, but only for a time. The Lord comes to Jerusalem's defense.

Verse 4 states that the LORD's feet "will stand on the Mount of Olives" in front of Jerusalem on the east side. And the Mount of Olives "will be split in its middle from east to west." Verse 5 declares that the Lord God will come with His holy ones, His heavenly army. Verses 6 and 7 also reveal that there will be cosmic signs. Verse 8 shows that at this time "living waters will flow out of Jerusalem." Half will flow toward the eastern sea and half to the western sea. This will be the case in both summer and winter. Thus, kingdom conditions will bring nourishment and prosperity to the area.

All of these events lead up to the statement in v. 9 that: "And the Lord will be king over all the earth." Thus, various events happen in connection with the Lord's kingdom over the earth:

- The nations will attack Jerusalem and cause temporary harm to the city (2).
- The Lord will fight against these nations that attack Jerusalem (3).
- The Lord will return to the Mount of Olives and cause major geographical changes to the area (4).

- There will be cosmic signs (6–7).
- Living waters will flow out of Jerusalem (8).
- The Lord will be king over the earth (9).

These events should be understood in a straightforward manner. As Merrill states, "There is no reason to take this in any but a literal way, unless one is prepared to deny a literal coming of YHWH as well."[23] These occurrences, individually and collectively have not yet happened in history. Therefore, we should expect a future fulfillment of them.

In sum, Zechariah 14:1–9 gives important information concerning the *timing* of God's kingdom. On a future day, when Jerusalem is under siege by the nations, the Lord will defend the city and its inhabitants, returning to the Mount of Olives. Cosmic signs and major topographical changes will take place. At that time, "The Lord will be king over all the earth" (14:9).

The Nature of the Kingdom (Zechariah 14:10–21)

Zechariah 14:10–21 reveals details about the nature of the kingdom in the aftermath of the Lord's return to earth. The kingdom involves even more changes to Jerusalem as v. 10 indicates: "All the land will be changed into a plain from Geba to Rimmon south of Jerusalem; but Jerusalem will rise and remain on its site from Benjamin's Gate as far as the place of the First Gate to the Corner Gate, and from the Tower of Hananel to the king's wine presses." Verse 11 also says "Jerusalem will dwell in security." Verses 12–15 describe what will happen to those who previously waged war against Jerusalem. Destruction, panic, and plague befall the enemies of Israel. Verses 16–19 then detail the relationship of the nations to the kingdom:

> Then it will come about that any who are left of all the nations that went against Jerusalem will go up from year to year to worship the King, the LORD of hosts, and to celebrate the Feast of Booths. And it will be that whichever of the families of the earth does not go up to Jerusalem to worship the King, the LORD of hosts, there will be no rain on them. If the family of Egypt does not go up or enter, then no rain will fall on them; it will be the

23 Merrill, *Haggai, Zechariah, Malachi* 343–44.

> plague with which the Lord smites the nations who do not go up to celebrate the Feast of Booths. This will be the punishment of Egypt, and the punishment of all the nations who do not go up to celebrate the Feast of Booths.

Several points from this section are significant. First, some people from the nations survive the judgments of the Lord (v. 16). Second, those who survive the judgments will go to Jerusalem to worship the King. The nations must come to worship the King in person as He rules from Jerusalem, His capital city. This shows that Jerusalem as a city and Israel as a nation have future prominence and significance. Third, survivors from the nations will celebrate the Feast of Booths. This feast was one of three on Israel's calendar when God's people presented themselves at the sanctuary (see Lev. 23:34–44). The purpose of the feast was to celebrate the Lord's provision for Israel during their wilderness journey.

So how will an Israelite feast relate to the nations when the Lord rules upon the earth? Merrill suggests "there is evidence that this was an occasion for some kind of recognition of the king as YHWH's son and representative." Thus, "For the nations to observe the Feast of Tabernacles was for them to come in submission before the King of all the earth and render to Him their expressions of subservience."[24] In short, the Feast of Booths will be an opportunity for the nations of the earth to express their allegiance to the Lord.

Fourth, nations that do not observe the Feast of Booths will experience negative consequences. The Lord will smite the nations that disobey. Egypt, for example, will not experience rainfall. During this phase of the Lord's reign over the earth, disobedience is still possible for some and the Lord's righteous reign involves punishment on occasion. Then vv. 20–21 indicate that everything during this period will be holy to the Lord, even those things usually considered mundane:

> In that day there will be inscribed on the bells of the horses, "HOLY IS THE LORD." And the cooking pots in the Lord's house will be like the bowls before the altar. Every cooking pot in Jerusalem and in Judah will be holy to the LORD of hosts; and all

24 Ibid., 362–63.

> who sacrifice will come and take of them and boil in them. And there will no longer be a Canaanite in the house of the LORD of hosts in that day.

In sum, this section reveals the Lord will reign from Jerusalem over the nations. The nations must show their allegiance by observing the Feast of Booths. Those nations that do not obey the Lord will experience negative consequences, including the withholding of blessings.

Theological Implications of Zechariah 14

Key theological implications arise from Zechariah 14. First, this chapter affirms a coming kingdom upon the earth (v. 9). God will rule over the planet He created. Merrill is correct that, "The God who led His people through spatial, temporal history will recreate the cosmos in those same categories."[25] Second, Zechariah 14 shows that the kingdom follows tribulation, including the siege and deliverance of Jerusalem. Third, Zechariah 14 shows the future significance of Jerusalem and the people of Israel. The Lord not only delivers Jerusalem, but Jerusalem also operates as the capital city of the Lord's kingdom. Jesus himself predicted a day was coming when Gentile domination over Jerusalem would come to an end (see Luke 21:24). Fourth, the coming kingdom has universal implications. The kingdom does not just involve Israel—it involves all nations. Egypt is one example. The concept of God's blessings being mediated through Israel to the Gentiles is affirmed once again (see Gen 12:2–3). Fifth, Zechariah 14 reveals an intermediate kingdom distinct from both the present age and the final eternal state. Wayne Grudem states the issue well:

> Here again the description [Zech 14:5–17] does not fit the present age, for the Lord is King over all the earth in this situation. But it does not fit the eternal state either, because of the disobedience and rebellion against the Lord that is clearly present.[26]

These conditions of Zechariah 14 can only occur in an intermediate kingdom between the present age and the eternal state. While people from all

25 Ibid., 357.

26 Grudem, *Systematic Theology*, 1129.

nations are being saved in this age, the nations do not obey our Lord (see Ps 2). In fact, they persecute those who belong to the Lord. In the coming kingdom, though, Jesus will rule the nations while He is physically present on earth. The nations will obey and submit to His rule, but as Zechariah 14 points out, whenever a nation does not act as it should there will be punishment. On the other hand, in the eternal state there is no disobedience from the nations. The activities of the nations in the eternal state are only positive. The nations with their kings bring contributions to the New Jerusalem (see Rev 21:24) and the leaves of the tree of life are for the healing of the nations (see Rev 22:2). To compare:

> Present Age: Jesus is in heaven and the nations do not yet submit to Jesus as King.
>
> Millennial Kingdom: Jesus rules the nations on earth and punishes those nations that do not act as they should.
>
> Eternal State: The nations act exactly as they should with no need of punishment.

OT Intermediate Kingdom Passages

OT Passage	Conditions in Intermediate Kingdom
Ps 72	A kingdom reign on earth with righteous judgments for the poor, afflicted, and needy
Isa 11:4	A kingdom reign with righteous decisions made for the poor and afflicted
Isa 24:21–23	Many days between initial and final punishment of wicked spiritual beings and human kings
Isa 65:20	Increased longevity of life yet death occurs for wicked actions; childbirth occurs yet no infant mortality
Zech 8	Peaceful and playful conditions in the streets with the presence of elderly who need help, and youth who are playing
Zech 14	A kingdom reign on the earth over nations who serve the Lord, yet people can sin and face negative consequences for disobedience

MALACHI

Malachi is the last book of the OT. The prophet, Malachi, offered an indictment against Judah and its priests. The prophet called on the people to turn from their sin. If they did not the Lord would bring a curse on the land.

Kingdom implications exist in Malachi. Twice in 1:11, God declared, "My name will be great among the nations." The Lord also revealed that a "messenger" would clear the way for His sudden coming to the temple (3:1). This was fulfilled with John the Baptist who prepared the way for Jesus. The coming of the Lord means purification for God's people as the Lord is likened to a "refiner's fire" and "smelter and purifier of silver" (see 3:2–4). The refining ministry of the Lord will mean that the "offering of Judah and Jerusalem will be pleasing to the Lord as in the days of old as in former years" (3:4). This points to a restoration of fallen Israel. There will also be "judgment" for the wicked, the sorcerers, adulterers, and those who mistreat the helpless (see 3:5). God promises Israel that if they return to Him He will return to them (3:7). When this occurs God will open the windows of heaven and pour out His blessings (3:10). These blessings for Israel will function as a witness to the nations: "All the nations will call you blessed, for you shall be a delightful land" (3:12). Again, Israel's actions involve more than just Israel. When Israel acts wickedly they disgrace the name of the Lord, but when they act rightly, they bring glory to His name.

The last chapter of the last book of the OT ends with a message of judgment and then blessing. The fiery judgment of the Day of the Lord is found in 4:1: "'For behold, the day is coming, burning like a furnace; and all the arrogant and every evildoer will be chaff; and the day that is coming will set them ablaze,' says the Lord of hosts, 'so that it will leave them neither root nor branch.'"

Yet the result is different for those who know the Lord. For them there are kingdom blessings: "But for you who fear My name, the sun of righteousness will rise with healing in its wings; and you will go forth and skip about like calves from the stall" (4:2). Righteousness will shine through like the sun and the "wicked... will be ashes under the soles of your feet" (4:3). This shows there is a triumph of the kingdom after the judgment of God's opponents.

There also is the promise that Elijah will be sent by God before the coming of the great and terrible Day of the Lord (4:5). Then the last verse of the OT ends on a positive note: "He will restore the hearts of the fathers to their children and the hearts of the children to their fathers, so that I will not come and smite the land with a curse" (4:6). The emphasis here, as Hill has pointed out, is "inter-generational reconciliation."[27] The hearts of the people of Israel are restored, something only God could accomplish. Thus, the last book of the OT ends with the promise of judgment followed by a restored kingdom for Israel.

SUMMARY OF THE KINGDOM IN THE PROPHETS

As the OT writings come to an end, Israel was taken captive by the nations for covenant disobedience. Return from exile occurred, but Israel still remained under Gentile powers, suffering the consequences for covenant failure. Yet the prophets continually proclaimed a coming kingdom in which Israel will be saved (Deut 30:6), restored (Amos 9:11–12), and experience both spiritual salvation and physical blessings. Gentiles, too, will participate in this kingdom under the ultimate Davidic King. The kingdom that the prophets predicted is spiritual in origin (from heaven) yet it will be earthly since it will be established on this earth. Yet there are also spiritual requirements for this kingdom. J. Dwight Pentecost sums up the message of all the prophets of Israel regarding the kingdom:

> Thus prophet after prophet gave comfort to the nation by reaffirming the hope of the Davidic covenant—that one of David's sons would sit on David's throne and rule over David's kingdom, and that under that reign Israel would experience the blessings of the Abrahamic covenant.[28]

27 Andrew Hill, *Haggai, Zechariah and Malachi*. Tyndale Old Testament Commentaries (Downers Grove: Inter-Varsity, 2012), 366.

28 J. Dwight Pentecost, *Thy Kingdom Come: Tracing God's Kingdom Program and Covenant Promises Throughout History* (Wheaton, IL: Victor Books, 1990), 153.

CHAPTER 14

A SUMMARY OF THE KINGDOM PROGRAM IN THE OLD TESTAMENT

We have surveyed many OT passages related to God's kingdom program. This chapter summarizes the main points of the kingdom storyline in the OT:

1. God as Sovereign and Universal King creates the universe and is King over all creation (Gen 1–2).

2. God creates man in His own image as a son and king so man can represent God on the earth and rule over God's creation on His behalf for His glory (Gen 1:26–28; Ps 8).

3. Man fails his task of ruling the creation for God's glory by sinning against his Creator (Gen 3); the vice-regent rebels against the King.

4. The fall results in a cursed creation in which man is subject to death, the creation is subject to futility, and Satan usurps authority (Gen 3).

5. God promises a future Savior, a Satan (serpent)-crusher and curse-remover from the seed of the woman who will save man and restore the creation (Gen 3:15).

6. God unleashes a global flood to judge wicked mankind, but since God has promised a Savior, He chooses Noah as the means to keep mankind preserved, the animal kingdom alive, and God's kingdom purposes intact (Gen 6–9).

7. Through the Noahic covenant God promises stability of nature as a platform for carrying out His kingdom plans (Gen 8:21–22).

8. Through the Tower of Babel incident God institutes ethnic diversity and nations to carry out His original plan for man to multiply and fill the earth (Gen 10–11).

9. God's plan for restoration and a worldwide kingdom is mediated through Abraham via the Abrahamic Covenant; Abraham and the developing people of Israel will be the vehicles for blessing the nations of the earth (Gen 12, 13, 15, 17, 22).

10. Through Abraham, Isaac, and Jacob the people of the kingdom program grow in number in Egypt where eventually they become enslaved.

11. God rescues His people, Israel, so they can be a kingdom of priests and a light to other nations; Israel, with its Promised Land, is the platform through which God will bless other nations (Exod 19:6; Deut 4:5–8).

12. The Mosaic Covenant is the means through which Israel could be set apart for God's purposes, and the way the nation could stay connected to the promises of the Abrahamic Covenant (Exod 20).

13. Israel is promised spiritual and physical blessings for keeping the Mosaic Covenant, and curses and dispersion for disobeying the Mosaic Covenant (Deut 28–29).

14. God predicts Israel will possess the land of promise only to be dispersed because of covenant disobedience. This will be followed by a restoration of Israel from the nations with both spiritual and physical prosperity. The basis of this restoration will be a circumcised heart (Deut 30:1–10).

15. God's kingdom on earth is mediated through Moses, and then Joshua, and then through the judges and eventually the kings of Israel (Joshua–Chronicles).

16. With the Davidic Covenant God promises David an eternal kingdom for Israel through David's descendants with physical blessings and rest from enemies; this covenant will also bring blessings to all mankind (2 Sam 7).

17. Israel flourishes under David and then Solomon with the kingdom promises of land, seed, and international blessings being on the verge of fulfillment (1 Kgs 1–10).

18. Solomon's idolatry (1 Kgs 11) puts the kingdom of Israel on a trajectory that eventually leads to dispersion. The tribes of Israel are taken captive by Assyria and Babylon. The glory of God departs from the temple signifying the end of the mediatorial kingdom in Israel (Ezek 8–11).

19. With the end of the kingdom in Israel the prophets became the spokespersons for God to Israel, and they proclaim both judgment for covenant disobedience and a future restoration in a kingdom under a Davidic leader (Isaiah; Jeremiah; Ezekiel).

20. Because of Israel's failure to be a kingdom of priests for God's glory, God will raise up an ultimate Israelite, a Servant, who will restore the nation Israel and bring blessings to the Gentiles (Isa 42; 49; 52–53).

21. God will mediate a New Covenant through Israel that grants a new heart and indwelling Spirit to God's people so they will obey God and allow God's people to experience kingdom blessings (Jer 31–34; Ezek 36–37).

22. The prophets reveal a coming Day of the Lord when God will judge the nations of the earth and purge His people Israel; this will be followed by the Davidic kingdom on earth, centered in Jerusalem, under the Messiah, in which both Israel and the nations will be God's people (Isaiah–Malachi).

23. The OT ends with the expectation God will fulfill His kingdom promises while His people wait for deliverance.

SUMMARY

The OT revealed God's plans to restore His creation that was marred at the fall. God's plans are holistic. He will restore all things material and immaterial. This includes individuals, the nation Israel, and the nations of the world. The kingdom plan will be carried out through the eternal and unconditional covenants—Noahic, Abrahamic, Davidic, and New. The Mosaic Covenant was a temporary and conditional covenant that Israel failed. Because Israel did not keep the Mosaic Covenant, God's kingdom did not come in its fullness and there is the need for the superior New Covenant, which will enable Israel (and others) to obey the Lord.

According to the prophets the restoration of all things will center upon an ultimate Israelite, the true Servant, who we now know as Jesus the Messiah. There is a coming Day of the Lord when the nations of the earth will be judged and Israel will be saved. Kingdom conditions will follow when the ultimate Davidic ruler will reign from Jerusalem over a restored Israel and the nations of the earth will be blessed. This is the kingdom message of the OT, a message that will continue for four hundred years and into the dawning of the NT era.

PART

3

THE KINGDOM PROGRAM IN THE NEW TESTAMENT

KINGDOM EXPECTATIONS AT THE TIME OF JESUS' BIRTH (MATTHEW 1–2 AND LUKE 1–2)

As the NT era arrives a new page is opened in the developing kingdom program. In the opening scenes of Matthew and Luke anticipation is electric concerning a coming Savior and King. Something big is about to happen and it does. The Messiah is about to burst on the scene.

One issue to grapple with is whether the NT affirms the literal expectation of the OT prophets, or whether it transcends and redefines it. Does the NT continue the kingdom storyline or does it change it? Does the coming of Jesus mean the literal fulfillment of the OT promises or the transcending of the promises? Matthew 1–2 and Luke 1–2 help answer these questions. As Messiah's arrival is on the brink, expectations concerning Him are consistent with the picture presented by the OT prophets.

THE BLOODLINE TO BE KING

Genesis 3:15 presented hope of a coming seed who would reverse the curse and defeat the power behind the serpent (Satan). Matthew 1 introduces the kingdom plan by showing that Jesus is the promised seed. He is the "Messiah" who has the bloodline to be the promised Davidic king.[1] As v. 1 states, "The record of the genealogy of Jesus the Messiah, the son of David, the son of Abraham." That David is mentioned first shows the importance of linking Jesus with David, the one to whom the Davidic Covenant was given. The mention of "Abraham" connects Jesus with Abraham and the

1 See Douglas R. Hare, *Matthew* (Louisville: John Knox, 1993), 8.

Abrahamic Covenant. Genesis 17:6 predicted kings would come from Abraham and the ultimate King would soon arrive.

Jesus is related to both Abraham and David. He meets the requirements of the promised Messiah. As J. Dwight Pentecost puts it, "Jesus legally and physically possesses all rights to David's throne."[2] For all the opposition Jesus will face from Israel's religious leaders, they never challenged his biological connection to David. Genealogical records were preserved in the temple and if Jesus was not in the line of David this could have been pointed out by Jesus' enemies. But no objection was offered.[3] As Jesus himself declared, "I am the root and the descendant of David" (Rev 22:16).

THE EXPECTATION OF MARY

Several people understood the coming of Jesus in relation to OT expectations. Their views are remarkably consistent with what the OT predicted. One of the first things said about Jesus was that He would fulfill the promise of a kingdom for Israel. The angel Gabriel declared to Mary:

> "And behold, you will conceive in your womb and bear a son, and you shall name Him Jesus. He will be great and will be called the Son of the Most High; and the Lord God will give Him the throne of His father David; and He will reign over the house of Jacob forever, and His kingdom will have no end" (Luke 1:31–33).

The language of "throne," "house," and "kingdom," is consistent with 2 Samuel 7's discussion of the Davidic Covenant. When Gabriel announced the coming of Jesus, he explicitly linked it with the kingdom promise made to David. The connection is straightforward with no transcending of the original meaning. As Saucy notes, "Mary could only have understood these words as announcing the coming of the prophesied kingdom."[4]

---

2 Pentecost, *Thy Kingdom Come*, 153.

3 Ibid., 154.

4 Robert L. Saucy, *The Case for Progressive Dispensationalism*, 82. According to A. B. Bruce, "The Messiah is here conceived in the spirit of Jewish expectation . . . ." A. B. Bruce, "The Synoptic Gospels," in *The Expositor's Greek New Testament*, ed. W. Robertson Nicoll (Grand Rapids: Eerdmans, 1951), 1:464.

This kingdom "reign" will be "over the house of Jacob forever." "Jacob" is a reference to Israel. Jesus will rule over Israel and His reign will not end. There is no redefinition of Israel. The message he gave and the message Mary understood was that Jesus would reign over the nation Israel. This understanding is consistent with Mary's famous Magnificat (Luke 1:46–55) where she states that God is fulfilling the Abrahamic Covenant with Israel:

> "He has given help to Israel His servant,
> In remembrance of His mercy,
> As He spoke to our fathers,
> To Abraham and his descendants forever" (Luke 1:54–55).

According to Mary, God is giving Israel help based on His mercy and His promises to Abraham. Isaiah had much to say about the "servant" concept. In his writings, the nation Israel itself was God's servant—"But you, Israel, My servant" (41:8). Mary draws upon the concept of Israel as God's servant to make the point that God's mercy is coming upon Israel. This mercy will come through her Son, Jesus, the ultimate Israelite, who will restore the nation Israel. As Isaiah 49:6 predicted, "He says, 'It is too small a thing that You should be My Servant, To raise up the tribes of Jacob and to restore the preserved ones of Israel.'"

Mary relies on what Gabriel stated and the OT understanding of the Abrahamic and Davidic Covenants and how they related to Israel. There is no indication that the OT expectation is transcended or redefined. As Robert Duncan Culver observed, "That wise and gentle young lady reflected quite a literal understanding of Gabriel's announcement in her 'Magnificat' several weeks later (see Luke 1:46–55). She took the announcement literally."[5]

THE EXPECTATION OF ZACHARIAS

Mary was not the only one with expectations grounded in the OT prophets. John the Baptist's father, Zacharias, was filled with the Spirit and prophesied the following:

> "Blessed be the Lord God of Israel,
> For He has visited us and accomplished redemption for His people,

5 Robert Duncan Culver, *Systematic Theology: Biblical & Historical* (Mentor: Great Britain, 2005), 625.

And has raised up a horn of salvation for us
In the house of David His servant—
As He spoke by the mouth of His holy prophets from of old—
Salvation FROM OUR ENEMIES,
And FROM THE HAND OF ALL WHO HATE US;
To show mercy toward our fathers,
And to remember His holy covenant,
The oath which He swore to Abraham our father,
To grant us that we, being rescued from the hand of our enemies,
Might serve Him without fear" (Luke 1:68–74).

Zacharias ties the coming of Jesus with the fulfillment of promises to Abraham and David. He speaks of both salvation and deliverance for Israel from her enemies. While many acknowledge that Jesus offered spiritual salvation for Israel, fewer recognize that God's plan also involves national deliverance for Israel from her enemies—"Salvation FROM OUR ENEMIES, And FROM THE HAND OF ALL WHO HATE US" (Luke 1:71). Zacharias relies on Psalm 106, which speaks of God's faithfulness to save and deliver the nation Israel even though Israel had not been faithful to God.[6] Also, Zechariah 14 predicted national deliverance for Jerusalem and Israel as a result of Messiah's coming and kingdom.

There is no need to spiritualize this promise of national deliverance for Israel. This is a promise Jesus will fulfill with His second coming to earth. Zacharias, therefore, viewed the coming of Jesus as being linked with the salvation and rescue of Israel. Since Zacharias is filled with the Spirit (see Luke 1:67) it is difficult to conclude that Zacharias was wrong about expecting deliverance for the nation Israel or that he was only operating as an OT saint who was not aware God was transcending the OT expectation. Robert Strimple's statements that both Mary and Zacharias "speak as they do here because they are Old Testament saints," and "we would not expect them to speak in the language of the apostle Paul,"[7] are difficult to accept. The better explanation is that Mary and Zacharias meant exactly what they said, and that they were affirming the literal meaning of the OT prophets.

6 His specific reference appears reliant on Psalm 106:10.

7 Robert B. Strimple, "Amillennialism," in *Three Views on the Millennium and Beyond*, 95.

So as the NT opens, the storyline in the OT continues; it is not reinterpreted or transformed.

With Luke 1:68–74 Zacharias affirmed that Messiah's coming means salvation and political deliverance for Israel. To conclude otherwise is to go contrary to what Zacharias declared under inspiration from the Holy Spirit. That this deliverance awaits Jesus' second coming does not make the fulfillment of Zacharias's words any less true or certain.

THE EXPECTATION OF THE MAGI

Matthew also reveals messianic expectations that were swirling at the time of Jesus' birth. With Matthew 2, kingdom hope comes from a surprising group—Gentile astrologers from the east. Certain "magi from the east" arrived in Jerusalem (2:1) declaring, "Where is He who has been born King of the Jews? For we saw His star in the east and have come to worship Him" (2:2). Most scholars think the "magi" belonged to a priestly caste of astrologers probably from Persia.[8] There are many questions about this mysterious group, but significantly, Gentiles from a faraway country were determined to travel a great distance and find the One who would be King of Israel. This is an early indicator that Jesus' mission would extend beyond Israel to Gentiles. This King of Israel will also be King of the entire world (see Zech 14:9), including this band of astrologers from Persia. This truth would challenge many Jews who were resistant to God's kingdom extending to Gentiles. This account of the magi testifies that Gentiles will be part of Messiah's kingdom. These Gentile astrologers from afar grasped what many inside Israel refused to see.

Also, God used a cosmic sign, a literal star to lead the magi in the direction of this King. Cosmic signs are often associated with major events in biblical history. Just as a cosmic body was involved with the Messiah's first coming, literal cosmic bodies will also give evidence of the nearness of the King and His kingdom with His second coming (see Matt 24:29–31).

8 Craig S. Keener, *The Gospel of Matthew: A Socio-Rhetorical Commentary* (Grand Rapids: Eerdmans, 1999), 99.

THE EXPECTATION OF THE RELIGIOUS LEADERS AND HEROD

The magi's quest for the King intersected with another ruler, Herod, who viewed himself as king of the Jews. Their arrival in Jerusalem indicated that they expected to find the King in the city of David. When Herod heard of the magi's quest he was disturbed (2:3) and inquired more information from the chief priests and scribes. Relying quite literally on the OT prophet, Micah, we are told:

> They said to him, "In Bethlehem of Judea; for this is what has been written by the prophet:
>
> 'AND YOU, BETHLEHEM, LAND OF JUDAH
> ARE BY NO MEANS LEAST AMONG THE LEADERS OF JUDAH; FOR OUT OF
> YOU SHALL COME FORTH A RULER
> WHO WILL SHEPHERD MY PEOPLE ISRAEL" (2:5–6).

The religious leaders of Israel viewed the coming King as a "ruler" over "Israel." Herod certainly had this understanding, viewing the coming child-king as a threat to his political position. They understood that the kingdom of Messiah would involve a political rule over Israel. No indication exists that the Jewish religious leaders were wrong in their understanding. The perception that the Messiah would be a political ruler over Israel is correct. Isaiah 9:6 predicted this: "the government will rest on His shoulders." Of course, Jesus would be more than a political ruler. He would also be a Savior from sin. But these two concepts are not mutually exclusive. They harmonize. A savior from sin can also be a political ruler over nations. So there is a political dimension to the coming Messiah. From our standpoint in history, Jesus became a spiritual Savior to all who believed on Him with His first coming, but a political rule awaits His second coming (Rev 19:15).

THE EXPECTATION OF SIMEON AND ANNA

Mary and Joseph presented the eight-day old Jesus for circumcision at the temple (Luke 2:21ff.). Present there was a "righteous and devout" man called Simeon (Luke 2:25a). Simeon "was looking for the consolation of Israel; and the Holy Spirit was upon him" (2:25b). The Holy Spirit revealed to Simeon that he would see the Messiah before he died. Significantly, Simeon's expectation of the Messiah was linked with his hope for the "consolation of Israel." As the OT revealed on many occasions, the coming of the Messiah also meant comfort for Israel. This was Simeon's expectation as well.

Filled with gratitude and awe for beholding Jesus, the Messiah, Simeon accepted his own impending death (2:29) and declared the following:

> "For my eyes have seen Your salvation,
> Which You have prepared in the presence of all people,
> A LIGHT OF REVELATION TO THE GENTILES,
> And the glory of Your people Israel" (Luke 2:30–32).

Relying on passages such as Isaiah 42:6 and 49:6, Simeon expressed the truth that salvation was connected with the One (Jesus) who would bring the light of salvation to Gentiles and glory to God's people, Israel.[9] This shows continuity with the OT expectation. The Savior is not coming to make Gentiles part of Israel but to bring salvation and light to both Israel and Gentiles.

The godly and aged prophetess, Anna, follows this encounter with Simeon. Luke 2:38 says that she "continues to speak of Him to all those who were looking for the redemption of Jerusalem" (2:38). Just as Simeon was looking for the "consolation of Israel," Anna spoke to those looking for "the redemption of Jerusalem." Jerusalem carries great significance since it is the capital city of Israel. It too will be restored.[10]

The Jewish expectations of Mary, Zacharias, Simeon, and Anna should not be glossed over or dismissed. Nor should we view their beliefs as needing to be transcended by later revelation. These people, under divine guidance or inspiration, believed the coming Messiah would bring salvation and national deliverance for Jerusalem and Israel. Their understanding is consistent with the message of the OT prophets and an important

9 See Luke Timothy Johnson, *The Gospel of Luke*, in Sacra Pagina, ed. Daniel J. Harrington, S. J. (Collegeville, MN: The Liturgical Press, 1991), 55.

10 As history shows, the great city has taken a long and arduous path toward this restoration, and experienced a major setback because of Israel's rejection of Jesus the Messiah (see Luke 19:41–44). But Jesus indicated the Gentile trampling of Jerusalem will come to an end and the city will be redeemed (see Luke 21:24; Matt 23:37–39).

indicator that the storyline begun in the OT is the storyline that the NT will build upon. Their expectation harmonizes well with that of the magi that Messiah's salvation would also extend to Gentiles. The hope of the OT prophets is also the hope of the people of God early in the gospels.

JESUS AS REPRESENTATIVE OF ISRAEL (MATTHEW 2)

Significant to the kingdom program is Jesus' identification with Israel. From Israel will come an ultimate Servant and representative of Israel. This is a major emphasis of Matthew 2. The prophet, Isaiah, revealed that a true Israelite would come who would restore the nation Israel and bring blessings to the Gentiles. For example, Isaiah 49:3, 6 declares:

> He said to Me, "You are My Servant, Israel,
> In Whom I will show My glory."...
> He says, "It is too small a thing that You should be My Servant
> To raise up the tribes of Jacob and to restore the preserved ones
> of Israel; I will also make You a light of the nations
> So that My salvation may reach to the end of the earth."

A coming "Servant" will restore Israel. Matthew reveals that Jesus is the true Israelite who will accomplish this. Matthew shows this by linking events in Israel's history with events in Jesus' life. Such parallels are not mere coincidences but divinely intended correspondences. For example, Matthew 2:13–14 states that Mary and Joseph took Jesus to Egypt to escape Herod's attempt to kill the child. Then verse 15 relates Jesus' return from Egypt with Israel's exodus journey centuries earlier:

> He [Jesus] remained there until the death of Herod. This was to fulfill what had been spoken by the Lord through the prophet: "OUT OF EGYPT I CALLED MY SON."

Jesus' return from Egypt is said to "fulfill" Israel's journey from Egypt at the time of the exodus. The natural question is, "How can Jesus' return from Egypt be a fulfillment of an historical event that happened centuries earlier?" Hosea 11:1 is referring to the past event of the exodus from Egypt. So how can a reference to an historical event hundreds of years earlier be fulfilled in Jesus? Some claim this is an example where a NT writer uses the OT out of context. Others say Matthew is reinterpreting Hosea 11:1 and changing a historical reference into a prophecy about Christ. Neither of these options is correct.

Matthew is not using Hosea 11:1 in a non-contextual or reckless manner. He knows what Hosea meant and is not overturning the meaning of Hosea 11:1. Instead, Matthew is connecting a significant event in Israel's history with an event in Jesus' life to show that Jesus is connected with Israel. This shows Jesus is the true representative of Israel.

A difference exists between interpreting a passage and showing how two events correspond to each other. Matthew is not so much explaining the words of Hosea 11:1 as much as He is showing a correspondence between Israel and Jesus. The Jews understood the concept of corporate solidarity in which "one" can represent "many," and the experience of the one can relate to the many. Such a connection is not as familiar to a modern audience, but it would be to the original Jewish readers of Matthew's gospel. As Craig Blomberg notes, "[F]or believing Jews, merely to discern striking parallels between God's actions in history, especially in decisive moments of revelation and redemption, could convince them of divinely intended 'coincidence.'"[11]

Also, the corporate connection between Israel and Israel's coming King in relation to Egypt is taught in the OT. Compare the following oracles of Balaam in Numbers 23 and 24:

> "God brings them [Israel] out of Egypt, He [God] is for them like the horns of the wild ox" (Num 23:22).

> "God brings him [Israel's king (see Num 24:7)] out of Egypt, He is for him like the horns of the wild ox" (Num 24:8).

Numbers 23:22 refers to Israel while Numbers 24:8 refers to Israel's king. Note that God brought both Israel and Israel's king out of Egypt, showing a corporate and typological connection between Israel and Israel's coming king. Perhaps Hosea had this connection in mind when he wrote Hosea 11:1. If he did then Hosea did have more in mind than just the actual

11 Craig L. Blomberg, "Matthew," in *Commentary on the New Testament Use of the Old Testament*, eds. G. K. Beale and D. A. Carson (Grand Rapids: Baker, 2007), 8.

exodus of Israel centuries earlier. He may have been thinking of Israel's coming King as well. When Matthew quotes Hosea 11:1 he could be drawing on a recognized OT type between Israel and her king.

In sum, Matthew's intent is not to give new meaning to Hosea 11:1 but to connect Israel's exodus from Egypt with an event in Jesus' life under the umbrella of corporate representation. Israel is God's son, and Jesus is God's Son. The fact that both have an experience of being called out of Egypt is no coincidence but a divinely intended correspondence. This is an indicator Jesus is the One who can save and restore Israel.

Matthew 2:17–18 is another example where an event in Israel's history corresponds to an event in Jesus' life to show Jesus' relationship to Israel. Matthew 2:16 records that Herod was enraged and unleashed a massacre on all male children in Bethlehem to extinguish a threat from another King. Matthew then links this wicked event with what Jeremiah discussed in Jeremiah 31:15:

> Then what had been spoken through Jeremiah the prophet was fulfilled:
>
> "A VOICE WAS HEARD IN RAMAH,
> WEEPING AND GREAT MOURNING
> RACHEL WEEPING FOR HER CHILDREN;
> AND SHE REFUSED TO BE COMFORTED,
> BECAUSE THEY WERE NO MORE."

Jeremiah 31 is a chapter of great hope for Israel and comes within the overall context of the Book of Consolation of Jeremiah 30–33 which details the New Covenant that will be given to Israel (see Jer. 31:31–34). Yet sandwiched in the middle of this chapter is v. 15 which refers to the deportation of the sons of Israel during the Babylonian captivity (586 B.C.). Ramah, just north of Jerusalem, was the place where Jewish exiles were gathered before departing for Babylon. The women of Jerusalem wept over the deportation of their young men.

But certain questions arise with Matthew's use of Jeremiah 31:15: (1) How can a first century A.D. event be a fulfillment of another event hundreds of years earlier?; (2) How can the slaughter of infants be a fulfillment of a deportation?; (3) How can an event in Ramah be a fulfillment of an event in Bethlehem?

Matthew is not saying that Ramah is really Bethlehem or that the Babylonian deportation is the slaughter of infants in the first century. Like Matthew 2:15, Matthew is showing a correspondence between an event in Israel's history and an event in Jesus' life to show the connection between Jesus and Israel. God intended for the deportation of the sons of Israel of Jeremiah's day to *correspond* to the slaughter of infants in Jesus' day. What happened in Jesus' day heightens what Israel experienced earlier. Both events involve sorrow in the midst of tragedy. In addition, Jeremiah 31:15 is a lament in the context of future hope. So, too, with Jesus' coming a sorrowful event (death of children) is occurring along an event of great hope (coming of Messiah). Matthew may be drawing attention to the hope element found in Jeremiah in an analogous way to the hope that Jesus brings His people. Thus, we see another example of divine correspondence between Israel and Jesus.

These examples show Jesus is God's Servant who can restore the nation Israel and bring blessings to the Gentiles. He is qualified to present the kingdom. This identification of Jesus as the true representative of Israel does not mean the non-significance of the nation Israel. The opposite is actually the case. The presence of Jesus as the true Israel will mean the restoration of the nation Israel as the Corporate Head (Jesus) restores the body (Israel) (see Isa 49:6).

CONCLUSION

The early chapters of Luke and Matthew reveal important expectations concerning the kingdom of God. There was hope concerning the coming King who was connected with the promises to Abraham and David. This King, whose name is Jesus, is the Son of David who will rule over Israel. He will fulfill the spiritual and national promises of the Abrahamic and Davidic Covenants and bring blessings to the Gentiles. These were the hopes of Mary, Zacharias, the magi, the Jewish religious leaders, Herod, Simeon, and Anna. Matthew also shows that Jesus is the true Israelite who can restore Israel and bring blessings to the Gentiles.

While some have claimed that the NT transcends the OT expectation from a physical/national kingdom to a spiritual/personal kingdom, the early chapters of Matthew and Luke show no such idea. *At this point in the development of the kingdom program there is no indication the OT expectation has been transcended or spiritualized. Instead, the literal OT expectation is affirmed.* This expectation sets the scene for the proclamations of John the Baptist and Jesus that—"the kingdom of heaven is near" (Matt 3:2; 4:17).

THE "AT HAND" KINGDOM (MATTHEW 3:2 AND 4:17)

With Matthew 3, the forerunner of the King, John the Baptist, arrived preaching in the wilderness of Judea. His message was, "Repent, for the kingdom of heaven is at hand" (3:2). Shortly thereafter, Jesus began His ministry with the same message—"Repent, for the kingdom of heaven is at hand" (Matt 4:17). What did John and Jesus mean by these words that summarized their ministries?

Before looking at the details of this statement, the OT background for this concept is important. On multiple occasions the OT prophets declared that national repentance on Israel's part would bring kingdom blessings and reinstatement to the blessings of the Abrahamic Covenant. Passages such as Leviticus 26:40–45; Jeremiah 3:12–18; and 2 Chronicles 7:13–14 reveal this:

> **Lev 26:40–45**:
> "*If* they [Israel] confess their iniquity...
>
> "*Then* I will remember my covenant with Jacob... and I will remember the land."

> **Jer 3:12–18**:
> "'*Return*, faithless Israel,' declares the LORD..."
>
> "*Then* I will give you... (shepherds to feed, prosperity in the land, God's presence, nations coming to Jerusalem, unification of Israel)

2 Chr 7:13–14:
"*If*... My people... humble themselves and pray and seek My face and turn from their wicked ways."

"*then* I will hear from heaven, will forgive their sin and will heal their land."

The cause and effect relationship is noticeable. If Israel repents then God blesses them. These passages assume Israel's disobedience and consequences for covenant betrayal. But hope exists. If Israel repents then kingdom blessings will arrive and a reversal of negative circumstances will occur. This restoration includes spiritual salvation and physical prosperity, including the land. As we will see, the declaration, "Repent for the kingdom of heaven is at hand," shows that Israel's Messiah was now in Israel's midst and the kingdom was on the brink. But repentance would be necessary for Israel to inherit this kingdom. What the OT prophets predicted was now an imminent reality and choice for Israel. What will they choose?

THE KINGDOM OF HEAVEN

The expression, "kingdom of heaven," is distinct to Matthew's Gospel[1] appearing thirty-two times.[2] While not found in the OT, it appears reliant on Daniel 2–7[3] and Daniel's message of a kingdom from heaven that will dramatically replace existing earthly kingdoms. The title "kingdom of heaven" does not mean the kingdom is "heaven" itself or that the kingdom has nothing to do with earth. Instead, the kingdom's *source* is heaven. Heaven is where it comes from although it takes a tangible earthly form.[4]

1 David L. Turner, *Matthew*, Baker Exegetical Commentary on the New Testament (Grand Rapids: Baker, 2007), 107.

2 Overall, Matthew uses *basileia* ("kingdom") fifty-five times. He uses "kingdom of God" four times.

3 Pennington states, "Matthew, drinking deeply at the waters of Daniel, has developed his kingdom of heaven language and theme from the same motif and similar language in Daniel 2–7." Jonathan T. Pennington, *Heaven and Earth in the Gospel of Matthew* (Grand Rapids: Baker, 2007), 289. He also argues that "kingdom of heaven" language comes from Daniel's "God of heaven" and kingdom language and is converted into the "kingdom of heaven" expression (291).

4 This may parallel the truth of the resurrection body of believers that is tangible and physical yet "spiritual" since its source is heaven (see 1 Cor 15).

Matthew and other NT writers will also use the phrase "kingdom of God." How related are the designations "kingdom of God" and "kingdom of heaven"? While some have claimed they are different, this is not the case. The same kingdom is in mind with both phrases. As Pennington points out, "In twelve instances, Matthew's kingdom of heaven is in direct parallel with Mark and Luke's 'kingdom of God' and it is clear that Matthew's phrase refers to the same thing as the other Evangelists, as well as other NT authors."[5] Also, the phrase "kingdom of God" parallels the phrase "kingdom of heaven" since the kingdom comes from God. Put together, the kingdom comes from heaven and God.

There are other important issues regarding this "kingdom of heaven" which is said to be "at hand." First, what specifically is this kingdom (*basileia*) of heaven? And second, in what sense was this kingdom "at hand"? Did it arrive with Jesus' first coming or was it impending being contingent on other factors? We turn now to these issues.

THE NATURE OF THE KINGDOM

Scholars do not agree on the nature of the kingdom that John and Jesus proclaimed. There are three main understandings. The first is the "full kingdom" view. This asserts that John and Jesus were proclaiming the nearness of the prophesied kingdom of the OT in all its dimensions. This included not only salvation and spiritual blessings, but physical and national blessings as well. This involved fulfillment of promises to Israel. Thus, the entire package of kingdom blessings was "at hand." With this perspective, the kingdom in all its dimensions was on the brink as John and Jesus proclaimed it. The qualification for its coming was repentance and belief on the part of Israel to whom the nearness of the kingdom was being presented. This perspective sees much continuity with the OT kingdom expectation and what the Jewish audiences of John and Jesus would have understood. The kingdom of the OT prophets was the same kingdom John and Jesus were proclaiming.

A second interpretation understands the "kingdom of heaven" as being spiritual in nature. So John and Jesus were not proclaiming an earthly kingdom for Israel but, instead, were announcing a spiritual kingdom of

5 Ibid., 140.

salvation to individuals. This perspective involves a major transcending and redefining of the OT expectation that spoke of material and national blessings alongside spiritual blessings.

A third view is that the kingdom proclaimed by John and Jesus was an "already/not yet" kingdom. Jesus inaugurated the Davidic/Messianic kingdom. However, consummation of the kingdom comes later. The details of what exactly was inaugurated are not always clear from those who espouse this view. But the presence of Jesus himself, His miracles, and the salvation He brought are often viewed as manifestations of an "already" or inaugurated Davidic kingdom of Jesus. But matters such as a restored creation and vindication of God's people await the second coming of Jesus. Thus, with this third view the Davidic kingdom actually arrived with Jesus' first coming but the full manifestation of the kingdom is still future with His second coming. In discussing the nearness of the kingdom in Matthew 3:2 and 4:17, one author states, "A common and helpful way to describe the dynamic nature of God's reign is to say that it has been inaugurated at Jesus' first coming and will be consummated when he returns."[6]

Which view is best? In our view, the spiritual kingdom only view must be dismissed. Since God's creation includes both spiritual and physical elements, the restoration of all things must include both spiritual and physical dimensions. According to Matthew 5:5 kingdom blessings include inheriting the land, which is a physical blessing. The view that Jesus is presenting a spiritual kingdom only appears more in line with a Platonic dualism between spirit and matter than a biblical worldview. This perspective has the least credibility and should be rejected.

The "already/not yet" perspective is probably the dominant view of Christian scholars today. This view has more going for it than the spiritual kingdom view since it understands that the kingdom presented by John and Jesus is more than just a spiritual kingdom. Yet it does not do justice to the full package of kingdom blessings presented by John and Jesus at the time of their pronouncements. Nor does it take into account the significance of Israel's response to the presentation of the kingdom at this time and the

6 David L. Turner, "Matthew Among the Dispensationalists: A Progressive Dispensational Perspective on the Kingdom of God in Matthew," unpublished paper for ETS Dispensational Study Group (Nov 2009), 5.

reality that more aspects of the kingdom could have arrived if Israel had repented (see Luke 19:41–44).

Also, with hindsight, we now know there will be two comings of Jesus and that kingdom blessings will be part of His second coming. But two comings of Jesus was not revealed until Matthew 13. The key issue concerns what is being presented at the time of Matthew 3:2 and 4:17.

The best understanding is that John's and Jesus' presentation of the kingdom involved the full package of kingdom blessings as foretold in the OT. As the kingdom message played out in real time, it would become evident there would be two comings of the King. But this does not negate the reality that the kingdom in its entirety was proclaimed as near when John and Jesus began their ministries. As early as Matthew 5:5 Jesus spoke of inheriting the "land/earth." In Luke 19 Jesus told the people of Jerusalem they could have had "peace" (v. 42), but, instead, catastrophic destruction of Jerusalem would occur because Israel "did not recognize the time of your visitation" (Luke 19:44). The potential for national peace must have been part of Jesus' original kingdom message to Israel since rejection of the King and His kingdom meant national destruction.[7] Plus Jesus "wept" when He saw the city of Jerusalem (41–42) showing a real offer of peace was presented to Israel. His emotions reveal the genuineness of the kingdom offer, which included peace for the people of Israel. Since Jesus grieved over the loss of national peace, the offer of national peace must have been genuine.

There is a fine line between the full kingdom view and the already/not yet perspective. The main difference lies in the intent of John and Jesus when they proclaimed the kingdom's nearness. The full package view sees more elements of the kingdom being presented early in the Gospels, including the full blessings of the promised kingdom for Israel. This involves physical and national promises in addition to blessings associated with personal salvation.

JOHN THE BAPTIST'S EXPECTATION

What did John the Baptist mean with his declaration that the kingdom of heaven was "at hand"? Most probably, John was anticipating and proclaiming an earthly kingdom consistent with what was predicted in the OT.

7 This destruction was fulfilled with the destruction of Jerusalem in A.D. 70.

Ellison rightly observes, "It is important that these physical aspects of the kingdom not be dismissed in John's introduction."[8] Even George E. Ladd, who held that Jesus redirected the OT expectation of an earthly kingdom, declared, "John the Baptist had announced the coming of the Kingdom of God (Matt. 3:2) by which he understood the coming of the Kingdom foretold in the Old Testament."[9] Also, A. B. Bruce stated, "We know what John meant when he spoke of the kingdom. He meant the people of Israel converted to righteousness, and in consequence blessed with national prosperity."[10]

That John proclaimed an earthly kingdom for Israel and not just a "spiritual" kingdom is evident from the context. John offered no explanation of this kingdom he announced, expecting his audience to understand its nature. Ridderbos points out this kingdom of heaven "was not unknown to those to whom this message was addressed, but was rather calculated to find an immediate response with them."[11] If the OT anticipated an earthly kingdom and John was now proclaiming a spiritual or 'already' kingdom, why is there no definition or redefinition of the kingdom? The lack of qualifying language shows the expectation of an earthly kingdom was correct. When the Jewish hearers of John's message heard the term, "kingdom," an earthly kingdom would come to mind, not a spiritual kingdom over the hearts of men. It seems unlikely John meant a spiritual kingdom knowing his hearers would be thinking of an earthly kingdom. We agree with McClain that, "The absence of any formal definition of the Kingdom in its initial announcement indicates that the Jewish hearers were expected to know exactly what Kingdom was meant."[12]

THE MEANING OF "AT HAND"

The next major issue in Matt 3:2 concerns the meaning of "at hand." How was the kingdom of heaven "at hand"? Does John mean the kingdom had

8 Stanley A. Ellisen, *Parables in the Eye of the Storm* (Grand Rapids: Kregel, 2001), 33.

9 George E. Ladd, *The Gospel of the Kingdom* (Grand Rapids: Eerdmans, 1959), 53–54.

10 A. B. Bruce, *The Kingdom of God* (Edinburgh: T & T Clark, 1904), 52.

11 Herman Ridderbos, *The Coming of the Kingdom* (Philadelphia, PA: Presbyterian and Reformed, 1962), 3.

12 McClain, *The Greatness of the Kingdom*, 276–77.

arrived? Or does he mean "drawn near," "imminent," or "impending"? If John meant "present" or "arrived" then there must be a sense in which the kingdom of God had actually arrived and was in operation when he made his proclamation. But if John meant "drawn near" then the kingdom is imminent or on the brink but had not actually arrived although its presence is very close. To use a common example, there is a difference between out-of-state relatives actually arriving at your house and these relatives being so near their arrival could occur at any moment.

The word John used for "at hand" is *engiken*. The verb is related to *engidzo* which means "to bring near," "to come near," or "draw close." The term is connected with the idea of imminence. Note other uses of *engiken*:[13]

> **Matt 26:45**: Then He came to the disciples and said to them, "Are you still sleeping and resting? Behold, the hour *is at hand* [*engiken*] and the Son of Man is being betrayed into the hands of sinners.
>
> **Matt 26:46**: Get up, let us be going; behold, the one who betrays Me *is at hand*!"
>
> **Luke 21:20**: "But when you see Jerusalem surrounded by armies, then recognize that her desolation *is near*."
>
> **Rom 13:12a**: The night is almost gone, and the day *is near*.
>
> **James 5:8**: You too be patient; strengthen your hearts, for the coming of the Lord *is near*.
>
> **1 Pet 4:7a**: The end of all things *is near*.

As these examples show, *engiken* is closely tied to the concept of imminence. The verb points to events that are imminent or impending, events that are on the brink but have not actually arrived. None of the examples above show the "near" events had occurred yet, but they were very close.

13 References to *engiken* are in italics.

Robert Gundry argues *engiken* "indicates nearness, right up to, but not including the point of arrival."[14] This rule of God "verges on arrival."[15]

All fourteen uses of *engiken* in the NT seem to carry this sense of imminence. This point is important for our understanding of the kingdom. When John and Jesus declare the kingdom as "at hand" (Matt 3:2; 4:17), they are not saying it has "arrived." They are saying it is "on the brink" or "impending." This supports the view that the kingdom did not arrive with their personal pronouncements at this point.

Some scholars have understood *engiken* to mean "arrived."[16] For them, the proclamation of the nearness of the kingdom was a statement that the kingdom had been established. But this is questionable for several reasons. First, this is not consistent with the usual sense of *engiken* in the NT. While imminence often leads to arrival, there are no clear cases where "arrival" seems to be a more accurate understanding than "at hand" or "near." Second, in regard to John, in what sense can the forerunner of the King bring the arrival of the kingdom? John did not have the authority to bring in the kingdom when Jesus' public ministry had not begun yet. So in the case of John the kingdom had not yet arrived. Third, how could the kingdom have arrived when Jesus' death, resurrection, ascension, exaltation to the right hand of the Father, and the coming of the Holy Spirit had not occurred yet? To believe the kingdom had arrived in Matt 3:2 is to affirm the kingdom of heaven could be established before the cross and other important events. Also, the Scripture indicates that the Day of the Lord and the events of the coming tribulation period must occur before the kingdom begins (see Matt 25:31).[17] If the kingdom arrived with John's message in 3:2, how then does one explain the presence of the kingdom before the earthly ministry of Christ?

---

14 Robert H. Gundry, *Matthew: A Commentary on His Handbook for a Mixed Church under Persecution* (Grand Rapids: Eerdmans, 1994), 43.

15 Ibid.,44.

16 See E. Earle Ellis, *The Gospel of Luke, Century Bible* (Camden, NJ: Thomas Nelson, 1966), 13, 202–203. Also, see C. H. Dodd, *The Parables of the Kingdom* (New York: Charles Scribner's Sons, 1961), 21. Regarding Jesus' statement that the kingdom was near, Dodd declared, "It is not, merely imminent, it is here," 33.

17 Blaising is correct when he states, "Throughout biblical theology, the eschatological kingdom is seen as coming in its fullness through a Day of the Lord." Blaising, "A Premillennial Response," 74.

The preferred view is that the earthly kingdom promised in the OT was on the brink with John's announcement. It was imminent. The people of Israel needed to repent and become spiritually qualified for its coming.

JESUS' VIEW ON THE KINGDOM

Matthew 4 introduces the public ministry of Jesus: "From that time Jesus began to preach and say, 'Repent, for the kingdom of heaven is at hand'" (4:17). Jesus' words are the same as John's in Matthew 3:2. John relied upon the OT understanding of an earthly kingdom with his message. But what does Jesus mean when He says the "the kingdom of heaven is at hand"?

While there is a consensus John was referring to the kingdom expectation of the OT, some think Jesus meant something different, a spiritual kingdom of personal salvation without any nationalistic elements. So when Jesus refers to the "kingdom" is this the kingdom foretold by the OT prophets? Or does Jesus transcend and reinterpret the kingdom?

The former is likely. There is continuity between Jesus' understanding and that of the OT prophets. The kingdom Jesus proclaims has both spiritual requirements and qualities along with physical and national elements. Jesus offers no redefinition of the kingdom of heaven, nor does he make a distinction between His view and John's view. As Saucy states, "Since He [Jesus] gave no explanation of the meaning of the kingdom in His early proclamation, it seems reasonable to conclude that Jesus assumed His audience knew the meaning of this term."[18] Plus, Jesus does not offer any correctives to those who were thinking of the kingdom in line with the OT expectation.[19] J. Ramsey Michaels observes Jesus' expectation of the kingdom is "well within the framework of contemporary Jewish messianic and apocalyptic expectations." This is a kingdom that is "*both* spiritual and national, *both* universal and ethnic."[20]

18 Robert Saucy, "The Presence of the Kingdom in the Life of the Church," *Bibliotheca Sacra* Jan–Mar (1988), 33.

19 Ibid., 87. "It is inconceivable that Jesus, knowing the understanding of his hearers, would not have immediately sought to correct their thinking if he in fact had another concept of the kingdom in mind."

20 J. Ramsey Michaels, "The Kingdom of God and the Historical Jesus," in *The Kingdom of God in 20th-Century Interpretation*, ed. Wendell Willis (Peabody, MA: Hendrickson, 1987), 114, 116.

Also, Jesus' followers did not view themselves as being in the kingdom at this time. Later in His ministry, Jesus gave the parable of the nobleman to convince the disciples that the kingdom would not "appear immediately" (see Luke 19:11). This shows that late in Jesus' earthly ministry the disciples thought Jesus would soon establish the kingdom, but they did not view themselves as currently being in the kingdom. It was something they were expecting. On the day of Jesus' ascension the disciples were asking Jesus *when* he would restore the kingdom to Israel (Acts 1:6). Even at this later time, they viewed the kingdom as a future entity.

Significantly, Jesus used nearness terminology again in Luke 21:31 when discussing the coming of the kingdom after the signs of the end-times events: "So you also, when you see these things happening [end-times events], recognize that the kingdom of God is *near* (*engus*)."[21] Kümmel is correct when he states that *engus* refers to "an event which is near, but has not yet taken place."[22] So, Jesus said signs of the end (i.e. tribulation events) will indicate the soon coming of the kingdom. If this is the case, then it is difficult to hold the kingdom was established before these end-times events.

THE KINGDOM AND ISRAEL

If the kingdom John and Jesus proclaimed was the promised kingdom of the OT prophets, and if it is true the kingdom was near or impending, what are the implications of this? The command ("repent") and the audience are significant. The message of repentance in light of the kingdom is proclaimed specifically to the people of Israel. What is strongly implicit here is explicitly stated in Matthew 10:5–7 where the proclamation of the nearness of the kingdom was limited only to Israel and not to Gentiles or Samaritans. The cities of Israel are also in view in Matthew 11:20–24. This point must not be missed. Early on, Jesus' kingdom proclamation was limited to Israel. This must mean more than simply a courtesy call to the OT people of God as if Israel gets the first shot at the kingdom before everyone else. If the kingdom were simply personal salvation why proclaim it only

21 Emphasis mine.

22 W. G. Kümmel, *Promise and Fulfillment*, Studies in Biblical Theology 23 (Naperville, IL.: Allenson, 1957), 19.

to Israel? There must be a national element—and there is. There was a real presentation of the kingdom to Israel in all its dimensions.

The prophesied kingdom was on the brink, so Israel needed to be ready; they needed to repent. It would not be bestowed simply based on ethnicity. Being a physical Jew was not enough (Rom 9:6). Repentance was the prerequisite for entrance into the kingdom. With John 3:3 Jesus declared, "unless one is born again he cannot see the kingdom of God." While there is a close relationship between salvation and the kingdom, the two are not the same thing. We cannot say "salvation is the kingdom," or "the kingdom is salvation." The kingdom of God is a broader concept than human salvation. One must be saved in order to enter the kingdom. Thus, *salvation is the qualification for entrance into the kingdom*. This idea is found in the Sheep-Goat judgment of Matthew 25 where those who are true followers of Christ are told, "Come, you who are blessed of My Father, inherit the kingdom prepared for you from the foundation of the world" (Matt 25:34). In this context, the saved people revealed their relationship to God by their good deeds. They then enter the kingdom that comes with Jesus' second coming.

In sum, the kingdom was the primary message of both John the Baptist, Jesus, and then the apostles. The kingdom they proclaimed was the kingdom prophesied by the OT prophets. This kingdom had not arrived but it was near or imminent. This kingdom would not just simply be given to Israel, though. Repentance was necessary for entrance into it.

If the kingdom was the prophesied kingdom of the OT. And if this kingdom was presented as imminent. And if the kingdom was presented to Israel at this point with the condition of repentance, what are the implications of all these factors? *There seems to be a presentation of the kingdom to Israel that is linked with Israel meeting the spiritual requirements of the Messiah*. The entire kingdom package was presented to Israel with the spiritual qualification of repentance. Such a scenario was presented in Leviticus 26:40–45 where God promised return and deliverance for the nation with the major condition of repentance.

JESUS' BAPTISM AND THE ANOINTING OF THE KING

With Matthew 3:11–17 the prophesied forerunner of the King identifies and explains the significance of the King. John the Baptist announces to the people of Israel that the One who is coming "will baptize you with the Holy Spirit and fire" (Matt 3:11b). This declaration is full of Davidic and New Covenant implications. The Davidic King will bring New Covenant Holy Spirit baptism for those who repent and identify with Him. And He will bring judgment by fire for those who do not.[23] This leads to the arrival of Jesus and the baptism of Jesus by John. John initially resists the idea of baptizing Jesus, acknowledging that he needed to be baptized by Jesus. Jesus responded—"Permit it at this time; for in this way it is fitting for us to fulfill all righteousness" (Matt 3:15). After Jesus was baptized John saw the Holy Spirit descend as a dove and come upon Jesus. Then the voice of God the Father announced from heaven—"This is my beloved Son, in whom I am well-pleased" (3:17).

Jesus said the baptism was a way for both He and John "to fulfill all righteousness." The word for "fulfill" is *pleroō* and was used strategically by Matthew in chaps. 1 and 2 to identify Jesus with Israel by connecting events and prophecies in Israel's experience with Jesus. Likewise the term "fulfill" is used here to connect John and Jesus with what the OT predicted concerning the righteous King and His kingdom. The OT had predicted a coming King and His forerunner. Now the time arrived for them to fulfill their destiny.

The baptism of Jesus by John has several dimensions of significance. First, John 1:33–34 indicates the baptism event allowed John to rightly identify Jesus as the Messiah. It brought together the messenger and the Messiah. Second, Jesus identified with sinners through His baptism. Third, the baptism allowed Jesus to identify with the believing remnant of Israel. Yet the fourth purpose may be the primary significance for Jesus' baptism. As Pentecost puts it, "[A]t His baptism Jesus Christ was anointed by the Holy Spirit of God to fulfill the functions of the messianic office."[24] So the fulfillment of righteousness involved the announcement and anointing of the righteous King of Israel who was now in Israel's midst offering a kingdom of righteousness (see Matt 4:17). Peter affirmed the kingly

23 From our perspective in time we know Jesus brought the baptizing ministry of the Holy Spirit with His first coming (as a result of the ascension), while the eschatological Day of the Lord judgment with fire coincides with His second coming (see 1 Thess 5; 2 Thess 2; 2 Pet 3).

24 Pentecost, *Thy Kingdom Come*, 201.

significance of Jesus' baptism in Acts 10:37–38: "after the baptism which John proclaimed. You know of Jesus of Nazareth, how God anointed Him with the Holy Spirit and with power." Peter viewed Jesus' baptism as an anointing, a ritual done for a king. Just as David and the kings in David's line were anointed, so too the ultimate Davidic King would be anointed. "At His baptism Jesus the Son was officially recognized by God the Father as Israel's King."[25]

Finally, righteousness was expected for both Israel and the kings of Israel in the line of David. Grisanti notes, "The Davidic ruler should epitomize the standards of the Mosaic Covenant."[26] Thus, the role of the Davidic king was to lead in righteous obedience to the Mosaic Covenant. According to the prophecy of Isaiah 9:7 the coming Messiah would bring righteousness: "There will be no end to the increase of His government or of peace, on the throne of David and over his kingdom, to establish it and to uphold it with justice and righteousness from then on and forevermore." Thus, the fulfilling of all righteousness will involve the righteousness of Jesus, the ultimate Israelite and Son of David, who expressed the heart-felt obedience to the Mosaic Covenant that God required.

Matthew 4 reveals three other significant developments: (1) Jesus' direct encounter with Satan; (2) the choosing of the first disciples; and (3) the proclamation of the kingdom with attending miracles. In our next chapter we will study Jesus' temptation from Satan and the battle between the kingdom of God and the kingdom of Satan.

25 Ibid., 202.

26 Michael Grisanti, "The Davidic Covenant," *The Master's Seminary Journal* 10 (1999): 246.

CHAPTER 17

THE KINGDOM OF GOD VS. THE KINGDOM OF SATAN (MATTHEW 4:1–11)

Satan opposes God's plans to establish a mediatorial kingdom on earth. It is no surprise, then, that the arrival of Jesus the King is met with fierce resistance from the god of this world. With Jesus' birth, Satan inspired a murderous attempt through Herod to remove the coming King. Yet a direct encounter between Satan and the Messiah must take place. And it does as Matthew 4 explains.

After Jesus' baptism He was "led up by the Spirit into the wilderness to be tempted by the devil" (4:1). This was a showdown. Many years earlier another showdown occurred between Satan and the head of mankind in the Garden of Eden. The opponent back then was Adam. Satan won. He duped God's image-bearer and mediatorial king, usurping authority on the earth. Now another Adam, a Last Adam, was on the scene to wrest that authority from Satan. Yet Satan's resistance is fierce. He will test this Last Adam beyond the first one. Will Satan maintain his earthly power, or will Jesus take it from him? The fate of the planet and mankind was at stake. Yet before looking at this encounter it is helpful to survey the cosmic battle between God and Satan in the OT.

THE COSMIC BATTLE IN THE OLD TESTAMENT

Ezekiel 28:12–17

It is difficult to give specifics on the first sin in the cosmos, the sin of the being we now know as Satan. But Ezekiel 28:12–17 seems to offer some details on his demise. This text is addressed to the king of Tyre (v. 12), yet what is described here goes far beyond just a mere human king. This being is one who was "the anointed cherub who covers" who was "on the holy mountain of God" (v. 14). Thus, he is an angelic being who had access to God. This being also "had the seal of perfection" and was "full of wisdom and perfect in beauty" (v. 12). Again, this description again seems to go far beyond any human leader. Then because his heart was lifted up with beauty he was cast to the ground (v. 17). This text best applies to Satan's fall.

Genesis 3:15

Man was created as God's image bearer to rule and subdue the earth in kingly fashion as God's mediator. But Adam and Eve listened to the voice of Satan through the serpent and disobeyed God. While God would still remain King over the universe man failed in his kingdom responsibilities to rule the earth on God's behalf. That a transfer of power to Satan took place is evident in the fact that Satan could rightfully offer Jesus the kingdoms of the world if Jesus would worship him (see Matt 4:8–9), something Jesus did not dispute.

Satan's victory in the Garden of Eden would not last forever, though. God would not allow Satan's intrusion into His kingdom plans to stand. Addressing Satan as the power behind the serpent, God declared,

> "And I will put enmity
> Between you and the woman,
> And between your seed and her seed;
> He shall bruise you on the head,
> And you shall bruise him on the heel" (Gen 3:15).

God is determined to reverse Satan's victory. Satan would not have final victory over God's very good creation (Gen 1:31). Nor would he have the final triumph over the pinnacle of God's creation—man. This battle will continue throughout generations, "between your seed [Satan] and her seed [mankind]." So every encounter between good and evil is part of this war. Eventually, this battle will culminate in a specific seed of the woman, a

"He" who will deliver a crushing head blow to Satan. This "He" is Jesus the Messiah, the ultimate seed (see Gal 3:16).

Job 1–2 and Daniel 10

The cosmic battle between God and Satan occurs in Job. In the halls of heaven Satan appeared before God seeking permission to test Job with calamity to see if Job would obey God (see Job 1–2). Job never was privy to the heavenly scenes that so affected his life, but the account of Job 1–2 is a startling window into heaven that shows events on earth are part of a great cosmic battle between God and Satan.

Cosmic warfare and its implications for nations is evident in the events of the book of Daniel. A demonic being identified as "the prince of the kingdom of Persia" hindered an angel of God for twenty-one days until another angel, Michael, brought assistance (10:13). A "prince of Greece" is referred to in v. 20. What is significant here is that representatives of Satan are delegated to nations of the earth. This suggests a strategic hierarchy in the kingdom of Satan. The presence of such territorial spirits may be a satanic imitation of the archangel, Michael, who is "prince" over Israel (see Dan 10:21; 12:1).

God is sovereign over Gentile nations and kingdoms, but in this fallen world before God restores all things, Satan and his adversaries have a presence and power among the Gentile nations. A close connection exists between Satan and the forces of darkness and the kingdoms of this world. Ephesians 6:12 refers to "world forces of this darkness" and "spiritual forces of wickedness in the heavenly places." Satan showed Jesus "all the kingdoms of the world" and offered Him "all these things" if Jesus would worship him (Matt 4:8–9). Jesus does not tell Satan he does not have such power. He says that only God alone should be worshiped (Matt 4:10).

Daniel 2 and 7 predicted the kingdom of God will come suddenly and violently to replace the existing Gentile kingdoms. The replacement of Gentile kingdoms with God's kingdom also involves the defeat and removal of Satan's power on the earth over the nations. This is specifically stated to be the case in Revelation 20 where the return of Jesus means Satan is bound and imprisoned in the abyss "so that he would not deceive the nations any longer" (Rev 20:2–3a).

Isaiah 24–27

In Isaiah's Little Apocalypse of chaps. 24–27 a staged defeat of the forces of darkness is referenced in connection with the coming of God's kingdom. Isaiah 24 describes a coming time of tribulation and destruction upon the entire earth. The inhabitants of the earth are terrified (v. 11) and the earth itself suffers violence (vv. 19–20). This Day of the Lord judgment leads to punishment:

> On that day the Lord will punish
> the host of heaven above
> and kings of the earth below.
> They will be gathered together
> like prisoners in a pit.
> They will be confined to a dungeon;
> after many days they will be punished
> (Isa 24:21–22) (HCSB).

Two groups experience this Day of the Lord judgment. The first is the "host of heaven" which are spiritual beings opposed to the Lord. This probably refers to Satan and his fallen angels. The second group is the "kings of the earth." These are leaders of the nations who are opposed to God. Thus, in connection with the Day of the Lord both evil spiritual powers and evil human leaders will suffer the wrath of God.

The last verse of Isaiah 26 and the first verse of Isaiah 27 also foretell the destruction of both humans and spiritual forces opposed to God:

> For behold, the LORD is about to come out from His place
> To punish the inhabitants of the earth for their iniquity (26:21a).
>
> In that day the LORD will punish Leviathan the fleeing serpent,
> With His fierce and great and mighty sword,
> Even Leviathan the twisted serpent;
> And He will kill the dragon who lives in the sea (27:1).

The "serpent" and "dragon" refers to evil spiritual powers. These designations are applied to Satan in Revelation 12:9 and 20:2.

In sum, the OT explicitly teaches that God's plan to establish His kingdom is tied to defeating the powers of darkness and Satan. God is dealing with evil human beings, but He is also defeating evil spiritual forces. It should be no surprise, then, that when Jesus appears on the scene His kingdom involves defeating Satan and his forces. Jesus' deliverance of people under demonic influence is not just a kind act for oppressed people, but a confrontation between the kingdom of God and the kingdom of Satan. Each victory over the powers of darkness is a taste of the coming kingdom.

As early as Genesis 3 God foretold the ongoing battle between the seed of the woman (God's people) and the seed of the serpent (Satan's offspring). The coming of God's kingdom must involve the defeat of Satan's kingdom.[1] Since the fall, Satan has operated as a usurper of God's kingdom program, duping mankind to follow him rather than God. This does not mean God's sovereign universal kingdom was forfeited to Satan.[2] For His own purposes and plan, God allows the satanic rebellion to take place. But as Arnold observes, "The presence of evil... demonstrates that God will need to assert his reign against those who would seek to oppose him and his people."[3]

The kingdom program after Genesis 3 is the process by which God brings this rebellious planet back into conformity with His perfect will. This must involve the defeat of Satan. This battle will continue until the establishment of the new heavens and new earth described in Revelation 21. The real battle, then, is not found primarily at the level of the seen, although it certainly includes it. Paul states our battle is not against flesh and blood but against the powers of darkness (see Eph 6:12).

JESUS, SATAN, AND EXORCISMS IN THE GOSPELS

The arrival of Jesus was an invasion of Satan's empire. This carpenter from Nazareth may not have seemed like much, but Satan knew the disastrous

1 Ladd is correct that "The theology of the kingdom of God is essentially one of conflict and conquest over the kingdom of Satan." George E. Ladd, *A Theology of the New Testament*, rev. ed. (Grand Rapids: Eerdmans, 1993), 48.

2 Arnold is right that "It would be wrong to assert that the Gospels teach that God once reigned but has been dethroned by Satan sometime before the coming of Jesus." Clinton E. Arnold, "The Kingdom, Miracles, Satan and Demons," in *The Kingdom of God*, ed. Christopher W. Morgan and Robert A. Peterson (Wheaton, IL: Crossway, 2012), 159.

3 Ibid., 160.

implications of His arrival. After Jesus was baptized by John (Matt 3:13–17) "Jesus was led up by the Spirit into the wilderness to be tempted by the devil" (Matt 4:1). The scene is strategic. Just as the first humans (Adam and Eve) were confronted by Satan, so the ultimate representative of man (Jesus) would be as well. Like Adam and Eve, Jesus would stand in the presence of Satan to face his deception. But this time the result would be different. Adam failed, but Jesus would not.

After Jesus' fasting for forty days Satan tried to exploit Jesus' hunger, tempting Jesus to turn stones into bread (Matt 4:3). Satan then tempted Jesus to jump off the temple to force God to deliver Him (Matt 4:6). The third temptation by Satan is particularly significant since Satan offered to give Jesus the kingdoms of the world if Jesus would worship him (Matt 4:8–9). Jesus did not dispute Satan's claim or say, "You don't have that power." Satan does possess some power over the kingdoms of the world since it was something he could offer to Jesus.

Jesus overcomes and refutes all three temptations by using the Word of God. In doing so, the Last Adam succeeds where the first Adam failed. Jesus wins this encounter. He does not buckle to temptation the way Adam and Eve did and soon He will publically announce His message of the kingdom (Matt 4:17). The battles between Jesus and Satan's kingdom will occur throughout the Gospels. In Matthew 8:28–34 Jesus cast demons out of two men. He then healed a mute man who was demon possessed. This authority over demons was then delegated to Jesus' twelve disciples: "Jesus summoned His twelve disciples and gave them authority over unclean spirits, to cast them out, and to heal every kind of disease and every kind of sickness" (Matt 10:1). These abilities, including the power to cast out demons, was part of the message of the nearness of the kingdom:

> These twelve Jesus sent out after instructing them: "Do not go in the way of the Gentiles, and do not enter any city of the Samaritans; but rather go to the lost sheep of the house of Israel. And as you go, preach, saying, 'The kingdom of heaven is at hand.' Heal the sick, raise the dead, cleanse the lepers, cast out demons. Freely you received, freely give."

As Jesus delegates His message of the kingdom, He also delegates the ability to heal diseases and cast out demons. Such healings and exorcisms were tangible proofs the kingdom of God was near to Israel. Such evidences should cause the cities of Israel to repent and believe on the Messiah. Again, the close connection between the kingdom of God and the defeat of Satan and his fallen angels is evident.

Sadly, Matthew 11–12 reveals that both the cities of Israel and Israel's leaders did not accept the kingdom message of Jesus and His ambassadors. The cities did not repent when they saw miracles (Matt 11:20–24). The leaders did not believe either. In Matthew 12:22 Jesus healed a demon-possessed man who was also blind and mute. The crowds wanted an answer as to what this meant, and the Pharisees responded by saying, "This man casts out demons only by Beelzebul the ruler of the demons" (12:24). This charge was extremely serious. They were calling Jesus' works the deeds of the devil. Jesus refuted the claim of the Pharisees and the logic behind it. First, Jesus said it made no sense for Satan to cast out Satan since no kingdom divided in this way could stand (12:24–27). Second, Jesus noted the Pharisees were inconsistent. They accepted the exorcisms of others but would not accept what Jesus did (12:27). Third, Jesus says His casting out of demons was evidence the kingdom of God had come upon the people of Israel:

> "But if I cast out demons by the Spirit of God, then the kingdom of God has come upon you. Or how can anyone enter the strong man's house and carry off his property, unless he first binds the strong man? And then he will plunder his house" (Matt 12:28–29).

These verses show the inherent connection between Jesus' power over Satan and the kingdom of God. Jesus' exorcisms were proof the kingdom of God had come upon the people. When the people and leaders of Israel saw healings and exorcisms they should have believed in Jesus as King. Jesus proved He could restore the creation and bring healing and wholeness including relief from Satan. The proper response should be faith and repentance, not hardened unbelief.

Note also that Jesus mentions the importance of binding the strong man (v. 29). The coming of the kingdom involves the binding of Satan. A kingdom cannot exist in which Satan is free to roam and destroy. In Luke's parallel account of Jesus' confrontation with the Pharisees after healing a demon-possessed man, Jesus declared, "But if I cast out demons by the finger of God, then the kingdom of God has come upon you" (Luke 11:20). Again, the same truth is affirmed. Jesus' casting out of demons means the presence of the kingdom has come upon the people of Israel.

Another relevant passage concerning demons and Satan is found in Luke 10:17–18:

> The seventy returned with joy, saying, "Lord, even the demons are subject to us in Your name." And He said to them, "I was watching Satan fall from heaven like lightning."

Here the disciples expressed joy that demons were subject to them in Jesus' name. As representatives of Jesus' kingdom message, they experienced success with victory over demons. Jesus then stated He witnessed Satan's sudden expulsion from heaven. The language is reminiscent of Isaiah 14:12: "How you have fallen from heaven, O star of the morning, son of the dawn!" Jesus also indicated that His nearing death also meant the casting out of "the ruler of this world" (John 12:31).

The battle and defeat of Satan occurs over the course of the two comings of Jesus. Satan experienced a fatal blow at the cross as Jesus broke Satan's power over mankind. Hebrews 2:14b states, "He Himself [Jesus] likewise also partook of the same, that through death He might render powerless him who had the power of death, that is, the devil." With Jesus' resurrection and ascension to the right hand of God Jesus has authority "far above all rule and authority and power and dominion" (Eph 1:20–21). Yet Satan is still active in his deception of the nations and there are major parts of the defeat of Satan that await the second coming. John says, "the whole world lies in the power of the evil one" (1 John 5:19b; Rev 12:9). Peter stated that Satan still prowls about seeking to devour people (1 Pet 5:8). The full armor of God must be donned to withstand him (see Eph 6:10–18). Paul told the Romans that "The God of peace will soon crush Satan under your feet" (Rom 16:20), indicating the crushing of Satan was still future. The second coming of Jesus will result in a binding of Satan in an abyss (Rev 20:1–3). Then after a thousand-year reign of Jesus, Satan is released, defeated decisively, and sentenced to the lake of fire, his ultimate destiny (Rev 20:7–10).

Barrick has rightly noted that Satan's attempt to thwart God's kingdom can be called the "anti-kingdom program."[4] Yet God confronts Satan's kingdom and triumphs over it. Barrick has documented a helpful chiastic structure to summarize how God deals with the anti-kingdom program of Satan from creation to new creation:

Genesis 1:1 **Creation**
Genesis 3:1 **Satan's Freedom**
Genesis 6–8 **Worldwide Judgment**
Genesis 10–11 **Babel/Babylon**
... etc.
... etc.
Revelation 17–18 **Babylon**
Revelation 19:11–19 **Worldwide Judgment**
Revelation 20:2–3 **Satan's Confinement**
Revelation 21:1 **New Creation**[5]

In sum, Jesus' encounters with evil spiritual forces were demonstrations of kingdom power and previews of what conditions on earth will be like in the millennial kingdom. That is why Jesus can say, "If I cast out demons by the Spirit of God, then the kingdom of God has come upon you" (Matt 12:28); and, "But if I cast out demons by the finger of God, then the kingdom of God has come upon you" (Luke 11:20). Such power encounters were evidence to the people and leaders of Israel that their Messiah was standing before them.

4 Barrick, "The Kingdom of God in the Old Testament," 178.

5 Ibid., 178.

MIRACLES AND PREVIEWS OF THE KINGDOM (MATTHEW 4:23–24)

In addition to the great cosmic battle between the kingdoms of God and Satan, Matthew 4 introduces the importance of miracles in the kingdom ministry of Jesus. Miracles reveal a major difference between the forerunner of the King (John the Baptist) and the King himself (Jesus). According to John 10:41: "John performed no sign." But Jesus did. Jesus' proclamation of the nearness of the kingdom is accompanied by many signs. As Matthew 4:23–24 declares:

> Jesus was going throughout all Galilee, teaching in their synagogues and proclaiming the gospel of the kingdom, and healing every kind of disease and every kind of sickness among the people. The news about Him spread throughout all Syria; and they brought to Him all who were ill, those suffering with various diseases and pains, demoniacs, epileptics, paralytics; and He healed them.

These miracles drew attention to the legitimacy of Jesus and His ministry. Clearly, this was no ordinary man for only a man of God could do such miraculous acts. As Nicodemus told Jesus, "Rabbi, we know that You have come from God as a teacher; for no one can do these signs that You do unless God is with him" (John 3:2). Miracles authenticated Jesus and brought great relief to those whom He touched. Mark's gospel in particular tells of the enthusiasm Jesus' healing ministry brought:

> When evening came, after the sun had set, they began bringing to Him all who were ill and those who were demon-possessed. And the whole city had gathered at the door. And He healed many who were ill with various diseases, and cast out many demons (Mark 1:32–34a).

The words "all who were ill," "the whole city gathered at the door," and "He healed many" show the extent of Jesus' miracles and the popularity of Jesus. Peter told Jesus, "Everyone is looking for You" (Mark 1:37). Jesus became so popular that, "Jesus could no longer publicly enter a city, but stayed out in unpopulated areas; and they were coming to Him from everywhere" (Mark 1:45). The results of these miracles must have been incredible. B. B. Warfield observes that, "Disease and death must have been almost eliminated for a brief season from Capernaum and the region which lay immediately around Capernaum as a center."[1]

But there is another dimension to the miracles. The miracles also gave Israel glimpses and previews of Messiah's coming kingdom. As John MacArthur states, "The New Testament miracle age was for the purpose of confirming the Word as given by Jesus and the apostles, of offering the kingdom to Israel, and of giving a taste, a sample, of the kingdom."[2] The OT prophets predicted messianic times would reverse the conditions of a fallen world. Isaiah 35 declared:

> Then the *eyes of the blind will be opened*
> And the *ears of the deaf will be unstopped.*
> Then the *lame will leap like a deer,*
> And the tongue of the mute will shout for joy.
> For waters will break forth in the wilderness
> And streams in the Arabah.
> The scorched land will become a pool
> And the thirsty ground springs of water.... (Isa 35:5–7a).

1 B. B. Warfield, *Christianity and Criticism* (New York: Oxford University Press, 1929), 54.

2 John F. MacArthur, *1 Corinthians: The MacArthur New Testament Commentary* (Chicago: Moody, 1984), 360.

Isaiah 25:6–8 predicted that kingdom conditions bring the removal of death. Healings and resurrections restore people to health and preview what life on earth will be like in the kingdom of God. In Matthew 11, John the Baptist sent his disciples to ask Jesus, "Are you the Expected One, or shall we look for someone else?" (11:3). Jesus responded by pointing to His miracles and how they connected with Isaiah 35:

> And Jesus answered and said to them, "Go and report to John what you hear and see: the blind receive sight and the lame walk, the lepers are cleansed and the deaf hear, and the dead are raised up, and the poor have the gospel preached to them" (Matt 11:4–5).

The proof was in the miracles. Jesus showed He was the Messiah by giving demonstrations of the kingdom. Miracles were glimpses of what the world would be like when His kingdom is established. Thus, miracles were demonstrations of kingdom power and proof Jesus truly was the Messiah of Israel.

Matthew 8–9 records many healings of Jesus. With 8:2–3 Jesus healed a leper. In 8:5–13 Jesus healed the servant of a Gentile centurion without even entering his house. Jesus then healed Peter's mother-in-law of a fever (8:14–15). Matthew 9:18–35 describes a cluster of miracles done by Jesus. A woman losing blood was healed; a dead girl was brought to life; two blind men were given sight; a demon-possessed and mute man was delivered and healed. Matthew 9:35 summarizes how these miracles related to the kingdom: "Jesus was going through all the cities and villages, teaching in their synagogues and proclaiming the gospel of the kingdom, and healing every kind of disease and every kind of sickness."

NATURE MIRACLES AND THE KINGDOM

Jesus' miracles extended beyond healings and exorcisms. They also included nature miracles. These, too, were demonstrations and glimpses of the kingdom. The first Adam was supposed to rule over the created realm yet he failed (see Gen 1:26–28). Not only did sickness and death enter because of this failure, but nature works against man as well. "Cursed is the ground because of you... Both thorns and thistles it shall grow for you" (Gen

3:17–18). Ever since the fall man struggles with nature which often overwhelms him.

Jesus' nature miracles show He is the One who can rule and subdue the earth. According to Matthew 8:23–27 Jesus and the disciples were on a boat when "a great storm in the sea" arose (8:24). The experienced fishermen feared for their lives and called out to Jesus for help. Jesus rebuked the winds and the sea and the waters became "perfectly calm" (8:26). The response of the disciples was astonishment: "What kind of a man is this, that even the winds and the sea obey Him?" (8:27).

This miracle demonstrated Jesus as King over nature. Likewise, when Jesus turned water into wine or multiplied bread and fish, He showed His mastery over creation. Nature miracles, therefore, were incredible attestations to Jesus and demonstrations of His kingdom power. They gave glimpses of a restored creation when the Messiah reigns on the earth. Yet, previews of the kingdom are not the same as the kingdom fully arriving. Saucy is correct that "miracles of Jesus were exertions of kingdom power, but not yet the kingdom."[3] Paul states in Romans 8 that the present creation is still subject to futility (8:20) and longs to be "set free from its slavery to corruption" (8:21). This freedom will occur alongside the glorification of God's people, which is still to come (8:19).

Eugene Merrill rightly suggests that Jesus' nature miracles are connected with His role as the "second" or "last" Adam. He says, "there is every reason to believe... that Jesus was exercising the God-given authority of Adam, an authority designed for the entire human race, forfeited by sinful Adam, and restored in and through Christ."[4] Jesus' nature miracles are linked with the kingdom mandate of Genesis 1:26–28, and show Jesus succeeding in the realm where Adam failed.

Yet in this age, Jesus' bodily presence in heaven means the complete fulfillment of the mandate to rule the earth awaits future fulfillment. Hebrews 2:8 says, "But now we do not yet see all things subjected to him [man]." Since this present age still experiences satanic deception, disease and death, and disharmony in nature, we know the kingdom of God has

3 Robert L. Saucy, *The Case for Progressive Dispensationalism*, 100.

4 Eugene H. Merrill, "Covenant and Kingdom: Genesis 1–3 as Foundation for Biblical Theology," in *Criswell Theological Review* 1 (1987): 300–01.

not been established. But Jesus will return and fully restore all things (see Acts 3:21).

DO JESUS' MIRACLES MEAN THE KINGDOM ARRIVED?

Some have claimed that Jesus' miracles reveal an "already" or "inaugurated" kingdom. It is true that when Jesus was on earth the kingdom was near in His person, and His confrontations with Satan and demons were tangible manifestations of the kingdom of God. But were Jesus' statements that "the kingdom of God has come upon you" proof that the kingdom of God had arrived to stay?

Jesus' miracles were tastes and previews of the coming kingdom. But they did not mean the messianic kingdom actually began and remained at this time. Hebrews 6:5 supports this. Looking back from his perspective in history, the writer of Hebrews said his readers "have tasted... the powers of the age to come." Some experienced the miracles of the apostles, and experiencing these miracles ("powers") was called a tasting of the "the powers of the age to come." Since miracles are foretastes of kingdom conditions, experiencing a miracle means getting a taste or glimpse of what the coming kingdom will be like. Experiencing miracles did not mean the kingdom had arrived to stay, but it did mean experiencing a sample of the kingdom.

Later in His ministry Jesus placed the kingdom's coming in the future (see Luke 19:11; Matt 19:28; Matt 25:31; Luke 21:31). He does not look back and say the kingdom began with His miracles. The kingdom is linked with Jesus' physical presence, thus the removal of Jesus' presence on earth will affect the kingdom's presence.

The miracles Jesus performed on earth at the time of His first coming were not permanent. The people He healed eventually died. Even those raised from the dead like Jairus' daughter (Mark 5:21–43) and Lazarus eventually died. But when Jesus establishes His kingdom at His second coming, it will be characterized by perpetual wholeness and restoration. Plus, the healings and resurrections Jesus performed are not occurring today. His miracles were public and undeniable. If the kingdom was inaugurated with Jesus' first coming we should expect these miracles to continue or increase as they did in the days of Jesus. But they do not. Lack of undeniable kingdom miracles today is evidence the kingdom awaits the future.

Two Views on the Significance of Jesus' Miracles for the Kingdom of God

View 1: Jesus' miracles mean His kingdom reign has been inaugurated.

View 2: Jesus' miracles are samples of kingdom blessings to come.

THE CONTEXT FOR MIRACLES

Miracles are God's direct supernatural interventions in the world where He overrides or suspends the laws of nature to accomplish His purposes. The miracles in the Bible include physical healings, resurrections, controlling nature, and casting out demons. They also involve cosmic signs and judgments like the plagues against Egypt. Miracles do not occur in a vacuum. They operate within the context of bigger themes. One such theme is God's sovereignty. As Pentecost states, "In reality, the question of miracles at its simplest is a question of whether an infinite, sovereign God has the power as well as the right to demonstrate that power within the sphere over which He rules."[5] The answer to that question is a resounding, Yes!

Another important theme that intersects with kingdom miracles is the fall of man. Miracles occur because of negative circumstances in a fallen and cursed world. For example, physical healings in the Bible occur because people are sick. Resurrections occur because people die. Nature miracles occur because creation threatens man (i.e. Jesus calming a threatening storm). Exorcisms were needed because Satan and demons harm people. Miracles were not needed before the fall when there was no sickness, death, nature run amok, or demon possession. Miracles also are not necessary in the eternal kingdom because nothing bad happens there.

Miracles are acts of restoration. They correct something gone wrong. They are tastes or glimpse of the restoration of all things (see Acts 3:19–21). Miracles, therefore, are inherently related to the kingdom of God and have

5 Pentecost, *Thy Kingdom Come*, 18.

kingdom implications. In Micah 7, the prophet foretold conditions that will occur with Messiah's kingdom: "Shepherd Your people with Your scepter" (7:14). Then a significant statement about miracles is made next: "As in the days when you came out from the land of Egypt, I will show you miracles" (7:15). Back when the Hebrew people were enslaved in Egypt, God performed mighty miracles to deliver them from Egypt:

> "But I will harden Pharaoh's heart that I may multiply My signs and My wonders in the land of Egypt. When Pharaoh does not listen to you, then I will lay My hand on Egypt and bring out My hosts, My people the sons of Israel, from the land of Egypt by great judgments. The Egyptians shall know that I am the LORD, when I stretch out My hand on Egypt and bring out the sons of Israel from their midst" (Exod 7:3–5).

The miracles at the time of the exodus were judgments on Pharaoh and Egypt. They also occurred within the larger context of God's plans to establish Israel as a kingdom. God's plan since the giving of the Abrahamic Covenant was for His people, Israel, to possess a kingdom with land. But this could not occur if the Hebrews remained forever enslaved in Egypt. After the exodus, God referred to the Hebrews as "a kingdom of priests and a holy nation" (Exod 19:6).

Miracles serve several purposes. They are acts of compassion. Also, miracles confirm God's messengers (see Heb 2:3–4). But miracles are also closely connected to God's kingdom plans. The coming of God's kingdom involves miracles. Just as miracles were associated with Israel's kingdom after the exodus, so too miracles will be associated with Messiah's reign. This was true with Jesus' first coming (see Matt 4:17, 23–24). It was also true for the apostles who performed miracles as part of their proclamation of Jesus and His kingdom in Acts 3. It will also be true in the future when the two witness of Revelation 11 perform miracles in light of the soon return of Jesus.

Miracles	Kingdom Implications
Plagues against Egypt/Miracles of Moses	Exodus from Egypt and Establishment of Israel as a kingdom
Jesus' healings/exorcisms/ resurrections/nature miracles	Nearness of the Kingdom to Israel
Apostles' miracles in Acts	Presentation of kingdom to Israel
Miracles by two witnesses in Rev 11	Nearness of Second Coming and Kingdom

CHAPTER 19

THE KINGDOM IN THE SERMON ON THE MOUNT (MATTHEW 5–7)

The nearness of the kingdom is the backdrop for Jesus' Sermon on the Mount found in Matthew 5–7. Yarbrough aptly notes, "the Sermon on the Mount in its entire sweep is suspended on a kingdom cord."[1] In these three chapters, Jesus mentions "kingdom" eight times (5:3, 5:10, 5:19 (twice), 5:20; 6:10, 6:33; 7:21).[2] The emphasis is on the futurity of the kingdom. Jesus says we are to pray for the coming of the kingdom so God's will can be done on earth like it is in heaven (6:10). And entrance into the kingdom is contingent on passing Jesus' judgment that is still future (7:21). Yet Jesus presents the kingdom as something that belongs to His followers in 5:3 and 5:10 ("theirs is the kingdom of heaven"). So the presence and futurity of the kingdom must be addressed.

The setting of the sermon is also significant. Just as Israel was declared a kingdom of priests at Mount Sinai (see Exod 19:5–6), the Messiah now offers His instruction on a mount, instruction that is part of the developing "law of Christ" (see Gal 6:2; 1 Cor 9:21).

DIFFERING VIEWS OF THE SERMON

Disagreement exists on the meaning of the kingdom in the Sermon on the Mount. Much of this centers on the applicability of the sermon to believers

1 Yarbrough, "The Kingdom of God in the New Testament: Matthew and Revelation," 113.

2 The number is nine if including the disputed reference in 6:13: "For Yours is the kingdom ..."

today. Another area of dispute is whether Jesus views the kingdom as a present or future reality. Before addressing these issues, it is helpful to summarize the four main approaches of the sermon's relationship to the kingdom.

Spiritual Kingdom View

First, there is the spiritual kingdom view in which Jesus allegedly proclaims a present spiritual kingdom. Much is made of Matthew 5:3 and 5:10 where Jesus says, "for theirs is the kingdom of heaven." The present tense "is" for some means the kingdom arrived to stay and believers enter Jesus' spiritual kingdom through faith. The kingdom is a current reality and so too are all the blessings described in 5:3–10.

Future Kingdom View

The future kingdom view is opposite from the spiritual kingdom view. Instead of the kingdom being present in this age and the sermon being applicable to today, some claim the kingdom is future and earthly, and the ethic Jesus describes will only be applicable to those living in the future earthly kingdom. With this view the sermon is not applicable to Christians in this age. It is for the Jews in the coming millennial kingdom. Some earlier dispensationalists like Lewis Sperry Chafer held this view.[3] Some later dispensationalists modified this view claiming that while the Sermon on the Mount would be fulfilled in the millennial kingdom, the sermon was still applicable and relevant for today.[4]

Inaugurated Kingdom View

Others claim the Sermon on the Mount promotes an inaugurated or "already/not yet" kingdom. Jesus inaugurated His kingdom rule with His first coming but the fullness of the kingdom of God and its blessings will be culminated with Jesus' return. Therefore, the kingdom is in operation now

---

3 Lewis Sperry Chafer held that the Sermon on the Mount was addressed to the Jew before the cross and in the coming kingdom, but was "not now in effect." L. S. Chafer, *Systematic Theology* (Dallas: Dallas Theological Seminary, 1948), 5:97.

4 See Charles Ryrie, *Dispensationalism Today* (Chicago: Moody, 1965), 107–108.

but this kingdom has a future element to it as well. Concerning this view, Charles Quarles writes:

> Perhaps the prevailing interpretive approach to the SM [Sermon on the Mount] among modern evangelical scholars is the "inaugurated eschatology" approach. This approach insists that the kingdom of God was inaugurated on earth through the ministry of Jesus. However, His kingdom will not be consummated until His return.[5]

With this view, the inauguration of the kingdom means the ethic of the sermon is the "goal and ideal of Christians here and now." But "disciples will not be fully characterized by the righteousness that the sermon describes until the kingdom is consummated at the time of the Second Coming."[6] Those who adopt this view often believe Matthew 5:3 and 5:10 indicate "already" aspects of the kingdom while Matthew 5:4–9 emphasizes the "not yet" benefits of the kingdom. Therefore, the kingdom of Jesus has been inaugurated now but the fullness of the kingdom and its blessings await a future consummation when Jesus returns. This is probably the majority view today.

Future Kingdom with Present Implications View

Another perspective is that the kingdom Jesus discussed was future at the time of the sermon. But the sermon is a required ethic for all who believe in Jesus and are citizens of the coming kingdom. The sermon presents a required ethic for Jesus' followers. They are "sons of the kingdom" because they are rightly related to the King and His kingdom.

Thus, the kingdom is future although Jesus' followers belong to it and should live in light of it. Keener points out, "the present significance of the future kingdom in early Christian teaching was thus that God's people

5 Charles Quarles, *The Sermon on the Mount: Restoring Christ's Message to the Modern Church* (Nashville, TN: B & H Academic, 2011), 10.

6 Ibid.

in the present age were citizens of the coming age."[7] This position affirms present applicability of the sermon to today while holding that the kingdom reign of the Messiah is still future.

Our position is this latter view. The kingdom presented by Jesus is future and earthly at the time of the sermon, but there is present applicability of its message to Jesus' followers. The discussion below will try to support this understanding.

THE BEATITUDES

In Matthew 5:3–10 Jesus emphasizes the spiritual characteristics necessary to meet the requirements of the King and His kingdom ("poor in spirit," "humble," etc.). Each spiritual requirement is followed by a blessing. The blessings of vv. 4–9 are presented as something realized in the future ("they shall be...). These future blessings are sandwiched by statements of a present possession concerning the kingdom of heaven in vv. 3 and 10:

> [3] "Blessed... for theirs *is the kingdom of heaven.* (present)
> [4] "Blessed... for they shall be comforted. (future)
> [5] "Blessed... for they shall inherit the earth. (future)
> [6] "Blessed... for they shall be satisfied. (future)
> [7] "Blessed... for they shall receive mercy. (future)
> [8] "Blessed... for they shall see God. (future)
> [9] "Blessed ... for they shall be called sons of God. (future)
> [10] "Blessed... for theirs *is the kingdom of heaven.* (present)[8]

An interpretive decision is needed at this point. The six blessings of vv. 4–9 are future-oriented—"they shall... ." But vv. 3 and 10 declare that the kingdom is a present possession ("is") for those who meet Jesus' requirements. The kingdom somehow belongs to believers presently but the blessings associated with the kingdom are presented as in the future. So how should these statements be understood? To answer this I will comment on the four views of the sermon mentioned earlier and how they relate to the Beatitudes.

7 Craig S. Keener, *The Gospel of Matthew: A Socio-Rhetorical Commentary* (Grand Rapids: Eerdmans, 2009), 69. We are not claiming Keener would formally adopt the view presented in this chapter.

8 Emphases mine.

There is little support for the spiritual kingdom view. On several occasions in the sermon itself Jesus emphasizes the futurity of the kingdom (see Matt 6:10; 7:21). Plus, Jesus offers no indication that the kingdom is only a spiritual entity. Inheriting the land/earth, a physical blessing, is promised to Jesus' followers (Matt 5:5). Jesus did not transform the kingdom to a purely spiritual kingdom of the heart.

The future kingdom only with no application for today view is also insufficient. While the kingdom is future at the time of the sermon, the sermon has applicability for Jesus' followers before the kingdom is established. Jesus mentions conditions that relate more to the present age than the coming kingdom. Matthew 5:11–12 states that Jesus' followers will be insulted and persecuted just like the prophets. These experiences do not coincide with those in the millennium where believers are reigning (see Rev 20:4). Jesus tells His followers to be "salt" and "light" (Matt 5:13–14) which seems more appropriate in a decaying and dark world. Also, Jesus discusses not resisting an evil person and how to respond if one is slapped on the cheek (5:39). He also talks about what to do if sued in court (5:40). One would not expect believers to be slapped or taken advantage of in the kingdom. But such circumstances occur in our present age. It is better to hold that Jesus is giving instruction to His followers that are immediately applicable as they seek the kingdom of God (see Matt 6:33).

The third view is that Jesus is speaking of "already" and "not yet" aspects of the kingdom in Matthew 5:3–10. While this view is possible it is not the best understanding. Supposedly, the word "is" in Matthew 5:3 and 10 shows that the kingdom is inaugurated even though the emphasis in 5:4–9 is future. But the "is" references in 5:3 and 5:10 can easily be harmonized with a futuristic understanding of the kingdom. As Gundry notes, "The present tense of 'is' (see also v 10) needs to be taken futuristically, since we read the future tense in the second halves of the following beatitudes and since in v 12 the phrase 'in heaven' almost demands a futuristic understanding."[9]

Jesus' use of "is" can refer to belonging or possession. If one is poor in spirit or persecuted for Christ the kingdom of heaven belongs to that person. This is true of other eschatological entities as well. We are positionally

9 Robert H. Gundry, *Matthew: A Commentary on His Handbook for a Mixed Church under Persecution* (Grand Rapids: Eerdmans, 1994), 68.

citizens of heaven (Phil 3:20) and have come to the New Jerusalem (Heb 12:22), but in both cases living Christians on earth are not actually in heaven or in the New Jerusalem. These great realities belong to us but our experience of them awaits the future.

Another issue with the inaugurated kingdom view concerns what was actually inaugurated at the time of the sermon. It is one thing to say Jesus was preaching an inaugurated kingdom, but it is another matter to state what exactly was inaugurated at this point. Jesus' death, resurrection, ascension and exaltation to the right hand of God had not occurred yet. The Day of the Lord had not arrived yet. Messiah's judgment of the nations had not occurred. These are prerequisites for the kingdom. Also, evidence is lacking that the disciples of Jesus or anyone else believed that they were operating within an inaugurated kingdom at the time of the Sermon on the Mount (see Luke 19:11; Acts 1:6).

The context of the sermon best coincides with the "future kingdom with present implications" view. Matthew 4:17 indicates the nearness but not arrival of the kingdom. Jesus is proclaiming the necessity of repentance in order for a person to enter the impending or imminent kingdom when it comes, but He has not proclaimed the kingdom's official arrival.

The futurity of the kingdom is seen in other sections of the Sermon on the Mount. Jesus taught His disciples to pray, "Your kingdom come. Your will be done, on earth as it is in heaven" (6:10). God's will is not always done on earth as it is in heaven, but it will be. God's will on earth and heaven will be accomplished. That Jesus told His disciples to pray for the coming of the kingdom reveals the kingdom had not arrived at the time of the sermon. If it had Jesus would not tell them to pray for its coming.

The futurity of the kingdom also is seen in Matthew 7:21 where Jesus declared, "Not everyone who says to Me, 'Lord, Lord,' will enter the kingdom of heaven, but he who does the will of My Father who is in heaven will enter." The mention of "will" puts the kingdom in the future. Jesus then says that it is "on that day" that those who cried "Lord, Lord," but practiced lawlessness will be told to depart from Him (7:22–23). "That day" refers to the judgment day when entrance into the kingdom of heaven is determined.

In sum, the Sermon on the Mount of Matthew 5–7 reaffirms that the kingdom of heaven is future and earthly (5:5). We pray for its coming (6:10) and it will be established in connection with coming judgment (7:21–22).

True believers possess a positional relationship to the King before the kingdom is established. They are to live by Jesus' kingdom ethic. Jesus' followers are related to the kingdom before its establishment. So then, the Sermon on the Mount reveals the standards by which those who belong to King Jesus should live.

THE KINGDOM AND LAND (MATTHEW 5:5)

One future blessing mentioned in the sermon is "earth/land." Jesus stated in Matthew 5:5: "Blessed are the gentle, for they shall inherit the earth (land)." Here we have a specific NT reference to land. The term Jesus uses for "earth" is *gēn*, a word that can be translated as "earth," "land," "soil," or "ground." Jesus' statement appears reliant on Psalm 37:11: "But the humble will inherit the land, and will delight themselves in abundant prosperity."[10] This certainly has ties to the Abrahamic Covenant blessings for Israel concerning land and prosperity (see Gen 12:6–7).

The concept of "land" or "earth" is important to the Bible's storyline. Genesis 1:1 stated that God created "the earth". God's image bearer—man—was created to rule and subdue the earth (Gen 1:26–28). Adam was tasked with cultivating and keeping the land in the Garden of Eden (Gen 2:15). When man fell the ground was cursed because of him (Gen 3:17). With the Noahic Covenant God promised He would never curse the ground and destroy it with water again (Gen 8:21). God also promised perpetuity of seasons for the earth (Gen 8:22). Genesis 10–11 describes how the mandate to fill the earth occurs through nations. The Abrahamic Covenant involves the promise of land (Gen 12:6–7) to Abraham's descendants. Specific boundaries for this land are detailed in Genesis 15:18–21. The exodus from Egypt occurred so the nation Israel could be a kingdom and nation for God (Exod 19:5–6) that lives in its own land. The book of Joshua details Israel's possession of the Promised Land. Even before Israel was in the land God promised physical prosperity in the land for obedience, but disobedience would lead to removal from the land. Repentance would result in reinstatement to the land of promise (see Lev 26:40–45 and Deut 30:1–8). The Davidic and

10 And Psalm 37:22, "For those blessed by Him will inherit the land." Also, Psalm 37:29: "The righteous will inherit the land, and dwell in it forever." Not only does Jesus use Ps 37 eschatologically, so too does one of the commentaries of the Dead Sea Scrolls (4Q171frags. 1–10, ii 8–10).

New Covenants emphasize the importance of land. God promised David, "I will also appoint a place for My people Israel and will plant them, that they may live in their own place and not be disturbed again" (2 Sam 7:10). With the New Covenant promises of Jeremiah 33:11 God declared, "I will restore the fortunes of the land as they were at first." With Jeremiah 33:15 we also see, "In those days and at that time I will cause a righteous Branch of David to spring forth; and He shall execute justice and righteousness on the earth."

Even during times of judgment, punishment, and removal from the land, the promise of restoration to the land was a strategic message of the prophets. After discussing the banishment of Israel to the nations, the Lord declared, "For I will restore them to their own land which I gave to their fathers" (Jer 16:15). What is significant about this statement in Jeremiah 16:15 is that the land promise remains alive many centuries after the initial giving of the Abrahamic Covenant. Even the last verse of the OT mentions the land—"He will restore the hearts of the fathers to their children and the hearts of the children to their fathers, so that I will not come and smite the land with a curse" (Mal 4:6). Thus, land for Israel begins and ends as a strong theme in the OT.

As the Gospels begin land is still significant. With Luke 1:32–33 Gabriel told Mary that her Son, Jesus, "will reign over the house of Israel forever." The prophetess Anna was "looking for the redemption of Jerusalem" (Luke 1:36, 38). Thus, when Jesus said His followers would "inherit the earth/land" (Matt 5:5) this coincided with the message of the prophets. That this land promise relates to Israel at this point is also no surprise. As Craig Evans puts it, "Jesus' third beatitude, then, speaks to Israel's hope for national renewal, which includes, in some instances, regaining the land itself."[11] Land, therefore, is part of the kingdom proclamation to Israel.

Yet the issue of land is a heavily debated topic among theologians. Not all think land promises to Israel will be fulfilled in a particular sense with the nation Israel. Some argue land promises of the Abrahamic Covenant were fulfilled in the OT or functioned as a type that points forward to Jesus so that He fulfills the land promises in His person. With this view the land

11 Craig A. Evans, ed., *The Bible Knowledge Background Commentary: Matthew–Luke* (Colorado Springs, CO: Cook Communications, 2003), 105.

promises are fulfilled or absorbed into Jesus. Others claim fulfillment in Jesus involves a universalization of the land so OT land promises to Israel no longer need to be fulfilled with Israel. Instead, land promises allegedly are expanded to the entire earth for all Christians with no need for a particular fulfillment with the nation Israel.[12] Allegedly, the particular (land for Israel) is skipped over for the universal (land for all). Romans 4:13 is sometimes used as support for this view. Here Paul says, "For the promise to Abraham or to his descendants that he would be heir of the world was not through the Law, but through the righteousness of faith." But is Paul expanding or universalizing the land promise of the Abrahamic Covenant in such a way that a particular fulfillment of the land promise with Israel is no longer necessary?

The answer is, No. Romans 4:13 is not evidence that OT land promises to Israel have been universalized to nullify particular fulfillment with Israel. In fact, the verse is not even primarily about land. The context of Romans 4 is about descendants of Abraham and involves Abraham's role as being the father of both believing Gentiles and Jews who have been justified through faith alone. This is the point of Romans 4:11–12. Since Abraham was reckoned righteous by faith before he was circumcised, he was qualified and positioned to be the father of both believing Jews and Gentiles. Romans 4:17 then points out Abraham's role as being the "father of many nations." It is in this sense of descendants that Abraham is "heir of the world." The issue here is not about land or transcending Israel's land promises, but about descendants.

That Paul uses the term *kosmos* for "world" and not *gē* in Rom 4:13 is relevant. The term *gē* always refers to physical earth in some way, whether land, soil, or ground. But Paul uses *kosmos*, a broader term which can refer to physical earth, but often refers to people in the world (see John 3:16).

12 Wellum and Gentry reference Romans 4:13 for this view: "Paul seems to be saying that Abraham did not understand the land promise as referring only to a specific geographical location; rather he viewed the promise as that which ultimately would encompass the entire created order." Gentry and Wellum, *Kingdom through Covenant*, 708.

Since the context of Romans 4 is people, Paul's use of *kosmos* most likely refers to descendants of Abraham, not land.[13]

Another issue to consider is that Romans 4:13 refers to "the promise to Abraham." What Paul is referring to involves something explicitly promised to Abraham, something of which Abraham would be aware. Yet, when the Abrahamic Covenant promises are examined in Genesis, we see Abraham was promised to be a blessing to the families of the earth and the father of many nations. He was also promised a land with specific borders—"From the river of Egypt as far as the great river, the river Euphrates" (Gen 15:18). But we don't see a specific promise that Abraham would be heir of the entire earth in a geographical sense. In sum, Abraham was not promised the geography of the entire earth explicitly but he was promised many descendants who would be blessed because of him.[14] Thus, the content of the original promises to Abraham can help our understanding of Romans 4:13 and this points to the view that Abraham is heir of the world in regard to descendants.

In sum, Romans 4:13 is primarily about Abraham's role as the father of many descendants. This verse does not transcend or universalize OT land promises to Israel to the exclusion of particular fulfillment with Israel. Yet it is true that fulfillment of land promises to Israel will benefit the whole world geographically. Since Israel and Israel's land are the platforms for physical and land blessings for all people groups, Israel's land will function as the basis for global blessings, including land for the nations. Just as Israel is a microcosm of what God will do for all nations, so too, Israel's land is a microcosm for physical and land blessings God will bring to all nations. Isaiah 27:6 states, "In the days to come Jacob will take root, Israel will blossom and sprout, and they will fill the whole world with fruit." As God blesses Israel He will also bless other nations. Romans 11:12, 15 indicates that greater blessings await Gentiles with Israel's future fulfillment (see

13 For a helpful discussion of the relationship of Romans 4:13 to land issues see Nelson Hsieh, "Abraham as Heir of the World: Does Romans 4:13 Expand the Old Testament Abrahamic Land Promises?" *The Master's Seminary Journal* 26 (2015): 95–110. Hsieh says Romans 4:13 "is about the worldwide nature of Abraham's descendants; it is not about the worldwide nature of Abraham's land promise. In fact, it simply has nothing to say about the land promise" (110).

14 We are not denying that the Abrahamic Covenant eventually has implications in regard to the whole earth, but the global promises to Abraham specifically emphasize descendants.

Rom 11:26). So the blessings via Abraham will eventually impact the entire world. But this will occur through God's plans for Israel and Israel's land. God does not skip over the importance of Israel.

Michael Vanlaningham observes the error of concluding that blessings to the world rule out fulfillment with the nation Israel. He notes, "It appears logically fallacious to argue that if Abraham and his diverse family inherit the world, the land of Israel is excluded for the Jewish believers."[15] He also says, "Even if one grants the universalizing of the land promise, this does not eliminate the possibility that Israel might still possess its Promised Land as its share in the inherited world."[16]

The best view is that fulfillment of the land promise takes place through Jesus who literally brings land blessings to Israel and then the nations of the world. Note the contrast:

It is not:

Land promises → Jesus → The nations

Instead, it is:

Land promises → Jesus → Israel → The nations

How does this all relate to Matthew 5:5? The promise of land at this time has specific reference to Israel. Jesus quotes Psalm 37, which concerns Israel and Israel's land. This is what Jesus' Jewish audience would have understood at that time. Also, Jesus' statement comes within the context of the presentation of the nearness of the kingdom to Israel, which includes physical blessings alongside spiritual blessings. This heightens the probability that the land of Israel is in view. So land promises to Israel cannot be divorced from Matthew 5:5. But since Israel is a microcosm of what God will do for all nations when Israel is restored and in their land, other nations will be blessed as well eventually. Since Israel and Israel's land are microcosms of what God will do on a global and universal scale, the land

15 Michael G. Vanlaningham, "The Jewish People according to the Book of Romans," in *The People, the Land, and the Future of Israel: Israel and the Jewish People in the Plan of God*, ed. Darrell L. Bock and Mitch Glaser (Grand Rapids: Kregel, 2014), 119.

16 Ibid.

promise can be applied to Israel and extended beyond Israel. Fulfillment of the particular promise to Israel will lead to global blessings.

This perspective avoids two errors. The first error is that the land/earth reference in Matthew 5:5 only has relevance for Israel. The second error is that land promises to Israel have been universalized in a way that no longer includes national Israel. The first view is too narrow and does not include Gentiles. The second perspective skips to universal fulfillment while not understanding that *particular* fulfillment with Israel (via Jesus the Messiah) is a vehicle for *universal* fulfillment.

JESUS AND THE FULFILLMENT OF ALL THINGS (MATTHEW 5:17–18)

Matthew 5:17–19 involves the kingdom since Jesus states all details and predictions found in the OT must come to completion. Verse 17 states, "Do not think that I came to abolish the Law or the Prophets; I did not come to abolish but to fulfill."

Jesus appears to address a misperception in a polemical way. When He says, "Do not think..." this must mean some were thinking erroneous things about Jesus' teachings on the Law and the Prophets. The religious leaders viewed Jesus' teaching on the Sabbath and ritual purity to be particularly scandalous (see Matt 12:1–8; 15:1–20). They were arguing Jesus disregarded the Law and the Prophets.

"The Law or the Prophets" refers to the OT, the entire Hebrew canon. Jesus states He did not come to "abolish" the Hebrew canon but to "fulfill" it. The term "fulfill" is *pleroō*. Depending on the context, the term can mean "to fill up," "to make full," or "to realize." Jesus uses the term in contrast to "abolish." Jesus did not come to disregard or nullify the OT; He came to complete it in all its details. In other words, Jesus did not come to discard anything in the OT. He came to fulfill everything.

Verse 18 continues Jesus' thought, "For truly I say to you, until heaven and earth pass away, not the smallest letter or stroke shall pass from the Law until all is accomplished." Jesus ties the fulfillment of the OT with the enduring nature of the universe. Nothing the OT taught or predicted can be done away with until "all is accomplished."[17]

One interpretive issue to grapple with is Jesus' second use of "Law." Is Jesus only referring to the Mosaic Law at this point or is Law also a reference to the entirety of the OT teaching. The latter is more likely. As Quarles argues, "the 'Law' in verse 18 is likely a shortened reference to the Law and Prophets mentioned in the preceding verse and thus refers to the entirety of the Hebrew Bible."[18] Jesus is not referring to the Mosaic Law only. The rest of the OT is also in view. *Thus, Jesus is saying heaven and earth cannot pass away until everything the OT stated and predicted comes to pass.* Since Jesus refers to "the smallest letter or stroke," He affirms *everything* in the OT must occur. Every last detail must be fulfilled. Quarles summarizes the point: "Jesus' point was that the authority and relevance of the OT would not wane until God fulfilled every promise and prediction in its pages."[19]

So what are the implications of this section for the kingdom? Everything the OT predicted, including all its prophecies of the kingdom of God, must come to fruition. No detail is too small to be fulfilled.

Considerable debate occurs concerning what it means for Jesus to "fulfill" the OT and what it means for "all" to be "accomplished." Some take what could be called an "absorption" or "embodiment" view of fulfillment where the details of OT prophecies are absorbed into Jesus or embodied by Him. Supposedly, the physical, national, and/or land promises of the OT find fulfillment, not by actually being fulfilled literally in history, but by being fulfilled in the person of Jesus who represents the highest ideal of these matters. But this view is not completely accurate. Yes, Jesus is the perfect embodiment of certain OT matters such as the Mosaic Law. Jesus embodied the essence of the Mosaic Law by loving God and others just as the law required (Rom 13:8–10). The Old Testament itself predicted that the Mosaic Law would be replaced by the superior New Covenant (Jer 31:31–34).

17 Quarles argues that *ginomai* could literally be translated "everything happens," *Sermon on the Mount*, 91.

18 Ibid., 94.

19 Ibid., 99.

But the promises and people involved with the covenants of promise are not transcended.[20] These must be fulfilled as stated. Prophecies concerning Israel, land, temple, and other matters in the OT will be fulfilled just as predicted. Jesus himself often refers to specifics of OT prophecy as needing to be fulfilled. For example, Jesus predicts the fulfillment of the abomination of desolation (Matt 24:15), cosmic signs (Matt 24:29), and the restoration of Israel (Matt 19:28). In Matthew 24:34 Jesus declared, "Truly I say to you, this generation will not pass away until all these things take place." The "these things" are details of the Olivet Discourse. When Jesus predicts matters beyond His first coming, He says these specific things will be fulfilled. The details of the prophecies are still significant and in need of fulfillment.

The comparison of the 'two approaches of fulfillment in Christ' can be seen below:

Details Accomplished	Absorption/Embodiment
Because of Christ all the details of the promises and covenants of the Old Testament will occur just as the inspired authors originally predicted. This occurs as a result of the two comings of Jesus.	The promises and covenants of the Old Testament find fulfillment in the person of Christ who embodies the true significance of them. No need to always look for literal fulfillment of all the details.

The "details accomplished" approach is preferred. If Jesus expects literal fulfillment of OT prophecies, so should we. Jesus does not encourage abandoning expectations of prophetic events because they are absorbed into Him. Thus, when Jesus says He will fulfill all things and that all things will be accomplished, this means Jesus brings the details of all things in the Scriptures to fulfillment just as the inspired writers predicted. Paul stated God will "bring everything together in the Messiah, both things in heaven and things on earth in Him" (Eph 1:10b) (HCSB). This includes what the prophets stated concerning the Messiah and what He would do.

20 This includes the Abrahamic, Davidic, and New covenants.

Many matters were fulfilled with Jesus' first coming, but many also await His second coming. Matthew 5:17–18 reveals nothing the OT predicted will fail—all will be accomplished. This includes kingdom promises in all their dimensions.

THE KINGDOM PRESENTED AND REJECTED (MATTHEW 8–12)

After presenting the requirements for entering His kingdom (Matt 5–7), Jesus continues His kingdom proclamation to Israel. This includes great miracles and the recruitment of His disciples to announce the kingdom to the cities of Israel. But the people and leaders of Israel resist. The kingdom presented in Matthew 8–10 becomes the kingdom rejected in Matthew 11–12.

GENTILE INCLUSION IN THE KINGDOM

Matthew 8–10 involves widespread kingdom proclamation to Israel. Yet Jesus also reveals Gentiles are included in the kingdom program. While the kingdom is mediated through the nation Israel, it is not only for Israel. The kingdom is open to all who believe.

With Matthew 8 Jesus honored the faith of a Gentile centurion who believed Jesus could heal his son. Jesus compares the centurion's faith with those in Israel: "Truly I say to you, I have not found such great faith with anyone in Israel" (8:10). This is an early hint the people of Israel were not expressing the required faith. The faith of this Gentile exceeded that of God's covenant people. Jesus then makes a startling statement to Jews who thought their ethnicity alone qualified them for kingdom entrance:

> I say to you that many will come from east and west, and recline at the table with Abraham, Isaac and Jacob in the kingdom of heaven; but the sons of the kingdom will be cast out into the

> outer darkness; in that place there will be weeping and gnashing of teeth (8:11–12).

This account offers three truths about the kingdom. First, it reveals something about its nature. Second, it has implications for the timing of the kingdom. And third, it addresses who will participate in the kingdom.

The nature of the kingdom is similar to the OT expectation of a literal earthly kingdom with fellowship and feasting for all people groups. Isaiah 25:6 states:

> The LORD of hosts will prepare a lavish banquet for all peoples on this mountain; A banquet of aged wine, choice pieces with marrow, and refined, aged wine.

Kingdom conditions will be joyous and include banquets and feasting. While the kingdom of God is not only about eating and drinking (see Rom 14:17) it certainly includes these matters. Food and drink, when used properly, are good gifts from God and often accompany relationships and fellowship (see Acts 14:17). At the Last Supper Jesus longed to eat a Passover meal with His friends again in the kingdom of God (see Luke 22:14–18). The kingdom of God, therefore, is not about asceticism and denial of all God-given pleasures. It will be a time of celebration, relationships, and food. The mention of Abraham, Isaac, and Jacob is also important since it draws attention to a Jewish element of this kingdom. As Toussaint notes, "That the Jewish kingdom is in view is well established by the naming of the three patriarchs."[1] He also notes the verb "to recline" (*anaklino*) "suggests a banquet, a term often used by the Jews to characterize the promised blessings of the prophesied kingdom."[2]

Next, Jesus' words show these kingdom conditions are future. This banquet was not currently happening but was future ("will come"). This reaffirms that the kingdom Jesus presented as "at hand" had not yet arrived. The judgment of those who will not be part of this kingdom is future as well ("will be cast out into the outer darkness").

1 Stanley D. Toussaint, *Behold the King: A Study of Matthew* (Portland, OR: Multnomah, 1980), 124.

2 Ibid.

Finally, this passage has implications for who will participate in this coming kingdom banquet. Jesus' statement that "many will come from east and west" reveals Gentiles from all parts of the earth will participate in the kingdom. This truth of Gentile inclusion should be no surprise. Isaiah 25:6 declared that the "lavish banquet" would be for "all peoples" which includes Gentiles. While the religious leadership of Israel was stunned by Jesus' inclusion of Gentiles in the people of God, this was no secret to the OT prophets.

Jesus said some physical descendants of the Jewish patriarchs would be barred from the kingdom, while Gentiles would participate in this blessed and joyful event. Thus, the kingdom not only will include believing Gentiles it will exclude unbelieving Jews. Jesus calls the Jews "sons of the kingdom" (Matt 8:12), which, according to Gundry, is "a Semitic expression for those who belong, or by privilege should belong, to the kingdom."[3] The "sons of the kingdom" in this context are Jews who have access to the revelation of God and His kingdom program. They should be the first to meet the spiritual requirements of the kingdom, but they will be "cast out into outer darkness" and not allowed to enter the kingdom. Here, being a 'son of the kingdom' does not mean one is presently in the kingdom. If this were the case then unbelieving Jews who are called "sons of the kingdom" would be in a present kingdom. One must be born again to enter the kingdom (see John 3:3), and they certainly had not done so.

THE APOSTLES AND THE NEARNESS OF THE KINGDOM TO ISRAEL

With Matthew 9, Jesus engaged the cities of Israel, performing miracles in connection with proclaiming the kingdom of God. With Matthew 10 He enlists His disciples for this proclamation. Kingdom authority over demons and diseases was delegated to the twelve disciples: "Jesus summoned His twelve disciples and gave them authority over unclean spirits, to cast them out, and to heal every kind of disease and every kind of sickness" (Matt

3 Robert H. Gundry, *Matthew: A Commentary on His Handbook for a Mixed Church under Persecution* (Grand Rapids: Eerdmans, 1994), 145.

10:1). The ability to perform miracles was in the context of the kingdom message to the cities of Israel:

> These twelve Jesus sent out after instructing them: "Do not go in the way of the Gentiles, and do not enter any city of the Samaritans; but rather go to the lost sheep of the house of Israel. And as you go, preach, saying, 'The kingdom of heaven is at hand.' Heal the sick, raise the dead, cleanse the lepers, cast out demons. Freely you received, freely give" (10:5–8).

The kingdom message at this point was not for "Gentiles" or "Samaritans." Rather it was for "the lost sheep of the house of Israel." The kingdom message was only for Israel at this point.

This shows a strong connection between the kingdom and Israel and that a presentation of the kingdom to Israel is occurring at this time. Such a restriction at this point makes no sense if only individual spiritual salvation is in view. As Saucy observes, "If Jesus proclaimed a kingdom consisting only of the spiritual salvation now present for all in the church, why was this message limited to the nation Israel?"[4] Instead, this message had great implications for Israel. There was a presentation of the kingdom that if positively received would bring kingdom blessings.[5]

Also, as part of the proclamation of the kingdom, the disciples were able to cast out demons and heal the sick. Such miracles would validate their ministry and give tangible demonstrations of kingdom power and evidence of the nearness of the kingdom. So how was this message of the kingdom received? The answer is revealed in Matthew 11–12.

REJECTION OF THE KINGDOM BY THE CITIES OF ISRAEL (MATTHEW 11)

Matthew 11–12 marks a significant development in the kingdom program. As Mark Saucy notes, "Matthew 11 and 12 show that the King and His kingdom were rejected by most of those to whom Jesus ministered." This

4 Robert L. Saucy, *The Case for Progressive Dispensationalism*, 88.

5 In Luke 19:41–44 Jesus indicated that blessings could have occurred for Israel, but since Israel did not believe, judgment would come.

does not mean opposition had not occurred earlier, but now "there is a particular climax of rejection of Jesus."[6] Rejection of the King and His kingdom dominates these chapters.

As noted, proclamation of the nearness of the kingdom accompanied by miracles occurred with the ministries of Jesus (Matt 9) and the twelve apostles (Matt 10). John the Baptist also proclaimed the kingdom (see Matt 3:2). The cities of Israel were saturated with the proclamation of the impending kingdom of God. The eradication of sickness and demon possession on a wide scale was clear testimony of this fact.

Matthew 11 begins with the news that John the Baptist had been imprisoned. From prison John sent his disciples to ask Jesus if He really was the "Expected One" (11:3). Perhaps John's incarceration caused John to wonder about Jesus. If the kingdom was "near" then why was John in prison? Jesus then told them to report back to John what they were seeing—the sick were being healed, the dead raised, and the gospel was preached (see 11:4–6). Such news should encourage John the Baptist.

Next, Jesus honored John and said Scripture predicted John's ministry (see Matt 11:10). Then in Matthew 11:11 Jesus tied John the Baptist to the kingdom: "Truly I say to you, among those born of women there has not arisen anyone greater than John the Baptist! Yet the one who is least in the kingdom of heaven is greater than he." Here Jesus praises John the Baptist and draws attention to the futurity of the kingdom. At this point in history Jesus affirms John is the greatest person who has ever lived.[7] Yet He also says everyone present in the kingdom is in a better position than John. The point here is that being in the kingdom is greater than not being in the kingdom. This shows the kingdom had not arrived yet or surely John would be in it. Toussaint notes, "Though John is as great as the greatest of the Old Testament saints, the least in the kingdom which is at hand is greater than John now. This statement further affirms that the kingdom was not then present, otherwise John would certainly have been in it."[8]

6 Mark Saucy, "The Kingdom-of-God Sayings in Matthew," *Bibliotheca Sacra* 151 (1994): 182–83.

7 The one clear exception to this would be Jesus himself.

8 Toussaint, *Behold the King*, 150.

Jesus then said: "From the days of John the Baptist until now the kingdom of heaven suffers violence, and violent men take it by force. For all the prophets and the Law prophesied until John." (Matthew 11:12–13). Something important was taking place in this unique and narrow period—"from the days of John the Baptist until now." On other occasions Jesus linked the actions of Israel with past generations,[9] but now He refers to a narrow window of time. What has been going on since John began his ministry that is so important? The answer is that the kingdom of heaven is suffering violence and violent men are somehow taking the kingdom by force.

What can this mean? In what sense is the kingdom "suffering violence"? The verb is *biadzetai*. Some say the verb is middle and refers to an intense striving needed to enter the kingdom. If this is the case then active striving is needed to enter the kingdom of God. Toussaint, though, rightly argues that the verb is passive which means something negative was being done to the kingdom by evil men.[10] Mounce, too, states, "it is better to take *biazetai* as passive and translate 'has been enduring violent assault.'"[11] So what does this mean? Nefarious men were doing violence or harm to the kingdom in some way. Blomberg translates this verse, "the kingdom of heaven suffers violence, and violent people attack it."[12] Evil people were damaging or negatively affecting the kingdom. They were hindering its

9 See Matthew 23:35–39. Jesus links the present generation of Israel with the killings of the prophets throughout history showing an inter-generational connection.

10 Ibid., First, he points out that the verb has no object. Second the use of *harpadzo* for "take it by force" indicates a violent snatching. Third, the feminine pronoun "it" "shows that the kingdom is that which is being seized."

11 Robert H. Mounce, *Matthew*, New International Biblical Commentary (Peabody, MA: Hendrickson, 1991), 104. Commenting on Matthew 11:12, in connection with the parallel account in Luke 16:16, Kümmel states, "So Matthew 11.12 must have the meaning: since the appearance of the Baptist until the present moment the Kingdom of God is being violently assaulted and violent men wish to rob it." W. G. Kümmel, *Promise and Fulfillment*, 122–23.

12 Craig L. Blomberg, *Matthew*, The New American Commentary (Nashville: Broadman, 1992), 188.

coming.[13] So as with other passages (see Matt 23:39; Acts 3:19–21), Matthew 11:12–13 shows that the kingdom is tied to Israel's response to her Messiah. In this case, the violent rejection of Jesus by the leaders of Israel means an attack on the kingdom.

In sum, Jesus announces that the religious leaders of Israel are harming the kingdom program. As the King and His emissaries herald its nearness, wicked men actively oppose the kingdom. Since the ministry of John began, the religious leaders and Herod intensely opposed John, Jesus, and the kingdom. Plus, Matthew 23:13 indicates the leaders of Israel were not allowing people to enter the kingdom. Jesus said: "But woe to you, scribes and Pharisees, hypocrites, because you shut off the kingdom of heaven from people; for you do not enter in yourselves, nor do you allow those who are entering to go in."

Matthew 11:11–13 reveals that the OT prophets predicted the coming of the king's forerunner and the kingdom. The response of the leaders, though, was doing violence to the kingdom. They were opposing it by resisting the messengers of the kingdom. There was a real presentation of the kingdom to Israel at this point in Matthew's Gospel, but wicked men were doing violence to it. As Toussaint says, "The King has declared the present condition of the kingdom—it is suffering violence at the hands of the violent men who were the leaders of Israel."[14]

The rest of Matthew 11 further discusses this rejection. With 11:14 Jesus states, "And if you are willing to accept it, John himself is Elijah who was to come." The conditional particle "if" (*ei*) indicates that if Israel would receive John and his message then John would be the fulfillment of the Malachi 4 prophecy concerning the coming of Elijah. "There is scarcely a

13 Turner writes, "It is best to understand this difficult passage . . . as teaching the difficult truth that John in prison is learning: the kingdom will not immediately judge God's enemies but will itself be oppressed by them for a time until God vindicates himself and his people." David L. Turner, *Matthew*, Baker Exegetical Commentary (Grand Rapids: Baker, 2008), 295. Turner lists Herod the Great, Herod the Tetrarch, and the religious leaders as enemies who do violence to the kingdom (see 294). Luz says, "it is most natural to think of the opponents of John and Jesus who take away the kingdom by force. The general formation includes both political opponents (Herod Antipas) and the religious establishment." Ulrich Luz, *Matthew 8–20* (Minneapolis, MN: Fortress, 2001), 141. See also, Matthew W. Bates who believes Matt 11:12 and Luke 16:16 are veiled references to Herod Antipas. "Cryptic Codes and a Violent King: A New Proposal for Matthew 11:12 and Luke 16:16," *Catholic Biblical Quarterly* (2013): 74–93.

14 Toussaint, *Behold the King*, 153.

passage in Scripture which shows more clearly that the kingdom was being offered to Israel at this time."[15]

Tragically, Matthew 11:16–19 shows there would be no acceptance of John or Jesus. This "generation" that John preached to concluded that "He [Jesus] has a demon" (18). They also stated that Jesus was "a gluttonous man and a drunkard, a friend of tax collectors and sinners!" (19). Matthew 11:20–24 confirms the national rejection of Jesus and the kingdom. Jesus "denounces" the cities of Israel "because they did not repent" (20). To show the wickedness of their rejection of Him, Jesus states Sodom would fare better on the Day of Judgment than the cities of Israel.

What is evident in Matthew 11 is that the cities of Israel did not repent and embrace the kingdom that was near. Their error was not in misunderstanding the nature of the kingdom, but in their lack of repentance to be ready for it.[16] They had not responded positively to the news of the impending kingdom thus the coming judgment day would not go well for them. So far, Israel was failing the test and missing its time of visitation (see Luke 19:44).

REJECTION OF THE KINGDOM BY THE LEADERS OF ISRAEL

The situation gets worse with the events of Matthew 12. This chapter highlights the intense hostility of the Jewish religious leaders against Jesus.

The Pharisees challenged Jesus when they saw His disciples eating heads of grain on the Sabbath (12:1–7). They also confronted Him for healing a man on the Sabbath (12:8–21). Jesus then healed a man who had been possessed by a demon (12:22). This was a strategic point in the ministry of Jesus because of the response of the crowds and the Pharisees. Matthew 12:23 states: "All the crowds were amazed, and were saying, 'This man cannot be the Son of David, can he?'" The title, "Son of David" refers to the Messiah. Seeing a dramatic miracle stimulated the crowd to ask whether this Jesus of Nazareth was truly the long awaited King of Israel. As the spotlight turns to the religious leaders they offer an emphatic—No! Not only is

15 Ibid.

16 "He [Jesus] did not condemn the crowds because of political or national notions about the kingdom. Instead, His condemnation was because they had failed to meet the spiritual demand of the kingdom by repenting." Mark Saucy, "The Kingdom-of-God Sayings in Matthew," 185.

Jesus not the Messiah, Jesus is under the influence of Satan. Jesus "casts out demons only by Beelzebul the ruler of the demons," they said (12:24).

The gravity of this response must be grasped. The Messiah of Israel was in their midst performing great miracles. But instead of believing in Him, the religious leaders, who represented Israel, accuse Him of teaming with Satan.

This false accusation cannot stand. Jesus responds, "But if I cast out demons by the Spirit of God, then the kingdom of God has come upon you" (Matt 12:28). Two points should be noticed. First, casting out demons is linked with the presence of the kingdom. This was the case in Matthew 9:35 with Jesus and Matthew 10:7–8 with the disciples. Direct suppression of Satan's realm characterizes the kingdom. The binding of Satan is directly connected with the establishing of the kingdom at Jesus' return (see Rev 20:1–3). The kingdom had come at this time in the person and work of the King who was standing in their midst.

Jesus' miracles were not evidence that He works for Satan. They show the kingdom has come upon Israel. Yet their hardened unbelief and distortion of the Messiah and His works was blasphemy against the Holy Spirit (12:31). This is an unforgivable sin (12:32). The unforgivable sin in this context is hardened and willful rejection of the Messiah who was standing before them doing miracles in the power of the Holy Spirit. It was an inexcusable rejection of the Messiah and His kingdom.

The leaders of Israel crossed a line of no return. This tragic event has devastating consequences not only for them but for the nation Israel. What was occurring was both an individual and national sin. And the consequences will be both individual and national. After this encounter with the Jewish religious leaders the die is cast. The cities and leaders of Israel will not believe. From this point onward *the kingdom will not be presented as "at hand" or "near."* In fact, shortly before His final entrance into Jerusalem Jesus would give a parable to show that the kingdom of God was *not* "going to appear immediately" (Luke 19:11). The kingdom would become "near" in the future with events associated with the coming tribulation period (see Luke 21:31).

As events unfold, it becomes evident the ministry of Jesus the Messiah will include two phases—a first and second coming. The first coming will emphasize the atoning work of the Messiah for sin, while the second will bring His kingdom (see Acts 3:18–21). The promised kingdom of the OT prophets would not be established soon because of the negative reception of it by Israel. But it would come in the future. New truths concerning the kingdom program will be offered with Matthew 13 as the necessity of two comings of the Messiah becomes manifest.

CHAPTER 21

MYSTERIES OF THE KINGDOM (MATTHEW 13)

In the aftermath of rebuking Israel's religious leaders for their unbelief, Jesus presented eight parables in Matthew 13 regarding the kingdom of heaven. Interpreters have differed greatly in their understandings of these kingdom parables. Some believe Jesus introduced a transformed and more spiritualized view of the kingdom than what the OT prophets predicted. Some hold Jesus is introducing a "mystery form" of the kingdom, which is Christendom or the believing church. Still others hold that Jesus is offering new truths about the kingdom while still maintaining the expectation of the earthly kingdom foretold by the OT prophets. This latter view is preferred. The kingdom Jesus proclaims in Matthew 13 is the same kingdom predicted by the OT prophets, but Jesus now offers new truths about it.

Before plunging into the details of this important chapter, I now present a summary of what I believe this chapter as a whole is affirming. *The purpose of Matthew 13 is to offer new truths about the kingdom program in light of Israel's rejection of Jesus. The kingdom will not be established with Jesus' first coming. Instead, an inter-advent age will occur where the kingdom program proceeds as the message of the kingdom and the growth of kingdom citizens occurs alongside the work of the devil. But when Jesus returns a second time in judgment, He will separate the sons of the kingdom from the sons of the evil one and then the sons of the kingdom will partake in Jesus' kingdom. With Matthew 13 we see clearly for the first time that the kingdom program involves two comings of Jesus and what this means for the period between these two comings.*

THE SETTING FOR MATTHEW 13

The parables of Matthew 13 must be understood within the larger story playing out in Jesus' ministry. As Matthew 3:2; 4:17; and 10:7 revealed, Jesus, John, and the apostles were proclaiming the nearness of the kingdom to Israel. The kingdom's arrival was conditioned on Israel's repentance and reception of Jesus as King. But as Matthew 11–12 showed, both the people and leaders of Israel were rejecting the King and His kingdom. The actual killing of the Messiah would occur later, but Israel had crossed a line of no return. Yes, a remnant of individual Jews had believed and others would come to salvation, but the nation as a whole, including its leaders, had made up its mind regarding Jesus and His kingdom. Their answer was No! An unforgivable sin occurred—rejecting Jesus the Messiah who was doing kingdom miracles in the power of the Holy Spirit. The events and statements from Jesus in Matthew 13 occur as a direct result of this development.

Jesus switches tactics because of the hardness of their hearts. He begins to speak in parables as He reveals "mysteries" or new truths about the kingdom of heaven in parable form. This shift is no incidental matter but a calculated response by Jesus in light of what has just occurred. No longer is Jesus speaking to the crowds with straightforward words. The simple clarity of the Sermon on the Mount is no more (see Matt 5–7). Now His words are shrouded in mystery to the crowds. This shift in approach was not lost on the disciples who asked him, "Why do you speak to them in parables?" (Matt 13:10). Something was different and they sensed it. Matthew 13:11–13 then states:

> Jesus answered them, "To you it has been granted to know the mysteries of the kingdom of heaven, but to them it has not been granted. For whoever has, to him more shall be given, and he will have an abundance; but whoever does not have, even what he has shall be taken away from him. Therefore I speak to them in parables; because while seeing they do not see, and while hearing they do not hear, nor do they understand."

The key phrase here is "mysteries of the kingdom of heaven." "Mysteries" in this context are new truths and these new truths concern the "kingdom of heaven." The purpose of these mysteries is to reveal new information to those who believe and to hide truth from those who have hardened their hearts. The "kingdom of heaven" is still the same kingdom proclaimed earlier. It is an earthly kingdom for those who trust in the Messiah. Yet new truths concerning this kingdom are being offered.

In addition to new truths about the kingdom, Jesus explains that the parables are in relation to divine judgment upon Israel for disobedience. In doing so He quotes Isaiah 6:9–10:

> In their case the prophecy of Isaiah is being fulfilled, which says,
> "YOU WILL KEEP ON HEARING, BUT WILL NOT UNDERSTAND;
> YOU WILL KEEP ON SEEING, BUT WILL NOT PERCEIVE;
> FOR THE HEART OF THIS PEOPLE HAS BECOME DULL,
> WITH THEIR EARS THEY SCARCELY HEAR,
> AND THEY HAVE CLOSED THEIR EYES,
> OTHERWISE THEY WOULD SEE WITH THEIR EYES,
> HEAR WITH THEIR EARS,
> AND UNDERSTAND WITH THEIR HEART AND RETURN,
> AND I WOULD HEAL THEM" (Matt 13:14–15).

These parables relate to Israel's unbelief. While other parables might help people understand certain truths, the parables of Matthew 13 are largely intended to hide truth. Divine judgment is occurring with Israel. Because the people would not receive the simple words of Jesus, now they would receive parables that hide truth from them. Such is the consequence for unbelief.[1]

This concealing of truth is linked with four parables told "out of the house" by Jesus (13:1) and four spoken in the house (13:36). The ones spoken out of the house by the sea are directed to the crowds while the ones in the house are only for Jesus' disciples. Thus, there are two audiences. There are parables spoken to the crowds with the disciples present and parables given only to the disciples.

Another distinction involves who receives an explanation of the parables. The crowds never receive explanations of Jesus' parables. They hear four parables but no interpretation is offered. On the other hand, the

1 Meier observes, "The parables portray a breach between Jesus and Israel widening to a breaking point. The very fact that Jesus now withdraws into a parabolic form of teaching is a sign of judgment upon Israel." John P. Meier, *The Vision of Matthew Christ, Church, and Morality in the First Gospel* (New York: Paulist, 1978), 90.

disciples receive an interpretation. In regard to the kingdom parables Mark 4:34 declares, "He was explaining everything privately to His own disciples."

Still another distinction relates to which parables are explicitly called kingdom parables. There are eight parables overall. The six parables in the middle are introduced by the phrases, "The kingdom of heaven may be compared to..." or "the kingdom of heaven is like..." But the first and last parables are not introduced in this manner. This does not mean these first and last parables are not related to the kingdom but it appears that the first parable—the parable of the sower—introduces the next six kingdom parables. And the eighth and last parable—the householder parable—sums up the parables and offers practical applications.

Parable of the Sower

The Parable of the Sower (13:3–9, 18–23) reveals there are various responses to the kingdom message. It explains how the message of the kingdom is not received by all. It could be baffling to contemplate how the Messiah and His message could be rejected by so many. How could Israel reject her Messiah? But this parable explains why. There is nothing wrong with the sower (Jesus) or the seed (the kingdom message). But there is something wrong with the hearts of men who hear the message. Some have no desire to believe while others have superficial responses. But others will believe the Word and bear spiritual fruit for God.

The seed on the road eaten by the birds represents people who have no interest or concern in the kingdom (13:19). The kingdom message is quickly removed from them. Next, the seed sowed on the rocky and thorny soils represents superficial responses (13:20–22). Only the seed on good soil bears fruit (13:23). These are true believers who bear fruit for God and are in a position to receive more kingdom truths. In sum, as the kingdom message is proclaimed many will reject it while only a few will believe.

Parable of the Wheat and the Tares

The parable of the wheat and the tares (13:24–30, 34–43) begins the explicit kingdom parables. Starting in 13:24 the kingdom of heaven is likened to "a man who sowed good seed in his field." This reveals that sons of the kingdom and nonbelievers will co-exist until Jesus comes again. Then Jesus will separate the tares (unbelievers) from the wheat (believers). The sons of the kingdom are not commanded to remove the sons of the devil in this age. That task belongs to the Messiah and His angels at Jesus' return. One of the key new truths here is that judgment is delayed until Jesus comes again.[2] This development is new since the OT did not clearly present a delay in judgment for the wicked after the Messiah first arrived. Also, remember that with earlier proclamations of the kingdom, John proclaimed imminent judgment. He declared, "The axe is already laid at the root of the trees; therefore every tree that does not bear good fruit is cut down and thrown into the fire" (Matt 3:10). John viewed the judgment of Messiah as being on the brink. Yet in light of recent events, Jesus now says judgment will not come for the wicked until a later period. The kingdom that was imminent in Matthew 3 is now viewed as arriving later.

An interpretive issue exists in 13:41. We are told the "Son of Man will send forth His angels, and they will gather out of His kingdom all stumbling blocks, and those who commit lawlessness." Because of the words, "out of His kingdom" some believe Jesus is returning to an already established kingdom. This is not an unreasonable view, but it is unlikely. Instead, the better view is that as the King comes His kingdom comes with Him. The initial act of the King is to remove the wicked from His newly arrived kingdom. As Alfred Plummer correctly states, "the Son of Man brings the Kingdom with Him, and at that consummation 'the sons of the evil one' may be said for the moment to be in the Kingdom; but they are immediately expelled, as having no right to be in it."[3]

When Jesus comes with His kingdom, His initial action is to remove "all stumbling blocks," i.e. all non-believers from His newly established kingdom. This is consistent with Matthew 25:31–46 which explains that

2 In reference to the parables of Matthew 13 Schreiner points out, "Perhaps the most surprising feature is that the kingdom arrives without an immediate final judgment." *The King in His Beauty*, 443.

3 Alfred Plummer, *An Exegetical Commentary on the Gospel According to S. Matthew* (Grand Rapids: Eerdmans, 1956), 196. Saucy agrees, "This [Matt 13:40–43] does not suggest that the righteous are presently in some inaugurated kingdom on earth but not 'shining.' The wheat and the weeds are growing in the same field—that is, the world, which is never identified as the kingdom. Furthermore, as we have seen, the weeds are cast out of the kingdom, but this is only with its coming at the end of the age with the return of Christ. They could not be said to be 'in the kingdom' today. It is preferable, therefore, to interpret this future 'shining' in the kingdom as relating to the future establishment of the kingdom." Robert L. Saucy, *The Case for Progressive Dispensationalism*, 100–01.

when Jesus returns He gathers and removes His enemies in connection with the establishment of His kingdom.

What is a "mystery" in this parable is the co-existence of "sons of the kingdom" (wheat) and "the sons of the evil one" (tares) (v. 38) in this age. Jesus allows both groups "to grow together until the harvest." In vv. 28–29 the slaves of the landowner ask if they may gather up the tares and get rid of them, but the landowner's response is, "No." The good wheat could be uprooted with the tares. Instead, they must wait until the "harvest" (i.e. Jesus' second coming) when the landowner tells His "reapers" (angels) to separate the wheat and the tares.

This parable of the wheat and the tares shows connections between the kingdom and this present age. First, there are people called "sons of the kingdom." They have believed in King Jesus and are related to His kingdom. Second, an era will exist in which the sons of the kingdom will co-exist alongside sons of the evil one in this world before the establishment of Jesus' kingdom. During this period there should be no attempt to forcibly remove unbelievers. Third, the kingdom comes with the second coming of Jesus when unbelievers will be removed from His kingdom. Kümmel is correct that with this parable "the emphasis is not on the growth of the Kingdom of God in the present, but on the separation taking place at the judgment, at the coming of the Kingdom of God."[4]

In sum, this parable affirms the kingdom predicted in the OT but adds new truths concerning two comings of the King and conditions in this inter-advent period.

Parables of Mustard Seed and Leaven

With Matthew 13:31–33 Jesus likened the kingdom of heaven to a mustard seed and leaven:

> He presented another parable to them, saying, "The kingdom of heaven is like a mustard seed, which a man took and sowed in his field; and this is smaller than all other seeds, but when it is full grown, it is larger than the garden plants and becomes a tree, SO THAT THE BIRDS OF THE AIR come and NEST IN ITS BRANCHES."

4 Kümmel, *Promise and Fulfillment*, 135.

> He spoke another parable to them, "The kingdom of heaven is like leaven, which a woman took and hid in three pecks of flour until it was all leavened."

These two brief parables come without explanation although Mark 4:34 indicates Jesus explained all of the parables to His disciples. So caution must be used as we interpret them. They link the kingdom with small beginnings that eventually explode into something grand. This growth of the kingdom could be linked with two developments. First, the message of the kingdom is spreading in this age. Second, the number of those who believe in the kingdom message is growing. Thus, while the kingdom itself awaits establishment at the second coming, the kingdom grows as the message of the kingdom and sons of the kingdom increase.

Parables of the Hidden Treasure and Costly Pearl

Jesus also likened the kingdom of heaven to a hidden treasure and a costly pearl in 13:44–46:

> The kingdom of heaven is like a treasure hidden in the field, which a man found and hid again; and from joy over it he goes and sells all that he has and buys that field. Again, the kingdom of heaven is like a merchant seeking fine pearls, and upon finding one pearl of great value, he went and sold all that he had and bought it.

These parables speak of the value of the kingdom and the intense desire that must accompany those who seek to enter it. One should value the kingdom above all else. Earlier, Jesus said, "But seek first His kingdom and His righteousness, and all these things will be added to you" (Matt 6:33).

Parable of the Dragnet

Matthew 13:47–50 then records the parable of the dragnet:

> "Again, the kingdom of heaven is like a dragnet cast into the sea, and gathering fish of every kind; and when it was filled, they drew it up on the beach; and they sat down and gathered

> the good fish into containers, but the bad they threw away. So it will be at the end of the age; the angels will come forth and take out the wicked from among the righteous, and will throw them into the furnace of fire; in that place there will be weeping and gnashing of teeth."

Here Jesus likens the kingdom of heaven to a dragnet cast into the sea that gathers both good and bad fish. Later, fishermen separate the bad fish from the good fish. This parable is similar to the wheat and the tares' parable. Both righteous and wicked will co-exist in this age until a coming day when the wicked are removed. The coming of the kingdom is not a joyous event for all. For the wicked it will be a time of judgment. Like the parable of the wheat and the tares, this parable reveals that Messiah's judgment is delayed. But the delay should not cause one to conclude judgment is not coming. The mixture of good and bad in this age will not continue forever.

SUMMARY

Matthew 13 reveals important new truths about the kingdom in the aftermath of Israel's rejection of Jesus. The kingdom will not be established with Christ's first coming. There must be an intervening age between His first and second comings and then the kingdom will be established. Yet this period between the two comings is related to the kingdom program. There exists a growing nucleus of people called "sons of the kingdom" who have believed the "word of the kingdom." But the kingdom itself will not be established until the second coming of Jesus. Later, Matthew 19:28 and 25:31 link Jesus' kingdom reign with the second coming, the transformation of the earth, and coming judgment. So even after Matthew 13 the kingdom is still presented as future and earthly by Jesus.

Two extremes must be avoided. First, it is wrong to deny any connection between the kingdom and the present age. The kingdom program is related to the present age in regard to the message of the kingdom and the growth of kingdom citizens. Second, it is incorrect to hold the kingdom reign itself has been established in this age. That will occur at Jesus' second coming.

Other Scriptures point to this balance. Colossians 1:13 indicates Christians have been transferred to Christ's kingdom, but this kingdom is linked with our "inheritance" in Colossians 1:12 which is future. In Revelation 5:10 we are told that the saints have been made a "kingdom" yet the reign of this kingdom is future ("and they will reign upon the earth").

Matthew 13 does not transform the nature of the kingdom presented in the OT, but it does present new truths about its timing and how it relates to this age. At the end of the chapter Jesus asked his disciples if they understood what He was talking about and their answer was "Yes" (13:51). Jesus then said, "Therefore every scribe who has become a disciple of the kingdom of heaven is like a head of a household, who brings out of his treasure things new and old" (13:52). His mention of things both "new and old" is significant. Jesus is not just restating previous revelation on the kingdom, nor is He only giving new information about the kingdom. He is doing both. There is information from the OT about the kingdom, and there is new information to be gleaned. The kingdom as prophesied would be established on the earth some day (i.e. the old), but there would also be an age between the two comings of Messiah with conditions never discussed before (i.e. the new).

A delay in the establishment of the kingdom does not mean the kingdom program has no connection with the present. Such a scenario is a mystery. While the OT predicted both a Suffering Servant and a Reigning Messiah, it did not explicitly state there would be two comings of the Messiah separated by a considerable period of time.[5] This may be hinted at in a couple of OT passages. Psalm 110:1–2 stated the Messiah would have a session at the right hand of God until the Messiah reigns from Jerusalem. This includes a gap that Peter said "must" occur in Acts 3:19–21. Also, Daniel 9:24–27 predicted Messiah would come and be "cut off" before all kingdom conditions were fulfilled. Events such as the destruction of Jerusalem in A.D. 70 needed to occur before the kingdom arrived (see Dan 9:26–27). But, as Pentecost puts it, "what the Old Testament had not revealed was that *an entire age would intervene between the offer of the kingdom by the Messiah and*

5 For example, Zechariah predicted a humble coming of the Messiah (Zech 9:9), followed by an earthly reign from sea to sea (Zech 9:10). Later revelation would show these events would be separated by a considerable period of time.

Israel's reception of the King and enjoyment of full kingdom blessings."[6] This age Jesus describes covers the period from Israel's rejection of Jesus through His return to earth at His second coming. The Messiah will suffer and die and then later come back to establish His kingdom upon the earth.

6 Pentecost, *Thy Kingdom Come,* 219. Emphases are in original.

CHAPTER

22

THE CHURCH, THE CROSS, AND THE KINGDOM PREVIEW (MATTHEW 14–17)

While the emphasis of Jesus' ministry focused on proclaiming the nearness of the kingdom and the call to repent in light of its imminence, the emphasis after Matthew 13 turns more to the cross. No longer do we find widespread presentations of the kingdom to the cities of Israel or declarations the kingdom is "near." The focus shifts to the coming suffering of the Messiah. The message of Daniel 9:26 that Messiah would be "cut off" followed by a destruction of Jerusalem comes to the fore.

With Matthew 14 we learn that the first herald of the kingdom's nearness, John the Baptist, was beheaded (14:10). Earlier Jesus declared, "If you are willing to accept it, John himself is Elijah who was to come" (Matt 11:14). But the people and leaders did not accept John's message. The messenger of the King was dead.

Then in Matthew 15 a Canaanite woman came to Jesus for mercy for her daughter who was possessed by a demon (15:22). Jesus granted her request but not before declaring, "I was sent only to the lost sheep of the house of Israel" (15:24). He also said "it is not good to take the children's bread and throw it to the dogs" (15:26). These words seem cold at first. Jesus is saying His ministry at this point was to Israel alone and not to the Gentiles. He likens Israel to "children" and Gentiles to "dogs." His ministry would eventually extend to Gentiles as well (see Matt 28:19), but at this point His focus was on Israel.

The woman offers a bold and shrewd answer that Jesus rewards. She does not declare, "That's not fair!" Nor does she challenge Jesus' statement or say He is wrong for thinking this way. Instead, she acknowledges the truth of what He said, but then argues for blessings within the framework Jesus established. She said, "Yes, Lord; but even the dogs feed on the crumbs which fall from their master's table." She acknowledges that the Messiah's ministry was to Israel, but hoped blessings could extend to her family. Jesus honors her by calling her a woman of great faith and then heals her daughter (15:28). The healing benefits of the King are extended to the family of a Gentile who shows great faith and perseverance. Yes, Jesus' kingdom message was focused on Israel at this point, but blessings to the Gentiles are also part of the kingdom plan. Blessings to this Gentile woman are a sample of blessings to come to other people groups. The kingdom will involve all peoples.

CHURCH AND KINGDOM

How do the cross and the kingdom intersect? For Christians who understand the significance of Jesus' death for sinners, it is easy to forget that most of Jesus' predictions concerning His death came late in His earthly ministry and were shocking to His followers. Jesus and His disciples spent much time proclaiming the kingdom but *it is not until Matthew 16 that Jesus explicitly brings up the cross.* When the cross is brought up, Jesus' followers are upset and don't understand how this could possibly be a part of God's plans. They were expecting a kingdom, not a crucifixion—a reigning Messiah, not a Suffering Servant. Jesus would have to instruct them how both worked together.

After warning the disciples about the ways of the Pharisees, Jesus and the apostles entered the district of Caesarea Philippi. Here the attention turned to Jesus' identity. Jesus asked the apostles what the people were saying about Him. The answers were varied—John the Baptist, Elijah, Jeremiah, or some other OT prophet (see Matt 16:13). Jesus then asked them who they believed He was. Peter responded, "You are the Christ, the Son of the living God" (16:15). This answer pleased Jesus and indicated that the Father revealed this truth to them (16:17).

Upon Peter's confession of Jesus as the Messiah, the Son of God, Jesus announced His plans for building His church—"you are Peter, and upon this rock I will build My church" (16:18). For the first time the concept of the church is introduced. That this church is future is evident by the future tense—"I will build." Jesus then tells Peter about authority in relation to the kingdom:

> "I will give you the keys of the kingdom of heaven; and whatever you bind on earth shall have been bound in heaven, and whatever you loose on earth shall have been loosed in heaven" (16:19).

There are several issues here. One concerns who the "you" is. Is this promise only directed to Peter? Or is this a promise to the twelve apostles of which Peter is the chief representative? Or does the "you" involve all believers in Jesus? Second, what do the keys represent? Third, what is the "kingdom of heaven" Jesus is referring to? Is this kingdom the church? Is it personal salvation? Is the kingdom God's reign from heaven? Or is it a future earthly kingdom? And fourth, what is this power of binding and loosing?

On the first issue, the "you" is probably a reference to Peter and the apostles. Since Peter is the leader among the apostles, an address to him can include the others as well. There is not enough reason to conclude this promise was to Peter alone. Later in Matthew 19:28 Jesus explicitly promises that the twelve apostles will sit on twelve thrones judging the twelve tribes of Israel at the time of the renewal of the earth.

Second, "keys" is a reference to authority. "The motif of keys," as Harrington notes, "is rooted in Isaiah's prophecy to Shebna that he would be replaced as chief steward over the royal household by Eliakim [see Isa 22:21–22]."[1] Jesus is granting Peter and the apostles an authority in relation to the kingdom of heaven. Later, Jesus would say the scribes and Pharisees "shut off the kingdom of heaven from people" and in doing so did not allow others to enter (Matt 23:13). The religious leaders used their authority for bad purposes, but the apostles are given authority in accord with Jesus' purposes. The ability to "bind" or "loose" probably refers to executive decisions made by the apostles. Because Jesus delegates kingdom authority to the apostles, they can know their decisions have the support of heaven. No one can overthrow their verdicts since they have the backing of God. As

1 Daniel J. Harrington, S. J. *The Gospel of Matthew,* Sacra Pagina, ed. Daniel J. Harrington, S. J. (Collegeville, MN: Liturgical Press, 2007), 251.

Harrington puts it, "The idea is that God will ratify and stand behind what Peter (and the others) enact."[2]

The "kingdom of heaven" to which Jesus refers is the same kingdom He discusses elsewhere—the coming messianic kingdom that will be established on the earth when He returns in glory with His angels (see Matt 19:28; 25:31). Because Jesus mentions the "church" in close proximity to His statements about the kingdom, some identify the church as the kingdom of heaven, but the two are distinct although related concepts.

To sum up, Jesus promises Peter and the apostles, special places of authority in the kingdom of heaven when it is established. According to Matthew 19:28 this involves positions of authority over a restored Israel in the *eschaton*. Later, Jesus also will promise members of the church positions of authority over the nations when Jesus returns and rules the nations (see Rev 2:26–27; 3:20–21). In 1 Corinthians 6:2, Paul also talks about a future reign of the saints—"Or do you not know that the saints will judge the world?" The King desires to share His kingdom reign with His faithful followers.

Another possible view is that the keys of the kingdom of heaven refer to the authority to offer the gospel message that allows people to be qualified to enter the kingdom. This authority is first given to Peter and the apostles, and then by extension, this authority could apply to others who like the apostles have believed in Jesus. Therefore, Jesus delegates the authority of the gospel message to His followers and in so doing gives them the keys to the salvation that qualifies one to enter the kingdom of heaven. Both of these last options are possible, although we lean toward the former view that the keys to the kingdom refer to the authority the apostles will have when the kingdom is established.

THE CROSS

The plot thickens with the events of Matthew 16:21. Jesus, for the first time, explicitly unveils His coming death. He must go to Jerusalem where He will suffer many things and be killed and then raised on the third day. Strategically, Matthew uses the phrase—"From that time" to introduce Jesus' statements about His sufferings. The only other time Matthew uses that

2 Ibid., 248.

phrase is in Matthew 4:17: "From that time Jesus began to preach and say, 'Repent, for the kingdom of heaven is at hand.'"

The use of this phrase tells us what Jesus emphasized at these times. It also shows an important shift in what Jesus was doing. From the time of Matthew 4:17 the nearness of the kingdom of heaven was the major theme of His ministry. Now, with Matthew 16:21, Jesus' emphasis shifts to His sufferings to come.[3] To compare:

Matt 4:17: "From that time"... the nearness of the kingdom.

Matt 16:21: "From that time"... the road to the cross.

Jesus' prediction of His sufferings and death were not received well. The disciples, who earlier were telling the cities of Israel the kingdom was at hand (see Matt 10:5–7) were now being told that the One they had declared as "Messiah" and "Son of the living God" must suffer an agonizing death. Peter rebuked Jesus for this idea and was himself rebuked by Jesus (16:22–23). At this point, Peter was not grasping the relationship of the kingdom and the cross. A kingdom preview from Jesus would be a source of comfort in times to come. The cross was coming soon, but the kingdom would come as well.

A KINGDOM PREVIEW

After the somber news of His coming suffering, Jesus makes statements concerning His return and kingdom:

> "For the Son of Man is going to come in the glory of His Father with His angels, and WILL THEN REPAY EVERY MAN ACCORDING TO HIS DEEDS. Truly I say to you, there are some of those who are standing here who will not taste death until they see the Son of Man coming in His kingdom" (16:27–28).

These words must have been assuring to the apostles who were expecting Jesus to reign over Israel. One natural question that may have arisen in the

3 Commenting on the two uses of "from that time," Toussaint says, "From now on a new emphasis on this fact characterizes the King's instructions. The fact that the Lord now begins to instruct His disciples in preparation for His death and resurrection bears strong testimony to the reaction of Israel to the presence of its King." Toussaint, *Behold the King*, 207.

midst of such sober discussion about Jesus' death was—"What about the kingdom?" After all, the kingdom had been the emphasis of their public ministry to Israel.

Jesus' words in 16:27–28 were an affirmation that in spite of coming suffering, God's kingdom program was still on track. Even though He must die, a time was coming when Jesus would come in glory.

With 16:28 Jesus declared that some standing before Him would not die until they saw the Son of Man coming in His kingdom. Several interpretations have been given concerning this statement. Some say Jesus was simply wrong. Others say the kingdom came with the resurrection of Jesus. Many interpreters, however, have rightly concluded that this "coming" of Jesus was fulfilled with the events of the Transfiguration six days later as described in Matthew 17:1–13. Here the disciples receive a 'kingdom preview'—not the full and final establishment of the kingdom, but a taste or glimpse of the kingdom as they see the glorified Messiah.

Jesus took Peter, James, and John "on a high mountain" where "He was transfigured before them" (17:1–2). Jesus' face "shone like the sun" and His garments became "white as light" (17:2). Moses and Elijah appeared and spoke with Jesus in the presence of the apostles (17:3). The presence of the two OT figures who most represent the Law (Moses) and the Prophets (Elijah) adds further confirmation that Jesus fulfills the message of the OT. According to Luke, both Moses and Elijah appeared "in glory" and "were speaking of His [Jesus'] departure which He was about to accomplish at Jerusalem" (Luke 9:31). This shows the intersection between the cross and the kingdom. Jesus along with Moses and Elijah appear in glory, yet their discussion includes Jesus' sufferings at the cross. This is fitting since Jesus' atoning ministry on the cross is the foundation for the kingdom. Not only is the salvation of people at stake with Jesus' death, but so too is cosmic reconciliation. Paul makes this connection in Colossians 1:20: "and through Him to reconcile all things to Himself, having made peace through the blood of His cross; through Him, I say, whether things on earth or things in heaven."

Peter's initial response to this transfiguration event is significant:

> Peter said to Jesus, "Lord, it is good for us to be here; if You wish, I will make three tabernacles here, one for You, and one for Moses, and one for Elijah" (Matt 17:4).

Peter's response is not that of a confused man who did not know what he was saying because of the magnitude of this event. The request to make three tabernacles for Jesus, Moses and Elijah reveals that Peter believed the kingdom in all its glory and power was now beginning. He wanted to construct booths for Jesus, Moses, and Elijah because he believed the kingdom was unfolding. The feast of Tabernacles has eschatological implications for the Jews. Zechariah 14, which discusses conditions when the Lord is King over all the earth (Zech 14:9), mentions the Feast of Tabernacles as being observed by the nations (see Zech 14:16).[4]

Of course, Peter was in error on the kingdom's timing. The discussion between Jesus, Moses, and Elijah was about Jesus' soon coming death, not the arrival of the kingdom. But such a display of kingdom glory would serve as an encouragement for Peter and the others. Peter's words in 2 Peter 1:16–18 verify that this transfiguration event was the fulfillment of what Jesus promised in Matthew 16:28 concerning His coming:

> For we did not follow cleverly devised tales when we made known to you the power and coming of our Lord Jesus Christ, but we were eyewitnesses of His majesty. For when He received honor and glory from God the Father, such an utterance as this was made to Him by the Majestic Glory, "This is My beloved Son with whom I am well-pleased"—and we ourselves heard this utterance made from heaven when we were with Him on the holy mountain.

When Peter looked back on the Transfiguration, he claimed this event was the "power" and "coming" of Jesus. Yet later in 2 Peter, Peter made clear that there is a future coming of Jesus in connection with the Day of the Lord (2 Pet 3:10–15). Thus, the Transfiguration of Matthew 17 was a preview of the kingdom that will be fully established at a later time. What comfort

4 The feast of tabernacles is so significant in the kingdom that Zechariah 14 speaks of consequences for nations that do not observe it as they should (see Zech 14:19).

that must have brought the apostles as they labored amidst persecution. A preview of the kingdom was evidence the kingdom would fully be established. As Harrington notes, "The disciples receive a preview of glory that will belong to Jesus in the eschaton and the fullness of God's kingdom."[5]

As if this event was not confirmation enough, the voice of God the Father interjected, "This is My beloved Son, with whom I am well-pleased; listen to Him!" (Matt 17:5). The apostles fell to the ground terrified, but Jesus came to them, and when they looked up the event was over and all they saw was Jesus. This then led to a discussion concerning the coming of Elijah.

Matthew 16 and 17 have important implications for the kingdom program. Peter recognized Jesus was Messiah. The reward for Peter and the apostles will be positions of authority in the coming kingdom. Yet the cross must occur first. This news of the cross, though, does not mean the kingdom program has been abandoned. Jesus is coming in glory and judgment and will establish His kingdom. The Transfiguration was a preview of this kingdom and it gave reassurance that suffering was not the end of God's kingdom plans. As McClain puts it:

> If the reader will observe carefully the order of events recorded in Matthew 16:21–17:8, it will become increasingly clear that against the dark background of our Lord's open announcement of His rejection and death, there was need for some reassurance as to the reality and nature of the Kingdom which the apostles had been preaching to the nation of Israel. And this reassurance was given to them on the Mount of Transfiguration.[6]

5 Harrington, *The Gospel of Matthew*, 253.

6 McClain, *The Greatness of the Kingdom*, 337.

GREATNESS AND REWARDS IN THE KINGDOM (MATTHEW 18–20)

The path to greatness in God's kingdom is not through deception and ruthless grabs for power. It is by service. This is the message of Matthew 18–20. Matthew 18 begins with the disciples asking Jesus, "Who then is greatest in the kingdom of heaven?" (18:1). Jesus responds by showing greatness is linked to being humble like a child:

> And He called a child to Himself and set him before them, and said, "Truly I say to you, unless you are converted and become like children, you will not enter the kingdom of heaven. Whoever then humbles himself as this child, he is the greatest in the kingdom of heaven" (Matt 18:2–4).

Like Matthew 5:3–10, both present and future tense verbs are together used concerning the kingdom in Matthew 18:1–4:

- "Who then is greatest in the kingdom of heaven?" (present)
- "Unless you are converted... you will not enter the kingdom of heaven" (future)
- "Whoever then humbles himself... he is greatest in the kingdom of heaven" (present)

Some think the present tense "is" means the kingdom arrived. However, Jesus is probably discussing the characteristics necessary for a person to enter the kingdom of God. It is best to view the disciples as asking what requirements are necessary for being great in the kingdom when it is established. If the kingdom were already in operation they would already know where they stood in relation to it. In fact, Matthew 20:20–28 will show that the disciples viewed positions of power in the kingdom as future from their standpoint. The message of Jesus is that now is the time to evidence humility and service. Doing so qualifies one to be great in the kingdom.

REWARDS IN THE COMING KINGDOM

Matthew 19:27–30 also reveals truths concerning rewards in the kingdom. The setting is Jesus' encounter with the Rich Young Ruler (see Matt 19:16–26). While the ruler desired eternal life, he had a heart issue since he was not willing to place God above his possessions. Jesus said it was easier for a camel to go through the eye of a needle than for a rich man to enter the kingdom of God (Matt 19:24).

With 19:27, Peter asked Jesus what reward he and others would have for following Jesus: "Then Peter said to Him, 'Behold, we have left everything and followed You; what then will there be for us?'" This question may seem self-serving, even inappropriate. But Jesus does not rebuke Peter for asking such a question or claim his motivations were wrong. Instead, Jesus offers an incredible promise in Matthew 19:28:

> And Jesus said to them, "Truly I say to you, that you who have followed Me, in the regeneration when the Son of Man will sit on His glorious throne, you also shall sit upon twelve thrones, judging the twelve tribes of Israel."

Jesus' promise is this—*when the renewal of the cosmos takes place and Jesus assumes the throne of David, the twelve apostles will have ruling positions over a united and restored nation of Israel.*

The word "regeneration" is *palingenesia* and is connected with the ideas of "re-creation" and "renewal."[1] In this context it refers to the coming

1 The NIV and NRSV translate this term as "the renewal of all things." "It was used by the Stoics to describe the renewal of each age in the endless cosmic cycle of destruction by conflagration and subsequent re-creation. In the writings of Philo it denoted either the restoration of human life or the regeneration of the world after the great flood." David C. Sim, "The Meaning of *paliggenesia* in Matthew 19:28," *Journal for the Study of the New Testament* (1993): 4.

eschatological renewal of the world. J. I. Packer says, "it denotes the eschatological 'restoration of all things' (Acts 3:21) under the Messiah for which Israel was waiting."[2] This "cosmic renewal" is future since it is linked with the time "when the Son of Man will sit on His glorious throne." This glorious throne is the throne of David mentioned by the angel Gabriel in Luke 1:32–33. Jesus' assumption of the Davidic throne coincides with the future renewal of the cosmos.

So Jesus places His Davidic throne and kingdom reign in the future. He does so again in Matthew 25:31 when He says, "But when the Son of Man comes in His glory, and all the angels with Him, then He will sit on His glorious throne." This is a reference to Jesus' second coming and judgment of the nations (see Matt 25:31–46). On two occasions, therefore, Jesus states when His throne will be occupied—in the future at the time of the renewal of the world and His second coming to earth with His angels.

Matthew 19:28 also reveals the kingdom involves a restored nation of Israel. On several occasions the OT prophets predicted a restored Israel with a unification of the twelve tribes (see Ezek 36–37). In the *eschaton* this restoration will occur and the twelve apostles will be a part of it with significant ruling positions. So there is a nationalistic element to Christ's kingdom. Israel as a nation is part of the kingdom.

Some have tried to bypass the natural meaning of this verse claiming that Israel is really the church. David Hill states, "The twelve tribes are the new Israel, probably the Church."[3] Also, Robert H. Mounce declares, "The symbolism of the twelve tribes is carried over into New Testament to represent the Christian church."[4] But such a conclusion is not justified. Other than just asserting it, what evidence is there that the church is the Israel of Matthew 19:28? At what point in Matthew has Israel not had a Jewish element to it? Harrington is correct that, "There is no reason to interpret the

2 J. I. Packer, "Regeneration," in *Evangelical Dictionary of Theology*, ed. Walter A. Elwell (Grand Rapids: Baker Book House, 1984), 925.

3 David Hill, *The Gospel of Matthew*, The New Century Bible Commentary (Grand Rapids: Eerdmans, 1972), 284.

4 Robert H. Mounce, *Matthew*, New International Bible Commentary on the New Testament (Peabody, MA: Hendrickson, 1991), 185.

twelve tribes of Israel as a symbol for the Church. Matthew meant Israel."[5] Blaising also summarizes the text well by affirming that Jesus' view of a coming kingdom for Israel was consistent with the OT tradition:

> In summary, we see that Jesus affirmed the tradition of Old Testament prophecy and apocalypticism and proclaimed a coming worldwide political kingdom in which He as Messiah of the house of David would rule Israel and all the nations. We see Him making preparations for the administration of that coming kingdom by promising His disciples ruling positions along with Him.[6]

In addition to positions of authority in the coming kingdom, another promise of Jesus in Matthew 19:27–30 concerns rewards in the future for those who follow Jesus now: "And everyone who has left houses or brothers or sisters or father or mother or children or farms for My name's sake, will receive many times as much, and will inherit eternal life" (19:29).

This answer is stunning. Jesus declares that great material rewards await those who sacrifice for Jesus now. And not just material rewards, but exponential material rewards. This includes both personal relationships ("brothers," "sisters," etc.), and possessions ("houses," "farms"). In this current age Jesus' followers must often give up material possessions for the cause of the gospel. Some forsake lives of luxury and comfort, or proximity to family and friends for little means, danger, and poverty. Doing so does not go unnoticed by our Lord. People who give up comforts will be greatly rewarded. If they give up relationships they will receive them. If they give up houses and farms, those things we will be theirs in abundance. Note how tangible these rewards are. Jesus does not say, "If you give up relationships and material possessions now you will get a cloud in the sky." Instead, the rewards are real and tangible.

This shows Jesus' kingdom will also have physical/material elements to it. The kingdom is not just about spiritual blessings; it also involves material blessings. There is no Platonic dualism in which material blessings are inferior to the spiritual. This is a "both/and" not an "either/or" scenario.

5 Harrington, *The Gospel of Matthew*, 279.

6 Craig A. Blaising and Darrell L. Bock, *Progressive Dispensationalism* (Grand Rapids: Bridgepoint Books, 1993), 238.

The Rich Young Ruler was not willing to follow Jesus and do this, and in the end he lost everything. But for those who give up everything now, they gain it all back and more.

THE PATH TO KINGDOM GREATNESS

In Matthew 20:20–28, the issue of being great in the kingdom of heaven arises again as the mother of James and John asks that her sons have prime positions of authority next to Jesus in the kingdom:

> Then the mother of the sons of Zebedee came to Jesus with her sons, bowing down and making a request of Him. And He said to her, "What do you wish?" She said to Him, "Command that in Your kingdom these two sons of mine may sit one on Your right and one on Your left" (Matt 20:20–21).

Mark's account of this incident does not mention the mother; Mark only mentions James and John. Harmonizing the two accounts indicates James and John were the instigators behind this request although the actual request itself came from the mother, who no doubt was also interested in securing high positions for her sons.

Several points are significant. First, as Blomberg puts it, the mother's request "picks up on the promise of [Matt] 19:28"[7] in which Jesus promised the disciples positions of authority over the twelve tribes of Israel. The mother was not privy to the actual words of Jesus, although it is likely James and John informed her of what Jesus said.[8]

Second, James and John and their mother perceived the kingdom consistently with the OT prophetic picture of an earthly kingdom with ruling positions. To ask for positions at the right hand and left hand was a request for the two sons to be the most important figures in Jesus' kingdom.

Third, they viewed the kingdom as being future from their standpoint. It is when the kingdom is established that they hoped for ruling positions. The disciples did not view themselves as existing in a present

7 Blomberg, *Matthew*, 306.

8 Ibid., 307. Blomberg says the mother's request "is further evidence that her sons had to have informed her and were in on the request."

kingdom since their question is geared toward a future time. If the kingdom had been inaugurated this was not known by James and John. Thus, this request reveals how the apostles viewed the kingdom and their relationship to it. The kingdom was future and involved real positions of authority. Jesus' response reveals more information concerning the kingdom:

> But Jesus answered, "You do not know what you are asking. Are you able to drink the cup that I am about to drink?" They said to Him, "We are able." He said to them, "My cup you shall drink; but to sit on My right and on My left, this is not Mine to give, but it is for those for whom it has been prepared by My Father" (Matt 20:22–23).

Jesus addressed a misconception of James, John, and their mother. But their error was not in how they viewed the nature of the kingdom.[9] Their error concerned how one becomes great in the kingdom. Jesus does not tell James and John their understanding of the kingdom is wrong. As Culver points out, "Jesus did not rebuke the mother of James and John for looking ahead to an earthly kingdom in which her two sons might have prominent positions, but for her selfish desires (Matt. 20:20–23)."[10]

Jesus affirms their expectation of the kingdom was correct. So at this late date in Jesus' ministry, Jesus and the disciples viewed the kingdom as a future reality. Jesus does not rebuke them for this belief or indicate His kingdom reign was a present reality. Nor does He say that positions of authority are a present reality for His followers. He does say the decision concerning positions of authority lies with the Father and that greatness comes through suffering. This is why Jesus challenges them concerning their willingness to suffer as He will suffer. They declare they "are able," a naïve answer no doubt. Jesus then indicates the time will come when they will suffer, but positions of authority in the future kingdom are decided by the Father.

9 Ibid., If we understand him correctly, our view disagrees with Blomberg's assertion that "In v. 22 Jesus tells mother and sons that they do not yet understand the nature of His kingdom." They did not err in understanding the nature of the kingdom, they were wrong concerning how to be great in God's kingdom.

10 Robert Duncan Culver, *Systematic Theology: Biblical & Historical* (Great Britain: Mentor, 2005), 625.

Where the three erred was thinking they could have exalted positions of authority in the kingdom by pursuing greatness like the world. In fact, when the other ten disciples caught on to their request, "the ten became indignant with the two brothers" (Matt 20:25). The other ten were worried that James and John were making a power move that would leave them out. Their motives probably were not much better than James and John's. Jesus tells them their focus was wrong and that the path to greatness was through service, of which He was the supreme example:

> But Jesus called them to Himself and said, "You know that the rulers of the Gentiles lord it over them, and their great men exercise authority over them. It is not this way among you, but whoever wishes to become great among you shall be your servant, and whoever wishes to be first among you shall be your slave; just as the Son of Man did not come to be served, but to serve, and to give His life a ransom for many" (Matt 20:25–28).

Greatness in the kingdom comes through humble service now. This was something Jesus' disciples needed to grasp. As Culver puts it, "The disciples were prepared for the coming of the kingdom, but not positions in it."[11]

11 Ibid., 233.

THE "IN YOUR MIDST" KINGDOM (LUKE 17:20–21 AND MATTHEW 12:28)

We now shift to the presence of the kingdom in Jesus' earthly ministry. Here we concentrate on two passages—Luke 17:20–21 and Matthew 12:28. In addressing Luke 17:20–21 there is a translation issue that affects how the kingdom will be understood. The New International Version translates this in a way that indicates the kingdom is an inner reality:

> Once, having been asked by the Pharisees when the kingdom of God would come, Jesus replied, "The kingdom of God does not come with your careful observation, nor will people say, 'Here it is,' or 'There it is,' because the kingdom of God is within you." (emphasis mine)

With this translation, the kingdom of God is a spiritual entity that resides within a person's soul or heart. But the New American Standard Bible translates this differently:

> Now having been questioned by the Pharisees as to when the kingdom of God was coming, He answered them and said, "The kingdom of God is not coming with signs to be observed; nor will they say, 'Look, here it is!' or, 'There it is!' For behold, the kingdom of God is in your midst." (emphasis mine)

With this translation the kingdom appears to be among or around Jesus' hearers, but not inside of them. Which understanding is correct?

Two questions are significant in looking at this passage. First, what does Jesus mean when He says the kingdom of God is not coming with signs to be observed? And second, is Jesus saying the kingdom of God is a spiritual kingdom that resides in the hearts of men ("within you"), or is He declaring a presence of the kingdom with His personal presence ("in your midst")? Or does some other understanding fit best?

We address the second issue first. Bible versions seem evenly divided on the translation. Several translate *entos humōn* as "within you" while others offer "in your midst" as the best translation. The first view has a long history of support. On the other hand, most of the modern versions opt for the "in your midst" understanding (NASB, HCSB, ESV). Walter Elwell, when discussing twentieth century discoveries and translations, stated: "Another example is that in *koine* Greek, the expression *entos humōn* (literally, 'inside of you') often meant 'within reach.' Thus, Jesus' statement in Luke 17:21 could mean, 'the kingdom is within reach.'"[1]

While not nearly as popular as the two main views another perspective also exists. In 1948, Colin Roberts offered an alternative understanding of Luke 17:21 that is not contrary to the two main views, but presents a different emphasis. Roberts claimed scholars addressing this verse often ask the wrong question. "To ask whether the Kingdom is external or internal, a state of mind or a state of society, a process or a catastrophic event is (in this context) to ask the wrong question."[2] The erroneous assumption or misconception "is that the Kingdom is something external to men, independent of their volitions and actions; it is a conditional possession."[3]

Roberts emphasizes the volitional and conditional element of the kingdom. It is connected to the original question, concerning "*when* the kingdom of God was coming" (Luke 17:20). He says, "To the question, *When is the Kingdom coming?* the answer is that it does not come at all if you strain your eyes to look for it, because it is with you, in your possession, if

1 Walter A. Elwell and Philip Wesley Comfort, *Tyndale Bible Dictionary* (Wheaton, IL: Tyndale House Publishers, 2001), 207.

2 Colin H. Roberts, "The Kingdom of Heaven (Lk. XVII.21)," in *Harvard Theological Review*, vol. XLI (January 1948, no. 1): 8.

3 Ibid.

you want it, now."[4] Roberts supports this understanding with other passages that link the kingdom with volitional choices:

> Elsewhere in the Gospels the Kingdom is something that can be received; something to be sought for like the pearl of great price; something that belongs to some people and not to others. "Ask and it shall be given unto you; seek and you shall find; knock and it shall be opened unto you. For everyone that asks receives and he who seeks finds, and to him that knocks it shall be opened."[5]

Which of the three views is accurate? In situations like this it is best to see if the context sheds light on which understanding is correct. There are three reasons for preferring the "in your midst" view over the "within you" perspective. First, the immediate audience to whom Jesus was speaking was the Pharisees ("He answered *them* and said"). Jesus probably would not say the kingdom of God was in their hearts. The Pharisees had wicked hearts, not hearts in which the kingdom resided. Some have claimed, though, that Jesus was speaking in a generic fashion and making a general statement that the kingdom is an inner spiritual reality for those who receive it without claiming the kingdom was presently in the heart of the Pharisees. But v. 20 makes it clear the Pharisees were the recipients of His words, an unlikely target for a present inner kingdom of the heart. As Geerhardus Vos puts it, "of the unbelieving Pharisees it could scarcely be said that the kingdom was '*within*' them."[6]

Second, the later passages of Luke 19:11–27 and 21:31 reveal the kingdom is not a present spiritual kingdom in the heart but a kingdom that will come in the future with Jesus' return. Jesus offers the parable of the minas to counter the idea that the kingdom would be established immediately (Luke 19:11–27). With Luke 21:31 Jesus indicates the kingdom would only be near with the cataclysmic events of the coming tribulation period. If

4 Ibid., 7–8.

5 Ibid.

6 Geerhardus Vos, *The Teaching of Jesus Concerning the Kingdom of God and the Church* (New York, NY: American Tract Society, 1903), 53. Emphases in original.

Jesus was preaching a spiritual kingdom of the heart why does He make it so clear after 17:21 that the kingdom was a tangible and future entity?

Third, the "within reach" or "in your midst" understanding aligns best with the *engiken* term that was used several times concerning the kingdom in passages like Matt 3:2; 4:17; and 10:7. This term is best translated "near" or "at hand" and indicates imminence but not arrival.

So Kümmel is correct that "the translation 'amongst you' must be preferred."[7] In addition, if Roberts is correct that the timing of the kingdom is linked with the volitional choice of Jesus' audience, which in this case is the leaders of Israel, this could coincide with other passages in which a presentation of the kingdom is being made to Israel on the condition of repentance (Matt 3:2; 4:17; Matt 23:37–39; Acts 3:20–21).

Concerning the first issue, why does Jesus tell His audience they should *not* look for signs of the kingdom in Luke 17:20? One possible reason is that the kingdom's presence will be so sudden that there is no gradual arrival to look for. At one moment it is not present and then in another it is. When the kingdom comes it will arrive rapidly, in a moment. This view is compatible with Jesus' words just a few verses later where He likens His coming to lightning: "For just like the lightning, when it flashes out of one part of the sky, shines to the other part of the sky, so will the Son of Man be in His day" (Luke 17:24).

This view of the kingdom's suddenness is possible. But we lean toward another view. The reason Jesus told the religious leaders not to look for signs of the kingdom is because the kingdom was present in Jesus' person as He stood before them at that time. To paraphrase, Jesus is saying something like, "Don't look for signs of the kingdom because, the kingdom is right in front of you with My presence." Why search for that which is standing before you?[8] Jesus' personal presence means a presence of the kingdom.

When Jesus foretells future events in Luke 21, He tells His apostles that cosmic signs and other future events are *signs* of the kingdom's nearness ("So you also, when you see these things happening, recognize that the

7 Kümmel, *Promise and Fulfillment*, 34.

8 Ibid., 35. "... there remains only the interpretation that the Kingdom of God has already become effective in advance in Jesus and in the present events appearing in connexion with his person."

kingdom of God is near"—Luke 21:31). Note the difference between Luke 17:21 and Luke 21:31:

> **Luke 17:20–21:** Jesus says not to look for signs concerning the kingdom.
>
> **Luke 21:31:** Jesus says to look for signs concerning the kingdom.

The best way to harmonize these two passages is to understand that Jesus' bodily presence carries with it a presence of the kingdom. Yet His presence changes when He ascends bodily to heaven. His physical presence awaits His second coming and kingdom.

So at the time of Luke 17:20–21 there was no need to look for signs of the kingdom. People were responsible to respond to Jesus who was standing before them. The kingdom was present at that time in His person. But when Jesus ascends to heaven and is bodily absent from the earth, circumstances change. One then can looks for signs of His return and the coming of the kingdom of God (Luke 21:31). When Jesus returns He will bring the kingdom with Him (Matt 25:31).

There is much debate over Luke 17:20–21, but context reveals that "in your midst" is a better translation than "within you." This passage does not teach the kingdom is only a present spiritual kingdom. Viviano warns against using this verse as a starting part for an overly spiritualized view of the kingdom:

> Unfortunately, this verse has been abused throughout history and led to an overly spiritual depoliticized and then trivialized interpretation of the Kingdom. It is a mistake to make this verse the starting point of our understanding of the Kingdom in the proclamation of Jesus.[9]

Matthew 12:28

Another verse addressing the presence of the kingdom is Matthew 12:28 where Jesus said: "But if I cast out demons by the Spirit of God, then the kingdom of God has come upon you." The stimulus for this statement was

9 Benedict. T. Viviano, *The Kingdom of God in History* (Wilmington: Michael Glazier, 1988), 27.

Jesus' healing of a demon-possessed man who was blind and mute (Matt 12:22). The Pharisees argued that Jesus' exorcisms were done through the power of Satan (12:24). Jesus responds by saying this claim was ridiculous since Satan would not fight himself. He then says the Pharisees were inconsistent since they accepted the exorcisms of others (12:26–27). Jesus says His demonstrations of power over demons by the power of the Holy Spirit showed that the kingdom of God had come upon them (12:28). So in what sense had the kingdom come upon Jesus' audience?

The kingdom came upon the people since the King and His kingdom works were manifested before them. His miracles were tastes and glimpses of the kingdom. The OT predicted that the kingdom involved judgment on evil forces (see Isa 24:21). It also predicted healing (Isa 35) as God brought wholeness and restoration to His people. Jesus' exorcisms were demonstrations of kingdom authority and showed the nearness of the kingdom.

So instead of the sinful response of the Pharisees who said Jesus was working for Satan, the right response was to recognize Jesus' miracles and exorcisms as proof He was the King and that the kingdom was upon them.

Together, Luke 17:20–21 and Matthew 12:28 reveal the kingdom was present among the people with Jesus' person and works. This should stir the people to repent and believe in Jesus. Yet rejection of Jesus also meant a rejection of His kingdom. The removal of Jesus' bodily presence will also mean the removal of the kingdom, yet only for a time. The return of Jesus brings the full arrival of the kingdom (see Acts 3:20–21).

THE KINGDOM AND JESUS' FINAL ENTRY INTO JERUSALEM (LUKE 19 AND MATTHEW 21–23)

THE SETTING FOR THE TRIUMPHAL ENTRY

Events associated with Jesus' entry into Jerusalem days before His death have important ramifications for the kingdom program. Jesus offers several statements concerning the kingdom's timing and its relationship to Israel. Israel's rejection of Jesus means the kingdom's arrival will be delayed. Also, Israel will face judgment for rejecting her Messiah, yet a day is coming when Israel will cry out to Jesus and experience national salvation and restoration.

THE KINGDOM DELAY

At the time of Luke 19:11 Jesus is on the brink of entering Jerusalem from Jericho. The kingdom of God was on His mind as He corrects a misperception concerning the timing of the kingdom:

> While they were listening to these things, Jesus went on to tell a parable, because He was near Jerusalem, and they supposed that the kingdom of God was going to appear immediately.

Jesus refutes the idea that the kingdom would "appear immediately." The audience ("they"), including the multitude and Jesus' disciples, heard Jesus' words regarding the salvation of Zaccheus (see Luke 19:1–10). Several points should be noted from Luke 19:11.

First, a strong expectation existed Jesus would soon establish the kingdom. His close proximity to Jerusalem and the manner in which He approached Jerusalem stimulated this thinking.

Second, neither Jesus nor His audience viewed the kingdom of God as established already. Both viewed the kingdom as future from their standpoints. If the crowd expected the kingdom to be established immediately this shows they did not view the kingdom as existing yet. Jesus' answer also reveals He did not perceive the kingdom as currently in operation.

Third, the purpose of the parable is to show the kingdom would not be established soon. The parable, therefore, is about the kingdom's *timing* not its *nature*. McClain notes, "The people were not wrong in looking for a very genuine appearing or manifestation of the Messianic Kingdom; but the error of which they needed to be cured was the supposition that the Kingdom could come at once without first a departure and a return on the part of the King."[1]

Moving on, Luke 19:12 then states: "So He [Jesus] said, 'A nobleman went to a distant country to receive a kingdom for himself, and then return.'" The historical background for this parable came from actual events in the political history of the times. "It was regular procedure for native princes to journey to Rome to receive their right to rule."[2] The case of Herod Archelaus, with whom Jesus' listeners would have been familiar, was one example.[3] His father, Herod the Great, and the army had proclaimed Archelaus a leader, but Archelaus did not have the right to rule until he first received official permission from Caesar Augustus in Rome. This involved traveling for many months. Some Jews followed Archelaus to Rome to contest his petition to rule over them. In 4 B.C. Caesar Augustus granted Archelaus authority over Samaria, Judea, and Idumea to the dismay of Archelaus's opponents. Thus, there was a process before Archelaus actually began to rule. Authority to rule was first given and then the kingdom reign began upon his return.

1 McClain, *The Greatness of the Kingdom*, 342.

2 Ibid., 341.

3 See Brian Schultz, "Jesus as Archelaus in the Parable of the Pounds in (Lk. 19:11–27)," *Novum Testamentum* 49 (2007): 105–27.

The "nobleman" of Luke 19:12 represents Jesus. He travels to a "distant country" (heaven) in order to "receive a kingdom" and then returns to begin his rule over his kingdom. The nobleman is not reigning before he travels to receive his kingdom. He travels to receive official authority to rule. When he receives this right to rule he will then return and begin the function of reigning.

The reason the kingdom is *not* going to appear immediately is because Jesus must receive kingdom authority first. The "distant country" appears to be heaven and is connected with Jesus' resurrection and ascension.[4] As Matthew's Gospel ends, Jesus says, "All authority has been given to Me in heaven and on earth" (Matt 28:18). Psalm 110 declares that David's Lord—the Messiah—must have a session at the right hand of God in heaven before He comes to earth to rule (see Ps 110:1–2). Acts 3:21 affirms this by noting, "heaven must receive" Jesus "until the period of restoration of all things."

Archelaus went to Rome to receive his kingdom from Caesar, but his kingdom reign began when he returned to Judea where he rewarded his servants and punished his enemies. Likewise, Jesus must travel to heaven to receive kingdom rights from the Father. He receives the right to rule there but His kingdom reign begins at His return. Luke 19:13–15 continues the parable:

> And he called ten of his slaves, and gave them ten minas and said to them, "Do business with this until I come back." But his citizens hated him and sent a delegation after him, saying, "We do not want this man to reign over us." When he returned, after receiving the kingdom, he ordered that these slaves, to whom he had given the money, be called to him so that he might know what business they had done.

The nobleman's slaves were each given a mina, which is the equivalent of one hundred days of pay. They were to "do business" and make a profit on behalf of the nobleman. These slaves represent servants of Christ. Christians are to use their gifts and talents for Jesus in this period before

4 "The kingdom of which our Lord speaks is received in heaven, but set up on earth." Henry Clarence Thiessen, "The Parable of the Kingdom and the Earthly Kingdom," *Bibliotheca Sacra* (1934): 184.

His second coming. The "citizens" who hate the nobleman are unbelievers who do not want Jesus to reign over them.

Verses 16–26 discuss how three of the servants used their minas. The first was productive. He took his mina and made ten minas. The second made his mina become five minas. But the third did nothing with his mina. He received a strong rebuke and his mina was taken from him and given to the one with ten. The citizens, however, who opposed the nobleman were slain (v. 27). Also significant are the positions of ruling authority given to the faithful slaves. The first servant was given "authority over ten cities" (v. 17). The second servant received authority over five cities (v. 18). The nobleman's servants participate in his reign by also having positions of authority. Faithful service now results in positions of authority later. Neither the nobleman nor the servants were reigning while the nobleman was traveling to the distant country but they reign when the nobleman returns. These truths fit with other passages where the reign of the saints coincides with the reign of the Messiah (see Rev 2:26–27; 5:10).

To summarize, Jesus' audience believed the kingdom of God would be established immediately. But the kingdom would not be established until Christ returned from heaven after He received authority from the Father. After that He will come and reward His servants abundantly giving more to those who were faithful and taking away from those who were not. The application for Jesus' followers is that they should be faithful, using their gifts and talents during this period between His two comings. When Jesus returns He will reward the faithful and grant them ruling authority. Yet their rewards will not be equal. Those who are most faithful will reap the most rewards. Unbelievers who resist Jesus' authority will be destroyed.

THE TRIUMPHAL ENTRY

Jesus' parable of the minas was soon followed by His entry into Jerusalem. Here the King of Israel presents himself to Israel. McClain is correct that many Christians celebrate this event but there is "little understanding of its relation to the history of the Kingdom of God" and why it is "of tremendous import."[5] Jesus' entry into Jerusalem is full of kingdom implications.

5 McClain, *The Greatness of the Kingdom*, 346.

This entry is not like His other visits into Jerusalem. Jesus commands the disciples to go into the village to acquire a donkey the Lord prepared (Luke 19:31). Jesus will come into Jerusalem on a donkey to fulfill the prophecy of Zech 9:9. As Matthew 21:4–5 states:

This took place to fulfill what was spoken through the prophet:

> "SAY TO THE DAUGHTER OF ZION,
> 'BEHOLD YOUR KING IS COMING TO YOU,
> GENTLE, AND MOUNTED ON A DONKEY,
> EVEN ON A COLT, THE FOAL OF A BEAST OF BURDEN.'"

This is a presentation of a King to His people in fulfillment of prophecy. It is, as Toussaint points out, "the final and official presentation of Jesus to Israel as its Messiah."[6] Luke states that as Jesus was approaching Jerusalem "near the descent of the Mount of Olives" (Luke 19:37) the crowd began shouting "BLESSED IS THE KING WHO COMES IN THE NAME OF THE LORD" (Luke 19:38a). The crowds recognized the messianic significance of this event. Matthew records, "Hosanna to the Son of David; Blessed is he who comes in the name of the Lord; Hosanna in the highest!" (Matt 21:9). Disturbed by this, some of the Pharisees told Jesus, "Teacher, rebuke Your disciples" (Luke 19:39). They did not want Jesus recognized as Israel's Messiah.

But while the crowds praised Jesus, days later some would shout "Crucify Him!"[7] Expecting a king to bring deliverance from Israel's enemies was not wrong. Zacharias expected this according to Luke 1:71. But the people and leaders were not willing to meet the spiritual requirements of the King who was in their midst. They, as the next passage will show, missed the time of their "visitation" (Luke 19:44). The results will be catastrophic.

CONSEQUENCES FOR MISSING VISITATION

Luke 19:41–44 is strategic for understanding the kingdom program in history. As Jesus approached Jerusalem, there are kingdom implications stemming from Israel's rejection of Jesus as their Messiah. Israel's refusal to

6 Toussaint, *Behold the King: A Study of Matthew*, 241.

7 We are not claiming the two crowds of Palm Sunday and Good Friday are exactly the same.

believe in Jesus means the kingdom would not be established at this time. Instead, judgment for Israel was around the corner.

Verse 41 states: "When He approached Jerusalem, He saw the city and wept over it." As Jesus approached Jerusalem from the Mount of Olives He was not rejoicing like the crowds. Verses 42–44 tell us why:

> (Jesus) saying, "If you had known in this day, even you, the things which make for peace! But now they have been hidden from your eyes. For the days will come upon you when your enemies will throw up a barricade against you, and surround you and hem you in on every side, and they will level you to the ground and your children within you, and they will not leave in you one stone upon another, because you did not recognize the time of your visitation."

The reason for this emotional display was Jesus' sorrow for Israel. He weeps for Israel like a parent weeping for a wayward child. Israel's rejection of their Messiah will result in terrible consequences even though they were blind to it.

Jesus declares the significance of "this day": "If you had known in this day, even you, the things which make for peace" (v. 42). The reference to "this day" is emphatic and reveals something unique about it. But why? This day had the potential to bring "things which make for peace." Jesus can bring the kingdom and its blessings. This "peace" must be more than just individual salvation. Jesus addressed Jerusalem, the capital city of Israel like a person—"You." "If you had known..." Also, the consequences for unbelief here are national and physical. If the consequences for unbelief are national and physical, so too must the offer of blessings be national and physical as well.[8]

Peace could have come to Israel but this will not happen now. Instead, peace will be "hidden" and judgment will come. Enemies will surround Jerusalem and utterly destroy the city. Why?—"because you did not recognize the time of your visitation" (19:44). Israel's visitation was the appearance of her Messiah. Yet they did not respond properly. Salvation and restoration were before her, but she turned her head and refused.

8 "In Luke's mind, this would have meant primarily equity among all people (1:48–53), a change of government (1:52 cf 19:38), a fulfillment of Isaiah's prophecy (4:21), restitution by the rich (3:10–14 cf 18:22) and a reversal of social roles (cf 22:24–27)." McGlory Speckman, "The Kairos behind the Kairos Document: A Contextual Exegesis of Luke 19:41–44," *Religion & Theology* 5 (1998): 214.

Some scholars have proposed that "this day" and "visitation" are connected with the fulfillment of the Daniel 9:25 prophecy where Messiah the Prince is predicted to come to Israel at the end of the sixty-ninth week of Daniel. Harold Hoehner claims the sixty-ninth week of Daniel expired exactly on the day of the Triumphal Entry of Jesus into Jerusalem.[9] If this is the case, "this day" could have prophetic significance back to Daniel 9 and Messiah's coming to Israel.

So how does Luke 19:41–44 relate to the kingdom of God? Previously, Jesus revealed the kingdom of God would not be established for a while (Luke 19:11–27). Now we are told there could have been "peace." Peace here refers to kingdom blessings promised in the OT. Of course, spiritual salvation would be at the heart of this peace, but this peace also included security and prosperity for Jerusalem and Israel, just as Zacharias, Simeon, and Anna expected (see Luke 1:67–79; 2:25–38).

Part of the reason physical peace and prosperity are in view with Jesus' words is because of the opposite consequences now facing Jerusalem because of unbelief. Since Israel rejected her Messiah, the result would be a literal destruction of its capital city. Thus, just as there would be a literal destruction of the city of Jerusalem for unbelief, there also could have been peace and security for Jerusalem if the people accepted their Messiah. To put it another way:

–National belief in Jesus would lead to national peace.
–National rejection of Jesus leads to national catastrophe.

In sum, Luke 19:41–44 reveals a genuine presentation of kingdom blessings to the people of Israel. Yet these kingdom blessings were conditioned on Israel's repentance and belief in their King. This must be the case because Jesus wept over Israel's choice and the consequences for her rejecting Him. Also, they are held responsible for not accepting their Messiah. As McClain asserts, "The historic fact that Israel did not receive Him, however, subtracts nothing from the reality of the offer and the divinely imposed obligation."[10]

9 See Harold W. Hoehner, *Chronological Aspects of the Life of Christ* (Grand Rapids: Zondervan, 1978).

10 McClain, *The Greatness of the Kingdom*, 353.

Yet as Brent Kinman points out, the judgment of Luke 19:41–44 is not permanent: "Jesus' announcement at 19:41–44 need not represent a definitive or final break between God and Israel—as in the Old Testament, the aim of chastisement visited upon Jerusalem is restoration."[11] As terrible as the coming judgment will be, hope for the restoration of Jerusalem remains (see Luke 21:24b).

WHAT IF ISRAEL BELIEVED?

Some resist the idea of a kingdom presentation to Israel or the idea that the timing of the kingdom's arrival is related to national Israel's reception of Jesus.[12] One objection is that such a scenario implies the cross of Christ would be unnecessary if Israel believed in Jesus at His first coming. After all, if Israel believed in Jesus then the kingdom would have come and the cross of Jesus would not have occurred. Another objection is that God knew Israel would not believe, so how could a genuine offer of kingdom blessings be given to a people whom God knew would not believe?

A few things can be said to these objections. First, God's kingdom and salvation purposes could only be accomplished by the death of Jesus. So the cross of Christ had to occur. Both human and cosmic reconciliation only happen through the atoning work of the Suffering Servant (see Isa 52–53; Col 1:20). Jesus' atonement is the basis for the kingdom. Thus, the suffering of the Messiah is not only predicted in the OT, it is necessary for the kingdom. Second, from our perspective in time we know it was not God's plan for the kingdom to arrive in connection with Jesus' first coming.

But these truths do not mean a genuine presentation of kingdom blessings were not offered to Israel by Jesus. God can extend genuine promises of blessing while knowing that the people to whom the promises were made would not respond positively. Leviticus 26:40–45 declared that Israel's reentry into the blessings of the Abrahamic Covenant is conditioned upon national repentance:

11 Brent Kinman, *Jesus' Entry into Jerusalem in the Context of Lukan Theology and the Politics of His Day* (New York: Brill, 1995), 132.

12 For example, Kim Riddlebarger states, "But the New Testament knows nothing of a kingdom offered and kingdom withdrawn according to the whims of unbelieving Israel." Riddlebarger, *A Case for Amillennialism*, 103.

> "If they confess their iniquity and the iniquity of their forefathers, in their unfaithfulness which they committed against Me, and also in their acting with hostility against Me... . then I will remember My covenant with Jacob, and I will remember also My covenant with Isaac, and My covenant with Abraham as well, and I will remember the land" (Lev 26:40–42).

This "if... then" scenario shows that "if" Israel believes "then" God will reestablish Israel to Abrahamic Covenant blessings. Thus, Israel's repentance and belief for kingdom blessings was part of the OT message.

Also, most acknowledge that a genuine offer of salvation and blessing can be extended to a person who God knows will not believe. Consider the presentation of the gospel to a person who refuses to believe. When a non-Christian is presented with the gospel there is a real offer of forgiveness and eternal life. The plea "Believe on the Lord Jesus Christ and you will be saved and go to heaven!" is a genuine call to salvation even to those who do not accept the message. Because God is sovereign and all knowing, He knows some will not respond to the gospel message and be saved. Yet this does not make the offer of forgiveness of sins and eternal life any less genuine or legitimate.

So what is true at the individual level can also be true at a national level. God can extend a genuine offer of kingdom blessings to Israel while knowing Israel would not believe and kingdom blessings would not occur at that time. Jesus said Israel missed its visitation and the things that make for peace (see Luke 19:41–44). This "peace" had to include real kingdom peace. In order to "miss" peace, the possibility for peace needed to exist. Jesus also said the cities of Israel would be held accountable at the judgment day for rejecting the kingdom (see Matt 11:20–24). We now know Israel did not repent, but the offer of blessing was legitimate and genuine. That is why there is accountability at the judgment.

Another example of a genuine offer involves the first man—Adam. In Genesis 2:15–17 Adam was offered a real choice. He could obey God and live by not eating of the tree of the knowledge of good and evil, or he could disobey God by eating of the tree and experience death. Adam's choice was real and God's offer to Adam of remaining in life or dying was genuine. Yet God in His omniscience knew Adam would sin. We also know God's plan from eternity past involved the saving work of Jesus and the necessity of the cross. So we could ask, "What if Adam did not sin? Would that make the cross unnecessary?" Of course, we know God's plan from the beginning involved the necessity of Jesus being the Savior. Thus, we can affirm two truths—(1) Adam was genuinely promised continuing life for obedience and death for disobedience; and (2) God's plan involved Adam's sin even though Adam had a real choice.

To use another example, God promised king Saul a permanent kingdom over Israel, but this did not occur since Saul disobeyed God (see 1 Sam 13:13–14). But how can this be? Wasn't it God's plan that David be the one through whom the eternal dynasty over Israel occurred? The answer is, Yes. From our standpoint we know that God decreed David, not Saul, as the vehicle for the eternal dynasty. But that does not make God's offer to Saul any less genuine.

So what if Israel had believed in Jesus as Messiah at His first coming? More on this will be said in our section on Acts 3:19–21. But in one sense, we don't really have to answer that question. It is a hypothetical scenario. All we need to know is that Israel was offered real kingdom blessings if they believed in Jesus, yet in God's sovereign plan this was not going to occur at this time. That generation of Israel will be held accountable for their unbelief (see Matt 11:20–24).

To conclude, the death of Jesus on the cross had to occur because it is absolutely necessary for salvation and because the OT predicted it. Yet this truth coincides with a genuine presentation of the kingdom to Israel.

ISRAEL'S COMING JUDGMENT FOR UNBELIEF

Matthew 21:23–32

With kingly authority Jesus entered the Jerusalem temple and drove out greedy moneychangers who turned His Father's house into a den of thieves (Matt 21:12–13). He also performed many healings (21:14). When Jesus entered the temple the next morning, the chief priests and elders challenged Jesus' authority (21:23). Refusing to fall into their trap, Jesus asked them by what authority John the Baptist functioned. Since they refused to answer His question, Jesus refused to answer their question. Jesus then offered the parable of the two sons. One son initially refused his father's command to work in the vineyard but later changed his mind and did so. On the other hand, the second son said he would do the work, but in reality did not. Likening this parable to Israel's religious leaders and sinners, Jesus said, "Truly I say to you that the tax collectors and prostitutes will get into the kingdom of God before you" (21:31). The shocking truth was that terrible sinners who repented would reach the kingdom of God while Israel's religious leaders would not.

Parable of the Landowner (Matthew 21:33–46)

The stinging rebuke by Jesus against the leaders was followed by the parable of the landowner (21:33–46). Here Jesus draws upon Isaiah's vineyard parable found in Isaiah 5. With this chapter, the "vineyard" of the Lord "is the house of Israel" (5:7). The Lord took care of this vineyard, expecting it to "produce good grapes," but "it produced only worthless ones" (Isa 5:2). Jesus likened the message of Isaiah 5 to the present leaders of Israel who beat the slaves and Son (Jesus) of the Landowner (God). The crowds admitted that the owner of the vineyard needed to remove the wicked vine-growers and replace them with other vine-growers (21:41). This leads to the truths of Matthew 21:43.

Matthew 21:43 has important implications concerning who will experience the kingdom: "Therefore I say to you, the kingdom of God will be taken away from you and given to a people, producing the fruit of it." This statement of Jesus has more to do with participants of the kingdom and not the kingdom's nature. But it does have ramifications regarding Israel's relationship to the kingdom.

There are at least three understandings of Jesus' words. First, some claim this verse reveals the kingdom of God was permanently taken from the nation Israel and given to the church. This is a replacement theology perspective. With this view custody of the kingdom is transferred from national Israel to the church. Jack Dean Kingsbury says, "God has withdrawn his Kingdom from Israel" and has "given it to the church (21:43)."[13]

A second view is that the kingdom is not taken from Israel as a whole but from the *current leadership* in Israel. Custody of the kingdom is removed

13 Jack Dean Kingsbury, *Matthew: Structure, Christology, Kingdom* (Philadelphia: Fortress, 1975), 157.

from the wicked religious leaders of Israel and transferred to the believing Jewish remnant who follows Jesus. As Turner explains: "'The nation' of 21:43 is the Matthean community as an eschatological messianic remnant whose leaders will replace the current Jerusalem religious establishment and lead Israel in bearing the fruit of righteousness to God."[14] The apostles who are earlier promised ruling positions over the twelve tribes of Israel in the future represent this believing Jewish remnant (see Matt 19:28):

> The transferal of the kingdom to a fruitful "nation" (21:43) is thus related to the foundational role of the apostles with Peter at the head in teaching and disciplining the messianic remnant of Israel.[15]

This position emphasizes Jesus' direct address to the Jewish leaders. Matthew 21:45 says the chief priests and Pharisees knew Jesus "was speaking about them." The religious leaders understood Jesus' words as a rejection of them as guides of Israel. Thus, with this view, Matthew 21:43 teaches that leadership is being removed from the current Jewish leaders and transferred to Jesus' apostles.

A third perspective is that the kingdom is being taken from the current generation of Israel, of which the religious leaders are representatives, and will be given to a future believing generation of Israel, the coming generation that will truly say, "Blessed is He who comes in the name of the Lord" (see Matt 23:39). This is the "all Israel" who will be saved according to Romans 11:26. Thus, the nation to whom the kingdom will be given is a future believing generation of Israel. In reference to Matthew 21:43, Pentecost states, "it seems better to understand it as a future generation in Israel that will repent as the Davidic form of the kingdom is instituted by the returning Messiah."[16]

So which of the three views is the best option? The first view, the church permanently replaces Israel perspective, is not viable. On several

14 Turner, *Matthew*, 518.

15 David L. Turner, "Matthew 21:43 and the Future of Israel," in *Bibliotheca Sacra* 159 (2002): 60. Turner also says, "The apostles were the new leaders of the nation; they would produce the fruit that the recalcitrant farmers refused to give the landowner" (60).

16 Pentecost, *Thy Kingdom Come*, 226.

occasions Jesus affirmed a future for national Israel (see Matt 19:28; 23:39). This would not only go against Jesus' own teaching, but the teaching of the OT and NT (see Deut 30:1–8; Zech 12:10; Luke 1:32–33; Rom 11:26).

The second view, that Jesus is announcing the removal of kingdom custody from the current Jewish leadership, has more to commend it. The strength of this view is that Matthew 21:45 specifically says the religious leaders knew Jesus was speaking about "them." As M. Eugene Boring states, "Who is represented by the 'you' from whom the kingdom is taken? Who is the 'nation' to whom it is given? In the context, the addressees are clearly the chief priests and Pharisees... i.e., the Jewish leadership, not the people as a whole."[17] Making a similar point, David D. Kupp writes, "Jesus' growing antipathy to the Jewish leaders has never spelled outright rejection of the Jewish crowds, the people of Israel. Even in 21.43 the target audience is explicitly the leaders, not the people."[18] Plus Matthew 19:28 explicitly promises that the apostles will rule over a restored national Israel when Jesus assumes the Davidic throne at His return.

The third view, that the kingdom will be given to a future generation of believing Israel, also has much going for it. In Matthew 23:39 Jesus said He would remove His presence from Israel until the day Israel cries out, "Blessed is He who comes in the name of the Lord." This affirms judgment for the present generation of Israel while predicting a future generation that would sincerely cry out to her Messiah. Fruchtenbaum observes, "The point is that the kingdom while taken from the present Jewish generation, will be given to a future generation of Israel."[19] We lean toward this third view. Jesus is removing the kingdom from the current generation of Israel until a future nation of Israel cries out to Him for salvation.

17 M. Eugene Boring, *The Gospel of Matthew: Introduction, Commentary, and Reflections*, The New Interpreter's Bible, vol. 8 (Nashville: Abingdon, 1995), 415.

18 David D, Kupp, *Matthew's Emmanuel: Divine Presence and God's People in the First Gospel* (Cambridge: Cambridge University Press, 1996), 95. Luz writes, "Is Jesus announcing the supersession of Israel by the Gentile Church in the history of mankind's salvation? . . . No, because in this context he is quite clearly speaking to Israel's leaders and to no one else. No, because *ethnos*—that same Greek word for 'people' that means, in the plural, 'nations' or 'Gentiles'—cannot simply be equated with 'church.'" Ulrich Luz, *The Theology of the Gospel of Matthew*, trans. J. Bradford Robinson (Cambridge: Cambridge University Press, 1995), 119.

19 Fruchtenbaum, *Israelology*, 405. This is also the view of McClain, *The Greatness of the Kingdom*, 296–97.

Parable of the Marriage Feast (Matthew 22:1–14)

Jesus continues with judgment parables in the final days before His death. In Matthew 22:1–14 He likens "the kingdom of heaven" to "a king who gave a wedding feast for his son" (22:2). This parable has important ramifications regarding presentations of the kingdom to Israel and Israel's rejection of the kingdom at this time. This also is important regarding Gentile inclusion in the kingdom program.

The "king" represents God the Father. The "son" is Jesus. And the "wedding feast" refers to the kingdom. A wedding feast is a time of joy, feasting, and celebration, and is an appropriate analogy for the kingdom. Isaiah 25:6 pictures the kingdom as "a lavish banquet." Jesus mentions a kingdom banquet in Matthew 8:11. Revelation 19:9 speaks of a "marriage supper of the Lamb." The kingdom is a joyous event with banquet celebration. In this parable, the king (God the Father) is throwing a celebration (kingdom) for his son (Jesus). And the king offers a series of calls to this joyous event.

With the first announcement, the king "sent out his slaves to call those who had been invited to the wedding feast" (3a). The king sends representatives to call a group who had already been invited to the wedding feast. There is a group who already received an invitation although the event had not occurred yet. This is consistent with the cultural practice for a wedding invitation to be offered although the specific date of the wedding was to come later.

Israel received the invitation as recipients of the OT kingdom promises. With the arrival of Jesus, Israel was called to the kingdom celebration. This first call probably refers to the message of John the Baptist and Jesus' disciples to the people of Israel (see Matt 3:2 and 10:5–7). Another possible view is that this first call was the message of the prophets to Israel, but it is probably best to view the prophets as giving the invitation that came prior to this first call.

The response of this first call is stunning—"and they were unwilling to come" (3b). Incredibly, the people invited to the wedding feast of the Son refused the invitation. The current generation of Israel rejected the offer of the kingdom. The king's restraint to this rejection is remarkable. He does not judge them immediately but offers another call to this group:

> Again he sent out other slaves saying, "Tell those who have been invited, 'Behold, I have prepared my dinner; my oxen and my fattened livestock are all butchered and everything is ready; come to the wedding feast'" (v. 4).

Conditions for the wedding feast are even further along now. McClain draws attention to the "everything is ready" statement and links this second call with "our Lord's finished work of redemption at Calvary."[20] "Such a call," he states, "could not have gone forth until after the Resurrection."[21] If this understanding is accurate, then this second call refers to the offer of the kingdom extended again to Israel by the post-Pentecost ministry of the apostles. This explicitly occurs in Acts 3:19–21. In this passage the "men of Israel" (Acts 3:12) are told that repentance leads to forgiveness of sins that leads to kingdom conditions and the return of Jesus.[22] So it is possible that Jesus' statement in 22:4 relates to the reoffer of the kingdom to Israel in Acts 3:19–21. But tragically, again, the people of Israel reject this second offer.

> But they paid no attention and went their way, one to his own farm, another to his business, and the rest seized his slaves and mistreated them and killed them (vv. 5–6).

Israel's rejection takes two forms. First, they "paid no attention." They treated the kingdom offer with contempt by ignoring it. The second response was more violent in that they mistreated and killed the messengers of the king. This occurred as the apostles continued to be persecuted.

Both responses of neglect and persecution draw the wrath of the king: "But the king was enraged, and he sent his armies and destroyed those murderers and set their city on fire" (v. 7). This appears to be a prediction of the A.D. 70 destruction of Jerusalem, which Jesus predicts in Luke 19:41–44 and 21:20–24. In Luke 21:22 Jesus refers to Jerusalem's desolation by armies as "days of vengeance."

20 McClain, *The Greatness of the Kingdom*, 406.

21 Ibid.

22 Ibid., "This [v. 4] points to the post-Pentecostal offer, as described in the Book of Acts." The kingdom conditions of Acts 3:19–21 are described as "times of refreshing" and "the restoration of all things."

As McClain puts it, "there is no *third* call for this generation of Israel."[23] Only judgment. With Matthew 22:8–10 another call will be offered, but this time it is a universal call that takes place in "the main highways" and "streets." This is a reference to the areas of the Gentiles where the invitation will reach. The messengers of the king "gathered together all they found, both evil and good" to such an extent that "the wedding hall was filled with dinner guests." The kingdom invitation extends to Gentiles. Israel, who possessed the original invitation, failed to respond to the kingdom call. They will be judged and others will be invited. This truth parallels Jesus' words in Matthew 8:11–12:

> "I say to you that many [believing Gentiles] will come from east and west, and recline at the table with Abraham, Isaac and Jacob in the kingdom of heaven; but the sons of the kingdom [unbelieving Jews] will be cast out into the outer darkness; in that place there will be weeping and gnashing of teeth."

The book of Acts reveals the message of the kingdom going to the Gentiles. Paul, himself, was an apostle to the Gentiles (Rom 11:13).

The rest of the parable reveals that not all who show up for the kingdom are worthy of experiencing it (vv. 11–14). But in regard to the kingdom, Matthew 22:1–14 reveals several important truths. First, Israel was invited to the kingdom via the OT prophets. Second, when the time came for Israel to be summoned to the kingdom, the people rejected the first call, which probably included the message of John the Baptist and Jesus' apostles (see Matt 11:20–24). Third, God extended a gracious second call to Israel, probably through the coming post-Pentecost ministry of the apostles. But this offer, too, was rejected. Fourth, national judgment would come upon Israel, as the capital city of Jerusalem will be destroyed by fire. This was fulfilled in A.D. 70 when Jerusalem was destroyed. Fifth, the kingdom offer will be extended to Gentiles. This occurs as the message of the kingdom is extended to Gentiles. In sum, the parable of the wedding feast stood as a sharp and dire warning to the leaders of Israel who continued in their stubborn rebellion against God and His kingdom program.

23 Ibid.

WOES TO THOSE WHO SHUT OFF THE KINGDOM (MATTHEW 23:1–36)

The religious leaders of Israel sought to trap Jesus into making a mistake. With Matthew 23, Jesus goes on offense by delivering eight stinging "woes" against the scribes and Pharisees. The first "woe" in v. 13 has special implications for the kingdom:

> "But woe to you, scribes and Pharisees, hypocrites, because you shut off the kingdom of heaven from people; for you do not enter in yourselves, nor do you allow those who are entering to go in."

This verse parallels Matthew 11:12–13 where the religious leaders were bringing violence to the kingdom program. Since they resisted the King they were hindering the kingdom's coming and the ability of the people to enter it. The rejection of Jesus by Israel's leaders "effectually shut the door to the Kingdom offered by God through His Son upon earth."[24] But what is the full significance of Jesus' statement? Are the scribes and Pharisees shutting off the kingdom by hindering people from being saved, or is there a sense in which they are negatively affecting the timing of the kingdom's arrival? By rejecting Jesus and His message the religious leaders of Israel were steering people away from the salvation found in Jesus. But what Jesus describes goes beyond this. Jesus' declaration goes beyond personal salvation. As McClain points out:

> It must be observed here that, if the teaching of verse 13 were limited to the matter of personal salvation through Christ, it could hardly be true. For in this sense the Pharisees could shut no one out of the Kingdom of God. But they could and did, by their obstinate rejection of the Messianic King, shut both themselves and all the Israel of that generation out of His promised Kingdom, in the sense that its establishment is now, by the course of events, set at a second advent of the King.[25]

24 Ibid., 357.

25 Ibid., 358.

Since the coming of the kingdom was contingent on Israel's repentance, the religious leaders were hindering the kingdom's arrival and not allowing those who wanted to enter it, to enter. This is consistent with the truth of Matthew 11:12 that wicked men were taking the kingdom by force and doing violence to it.

HOPE FOR JERUSALEM (MATTHEW 23:37–39)

Coming off His eight woes to the religious leaders of Israel, Jesus presents a picture of both judgment and hope for Jerusalem. Jesus rebukes the people of Jerusalem for killing the prophets. This was tragic since Jesus, in tenderness, said He wanted to gather the Jewish people "the way a hen gathers her chicks under her wings." This shows Jesus presented a genuine offer of blessing to the Jewish people. The problem, though, rested with the obstinate people—"You were unwilling" (Matt 23:37). This unwillingness points to Israel's volitional refusal to believe in Christ and parallels Jesus' statement in Luke that Israel missed its "time of visitation" (Luke 19:44).

Because Israel killed the prophets and now were rejecting the Messiah, destruction would come: "Behold your house is being left to you desolate!" (Matt 23:38). Like Luke 19:41–44, this too is a prediction of the coming destruction of Jerusalem and its temple. This occurred in A.D. 70 when the Romans destroyed Jerusalem.

Jesus' next statement is strategic concerning the kingdom program and Israel's place in it. This judgment for Israel's unbelief will someday be reversed: "For I say to you, from now on you will not see Me until you say, 'BLESSED IS HE WHO COMES IN THE NAME OF THE LORD!'" This statement has been understood in three main ways. The first is that "Blessed is He..." is a cry of a reluctant and unsaved Israel at the time of its judgment. Allegedly, Israel will be forced to acknowledge Jesus is the Messiah. John Calvin stated, "He [Jesus] will not come to them [the Jews] until they cry out in fear—too late—at the sight of His Majesty."[26]

But this view is unnecessarily pessimistic. As Graham Stanton points out, "the difficulty with this interpretation is that Psalm 118.26 which is

26 John Calvin, *A Harmony of the Gospels Matthew, Mark and Luke, and James and Jude* vol. 3, trans. A.W. Morrison (Edinburgh: The Saint Andrews Press, 1972), 71.

cited in Matthew 23.39 is surely an expression of joyful praise rather than of fear or mourning."[27] Jesus quotes Psalm 118:26a, which is positive concerning Israel's relationship to God. The last part of Psalm 118:26 states, "We have blessed you from the house of the LORD." This is a happy and willing declaration from people who know the Lord, not the words of a reluctant group on their way to judgment. Craig Evans claims, "The rabbis understood Psalm 118:26 in reference to the day of redemption."[28] This negative judgment view also conflicts with various Scripture passages like Zechariah 12:10 and Romans 11:26–27 which speak of a coming positive response of the nation Israel to her Messiah.

A second view is that Jesus' words are an unqualified, straightforward prediction of Israel's salvation in a coming day. While the current generation had not believed and was facing national calamity, a coming generation of Israel will cry out in embracement of her Messiah. Craig S. Keener notes the hope in this passage:

> This passage reminds us that God does not forget his promises to his people.... Matthew places it among the woes of coming judgment, but in so doing transforms this into a promise of future hope.... Israel's restoration was a major theme of the biblical prophets and reappeared at least occasionally in early Christianity (Rom 11:26), though the emphasis of early Christian apologetic came to focus on the Gentile mission.[29]

This view has more going for it than the first. Other passages of Scripture predict a future salvation and restoration of Israel.

But there is another perspective, a third option that fits even better. In his study of Matthew 23:39 and Luke 13:35b, Dale Allison argues that Jesus' words include a "conditional" element and are more than an

27 Graham Stanton, *A Gospel for a New People: Studies in Matthew* (Edinburgh: T&T Clark, 1992), 249.

28 Craig Evans, "Prophecy and Polemic: Jews in Luke's Scriptural Apologetic," in *Luke and Scripture: The Function of Sacred Tradition in Luke–Acts*, ed. Craig A. Evans and James A. Sanders (Minneapolis: Fortress, 1993), 179 n. 33.

29 Craig S. Keener, *Matthew*, The IVP New Testament Commentary Series (Downers Grove, IL: InterVarsity, 1997), 341.

unqualified and straightforward declaration of salvation for Israel.[30] Yes, the deliverance of Israel would occur, so there is similarity with the second view above. But there also is a contingency element to this statement that highlights the importance of Israel's belief as a condition for Jesus' return and kingdom blessings. This view does more justice to the context and what God expects from Israel (Lev 26:40–45). Jesus' declaration of judgment for unbelief is probably not followed by an unconditional statement of salvation. But it is a call for belief so Israel can experience Jesus' return and presence. As Allison puts it:

> The text then means not, when the Messiah comes, his people will bless him, but rather, when his people bless him, the Messiah will come. In other words, the date of the redemption is contingent upon Israel's acceptance of the person and work of Jesus.[31]

Jesus' coming is contingent on Israel's acceptance of Jesus. Allison offers several reasons for this contingency perspective. The first is that "belief in the contingency of the time of the final redemption is well-attested in Jewish sources of the second century and later."[32] Second, the word "until" (*eos*) "can indicate a contingent state in Greek sentences in which the realization of the apodosis is dependent upon the realization of the protasis."[33] This means the Greek term *eos* "is not simply temporal" as in the sense of "until" but "properly conditional," more in the sense of "unless."[34] Thus, the people of Jerusalem will not see Jesus "unless/until" they say "Blessed is He..." Third, Allison holds that the structure of Matthew 23:39 "argues for the conditional interpretation."[35] He points out that several Jewish

30 Dale C. Allison Jr., "Matt. 23:39 = Luke 13:35b as a Conditional Prophecy," *Journal for the Study of the New Testament* 18 (1983): 81.

31 Ibid., 77.

32 Ibid. He lists many examples in pages 77–78.

33 Ibid.

34 Ibid.

35 Ibid., 79.

eschatological passages carry a conditional element along with an eschatological event. The structure is:

> (a) statement about the messianic advent with adverbial particle of negation attached ("The Son of David will not come")
>
> (b) conditional particle (עד)
>
> (c) condition to be met (in Israel) for fulfillment of the messianic advent (e.g., "no conceited men in Israel")[36]

He then says Matthew 23:39 (along with Luke 13:35b) "can be analyzed as having precisely the same structure":

> (a) statement about the messianic advent with adverbial particle of negation attached ("You will not see me," "me" being Jesus, the Messiah)
>
> (b) conditional particle (εως)
>
> (c) condition to be met (in Israel) for fulfillment of the messianic advent (those in Jerusalem utter, "Blessed is he who comes in the name of the Lord," and thereby acknowledge the person and work of Jesus).[37]

Allison then summarizes this point: "It therefore appears that the synoptic verse sets forth, in a traditional fashion, a condition for the great redemption."[38]

Fourth, Allison argues that the conditional view avoids the "pitfalls" of the other two options and is a better fit contextually. A permanent rejection of Israel does not fit the context of Matthew or the Bible. Also, an unqualified statement of future salvation is not satisfactory because just as there was a volitional rejection of Jesus, there must be a willing acceptance of Him to experience the blessings of His return.

36 Ibid., On this page he offers several such examples.

37 Ibid., 78-79.

38 Ibid., 80.

Thus, the better view is the "contingency" perspective in which Israel's restoration is dependent on Israel's belief in Jesus. As Allison states, "For Jesus affirms that, if she will, Jerusalem can, in the end, bless in the name of the Lord the one who will come, and her doing so, that is, her repentance, will lead to deliverance."[39]

The necessity of belief for eschatological blessing is found in Leviticus 26:40–45; Luke 19:41–44 and Acts 3:19–21. Acts 3 links Israel's belief with the return of Jesus and the "restoration of all things." Or as Allison puts it, Peter's words to the men of Israel "make the time of the Kingdom's coming hinge upon the repentance of God's people."[40] So there are other examples of contingency in connection with eschatological blessings for Israel.

Matthew 23:39 predicts a future salvation and deliverance of Israel. This coincides with the truth that Jesus' return is linked with Israel's belief in Him. The abandonment of Jerusalem will come to an end "when Jerusalem genuinely understands Psalm 118:26, the text shouted by the crowd at the triumphal entry."[41] Just as sinful rebellion against God's Messiah will result in terrible judgment, so too, embracement of the Messiah will lead to blessings and reversal of judgment.

Contingency in Matthew 23:39 exists. As Charles H. Talbert concludes in regard to this verse, "When his [Jesus'] people bless him, the messiah will come (cf. Acts 3:19–21). The date of redemption for the Matthean Jesus, then, is *contingent* on Israel's acceptance of him."[42]

39 Ibid.

40 Ibid., 81.

41 Turner, *Matthew*, 561.

42 Charles H. Talbert, *Matthew, in Commentaries on the New Testament* (Grand Rapids: Baker Academic, 2010), 260. Emphasis is mine.

Passages that Affirm Contingency in Regard to the Kingdom

Lev 26:40–45: Israel's dispersion will be reversed and reinstatement to the Abrahamic Covenant and the land will occur if/when national Israel repents.

Jer 3:12–18: Israel's repentance can lead to faithful shepherds, prosperity in the land, God's presence, nations coming to Jerusalem, and unification for the tribes of Israel.

Jer 18:1–10: God will change His plans for good or evil against a nation if it changes its ways.

1 Sam 13:13–14: If Saul obeyed, God would establish his kingdom forever, but disobedience removed this possibility.

2 Chron 7:14: God promises that if Israel will seek God, He will forgive Israel's sin and heal its land.

Matt 3:2; 4:17 10:5–7: The kingdom is presented as imminent to the people of Israel upon the condition of repentance.

Matt 11:14: If Israel will accept him, John the Baptist can fulfill the prophecy of Elijah's coming to restore the hearts of the fathers (Mal 4:5–6).

Luke 19:41–44: Israel could have "peace" on "this day" but missed its "time of visitation" resulting in coming national catastrophe.

Matt 23:39/Luke 13:35: Israel will not experience the presence of Jesus until the nation cries out to Him.

Acts 3:19–21: Israel's repentance and belief leads to kingdom conditions, the return of Jesus, and the restoration of all things.

Rom 11:11–15: Israel's belief results in greater world blessings.

CHAPTER 26

THE KINGDOM IN THE OLIVET DISCOURSE (MATTHEW 24–25 AND LUKE 21)

Jesus' most extended discussion of future events occurs in the Olivet Discourse. His message from the Mount of Olives is found in Matthew 24–25; Mark 13; and Luke 21. Here Jesus discusses the signs of His coming and the end of the age (Matt 24:3). These sections contain strategic information concerning the kingdom of God, particularly its timing. The contents of the Olivet Discourse are highly debated with almost every verse contested and interpreted differently by Bible scholars. I will not explain all the details or address every point of debate. Instead, this chapter will focus on how the Olivet Discourse directly intersects with the kingdom program. In sum, this chapter will argue that the kingdom in the Olivet Discourse is consistent with the kingdom program presented in the OT and the gospels. The kingdom is an earthly kingdom that comes to earth after a period of tribulation and after Jesus' second coming.

Much debate concerning the Olivet Discourse centers on the timing of its fulfillment. Some argue that all or most of the events in the Olivet Discourse were fulfilled with the destruction of Jerusalem in A.D. 70. Others emphasize a future fulfillment. And some see a combination of both A.D. 70 fulfillment and future fulfillment.[1] This latter perspective is our view although we believe the emphasis as a whole is on future fulfillment.

Several elements in the discourse are relevant to the kingdom program. In harmony with the OT expectations Jesus reveals the following scenario:

1 I see most of the discourse being fulfilled in the future with the exception of Luke 21:12–24a, which had a first-century fulfillment.

1. A unique period of tribulation is coming for Israel and the world.
2. This tribulation is followed immediately by the return of Jesus the Messiah.
3. The return of Jesus the Messiah means the rescue of Israel and the judgment of the nations.
4. After tribulation and judgment the kingdom is established and the righteous inherit the kingdom.

The stimulus for the Olivet Discourse was the disciples' comments about the beauty of the temple. This is followed by Jesus' startling statement that the temple would be destroyed. The curious disciples asked Jesus when that would occur and what would be the sign of His coming and the end of the age (Matt 24:3). The word for "coming" is *parousia*, which means "arrival" or "presence." Since the disciples were not anticipating Jesus' death they were not thinking explicitly of Jesus' second coming, but instead were asking Jesus when He would manifest himself as Israel's Messiah in power and glory. The manifestation of the Messiah would also mean the end of the present evil age and the inauguration of Messiah's kingdom and the blessings promised in the OT prophets.

The disciples were likely thinking of Zechariah 14 when they asked their question. This passage describes a coming siege of Jerusalem by the nations followed by the Lord's return to the Mount of Olives to rescue Jerusalem and establish His kingdom upon the earth. In Zechariah 14 the pattern is tribulation for Israel *then* the return of the Lord to rescue the people of Israel, and *then* God's kingdom.

Jesus discusses events such as wars, rumors of wars, famines and earthquakes. These events are "birth pangs" in that the end is near but not quite yet (see Matt 24:4–8). Jesus then tells of great persecution and the necessity of the gospel being preached to all nations before the end comes (Matt 24:9–14).

Next, Jesus speaks of an important event first spoken of in Daniel—the "abomination of desolation." Jesus said, "When you see the ABOMINATION OF DESOLATION which was spoken of through Daniel the prophet, standing in the holy place" (Matt 24:15). Daniel mentioned "abomination of desolation" in Daniel 11:31 and 12:11. He also referred to "abominations" in Daniel 9:27. This event is extremely perilous for Israel and its temple. This abomination of desolation leads to persecution for Israel since Jesus says, "then those who are in Judea must flee to the mountains" (24:16). No one in Judea should delay or return to gather their belongings. Women who are pregnant or nursing are particularly vulnerable to the dangers of this time. If this abomination occurs on the Sabbath or on winter this would make escape even more difficult (Matt 24:17–20). The language here is very Jewish. He then identifies this coming period as "great tribulation," one that is worse than any other in human history (24:21). If this period were to continue without God intervening no one would survive (24:22).

Significantly, Jesus expects a literal fulfillment of OT prophecies. He relies literally on the prophet Daniel and his predictions concerning a coming "abomination of desolation" and what this means for Israel. Jesus refers to persecution in the land of Israel and gives instruction to the people of Israel. Observe the Jewish elements so far:

- "Those who are in Judea"
- The "abomination of desolation" persecution of Israel spoken of by Daniel
- The "holy place" (i.e. Jewish temple)
- Praying that escape from persecution does not occur on the Sabbath

These points show Israel and Israel's land have future theological significance or Jesus would not mention them. Jesus sees the details of OT prophecy as still in need of literal fulfillment. He does not rule out the significance of the nation Israel or the temple. Instead, He sees the necessity of OT prophetic events occurring.

Certain cosmic signs and Jesus' return occur "immediately after the tribulation of those days" (24:29a). The sun and moon are darkened and stars fall from the sky (24:29b). Again, Jesus relies literally on passages like Isaiah 13 which predicted cosmic signs associated with the Day of the Lord. This then leads to the coming of Jesus—"And then the sign of the Son of Man will appear in the sky, and then all the tribes of the earth will mourn, and they will see the SON OF MAN COMING ON THE CLOUDS OF THE SKY with power and great glory" (24:30). This refers to Jesus' return to earth. Some hold that this concerns a coming of Jesus through the armies of Rome that destroyed Jerusalem in A.D. 70, but this cannot be the case. This is a direct, personal, and bodily return of Jesus, the kind of coming that the angels in Acts 1:11 predicted: "They [the angels] also said, 'Men of Galilee, why do you stand looking into the sky? This Jesus, who has been taken up from you into heaven, will come in just the same way as you have watched Him go into heaven.'"

That this must be a reference to Jesus' personal coming from heaven to earth also is seen in the *results* of this coming. The rest of the discourse reveals that the coming of Jesus in power and great glory involves the rescue of Israel and the judgment of the nations—events that occur on the earth.

Matthew 24:30 also states that with the coming of the Son of Man, "then all the tribes of the earth will mourn." Many understand the "tribes" to be all people groups of the earth. With this understanding all people groups on the earth will respond to Jesus' coming. Yet the term for "earth" is *gēs*, which can also be translated "land." Since the context is Jewish and Jesus already referred specifically to the land of Judea, He probably has the land of Israel in mind. If the proper translation is "all the tribes of the land will mourn" this could be an explicit reference to the salvation of the tribes of Israel predicted in Zechariah 12:10:

> "I will pour out on the house of David and on the inhabitants of Jerusalem, the Spirit of grace and of supplication, so that they will look on Me whom they have pierced; and they will mourn for Him, as one mourns for an only son, and they will weep bitterly over Him like the bitter weeping over a firstborn."

Zechariah 12:11–13 also describes how the various families within Israel will mourn for the returning Lord. So Zechariah 12 predicts a day when the families and clans of Israel will mourn over their Messiah. Since the context of Zechariah 12–14 is the salvation and rescue of Israel—"I will pour out... the Spirit of grace"—the mourning is from a repentant and saved Israel. Thus, Jesus probably has the salvation of Israel described in Zechariah 12 in mind.

Matthew 24:31 then states: "And He will send forth His angels with A GREAT TRUMPET and THEY WILL GATHER TOGETHER His elect from the four winds, from one end of the sky to the other." Earlier the people of Israel had been scattered because of persecution (24:9–22). This happens when the abomination of desolation in Jerusalem occurs. But with His coming, Jesus will use His angels to gather His elect ones, which in this context is Israel.

With Matthew 24:32–34 Jesus uses the example of a fig tree to alert His people concerning the timing of these events. Just as an observant person can know that a tender branch and the bearing of leaves of a fig tree means summer is near, so too, those who see the events Jesus is referring to can know that Jesus' coming is "near." The "generation" that sees the unfolding of the events described in Matthew 24 is the generation that will see the return of Jesus to earth. But according to Jesus, no one knows when this period of tribulation will break onto the scene—"But of that day and hour no one knows, not even the angels of heaven, nor the Son, but the Father alone" (Matt 24:36). No one knows when this period of tribulation that culminates in the coming of Jesus will take place, but when it does the generation who sees these events can grasp they are the ones who will see the coming of Jesus.

The sudden coming of this period will be like the days of Noah when judgment overcame the world (24:37–40). One should be "alert" (24:42) and act as a sensible slave and not a reckless one who acts wickedly and meets sudden awful judgment from the returning Lord (Matt 24:43–51).

JUDGMENT THAT FOLLOWS THE RETURN OF JESUS

Matthew 24 describes a unique period of tribulation immediately followed by the return of Jesus and the rescue of Israel. Then Matthew 25 focuses on the judgment and kingdom following these events. With 25:1 Jesus says, "Then the kingdom of heaven will be comparable to ten virgins who took their lamps, and went out to meet the bridegroom." Five of these virgins are wise, prepared for the bridegroom's coming, but five are foolish and are not prepared (see Matt 25:1–13). This parable shows that Jesus' return means blessings for those ready for Him, and exclusion from His presence for those who are not. Some will be ready for His kingdom and others will not. Then Jesus gives another parable, the parable of the talents, to reveal that rewards await those who use their resources for Him and judgment for those who do not (Matt 25:14–30).

Matthew 25:31 is strategic since it links the coming of the kingdom and Jesus' reign from the Davidic throne with the second coming of Jesus to earth: "But when the Son of Man comes in His glory, and all the angels with Him, then He will sit on His glorious throne." The "when... then" formula is significant here. *When* one thing occurs *then* another will occur. What is the when? It is the coming of the Son of Man (Jesus) to earth. It is a future coming in "glory" and with "all the angels." The *then* is Jesus' sitting "on His glorious throne." This glorious throne is Messiah's Davidic throne, the same throne the angel Gabriel said Jesus would reign upon forever (Luke 1:32–33).

This verse has great implications concerning the timing of the kingdom since Jesus explicitly states when His kingdom will begin. *It is at His second coming, and not before, when Jesus assumes the Davidic throne.* As Pond observes, "Matthew's use of ὅταν [when] followed by τότε [then] links two events in temporal sequence: after one thing happens, then the second thing happens. The Son of Man will not sit on His glorious throne until He comes in His glory."[2] This shows that "Jesus' reign on His throne is yet future; the present age is not the age of the messianic kingdom."[3]

We do not have to speculate concerning the timing of Jesus' assumption of the Davidic throne since Jesus tells us when this will happen. It follows His second coming to earth in glory. At this time "all the nations will be gathered before Him" (25:32), another event that is future. Jesus will judge the nations of the earth right after He returns. The prophet Joel predicted such a judgment:

> "For behold, in those days and at that time,
> When I restore the fortunes of Judah and Jerusalem,
> I will gather all the nations
> And bring them down to the valley of Jehoshaphat.
> Then I will enter into judgment with them there
> On behalf of My people and My inheritance, Israel,
> Whom they have scattered among the nations;
> And they have divided up My land" (Joel 3:1–2).

2 Eugene W. Pond, "The Background and Timing of the Judgment of the Sheep and the Goats," *Bibliotheca Sacra* 159 (2002): 212.

3 Ibid., 213.

At the time of Israel's restoration God will judge the nations on behalf of Israel. Never before in history have the nations of the earth been gathered to be judged by the Messiah. This judgment will take place when Jesus returns.

Matthew 25:34 states that those who pass the judgment will "inherit the kingdom" prepared for them. These believers were not in the kingdom before this judgment but they will enter it *after* this judgment. This too indicates a future kingdom, not a present one.

In sum, the Olivet Discourse of Matthew 24–25 places the establishment of the kingdom after the events of the tribulation, the second coming of Jesus, the rescue of Israel, and the judgment of the nations. This is consistent with the picture offered in the OT.

LUKE AND THE OLIVET DISCOURSE

Luke 21 offers additional details relevant to the kingdom program in Jesus' Olivet Discourse. For example, Luke 21:20–24 gives specific information concerning the coming destruction of the temple in A.D. 70. But first, let us start with Luke 21:10–11.

Like Matthew 24:4–8, Luke 21:10–11 details events concerning the future tribulation period which include wars, earthquakes, famines, plagues, and cosmic signs. Jesus offers an important chronological indicator, though, with v. 12, "But before all these things..." Jesus says certain events take place *before* the tribulation period. Luke 21:12–24 probably describes events of the first century leading up to and including the destruction of Jerusalem by the Romans in A.D. 70. Verses 12–19 predict persecution and then vv. 20–24 detail the destruction of Jerusalem.

Jesus says, "But when you see Jerusalem surrounded by armies, then recognize that her desolation is near" (Luke 21:20). The presence of armies surrounding Jerusalem means the destruction of the city is at hand. Those who are in Judea or Jerusalem must leave and those outside the city should not try to enter it (Luke 21:21). Jesus describes this period when Jerusalem is destroyed as "days of vengeance" (v. 22). With v. 23 Jesus also says "there will be great distress upon the land and wrath to this people." This leads to the destruction of Jerusalem:

> "and they will fall by the edge of the sword, and will be led captive into all the nations; and Jerusalem will be trampled under

foot by the Gentiles until the times of the Gentiles are fulfilled" (Luke 21:24).

This period of "vengeance," "distress," and "wrath" in Luke 21:20–24 that results in the destruction of Jerusalem is distinct from the period described in Matthew 24, which results in the salvation and rescue of Israel. Matthew 24:31 speaks of the elect being gathered by the angels. Thus, there is a distinction between the "days of vengeance" upon Israel described in Luke 21:20–24 and the rescue of Israel detailed in Matthew 24.

The last part of Luke 21:24 says Jerusalem falls by the sword, is led captive to all the nations, and is trampled by the Gentiles. But this awful experience is not permanent. The word "until" [*achris hou*] indicates reversal and places a time limit on this period of wrath and distress—"until the times of the Gentiles are fulfilled." The "times of the Gentiles" is the period of Gentile domination over Israel and Israel's land. This period will come to an end. Gentile oppression must be reversed and Jerusalem restored. Eric Franklin rightly asserts the destruction of Jerusalem spoken of in 21:24 "is not the last word"[4] for the nation Israel. In fact, its restoration is still to come:

> In Jesus, the promises to David have received their guarantee (1.32–33) so that the restoration of the kingdom to Israel is still part of the Christian hope (Acts 1:6). At the moment, Jerusalem's house is forsaken (13.35), but this is only until 'the times of the Gentiles are fulfilled' (21.24) when, at the day of her restoration, she will cry, 'Blessed be he who comes in the name of the Lord' (13.35). The destruction of Jerusalem in no way contradicts Luke's theme, for he is confident of her restoration and future supremacy.[5]

Jerusalem is important in God's future plans. Luke 21:20–24 speaks of a severe destruction of Jerusalem with long-lasting negative consequences for Israel. But the time of Gentile domination of Israel and Jerusalem is temporary. A day is coming when Jerusalem will be restored and established as the

4 Eric Franklin, *Christ the Lord: A Study in the Purpose and Theology of Luke–Acts* (London: SPCK, 1975), 130.

5 Ibid.

capital city of God's earthly kingdom. "The implication," as Buzzard notes, "is that Jerusalem, as capital of the Messiah's kingdom, will not remain under Gentile control indefinitely.... the time for Jerusalem's redemption will have arrived."[6]

THE NEARNESS OF THE KINGDOM—AGAIN! (LUKE 21:31)

So you also, when you see these things happening, recognize that the kingdom of God is near (Luke 21:31).

With Luke 21:31 Jesus says certain events must transpire before the kingdom would be near again. Jesus predicted false christs, wars, earthquakes, famines, and cosmic signs (8–11). With v. 12, He speaks of events that will take place *before* the events of 8–11. He says, "But before all these things," and then predicts persecution (12–19) and the destruction of Jerusalem (20–23). The destruction here is a reference to A.D. 70 when the Romans destroyed Jerusalem. Thus, what Jesus discusses in 12–23 will occur before the events mentioned in vv. 8–11. The "times of the Gentiles" mentioned in v. 24 covers the time period between the destruction of the temple in A.D. 70 and the Gentile domination of Jerusalem until Jesus comes again and Jerusalem is restored. With vv. 25–27, Jesus again discusses events in the coming tribulation. This period involves cosmic signs, terrifying waves, and the Son of Man coming in a cloud with power and great glory.

The Fig Tree Example

With Luke 21:29–30 Jesus gives the parable of the fig tree: "Then He told them a parable: 'Behold the fig tree and all the trees; as soon as they put forth leaves, you see it and know for yourselves that summer is now near.'" Seeing certain things reveals something else is soon to happen. Just as observing a fig tree putting forth leaves reveals summer is near, so too the presence of certain events reveals the kingdom's coming is imminent:

6 Anthony Buzzard, "Acts 1:6 and the Eclipse of the Biblical Kingdom," *Evangelical Quarterly* 66 (1994): 206.

> So you also, when you see these things happening, recognize that the kingdom of God is near (Luke 21:31).

The mention of "these things" refers to the eschatological events Jesus just discussed in Luke 21. When one sees cosmic signs, oceanic disturbances, and other occurrences, one can know the kingdom is near. Until these events occur the kingdom is not near. This shows *the kingdom of God is future and will be near again only after the eschatological events of Luke 21*.

SUMMARY OF THE KINGDOM IN THE OLIVET DISCOURSE

How does the kingdom program relate do the Olivet Discourse? Jesus restates key OT prophecies to show that what the prophets wrote about the kingdom is still in effect. Jesus' death is just a few days away but the earthly kingdom of the Messiah will still be established. Matters such as tribulation, destruction of the Jerusalem temple, persecution of Israel, cosmic signs, the coming of Messiah, the judgment of Israel, the judgment of the nations, and the establishment of the kingdom of God must take place first. In harmony with other kingdom passages, the Olivet Discourse presents the kingdom as both future and earthly and coincides with the return of Jesus the Messiah.

CHAPTER 27

THE KINGDOM AND THE MESSIAH'S PASSION

THE KINGDOM AND THE LAST SUPPER

The kingdom was a major emphasis for Jesus in the days leading to His death. In an upper room at the Last Supper the kingdom was very much on Jesus' mind. He mentions "kingdom" five times–Luke 22:16, 18; Mark 14:25; Luke 22:29, 30. Two references occur during the prelude to the supper and three during it. We start with the first two references in Luke's account:

> When the hour had come, He reclined at the table, and the apostles with Him. And He said to them, "I have earnestly desired to eat this Passover with you before I suffer; for I say to you, I shall never again eat it until it is fulfilled in the kingdom of God" (Luke 22:14–16).

> And when He had taken a cup and given thanks, He said, "Take this and share it among yourselves; for I say to you, I will not drink of the fruit of the vine from now on until the kingdom of God comes" (Luke 22:17–18).

Jesus desired to eat the Passover meal with His disciples before He suffered. He then connects the Passover with the kingdom by saying He would never again eat the Passover with the disciples "until it is fulfilled in the kingdom of God" (22:16) and "until the kingdom of God comes" (22:18). This reveals that time would pass before He would celebrate a Passover feast again with His followers. The two uses of "until" in vv. 16 and 18 point to a time period before the kingdom of God is fulfilled or comes. Again, this shows the kingdom of God was not inaugurated yet. If the kingdom already arrived Jesus would not be speaking of it as a future occurrence. This is reinforced later when Jesus links the kingdom with the apostles ruling over the twelve tribes of a restored Israel, which is also a future event (22:30).

Jesus broke bread and gave it to His disciples, and then offered them the cup saying, "This cup which is poured out for you is the new covenant in My blood" (Luke 22:20). The "new covenant" harkens back to the covenant's initial promise in Jeremiah 31:31–34. Jesus' death establishes the New Covenant. Jesus' wording indicates a gap in time between the establishing of the New Covenant and the kingdom of God. The New Covenant would be established with Jesus' death in a few hours, but the kingdom's coming is distant at this point. This shows the arrival of the New Covenant's inauguration cannot be equated with the coming of the kingdom, since the arrival of the former did not mean the arrival of the latter. This is similar to Acts 1:5–7 in which Jesus promised the arrival of the New Covenant ministry of the Holy Spirit in a few days, while indicating the kingdom's arrival was in the distant future.

Jesus' references to the kingdom at the Last Supper seemed to spark a controversy among the disciples who wanted to establish prestigious positions for themselves in it:

> And there arose also a dispute among them as to which one of them was regarded to be greatest. And He said to them, "The kings of the Gentiles lord it over them; and those who have authority over them are called 'Benefactors.' But it is not this way with you…." (Luke 22:24–26a).

Jesus instructed the disciples that greatness in the kingdom is not granted the world's way. Greatness in God's kingdom comes through humble service, the kind of service Jesus will soon exemplify at the cross. So not only is Jesus thinking of the kingdom, the apostles are too, although their conception of how to be great in it is skewed. Yet, even as Jesus corrects the misconception concerning greatness, He affirms that the kingdom of God is future and earthly:

> "You are those who have stood by Me in My trials; and just as My Father has granted Me a kingdom, I grant you that you may

> eat and drink at My table in My kingdom, and you will sit on thrones judging the twelve tribes of Israel" (Luke 22:28–30).

The message here is similar to Matthew 19:28 when Jesus told the twelve apostles they would rule over the twelve tribes of Israel when the world is regenerated. With Matthew 19:28 the reigning on twelve thrones was clearly in the future, in the age to come. Now Jesus again reaffirms this promise on the brink of His death. The nation Israel will be united and restored in Messiah's kingdom, and the apostles will have key positions of authority in the kingdom.

Jesus also declared, "Just as My Father has granted Me a kingdom." This shows Jesus' kingdom authority comes from the Father and harkens back to Luke 19:12 where Jesus likened himself to a "nobleman" who "went to a distant country to receive a kingdom for himself, and then return." The Father grants Jesus authority for a kingdom reign when Jesus returns to earth.

Jesus then says He will do for His followers what the Father has done for Him: "I grant that you may eat and drink at My table in My kingdom." Just as the Father granted Jesus His kingdom, Jesus grants the apostles benefits of this kingdom, a banquet that includes eating and drinking. Peter Nelson says, "Subjunctive ἔσθητε [may eat] and πίνητε [drink] clearly anticipate *a future* meal at Jesus' table in his kingdom."[1] This reaffirms the truth that the future kingdom of the Messiah involves the reign of His followers.

The mention of eating and drinking in Jesus' kingdom is not metaphorical. Just moments before, Jesus said He would not eat and drink with the apostles again until the coming of the kingdom of God (22:14–18). He was referring to a tangible Passover meal. Just as Jesus' kingdom is a tangible earthly kingdom, so too will the celebration banquets in it be real and tangible as well. No Platonic dualism between spirit and matter is present in Jesus' kingdom. The kingdom is not only about eating and drinking (see Rom 14:17), but it certainly includes it.

Then Jesus mentions that the apostles "will sit on thrones judging the twelve tribes of Israel." The future sense of "will sit" again confirms that the

1 Peter K. Nelson, "Luke 22:29–30 and the Time Frame for Dining and Ruling," *Tyndale Bulletin* 44 (1993): 352. Emphasis is in the original.

kingdom Jesus is discussing is future and points to a future age.[2] Their position on "thrones" leads to judging the tribes of Israel. Again, this is not metaphorical language, but fitting positions for the twelve apostles as reward for following Jesus in the present. Standing by Jesus in His trials results in judicial positions of authority over Israel when the kingdom comes.

Some have tried to downplay the straightforward language of this passage by claiming the twelve tribes of Israel is really a reference to the church. But as Nelson has observed, the reference to the "twelve tribes" in 22:30 refers to the Jewish people. There is no use of "Israel" in the Synoptics or Acts "which does not refer to the Jewish people/nation, the Israel of the OT.... Thus it does not appear that Luke attaches a new Christian meaning to the various terms and phrases that have traditionally been used to describe Israel of old...."[3] In light of Luke's literal sense of "Israel," Luke 22:30 is speaking of national Israel:

> It is best to take the "twelve tribes of Israel" in Luke 22:30b as referring to the Israel of the OT, the people of God. Luke does not envision a new Israel which becomes marked off from Israel of old, but an Israel which has returned to its roots and whose Messiah has come welcoming all who would repent and believe.[4]

In a similar way, Lewis and Demarest conclude Luke 22:29–30 has implications for restored institutional Israel: "Does this activity not presume the future restoration of the twelve tribes in institutional Israel?"[5]

What follows shortly after the promise of reward concerns how the apostles should operate in the period between Jesus' death and His coming again:

> And He said to them, "When I sent you out without money belt and bag and sandals, you did not lack anything, did you?" They

2 "Moreover, καθήσεσθε [you will sit] necessarily anticipates a future realisation, and the timing for the present participle κρίνοντες [judging] is contemporaneous with καθήσεσθε [you will sit]." Ibid.

3 P. K. Nelson, *Leadership and Discipleship: A Study of Luke 22:24–30*, SBL Dissertation Series 138 (Atlanta: Scholars Press, 1994), 221–22.

4 Ibid., 223.

5 Gordon R. Lewis and Bruce A. Demarest, *Integrative Theology: Historical, Biblical, Systematic, Apologetic, Practical* (Grand Rapids: Zondervan, 1994), 3:411.

> said, "No, nothing." And He said to them, "But now, whoever has a money belt is to take it along, likewise also a bag, and whoever has no sword is to sell his coat and buy one. For I tell you that this which is written must be fulfilled in Me, 'AND HE WAS NUMBERED WITH TRANSGRESSORS'; for that which refers to Me has its fulfillment." They said, "Lord, look, here are two swords." And He said to them, "It is enough" (Luke 22:35–38).

Jesus tells His followers they need money belts and swords. He also asks the apostles if they remember earlier when He sent them out *without* money belts, bags, and sandals. They affirmed this and their understanding that they had everything they needed back then. This situation refers back to Matthew 10 when Jesus told the apostles not to take these basic items with them when they proclaimed the nearness of the kingdom to Israel. After being told not to enter the towns of the Samaritans and Gentiles, but only the cities of Israel (Matt 10:5–7), Jesus said:

> Do not acquire gold, or silver, or copper for your money belts, or a bag for your journey, or even two coats, or sandals, or a staff; for the worker is worthy of his support (Matt 10:9–10).

Note the change in conditions for the apostles from Matthew 10 to Luke 22:

> **Matthew 10**: Jesus tells apostles they do not need money belts, bags, coats, sandals or staff.
>
> **Luke 22**: Jesus tells the apostles they need money belts, bags, and a sword.

Why the dramatic shift? Why does Jesus now say they need food supplies and a sword when earlier they did not? *It is because of the radically different conditions that will soon arrive.* McClain notes, "These are radical words from the lips of Christ, suggesting a radical change of conditions just at hand.... What He had formerly commanded them *not* to take (Matt 10:9–10), He now commands them to take!"[6] But why this change? The early commissioning of the apostles for kingdom proclamation to Israel operated under divine protection and blessing since the Messiah was personally with them.

6 McClain, *The Greatness of the Kingdom*, 372.

No illness happened and they needed nothing. "For friends and relatives, healing was available without reserve (Matt. 8:14–16)."[7] Also, "If food and drink were lacking, the miracle-working power of the King was sufficient for the emergency (John 2:1–11; 6:1–15)."[8]

But the removal of Jesus' presence will change matters significantly. As McClain explains, "What our Lord here enjoins upon His disciples is simply the duty of *self-preservation* as the need may arise under the new conditions."[9] This shows conditions will be quite different for the apostles compared to their earlier ministry.

So the kingdom is a major theme at the Last Supper. Even on the brink of His death, Jesus looks beyond the cross to the glories of the kingdom and a restored Israel and how His friends will be there fellowshipping and ruling with Him. Yet he also prepares them for more difficult conditions between His two comings.

THE KINGDOM AND JESUS' TRIALS

The kingdom of God topic also arises in the trials of Jesus. At His religious trial, Caiaphas the high priest demanded Jesus answer whether He was the Messiah, the Son of God (Matt 26:63). Jesus' answer was both dramatic and stunning:

> Jesus said to him, "You have said it yourself; nevertheless I tell you hereafter you will see THE SON OF MAN SITTING AT THE RIGHT HAND OF POWER AND COMING ON THE CLOUDS OF HEAVEN" (26:64).

Yes. Jesus is the Messiah, the Son of God. Jesus appeals to the messianic passage of Daniel 7:13 that tells of Messiah's coming kingdom. But not only this, Caiaphas will one day see the coming of Jesus' kingdom.

Next, according to John's account, Pilate asked Jesus, "Are you the King of the Jews?" (John 18:33). Jesus responded:

---

7 Ibid., 371.

8 Ibid.

9 Ibid., 372. Emphasis in original.

> "My kingdom is not of this world. If My kingdom were of this world, then My servants would be fighting so that I would not be handed over to the Jews; but as it is, My kingdom is not of this realm" (John 18:36).

Some have understood Jesus' answer to mean Jesus' kingdom is only a spiritual kingdom. Yet this is a misunderstanding. When Pilate asked his question, he was not looking at this issue from a Jewish theological standpoint, and Jesus' answer was not the same as the one He offered to Caiaphas. Jesus does not bring up the kingdom passage of Daniel 7.

Pilate's concerns are solely political. He wants peace. He wants to know if Jesus is an immediate political threat to Rome. The religious leaders told him this was the case but he wants to know for himself. Jesus is aware of this. So when He addressed Pilate Jesus was not answering the procurator in the same way He answered the Jew, Caiaphas. Jesus answers Pilate's concern by informing him that He is not attempting a political takeover with His followers at this time.

Jesus' statement, "My kingdom is not of this realm," must be understood correctly. The preposition *ek* ("of" or "out of") refers to "source." The source of Jesus' kingdom is not found in this earthly realm because if it were, Jesus' followers would be fighting. Hours earlier Jesus told Peter to put his sword away after Peter struck a person involved with Jesus' arrest (see John 18:10–11). On the other hand, with Jesus' second coming His kingdom will have heaven as its source (see Matt 25:31). At that time Jesus will come as a political and military conqueror and use a sword to smite the nations that challenge Him (see Rev 19:15).

So at this point Pilate need not worry about a political takeover from Jesus. Pilate told the Jewish leaders, "I find no guilt in Him" (John 18:38). Pilate even "made efforts to release Him" (John 19:12). Jesus' statement that His kingdom is not of this world does not mean Jesus will never establish an earthly kingdom or that His kingdom is only spiritual. Concerning John 18:36, Middleton correctly notes, "A careful reading... suggests that Jesus is not identifying his kingdom with heaven; rather, he is locating the origin of his power.... Jesus's kingdom... is *from* God, who reigns from heaven, but it is *for* the earth."[10]

AUTHORITY AND THE GREAT COMMISSION

The King goes to the cross and dies. He completes His role as the Suffering Servant and Lamb who dies for His people (see Isa 53). His blood brings atonement and is the basis for human salvation and cosmic reconciliation (see Col 1:20). His resurrection then vindicates who He is. With Matthew 28, Jesus appears to His disciples and friends. In 28:18 He declares, "All authority has been given to Me in heaven and on earth." The word for "authority" is *exousia* and refers to the right to rule. Jesus' death, resurrection and ascension result in Jesus having sovereign authority over everything in heaven and earth. This authority also is the basis for the disciples' mandate to "make disciples of all the nations" (19). Jesus' authority is linked with His resurrection and position at the right hand of the Father predicted in Psalm 110:1. As McClain observes, "It is in this glorious capacity that our Lord Jesus Christ sits today upon the throne of the universe."[11] Jesus' assumption of the Davidic throne on earth is still future (see Matt 19:28; 25:31), yet His authority to rule as Messiah is granted to Him. The authority to rule will culminate in a kingdom reign.

THE KINGDOM AT THE END OF THE GOSPELS

The early chapters of the Gospels contained several proclamations of the nearness of the kingdom because the Son of David appeared (Matt 3:2; 4:17: 10:5–7; Mark 1:15; Luke 4:43). Along with this proclamation were widespread miracles to the cities of Israel accomplished by both Jesus and His apostles. But with the rejection of the Messiah by the people and leaders of Israel, these proclamations gave way to Jesus' emphasis on the cross. Discussions concerning the kingdom became future-oriented (see Matt 25:31; Luke 19:11; 21:31). Thus, the kingdom that started out as "at

10 Middleton, *A New Heaven and a New Earth*, 247.

11 McClain, *The Greatness of the Kingdom*, 33.

hand" or "near" transitioned to being more distant. As Herman Ridderbos pointed out,

> While at the beginning of his preaching all emphasis is laid upon the presence of the fulfillment, as is seen in connection with his miracles; at the end of the synoptic kerygma everything is again focused upon the future. The coming of the kingdom is then referred to in such an absolutely future sense as if it *had not* yet come....[12]

The drama of the kingdom program continues. The story now shifts to the book of Acts.

12 Ridderbos, *The Coming of the Kingdom*, 468. Mark Saucy states, "Kingdom sayings at the beginning of Matthew's Gospel should not be 'leveled' with those of the end and vice versa." "The Kingdom of God Sayings in Matthew," 175.

CHAPTER

28 THE KINGDOM IN ACTS

With Acts the kingdom program transitions from Jesus' earthly ministry to His exaltation to the right hand of God and the spread of the gospel through His church. Yet the necessity of a kingdom for Israel is still explicitly taught. The term "kingdom" is found eight times in Acts—1:3, 6; 8:12; 14:22; 19:8; 20:25; 28:23, 31. While this is not an insignificant amount of uses, it is much less than the many references found in the gospels, including the forty-four references in Luke's Gospel. Acts begins with Jesus emphasizing the kingdom (1:3) and ends with Paul proclaiming the kingdom to Jewish leaders (Acts 28:17–31). The starting point for the kingdom program in Acts is the Mount of Olives and Jesus' last words to His disciples before His ascension to heaven.

THE TIMING OF THE RESTORATION OF THE KINGDOM TO ISRAEL (ACTS 1:3–8)

We are often fascinated by 'famous last words' of important people. With Acts we have the last words of Jesus before He ascends to heaven. As Acts 1 opens, the kingdom is on the minds of both Jesus and the apostles. Jesus is teaching about it and the apostles are asking about it. The exchange here reveals how the apostles and Jesus view the kingdom's timing and relationship to Israel at this crucial time in history.

Luke begins by saying Jesus "presented Himself alive after His suffering, by many convincing proofs... over a period of forty days" (Acts 1:3a). The primary issue Jesus instructed the apostles on was the kingdom—"speaking of the things concerning the kingdom of God" (Acts 1:3b). We are not privy to what Jesus specifically said but He spent precious time on this topic. Jesus remained forty days with His disciples and His message could be encapsulated into one main thing—the kingdom.

Jesus commanded the disciples to stay in Jerusalem and wait for the baptism with the Spirit that would occur "not many days from now" (Acts 1:4–5). The coming of the New Covenant ministry of the Holy Spirit was just days away. This promise may have stimulated the question of the apostles that also concerned timing—"Lord, is it at this time You are restoring the kingdom to Israel?" (1:6). Since the coming of the Holy Spirit was very close, perhaps the kingdom was near too. This question carries several important implications and offers a glimpse into how the apostles viewed the kingdom of God.

First, the apostles expected a restoration of the kingdom to Israel. Even opponents of a restoration of national Israel often admit this. On the day of Jesus' ascension the apostles are thinking of the kingdom and Israel. This is not surprising since earlier they spent much time proclaiming the nearness of the kingdom specifically to Israel (see Matt 10:5–7). Whatever view one holds of the kingdom, this fact must be grappled with. The apostles who had their eyes opened and received forty days of kingdom instruction from Jesus were expecting a literal restoration of the kingdom to Israel.

Second, the word "restore" (*apokathistemi*) reveals the apostles expected continuity with Israel's prior kingdom. This term means "to bring or restore something to its former state." Restoration implies prior existence for only that which once existed can be restored. Israel was a kingdom but the kingdom ended because of disobedience. Yet it will be brought back. Insight into the term "restore" can also be gleaned from Acts 3:21 which also mentions "restoration" ("restoration of all things") in a heavily future context associated with the second coming of Jesus. The restoration that the apostles expected is the restoration that will occur with Jesus' return.

Third, the question of the apostles concerned the *timing* of the kingdom—"Lord, is it *at this time* You are restoring the kingdom to Israel?" This is a "when" question, not a "what" question. The apostles are not asking Jesus to define the kingdom or to explain its nature. They want to know *when* it was coming.

Fourth, the apostles did not view the kingdom as being in operation or inaugurated at this point. Instead, they were looking for its coming. This highlights a theme found in Luke/Acts that God's people are expecting a restored kingdom for Israel that is still to come. This is true at the beginning and end of Jesus' earthly ministry:

Expectations Before Jesus' Ministry	Expectations at End of Jesus' Ministry
Zacharias was anticipating "Salvation FROM OUR ENEMIES, And FROM THE HAND OF ALL WHO HATE US" (Luke 1:68).	Joseph of Arimathea was one "who was waiting for the kingdom of God" (Luke 23:51).
Simeon was "looking for the consolation of Israel" (Luke 2:25).	Two men on the way to Emmaus stated, "But we were hoping that it was He who was going to redeem Israel" (Luke 24:21).
Anna was speaking to "all those who were looking for the redemption of Jerusalem" (Luke 2:38).	The apostles ask, "Lord is it at this time You are restoring the kingdom to Israel?" (Acts 1:6).

In Acts 3:19–21 Peter will announce that the kingdom awaits Israel's belief in Jesus. It is at that time the hope of the kingdom becomes a reality.

This question concerning the timing of the kingdom in Acts 1:6 also confirms that when the apostles preached the nearness of the kingdom earlier, they were not teaching the kingdom had arrived (see Matt 10:5–7). If they had, they would not now be asking a question concerning when it would come. Why ask about the coming of something that had already arrived?

It is highly probable after forty days of instruction from the risen Jesus that the apostles had a proper grasp on the nature of the kingdom of God. They were not misguided as some have claimed. Raymond O. Zorn, for example, states that Acts 1:6 indicates "the last flicker on the apostles' part... concerning their hope that national Israel would once again be a political theocracy."[1] According to N. T. Wright, Acts 1:6 shows the disciples "had

1 Raymond O. Zorn, *Christ Triumphant: Biblical Perspectives on His Church and Kingdom* (Carlisle, PA: Banner of Truth Trust, 1997), 50.

not grasped the radical nature of Jesus' agenda."[2] But such assertions could only be true if the disciples totally missed the nature of the kingdom of God after forty days of instruction from the risen Jesus, and if Jesus was not effective in His instruction to them. Had not Jesus already opened their eyes concerning how the scriptures pointed to Him? (see Luke 24:27, 31). Were the forty days of kingdom instruction by Jesus a failure? The apostles were not misguided. They were not ignorant on this topic. We cannot look down on them and say, "How ignorant! The apostles still think the kingdom is political and national." Instead, the apostles properly understood the nature of the kingdom and Jesus was effective in communicating this to them. We do not need to question the intelligence of the disciples. Nor do we need to doubt the instructional ability of Jesus. McKnight is correct when he states, "Since Jesus was such a good teacher, we have every right to think that the impulsive hopes of his audience were on target."[3] Paul W. Walaskay rightly notes Jesus said nothing that "dampened the hope of his disciples for a national kingdom."[4]

As the exchange continues, the issue that was not known at this point was the *timing* of the kingdom:

> He [Jesus] said to them, "It is not for you to know times or epochs which the Father has fixed by His own authority; but you will receive power when the Holy Spirit has come upon you; and you shall be My witnesses both in Jerusalem, and in all Judea and Samaria, and even to the remotest part of the earth" (Acts 1:7–8).

Several points are worthy of note here. First, Jesus assumes the accuracy of the apostles' understanding. The apostles were expecting the restoration of the kingdom to national Israel, and Jesus gives no indication their understanding is incorrect. If the apostles were wrong would not Jesus correct

2 N. T. Wright, *Jesus and the Victory of God* (Minneapolis, MN: Fortress Press, 1996), 463.

3 Scot McKnight, *A New Vision for Israel* (Grand Rapids: Eerdmans, 1999), 130–31.

4 Paul W. Walaskay, *'And So We Came to Rome': The Political Perspective of St Luke* (Cambridge: Cambridge University Press, 1983), 17. Blaising writes, "The national hope of Israel in their question appears as a given. The question has to do only with the time of fulfillment." Blaising and Bock, *Progressive Dispensationalism* (Grand Rapids: Bridgepoint Books, 1993), 237. See also David L. Tiede, "The Exaltation of Jesus and the Restoration of Israel in Acts 1," *Harvard Theological Review* 79 (1986): 278.

their misunderstanding? Jesus often corrected erroneous thinking. Would this not be the perfect time, just before His ascension, to calibrate an erroneous view? If He does not, He will ascend to heaven with His trusted disciples being misguided on a topic of great importance. But no correction occurs.

Second, the apostles were not to know the timing of the restoration of the kingdom to Israel. That was only for the Father to know. This is similar to what Jesus said concerning the time period of His coming in the Olivet Discourse: "But of that day and hour no one knows, not even the angels of heaven, nor the Son, but the Father alone" (Matt 24:36).

Third, Jesus tells the apostles what they were to focus on—"but you will receive power when the Holy Spirit has come upon you; and you shall be My witnesses both in Jerusalem, and in all Judea and Samaria, and even to the remotest part of the earth" (1:8). Since the timing of the kingdom is not to be known and is in the indefinite future, the apostles needed to focus their attention to the immediate task at hand—the proclamation of the gospel to the ends of the earth. The Father will restore the kingdom to Israel according to His timetable, but the apostles needed to focus on their responsibility. This indicates that there will be a gap of time between the proclamation of the gospel to the nations and the establishment of the kingdom on earth. The former was to be their focus while the latter would come in the Father's timing.

Some who deny the concept of a restoration of national Israel have offered a different understanding of Jesus' response in Acts 1:8. Some believe that Jesus redefines the kingdom expectation, linking it with Spirit-filled gospel proclamation. For example, O. Palmer Robertson states, "The kingdom of God would be restored to Israel in the rule of the Messiah, which would be realized by the working of the Holy Spirit through the disciples of Christ as they extended their witness to the ends of the earth."[5] Allegedly, as the kingdom message was carried to the world through the Holy Spirit, Israel's kingdom was being restored. To support this view, Robertson ties the question of the disciples in Acts 1:6 with Jesus' statement in 1:8 that the disciples would receive the power of the Holy Spirit and they would be

5 O. Palmer Robertson, *The Israel of God: Yesterday, Today, and Tomorrow* (P&R Publishing, 2000), 134. Wright states that "Jesus reaffirms the expectation, but alters the interpretation." N. T. Wright, *The New Testament and the People of God* (Minneapolis: Fortress, 1992), 374.

Jesus' witnesses throughout the earth: "This statement [in 1:8] should not be regarded as peripheral to the question asked by the disciples. Instead, it is germane to the whole issue of the restoration of the kingdom to Israel."[6]

But this view that Jesus redefines the kingdom expectation to worldwide proclamation of the gospel is not accurate. The apostles asked about the timing of the kingdom for Israel and Jesus responds in two ways. The first response addresses timing and the second addresses what they were to be concerned with. In regard to timing—"It is not for you to know times or epochs." Jesus does not avoid their question. But this is not information they needed to know right now. He then tells them what they should focus on—gospel proclamation to the world. *But a statement concerning what they should focus on is not a redefinition of their expectation.* To use an example, imagine a father who tells his two teenage sons that he has a camping trip planned for them as a reward, but it will be a surprise as to when it happens. One day the sons say, "Dad are we going camping now?" The father's response is "I'm not telling you when we are going. It's a surprise. But what I want you to focus on now is doing your chores and schoolwork well." The father's statement is not a dodging of the question. Nor does it mean the camping trip is redefined to be chores and schoolwork. The father's response is a statement that chores and schoolwork are to be their focus until the camping trip arrives. The same is true for the kingdom. The apostles were to focus on the task at hand and the Father would determine the kingdom's timing. Or to put another way:

> <u>Question of Apostles:</u> When is the kingdom being restored to Israel?
>
> <u>Answer of Jesus:</u> That's not for you to know. Only the Father knows.
>
> <u>Present Implication for Apostles:</u> Focus on the task of gospel proclamation to the world.

There is another problem with the view that Jesus corrected or redefined the kingdom expectation of the apostles. If the disciples' concept of the kingdom was misguided or wrong then their earlier message of the kingdom

6 Ibid., 133.

to the cities of Israel (see Matt 10:5–7) was uninformed too. If the apostles expected a restored kingdom to Israel at the time of Acts 1 they certainly expected a restored kingdom to Israel earlier when they proclaimed the kingdom at Jesus' request. But would Jesus send His apostles out with an erroneous message then? And why wait until the day of His ascension to correct their view? There are too many problems with the idea that Jesus redefined the kingdom in Acts 1 to be just Spirit-filled gospel proclamation. The apostles believed in a restoration of the kingdom to national Israel.

Fourth, the coming of the Holy Spirit does not mean the kingdom has arrived. In v. 5, Jesus told the apostles they would be baptized with the Holy Spirit in a few days—"but you will be baptized with the Holy Spirit not many days from now." Yet right after this Jesus said the timing of the kingdom was not for them to know (v. 7). If the coming of the Holy Spirit meant the coming of the kingdom then Jesus' answer about the kingdom's coming should be the same—in a few days. But it is not. The timing of the Holy Spirit's baptizing ministry and the timing of the kingdom are distinguished in Acts 1:5–7. This shows they are not the same thing. Note the contrast from the standpoint of the apostles based on Jesus' instruction:

> Timing of the Holy Spirit's baptizing ministry: Not many days from now.
>
> Timing of the Kingdom: Not for you to know.

The baptism with the Spirit would take place very soon but the coming of the kingdom of God was in the indefinite future. While a close relationship certainly exists between the New Covenant ministry of the Holy Spirit and the kingdom of God they are not the same.[7] Since fulfillment of the kingdom program includes two comings of Jesus we can conclude that the inauguration of the New Covenant is occurring in this age while the restoration of the kingdom awaits the future.

7 I respectfully disagree with Storms when he says, "Although the connection between the two is not as explicit as one might hope, it is hard not to conclude that the coming of the kingdom is in some sense directly related to, if not identified with, the outpouring of the Spirit at Pentecost and the globally expansive evangelistic work to which Jesus commissions them in Acts 1:8." Sam Storms, *Kingdom Come: The Amillennial Alternative* (Ross-shire, Scotland: Mentor, 2013), 284.

In sum, Acts 1:3–8 is significant for the kingdom program. After Jesus' earthly ministry, resurrection, and forty days of instruction, the apostles still believed the kingdom would be restored to Israel. Jesus does not correct their perception but tells them the timing of this restoration is only for the Father to know. This is evidence Jesus and the apostles did not reinterpret the expectation of a kingdom for Israel. Instead, they affirmed it. Worldwide gospel witness will lead to many people becoming saved and qualified to enter the kingdom when it is restored in the future.

PROVING THE IDENTITY OF THE MESSIAH (ACTS 2:22–36)

Acts 2 is one of the most exciting chapters in the Bible. It is also one of the most debated. There are many important issues to think through here. On the Day of Pentecost the Holy Spirit filled the followers of Jesus, evidenced by speaking in tongues (Acts 2:4). These "tongues" were foreign languages (see Acts 2:7–11) testifying that the gospel of Jesus and the kingdom message were going worldwide. Genesis 10–11 highlighted the importance of nations and people groups in God's plans, now these peoples would have the gospel taken to them. Acts 2:14–21 reveals that the coming of the Spirit from the Messiah is a fulfillment of what the prophet Joel predicted (see Joel 2:28–32).[8] But our main focus here will be on how Acts 2:22–36 relates to the kingdom program.

The speech by Peter in Acts 2:22–36 begins in 2:14 when Peter addressed how speaking in tongues was connected with what the prophet Joel predicted. His speech is directed to the "men of Israel," including those involved with killing Jesus. How things have changed! The man who denied Jesus and fled in fear for his life was now boldly proclaiming Jesus as Messiah in fulfillment of the OT prophecies. This is evidenced by Peter's summary statement in 2:36:

> "Therefore let all the house of Israel know for certain that God has made Him both Lord and Christ—this Jesus whom you crucified."

8 This does not mean the entirety of the Joel 2 prophecy was fulfilled. Several aspects of the prophecy await fulfillment with Jesus' second coming. What is emphasized in Acts 2 is fulfillment of the New Covenant ministry of the Holy Spirit.

Peter argues for Jesus' identity as Lord and Christ (Messiah) by appealing to the "wonders and signs" God did through Jesus (v. 22). Peter then tells the Jews that this Jesus whom they killed was raised from the dead. He quotes David's words from Psalm 16 to show that the resurrection of Jesus was foretold in the OT (2:25–28). Then Peter connects David's understanding of the Davidic Covenant with the necessity of the Messiah's resurrection from the dead:

> And so, because he [David] was a prophet and knew that God had sworn to him with an oath to seat one of his descendants on the throne, he looked ahead and spoke of the resurrection of the Christ, that He was neither abandoned to hades, nor did His flesh suffer decay (Acts 2:30–32).

Peter quotes Psalm 132:11 to prove God promised David a descendant who would sit on his throne. This is combined with a quote from Psalm 16 to show that God's ultimate Holy One could not be held by the grave and suffer decay. *Peter's point is that Jesus is this promised descendant of David who will be placed on David's throne. And since this promised descendant needs to be alive to rule from David's throne He cannot remain dead. He must be raised from the dead.*

With Acts 2:33–35, Peter links Jesus with Psalm 110: "Therefore having been exalted to the right hand of God, and having received from the Father the promise of the Holy Spirit, He has poured forth this which you both see and hear" (Acts 2:33). The reference to Jesus being "exalted to the right hand of God" is an explicit reference to Psalm 110:1 which Peter will also quote in Acts 2:34–35. Psalm 110:1 indicated that God's man, this King/Priest, would have a session of authority and privilege at the right hand of God in heaven "until" the time came for God to extend this King's authority from Jerusalem. Peter declares that Jesus is this King/Priest of Psalm 110. He is the Messiah who has been exalted to the right hand of God. And being at the "right hand of God," Jesus received the promise of the Holy Spirit. As a result, He is the One responsible for the pouring out of the Spirit. Peter then offers his second reference to Psalm 110:

> For it was not David who ascended into heaven, but he himself says:
>
> "The Lord said to my lord,
> 'Sit at my right hand,

UNTIL I MAKE YOUR ENEMIES A FOOTSTOOL FOR YOUR FEET'" (2:34–35).

As important as he was, David cannot fulfill the promise of Psalm 110. David did not ascend into heaven and sit at the right hand of God. But Jesus does. By connecting the events of Acts 2 with promises of resurrection and the Davidic Covenant, Peter makes the case that Jesus is "both Lord and Christ [Messiah]" (2:36).

Since Acts 2 is interpreted in various ways it is necessary to grasp what it reveals about God's kingdom program. *Peter is stressing Jesus' identity as Messiah.* Peter is proving *who* Jesus is based on what the OT predicted. This Jesus is Lord and Messiah. And this Jesus who has been raised from the dead is exalted to the right hand of God where He pours out the Holy Spirit on His followers.

Peter does not say Jesus is currently ruling from Jerusalem. There is no quotation of Psalm 110:2 in which Yahweh stretches forth the Messiah's strong scepter from Zion (Jerusalem). That had not occurred yet since Jesus was in heaven, and the judgment of God's enemies and the reward of Jesus' followers has not happened. The context of Psalm 110:1–2 shows that God's King/Priest would have a session at the right hand of God before the Messiah's reign from Jerusalem begins. The Messiah sits at the right hand of God "until" the Lord stretches His scepter from Zion. Jesus' ascension places Him in a position of power and authority at the right hand of God but the reign of Messiah from Jerusalem awaits a future fulfillment. Acts 3:21 presents this timeline scenario when it states that "heaven must receive" Jesus "until the period of restoration of all things." This, too, affirms that Jesus must remain in heaven "until" the time comes for Him to restore all things including His kingdom rule from Jerusalem.

DOES THE RESURRECTION AND ASCENSION MEAN AN 'ALREADY' DAVIDIC REIGN?

Does Jesus' resurrection and ascension mean He is currently reigning from David's throne either in a full Davidic reign or an 'already/not yet' reign.[9]

9 Sam Storms states, "The resurrection of Jesus from the dead, followed by his exaltation and enthronement at the right hand of the Father, is the inaugural step in the restoration of the fallen booth of David..." *Kingdom Come*, 301.

If so, is David's throne no longer an earthly throne but a throne in heaven? We do not think so. The preferred view is that the resurrection and ascension of Jesus means that Jesus currently shares all authority and power with the Father at the Father's right hand, but the Davidic/Messianic reign awaits Jesus' second coming to earth. Or to put it another way:

> It is not: The resurrection and ascension means Jesus' Davidic/ Messianic reign is inaugurated or entirely fulfilled from heaven.
>
> Instead, it is: The resurrection and ascension means Jesus shares the throne of deity at the right hand of the Father in heaven and is exalted as Messiah, but the Davidic/Messianic reign on earth comes with Jesus' return.

Several reasons support this view. First, Psalm 110 tells of two phases of the ministry of the Messiah—a session of the Messiah at the right hand of the Father and then a kingdom rule from Jerusalem. A session at the throne of deity precedes a Davidic reign. Second, Jesus himself makes a distinction between the Father's throne and His own throne in Rev 3:21: "He who overcomes, I will grant to him to sit down with Me on My throne, as I also overcame and sat down with My Father on His throne." When Jesus gives this promise in the 90s A.D. He currently was at the right hand of the Father. As He assesses His current situation, He refers to His place as being on the Father's throne. But when He projects to the future He speaks of "My throne," a throne He will share with His followers in the future. The fact that Jesus speaks of the Father's throne and then His own throne shows these are two different thrones that occur at different times. Jesus' own throne is the Messianic/Davidic throne, a throne He will assume when He returns.

Third, Jesus places His throne and kingdom reign in the future beyond His resurrection and ascension. For example, Jesus himself predicted that His own placement on the "throne" would take place at the time of His second coming in Matthew 19:28:

> And Jesus said to them, "Truly I say to you, that you who have followed Me, in the regeneration when the Son of Man will sit on His glorious throne, you also shall sit upon twelve thrones, judging the twelve tribes of Israel."

Jesus will "sit on His glorious throne" (i.e. the Davidic throne) at the time of the renewal of the cosmos ("regeneration") and the restoration of the "twelve tribes of Israel." Since the renewal of the cosmos and the restoration of Israel are still future, so too must Jesus' sitting on His glorious throne. Jesus declared a similar truth in Matthew 25:31–32:

> "But when the Son of Man comes in His glory, and all the angels with Him, then He will sit on His glorious throne. All the nations will be gathered before Him; and He will separate them from one another, as the shepherd separates the sheep from the goats."

The context of Matthew 24–25 is the Olivet Discourse and the tribulation that is coming upon Israel and the entire world. And with 25:31 Jesus again mentions that "He will sit on His glorious throne" (see Luke 1:32–33). This event of sitting on His throne is linked with His coming "in His glory" and with the coming of "all the angels." It is also linked with all the nations being gathered before Him for judgment. These events are clustered together and occur around the same time. And like Jesus' second coming, the coming of all the angels, and the judgment of the nations are all future, so too must the assumption of Jesus' glorious throne. Jesus' assumption of the Davidic throne being a future and earthly event is an explicit teaching of Jesus himself.

Fourth, as discussed earlier, on Jesus' day of ascension, the apostles specifically asked Jesus when the kingdom would be restored and His answer was that only the Father knew (Acts 1:6–7). If the ascension caused a kingdom reign that would have been a good time for Jesus to let His followers know that the kingdom was indeed beginning. But He did not. What He did say was they would receive the Holy Spirit in a few days (see Acts 1:5). What is fulfilled in this age as a result of Jesus' resurrection and ascension is Messiah's session at the right hand of the Father. The Davidic reign occurs at Jesus' return.

Perhaps the chief evidence offered for the view that the resurrection and ascension shows Jesus is currently on David's throne is Acts 2:30–31a: "And so, because he [David] was a prophet and knew that God had sworn to him with an oath to seat one of his descendants on his throne, he looked ahead and spoke of the resurrection of the Christ." Some hold that if Jesus' resurrection is connected with the Davidic throne this means Jesus is on David's throne in heaven now. But this is not Peter's point. Peter explains that David understood that one of his [David's] descendants needed to sit on his throne. For this to occur, this ultimate descendant of David cannot stay dead since a dead Messiah cannot reign from David's throne. So the Messiah must be resurrected. The connection between the resurrection and David's throne is that the Messiah must be alive to assume the Davidic throne. Peter is not claiming that Jesus is currently on or ruling from David's throne.

ISRAEL'S BELIEF AND THE COMING OF THE KINGDOM (ACTS 3:12–26)

Acts 3:12–26 discusses the relationship of Israel to the return of Christ and the kingdom. This comes after Jesus' ascension and the sending of the Holy Spirit. This section also lays out what could be called "the official reoffer of the Messiah and His Kingdom."[10]

The healing of a lame beggar at the temple by Peter led to the apostle addressing the "Men of Israel" (Acts 3:12). Because of the Feast of Pentecost, many Jews were present in Jerusalem including the same Jewish leadership that put Jesus to death (see Acts 4:1, 6). The setting of Jerusalem, the temple, the Jewish people, and the Jewish leadership makes this address by Peter an event with great national implications.

Peter states that the God of Abraham, Isaac, and Jacob made Jesus His Servant, and this Jesus has fulfilled the OT prophecies concerning His suffering (see Acts 3:13, 18). But Peter tells the Jewish audience they "disowned the Holy and Righteous One" and "put to death the Prince of life" (3:13–15). It is this same Jesus who gave "perfect health" to the lame beggar (3:16).

Peter does not proclaim irreversible judgment for Israel's rejection of her Messiah. Instead, he softens his accusation by saying the people and leaders of Israel "acted in ignorance" (3:17). What he offers now is a second chance or offer to believe in the Messiah:

> "Therefore repent and return, so that your sins may be wiped away, in order that times of refreshing may come from the

10 McClain, *The Greatness of the Kingdom*, 403.

> presence of the Lord; and that He may send Jesus, the Christ appointed for you, whom heaven must receive until the period of restoration of all things about which God spoke by the mouth of His holy prophets from ancient time" (Acts 3:19–21).

This section includes two cause and effect situations. Peter calls on the Jews to "repent and return." His call is similar to the calls of the OT prophets for rebellious Israel to repent. And it is a summons to salvation. The Jews are encouraged to turn from their sins and believe in Jesus the Messiah, whom they have rejected so far.[11] If they do, something positive will happen. The words "so that" (*prōs ta*) indicate purpose. Repentance will lead to their sins being "wiped away." Thus, Israel's acceptance of Jesus the Messiah will lead to the removal Israel's sins. More than just individual sins and repentance are in view here. The national sin of rejecting the Messiah must be reversed by national repentance (see Lev 26:40–45).

But Peter does not stop there. Forgiveness is not the only result of repentance. Peter then mentions "in order that" (*hopōs an*) which also indicates another purpose. Repentance leads to forgiveness but then forgiveness of sins also leads to something called "the times of refreshing" which results from the Lord's presence (3:19).

This phrase, "times of refreshing," which only occurs here in the NT, involves the ideas of rest and refreshment. In this context it refers to an eschatological refreshment from God. There is some debate concerning what this "times of refreshing" is and when it occurs. Some see "times of refreshing" as forgiveness of sins and the experience of the Holy Spirit in this age. Others see "times of refreshing" as the kingdom itself that comes when Jesus returns. The latter option is more likely. The "times of refreshing" refers to the kingdom and is connected with the return of Jesus and the "restoration of all things" (v. 21). Toussaint argues the grammar supports this link between "times of refreshing" and the return of Jesus:

> The two clauses that follow *hopōs* go together. In other words, "that the times of refreshing may come from the presence of the Lord" must be taken with the words "and that He may send

11 The sins to be wiped away probably include both individual sins and the corporate sin of rejecting the Messiah.

> Jesus." As Haenchen puts it, "But the two promises are complementary statements about one and the same event." Nothing grammatically separates the promises: in fact, they are joined together by the connective *kai*.[12]

So then, this refreshing period is future and refers to coming kingdom conditions. James Montgomery Boice rightly links this with national blessings for Israel in connection with the return of Jesus. He says, "['times of refreshing'] probably concerns a future day of blessing when the Jewish people will turn to Christ in large numbers and a final age of national blessing will come."[13] Experiencing the "times of refreshing" means experiencing the blessings of Messiah's kingdom when He comes again. If "times of refreshing" refers to Messiah's kingdom on earth, then Peter is saying that if Israel repents their sins will be forgiven and the kingdom will come.

So are kingdom conditions contingent or reliant on Israel's response to Jesus? It appears so from this text. The near context of 3:19 has already revealed a clear statement of contingency. If Israel would repent then their sins would be forgiven. This is cause and effect. So why couldn't contingency in regard to the next purpose statement regarding the coming of the kingdom be present as well? As Toussaint states, "Peter had just said that removal of their sins was contingent on their repentance (v. 19). If contingency exists here, then it is certainly also present in verses 20–21."[14]

In addition to "times of refreshing," Israel's repentance also means "He [God] may send Jesus, the Christ appointed for you." This is a specific reference to the second coming of Jesus. The context and grammar make it difficult to avoid the conclusion that the return of Jesus is linked with

---

12 Toussaint, "The Contingency of the Coming of the Kingdom," 229–30.

13 James Montgomery Boice, *Acts: An Expositional Commentary* (Grand Rapids: Baker, 1997), 69. Boice also says there may be a sense in which the phrase may include blessings for God's people now. Walker also agrees that "times of refreshing" is a reference to a future kingdom: "The expression probably looks on ultimately to the time when Christ shall come again and when those Messianic promises which still remain unfulfilled shall be perfectly consummated.... That will be the golden age of blessing for the Jewish nation, and, through them, a period of spiritual quickening to the world at large (Romans xi. 11–36)." Thomas Walker, *Acts of the Apostles*. Kregel Expository Commentary Series (Grand Rapids: Kregel, 1965), 106–07.

14 Stanley D. Toussaint and Jay A. Quine, "No, Not Yet: The Contingency of God's Promised Kingdom," *Bibliotheca Sacra* 164 (2007): 144.

Israel's belief and repentance. The term for "may send" (*aposteilei*) is an aorist active subjunctive emphasizing possibility and a contingent element to this promise. If Israel believes, then God will send Jesus the Messiah. As John Phillips puts it:

> If the Jews had repented then and there, the initial fulfillment of such prophecies, as were evidenced at Pentecost, would have blossomed into a complete fulfillment, and the return of Christ could have taken place within a generation.[15]

That Peter states "the Christ appointed for you," is also significant. This highlights the continuing close relationship between Israel and the Messiah. Even the death of the Messiah at the hands of the Jewish leadership does not change this fact. Jesus is Savior and Messiah of all the world, but there is still a sense in which He is the Messiah of Israel. The crucifixion does not change this. Jesus is appointed for Israel because of the covenants and the promises (Rom 9:4). This also shows the close connection between Israel's response to her Messiah and the Messiah's coming.[16]

Peter then offers an extra truth about Jesus. Jesus is the One "whom heaven must receive until the period of restoration of all things" (3:21a). Jesus' session in heaven is not a last second addition to God's plans. It "must" occur. That heaven must receive the Messiah until the kingdom is established was predicted in Psalm 110:1–2 when Yahweh told the Messiah, that He [Messiah] will sit at His right hand until the time comes for the Messiah to rule over His enemies. A session for the Messiah at the right hand of God must precede Messiah's kingdom reign from Jerusalem (see Ps 110:1–2). That Peter has Psalm 110 in mind is likely since he quoted this psalm in Acts 2:30–36.

In addition to "times of refreshing" and the sending of the Messiah, Peter then introduces "the restoration of all things," of which the OT

15 John Phillips, *Exploring Acts: An Expository Commentary*. The John Phillips Commentary Series. (Grand Rapids: Kregel, 1986), 75.

16 In regard to the "appointed for you," Peter Goeman observes, "The dative 'you'. . . is likely a dative of possession and brings out the fact that this was the Jewish Messiah, He belonged to them. Thus, Peter's argument appears to focus on the necessity of Jewish repentance so that their Messiah would be sent back." Peter Goeman, "Implications of the Kingdom in Acts 3:19–21," *The Master's Seminary Journal* 26 (2015): 78.

prophets spoke. The word for "restoration" is *apokatastasis*, a term used in verb form in Acts 1:6 when the disciples asked Jesus about when the kingdom would be restored to Israel.[17] To restore something is to take a marred entity and renew it, to fix what has been broken. The close connection of "restore" in Acts 1:6 and 3:21 is no coincidence. The promised coming restoration of Acts 3:21 includes the restoration of Israel. As Beverly Roberts Gaventa observes, "Given that the apostles have already inquired about the 'restoration' of the kingdom... the 'restoration of all' surely includes restoring the kingdom of Israel."[18] OT prophets who often predicted a restoration of Israel reinforce this idea. Jeremiah 16:15 states, "For I will restore them to their own land which I gave to their fathers."[19] Keener observes that when the connection with Acts 1:6 and the OT prophets is considered, the restoration of Acts 3:21 includes a restored Israel:

> In view of the cognate usage in Acts 1:6 and the texts' claim that the object of restoration is what all the prophets spoke about, the restoration of Israel is the likeliest interpretation. Israel's restoration appears repeatedly in the biblical prophets (Amos 9:14; Ezek 39:25; Acts 1:6), a significant point here given that the restoration of what "the prophets predicted" (Acts 3:21).[20]

So the coming restoration of all things includes Israel. Yet there is no reason to limit this restoration to just national Israel. The prophets portrayed Israel as a microcosm for what God would do for the whole world. Isaiah 27:6 declares, "In the days to come Jacob will take root, Israel will blossom and sprout, and they will fill the whole world with fruit." In Romans 11:12, 15 Paul said that Israel's coming salvation and "fullness" would bring even greater blessings to the world. The restoration of Israel will lead to global

17 I. Howard Marshall also says the reference to "times" in 3:19 may have links with Jesus' statement that the disciples were not to know times or epochs in regard to Israel's restoration: "There may be a link with the 'times' in 1:7 associated with the restoration of the rule of God for Israel." I. Howard Marshall, *Acts*. Tyndale New Testament Commentary (Grand Rapids: Eerdmans, 1980. Reprint 1989), 93.

18 Beverly Roberts Gaventa, *Acts* in Abingdon New Testament Commentaries (Nashville, TN: Abingdon Press, 2003), 88.

19 See also Jeremiah 23:8; 24:6; Hosea 11:11.

20 Craig S. Keener, *Acts: An Exegetical Commentary* (Grand Rapids: Baker Academic, 2013), 2:1112.

blessings on a wide scale and includes cosmic renewal and harmony in the animal kingdom (Isa 11:6–9). Again, this is a case where both the *particular* and a *universal* work together in harmony. The restoration of all things centers on the restoration of Israel (Acts 1:6) but the results of this restoration are global and holistic. Thus, the "restoration of all things" involves kingdom blessings for Israel but also expands to the whole earth and all nations.

To summarize, a significant cause and effect scenario arises according to Acts 3:19–21. If Israel believes in Jesus Israel will be saved and her national sin of rejecting the Messiah will be forgiven. This salvation will lead to the arrival of the kingdom ("times of refreshing"), the return of the Messiah, and the restoration of all creation. The "times of refreshing" and "restoration of all things" is the kingdom, while the return of Jesus focuses on the return of the King. These three are inseparably connected. Thus, the scenario below (→ = "leads to"):

Israel's repentance → Israel's forgiveness → Return of Christ and kingdom of God

This cause and effect scenario has not gone unnoticed by scholars. F.F. Bruce righty pointed out the "call" to Israel in Acts 3:19–21 had the opportunity to change the course of world history. If only Israel had believed the kingdom would have come "much more swiftly":

> The exact meaning of these words of Peter has been debated from various points of view. This at least may be said with assurance: the whole house of Israel, now as on the day of Pentecost, received a call to reverse the verdict of Passover Eve and to accord Jesus united acknowledgement as Messiah. Had Israel as a whole done this during these Pentecostal days, how different the course of world history and world evangelization would have been! How much more swiftly (we may imagine) would the consummation of Christ's kingdom have come![21]

Bruce even used the word "offer" in regard to Peter words to Israel at this time. The refusal of Israel to heed the offer delays the coming of Jesus:

21 F. F. Bruce, *Commentary on the Book of the Acts*, The New International Commentary on the New Testament (Grand Rapids: Eerdmans, 1971), 91–92.

> Israel as a whole declined the renewed offer of grace and refused to recognize Jesus as Messiah.... The grand consummation and the *parousia* of Jesus lie still in the future: "we see not yet all things subjected to him" (Heb. 2:8).[22]

Others have noted a contingency element regarding the coming of the kingdom and the second coming of Jesus in Acts 3. I. Howard Marshall sees the future kingdom of God as "dependent" on the belief of the Jews: "That is to say, the coming of the 'messianic age' or the future kingdom of God, for which the Jews longed, was dependent upon their acceptance of Jesus as the Messiah."[23] Ben Witherington also states, "Christ's second coming is seen as in some sense dependent on Israel's repentance (cf. Rom. 11:12, 15, 26)."[24] David Peterson notes, "Peter's point in vv. 19–20 is that the previously rejected Messiah will return only if Israel repents."[25] Richard L. Longenecker sums up the message of Acts 3:19–21 well when he states, "Peter goes on to say that if his hearers repent, their repentance will have a part in ushering in the great events of the end time."[26]

Also important is the repeated emphasis that the restoration of the kingdom to Israel is based on the OT: "until the period of restoration of all things about which God spoke by the mouth of His holy prophets from ancient time" (Acts 3:21). Indeed, the prophets of the OT on several occasions promised kingdom conditions linked with Israel's repentance:

22 Ibid. Underline emphasis is mine.

23 I. Howard Marshall, *Acts* in Tyndale New Testament Commentaries (Grand Rapids: Eerdmans, 1980), 94.

24 Ben Witherington III, *The Acts of the Apostles: A Socio-Rhetorical Commentary* (Grand Rapids: Eerdmans, 1998), 187.

25 David G. Peterson, *The Acts of the Apostles* (Grand Rapids: Eerdmans, 2009), 181. Munck states, "Both Jews and Christians knew that there would be human participation in the fulfillment of salvation. The Jews maintained that Israel must first be converted, otherwise the Messianic age could not occur." Johannes Munck, *The Acts of the Apostles*: The Anchor Bible (Garden City, NY: Doubleday & Company, 1967), 29.

26 Richard N. Longenecker, "The Acts of the Apostles," in *The Expositor's Bible Commentary*, vol. 9., ed. Frank E. Gaebelein (Grand Rapids: Zondervan, 1981), 297.

- Leviticus 26:40–45 predicted a dispersed Israel would be brought back into the blessings of the Abrahamic Covenant "if" repentance occurred.
- Deuteronomy 30:1–10 declared a changed heart would lead to regathering from dispersion and spiritual and physical blessings for Israel.
- Jeremiah 18:7–10 revealed that promises of blessings or calamity can be affected by a nation's response to God.
- In 2 Chronicles 7:14 God stated, "and My people who are called by My name humble themselves and pray and seek My face and turn from their wicked ways, then I will hear from heaven, will forgive their sin and will heal their land."

The wording of Acts 3:21 closely parallels the words of the Spirit-inspired Zacharias in Luke 1:70:

> "As He spoke by the mouth of His holy prophets from of old" (Luke 1:70).
>
> "... about which God spoke by the mouth of His holy prophets from ancient time" (Acts 3:21).

And like Acts 3:21, the content of Luke 1:70 involves the restoration of national Israel:

> As He spoke by the mouth of His holy prophets from of old—
> Salvation FROM OUR ENEMIES,
> And FROM THE HAND OF ALL WHO HATE US;
> To show mercy toward our fathers,
> And to remember His holy covenant,
> The oath which He swore to Abraham our father,
> To grant us that we, being rescued from the hand of our enemies,
> Might serve Him without fear.

Peter then says the prophets taught these truths since Samuel (Acts 3:24). Then with Acts 3:25 Peter tells the leaders of Israel, "It is you who are the sons of the prophets and of the covenant which God made with your fathers, saying to Abraham, 'AND IN YOUR SEED ALL THE FAMILIES OF THE EARTH SHALL BE BLESSED.'" These words refute the idea that the Jewish nation is no longer significant in God's kingdom plans. Even after killing the Messiah and after Jesus' ascension and pouring out of the Holy Spirit, Israel is still important to God. Peter affirms Israel's continuing relationship to the Abrahamic Covenant. And he singles out the promise of Genesis 12:3 and 22:18 concerning Israel bringing universal blessings. This occurs through Israel's Messiah even if the people refused to believe.

In sum, Acts 3:19–26 is a strategic passage for the kingdom program. McClain says with this section, "we have something better than a term," we actually have "a *definition* of the Kingdom."[27] And this definition has three components. First, in regard to "content," the kingdom brings "the restoration of all things." Second, as for "timing," the kingdom comes when God sends the Christ appointed for Israel after Jesus' session at the right hand of the Father. And third, the condition for the kingdom's coming is "contingent upon the repentance and conversion of Israel."[28]

ACTS 8:12; 14:22

The kingdom also is mentioned in Acts 8:12 when Philip was preaching in Samaria: "But when they believed Philip preaching the good news about the kingdom of God and the name of Jesus Christ, they were being baptized, men and women alike." As the gospel goes beyond Jerusalem to Samaria, the preaching of "Jesus Christ" is linked with preaching "the good news about the kingdom." Entrance into the kingdom only comes via Jesus. Thus, when one preaches the gospel of Jesus Christ he is preaching about the kingdom of God.

The kingdom of God is then mentioned in Acts 14:22. After Paul was stoned and left for dead, he and Barnabas were "strengthening the souls of the disciples, encouraging them to continue in the faith, and saying, 'Through many tribulations we must enter the kingdom of God.'" Tribulations in the world precede the kingdom, and faithfulness through tribulations shows one is qualified to enter Jesus' kingdom when it comes.

27 McClain, *The Greatness of the Kingdom*, 406. Emphasis is in the original.

28 Ibid.

As Farnell states, "Here the emphasis is on the 'futurity' of the kingdom that involves great conflict."[29] The rewards associated with the kingdom will come someday, but for now Christians show themselves to be worthy of it by suffering for Jesus.

GENTILE INCLUSION IN THE PEOPLE OF GOD BECAUSE OF THE MESSIAH (ACTS 15)

With Acts 15:16–18, an OT kingdom passage, Amos 9:11–12, is quoted concerning a specific controversy regarding the salvation of Gentiles. In Acts 15, Luke described events surrounding the Jerusalem Council. The issue at hand involved what should happen to Gentiles who believed in Jesus. Do they need to be circumcised and keep the Law of Moses? Do they need to come under the umbrella of Israel? These issues are evident from 15:1:

> Some men came down from Judea and began teaching the brethren, "Unless you are circumcised according to the custom of Moses, you cannot be saved."

Some Jews from Judea were saying circumcision and adherence to the Mosaic Law were necessary for converted Gentiles. This caused "great dissension," so it was determined Paul, Barnabas, and others needed to go to Jerusalem and meet with the apostles and elders there to settle this matter (15:2). After they arrived, Paul and Barnabas told the group in Jerusalem the great things God was doing among the Gentiles. But some from "the sect of the Pharisees" insisted "it was necessary to circumcise them [Gentiles] and direct them to observe the Law of Moses" (15:5).

Peter passionately argued it was God's plan to save Gentiles by faith just like Jews, and placing Gentiles under the law was not wise (15:7–11). Barnabas and Paul then related that God was performing signs and wonders among the Gentiles (15:12). With v. 13 James takes center stage in the discussion:

> After they had stopped speaking, James answered, saying, "Brethren, listen to me. Simeon has related how God first concerned Himself about taking from among the Gentiles a people

29 F. David Farnell, "The Kingdom of God in the New Testament," in *The Master's Seminary Journal* 23 (2012): 205.

for His name. With this the words of the Prophets agree, just as it is written,
'AFTER THESE THINGS I WILL RETURN,
AND I WILL REBUILD THE TABERNACLE OF DAVID WHICH HAS FALLEN
AND I WILL REBUILD ITS RUINS,
AND I WILL RESTORE IT,
SO THAT THE REST OF MANKIND MAY SEEK THE LORD
AND ALL THE GENTILES WHO ARE CALLED BY MY NAME
SAYS THE LORD, WHO MAKES THESE THINGS KNOWN FROM LONG AGO'"
(Acts 15:13–18).

James appeals to what Peter said about God making Gentiles His people (v.13). He then refers to the OT prophets for support of this idea. He quotes Amos 9:11–12. James uses the word "prophets" in the plural and not the singular "prophet." He does not say, "This is what Amos says." Instead, it is more like, "This is what the prophets as a whole say." God's act of making Gentiles His people without becoming part of Israel was the message of several prophets, one of which is Amos. Several OT passages announced God would save Gentiles without them becoming part of Israel. Isaiah 19:24–25, for example, predicted Egypt and Assyria would become God's people alongside Israel. Isaiah 49:3–6 revealed the Servant of the Lord would restore the nation Israel and bring blessings to Gentiles. Zephaniah 3:9 declared Gentiles from the nations would call on the name of the Lord. Amos, too, makes this point.

So how should Acts 15:13–18 be understood? Here an OT kingdom passage is linked with current Gentile salvation. Some think this is an example of an OT kingdom passage (Amos 9) being reinterpreted or fulfilled non-literally. Anthony Hoekema, for example, argues the Amos passage "is being fulfilled right now, as Gentiles are being gathered into the community of God's people."[30] To him, this is "a clear example in the Bible itself of a figurative, nonliteral interpretation of an Old Testament passage dealing with the restoration of Israel."[31]

30 Anthony A. Hoekema, *The Bible and the Future* (Grand Rapids: Eerdmans, 1979), 210.

31 Ibid.

Acts 15:13–18, however, is not an example of a non-literal fulfillment of an OT kingdom passage. Nor does it set a pattern for reinterpreting other OT kingdom passages in a spiritual or non-literal way. There is a partial literal fulfillment of Amos 9:11–12, yet there are parts of this prophecy awaiting future fulfillment.

As mentioned in our earlier section on Amos, the main point of Amos 9:11–15 is the restoration of the Davidic kingdom under the Messiah and what this restoration means for Gentiles and the world. In much of his book, Amos wrote about the declining monarchy in Israel and coming captivity. He warned that Israel would be judged by God for breaking His covenant, but after judgment there would be a glorious restoration of the Davidic kingdom to Israel under the Messiah. This would result in blessings to the nations who would also be called by God's name (Amos 9:12). So as David King notes, "The incorporation of the Gentiles into the believing community of God was present in the Hebrew text of Amos."[32]

The point of Amos 9:11–12 is this—*a restored kingdom of Israel under the Messiah results in blessings to Gentiles.* Thus, messianic times include blessings for both Israel and Gentiles. James draws upon this truth in Acts 15 when discussing how Gentiles should be considered in light of Jesus' first coming.

But what about the fact that Israel and the Davidic kingdom had not been literally restored yet at the time? Rome was still in charge and Israel was not functioning as a united political entity as it did in the days of David and Solomon. It is unlikely the Jewish Christians in Jerusalem would be convinced they were in a restored Davidic kingdom. Earlier, when the apostles asked Jesus about when He was going to restore the kingdom to Israel, Jesus' response was that the kingdom's timing was unknown. The Father would restore the kingdom to Israel on His own timetable (see Acts 1:6–8). In Acts 3:19–21 Peter indicated the second coming of Jesus and the kingdom would occur in connection with the salvation of Israel. So the actual restoration of Israel awaits the second coming of Jesus.

The answer is found in what Jesus fulfilled with His first coming and what needs to be fulfilled at His second coming. What already has been fulfilled is the arrival of the Messiah, Jesus, who is the centerpiece of the

32 David M. King, "The Use of Amos 9:11–12 in Acts 15:16–18," in *Ashland Theological Journal* 21 (1989): 8.

restored Davidic kingdom. This Messiah has brought messianic salvation to Gentiles as Gentiles. This was predicted in Amos 9:11–12 and this has been fulfilled with the events in Acts. So there is literal partial fulfillment of Amos 9:11–12 in Acts 15. *Because of the Messiah, Gentiles are now becoming the people of God without needing to merge into Israel.* James draws upon this literal truth from Amos.

What still awaits fulfillment, however, is the restoration and unification of the nation Israel and the physical blessings Amos 9:13–15 predicts:

> "Behold, days are coming," declares the Lord,
> "When the plowman will overtake the reaper
> And the treader of grapes him who sows seed;
> When the mountains will drip sweet wine
> And all the hills will be dissolved.
> "Also I will restore the captivity of My people Israel,
> And they will rebuild the ruined cities and live in them;
> They will also plant vineyards and drink their wine,
> And make gardens and eat their fruit.
> "I will also plant them on their land,
> And they will not again be rooted out from their land
> Which I have given them,"
> Says the Lord your God.

It is significant that James only quotes Amos 9:11–12 to make his point and not 9:13–15 since all of this latter section awaits the return of Jesus.

Some might object to our proposed "partial fulfillment" view of Amos 9:11–12 in Acts 15, but partial fulfillments of OT prophecies are to be expected with the reality of two comings of Jesus. If one insists Amos 9:11–12 is reinterpreted and entirely fulfilled in the church, one must also spiritualize the physical blessings promised in Amos 9:13–15 and say these are all fulfilled in the church. If Amos 9:11–12 is spiritualized, so too must Amos 9:13–15.

So there is *initial fulfillment* of Amos 9 with the events described in Acts 15. Gentile inclusion in salvation as a result of the Messiah is a fulfillment of what was predicted in Amos 9 and the OT. But as Darrell Bock points out, "Initial fulfillment is not exhausted fulfillment."[33] The restoration of Israel is still future (see Acts 1:6).

But how can Gentile inclusion in the messianic plan precede the salvation and restoration of Israel? Romans 11:25–27 helps answer this. Paul explicitly declared the "mystery" or new truth that a period of Gentile salvation would precede the salvation of Israel:

> For I do not want you, brethren, to be uninformed of this mystery, lest you be wise in your own estimation, that a partial hardening has happened to Israel until the fullness of the Gentiles has come in; and thus all Israel will be saved; just as it is written, "The Deliverer will come from Zion, He will remove ungodliness from Jacob." "And this is My covenant with them, When I take away their sins."

One of the unforeseen mysteries revealed in the NT era is that the salvation of many Gentiles will precede the salvation and restoration of Israel. This was not predicted in the OT prophets but it occurred in connection with Israel's rejection of her Messiah. Paul says this situation will be used by God to make Israel jealous (see Rom 11:11). But the salvation of Gentiles should not be taken to mean believing Gentiles are part of a "new Israel" or that the Davidic kingdom and restoration of Israel are fulfilled in the present age between the two comings of Christ. According to Romans 11:25–27, the period between the two comings of Christ is characterized by Gentile salvation, but when Jesus comes again, the nation Israel will be saved and restored. In fact, even greater blessings to the world will occur when Israel as a nation believes in the Messiah (see Rom 11:12, 15).

So James does not reinterpret or transform the OT expectation for Israel with his words in Acts 15. Heater is correct when he declares, "I would hold that the citation [from James] is merely to show that the tenor of Old Testament Scripture supports the idea of Gentiles coming to God without losing their identity. James was not ignoring the future restoration of Israel and equating the 'hut of David' with the church; he merely said that one element of what will happen in the future was happening in this

---

33 Darrell L. Bock, "Evidence from Acts," in *A Case for Premillennialism: A New Consensus*, ed. Donald K. Campbell and Jeffrey L. Townsend (Chicago: Moody, 1992), 197.

day."[34] Or to put another way: *Messianic salvation because of Jesus the Son of David brings salvation of Gentiles on equal footing with believing Jews. This is a present fulfillment of the Amos 9 prophecy. But the restoration of the kingdom to Israel and physical blessings to the world await the second coming of Jesus* (see Acts 1:6; 3:19–21). Messianic salvation for Gentiles is now occurring, but the reign of the Messiah over a restored Israel with physical blessings on the earth is still future.

In sum, James argues that Gentiles do not need to become converts to Judaism to be saved. He appeals to the prophets, including Amos, to show Gentile inclusion in the people of God alongside Israel is part of God's plan and has occurred because of Jesus. Because Gentile inclusion into the people of God was prophesied for messianic times in the OT, and messianic salvation has been inaugurated with Jesus, the Gentiles should not be forced to convert to Judaism by being circumcised and observing the Law of Moses.

THE KINGDOM PROGRAM AT THE END OF ACTS

The last chapters in Acts reveal national Israel's importance to the kingdom. As Vittorio Fusco points out, "Right up to the last page, Luke-Acts refers repeatedly and with insistence to the 'hope of Israel', the 'hope in the promise made to the fathers' (28:20; cf. 23:6; 24:15, 21; 26:6f., 22f.). Though this hope has as its primary object the resurrection of the dead, it retains an aspect of nationalism. It is this hope that animates the incessant eschatological prayer of the twelve tribes."[35]

According to Acts 19:8 Paul went to the Jews with the message of the kingdom: "And he entered the synagogue and continued speaking out boldly for three months, reasoning and persuading them about the kingdom of God." Note Paul still devoted considerable attention to persuading the Jews. Then in 20:25 Paul reminded the elders at Ephesus that he had preached the kingdom to them. With Acts 26, Paul offered a defense of his ministry before Agrippa. In verse 2 Paul explained why the Jews were accusing him. They knew he was a "Pharisee according to the strictest sect of our

34 Homer Heater, "Evidence from Joel and James," in *A Case for Premillennialism*, 156–57.

35 Vittorio Fusco, "Luke-Acts and the Future of Israel," *Novum Testamentum* 38 (1996): 3.

religion." Thus, his credentials as a Jew were beyond dispute (v. 5). Then he mentioned how God's promise relates to the twelve tribes of Israel:

> And now I am standing trial for the hope of the promise made by God to our fathers; the promise to which our twelve tribes hope to attain, as they earnestly serve God night and day. And for this hope, O King, I am being accused by Jews (Acts 26:6–7).

Paul is standing trial "for the hope of the promise made by God to the fathers." Thus, Paul's message has roots back to the patriarchs of Israel and what God revealed to them. The promise God made to Abraham, Isaac, and Jacob is the same promise Paul is proclaiming. There is no indication this "promise" has been transcended or spiritualized or redefined into something different. This is the literal hope to Israel as found in the Abrahamic Covenant given to Abraham, Isaac, and Jacob.

Second, this promise was something "our twelve tribes hope to attain." Since the context is Paul's ministry to the Jews, the "twelve tribes" refers to the historical twelve tribes of Israel. This is what his audience would have understood. Paul is on trial for proclaiming the very promise the twelve tribes of Israel were hoping to attain. The promise made to the patriarchs is still relevant to the twelve tribes of Israel and there is hope for them. Some deny the significance of the literal twelve tribes of Israel and believe the twelve tribes are transcended by the church that is now the new Israel. Others want to say because Jesus Christ is the "true Israel" there is no significance for the literal twelve tribes of Israel. Paul does not argue this way. His message was related to the ethnic tribes of Israel.

Paul says his message to the Jews was in accord with the prophets and Moses:

> So, having obtained help from God, I stand to this day testifying both to small and great, stating nothing but what the Prophets and Moses said was going to take place; that the Christ was to suffer, and that by reason of His resurrection from the dead He would be the first to proclaim light both to the Jewish people and to the Gentiles" (Acts 26:22–23).

Paul's message was "nothing but what the Prophets and Moses declared." He is not saying something new. He is not transcending the OT or giving new revelation as an apostle. He is simply restating what the prophets and Moses had predicted—namely the death and resurrection of Christ and the proclamation of light to the Jews and Gentiles. He also keeps the distinction between Jews and Gentiles. He does not claim Gentiles in Christ are now spiritual Jews. Paul at the end of Acts relied strongly on the contextual meaning of the OT prophets.

The last chapter of Acts finds Paul in Rome. He "called together... the leading men of the Jews" and told them, "I am wearing this chain for the sake of the hope of Israel." Again, there is no indication here that Paul is telling these Jews about an alleged "new Israel." He is discussing the hope of national Israel, a hope rooted strongly in the OT.

Acts 28:23 states what happened when the Jews came to him on another occasion:

> When they had set a day for Paul, they came to him at his lodging in large numbers; and he was explaining to them by solemnly testifying about the kingdom of God and trying to persuade them concerning Jesus, from both the Law of Moses and from the Prophets, from morning until evening.

Paul's message to these Jews was "the kingdom of God" and "Jesus." Like he did with his encounter before Agrippa in Acts 26, he argues from the Law and the Prophets. As Acts ends, the last two verses show that Paul's message was preaching the kingdom:

> And he stayed two full years in his own rented quarters and was welcoming all who came to him, preaching the kingdom of God and teaching concerning the Lord Jesus Christ with all openness, unhindered (Acts 28:30–31).

At the end of Acts, hope for Israel remained. Regarding Paul's words in Acts 28, Göran Lennartsson points out, "The apostle Paul's cling to the hope of Israel... is hardly abandoned or reinterpreted by Luke."[36]

36 Göran Lennartsson, *Refreshing & Restoration: Two Eschatological Motifs in Acts 3:19–21* (Lund Sweden: Lund University, 2007), 285.

The kingdom program in Acts can be summarized:

1. In the forty days prior to Jesus' ascension the primary focus of Jesus' instruction to the disciples was the kingdom of God (Acts 1:3).
2. Just prior to Jesus' ascension the disciples of Jesus expected the restoration of the kingdom to the nation Israel (Acts 1:6).
3. Jesus affirms their understanding but says they were not to know the timing of the restoration of the kingdom to Israel; instead, their concern was to be proclamation of the gospel to the world (Acts 1:7–8).
4. Peter and the apostles affirmed to the Jewish nation that Jesus was the Messiah of Israel who had ascended to the right hand of the Father (Acts 2).
5. Peter told the people of Jerusalem that repentance and belief in Jesus would lead to forgiveness of sins, the coming of Jesus, and the restoration of all things that the OT prophets predicted (Acts 3:19–25).
6. As the apostles proclaimed the gospel of Jesus they were proclaiming the kingdom (Acts 8:12).
7. Suffering for Jesus shows one worthy of the kingdom (Acts 14:22).
8. Part of the kingdom program was in operation as Gentiles were being saved as they believed in the Messiah (Acts 15).
9. The kingdom of God was still proclaimed to the Jewish people (Acts 19:8; 28:23).

CHAPTER

29 THE KINGDOM IN PAUL'S EPISTLES

Compared to the Gospels, references to the kingdom in Paul's letters are considerably less. As Douglas Moo points out, "Paul does not often refer to the kingdom of God."[1] Paul's letters contain fourteen references to God's "kingdom." This compares with 121 references to "kingdom" in Matthew, Mark, and Luke. The Pauline references are Romans 14:17; 1 Corinthians 4:20; 6:9, 10; 15:24, 50; Galatians 5:21; Ephesians 5:5; Colossians 1:13; 4:11; 1 Thessalonians 2:12; 2 Thessalonians 1:5; and 2 Timothy 4:1, 18. These few references, however, do not mean the kingdom is insignificant to Paul. Kingdom truths are important in his writings.

When Paul uses "kingdom," he does not define the term, indicating his audiences probably understood its meaning.[2] Several of Paul's references indicate who will not enter God's kingdom. For example, Paul states "the unjust will not inherit God's kingdom" (1 Cor 6:9). Galatians 5:21 and Ephesians 5:5 declare that ungodly people will not inherit God's kingdom. In addition, Paul says those who worked with him were "co-workers for the kingdom of God" (Col 4:11). These verses reveal a strong connection

1 Douglas Moo, *The Epistle to the Romans*, The New International Commentary on the New Testament (Grand Rapids: Eerdmans, 1996), 857. According to George Ladd, "Paul says almost as little about the Kingdom of God as he does about the messiahship of Jesus." *A Theology of the New Testament* (Grand Rapids: Eerdmans, 1974), 450.

2 In regard to Paul's sole mention of "kingdom" in Romans with Romans 14:17, Yarbrough notes, "The fact that Paul can use the expression with no introduction or explanation suggests that both for him and his readers, the term is already familiar." Robert W. Yarbrough, "The Kingdom of God in the New Testament: Mark through the Epistles," in *The Kingdom of God*, ed. Christopher W. Morgan and Robert A. Peterson (Wheaton, IL: Crossway, 2012), 144.

between the kingdom and soteriology.[3] One must be saved and evidence righteous behavior to enter the kingdom. On the other hand, those characterized by evil deeds show the kingdom does not belong to them. These truths do not indicate kingdom entrance is based on works, but they show kingdom citizens have the power of the Holy Spirit in their lives bringing forth righteous behavior.[4]

Also, for Paul, the heart of the kingdom program is the resurrected Jesus who is the "descendant of David" (Rom 1:3; cf. 2 Tim 2:8). Thus, any kingdom truths in Paul are ultimately tied to Jesus the Messiah, the center of the kingdom program, and the One who brings fulfillment of the Davidic Covenant (see 2 Sam 7:12–16) over His two advents.

But is there anything in Paul's letters that reveals his views on the nature and timing of the kingdom? Was his concept of the kingdom spiritual or physical, or both? Was the kingdom present or future, or both? Much debate surrounds these questions. Our understanding is that Paul's ideas on the kingdom are consistent with those found earlier in the Gospels and Acts. *The kingdom of God will come in the future after the return of Jesus.*[5] *Christians are positionally related to the King and His kingdom and are to exhibit kingdom righteousness in their lives. Yet the kingdom and reign of Jesus the Messiah await the future.*

The futurity of the kingdom is stated explicitly on several occasions. In 1 Thessalonians 2:12 Paul stated, "we encouraged, comforted, and implored each one of you to walk worthy of God, who calls you into His own kingdom and glory."[6] The link with "glory" here shows the kingdom is future.

With 2 Thessalonians 1:5 Paul declared, "It is a clear evidence of God's righteous judgment that you will be counted worthy of God's kingdom, for

---

3 Vickers is correct that "Soteriology and kingdom go together." Brian Vickers, "The Kingdom of God in Paul's Gospel," *The Southern Baptist Journal of Theology* 12 (2008): 57.

4 Ibid., 58. Vickers aptly notes that the fruit of the Spirit is linked to the kingdom, "It could justly be called the 'fruit of the kingdom'". In my estimation this is true because of the close connection between the New Covenant and the kingdom.

5 See Moo, *The Epistle to the Romans*, 857 n.40.

6 "Paul here speaks about the future of this *kingdom*, the time when God's glory will be revealed " Gene L. Green, *The Letters to the Thessalonians*, The Pillar New Testament Commentary (Grand Rapids: Eerdmans, 2002), 138. Emphasis in original.

which you also are suffering." The current experience of the Thessalonians was "suffering." But suffering makes them worthy of the "kingdom" they will be entering. Kingdom follows suffering. As Furnish notes, Paul "focuses on the eschatological future, assuring believers that through their sufferings God is qualifying them to enter that coming kingdom."[7]

Second Timothy 2:12 also presents the kingdom as future. Paul does not mention the term, "kingdom," but he does indicate that faithful endurance by Christians now will lead to a future "reign" in Jesus' kingdom—"If we endure, we will also reign with Him." This present age is characterized by trials, but for those who endure, the kingdom is their reward. The future tense used here ("will... reign") shows reigning was not the current experience of his readers.[8] This present age is one of enduring hardship for the sake of Jesus. If this occurs then reigning with Jesus will result when His kingdom begins.[9]

Then, in 2 Timothy 4:1, Paul says, "I solemnly charge you in the presence of God and of Christ Jesus, who is to judge the living and the dead, and by His appearing and His kingdom." Here Paul links the "kingdom" with Jesus' "appearing." Since Jesus' "appearing" is future "His kingdom" is future as well. This is soon followed by: "The Lord will rescue me from every evil work and will bring me safely into His heavenly kingdom. To Him be the glory forever and ever! Amen" (2 Tim 4:18). Paul again refers to the Lord's "heavenly kingdom" as future and something the Lord "will" bring him to. Paul did not view himself as presently in the kingdom. He longed, though, for the day when the Lord would take him there. Farnell is correct that "in the epistles, the dominant teaching of the 'kingdom of God' centers on a future kingdom and not a present one."[10]

7 Victor Paul Furnish, *1 Thessalonians, 2 Thessalonians*, Abingdon New Testament Commentaries (Nashville, TN: Abingdon Press, 2007), 147.

8 Knight points out, "The future tense of συμβασιλεύσομεν [we shall reign with] refers to an end-time situation that comes after the responsibility of the present tense ὑπομένομεν [enduring] has ceased, since this state of existence for Christians has ended." George W. Knight III, *The Pastoral Epistles: A Commentary on the Greek Text*, The New International Greek Testament Commentary (Grand Rapids: Eerdmans, 1992), 405.

9 Collins says that with 2:11–13 Paul speaks of a "future kingdom" and "future reign." Raymond F. Collins, *I and II Timothy and Titus: A Commentary* (Louisville, KY: Westminster John Knox Press, 2002), 184.

10 Farnell, "The Kingdom of God in the New Testament," 205.

THE FUTURE REIGN OF THE SAINTS (1 CORINTHIANS 4 AND 6)

First Corinthians contains the most kingdom information of any Pauline epistle.[11] Our focus here is on chaps. 4 and 6. In 1 Corinthians 4:8 Paul addressed the pride of the Corinthians: "You are already filled, you have already become rich, you have become kings without us; and indeed, I wish that you had become kings so that we also might reign with you." The Corinthians were acting like they were in God's kingdom reigning already. As Hughes, puts it, "In 4:8, the Corinthians were already reigning in a kingdom of their own making."[12] But Paul chided their attitude. He played along and said they had become "filled" and "rich." He then said, "You have become kings without us." Paul then switched back to reality by telling them, "I wish that you had become kings so that we also might reign with you." He then contrasts this with his own experience of suffering. So contrary to how the Corinthians were acting, they were not kings and they were not reigning already. It would be nice if they were reigning, but they were not. In fact, Paul says he wishes he and others were reigning too. As Knight observes, "Paul criticizes those who think and act as if they are already reigning with Christ. He wishes that it were so ..."[13] This shows Paul did not view himself or his readers as reigning in a kingdom yet.

Paul then challenges and contrasts his ministry with those who were arrogant. All they had were words (1 Cor 4:19), but Paul had the power of the kingdom as his source: "For the kingdom of God does not consist in words, but in power" (1 Cor 4:20). While the reign of the Messiah and the saints had not begun yet, Paul possesses the power of the Holy Spirit that can transform his life. This is evident in what he said earlier in 1 Corinthians 2:4–5: "And my message and my preaching were not in persuasive words of wisdom, but in demonstration of the Spirit and of power, that your faith should not rest on the wisdom of men, but on the power of God." This

11 Yarbrough says this is true of any epistle in the New Testament. See Yarbrough, "The Kingdom of God in the New Testament: Mark through the Epistles," 145.

12 Robert B. Hughes, *First Corinthians*, in Everyman's Bible Commentary (Chicago: The Moody Bible Institute of Chicago, 1985).

13 Knight, *The Pastoral Epistles*, 405.

kingdom power, no doubt, will manifest itself with characteristics of "righteousness, and peace and joy in the Holy Spirit" (see Rom 14:17).

In 1 Corinthians 6:1–11, Paul addressed lawsuits among Christians. He used truths concerning the future kingdom of God and then applied them to a present situation. With v. 1 Paul rebuked those who "dare to go to law before the unrighteous and not before the saints." Paul is disappointed some Christians were going to governing authorities with their problems instead of settling matters within the people of God. To counter this approach he said, "Or do you not know that the saints will judge the world? If the world is judged by you, are you not competent to constitute the smallest law courts? Do you not know that we will judge angels? How much more matters of this life?" (1 Cor 6:2–3).

Here Paul appeals to the eschatological truth that the saints will judge the world and the angels.[14] This should have practical implications now for lawsuits among Christians. Paul's point is this—since Christians are destined to judge the world and angels, certainly they should be able to solve personal issues among themselves. This is an opportunity for citizens of the kingdom to apply kingdom principles to their lives now. In this sense the future should impact the present.[15] As Ciampa and Rosner rightly note, "From the perspective of the everlasting kingdom, the Corinthian litigation is 'trifling'... and totally insignificant."[16]

Paul views the activity of judging the world and angels as future—"the saints will judge the world." The saints are not currently judging or reigning in Christ's kingdom because that is a future event associated with Jesus' second coming. If the saints are not ruling over angels then we can know the kingdom awaits the future.

With 6:9 Paul states, "the unrighteous will not inherit the kingdom of God." After listing those who practice certain sinful activities, he then states they will not inherit the kingdom of God (10–11). The concept of

14 This principle is found in other passages. Jesus explicitly promised positions of authority in Revelation 2:26–27 and 3:21. When Christ returns to earth and establishes His kingdom, Revelation 20:4 states, "Then I saw thrones, and they sat on them, and judgment was given to them."

15 "The future carries weighty implications for conduct in the present." Roy E. Ciampa and Brian S. Rosner, *The First Letter to the Corinthians*, The Pillar New Testament Commentary (Grand Rapids: Eerdmans, 2010), 228.

16 Ibid.

"inheritance" in the Bible often refers to future rewards for the people of God (Col 1:12; 1 Pet 1:4). As Yarbrough points out, "By connecting inheritance with the kingdom, Paul indicates that he is using 'kingdom' in its eschatological sense."[17]

Paul's point is when the kingdom of God comes in the future those who act wickedly will not enter or participate in it. Thus, 1 Corinthians 6:1–11 has important implications for the kingdom program. It reveals: (1) the kingdom is future; (2) the future kingdom should impact how we live today; and (3) unbelievers will not inherit the kingdom.

THE KINGDOM OF THE SON (1 CORINTHIANS 15:20–28, 50)

First Corinthians 15 is about resurrection. Yet, it also intersects with the kingdom. Some view this chapter as evidence Jesus' kingdom reign is spiritual from heaven in this age, while others see it as evidence for a future kingdom reign of Jesus over the earth. Our view is the latter. First Corinthians 15 indicates an intermediate kingdom after the return of Jesus but before "the end" when Jesus presents the kingdom to God the Father and the eternal state beings. This passage also reveals the Son's role concerning the kingdom program. The Son's role, as commissioned by the Father, is to bring this wayward world back into conformity with God's perfect will. When the Son completes His mission, which was originally tasked to Adam (Gen 1:26–28), He then will hand His kingdom to the Father, and the transition to the eternal state will commence.

The Kingdom after the Return of Jesus

A proper interpretation 1 Corinthians 15:20–28 involves understanding key terms and quotations of OT passages. Paul begins by saying that Christ's resurrection is "the first fruits of those who are asleep" (15:20). Since Jesus is raised from the dead, so too will those who are in Him. Then in 1 Corinthians 15:22–24 Paul declares:

17 Yarbrough, "The Kingdom of God in the New Testament: Mark through the Epistles," 156. Fee states, "This of course refers to the eschatological consummation of the kingdom." Gordon D. Fee, *The First Epistle to the Corinthians*, in The New International Commentary on the New Testament (Grand Rapids: Eerdmans), 266.

> For as in Adam all die, so also in Christ all will be made alive. But each in his own order: Christ the first fruits, after that those who are Christ's at His coming, then comes the end, when He hands over the kingdom to the God and Father, when He has abolished all rule and all authority and power.

Here Paul gives a timeline of the "order" of the resurrection program by pointing out three events and their relation to the kingdom. First, he says Christ is "the first fruits" (v. 23a). This refers to the bodily resurrection of Christ. Christ's resurrection is the pattern and guarantee the resurrection of others will occur. Second, "after that" there is a resurrection of "those who are Christ's at His coming" (v. 23b). This second stage is future. When Jesus returns those who belong to Him also will be resurrected. At least two thousand years separate these first and second phases of the resurrection program. Third, Paul states, "Then comes the end," when Jesus "hands over the kingdom to God the Father" (v. 24a). This period of "the end" appears to be a third phase in the resurrection program. To summarize, there are three stages of the resurrection according to 1 Corinthians 15:23–24a:

1. "Christ the first fruits"
2. "after that those who are Christ's at His coming"
3. "then comes the end... ."

While there is not much debate concerning the first two stages, there is considerable disagreement concerning the "end" and whether this is a third stage of resurrection or not. Those who hold to an intermediate kingdom after the return of Jesus but before the eternal state believe Paul's words ("then comes the end") indicate a period of time between events 2 and 3. An era exists between the resurrection of those at Christ's coming and the "end" when Jesus hands the kingdom over God the Father. The "end" does not occur immediately after Jesus returns but occurs after the kingdom reign of Jesus. As Craig Blaising argues, "Christ's coming marks the second stage, not the third (in which the end occurs)."[18] This view is consistent with premillennialism.

18 Blaising, "A Premillennial Response," 79.

Those who do not agree with an intermediate kingdom of Christ after His second coming believe "the end" follows immediately after Jesus' coming. Thus, "the end" occurs as a result of the second coming of Christ. There is no third stage of the resurrection program, and no room for an intermediate kingdom or millennium after the return of Christ. When Jesus returns and His people are resurrected, the end comes at that time and the eternal state begins.[19]

So which understanding is correct? Our view is that Paul is speaking of a three-stage resurrection program that leaves room for a kingdom reign between Jesus' return and the "end," the kind of kingdom John speaks of in Revelation 20:1–6.

First, Paul's use of "order" (*tagma*), a word sometimes used of military troops, seems to hint at a progression of more than two events. While an "order" of events could apply to only two resurrections, more than two seems likely. Also, a considerable gap of time exists between the first and second resurrections—at least two thousand years.

Paul refers to Christ as the "firstfruits" of the resurrection and then uses the temporal adverb *epeita* ("afterward") to discuss the resurrection of those who belong to Christ at His coming. Then, in what D. Edmond Hiebert has referred to as "the crux of the millennial issue,"[20] Paul begins v. 24 with the indefinite phrase, *eita to telos* ("then comes the end"). The temporal adverb *eita* "likely implies an interval time between the coming of Christ and the end."[21] Thus, just as there is a considerable time gap between Christ's resurrection and the resurrection of those who belong to Jesus (events 1 and 2), there will be a time gap between the resurrection of the people of God and the end when Jesus hands the kingdom over to the Father (events 2 and 3).

That such a gap exists is implied from the *epeita... eita* construction in 23b–24a which shows one event being followed by another. It is also

19 For a detailed defense of this view see Storms, *Kingdom Come*, 143–48.

20 D. Edmond Hiebert, "Evidence from 1 Corinthians 15," in *A Case for Premillennialism: A New Consensus*, ed. Donald K. Campbell and Jeffrey L. Townsend (Chicago: Moody, 1992), 229.

21 Ibid., 230. Leon Morris states, "*Then* (*eita*) does not necessarily mean 'immediately after'. It indicates that what follows takes place at some unspecified time after the preceding." Leon Morris, *1 Corinthians*, Tyndale New Testament Commentaries (Grand Rapids: Eerdmans, 1985), 211.

supported by a similar *epeita... eita* formula earlier in 1 Corinthians 15:5-8. Here Paul lays out a chronological order of events concerning Jesus' resurrection appearances. After stating Jesus was raised on the third day (v. 4), he says,

> and that He appeared to Cephas, then [*eita*] to the twelve. After that [*epeita*] He appeared to more than five hundred brethren at one time, most of whom remain until now, but some have fallen asleep; then [*epeita*] He appeared to James, then [*eita*] to all the apostles; and last of all, as to one untimely born, He appeared to me also.

Paul offers a chronological progression of resurrection appearances,[22] and his uses of *epeita* and *eita* reveal a progression of appearances. Verse 7 is particularly significant since, like 1 Corinthians 15:23b–24a, this verse also offers the *epeita ... eita* formula and shows chronological progression with a time gap. Jesus appeared to James and then appeared to all the apostles.[23] And in both cases the formula indicates a similar time gap:

> 1 Cor 15:7: *epeita... eita* indicates a time gap of days
>
> 1 Cor 15:23b–24a: *epeita... eita* indicates a time gap of which we now know includes thousands of years (at least two thousand–one thousand)[24]

That the *epeita... eita* formula indicates a gap of similar time in 1 Corinthians 5:7 (days) reveals the likelihood that the formula in 1 Corinthians 15:23b–24a also indicates a gap of similar time (many years). Remember, that the main issue is whether the *epeita... eita* formula allows or indicates a time gap between the resurrection of those at the time of Jesus' coming and the "end." The evidence indicates it does, not only from the

22 "He [Paul] indicates that he is listing the appearances in chronological order." Ciampa and Rosner, *The First Letter to the Corinthians*, 749.

23 Ciampa and Rosner point out that Christ appears to two individuals who are leaders of two groups. Jesus appears to Peter and then the group that Peter is the leaders of–the twelve. Likewise, Jesus appears to James and then the "slightly enlarged group of apostles" related to him in Jerusalem (749).

24 The "one thousand" is taking into account the thousand-year period mentioned several times in Revelation 20:1–10.

immediate context of 1 Corinthians 15:22–24, but from a similar grammatical construction in 1 Corinthians 15:5–8.

In sum, 1 Corinthians 15:22–24 reveals a three-stage resurrection program with a gap of time between the second and third stages that allows for a considerable period of time for a kingdom reign of Jesus before the "end" comes.

The Son's Mission from the Father

Not only does Paul give significant information about the kingdom concerning the resurrection program, he also reveals how the kingdom program relates to the Son. As 1 Corinthians 15:24b–28 shows, the Father has a mission for Jesus, and when Jesus fulfills this mission a transition takes place in the kingdom program:

> then comes the end, when He hands over the kingdom to the God and Father, when He has abolished all rule and all authority and power. For He must reign until He has put all His enemies under His feet. The last enemy that will be abolished is death. For he has put all things in subjection under his feet. But when He says, "All things are put in subjection," it is evident that He is excepted who put all things in subjection to Him. When all things are subjected to Him, then the Son Himself also will be subjected to the One who subjected all things to Him, so that God may be all in all.

Verse 24 says when "the end" comes Jesus will hand the kingdom over to God the Father. So there comes a point when a handing of Jesus' kingdom to the Father follows the kingdom reign of Jesus. *Some transition occurs.* This transition only happens, though, after the Son has successfully "abolished all rule and all authority and power." Jesus must reign and stamp out all opposition and then the eternal kingdom can begin. Any authority or power opposed to God must be fully and finally defeated. Paul uses two OT passages—Psalm 110 and Psalm 8—to confirm he is referring to a future earthly reign of Jesus. Seth Turner rightly notes that "1 Corinthians 15.24 shows that this kingdom is not permanent, but will be handed back to the

Father. It is an *interim* reign on earth of the Messiah that begins with Jesus' return and the resurrection of Christians."[25]

With 15:25 Paul says, "He must reign until He has put all His enemies under His feet" (25). The "must" means it is necessary that Jesus reigns. Paul's wording in v. 25 is a reference to Psalm 110:1–2 which states:

> The LORD says to my Lord:
> "Sit at My right hand
> Until I make Your enemies a footstool for Your feet."
> The LORD will stretch forth Your strong scepter from Zion, saying,
> "Rule in the midst of Your enemies."

This allusion to Psalm 110:1–2 is evidence the "reign" of Jesus is a future earthly reign. The context of Psalm 110 is David's Lord, the Messiah, sitting at the right hand of God for a session in heaven "until" He begins His earthly reign over His enemies from "Zion" in Jerusalem. In reference to Psalm 110:1, the author of Hebrews says Jesus is "waiting" at the right hand of the Father (see Heb 10:12–13). When the heavenly session is over, God installs His Messiah on the earth to reign over it. From our current historical perspective, Jesus is currently at the right hand of God the Father, but this will be followed by a reign upon the earth. Thus, Jesus "must" reign from earth because Psalm 110 says this must happen. In Acts 3:21, Peter also uses "must" in regard to Jesus and His heavenly session before He returns to earth to restore everything:

> whom heaven <u>must</u> receive until the period of restoration of all things about which God spoke by the mouth of His holy prophets from ancient time.[26]

Peter's point is that heaven must receive Jesus "until" the "period of the restoration of all things" occurs. This restoration has not occurred yet, but it will when Jesus returns to earth (see Acts 3:20). What Peter speaks of is similar to Paul's point in 1 Corinthians 15:25.

25 Seth Turner, "The Interim, Earthly Messianic Kingdom in Paul," *Journal for the Study of the New Testament* (2003): 334. Emphasis in original.

26 Emphases are mine.

Note also there is a "reign" of Jesus. This "reign" involves more than the second coming event (see Rev 19:11–21). The second coming is a swift event but a "reign" involves a considerable period of time. Jesus the Son and Messiah must have a sustained reign in the realm where the first Adam failed (see Gen 1:26, 28; 1 Cor 15:45).

With 1 Corinthians 15:27, Paul quotes Psalm 8:6: "FOR HE HAS PUT ALL THINGS IN SUBJECTION UNDER HIS FEET." Paul interprets Psalm 8:6 both literally and christologically. The psalm refers to man's right to rule God's creation. So how does this apply to both mankind and Jesus? Corporate personality is in view here. Psalm 8 is addressed to man in a general sense, but since Jesus is the ultimate Man and Last Adam, He represents man. As Mark Stephen Kinzer notes, "The psalm is read in both an individual and a corporate sense."[27]

His use of Psalm 8 confirms Paul is thinking of a future earthly reign of Jesus. Psalm 8 explains and expands upon Genesis 1:26–28 and its truth that God created man to rule successfully over the earth. *Since the Last Adam, Jesus, must succeed from and over the realm where the first Adam failed, Jesus must reign over the earth.* The Last Adam's destiny is not to rule from heaven in a spiritual kingdom. Instead, He is to rule *from* and *over* the earth just like the first Adam was supposed to do. But unlike Adam, Jesus will succeed. Those who place Jesus' kingdom reign in this age from heaven over a spiritual kingdom are not giving justice to an important part of God's kingdom program—man must reign over the earth. Jesus as the ultimate man and representative of mankind will fulfill this task. A spiritual reign from heaven does not complete what God requires in Genesis 1:26–28 and Psalm 8.

With v. 28, Paul says all things will be subject to Jesus, yet he notes one exception—God the Father. The Father commissioned the Son to reign over the earth, so the Father is not subject to the Son. When everything has been subjected to Jesus, Jesus will willingly subject himself to the Father so the Father can be "all in all." The language here finds a cultural parallel in a Roman emperor who sends a trusted general with the task of squashing and fixing a rebellion in the empire. The emperor would grant the full authority and force of Rome to the general who would act on his behalf. When

27 Mark Stephen Kinzer, "'All Things Under His Feet': Psalm 8 in the New Testament and in Other Jewish Literature of Late Antiquity," Ph.D. diss., The University of Michigan, 1995, 261.

the trusted general succeeded in his mission and vanquished the enemies, he would then return to the emperor, not to challenge the emperor, but to show his subjection to him. The general acted with the full authority of the emperor and when victory occurs, he returns in victorious yet humble submission to the one who commissioned him.

This is similar to what Jesus does on behalf of the Father. The Father sends Jesus to conquer and restore this fallen world on His behalf, and when Jesus accomplishes this task He then will subject himself to the Father. Jesus' mission is accomplished and the Father is pleased with His reign. Every square inch of the universe has been restored. At this point the reign of Jesus is followed by the universal reign of God the Father. This does not mean Jesus ceases to reign. Revelation 11:15 says Jesus "will reign forever and ever." So as McClain notes, "This does not mean the end of our Lord's regal activity, but rather that from here onward in the unity of the Godhead He reigns with the Father as the eternal Son."[28] Messiah's kingdom is blended into the universal kingdom. Jesus' prayer, "Thy kingdom come, Thy will be done, on earth as it is in heaven" (Matt 6:10) is fully accomplished. Jesus' kingdom does not end like earthly kingdoms do by defeat but by fulfillment of its mission.

Look closely at the statements that the Son "hands over the kingdom to the God and Father" (v. 24), and "the Son himself also will be subjected to the One [the Father] who subjected all things to Him, so that God may be all in all" (v. 28). *These statements indicate a distinction between the Son's kingdom and the Father's kingdom*. Of course, these two phases of the kingdom plan work in perfect harmony. It is the Father's will that the Son's kingdom happen and succeed. It is the Son's desire to fulfill the Father's mandate for man to rule and subdue the world for God's glory. Yet there is a distinction. It is during the Son's reign that Jesus, the ultimate Man and King, fulfills all the prophecies, covenants, and promises concerning God's mediatorial kingdom program. When this occurs then the eternal kingdom of the Father will commence. This truth again indicates the need for an era distinct both from this present age and the eternal kingdom. One should not simply assume that unfulfilled promises awaiting fulfillment will be fulfilled

28 McClain, *The Greatness of the Kingdom*, 513.

in the eternal state. In doing so this would put fulfillment outside of the direct reign of Jesus the Messiah to whom the task of fulfillment belongs.[29]

In sum, 1 Corinthians 15:20–28 reveals three phases of the resurrection program and that Jesus' kingdom occurs between His return and the "end." At the time of the third phase of God's resurrection plan, which comes after the intermediate kingdom, Jesus will hand the kingdom over to God the Father. The Son fulfills the kingdom mandate given to man to rule over the earth, and when this occurs the transition to the Father's eternal kingdom begins.

As presented above, the grammar of 1 Corinthians 15:20–28 indicates a future reign of Jesus after His second coming to earth. Yet the context of 1 Corinthians also strengthens this understanding. Paul viewed the kingdom reign as future in 1 Corinthians 4 and 6. With 1 Corinthians 4:8 he scolded the Corinthians for thinking they were reigning already when they were not ("I wish that you had become kings so that we also might reign with you"). And in 1 Corinthians 6:2–3 he stated that the kingdom reign of the saints involves judging angels, something that was not happening in the present.

A close connection exists between the kingdom reign of Messiah and the reign of those who belong to Messiah. So if Paul clearly places the kingdom reign of the saints in the future in 1 Corinthians 4 and 6, this adds support to the view that the kingdom reign of the Son described in 1 Corinthians 15:20–28 is future as well.

Inheriting the Kingdom (1 Corinthians 15:50)

After 1 Corinthians 15:20–28 Paul explains the nature and necessity of a physical resurrection of believers. He then returns to the kingdom in v. 50: "Now I say this, brethren, that flesh and blood cannot inherit the kingdom of God; nor does the perishable inherit the imperishable." This statement is not

29 To offer an example, the amillennialist, Anthony Hoekema, rightly insisted that the promised harmony among nations promised in Isaiah 2:2–4 will occur in the future and is not fulfilled in the church. See Hoekema, *The Bible and the Future*, 205–206. But Hoekema put its fulfillment in the eternal state and not Jesus' millennial kingdom. Yet the prophecies of Isaiah are linked with the "child" and "son" upon whom "the government will rest on His shoulders" (Isa 9:6). This refers to Jesus. He is the one who will rule the nations. With Hoekema's scenario the reign over the nations of Isaiah 2:2–4 would not take place under the direct reign of the Messiah in His millennial kingdom. But this goes against the message of Isaiah. It is better to view Isaiah 2:2–4 and other passages that are not fulfilled yet as coming to fulfillment in a coming intermediate kingdom under the direct rule of the Messiah.

a claim physical bodies do not exist in the kingdom of God or that believers are only spirits. He has already explicitly affirmed the resurrection of the body (see Rom 8:23). Instead, his point is that human beings in their fallen, perishable bodies cannot inherit God's imperishable glorious kingdom.

How does this relate to the kingdom? Paul already discussed the kingdom in 1 Corinthians 15:20–28. In addition to a three-stage resurrection plan, he refers to two phases of the kingdom. First, there is a kingdom of Jesus. After this, Jesus hands His kingdom over to the Father and the eternal kingdom begins. So what phase of the kingdom is Paul referring to in 15:50? The Father's eternal kingdom is probably in view. Why? If the kingdom solely refers to Jesus' kingdom, the conditions Paul offers in v. 50 do not fit with the truth that some non-glorified saints will exist in Messiah's kingdom. This is true whether one holds a premillennial, amillennial, or postmillennial view of the kingdom. Premillennialism holds that Jesus' kingdom includes non-glorified saints. Postmillennialism and amillennialism believe Jesus' millennial kingdom occurs between His two comings, but they also affirm that Jesus' kingdom includes non-glorified saints, whether the church on earth or believers in heaven in the intermediate state. So all three camps have non-glorified saints in Jesus' millennial kingdom.

But Paul states "flesh and blood" (i.e. non-glorified humans) cannot inherit the kingdom of God. If he is referring to Jesus' messianic/millennial kingdom then none of the three millennial camps can be accurate since all three claim Christians currently participate in Jesus' kingdom in a non-glorified state. What does fit, though, is if Paul is referring to the Father's eternal kingdom, or what we call the eternal state. The Father's eternal kingdom contains only people in glorified bodies.

While 1 Corinthians 15:50 offers all interpreters challenges, the kingdom Paul presents in this verse is a future kingdom, one in which all will have glorified bodies. Since no believers have been glorified yet, we can know the kingdom Paul discusses is still future.

JESUS AND THE SUMMATION OF ALL THINGS (EPHESIANS 1:10, 19–22)

Kingdom truths exist in Ephesians 1, particularly with v. 10 and vv. 19–22. After explaining the great blessings Christians have in Christ (Eph 1:1–8),

Paul says God is making known the mystery of His will (v. 9), "with a view to an administration suitable to the fullness of the times, that is, the summing up of all things in Christ, things in the heavens and things on the earth" (1:10). Everything God is doing has a forward-looking goal. There is a coming "administration" or dispensation, "a fullness of times" where God will head up or sum up all things in Christ. This fullness of times, as Hoehner states, "is that future earthly messianic kingdom" that "had been promised in the OT."[30] When this kingdom occurs "all things" are summed up or headed up "in Christ." This involves all things in the universe, whether in heaven or on earth. Whether it is angels or humans, spiritual things or material matters, all things will come under the headship of Christ.

This is the "restoration of all things" Peter spoke of in Acts 3:21. Paul's point in Ephesians 1:10 is also similar to his argument in Colossians 1:20 that God was reconciling all things to Himself through Jesus and His cross, "whether things on earth or things in heaven." Here we see the intersection between Jesus, the cross, and the kingdom. Jesus is the one who restores and reconciles a fallen world through His death. Thus, not only does Jesus' death atone for the sins of God's image-bearers, it is the basis for the reconciliation of all things in His kingdom.

With Ephesians 1:19–22 Paul explains the authority the exalted Jesus currently possesses at the right hand of God in heaven:

> And what is the surpassing greatness of His power toward us who believe. These are in accordance with the working of the strength of His might which He brought about in Christ, when He raised Him from the dead and seated Him at His right hand in the heavenly places, far above all rule and authority and power and dominion, and every name that is named, not only in this age but also in the one to come. And He put all things in subjection under His feet, and gave Him as head over all things to the church.

Paul wants the Ephesians to understand the great power of God at work in them. This incredible power that raised Jesus from the dead and seated Him at God's right hand is the same power that God works "toward us who believe" (1:19). The "right hand" language in v. 20 alludes to Psalm 110:1,

30 Harold W. Hoehner, *Ephesians: An Exegetical Commentary* (Grand Rapids: Baker, 2002), 219.

which discusses God's king, the Messiah, sitting at the right hand of God. Jesus' session at the right hand of God has certain ramifications according to Ephesians 1:20–22. First, it means Jesus is "far above all rule and authority and power and dominion." Hoehner asserts that the "all" is better translated "every" and means that "Christ's position in the heavenlies is above 'every kind of' power that exists."[31] The cluster of entities Jesus is above involves every "rule," "authority," "power," and "dominion."

There is debate as to whether these categories are human or angelic. If angelic, are they evil or good, or both? Hoehner asserts all four refer to evil angelic powers.[32] If so, Jesus' session at the right hand of God relates especially to evil spiritual forces. This view appears well supported by the context of Ephesians. Paul refers to "the prince of the power of the air" (Eph 2:2). He also says Christians struggle "against the rulers, against powers, against the world forces of this darkness, against the spiritual forces of wickedness in the heavenly places" (Eph 6:12). So Paul is explicitly conscious of evil spiritual forces that oppose Christians in this age as he writes this epistle.

Second, Jesus' session at the "right hand" of God means Jesus' name is above every other name for all time whether in this present age or the age to come. There will never be a time when Jesus loses His position of authority. Third, Jesus being at the right hand of God means God has subjected all things under Jesus. Paul relies on Psalm 8:6 and man's right to rule over the creation. There is nothing in creation outside His authority. Fourth, Jesus is "head" over all things related to the church.

With Ephesians 1:19–22 we see Jesus exalted and enthroned at the right hand of Father where He shares the throne of deity with the Father in heaven, a fulfillment of Psalm 110:1. Christians should be encouraged that the same power that raised Jesus from the dead and seated Him with authority in heaven is the same power at work in their lives. While some understand this passage to teach a spiritual messianic reign of Jesus in this age, the emphasis here is on Jesus' exaltation and the authority He has that will be fully exercised at His return to earth (see Matt 19:28; 25:31).

31 Harold W. Hoehner, *Ephesians: An Exegetical Commentary* (Grand Rapids: Baker Academic, 2002), 276.

32 Ibid., 280. "Hence, these powers most likely are angelic and evil and wish to rob us of our spiritual benefits."

RELATIONSHIP OF THE KINGDOM TO TODAY (ROMANS 14:17 AND COLOSSIANS 1:13)

For Paul the kingdom is a future event. The Messiah exalted in heaven now will come again to rule the world directly with His saints. But Paul also teaches present implications of the kingdom for Christians. For example, Romans 14:17 declares, "for the kingdom of God is not eating and drinking, but righteousness, peace, and joy in the Holy Spirit." Also, Colossians 1:13 states: "For He has rescued us from the domain of darkness, and transferred us into the kingdom of His beloved Son."

At first glance, Romans 14:17 seems to contradict the connection between eating and drinking and the kingdom.[33] But the context concerns Christian liberty and instruction for Christians who disagree over matters like observance of days and eating unclean foods. Paul responds by highlighting the priority of "righteousness" "peace" and "joy" over observing days or which foods to eat. Spiritual characteristics are at the heart of the kingdom and it is these Christians should emphasize. But emphasizing these matters does not mean the kingdom of God has nothing to do with the physical realm or that eating and drinking will not occur. Jesus declared drinking from "the fruit of the vine" would take place in "the kingdom of God" (Luke 22:18). Paul wrote that the creation itself would one day be glorified (see Rom 8:19–23). So it is unlikely that Paul, in Romans 14:17, was promoting some Platonic understanding of the kingdom divorced from physical elements. Instead, he prioritizes the importance of righteousness, peace, and joy. If one gets these areas right, then the other issues will fall in line. So Paul is not discussing the nature of the kingdom as much as he is stressing what is most important in it. While food is necessary, the spiritual requirements of fellowship and harmony are what are most important. Paul's readers should not act like Pagan hedonists who place physical pleasures and desires above love of others.

In Colossians 1:13 Paul teaches that Christians have been transferred from the domain of darkness to the kingdom of God's Son. Some say this indicates a present kingdom of Christ. Curtis Vaughan, for instance, claims

---

33 For example, Smit observes, "At first sight, there can be no greater discrepancy, than between Paul's claim in Rom 14:17, that the Kingdom of God is not about eating and drinking, but rather about righteousness, peace and joy in the Holy Spirit, and traditions found in the synoptic Gospels." Peter-Ben Smit, "A Symposium in Rom. 14:17? A Note on Paul's Terminology," *Novum Testamentum* 49 (2007): 43.

that "kingdom" in this verse "is not to be interpreted eschatologically. It was for the Colossians a present reality."[34] Likewise, O'Brien claims that the "aorist tenses [ἱκανώσαντι, ἐρρύσατο, μετέστησεν] point to an eschatology that is truly realized."[35] Saucy, though, observes that the context of Colossians 1:13 "favors an eschatological meaning for the kingdom."[36] Verse 12 states, "giving thanks to the Father, who has qualified us to share in the inheritance of the saints in Light." The term "inheritance" has eschatological overtones and may indicate that the kingdom reference in Colossians 1:13 is also future-oriented even though there are present implications. Saucy may be correct when he concludes, "Although the blessings of the salvation of the kingdom are present, it is difficult to see in Paul's words any idea of a present kingdom of Christ in which believers share in his reign."[37] In response to O'Brien's grammatical argument for Colossians 1:13, Farnell says the grammar of Colossians 1 is consistent with a futuristic understanding of the kingdom:

> However, these verses may be easily understood as futuristic aorists that emphasize the certainty of the future event, especially since inheritance is in Paul's mind in the immediate context which points to the accompanying blessings of that kingdom (Col 1:12). While believers have been transferred to citizenship in the future kingdom, they also experience spiritual blessings while they await its appearance, as Colossians 1:14 goes on to stress.[38]

Those who believe in Jesus the King have been transferred from the realm of Satan to the authority of Jesus. They have a present relationship to His kingdom, even before it arrives. McClain puts it, "we have been (aorist tense) transferred *judicially* into the Kingdom of our Lord even before

34 Curtis Vaughan, "Colossians," in *The Expositor's Bible Commentary*, ed. Frank E. Gaebelein (Grand Rapids: Zondervan, 1978), 11:180.

35 Peter T. O'Brien, *Colossians and Philemon*, vol. 44. Word Biblical Commentary (Waco, TX: Word, 1982), 28.

36 Robert L. Saucy, *The Case for Progressive Dispensationalism*, 108.

37 Ibid., 105.

38 Farnell, "The Kingdom of God in the New Testament," 206.

its establishment."[39] Paul does not view Christians as currently reigning with Jesus. In fact, Paul already chided the Corinthians for acting as if they already were reigning (see 1 Cor 4:8). Instead, Christians are positionally transferred to Christ's kingdom even though the actual establishment of the kingdom awaits His second coming.[40]

Thus, while not reigning in the kingdom, members of the church have an important relationship to the kingdom. Erich Sauer summarizes this well: "As to their persons they are citizens of the kingdom; as to their existence they are the fruit of the message of the kingdom; as to their nature they are the organism of the kingdom; as to their task they are the ambassadors of the kingdom."[41]

THE KINGDOM AND ISRAEL (ROMANS 9–11)

Romans 9–11 is Paul's treatise on why God's word has not failed even though Israel did not believe in her Messiah. Paul emphatically denies God has rejected His people Israel (see Rom 11:1). This cannot occur because of God's "choice" and the fact that Israel is "beloved for the sake of the fathers" (11:28). Also God's "calling" is "irrevocable." There is coming a day when "all Israel will be saved" (Rom 11:26). The timing of Paul's words is important. Not only is Israel's rejection of Jesus established but the church as an entity is well established too. If there ever were a chance to declare national Israel's place in the plan of God had been forfeited or the church had replaced Israel this was it. Instead, Paul affirms Israel's place in God's plans.

Romans 9:4 is strategic as Paul declares certain truths concerning his "kinsmen" (v. 3). Even though Israel is in a state of unbelief Paul states that certain important things are still the present possession of Israel: "who are Israelites, to whom belongs the adoption as sons, and the glory and the covenants and the giving of the Law and the temple service and the promises." Although Israel is not experiencing these things in their current state

39 McClain, *The Greatness of the Kingdom*, 435.

40 This would parallel what John said in Revelation 5:9–10 where the people of God are said to be a "kingdom" even though their reign over the earth was still viewed as future. It would also parallel the truth that living Christians are citizens of heaven even though they currently are not in heaven yet (Phil 3:20).

41 Erich Sauer, *From Eternity to Eternity* (London: Paternoster, 1954), 92–93.

of unbelief, they have not been cut off from these matters either. They still possess "adoption as sons" which shows God's fatherly relationship to them has not been forfeited. The "covenants" still belong to Israel. This must include the Abrahamic, Davidic, and New Covenants. Israel is also related to the "temple service" and the "promises." These issues such as Israel's relationship with God, the covenants of promise, temple service, and the promises of God all have a direct relationship to the kingdom of God.

A section that also has implications for the kingdom of God is Romans 11:11–15:

> I say then, they [Israel] did not stumble so as to fall, did they? May it never be! But by their transgression salvation has come to the Gentiles, to make them jealous. Now if their transgression is riches for the world and their failure is riches for the Gentiles, how much more will their fulfillment be! But I am speaking to you who are Gentiles. Inasmuch then as I am an apostle of Gentiles, I magnify my ministry, if somehow I might move to jealousy my fellow countrymen and save some of them. For if their rejection is the reconciliation of the world, what will their acceptance be but life from the dead?

Here Israel's unbelief and then later belief relate to world blessings. Israel's current "transgression" and "failure" brought "riches" for "the world" and "Gentiles" (v. 12). So Israel's unbelief has not halted God's plans, for God is using Israel's unbelief to bless the world. But more is to come with Israel's belief. As Schreiner states concerning v. 12, "If the trespass of Israel has led to worldwide blessing, then their belief will bring even greater blessing to the world."[42]

Yet Paul offers more. Verse 15 reveals Israel's "acceptance" will mean even greater blessings—"life from the dead." Life from the dead is kingdom blessings, and probably includes the glorification of the creation discussed earlier in Romans 8:18–25. Salvific blessings in this age will be followed by a holistic restoration of creation, what Acts 3:21 called the "restoration of all things." The point is that blessings now lead to much greater blessings to

42 Thomas R. Schreiner, *Romans*, in Baker Exegetical Commentary on the New Testament (Grand Rapids: Baker, 1998), 596. We are not saying Schreiner agrees with all our conclusions in this chapter.

come. If God can use Israel's current unbelief to bring world blessings, what greater blessings will follow for the world when Israel believes (see Rom 11:26)? What happens now is good, but it gets much better.

Another issue is Paul's references to "their rejection" and "their acceptance" in v. 15. Do these refer to God's rejection and then God's acceptance of Israel? Or do they refer to Israel's rejection of Christ and the gospel and then Israel's acceptance of Christ and the gospel? Or to put another way, does God first reject and then accept Israel, or does Israel first reject the gospel and then believe later?[43]

There certainly is room for debate on this issue with fine scholars who argue on both sides.[44] Perhaps the strongest argument for the "God's rejection of Israel" view is that Romans 9–11 is a section emphasizing God's sovereignty. Yet Romans 9–11 also indicts Israel for their unbelief. Israel stumbled over Christ choosing to try to work their way unto salvation instead of trusting in Christ through faith (see Rom 9:30–10:4). Certainly, the "transgression" of v. 11 and v. 12 is Israel's volitional choice of unbelief. Since vv. 12 and 15 parallel each other, the "transgression" probably parallels "rejection" in v. 15. Just as Israel committed "transgression" they probably are the ones committing the "rejection." If Israel's rejection of the gospel is in view, which is likely, this is evidence Israel's repentance and belief are linked with kingdom blessings, since v. 15 states, "what will their acceptance be but life from the dead?" Israel's belief leads to kingdom blessings for the world.

So not only does Romans 11:26 speak of a future salvation of Israel at the time of Jesus' second coming, it also indicates that national Israel's salvation results in greater worldwide blessings. Paul affirms that Israel's restoration under the reign of the Messiah results in global blessings beyond what is taking place in the present age (see Isa 2:2–4; Amos 9:11–15). So while the term "kingdom" is not explicitly mentioned, this text affirms significant kingdom truths—namely God will restore Israel under Messiah and the world will be blessed to an even greater degree when that happens.

43 The former view argues for an objective genitive. The latter argues for a subjective genitive—Israel's rejection of God and the gospel by not believing in Jesus.

44 See Jim R. Sibley, "Has the Church Put Israel on the Shelf? The Evidence from Romans 11:15," in *Journal of the Evangelical Theological Society* 58 (2015): 571–81.

CONCLUSION

While the kingdom theme is not as prominent in Paul's letters as other sections of the NT, Paul still offers significant information about the kingdom program. For Paul the kingdom is future with present implications. Christians today are related to the kingdom and are to evidence kingdom righteousness in their lives even now. Those characterized by wickedness are not qualified to enter it.[45] Also, the kingdom reign of Jesus and His saints awaits His second coming. Jesus must reign in His kingdom over the earth. When He, the Last Adam, succeeds in reigning from and over the earth, His kingdom will transition to the kingdom of the Father and the eternal state will commence.

45 Kee strikes the right balance between Paul's view of a future kingdom with present implications: "The future kingdom of God... has a significant role in the thought of Paul. He asserts the qualities that characterize those who will share in the new circumstances when God's rule takes on its encompassing role over God's people and the world as a whole. That context will be characterized by righteousness, peace, and joy in the Holy Spirit.... Yet moral failures will result in disqualification for sharing in the kingdom." Howard Clark Kee, *The Beginnings of Christianity: An Introduction to the New Testament* (Madison Square Park, NY: T&T Clark, 2005), 483.

CHAPTER

30 THE KINGDOM IN HEBREWS

Hebrews is a book of exhortation (13:22) that extols the superiority of Jesus Christ and His priesthood. It also discusses the temporary nature of the Mosaic Covenant and how it is replaced by the superior New Covenant. While there are only two explicit references to "kingdom" in Hebrews there are several important truths about God's kingdom program in this document.

Our discussion of Hebrews will come in two sections. First, it will survey various passages in Hebrews that mention "kingdom" or have a relationship to the kingdom. Second, we will look specifically at references to Psalm 110 in Hebrews. Hebrews has the most references to Psalm 110 of any book in the NT so we will study how this book treats this important psalm.

In chap. 1, the author affirms the superiority of Jesus. Jesus is "heir of all things" (v. 2), and upholds all things (v. 3a). He is also the One who after making purification for sins "sat down at the right hand of the Majesty on high" (v. 3b). This reference to sitting at God's right hand is an allusion to Psalm 110:1. Then we are told Jesus is "better than the angels" (v. 4). With v. 8, God the Father speaks of the kingdom in relation to Jesus:

> But of the Son He says,
> "YOUR THRONE, O GOD, IS FOREVER AND EVER,
> AND THE RIGHTEOUS SCEPTER IS THE SCEPTER OF HIS KINGDOM."

Here God the Father calls the Son, "God," showing the deity of Jesus. The quotation comes from Psalm 45:6–7, a love or wedding psalm. Debate exists whether the referent in the psalm is Solomon or the Messiah, or both.

Whichever is most accurate, the writer of Hebrews shows that Jesus the Messiah is ultimately in view. This highlights the forever nature of Jesus' reign.

RULING MANDATE FULFILLED IN 'WORLD TO COME' (HEBREWS 2:5–8)

Hebrews 2 addresses the implications of Psalm 8, which details man's dignity and right to rule over God's creation. Psalm 8 is one of the most quoted OT passages in the NT, yet it is Hebrews 2:5–8 that offers the most extended discussion of this important psalm. In Hebrews 2:5 the author states there is a "world to come" that will be subjected to man, not angels. This is one example of futuristic eschatology by the writer and shows that His emphasis here is on the future. He then quotes Psalm 8:4–6 which tells of man's right to rule over God's creation—"AND HAVE APPOINTED HIM [MAN] OVER THE WORKS OF YOUR HANDS; YOU HAVE PUT ALL THINGS IN SUBJECTION UNDER HIS FEET" (Heb 2:7b–8a). The author affirms the truth of Psalm 8 that even in a fallen world man still possesses the right to rule God's creation.[1] This responsibility has not been forfeited. Yet, he also states this present age is not the era for the fulfillment of the ruling mandate—"For in subjecting all things to him, He left nothing that is not subject to him. But now we do not yet see all things subjected to him" (Heb 2:8b). The words "not yet" show that the rule over creation given to man is not happening yet. Wallis says this subjection, which is not yet, reveals that "the subjugation has not been begun nor has it been completed."[2]

The reason for this delay in fulfillment is the fall of man. Since man is in a sinful state (see Gen 3) and separated from God, he is unable to rule the earth successfully on God's behalf. So fulfillment of the ruling mandate awaits the future. Commenting on Psalm 8's use in Hebrews 2, Mark

1 Many have noted that Psalm 8:4–8 appears to be a commentary on the kingdom mandate of Genesis 1:26–28.

2 Wilber B. Wallis, "The Use of Psalms 8 and 110 in I Corinthians 15:25–27 and in Hebrews 1 and 2," in *Journal of the Evangelical Theological Society* 15 (1972): 28. "The perfect participle *hypotetagmenon* [having subjected, Heb 2:8b], looking at both ends of the action, would imply that the subjugation has not been begun... . the subjection of all things is yet future" (Ibid.).

Stephen Kinzer states, "The psalm must be intended for the eschaton, for it does not describe the current state of affairs."[3]

While mankind is the immediate focus in 2:5–8, the ultimate man, Jesus, is the subject of 2:9 and here we see how Jesus fits into God's plans: "But we do see Him who was made for a little while lower than the angels, namely, Jesus, because of the suffering of death crowned with glory and honor, so that by the grace of God He might taste death for everyone." This reveals a connection between Jesus' cross and kingdom. Because of His suffering, Jesus is now "crowned with glory and honor." This is consistent with passages such as Psalm 110:1; Matthew 28:19; and Ephesians 1:20–22 that picture Jesus as currently exalted as Messiah at the right hand of the Father in heaven. Because of His sufferings and cross, Jesus is the One who can fulfill the kingdom mandate on man's behalf in "the world to come." This truth is also found in Revelation 5 where the Lamb who suffered is worthy to take the world back for God and reign upon the earth (Rev 5:9–10).

Put together, man's present and future relationship to creation can be expressed as follows:

> Present: Man still possesses the right and responsibility to rule over God's creation, but this is not occurring yet.
>
> Present: Jesus, who is representative of mankind, is crowned with glory and majesty at the right hand of God.
>
> Future: In the world to come all things will be subject to man because of Jesus.

Jesus is also the One who can defeat Satan and deliver man from death. Although it was man's sin that transferred authority to Satan and introduced death, Jesus defeated these foes with His death (see Heb 2:14–15). This is the basis for man's rule in the coming world. Man cannot fulfill His destiny as ruler of this world while Satan and death remain obstacles.

3 Mark Stephen Kinzer, "'All Things Under His Feet': Psalm 8 in the New Testament and in Other Jewish Literature of Late Antiquity," Ph.D. diss., The University of Michigan, 1995, 261.

Jesus will fulfill the creation mandate to rule the world. He will accomplish this after His present session at the right hand of the Father.[4] Jesus will also empower those who belong to Him to do so. Thus, the fulfillment of the creation mandate given to man in Genesis 1:26–28 and reaffirmed in Psalm 8 is fulfilled in an individual and corporate sense. As the ultimate Man, Jesus, fulfills the mandate. And then He empowers those who belong to Him to rule as well. The foundation for the rule is the death of Christ, but the actual rule over the world awaits the future.

In sum, Hebrews 2 affirms the importance of the creation in God's plans and man's role in it. Just as man originally was delegated with authority over the world, so too, man will exercise authority over "the world to come." Man and the creation are forever linked, and God has not abandoned His plan for man to exercise his role over creation. Jesus will make this happen.

THE FUTURE KINGDOM AS PRESENT POSSESSION (HEBREWS 11–12)

As Hebrews unfolds, the superiority of Christ is further amplified. Christ's priesthood is superior to the Levitical priesthood of the Mosaic Covenant (ch. 7). The New Covenant Christ instituted is superior to the Mosaic Covenant (ch. 8). In Hebrews 11–12, the author offers key information regarding the kingdom and how it fits with the coming New Jerusalem.

Hebrews 11:8–10

With Hebrews 11:8–10 we learn the significance of the faith and hope that Israel's patriarchs had regarding the land of promise:

> By faith Abraham, when he was called, obeyed by going out to a place which he was to receive for an inheritance; and he went out, not knowing where he was going. By faith he lived as an alien in the land of promise, as in a foreign land, dwelling in tents with Isaac and Jacob, fellow heirs of the same promise; for

4 Since Jesus' miracles during His earthly ministry were tastes and glimpses of the kingdom, Jesus' nature miracles were samples of His dominion over nature. Yet the fulfillment of the mandate to rule over nature awaits the coming kingdom reign of Jesus.

> he was looking for the city which has foundations, whose architect and builder is God.

This account takes us back to Genesis 12 when Abraham [then Abram], the son of an idol worshiper, was called to leave his homeland in Mesopotamia for a land God promised him. By faith Abraham left the comforts of his previous home for an unknown place. Yet when he arrived he "lived as an alien in the land of promise." Abraham did not yet experience the full blessings promised to him. In fact, Stephen declared that God "gave him [Abraham] no inheritance in it, not even a foot of ground" (Acts 7:5). That would come later. As a result, Abraham "was looking for the city which has foundations, whose architect and builder is God" (Heb 11:10).

Abraham was looking for something greater than his own experience in the land. He was looking for a permanent "city" with foundations made by God. Hebrews 12:22 identifies this "city" as the "heavenly Jerusalem." Other writers call it the "new Jerusalem" (Rev 21:2) or the "Jerusalem above" (Gal 4:26). In addition, Hebrews 13:14 indicates that this "city" is "the city which is to come." This is significant since the writer of Hebrews is telling us that this city has not arrived yet. Hebrews 12:22–23 states God's people are related to this city, although its coming is still future.

Hebrews 11:13–16 says OT saints "died in faith, without receiving the promises" but they "welcomed them from a distance" (13). They were "looking for a country of their own" and because of this they refused to return to their original dwelling places (14–15). They had opportunities to go back, but they stayed looking for God's promise. Hebrews 11:16 then says they desired a better country, "a heavenly one." This is again linked with "a city" that God "prepared" for them.

Understanding the word "heavenly" is important. Some have taken "heavenly" to mean the OT saints were really looking for heaven, and not land on the earth. This would indicate a strong reality shift from an earthly hope to a spiritual expectation. This seems to be what Burge holds, "But Hebrews says that our 'homeland' has changed. It is not on earth. The argument is sustained in 11.16 where Hebrews continues, 'But as it is, they longed for a better *patris*—which belongs to heaven.'"[5] But this is a misunderstanding. "Heavenly" is not opposed to "earthly" or "physical." There is no Platonic dualism between spirit and matter here. The concept of "heavenly" here has more to do with source and power than with pure spirit as opposed to matter. The "city" the writer is referring to is a literal, physical city, a city that "is to come" (13:14). This city is upon the earth. What is heavenly about the city is its origin—its source is heaven.[6]

Likewise, the New Jerusalem is a real, tangible city that is still future. The city Abraham and other OT saints were searching for was a literal city made by God that would someday exist upon the earth. Abraham was looking for a glorious city in the land of promise, a majestic city from God with permanence.

Hebrews 12:18–24

Hebrews extols the superiority of Jesus the Messiah and how the New Covenant, established by Jesus, is superior to the Mosaic Covenant. In 12:18–24, the writer contrasts the two covenants via the illustrations of Mount Sinai and Mount Zion. The Mosaic Covenant is linked with Sinai and the New Covenant with Zion. Mount Sinai was the place where the Mosaic Law was given to Moses and the Israelites. It is associated with "darkness and gloom and whirlwind" (18). It was also linked with "fear and trembling" (21). But New Covenant saints are not related to Sinai, they "have come to Mount Zion" as 12:22–24 indicates:

> But you have come to Mount Zion and to the city of the living God, the heavenly Jerusalem, and to myriads of angels, to the general assembly and church of the firstborn who are enrolled in heaven, and to God, the Judge of all, and to the spirits of the righteous made perfect, and to Jesus, the mediator of a new

5 Gary M. Burge, *Jesus and the Land: The New Testament Challenge to "Holy Land" Theology* (Grand Rapids: Baker, 2010), 101. The claim that our homeland "is not on earth" seems dangerously close to anti-material Platonist thinking.

6 "... we are not going 'up' to the heavenly city; rather, the heavenly city is coming here, and it will be unveiled at the last day." Middleton, *A New Heaven and a New Earth*, 219.

> covenant, and to the sprinkled blood, which speaks better than the blood of Abel.

"Mount Zion" was a hill on the capital city of Jerusalem. It is called "the heavenly Jerusalem" (12:22). Since Mount Zion replaces Mount Sinai, this means that the New Covenant replaced the old Mosaic Covenant. God's people are no longer under the Mosaic Covenant but are under the New Covenant.

Those associated with the "heavenly Jerusalem" are "angels," the "church," "God," OT saints ("spirits of the righteous made perfect"), and "Jesus." So in what sense have Christians come to Mount Zion, the heavenly Jerusalem? Since this city is a city that "is to come" (13:14), Christians are not actually present in the city although they have a positional relationship to it. Revelation 21:1–2 says the New Jerusalem comes down to the new earth after the second coming of Jesus and the millennial kingdom. Christians are related to this city even though they are not experiencing it yet. This is seen in the statement that the "church" is "enrolled in heaven" (12:23). Living church saints are carrying out the Great Commission on earth, but they are "enrolled" or citizens of the heavenly Jerusalem. This is similar to the truth of Philippians 3:20 that "our citizenship is in heaven." Paul is not saying Christians are presently in heaven, but heaven presently belongs to them. So then, New Covenant Christians are citizens of the New Jerusalem, although the city's arrival is still future from our standpoint. This passage offers no support for a spiritual Jerusalem not related to the earth.

Hebrews 12:25–29

Hebrews 12:25–29 tells of coming judgment and kingdom. After warning the readers not to "refuse" God (12:25), they are reminded God "shook the earth" at the time of the giving of the law (12:26a). Exodus 19:18 says, "and the whole mountain quaked violently." But this would not be the last time God shakes the earth: "but now He has promised saying, 'yet once more I will shake not only the earth, but also the heaven'" (12:26b).[7] The "yet once more" indicates futurity. From his current standpoint, the writer of Hebrews sees a future shaking coming. This coming shaking will not just

7 The quotation comes from Haggai 2:6.

be limited to the earth; it will include "the heaven" as well. This indicates an increase from what occurred at Sinai, which was primarily related to the "earth." The purpose of this shaking is to remove things that can be shaken, so that things that cannot be shaken remain (12:27).

The shaking of the earth and heaven is both literal and future from our standpoint. It will be literal just as the violent quaking at Mount Sinai was a real shaking. As Homer Kent puts it:

> The first shaking was physical and geographical at Sinai. There is no good reason to take this second shaking of the earth and the heavens above in any less literal sense. The reference then is to the second coming of Christ, which will involve great physical judgments as foretold by the prophets in both the Old Testament and the New Testament.[8]

Such a picture is consistent with other passages that foretell a future shaking in the end times as part of the Day of the Lord judgments that precede the coming of the kingdom of God. Revelation 6:12–14 speaks of a "great earthquake" that will affect "every mountain and island" along with "the sky" being "split apart like a scroll." Isaiah 24 graphically states the earth will be "shaken violently" and "reel to and fro like a drunkard" (24:19–20) before the kingdom is established (Isa 25).

The "kingdom" is specifically referred to in Hebrews 12:28: "Therefore, since we receive a kingdom which cannot be shaken, let us show gratitude, by which we may offer to God an acceptable service with reverence and awe." Christians "receive" or "are receiving" an unshakeable kingdom. Monteforie observes that *paralambanontes* ("receiving") "suggests that the readers are in process of receiving, not that they have already received the kingdom. If the kingdom had actually been received, there would have been no need of this final exhortation."[9] The actual arrival of the kingdom is connected with the coming shaking of the earth.

8 Homer A. Kent, Jr., *The Epistle to the Hebrews: A Commentary* (Winona Lake, IN: BMH Books, 1972), 275–76.

9 Hugh Montefiore, *A Commentary on the Epistle to the Hebrews*. Black's New Testament Commentaries (London: Adam & Charles Black, 1964), 229. This "receiving" should be understood in a futuristic or proleptic sense.

Christians are receiving the kingdom because of their relationship to the King even though its arrival is still future. As with heaven and the New Jerusalem, the kingdom is something Christians currently receive since faith makes one a citizen of the kingdom before its actual arrival. Christians belong to Messiah's kingdom that will be established when Jesus returns to earth. Donald Hagner says the wording of Hebrews 12:28 reflects "a careful balance between present and future eschatology. We are in the process of receiving the kingdom now; we will receive it finally in the future."[10] Farnell points out how the grammar supports a future understanding of the kingdom:

> Although a temporal aorist participle is used ["receive"], the context places that reception at a future time of judgment and contrasts the temporary nature of earthly kingdoms with the permanence of that future kingdom (Heb 12:26–27).[11]

Hebrews 11–12 reveals important kingdom truths about the present and future. Presently, Christians today are related to both the New Jerusalem and the kingdom itself. Yet, the arrival of the New Jerusalem and the kingdom of God await the coming Day of the Lord with its shaking of the earth. Thus, Hebrews is consistent with other passages where the people of God lay claim to God's kingdom, yet the arrival of this kingdom follows God's judgment of the world.

THE RIGHT HAND OF GOD

We now survey the several references to Psalm 110 in Hebrews. Hebrews has more citations and allusions to Psalm 110 than any other NT book, which is significant since Psalm 110 is the most quoted and alluded to passage in the NT. Much of Hebrews stems from the author's emphasis on Psalm 110:1 and 110:4. He will quote Psalm 110:1 on several occasions to discuss Jesus' current session at the right hand of God. He will also refer to Psalm 110:4 to explain Jesus' priestly activity from heaven.

10 Donald A. Hagner, *Hebrews*. Understanding the Bible Commentary Series (Grand Rapids: Baker, 1990), n. p., section 38.

11 Farnell, "The Kingdom of God in the New Testament," 207.

Psalm 110:1 declares, "The Lord says to My Lord, 'Sit at My right hand until I make Your enemies a footstool for Your feet.'" This verse has great implications for God's kingdom program since it indicates that God's chosen King will enjoy a session at God's right hand in heaven before this King rules over His enemies from Jerusalem (see 110:2).

Hebrews explicitly refers to Psalm 110:1 on five occasions—1:3, 13; 8:1; 10:12; and 12:2. Mark Saucy observes that Psalm 110:1 "functions" in Hebrews "as a divine accolade of the Son because of his redemptive work."[12] The exaltation and session of Christ at the Father's right hand are about glory and honor. This status of being at the right hand is not stated in terms of an active reign.[13] While Psalm 110:1 and 110:4 are heavily emphasized in Hebrews there are no quotations of Psalm 110:2 which discusses the Messiah's reign from Jerusalem. While some may see this as an argument from silence it does seem odd that if the author of Hebrews wanted to emphasize a current messianic reign of Jesus from heaven he does not quote Psalm 110:2.[14] Instead, what is emphasized is the Messiah's session at the right hand of God (Ps 110:1) and His priestly ministry in the order of Melchizedek (Ps 110:4).

Hebrews 1:3

Hebrews 1:3 links Jesus' purification of sins with His sitting at the right hand of God:

> And He [Jesus] is the radiance of His glory and the exact representation of His nature, and upholds all things by the word of His power. When He had made purification of sins, He sat down at the right hand of the Majesty on high.

This is a contextual use of Psalm 110 because Psalm 110:4 links the King of Psalm 110:1 with a priesthood—"You are a priest forever, according to the

12 Mark Saucy, "Exaltation Christology in Hebrews: What Kind of Reign?" *Trinity Journal* 14 NS (1993): 47.

13 Ibid. "The Son's status is not characterized as an active reign or rule."

14 Ibid., 48. "This absence of Ps 110:2 is all the more noteworthy in the case of Hebrews, which is so dominated by Psalm 110 and concerned with the present ministry of the ascended Christ."

order of Melchizedek" (Ps 110:4). When Jesus made purification for sins He then sat down at the right hand of God. Jesus' sin offering on the cross led to His exaltation to the right hand of God. Thus, the emphasis here is on Jesus' priesthood in relation to God's right hand.

Hebrews 1:13

Hebrews 1:13 states:

> But to which of the angels has He ever said, "SIT AT MY RIGHT HAND, UNTIL I MAKE YOUR ENEMIES A FOOTSTOLL FOR YOUR FEET"?

The context of this verse concerns the superiority of Jesus. The main point is Jesus is superior to angels because no angel has been promised the exalted position of being at the right hand of God that leads to a reign over the earth.

What are the kingdom implications? Jesus is currently at the right hand of the Father. Mark Saucy argues, "The use of Psalm 110:1 at 1:3 and 13 fosters notions of glory, honor, and protection, but the absence of 110:2 suggests *ex silentio* that the process of ruling is not in the view of our author."[15] The lack of Psalm 110:2 in Hebrews, which discusses the active reign of the Davidic King, appears significant:

> This absence of Ps 110:2 is all the more noteworthy in the case of Hebrews, which is so dominated by Psalm 110 and concerned with the present ministry of the ascended Christ. If Christ were ruling now and even progressively subjecting his enemies, the author had an easy opportunity to say so from the Psalm which is so influential for his work. Instead, we are left with the Son seated at the right hand (1:3, 13), which, as W. O. E. Oesterley comments, ".... is a poetical way of expressing the truth that he is under divine protection, as well as being honored. But, further, he is to *sit*, an attitude which throughout the East... implies inactivity."[16]

15 Ibid. "The command to rule in Ps 110:2 is also absent from the NT through either allusion or citation. This is significant, considering the overall importance of Psalm 110 to the NT."

16 Ibid.

Hebrews 8:1

> Now the main point in what has been said is this: we have such a high priest, who has taken His seat at the right hand of the throne of the Majesty in the heavens.

Like Hebrews 1:3 the connection here is with Jesus' ministry as "high priest." As the high priest, Jesus has taken His seat at the right hand of God. This exaltation of Jesus is the basis for His priestly intercessory role. Again, this is a contextual use of Psalm 110 since the one at the right hand of God in Psalm 110 is also a priest.

Hebrews 10:12–13

> But He, having offered one sacrifice for sins for all time, sat down at the right hand of God, waiting from that time onward until his enemies be made a footstool for his feet.

Like Hebrews 1:3 and 8:1, this passage links Jesus' "sacrifice for sins" with sitting at the right hand of God. But v. 13 adds significant information. It states that Jesus is "waiting" (*ekdechomenos*) to subdue His enemies. This shows Jesus' current session at the right hand of God is not that of actively ruling over His enemies on earth as Davidic King. That day will come, but for now He is "waiting from that time onward until" He conquers His enemies. As Mark Saucy notes, "Far from initiating an active rule from his exalted position, the Session [at the right hand of God] leads instead to the Son's inactive waiting for the promise of the Father in Ps 110:1c."[17]

This waiting to rule does not mean the Messiah is altogether inactive since His priestly intercessory ministry is occurring and He shares the throne of the Father's universal kingdom. But Messiah's reign over His enemies on earth awaits the future.[18] When Jesus returns a second time, God will stretch forth His strong scepter from Zion (i.e. Jerusalem) (see 110:2). Psalm 110:1–2 did not indicate how long a gap would occur between the

17 Ibid., 50.

18 Ibid., 52. Saucy says, "according to our writer, the activity of the exalted Christ is of an intercessory character, more than a reigning one. Assuredly, the Son is not currently inactive, but his activity is directed specifically towards his people, not his enemies."

session of God's King at His right hand and the reign of this King from Zion, but such a gap is there. In sum, after making one sacrifice for sins, Jesus sat down at the right hand of God "waiting" until the day comes when He will actively reign over His enemies.

Hebrews 12:2

> Fixing our eyes on Jesus, the author and perfecter of faith, who for the joy set before Him endured the cross, despising the shame, and has sat down at the right hand of the throne of God.

This verse indicates Jesus' humiliation at the cross was followed by exaltation as He "sat down at the right hand of the throne of God." This verse is consistent with other uses of Psalm 110 in Hebrews that align with the original meaning of the psalm.

Summary of "Right Hand" Passages

The five "right hand" passages in Hebrews reveal key truths. First, Jesus is the King/Priest that Psalm 110 predicted. Second, the author focuses on the application of Psalm 110:1 and Psalm 110:4 to Jesus' present ministry in heaven. The uses of Psalm 110:1 show Jesus is currently at the right hand of the Father sharing the throne of deity with the Father. Jesus is at this position waiting for the time when God will install Him as King in Jerusalem. The uses of Psalm 110:4 emphasize Jesus' current role as Priest who makes intercession for His people.

SUMMARY OF THE KINGDOM PROGRAM IN HEBREWS

Hebrews is important for understanding the kingdom program. Christians currently are looking for the world to come (2:5) and the city to come (13:14). Jesus is currently exercising His priestly role from the right hand of God but is waiting for the day when He will reign as messianic King, putting His enemies under His feet (Heb 10:12–13). The kingdom has not arrived yet but it will come in connection with divine judgments to come (12:26, 28). But like Abraham, Christians are looking for the coming heavenly Jerusalem, a literal city that will exist on the earth. While the heavenly

Jerusalem has not been established on earth yet, members of the church "are enrolled in heaven" (12:23), showing they are related to the kingdom and the heavenly Jerusalem.

KINGDOM IN OTHER GENERAL EPISTLES

Most references to "kingdom" in the general epistles are found in Hebrews. Yet there are two other references—one in James and the other in 2 Peter. James uses the term in 2:5:

> Listen, my beloved brethren: did not God choose the poor of this world to be rich in faith and heirs of the kingdom which He promised to those who love Him?

James asserts the poor of the world are often rich in faith. This is not a statement that all poor people have faith or that no rich people have faith. But the poor often experience faith more since they are not trusting in their riches. In regard to the kingdom, those who are poor and express faith are "heirs of the kingdom." Being poor now does not mean being poor forever. They will inherit the kingdom when it comes. Thus, James 2:5 indicates a futuristic view of the kingdom. As Yarbrough observes, "James speaks of a kingdom in the same futuristic way that Jesus sometimes did."[19]

The other reference to the kingdom is 2 Peter 1:10–11:

> Therefore, brethren, be all the more diligent to make certain about His calling and choosing you; for as long as you practice these things, you will never stumble; for in this way the entrance into the eternal kingdom of our Lord and Savior Jesus Christ will be abundantly supplied to you.

Peter's point is one should verify God's calling by practicing what is right. For those who do this "entrance into eternal kingdom" of Jesus "will be abundantly supplied." Peter speaks of the kingdom as future here. The "entrance" into the kingdom refers to something that "will be" (future tense) supplied to those who qualify. Christians are not experiencing the

19 Yarbrough, "The Kingdom of God in the New Testament: Mark through the Epistles," 150.

kingdom now but they will. The reward of Jesus' coming kingdom is motivation for living right and persevering in this present age.

Although not mentioning "kingdom," another general epistle passage with kingdom implications is 1 Peter 3:22 which says Jesus "is at the right hand of God, having gone into heaven, after angels and authorities and powers had been subjected to Him." This is another reference to Psalm 110:1 and shows that angelic forces are subject to Jesus. What is described here parallels Colossians 2:15 which states, "When He [Jesus] had disarmed the rulers and authorities, He made a public display of them, having triumphed over them through Him." With these passages, the emphasis is on Jesus' authority over evil angelic powers as a result of being at God's right hand.

Jesus possesses all authority over heaven and earth, and the emphasis in 1 Peter 3:22 is on subjection of evil spiritual forces. This subjection of evil spiritual forces is not complete in this age. Satan and his forces still exercise authority and influence. Ephesians 6:12 says the struggle with "rulers," "powers," and "world forces of this darkness," takes place "in the heavenlies." Satan also is referred to as "the prince of the power of the air" (Eph 2:2). The full exercise of Jesus' authority awaits His second coming. It awaits the "administration" which is "the summing up of all things in Christ, things in the heavens and things on the earth" (Eph 1:10).

CHAPTER

31 THE KINGDOM IN REVELATION 1–18

The cosmic battle between good and evil has raged throughout history. It is fitting that the last book of the Bible describes the final battles between God's kingdom and Satan's kingdom.[1] The first book of the Bible introduced us to the cosmic battle (see Gen 3), now Revelation gives us the culmination of the war. Through a series of dramatic events the kingdom of Satan will be violently removed by the kingdom of God through the Day of the Lord judgments and the return of Jesus the Messiah. Because Revelation is so strategic to God's kingdom the following three chapters, starting with this one, are devoted to the kingdom program in the book of Revelation. Instead of avoiding what Revelation has to say about the kingdom, we should run to it for its truths.

SUMMARY OF THE KINGDOM PROGRAM IN REVELATION

The argument of Revelation is this: Jesus sits on the Father's throne in heaven with power and authority over the nations and kings of the earth (Rev 1:5; 3:21). Those who follow Jesus in this age are positionally a kingdom and form the nucleus of the coming kingdom reign (Rev 1:6; 5:10). Yet the followers of Jesus face intense opposition and persecution from the world and Satan. This is true for churches now (see Rev 2–3) and for the

1 "The last book of the Bible is pre-eminently *the Book of the Kingdom of God* in conflict with, and victory over, the kingdoms of this world." McClain, *The Greatness of the Kingdom*, 442.

followers of God during the unique hour of testing that will come upon the whole world (see Rev 3:10). The kingdoms of this world, with their capital city of Babylon, operate under the authority of Satan. Yet God has a plan to take this planet back and establish His kingdom on the earth (see Rev 4–5). The plan is for Jesus to take the title deed of the earth and unleash divine wrath upon an unbelieving world through a series of judgments (seals, trumpets, bowls) that will bring unparalleled calamity upon the earth. Satan, who knows his time is short, will intensify His evil rule upon the earth through the "beast" and "false prophet." They will persecute the saints but God will intervene on their behalf. Jesus, the Lamb and King of kings, will bodily and visibly return to defeat both evil human and spiritual forces. The beast and the false prophet will be sent to the lake of fire and Satan will be personally removed to a place called the abyss where his influence over the earth ceases. After that Satan will be sentenced to the lake of fire.

At His return, Jesus rewards His followers with ruling authority. He also resurrects His saints who died under Satan's persecution in the tribulation period. They are vindicated and granted ruling positions in His kingdom. This kingdom will last one thousand years. When this period expires Satan will be released to rally one final opposition against God at the beloved city of Jerusalem. Satan and his forces will be dramatically defeated as fire from heaven consumes them. A final judgment of the wicked ensues and then the eternal kingdom will commence in which both God and Jesus are on the throne from the New Jerusalem, the capital city of the new earth, and all remnants of the curse and sin are forever removed. The nations of the earth bring their contributions to the New Jerusalem in acts of worship. The kingdom program is fully accomplished as the Father and Jesus are on the throne and the saints are reigning. God's full presence is among His people along with the tree of life and the river of life.

KINGDOM LANGUAGE

Kingdom language permeates the book of Revelation. Observe the following:

- "throne" (*thronos*) occurs 41 times—38 for the divine kingdom and 3 for Satan's kingdom.

- "kingdom" (*basileia*) occurs 7 times—3 for God's kingdom and 4 for the kingdom of evil.
- "crown" (*diadema* and *stephanos*) occurs 11 times—applied to Christ, Satan, beast, Christian believers, rider on the white horse, demonic hosts, Israel, the Son of Man.
- "reign" (*basileuo*) occurs 7 times—applied to the divine kingdom.
- "power" (*exousia*) occurs 20 times—used evenly of two opposing kingdoms.
- "rule" (*poimaino*) occurs 4 times of Christ's activity.
- "judge" (*krino*) occurs 8 times in regard to divine government.
- "judgment" (*krisis* and *krima*) occurs 6 times in regard to divine government.
- "wrath" (*thumos* and *orge*) occurs 15 times in regard to divine judgment (once of satanic anger).[2]

The kingdom theme in Revelation intersects with another major emphasis of Revelation—the second coming of Jesus the Messiah. Jesus is the One who brings the kingdom with His return. The book opens and ends with:

- "BEHOLD, HE IS COMING WITH THE CLOUDS, and every eye will see Him" (Rev 1:7).
- He who testifies to these things says, "Yes, I am coming quickly." Amen. Come, Lord Jesus" (Rev 22:20).

The return of Jesus means the coming of the kingdom of God and its replacement of the kingdoms of this world inspired by Satan.

THE COMING "RULE"

Helpful clues for understanding the timing of the kingdom in Revelation are found in the references to "rule" or "ruler." In Revelation 1:5 Jesus is

2 Ibid., 442-43.

called "the ruler of the kings of the earth." Yet the next three references place His ruling function in the future:

> **Revelation 2:26–27**: He who overcomes, and he who keeps My deeds until the end, TO HIM I WILL GIVE AUTHORITY OVER THE NATIONS; AND HE SHALL RULE THEM WITH A ROD OF IRON, AS THE VESSELS OF THE POTTER ARE BROKEN TO PIECES, as I also have received authority from My Father.

> **Revelation 12:5**: And she gave birth to a son, a male child, who is to rule all the nations with a rod of iron; and her child was caught up to God and to His throne.

> **Revelation 19:15**: From His mouth comes a sharp sword, so that with it He may strike down the nations, and He will rule them with a rod of iron; and He treads the wine press of the fierce wrath of God, the Almighty.

These three passages refer to Psalm 2 where God's King and Son will rule the nations with a rod of iron after a period of rebellion. Revelation 12:5 and 19:15 reiterate this truth that Jesus will rule the nations with a rod of iron. Revelation 2:26–27 states Jesus will share His ruling function with those who know Him and overcome the world in this age.

Jesus' rule over the nations is future. With Revelation 2:26–27 the promise of ruling the nations is offered as a future reward to overcomers in the church. Jesus tells the church of Thyatira, "hold fast until I come" (2:25). If they "hold fast" until the coming of Jesus they will be rewarded with ruling functions in the kingdom of Christ. Revelation 19:15 says Jesus will "strike down the nations" and "rule them with a rod of iron" in connection with His second coming (Rev 19:11–21).

PROMISES OF FUTURE REWARD (REVELATION 1–3)

As John begins his message to the seven churches in Asia he declares that Jesus is "the firstborn of the dead, and the ruler of the kings of the earth" (1:5). Jesus is in control. He is alive and possesses authority over the kingdoms of the world. Revelation 1:6–7 then states,

> and He has made us to be a kingdom, priests to His God and Father—to Him be the glory and the dominion forever and ever. Amen. Behold, HE IS COMING WITH THE CLOUDS, and every eye will see Him, even those who pierced Him; and all the tribes of the earth will mourn over Him. So it is to be. Amen.

John says Christians are "a kingdom." Then with Revelation 5:10 he says those who make up the nucleus of this "kingdom" "will reign upon the earth." As Koester notes, "The faithful constitute *a* kingdom now by resisting the purported authority of evil, but *the* kingdom comes when evil is overthrown and the world recognizes the power of God and his Messiah (11:15; 12:10)."[3]

Jesus' messages to the seven churches of Revelation 2–3 reveal information concerning the timing of the kingdom of God. As Jesus addresses His churches, each is evaluated for its performance. Then Jesus offers promises of future blessings for persevering during present trials:

- Ephesus: right to eat of the tree of life in the Paradise of God (2:7)
- Smyrna: will not be hurt by the second death (2:11)
- Pergamum: given hidden manna, a white stone, and a new name written on the stone (2:17)
- Thyatira: granted authority and rule over the nations (2:26–27)
- Sardis: clothed in white garments, name in book of life, and confessed before the Father and the angels (3:5–6)
- Philadelphia: given pillar in the temple of God; the name of God and the New Jerusalem (3:12)
- Laodicea: sit down with Jesus on His throne (3:21)

Jesus' churches are facing difficult times. Some are doing better than others but all need encouragement. Jesus offers rewards for faithful service.

3 Craig R. Koester, *Revelation*, The Anchor Yale Bible (New Haven: Yale University Press, 2014), 389.

These rewards are not the current experience of these churches. Instead, they will be received when Jesus returns to earth and establishes His kingdom. Jesus does not tell the churches His kingdom is currently in operation or that the kingdom is their present experience. Instead, His message is about remaining faithful to reap the blessings of the coming kingdom. Jesus' message to the church at Thyatira highlights this point:

> He who overcomes, and he who keeps My deeds until the end, TO HIM I WILL GIVE AUTHORITY OVER THE NATIONS; AND HE SHALL RULE THEM WITH A ROD OF IRON, AS THE VESSELS OF THE POTTER ARE BROKEN TO PIECES, as I also have received authority from My Father (Rev 2:26–27).

Two points regarding the kingdom can be gathered here. First, when Jesus' kingdom reign begins, He will share His authority with those who are part of His church. In an ironic reversal of circumstances, those who were persecuted will rule. Daniel 7 revealed that the coming kingdom is closely associated with the reign of His saints. The "Son of Man" is given "dominion" and a "kingdom" (Dan 7:13–14). All the "peoples" and "nations" will "serve Him" (Dan 7:14). Yet later in the chapter we are told that after a time of tribulation "the saints took possession of the kingdom" (7:22). Then 7:27 links the reign of the saints with the reign of the Son of Man:

> Then the sovereignty, the dominion and the greatness of all the kingdoms under the whole heaven <u>will be given to the people of the saints of the Highest One</u>; His kingdom will be an everlasting kingdom, and all the dominions will serve and obey Him.

So when the Messiah rules, those who belong to Him also participate in His rule. The kingdom is future and the saints' participation in this kingdom reign is also future.

Second, these positions are real positions of authority over literal nations. Jesus will rule the nations of the earth (Rev 19:15). This is what passages like Isaiah 2:2–4 and Zechariah 14 predicted. National entities will exist in the kingdom and they will be ruled over by the Messiah and His people. Isaiah 19:24–25 lists Egypt, Assyria, and Israel as nations in the kingdom.

One reason we can know Messiah's kingdom is future is His people are not ruling the nations yet. Now is a time for faithfulness amid the nations who persecute Christ's followers. But the saints will reign over the nations.

Jesus' message to the church at Laodicea also reveals how the church relates to the kingdom program. In Revelation 3:21, Jesus states, "He who overcomes, I will grant to him to sit down with Me on My throne, as I also overcame and sat down with My Father on His throne." Similar to Revelation 2:26–27, this verse promises authority for the overcomer. Jesus mentions two distinct thrones—the Father's throne and Jesus' throne.

Jesus mentions the Father's throne of which He is now sharing. This is consistent with Psalm 110:1 that David's Lord, the Messiah, would sit at the right hand of God for a time until David's Lord reigns on earth (Ps 110:2). This is reaffirmed in Hebrews 10:12b–13 where we are told Jesus is currently sitting at the right hand of God "waiting from that time onward UNTIL HIS ENEMIES BE MADE A FOOTSTOOL FOR HIS FEET." Jesus waits at the right hand of Father "until" the time comes for Him to rule from David's throne on the earth (see Matt 25:31).

The authority Jesus possesses at the right hand of God is the pattern for how the followers of Jesus will share His throne. Just as Jesus now shares the throne of the Father, when Jesus comes again His followers also will share His throne. The churches that currently face persecution and attacks from Satan will become rulers under the authority of their Messiah. The persecuted ones will become the ruling ones.

Revelation 2–3 refutes the view that Jesus' millennial kingdom is now in effect. There are two things we know about the thousand-year kingdom of Revelation 20—Satan is bound (vv. 1–3) and the saints are reigning (v. 4). These conditions do not exist with the churches of Revelation 2–3. Satan is active and persecutes the churches. The church at Smyrna was told, "Do not fear what you are about to suffer. Behold, the devil is about to cast some of you into prison, so that you will be tested, and you will have tribulation for ten days" (2:10). Likewise, Jesus told the church of Pergamum, "I know where you dwell, where Satan's throne is; and you hold fast My name, and did not deny My faith even in the days of Antipas, My witness, My faithful one, who was killed among you, where Satan dwells" (2:13). It is highly unlikely that the churches of Revelation 2–3 viewed Satan as being bound. Their experiences indicated otherwise. Also, there is no proof the churches of Revelation 2–3 viewed themselves as reigning. Most were facing trials and opposition from Satan. They were not reigning in Messiah's kingdom yet; they needed to persevere so they could reign when Jesus comes.

The significance of Revelation 2–3 is great. About sixty years after Jesus' ascension to the right hand of the Father, Jesus addresses His churches. He presents His kingdom rule as future and offers rewards of His coming kingdom to those who overcome in the present.

HEAVENLY SETTING FOR AN EARTHLY KINGDOM (REVELATION 4–5)

Revelation 4–5 describes a heavenly throne room scene that leads to the establishment of Messiah's kingdom on earth. As the section begins, John hears a heavenly voice that declares, "Come up here, and I will show you what must take place after these things" (Rev 4:1b). The use of *meta tauta* ("after these things") reveals that what is to be fulfilled is subsequent to the conditions described in Revelation 2–3 and coincides with the last of the three stages mentioned in Revelation 1:19—"Therefore write the things which you have seen, and the things which are, *and the things which will take place after these things.*"[4]

The members of the Trinity are present in Revelation 4–5 as God plans to take back planet earth with a successful mediatorial kingdom. The language here closely parallels Daniel 7:13–14 concerning the Son of Man who appears before the Ancient of Days to receive kingdom power which then leads to a defeat of God's enemies and the reign of the saints on earth (see Dan 7:24–27). With Revelation 4 and 5, heaven is the headquarters for the unleashing of divine wrath that will lead to the replacing of Satan's kingdom with Messiah's rule. God's Messiah is granted kingdom authority that will lead to a kingdom reign on earth involving the saints.

As those who surround the throne testify, God is worthy to receive all glory, honor, and power because He created all things and all things exist because of Him. In the right hand of God is a book (or scroll) with seals on it (5:1). This book connects God's universal kingdom in heaven with

4 Emphases mine. "After these things" is also *meta tauta* showing that John is to write concerning events after the conditions of the churches in chapters 2–3 ("the things which are"). See Robert L. Thomas, *Revelation 1–7: An Exegetical Commentary* (Chicago: Moody, 1992), 337.

the coming mediatorial kingdom on earth. That this book is in the hand of God the Father shows the divine origin of its contents. The two best options for what the book represents are (1) the title deed to the earth, and (2) divine judgments to take the earth. Both harmonize here. The book certainly contains divine judgments, but these judgments are for the purpose of judging the earth and establishing Jesus' kingdom. Thus, the book is the title deed to the earth that contains the judgments necessary to make the kingdoms of this world become the kingdom of Christ.

An angel asks the question, "Who is worthy to open the book and to break its seals?" (5:2). In other words, who is worthy to judge and rule the earth? John weeps when no one was found worthy to take the book from the right hand of God. But then the Lamb, Jesus Christ, comes. He is worthy and able to take the book from God's hand and open its seals (5:4–7). The reason Jesus, who is both Lion and Lamb, is worthy, is because of His sufferings. Jesus by His blood purchased people "from every tribe and tongue and people and nation" (5:9). As with Colossians 1:15–20 and Hebrews 2:5–9, Revelation 5:9–10 connects the cross of Jesus with His coming kingdom. The reason why Jesus is worthy to take the book and establish God's kingdom on earth is because He has been slain and has purchased His people with His blood.[5] Cross and kingdom work in perfect harmony.

An explicit reference to the kingdom is found in Revelation 5:10: "You have made them to be a kingdom and priests to our God; and they will reign upon the earth." This verse reveals five key truths about the kingdom.

First, there is a relationship and a distinction between God's kingdom in heaven and the coming kingdom upon the earth. The heavenly throne room scene in Revelation 4–5 anticipates a coming kingdom upon the earth. Jesus takes the book from the Father on the Father's heavenly throne [Universal Kingdom] so a "reign upon the earth" [Davidic/Millennial Kingdom] can occur. Earlier with Revelation 3:21, Jesus distinguished the Father's throne from His own throne even though they work together. A kingdom of the Father in heaven exists. Revelation 4:2 tells of "One sitting on the throne." Also, the word "throne" is found at least seventeen times

5 Ibid., 394. Thomas says, "By permitting the Lamb to take the scroll, the one sitting upon the throne authorizes Him in a symbolic way to execute His plan for the redemption of the world. The Lamb and only the Lamb is qualified to do this because of His victorious death on the cross and the redemption secured thereby."

in Revelation 4–5. So a kingdom exists in heaven, a universal kingdom of the Father as He rules over all. But this heavenly kingdom is not all there is to the kingdom program. It anticipates a kingdom that must be established "upon the earth" (Rev 5:10). This is the kingdom of the Messiah, the Davidic kingdom predicted by Gabriel (see Luke 1:31–33) and Jesus (see Matt 19:28; 25:31).

Second, the people Jesus purchased with His blood are "a kingdom." Believers form the nucleus of Messiah's kingdom (see Rev 1:6). This shows a connection of the kingdom to the present, not in the form of a reign yet, but a growing group of followers who are qualified to enter Jesus' kingdom.

Third, the saints of God are destined to reign with Christ. When Jesus reigns, the saints will also reign. Jesus will share His kingdom authority with His followers. In Revelation 2:26–27, Jesus promised His people they would share in His reign over the nations. This was motivation for those currently facing difficult times. Because Jesus has authority as "ruler of the kings of the earth," (Rev 1:5) the saints can know they will reign with Him.

Fourth, this kingdom reign is future—"they will reign."[6] The kingdom reign of Jesus is still to come. At the time of the heavenly throne room scene the kingdom reign of Revelation 5:10 had not started yet. But this reign will occur after the second coming of Jesus (see Rev 19) as described in Revelation 20:4:

> Then I saw thrones, and they sat on them, and judgment was given to them. And I saw the souls of those who had been beheaded because of their testimony of Jesus and because of the word of God, and those who had not worshiped the beast or his image, and had not received the mark on their forehead and on

---

6 G. K. Beale opts for a minority textual reading that puts the reign of Revelation 5:10 in the present as opposed to the future (see *The Book of Revelation*, in The New International Greek Testament Commentary [Grand Rapids: Eerdmans, 2013], 361–64). Beale restates this view in his *A New Testament Biblical Theology: The Unfolding of the Old Testament in the New* (Grand Rapids: Baker, 2011), 348. Beale's conclusion goes against the majority of translations that translate Revelation 5:10 as "will reign" or "shall reign" including NASB, NIV, NLT, HCSB, ESV, KJF, ISV, NET Bible. Two translations that support Beal's understanding are ASC, and the ERV. Hoekema argued for the future tense: "the best texts have the future tense" (*The Bible and the Future* 283). We are not seeing enough evidence to go against the consensus that the best translation is "will reign." In addition, Beale argues that context makes him lean toward the present view of Revelation 5:10 but this is difficult to go with since this verse speaks of the saints reigning on the "earth." In what sense are saints reigning on the earth when the conditions of Revelation 2–3 and 6–19 describe intense persecution from Satan and the world?

> their hand; <u>and they came to life and reigned with Christ for a thousand years.</u>
>
> So then, Revelation 5:10 and Revelation 20:4 are connected.
>
> <u>Revelation 5:10:</u> "they will reign upon the earth." (promise of reward)
>
> <u>Revelation 20:4:</u> "they came to life and reigned with Christ for a thousand years." (promise actualized)

Revelation 5:10 is the *promise* of a coming reign of the saints while Revelation 20:4 is the *actualization* of that kingdom reign. The condition of the saints before the return of Jesus is not that of reigning. It is persecution and trial (see Rev 2–3; 6–19). As Herman Ridderbos points out, "Nowhere are the disciples or coming church given the role of conquerors or rulers of the world."[7] Yet these conditions will give way to a kingdom reign in the future. Koester is correct that Revelation 5:10 shows the saints "can expect to reign only in the future."[8]

Fifth, this coming reign of the saints is "upon the earth."[9] Messiah's kingdom is on earth, not heaven. The reign of Jesus and the saints must be in the realm of the original creation given to man in Genesis 1–2.[10] It is not the case that Adam was tasked with ruling the earth while the Messianic/Davidic rule of Jesus and the saints is in heaven. Jesus will succeed in the realm where Adam failed—earth.

Also, Russell Moore notes that Revelation 5:10 is evidence for an age of time distinct from both the present age and the final consummation:

7 Ridderbos, *The Coming of the Kingdom*, 470.

8 Koester, *Revelation*, 380.

9 In referencing Revelation 5:10 as evidence for "a distinct, future reign with Christ on earth," Lewis and Demarest point out "the new heavens and earth are not in this context." The millennium of Revelation 20 is. See Gordon R. Lewis and Bruce A. Demarest, *Integrative Theology: Historical, Biblical, Systematic, Apologetic, Practical* (Grand Rapids: Zondervan, 1994), 3:408.

10 Treat is correct that "The creation mandate to rule over the earth (Gen 1:28) clearly echoes in the last line of the hymn: 'and they shall reign on the earth' (Rev 5:10)." Jeremy R. Treat, *The Crucified King: Atonement and the Kingdom in Biblical and Systematic Theology* (Grand Rapids: Zondervan, 2014), 124.

> The "reign" that Christ promises to His believers, furthermore, is not a "spiritual" reign through the church. It is instead a coercive rule over the cosmos (Rev. 5:10), a reign that is impossible in either the "already" of the present age or the "not yet" of the final consummation.[11]

MARTYRED SAINTS (REVELATION 6)

Important truths about the kingdom's timing can be gleaned from the martyrs of Revelation 6. With Revelation 6:9–11 the souls of martyred saints appear in heaven. They died because of their commitment and testimony for Jesus in a hostile, God-hating world. These martyrs enter what is often called the 'intermediate state'—the state of believers in heaven who experienced physical death but have not yet received glorified bodies. These martyred saints in heaven are not ruling with Christ yet. That will occur with the events of Revelation 20:4 when these saints sit on thrones after the second coming of Jesus. Instead, they appear restless and are crying out for the Lord to avenge their blood:

> and they cried out with a loud voice, saying, "How long, O Lord, holy and true, will You refrain from judging and avenging our blood on those who dwell on the earth?"

These martyrs want justice for their executors. They cry out "How long?" but are told to wait a little while longer. The enemies of the saints are having their way on the earth, but that will end when Jesus returns to crush them and vindicate His people. That will come with the events of Revelation 19 and 20.

Some have taught that deceased saints are currently ruling with Jesus in His millennial kingdom in heaven. But Revelation 6:9–11 does not support this conclusion. The situation of these intermediate saints is not ruling with Christ but anticipating future justice. As Middleton states, "These righteous dead are clearly not at peace."[12] They are safe in a bodiless

---

11 Russell D. Moore, *The Kingdom of Christ: The New Evangelical Perspective* (Wheaton, IL: Crossway, 2004), 64.

12 Middleton, *A New Heaven and a New Earth*, 232.

intermediate state beyond the reach of their enemies, but their reign awaits the future (see Rev 20:4).

In sum, these saints in Revelation 6:9–11 are not reigning; they are waiting. And they are calling for vindication in the realm where their murders took place. The earth is the realm where the wicked took their lives, and this same earth is the sphere where the vindication of these saints must occur. Thus, Revelation 6:9–11 is important evidence the kingdom reign of Jesus and the Messiah is future and will be on the earth.

ISRAEL AND THE NATIONS (REVELATION 7)

Revelation 7 does not explicitly refer to a kingdom but implications concerning who will participate in the kingdom are given. Revelation 7:4–8 mentions "one hundred and forty-four thousand sealed from every tribe of the sons of Israel" and then lists twelve thousand from each tribe of Israel. This group consists of ethnic Jews as representative of the nation Israel and points to Israel's salvation and restoration during the coming tribulation period. Pate observes, "It seems that the purpose of the Great Tribulation is to win the nation of Israel to its Messiah."[13]

Again, the significance of national Israel in God's kingdom program is affirmed. Not only does John mention "Israel" he brings up their tribal affiliations, which has implications for the unification of Israel. The idea of a restoration of the tribes of Israel is also found in Matthew 19:28; Luke 22:30; Acts 26:7; Revelation 21:12.

That ethnic and national Israel is in view is also evident from the group mentioned next—Gentiles: "a great multitude which no one could count, from every nation and all tribes and peoples and tongues" (7:9a). The natural understanding is that the kingdom program includes Israel as Israel (7:4–8) and Gentiles from the nations (7:9–11). Both Jews and Gentiles are God's people but there are still ethnic distinctions among them.

There is no contextual reason to view the twelve tribes as a reference to the church. As Paige Patterson observes, "The distinction between the two groups would hardly allow for any other interpretation except for

13 C. Marvin Pate, "A Progressive Dispensationalist View of Revelation," in *Four Views on the Book of Revelation*, ed. C. Marvin Pate (Grand Rapids: Zondervan, 1998), 165.

one that sees the 144,000 as actually Jews."[14] The nucleus of the kingdom includes those from Jews and Gentiles who are both the people of God yet maintain their unique identities.[15]

THE COMING REIGN OF MESSIAH (REVELATION 11–12)

Deep into the tribulation period several declarations announce the coming reign of Jesus. These happen while Satan's deception of the nations pervades the entire earth. Revelation 11:15 states: "Then the seventh angel sounded; and there were loud voices in heaven, saying, 'The kingdom of the world has become the kingdom of our Lord and of His Christ; and He will reign forever and ever.'" Then with Verse 17 the twenty-four elders in heaven declare, "We give You thanks, O Lord God, the Almighty, who are and who were, because You have taken Your great power and have begun to reign."

Preceding these statements was the ministry, death, resurrection, and translation to heaven of God's two witnesses in the city of Jerusalem (Rev 11:1–13). While the earth-dwellers continued in their rebellion under the power of Satan, the seventh angel announced that the Messiah has "begun to reign" (v. 17) and "He will reign forever and ever" (v. 15). Verses 15 and 17 show the imminence of Messiah's kingdom. While some events must play out including the severe bowl judgments and the return of Jesus, the announcement that the kingdom of the world has become the kingdom of Christ is declared. As McClain has put it, "This is the *de jure* announcement of what in a short time will be made *de facto*."[16]

That Jesus' kingdom reign is still future at this point in Revelation 11 is evident since v. 18 states, "and the time came for the dead to be judged, and the time to reward Your bond-servants the prophets and the saints and those who fear Your name." These two events of judgment and reward had not transpired just yet, but they were on the brink of fulfillment. Put

14 Paige Patterson, *Revelation*, The New American Commentary (Nashville: B&H, 2012), 194. For a fuller discussion of the identity of the two groups mention in Revelation 7:4–11 see Patterson, 193–99.

15 Attempts to claim that 144,000 is a number of completion that means this is a reference to the church and not national Israel are not justified.

16 McClain, *The Greatness of the Kingdom*, 473.

together, judgment, reward, and kingdom reign are imminent, so much so that their arrival can be declared as fact. What is announced as reality in Revelation 11:15, 17 will be actually realized with the second coming event of Revelation 19.

Revelation 12 reveals more information concerning the cosmic battle between God and Satan. Verse 5 states: "And she [Israel] gave birth to a son, a male child, who is to rule all the nations with a rod of iron; and her child was caught up to God and to His throne." Israel is pictured as a woman giving birth to the Messiah who is depicted as a "son." This son is said to be one who will "rule all the nations with a rod of iron." This idea of ruling with an iron rule harkens back to Psalm 2:9 and Revelation 2:26–27.

Revelation 12:7–9 tells of a war in heaven in which Michael the archangel and the good angels waged war with Satan and his angels. Satan loses the battle and is thrown down to the earth. There is debate among scholars concerning the timing of this cosmic battle. Does it refer to the original fall of Satan as described in Ezekiel 28? Does it refer to the cosmic victory Jesus experienced over Satan at the cross? Or does it refer to a battle during the coming tribulation? The probable view is a battle and defeat of Satan connected with the coming tribulation period. The mention of a three and one-half year period in 12:14 makes this view likely.[17]

A loud voice in heaven then declares, "Now the salvation, and the power, and the kingdom of our God and the authority of His Christ have come, for the accuser of our brethren has been thrown down, he who accuses them before our God day and night" (12:10). This victory over Satan gives rise to another declaration that the "power" and" kingdom" and "authority" of Christ have come. Like 11:15, 17 this verse shows the imminence of Jesus' kingdom at this time.

THE FALSE TRINITY (REVELATION 13)

Revelation 13 describes the false trinity's authority before the return of Jesus. First, Satan is depicted as a "dragon" (13:1). Then there is a "beast" who is given authority from Satan (13:2). This beast appears to be an "antichrist" figure who does the work of Satan. Lastly, there is another beast that

17 Revelation 12:14 refers to "a time and times and half a time" which is 3.5 years.

makes the earthdwellers worship the first beast (13:12). This second beast has often been called a "false prophet."

The authority these three members of the false trinity have before the kingdom of Christ is established is significant. The first beast is described as possessing "ten horns" and "ten diadems"—symbols of kingdom authority (13:1). The dragon, Satan, gives the first beast "his power and his throne and great authority" (13:2). In 13:3 we are told "the whole earth" "followed after the beast" and worshiped the dragon and the beast (13:3–4a). The beast is given "authority to act" for a period of forty-two months. This beast uses his authority "to make war with the saints" and "overcome them" (13:7a). His authority extends globally over all—"and authority over every tribe and people and tongue and nation was given to him" (13:7b).

The language indicates Satan exercises kingdom authority over the earth through these two other persons. He is deceiving the nations before Jesus' second coming. While this kingdom is in force, the kingdom of Christ has not arrived, at least not yet. With the events of Revelation 19 and 20, though, Jesus comes to earth and sends the beast and false prophet to the lake of fire and then has Satan bound in a prison called "the abyss." The kingdom of Jesus the Messiah replaces the kingdom of Satan. Those who assert Jesus' Davidic and millennial kingdom are now in operation must deal with the conditions described in Revelation 13, which indicate a dominant and pervasive satanic kingdom before the return of Jesus. Satan is active and deceptive in this age before Jesus comes again.

CONDITIONS BEFORE THE KINGDOM (REVELATION 14–18)

Revelation 15 presents a scene in heaven in which seven angels carry seven plagues. With these plagues "the wrath of God is finished" (15:1). The purpose of the Lamb taking the book from the Father in Revelation 5 was so planet earth could be taken back for God. This involved the wrath of God through seal, trumpet, and bowl judgments. Now the end is near. Near the culmination of God's wrath, a song of praise to God proceeds from those who experienced victory over the beast and his image and number:

> "Great and marvelous are Your works,
> O Lord God, the Almighty;

> Righteous and true are Your ways,
> King of the nations!
> Who will not fear, O Lord, and glorify Your name?
> For You alone are holy;
> For ALL THE NATIONS WILL COME AND WORSHIP BEFORE YOU,
> FOR YOUR RIGHTEOUS ACTS HAVE BEEN REVEALED" (Rev 15:3–4)

God is called "King of the nations!" and then we are told, "all nations will come and worship before you." At the time of this scene the nations are still in rebellion against God. But the One who possesses authority as "King of the nations" will soon receive worship from the nations.

Revelation 17 refers to a harlot with the name on her forehead: "BABYLON THE GREAT, THE MOTHER OF HARLOTS AND OF THE ABOMINATIONS OF THE EARTH" (Rev 17:5). Verse 18 says the woman represents "the great city which reigns over the kings of the earth." The woman, therefore, refers to the city called Babylon. The chapter also refers to ten kings who give their authority to the beast (Satan):

> The ten horns which you saw are ten kings who have not yet received a kingdom, but they receive authority as kings with the beast for one hour. These have one purpose, and they give their power and authority to the beast (Rev 17:12–13).

These kings "wage war" against Jesus the King:

> These will wage war against the Lamb, and the Lamb will overcome them, because He is Lord of lords and King of kings, and those who are with Him are the called and chosen and faithful (Rev 17:14).

There is a battle of kingdoms here. The kings wage war against Jesus the Lamb who is "King of kings." As this occurs the beast has a reign upon the earth, but this reign is futile and short-lived because the "King of kings" who is also "the Lamb" "will overcome them." A real evil kingdom on earth fights against Jesus, yet this occurs under the sovereignty of God: "For God has put it in their hearts to execute His purpose by having a common purpose, and by giving their kingdom to the beast, until the words of God will be fulfilled" (17:17). This kingdom under the authority of the beast only exists while God allows it.

A battle of kingdoms transpires. The city of Babylon is inspired by Satan and this kingdom is opposed to Jesus who is the King of kings. Yet this kingdom cannot prevail and will be replaced by the kingdom of Jesus. With 18:9–10 the "kings of the earth" who committed immorality with Babylon are facing judgment along with Babylon. This leads to the climactic section of Revelation 19–20 where Satan and the nations opposed to God are forcefully destroyed by Jesus who returns to earth from heaven. The One who is "ruler of the kings of the earth" (Rev 1:5) now exercises His reign over the earth, destroying His enemies and vindicating those who belong to Him in the realm of their persecution (i.e. earth).

THE MILLENNIAL KINGDOM (REVELATION 19–20)

We now come to one of the most important kingdom passages—Revelation 19 and 20. It is also one of the most debated. Because of its significance we will set the background for this section that describes an intermediate kingdom of Jesus on earth for a thousand years before the eternal kingdom.

Revelation 19:11–21 describes the second coming of Jesus. Jesus returns with power and glory and destroys His enemies. Also destroyed are the beast and false prophet (20–21). The kingly implications of Jesus' coming are evident in Revelation 19:15–16:

> From His mouth comes a sharp sword, so that with it He may strike down the nations, and He will rule them with a rod of iron; and He treads the wine press of the fierce wrath of God, the Almighty. And on His robe and on His thigh He has a name written, "KING OF KINGS, AND LORD OF LORDS."

Striking the nations and ruling them with "a rod of iron" brings what God promised for His Messiah in Psalm 2:9 (see also Rev 2:26–27). The nations that scoffed at the Messiah are brought into subjection to the King of kings and Lord of lords.

With Revelation 20:1–10 the events of the second coming of Jesus unfold and an intermediate kingdom of a thousand years is explicitly revealed.

This section can be summarized as follows:

1. Satan will be bound and all his activities are completely ceased for a thousand years (1–3).
2. Positions of kingdom authority are granted to God's people and previously martyred saints (4).
3. The martyrs who were slain for the testimony of Jesus are resurrected and reign with Christ for a thousand years (4).
4. Another group, "the rest of the dead," comes to life a thousand years later (5).
5. Those who are part of the first resurrection are priests of God and Christ and will reign with Him for a thousand years (6).
6. At the end of the thousand years Satan is released and leads a rebellion that is immediately defeated with fire from heaven (7–10).

Before looking at this section, though, some information about the literary structure of Revelation must be understood. This is necessary since some claim Revelation 20 does not follow the events of Revelation 19, and claim that Jesus' kingdom does not follow His return but exists before it. But the kingdom of Revelation 20 does indeed follow the second coming of Jesus described in Revelation 19. The King returns and brings His kingdom.

LITERARY STRUCTURE

Where do the events of Revelation 20 fit within the overall structure of Revelation? Below is a listing of the major sections of Revelation:

Prologue	1:1–1:8
Letters to Seven Churches	1:9–3:22
Heavenly Court and Its Judgment	4:1–11:19
Prophetic/Apocalyptic Narrative	12:1–16:21
Fall of Babylon	17:1–19:10
Prophetic/Apocalyptic Narrative	19:11–21:8
New Jerusalem Established	21:9–22:9
Epilogue	22:10–22:21

John's discussion of the millennium comes within the section of 19:11–21:8 that describes the return of Jesus and events after His coming. John uses the expression *kai eidon* eight times (19:11, 17, 19; 20:1, 4, 11, 12; 21:1). *Kai eidon* can be translated "and I saw" or "then I saw." Together, these words can refer to chronological progression, which seems to be the case here. As Robert Mounce observed, "It should be noted that the recurring 'and I saw' of 19:11, 17, 19; 20:1, 4, 12; and 21:1 appears to establish a sequence of visions which carries through from the appearance of the Rider on the white horse (19:11) to the establishment of the new heaven and new earth (21:1ff)."[1]

As the events within 19:11–21:8 unfold John tells of several things he saw in succession:

> **19:11–16**: John saw ("And I saw") the return of Christ with the armies of heaven to strike down Christ's enemies and rule the nations.
>
> **19:17–18**: Then John saw ("Then I saw") an angel in heaven calling to the birds to eat the flesh of the enemies of Christ.
>
> **19:19–21**: Then John saw ("And I saw") the beast and the armies of the earth wage war against the returning Christ; the beast and the false prophet are seized and thrown into the lake of fire, and the rest of the enemies are slain.
>
> **20:1–3**: Then John saw ("Then I saw") an angel coming from heaven with a great chain to bind Satan and throw him into the pit where his evil activities totally cease.
>
> **20:4–10**: Then John saw ("Then I saw") thrones established, the resurrection of the martyrs and their reigning with Christ for a thousand years, and the rest of the dead coming to life after the thousand years are completed. After the thousand-year period

1 Robert H. Mounce, *The Book of Revelation*, New International Commentary on the New Testament (Grand Rapids: Eerdmans, 1977), 352. See also Waymeyer who says, "There is nothing in Revelation 20:1 that indicates a chronological break between the two chapters...." Matthew Waymeyer, "What About Revelation 20?," in *Christ's Prophetic Plans: A Futuristic Premillennial Primer*, ed. John MacArthur and Richard Mayhue (Chicago: Moody, 2012), 136

is over, Satan is released from his prison and leads a rebellion against God's people and the holy city. Satan is defeated and thrown into the lake of fire.

20:11: Then John saw ("Then I saw") a Great White Throne established that could not be escaped.

20:12–15: Then John saw ("And I saw") the great and the small judged, with those whose names were not found in the book of life being cast into the lake of fire; death and Hades were thrown into the lake of fire.

21:1–8: Then John saw ("Then I saw") a new heaven and a new earth and the coming of the New Jerusalem.

The main point is this—with Revelation 19:11–21:8 John describes the second coming of Jesus and the events that follow it. This includes the thousand-year reign of Christ of Revelation 20:1–10. The events of Revelation 20:1–10 follow the second coming of Jesus described in Revelation 19:11. There is sequential progression, not recapitulation in this section. As Craig Blaising observes, "It is noteworthy... that when the issue of theological-historical significance is suspended and the question is strictly literary, there is general agreement that the events in the visions of 19:11–21:8 are correlative with or consequent to the Parousia of 19:11."[2]

There are solid reasons for this understanding. Six of the eight visions that start with "and/then I saw" in 19:11–21:8 are commonly viewed as being future, happening at the time of or after the events of the *parousia* described in 19:11. The two debated ones are 20:1–3 and 4–7, which describe the binding of Satan and the reign of the saints. Amillennialists and postmillennialists place these sections between the two comings of Jesus. But it is better to understand all eight sections as describing events *after* the coming of Jesus. It appears arbitrary to claim six of these are post-*parousia*, but then assert that two of them recapitulate and describe conditions pre-*parousia*. Blaising is correct that, "The presumption is in favor of

2 Blaising, "Premillennialism," 213.

viewing the remaining two visions [found in 20:1–6] in a similar manner."[3] Mounce is also accurate that "The interpretation that discovers recapitulation for the segment 20:1–6 must at least bear the burden of proof."[4]

Also, the chronological understanding makes most sense of what is described in Revelation 19 and 20. This section tells of the defeat of the false trinity opposed to God—Satan, the beast, and the false prophet. As the returning Christ defeats the beast and the false prophet (19:19–21), the natural issue involves what will happen to Satan who is the power behind the beast and the false prophet. A chronological view understands that at the time of Christ's return Satan will be dealt with too. Right after the defeat of the beast and false prophet, Revelation 20:1–3 reports Satan being incarcerated. This means all three primary enemies are defeated with the return of King Jesus. But if one insists Revelation 19 is about the second coming of Jesus, but Revelation 20:1 kicks the reader back to the beginning of the church age, then there is a disconnect in when God deals with His ultimate enemies. In this odd scenario, Satan is bound at the beginning of the church age (sort of), but the beast and the false prophet who are empowered by Satan are not defeated until the second coming of Jesus. It seems better to view all three members of the false trinity defeated at the same time. Thus, Christ appears from heaven (19:11–19), He destroys His enemies including the beast and the false prophet (19:20–21), and then He deals with the third and leading member of the false trinity, Satan, by binding him and casting him into the abyss (20:1–3). Blomberg summarizes this point well:

> In the process, we are told about the fate of two of the three members of the so-called satanic trinity introduced in 12:1–13:18. The beast and the false prophet, parodies of Jesus and the Holy Spirit, are captured and thrown alive into the lake of fire (19:20). Readers expect to hear next about the fate of the ringleader of the three, Satan himself, the one who wanted to usurp the place of God the Father, and they are not disappointed. Revelation 20:1 continues seamlessly, describing Satan's confinement to

3 Ibid., 216.

4 Mounce, *The Book of Revelation*, 361.

> the abyss until the very end of the millennium. The rest of the chapter follows equally inexorably from there on.[5]

So sequential progression is preferred. As Ladd puts it, "There is absolutely no hint of any recapitulation in chapter 20."[6] Blomberg also aptly states, "No matter how many flashbacks or disruptions of chronological sequence one might want to argue for elsewhere in Revelation, it makes absolutely no sense to put one in between Revelation 19 and 20 as both amillennialists and postmillennialists must do."[7]

THE BINDING OF SATAN

Another reason for holding to a future and earthly understanding of the millennium of Revelation 20 involves the nature of Satan's binding as described in Revelation 20:1–3. This passage describes an incarceration of Satan as a person that results in a complete cessation of his activities:

> Then I saw an angel coming down from heaven, holding the key of the abyss and a great chain in his hand. And he laid hold of the dragon, the serpent of old, who is the devil and Satan, and bound him for a thousand years; and he threw him into the abyss, and shut it and sealed it over him, so that he would not deceive the nations any longer, until the thousand years were completed; after these things he must be released for a short time.

The language here is powerful. Note what happens to Satan:

1. Satan is "bound."
2. Satan is thrown into the abyss.
3. The abyss is "shut" and "sealed."

---

5 Craig L. Blomberg, "The Posttribulationism of the New Testament," in *A Case for Historic Premillennialism: An Alternative to 'Left Behind' Eschatology*, ed. Craig L. Blomberg and Sung Wook Chung (Grand Rapids: Baker, 2009), 68.

6 George Eldon Ladd, "An Historical Premillennial Response," in *The Meaning of the Millennium: Four Views*, ed. Robert G. Clouse (Downers Grove: InterVarsity, 1977), 190.

7 Blomberg, "The Posttribulationism of the New Testament," 67.

Much attention focuses on whether the activities of Satan are curtailed or ceased at this time. But before one even considers the activities of Satan, one must recognize what is happening to Satan himself. Satan is incarcerated and confined in a real place called "the abyss." So then, *more than a specific function of Satan (i.e. deceiving nations) is hindered; Satan himself is absolutely confined to a place that results in a complete cessation of all he does.*

Satan is imprisoned. He used to inflict his evil ways on the earth, but now he cannot because his personal presence is transferred to the abyss. In Revelation 9:1–3 the "bottomless pit" or "abyss" is a real place, a spirit-prison, where locust-like beings were confined. Their release from the abyss frees them to inflict damage "upon the earth" (9:3). While they were in the abyss they were not free to do anything on the earth. Also, with the demoniac in Luke 8, many demons pleaded with Jesus to avoid being sent to the "abyss" (8:31). They were afraid of being removed from the earth, not just a curtailing of their activities. Being in the abyss means no access to the earth. With this understanding that Satan will be imprisoned certain conclusions can be made concerning his activities.

Since Satan is confined to the abyss his ability to deceive the nations ceases. *Thus the main reason Satan is no longer able to deceive the nations is because he is in prison with no access to the earth.* Imprisonment of a person means cessation of that person's works. To use an example, if a police officer arrests a serial killer who terrorized a city and puts him in prison we could say, "This wicked person has been jailed so that he cannot continue his murdering ways." This does not mean his murdering activities are merely curtailed. Nor does it mean he is free to rape and rob. That would be absurd. His incarceration as a person means his wicked ways have totally stopped. Likewise, the binding of Satan means for the first time in history mankind will not have to deal with Satan's deceptive tactics. As Mounce states: "The elaborate measures taken to insure his [Satan's] custody are most easily understood as implying the complete cessation of his influence on earth (rather than a curbing of his activities)."[8] Put another way:

Satan's incarceration in the abyss → cessation of all his activities

8 Mounce, *The Book of Revelation*, 353.

Satan's imprisonment during the millennium is not compatible with the views of amillennialism and postmillennialism. Those positions assert the millennium is present during this current age and Satan is present and active. His limitation, allegedly, is his inability to stop the gospel from going to the nations. But Scripture indicates Satan's ability to deceive is alive and well in this present age:

> **2 Corinthians 4:4**: And even if our gospel is veiled, it is veiled to those who are perishing, in whose case the god of this world has blinded the minds of the unbelieving so that they might not see the light of the gospel of the glory of Christ, who is the image of God.
>
> **1 Peter 5:8**: Be of sober spirit, be on the alert. Your adversary, the devil, prowls around like a roaring lion, seeking someone to devour.
>
> **1 John 5:19**: the whole world lies in the power of the evil one.

These passages, written by three apostles after Jesus' first coming, reveal Satan is actively involved in worldwide deception. Plus, the book of Revelation says Satan is actively deceiving the nations with much success before Jesus' return. Revelation 12:9 declares:

> And the great dragon was thrown down, the serpent of old who is called the devil and Satan, who deceives the whole world; he was thrown down to the earth, and his angels were thrown down with him.

The sphere of Satan's deception before Jesus returns is "the whole world." This worldwide deception over the nations is again discussed in Revelation 13:2, 7–8:

> And the dragon [Satan] gave him [The Beast] his power and his throne and great authority... . It was also given to him [The Beast] to make war with the saints and to overcome them, and authority over every tribe and people and tongue and nation was given to him. All who dwell on the earth will worship him.

Satan is the energizing power behind the beast who has authority over "every tribe and people and tongue and nation." Thus, in the period between the two comings of Jesus, Satan is deceiving every people group. This is why the binding of Satan described in Revelation 20:1–3 is so dramatic and historic. Before Jesus returns Satan's deceptive power over the nations is strong, but in one dramatic moment his ability to deceive the nations ends. This contradicts the idea that only Satan's ability to deceive the nations is in view. As Wayne Grudem points out, "It seems more appropriate to say that Satan is *now* still deceiving the nations, but at the beginning of the millennium this deceptive influence will be removed."[9]

Those who assert the binding of Satan is taking place in this present age often link the events of Revelation 20:1–3 with Jesus' victory over Satan at the cross. Jesus was victorious over Satan at the cross. Yet the cosmic battle between God and Satan includes a series of events that eventually lead to Satan's imprisonment in the lake of fire (see Rev 20:10). Just as a war between nations can involve many battles, so too, the battle between God and Satan involves several battles:

1. Satan judged and cast down from heaven before the fall of man (Isa 14:12–15 and Ezek 28:11–19).
2. Jesus demonstrates power over Satan's realm through His casting out of demons (Matt 12:28).
3. Jesus' victory over Satan at the cross (Col 2:15).
4. Satan thrown to the earth for a short time shortly before the return of Jesus (Rev 12).
5. Satan bound in the pit for a thousand years at the return of Jesus (Rev 20:1–3).
6. Satan sent to the lake of fire forever after the thousand-year reign of Jesus (Rev 20:7 –10).

These events are separate but interrelated in the great cosmic war. Just as major wars in human history such as World War II can involve

9 Grudem, *Systematic Theology*, 1118. Emphasis in original.

several battles, so too the great cosmic battle can as well. So the binding of Satan described in Revelation 20:1–3 occurs after Jesus returns to earth, not before.

THE REIGN OF THE SAINTS (REVELATION 20:4)

The return of Jesus in Revelation 19 and the binding of Satan in Revelation 20:3 are connected with the reign of God's people in Revelation 20:4:

> Then I saw thrones, and they sat on them, and judgment was given to them. And I saw the souls of those who had been beheaded because of their testimony of Jesus and because of the word of God, and those who had not worshiped the beast or his image, and had not received the mark on their forehead and on their hand; and they came to life and reigned with Christ for a thousand years.

"Thrones" contain ideas of a kingdom reign, including ruling and judging. This reign will be carried out by more than one person since the plural "thrones" is used. But who are the "they" who will sit on these thrones? We are not told explicitly. Is this a reference to the twenty-four elders sitting on thrones in Revelation 4:4? The different contexts between chaps. 4 and 20 make this understanding improbable. As Robert Thomas observes, "The absence of this group [twenty-four elders] from this context and the absence of an indication that the thrones are twenty-four in number are strong objections to this theory."[10]

The most probable view is "they" refers to the armies that return with Jesus at His second coming in Revelation 19:14, 19. This group is the nearest antecedent of the "they" in 20:4. Christ reigns for a thousand years (20:4b), and it makes perfect sense that the armies who come with Christ will reign as well. This army is probably the church, who in Revelation 2:26–27 and 3:21, was promised ruling positions over the nations with Christ on His Davidic throne when He returns. The promise of a future kingdom reign in those texts finds fulfillment with what is described in 20:4.

10 Robert L. Thomas, *Revelation 8–22: An Exegetical Commentary* (Chicago: Moody, 1995), 413.

That the church returns with Christ at His return shows that it was removed before the time of wrath upon the earth as Revelation 3:10 promised. The church comes with Him from heaven to participate in the destruction of Jesus' enemies and reign with Jesus upon the earth (Rev 5:10).

The connection of "they" who sit on thrones in 20:4 with the returning armies of Revelation 19:14, 19 also shows a close chronological connection between the events of Revelation 19 and 20. The armies that return with Jesus at His coming in chap. 19 will reign as a result of His return in Revelation 20:4.

Yet there is a second group in Revelation 20:4 also destined to reign—"the souls of those who had been beheaded because of their testimony of Jesus and because of the word of God." These martyrs, who were discussed earlier in Revelation 6:9–11, "came to life and reigned with Christ for a thousand years." So not only will the church reign with Christ for a thousand years, so too will saints who died during the tribulation period. The first group arrives from heaven with the returning Christ, while the second group experiences resurrection after the return of Jesus. While their arrivals are different, they both share the same destiny—an earthly kingdom reign with Jesus for a thousand years.

TWO PHYSICAL RESURRECTIONS

Evidence for a future millennium also exists in the two resurrections of Revelation 20:4–5. The fulfillment of these two resurrections must be future from our standpoint in history. Since neither has occurred yet this demands that the millennium is future as well.

In v. 4, John says "the souls of those who had been beheaded because of their testimony of Jesus... came to life and reigned with Christ for a thousand years." These souls who were beheaded are the same martyrs who came out of the great tribulation into heaven as described in Revelation 6:9–11. Thus, there is an inherent connection between the martyrs of Revelation 6:9–11 and the resurrected martyrs in Revelation 20:4.

Revelation 6:9–11 describes the fifth seal and the martyrdom of God's people who were slain because of their commitment to the Word of God and their testimony for Jesus (see Rev 6:9). This solemn passage tells of the condition of the souls of these martyred saints. Their state is not that of "reigning." Instead, they cry out to the Lord for vengeance. These saints were killed for their testimony on the earth. Now their souls are in heaven and they cry out, "How long, O Lord, holy and true, will You refrain from judging and avenging our blood on those who dwell on the earth?" (6:10). Verse 11 then states these martyrs were clothed in white and told to "rest for a little while longer" until the full number of martyred saints was completed. The response given to them is to wait.

Their frustration ends, though, with the events of Revelation 19 and 20. Revelation 5:10 promised a coming day when the saints will reign upon the earth: "You have made them to be a kingdom and priests to our God; and they will reign upon the earth." The events of Revelation 20 fulfill this promise. The enemies of Jesus receive judgment. And with the Lord's return, His saints reign with Him on the earth. This is the message of Revelation 20:4–6.

Revelation 19:11–21 explains the return of Jesus and the vanquishing of His enemies. Then Revelation 20:1–3 details the complete cessation of the activities of Satan. Verse 4 says thrones are established, indicating a kingdom reign. Then martyred saints "came to life and reigned with Christ for a thousand years." These people who come to life are those who lost their physical lives in Revelation 6:9–11. But now they come to life.

The term for "came to life" is *ezesan*, a word used of Jesus' bodily resurrection in Revelation 2:8. There Jesus referred to himself as, "The first and the last, who was dead, and has come to life (*ezesan*)." Jesus' coming to life is not spiritual salvation since Jesus did not need to be saved. Instead, His was a physical resurrection, a bodily coming to life. The Jesus who was killed physically is the One raised physically from the dead. Likewise, these martyrs who physically died (Rev 6:9–11) are now physically made alive (Rev 20:4).

Verse 5 then states, "The rest of the dead did not come to life until the thousand years were completed." This introduces another group called "the rest of the dead." This is a different and broader group than the one mentioned in v. 4. It is said of this second group that they did not "come to life" until the thousand years were over. Again, the term for "come to life," *ezesan*, is used. Since *ezesan* referred to physical resurrection in v. 4 it is highly likely *ezesan* refers to physical resurrection in v. 5. Such a conclusion is based on strong contextual considerations since it is most probable that the term *ezesan* would be used similarly in such close proximity. *Thus, a thousand years after the first group was physically resurrected this second group experiences physical resurrection.*

For the second group, though, this physical resurrection is unto eternal judgment. Verse 6 states, "Blessed and holy is the one who has a part in the first resurrection; over these the second death has no power, but they will be priests of God and of Christ and will reign with Him for a thousand years." Those who experience the first resurrection will not experience "the second death." But those who are part of the second resurrection after the thousand years are affected by "the second death." This second death is linked with the lake of fire (20:14) that comes after the Great White throne judgment of Revelation 20:11–15.

Amillennialists and postmillennialists often claim the first reference to *ezesan* ("came to life") is a spiritual resurrection while the second reference to *ezesan* is a physical resurrection. The problem with this understanding is evident. That *ezesan* would be used in two different senses (spiritual then physical) in such close proximity seems most improbable. Plus, martyrs who died for Christ no longer need spiritual resurrection. They are already saved—that is why they gave their lives for Jesus in the first place. They give their physical lives for Jesus because they already are spiritually alive. But martyrs who died are in need of a physical resurrection, which Revelation 20:4 promises. Amillennialists and postmillennialists admit the second resurrection of Revelation 20:5 cannot be a spiritual resurrection for if it did, this would teach universalism, the view that all people will be saved. But if the second resurrection is a physical resurrection what contextual reasons are there for claiming that the first resurrection of 20:4 is spiritual? The claim that the resurrection of v. 4 is spiritual but the resurrection of v. 5 is physical is difficult to maintain, especially since the first resurrection involves believers who lost their physical lives for their testimony for Jesus.

Some have asserted that concerning the two resurrections chronology is not in view but the *quality* of the resurrections. Allegedly, the first resurrection is a kind of resurrection in which the focus is on spiritual salvation, while the second resurrection is in the category of physical resurrection. Yet such a view does injustice to the immediate context that is time-oriented. The eight "and I saw" (*kai eidon*) markers in Revelation 19:11–21:8 indicate chronology. And the second resurrection follows the first resurrection by a "thousand years," showing time is in view. So to deemphasize chronology here is a violation of the context.

The correct view is that martyrs who died for Jesus receive a physical resurrection, while a thousand years later a physical resurrection for another group occurs. All of this argues for a future millennium. *If the first resurrection of Revelation 20:4–5 is a physical resurrection then the millennium of Revelation 20 must be future, following the second coming of Jesus in Revelation 19. Since physical resurrection of the saints has not occurred in history, such a resurrection must be a future event.* Thus, Revelation 20:4–5 is powerful evidence for a millennium after the second coming of Jesus but before the eternal state.

RELEASE OF SATAN (REVELATION 20:7–10)

Revelation 20:7 states that after the thousand-year reign of Christ "Satan will be released from his prison." Earlier, Satan was bound and cast into "the abyss" (see Rev 20:2–3). He and his influence were removed from the earth for this period as Jesus ruled the nations with a rod of iron. But now he gets one more shot. Upon his release from the abyss he comes "to deceive the nations which are in the four corners of the earth" (Rev 20:8). Satan gathers the nations together for what John refers to as "the war." The number of those assembled by Satan is said to be "like the sand of the seashore" (20:8).

There is much debate concerning the timing of this Satan-led rebellion. Many hold this rebellion describes the same battle of Revelation 19:11–21 based on similarity of language from Ezekiel 38–39 and the parties involved in the battle. Certainly, there are similarities since both describe a cosmic battle and a defeat of Satan. But the differences indicate different battles at different times. To use an example, one could offer a long list of similarities between World War I and World War II but these would not mean they are the same event. Both occurred at different times and there are key differences that separate them.

The battle of Revelation 20:7–10 occurs after "the thousand years are completed," unlike the battle of Revelation 19:11–21 which occurs before the thousand year reign. How Satan is treated also differs. In Revelation 19 there is no mention of Satan being confined to the lake of fire. Instead, he is chained and placed in the abyss. So while similarities exist the differences indicate a different battle at a different time.

The presence of a great multitude that flock to Satan's final rebellion reveals the presence of unbelievers during the millennial reign of Jesus. While only true believers are allowed to enter the kingdom, some will be born who have not been regenerated. As McClain notes, "regenerated parents are no guarantee of regenerated progeny."[11]

Even with the presence of Satan's tempting influence removed and the glorious reign of Jesus present, some refuse to believe. Outward conformity to the reign of the Messiah during the millennium gives way to overt rebellion for some when Satan is released and the opportunity exists for unbelievers to flock to their spiritual father, the devil. "For a brief season the divine restraint will be relaxed for the purpose of providing one last and supreme demonstration of the appalling wickedness of the unregenerated human heart."[12] It is difficult to grasp how some people could remain in unbelief with the visible and reigning Jesus in their midst. But when has sin ever made sense? Why did Satan sin after being in God's presence? Why did most of Israel reject Jesus at His first coming? This rebellion after the millennium testifies that man's problem is not environmental or lack of evidence. The problem is his heart. Even with perfect societal conditions, some will rebel against God if their hearts are not changed.

The target of Satan and the wicked people of the nations is the capital city of Jerusalem—"they came up on the broad plain of the earth and surrounded the camp of the saints and the beloved city" (20:9). Not every believer in Jesus is actually in the city of Jerusalem but as the capital city of the millennial kingdom, Jerusalem is the natural target of the enemies of God. The result of this rebellion is not a lengthy war with both sides taking great casualties. This is a one-sided affair as "fire came down from heaven and devoured them" (20:9b). This is more like an execution. Satan may have intended a great, prolonged war but his defeat is swift and final. As

11 McClain, *The Greatness of the Kingdom*, 508.

12 Ibid.

McClain points out, "Though Satan gathers the rebels 'to battle,' there is no battle." Instead, "The end is by the fire of divine *execution*."[13]

Perhaps the most somber scene in the Bible is found in Revelation 20:11–15. After the millennial kingdom and the squashing of the final rebellion, there occurs a judgment scene from One who sits on a white throne. The "dead" both "great" and "small" stood before the throne. Books were opened, one being the book of life. Whoever's name was not found written in the book of life "was thrown into the lake of fire" (20:15). The wicked are forever banished from God's kingdom, soberly testifying to the fact that the story does not end well for everyone.

13 Ibid. Emphases in original.

CHAPTER

33

THE ETERNAL KINGDOM (REVELATION 21:1–22:5)

With Revelation 21 and 22, we come to the culmination of God's kingdom program and the goal of all history. Ever since the fall God's plan has been to restore His creation through the Son. This involves fulfilling the rule and subdue mandate of Genesis 1:26–28. At this point, Jesus' prayer that God's will be done on earth as it is in heaven (Matt 6:10) is a perfect reality. God is all in all (see 1 Cor 15:28). The Son's commission to reign until all His enemies have been defeated has occurred. Messiah's reign upon the earth has taken place and the Father's verdict is, "Mission Accomplished!" The transition to the eternal kingdom commences. The Messiah's mediatorial reign does not end as much as it transitions and merges into the Father's kingdom. Both Father and Son are on the throne (see Rev 22:3).

All three relationships God placed man into at creation are fully restored. First, man is in proper relationship with his Creator. Second, man is in complete fellowship and harmony with other human beings. And third, man's relationship with the creation is restored. All three relationships were marred at the fall, but now all three are complete.

While Genesis 1–2 was the original "Once upon a time," with Revelation 21–22 we see the ultimate "And they lived happily ever after." In one sense this is the end. Yet in another it is the beginning. This is the start of a new world inhabited only by lovers of God who will live forever confirmed in holiness and love in a world never again tainted by sin. They will spend the "ages to come" (Eph 2:7) worshiping God, reigning, and discovering the adventures of the new earth. The words of C.S. Lewis, from *The Last Battle*, capture this idea well:

> All their life in this world and all their adventures had only been the cover and the title page: now at last they were beginning Chapter One of the Great Story which no one on earth has read: which goes on forever: in which every chapter is better than the one before.

THE TIMING OF THE NEW EARTH

The most detailed discussion of the eternal kingdom is found in Revelation 21:1–22:5. There is much described here but our focus is mostly on how this section relates to the kingdom's timing and nature. As for timing, what is described starting in Revelation 21:1 occurs chronologically after the thousand-year reign of Christ on the earth, the final rebellion and defeat of Satan, and the Great White Throne judgment of Revelation 20. These events are followed by, "Then I saw a new heaven and a new earth" (Rev 21:1). The "new heaven and a new earth" language of Revelation 21:1 is first found in Isaiah 65:17—"For behold, I create new heavens and a new earth," and then again in Isaiah 66:22. Second Peter 3:13 declares: "But according to His promise we are looking for new heavens and a new earth, in which righteousness dwells." The final hope and destination of the believer is not the intermediate state in heaven, or even the millennium of Revelation 20:1–6, but the eternal state as described in Revelation 21 and 22.

THE CONNECTION WITH GENESIS 1–2

Before looking at Revelation 21:1–22:5, note the connection between the beginning and end of the Bible's story. The first chapters of Genesis and the last chapters of Revelation reveal divinely intended connections between first things (protology) and last things (eschatology). The comparisons are striking and show God's intent to restore the fallen creation:

Connections between Creation and New Creation

	Creation Gen 1–2 (with some 10–11)	New Creation Rev 21–22
God as Creator/Maker	"God *created*" (1:3); "in the day that the LORD God *made* earth and heaven" (2:4)	"I *am making* all things new" (21:5)
Heavens and Earth	"In the beginning God created *the heavens and the earth*" (1:1)	"Then I saw a *new heaven and a new earth*" (21:1)
Light	"Then God said, 'Let there be *light*'; and there was *light*" (1:3)	"they will not have need of the *light* of a lamp... the Lord God will *illumine* them" (22:5)
Holy Space	Holy space on the earth: *Garden of Eden* (2:8)	Holy space on the New Earth: *New Jerusalem*
Presence of God with man	"the LORD God walking in the garden in the cool of the day... the presence of the LORD God among the trees of the garden." (3:8);	"Behold, the tabernacle of God is among men, and He will dwell among them" (21:3)
Death	"in the day that you eat from it you will surely *die*" (2:17)	"there will no longer be *any death*" (21:4)
Curse	"*Cursed* is the ground because of you" (3:17)	"There will no longer be any *curse*" (22:3)
River	"Now a *river* flowed out of Eden to water the garden" (2:10)	"Then he showed me *a river of the water of life*, clear as crystal, coming from the throne of God and of the Lamb" (22:1)
Tree of Life	"the *tree of life* also in the midst of the garden" (2:9)	"On either side of the river was the *tree of life*, bearing twelve kinds of fruit" (22:2)
Rule/Reign	"*subdue* it [the earth]; and *rule* over..." (1:28)	"they will *reign* forever and ever" (22:5)
Satan	Satan free: "Now the *serpent* was more crafty than any beast of the field" (3:1)	Satan sentenced: "And the *devil* who deceived them was thrown into the lake of fire" (20:10)

Nations on the earth	Nations on the earth: Table of Nations (Gen 10–11)	"The *nations* will walk by its light, and the kings of the earth will bring their glory into it" (21:24)
Nations in harmony	Nations in conflict (Gen 10 onward)	Nations at peace: "the leaves of the tree were for the healing of the *nations*" (22:2)

THE NATURE OF THE NEW EARTH

What is the nature of the new earth conditions described in Revelation 21–22? Are the descriptions literal or figurative? Is the new earth an entirely new planet or a restored planet earth?

Literal or Figurative?

Concerning the nature of the new heaven and new earth there are two possibilities. One is that John is describing a tangible universe, i.e. a real physical planet. The second is he is describing spiritual realities for Christians now—the emphasis is on people, not place. Those who take the second view point to passages saying Christians are a new creation (see Gal 6:15) and new creatures (see 2 Cor 5:17). So the descriptions of the new earth in Revelation 21–22 allegedly are figurative descriptions of salvation.

The evidence lies heavily with the first view. John is describing a real universe where God's people will dwell, not just spiritual realities for Christians. Since the events of Revelation 21–22 follow the second coming and the millennial reign of Jesus, these events must be future from our standpoint. Also, Genesis 1–2 describes the creation of a real heaven and earth which is followed by a real fall (Gen 3). Since God is pursuing the "restoration of all things" (Acts 3:21), the "new heaven and new earth" of Revelation 21:1 is a restored physical entity as well. Just as Genesis 1–2 describes a literal creation, Revelation 21–22 describes a literal restoration of that creation. Certainly, in Christ, Christians are a new creation, but they also still await the resurrection. This is true for both believers and the creation (see Rom 8:19–23). Resurrected believers will inhabit the new earth still to come. We affirm a future and literal understanding of this passage.

Annihilation or Renewal?

Among those who hold to a coming physical new earth, debate exists as to whether the new earth will be a renovation of the current planet earth or an entirely new planet, an *ex nihilo* ("out of nothing") creation.[1] Is our present earth heading for *renewal?* Or is it annihilated and heading toward *replacement* with another earth? This latter view of annihilation with replacement relies on the wording of Revelation 21:1 that "the first heaven and the first earth passed away." This describes discontinuity between the former earth and the latter earth. But such language does not necessarily mean the first heaven and first earth were annihilated and replaced with a second heaven and earth. The better view is that the new earth is a renewal of the present earth, or as Turner states, "The new universe in Christ is none other than the old Adamic universe gloriously liberated from its cacophonous groan to a harmonious song of praise to the One who sits on the throne."[2] Several reasons supports this renewal view.

First, the renewal view fits the Bible's storyline. God's original creation was deemed "very good" (Gen 1:31). God's image bearers were supposed to rule and subdue God's world. But their sin caused the creation to be cursed. Yet hope remained. The storyline from Genesis 3 onward is that an ultimate seed of the woman (Jesus) would come and defeat the power behind the serpent (Satan) and reverse the curse covering creation (see Gen 5:28–29). What God is seeking is the "restoration of all things" marred by the fall (see Acts 3:21), not the "annihilation of all things." Satan does not get the victory over God's creation. God does. As Anthony Hoekema puts it, "If God would have to annihilate the present cosmos, Satan would have won a great victory."[3]

1 For lists of adherents of both sides see David J. MacLeod, "The Seventh 'Last Thing': The New Heaven and the New Earth (Rev. 21:1–8)" in *Bibliotheca Sacra* 157 (2000): 441 n.11, 12. MacLeod holds to an annihilation view.

2 David L. Turner, "The New Jerusalem in Revelation 21:1–22:5: Consummation of a Biblical Continuum," in *Dispensationalism, Israel and the Church: The Search for Definition*, ed. Craig A. Blaising and Darrell L. Bock (Grand Rapids: Zondervan, 1992), 265. For a fine discussion of this issue and a defense for the renewal view see Michael J. Svigel, "Extreme Makeover: Heaven and Earth Edition—Will God Annihilate the World and Re-create it Ex Nihilo?" *Bibliotheca Sacra* 171 (2014): 401–17.

3 Hoekema, *The Bible and the Future*, 280. Seiss points out, "for if the redemption does not go as far as the consequences of sin.... Satan's mischief goes further than Christ's restoration." J. A. Seiss, *The Apocalypse* (London: Marshall, Morgan, & Scott, n.d.), 483.

Thus, the story line is not:

Creation (out of nothing) → Fall → Annihilation → Creation (out of nothing)

Instead, the story line is:

Creation → Fall → Restoration[4]

Second, Romans 8 shows creation longs for renewal, not annihilation and extinction. The creation has been subjected to futility because of the fall but this is "in hope" (Rom 8:21). If creation is headed for annihilation how could it be hopeful? Instead, creation is longing for a reversal of fortune.

Third, the fate of creation parallels the fate of man, which is resurrection and renewal, not annihilation with a start-over. According to Romans 8:19: "the anxious longing of the creation waits eagerly for the revealing of the sons of God." Paul personifies the "creation" and says it eagerly anticipates the glorification of the children of God. It does so because the glorification of man brings the glorification of creation. In 8:21 Paul says, "the creation itself also will be set free from its slavery to corruption into the freedom of the glory of the children of God." Paul does not say creation is headed toward annihilation. Instead, it will be delivered from its current "corruption" as it enters the "freedom of the glory of the children of God." Glorification for man leads to glorification for creation, and there is a symmetrical relationship between man's fate and creation's destiny. Just as man has fallen and will be glorified, so too the fallen creation will be glorified. Note the parallel:

Fall of Man → Fall of Creation
Glorification of Man → Glorification of Creation[5]

Romans 8 shows a correspondence between creation now and in the future. The creation that is fallen is the same creation that will be renewed. There will be purging and transformation by fire (2 Pet 3:7) but a continuity exists. This is similar to believers in Jesus who are decaying physically but are longing for resurrection. Believers in Jesus will be resurrected and glorified in

4 The symbol "→" represents "then."

5 The symbol "→" represents "leads to." Also, by "glorification of man" I am referring to believers.

connection with His coming. Also, the glorified Jesus, who is the firstfruits of the resurrection (1 Cor 15:20), is the same Jesus who walked the earth. In these cases there is a transformation but a one-to-one correspondence between now and then still exists.

Fourth, the language of Scripture indicates renewal rather than annihilation. In Matthew 19:28 Jesus referred to "the regeneration" (NASB) or "renewal of all things" (NIV) that would take place.[6] Acts 3:21 speaks of the "restoration of all things" foretold by the OT prophets. The word for "restoration" here is related to the term "restoring" in Acts 1:6 concerning Israel's kingdom. The disciples expected a correspondence between the kingdom that belonged to Israel in the OT and the one that would be restored to Israel in the *eschaton*. In Colossians 1:20, Paul says Jesus will "reconcile all things to Himself." This reconciliation involves "all things" that "were created, both in the heavens and on earth, visible and invisible" (Col 1:16). Colossians 1 is explicit evidence God will reconcile everything He created.[7] As Randy Alcorn points out, the vocabulary of the Bible shows that God plans a renewal of the planet:

> God has never given up on his original creation. Yet somehow we've managed to overlook an entire biblical vocabulary that makes this point clear. *Reconcile. Redeem. Restore. Recover. Return. Renew. Regenerate. Resurrect.* Each of these biblical words begins with the re-prefix, suggesting a return to an original condition that was ruined or lost.[8]

In this debate over renewal vs. annihilation, much hinges on 2 Peter 3:10–13 with its language of fiery destruction for the earth. Those on both sides believe this section aligns with their view—either for annihilation or renovation of the planet. The passages declares:

> But the day of the Lord will come like a thief, in which the heavens will pass away with a roar and the elements will be destroyed with intense heat, and the earth and its works will be burned up.

6 The International Standard Version calls it "the renewed creation."

7 Universal reconciliation should not be confused with universal salvation.

8 Alcorn, *Heaven*, 88.

> Since all these things are to be destroyed in this way, what sort of people ought you to be in holy conduct and godliness, looking for and hastening the coming of the day of God, because of which the heavens will be destroyed by burning, and the elements will melt with intense heat! But according to His promise we are looking for new heavens and a new earth, in which righteousness dwells.

Those who hold the annihilation view of the present earth emphasize the following:

- "heavens and earth will pass away with a roar"
- "the elements will be destroyed with intense heat"
- "the earth and its works will be burned up"
- "all these things are to be destroyed"
- "heavens will be destroyed by burning"
- "elements will melt with intense heat"

Some believe such intense language means the current universe will be obliterated with fire, making an entirely new heaven and earth necessary.

Advocates of renewal, though, have a different understanding. First, they argue this fiery judgment is compared to an earlier global judgment—the flood of Noah's day (2 Pet 3:6) in which the planet was "destroyed" by water but was not annihilated.[9] The watery judgment of the global flood did not make the earth disappear. So if there can be a global destruction by water that did not annihilate the world then there can be a global destruction by fire that purifies but does not remove the planet.

This understanding is bolstered by a proper understanding of 2 Peter 3:10 and its declaration, "the earth and its works will be burned up." The Greek term translated "burned up" or "will be burned up" is *eurethesetai* which is best translated "will be found" or "will be laid bare." Daniel Wallace observes that "the meaning of the term is virtually the equivalent of 'will be disclosed,' 'will be manifested.' Thus, the force of the clause would be that 'the earth and the works [done by men] in it will be stripped

9 2 Peter 3:6: "the world at that time was destroyed, being flooded with water."

bare [before God].'"[10] Contextually, this term is used in a positive sense of believers just four verses later: "Therefore, beloved, since you look for these things, be diligent to be found [*eurethenai*] by Him in peace, spotless and blameless" (2 Pet 3:4). Also, this term is found in a fiery judgment setting in 1 Peter 1:7: "so that the proof of your faith, being more precious than gold which is perishable, even though tested by fire, may be found [*eurethe*] to result in praise and glory and honor at the revelation of Jesus Christ." Here judgment by fire involves a positive result for the Christian.[11]

So could 2 Peter 3:10 indicate a positive fate for planet earth? We think so. Purification not annihilation is in view. Middleton argues that "the image of judgment by fire in 2 Peter 3 is not purely destructive, but instead may be understood as a smelting process by which the dross of human sinfulness is burned off so that 'found' means something like 'standing the test' or 'showing one's mettle.... The fire of judgment might then be compared to a 'foundry,' where metals are melted down and reshaped into useful products."[12] In a similar way, Svigel claims that "the fires pictured in 2 Peter 3:10, 12–13 are best interpreted as purifying fires, likely drawing on metallurgical imagery of heating for the sake of purifying and strengthening, not annihilating."[13] In Malachi 3–4, which also discusses a coming Day of the Lord, fire can refine precious metals like silver that belong to God (Mal 3:2–3) and remove those things that do not (Mal 4:1). So 2 Peter 3 is not teaching an annihilation of earth. As Alcorn states:

> Therefore, they misinterpret words such as *destroy* to mean absolute or final destruction, rather than what Scripture actually teaches: a temporary destruction that is reversed through resurrection and restoration.[14]

10 Daniel B. Wallace, "A Brief Note on a Textual Problem in 2 Peter 3:10," http://bible.org/article/brief-note-textual-problem-2-peter-310 (accessed 12/28/2012).

11 A similar concept is found in 1 Corinthians 3:12–15 where the works of Christians are put through fiery judgment to see what remains.

12 Middleton, *A New Heaven and a New Earth*, 194.

13 Svigel, "Extreme Makeover," 413.

14 Alcorn, *Heaven*, 152.

Another argument for the annihilation view is the wording of Revelation 21:1: "Then I saw a new heaven and a new earth; for the first heaven and the first earth passed away, and there is no longer any sea." Doesn't the fact that the first earth "passed away" indicate an annihilation? Not necessarily. Gale Heide asserts, "The words 'passed away' in our English translation are commonly used in conversation to describe the death of a person. But the verb here, *aperchomai*, more frequently means 'to depart, go away.'"[15] Thus, John may simply mean "the first heaven and earth had gone from his sight," and is not describing how this occurred.[16] Svigel believes the things that pass away are "Not elements, atoms, or molecules, but the evil order of things: death, wickedness, grief, suffering, pain, degeneration, and deterioration that had long held all of these physical and spiritual elements in bondage. Those are the first things that had 'passed away.'"[17]

The words "passed away" does not mean annihilation of the earth but a transition from the old order of the fallen world to the new. What God does for His people supports this conclusion. A believer in Jesus becomes a new creation and experiences a passing away (2 Cor 5:17) but not in the sense of annihilation. This could also be true for creation:

15 Gale Heide, "What's New About the New Heaven and the New Earth? A Theology of Creation from Revelation 21 and 2 Peter 3," in *Journal of the Evangelical Theological Society* 40 (1997): 43.

16 Ibid.

17 Svigel, "Extreme Makeover," 416.

Category	Scripture	Implication
Man	2 Cor 5:17 "Therefore if anyone is in Christ, he is a new creature; the old things passed away; behold, new things have come."	A transition has occurred as a sinful person becomes a new creature in Christ. The new has come and old things have "passed away" but the person is still the same. There is a one-to-one correspondence.
Heaven and Earth	Rev 21:1 "Then I saw a new heaven and a new earth; for the first heaven and the first earth passed away."	A transition occurs as the first heaven and earth pass away and are replaced by a new heaven and new earth. Yet there is still a one-to-one correspondence between the first heaven and earth and the new heaven and earth.

Concerning His people God can say "old things passed away" but that does not mean annihilation and a start-over. Instead, the new comes by resurrection. The same is true for the earth. The earth as affected by the fall passes away, but God restores and resurrects the current planet. Middleton argues God's purposes do not involve doppelgängers:

> Are we to believe that Paul thinks that the passing away of the old life is equivalent to the obliteration of the person, who is then replaced by a doppelgänger? All the Pauline writings, not to mention common sense, suggest that no matter how radical the shift required for conversion to Christ, this describes the transformation rather than obliteration of the person. By analogy, then, the passing away of the present heaven and earth to make way for the new creation is also transformative and not a matter of destruction followed by a replacement.[18]

Most Christians would not be happy knowing they would were heading for annihilation. Such also is the case for the creation that Paul says is looking for glorification "in hope" (Rom 8:20). This present creation is not looking for annihilation but permanent glorification.

18 Middleton, *A New Heaven and a New Earth*, 206.

NO SEA

Revelation 21:1 reveals a significant transition from the millennial kingdom to the eternal kingdom. While it is not a transition from one planet to an entirely new planet, there are major changes. One such change is found in 21:1b which reads, "and there is no longer any sea." This is a challenging statement. The "seas" and water were part of the original "very good" creation (Gen 1:1–9, 31). Aquatic life was also part of the creation (1:20–22). A river once flowed out of Eden to water the garden and became divided into four rivers (Gen 2:10).

Water also plays an important role in the future millennial kingdom. Ezekiel 47 discusses a positive function for water in connection with a coming temple. Water from the temple starts as a trickle and then eventually becomes a gushing river that cannot not be crossed (47:5). As in the creation account, the water is linked with life and vibrant vegetation. The river brings an abundance of trees—"on the bank of the river there were very many trees on the one side and on the other" (47:7). These trees are linked with fruit. The fruit will be for food and the leaves for healing (47:12). As one ponders the importance of water in the original creation and its future significance in the millennium, it seems puzzling that water and aquatic life might not be part of the eternal kingdom.

So what does the "no sea" reference mean? Several options exist. First, it could mean there are no bodies of water at all and no aquatic life. The new earth is simply one big land mass and creatures like whales, fish, and all other water life are extinct. Second, "no sea" could be taken figuratively and refer to the absence of negative influences on the new earth. In the book of Revelation the "sea" is sometimes viewed negatively. John "saw a beast coming out of the sea" (Rev 13:1). The "harlot" sat on "the waters (17:15). Plus, in ancient times, the sea was viewed as a treacherous entity and a grave for many who tried to cross it. On the island of Patmos, the prisoner John certainly would have viewed the sea as a barrier to previous relationships. So some hold that "no sea" means lack of negative influences.

A third alternative is that "no sea" refers to the removal of vast salt-water oceans and seas that separate people. Yet it is not a statement that all bodies of water or even large bodies of fresh water lakes and rivers do not exist. Revelation 22:1–2 speaks of a river that flows from the throne of God:

> Then he showed me a river of the water of life, clear as crystal, coming from the throne of God and of the Lamb, in the middle of its street. On either side of the river was the tree of life, bearing twelve kinds of fruit, yielding its fruit every month; and the leaves of the tree were for the healing of the nations.

The "river of the water of life" in Revelation 22:1 shows the presence of water in the New Jerusalem. As with Ezekiel 47, the presence of a river means vegetation abundance, in this case "twelve kinds of fruit." Ezekiel 47 also says the gushing river that flows from the temple makes its way to the sea so "the waters of the sea become fresh" (47:8). Not only this, but "every living creature which swarms in every place where the river goes, will live" and "there will be very many fish" (47:9). Again, the description of Ezekiel 47 best fits the intermediate millennial kingdom, but the similar language of Revelation 22:1–2 indicates a positive function for water in the eternal state. Thus, there might be bodies of fresh water, perhaps even large rivers and lakes, and aquatic life on the new earth. God may cause salt-water creatures to be able to thrive in fresh water. In sum, "no sea" could mean large salt-water oceans that separate people will be removed, but water will probably still exist on the new earth.

THE NEW JERUSALEM

After John saw the coming of the new heaven and new earth, He then "saw the holy city, new Jerusalem, coming down out of heaven from God" (Rev 21:2). Just as the new earth is connected with the old earth, so too, the New Jerusalem is related to the former Jerusalem. As Alan Johnson puts it, "Since the Jerusalem from above is the 'new' (*kaine*) Jerusalem, we may suppose that it is connected in some manner with the old one so that the new is the old one renewed."[19] Like believers and the earth, the city of Jerusalem undergoes a resurrection and renewal. Just as the new earth is a real tangible planet, so too is the New Jerusalem. The city, while heavenly in origin, is a tangible city that resides on the new earth.

19 Alan F. Johnson, "Revelation," in *The Expositor's Bible Commentary*, ed. Frank E. Gaebelein, (Grand Rapids: Zondervan, 1982), 593.

The New Jerusalem is the capital city of the new earth. Some have speculated that the New Jerusalem is the new earth so the New Jerusalem and the new earth are the same. Allegedly, there is no part of the new earth outside the New Jerusalem. But John distinguishes the two. He saw a new heaven and a new earth (21:1) and then he saw the New Jerusalem (21:2). Just as Jerusalem in the past was the capital city of Israel and later will be the capital city of the world in the millennium (see Isa 2:2–4; Zech 14:9), the New Jerusalem is the capital city of the new earth. According to Revelation 21:10 John was carried by an angel in the Spirit to "a great and high mountain" so he could see the New Jerusalem coming from heaven. It seems that John is on a mountain perch outside the New Jerusalem when the city descends to earth which hints at its locale on the earth outside the city.

The dimensions also point to it being a city on the new earth. The length and width of the city are about 1500 miles. This is an enormous city that is roughly half of the size of the United States. But 1500 miles long and wide is not big for the earth. The length of the current circumference of the earth is nearly 25,000 miles. If the New Jerusalem is the new earth then the dimensions of this new earth will be dramatically smaller than the present planet. Such a shrinking of the planet, while not impossible, seems unlikely.

Also, activity exists outside of the New Jerusalem. Revelation 21:24 states that, "The nations will walk by its light, and the kings of the earth will bring their glory into it." If kings of the earth are bringing their "glory" or contributions into the city, activity is taking place outside the New Jerusalem. The direction of the kings of the earth into the city indicates geography outside the New Jerusalem. Therefore, the New Jerusalem is a city on the new earth and there are geographical locales outside this great city.

DESCRIPTION OF THE NEW JERUSALEM

The description of the New Jerusalem is mind-boggling yet what is described is not so 'other than' that any contemplation of it is futile. The city has a great and high wall with twelve gates. Twelve angels are at the gates. The names of the twelve tribes of Israel are written on the gates (21:12), showing the continuing relevance of national Israel in the New Jerusalem. There are also three gates at each direction–North, South, East, and West (21:13).

So human directions still exist and can be observed on the traditional four points of the compass. This shows continuity with the present earth.

Next, the wall of the city has twelve foundation stones with the names of the twelve apostles (21:14). The city and wall can be measured (21:15). The city is laid out as a square with length, width and height being equal, fifteen hundred [or fourteen hundred] miles each (21:16). Before looking at these dimensions more closely, note the measurements are literal—"human measurements which are also angelic measurements" (21:17). God seems to warn against spiritualizing this passage, emphasizing that the city is measured according to human measurements.

Next, the city is "laid out as a square." The length, width, and height of the city are equal. Concerning the shape of the city three understandings have been offered. First, many hold the city is in the shape of a cube. In OT times the Most Holy Place in the temple was in the shape of a cube. So if the New Jerusalem were modeled after the Most Holy Place, then the New Jerusalem would be like an encased temple or building. This includes a building reaching many miles into the air.

Another understanding is that the city is in the shape of a pyramid. And third, others believe the shape is that of a square. If so, the city is a large landmass—a garden-city with no encasing at the top of it. The city is not primarily a big skyscraper or large temple building but a very large land mass.

The shape of the city is influenced by another dimension, the declaration that there is a wall of 72 yards (21:17). But is the wall 72 yards thick? Or is it 72 yards high? Some who say it is 72 yards thick think that this wall serves as the outer casing for the cubed city. Others say the wall is 72 yards high and functions as a surrounding wall for the city.

So how big is the city? The prevailing view is that the city is 1500 miles wide, 1500 miles long, and 1500 miles high. This means an estimated area of 2,250,000 square miles. If correct, the size of this city would reach from Canada to Mexico and from the Appalachian Mountains to the California border. This would be roughly half the size of the United States and forty times bigger than England.[20]

A lesser-held but possible view is that the perimeter of the city is about 1500 miles. Since Jerusalem is laid out as a square, each side could be 375

20 See Alcorn, *Heaven*, 250.

miles long and the city has an area of 140,625 square miles. This is smaller than that proposed by the other view, but still very large. If this understanding is correct, the size of the city would be more like a large state in the United States. The county of Los Angeles, which has 9,818,605 people (2010 census), is 4,752 square miles. The New Jerusalem according to this projection would be about 30 times bigger in size than Los Angeles County as it currently exists.

NATIONS

Nations have been important in God's plans since Genesis 10–11. So it is no surprise that nations are important in the eternal kingdom and show a point of continuity with conditions in this present age. On three occasions "nations" are mentioned on the new earth. The first two occur in Revelation 21:24–26:

> The nations will walk by its light, and the kings of the earth will bring their glory into it. In the daytime (for there will be no night there) its gates will never be closed; and they will bring the glory and the honor of the nations into it.[21]

A third reference to "nations" is found in Revelation 22:2 where they are said to exist in harmony. So nations as geo-political entities exist on the new earth. In Revelation, the nations often are viewed negatively under the leadership of Satan and followers of the Beast.[22] But nations are now viewed positively. Not only is Israel restored, so too are many nations.

Some believe the "nations" are simply redeemed humanity in a generic sense without any ethnic and national diversity, but this is not accurate. After mentioning "nations" in Revelation 21:24, John also mentions

---

21 Emphases are mine.

22 David Mathewson writes, "so that now the nations and kings of the earth, formerly in compliance with Babylon and the beast, come to the New Jerusalem to render allegiance to God in fulfillment of Isaiah 2:2–5; 60." "The Destiny of the Nations in Revelation 21:1–22:5: A Reconsideration," *Tyndale Bulletin* 53 (2002): 132.

"kings of the earth." These nations have leaders—kings who represent their nations as they bring their glory into the New Jerusalem.[23]

The language here is similar to Isaiah 60: "Nations will come to your light, and kings to the brightness of your rising" (Isa 60:3). And, "The wealth of the nations will come to you" (Isa 60:5). Such a picture is consistent with OT passages such as Isaiah 19:24–25 that foretold nations in the future alongside Israel. Mathewson is correct that these nations represent a "third group" in addition to national Israel and the church:

> Therefore, in addition to the OT people of God indicated by the twelve gates named after the twelve tribes of Israel (21:12) and the NT people of God indicated by the twelve foundations inscribed with the twelve apostles, the reader is meant to distinguish a third group: *the nations who will be converted in the future in fulfillment of the OT prophecies* (Is. 2:2–5; 60) will also inhabit the new Jerusalem and become, along with the former two groups, the one people of God (21:24; cf. v. 3).[24]

Twice it is stated that the nations will bring their "glory" into the New Jerusalem. This "glory" probably refers to cultural contributions. There is no need here to limit "glory" simply to the nations bringing themselves with no reference to their wealth.[25] Both are in view here. We are not told what these contributions are, but they probably involve the best these nations have to offer regarding wealth, art, music, architecture, agriculture, etc. As Hoekema states, "Is it too much to say that, according to these verses [Rev

23 David E. Aune states, "The pilgrimage of the kings of the earth to the New Jerusalem presupposes the existence of the nations of the world and their rulers as well as the location of the eschatological Jerusalem on the earth." *Revelation 17–22*, in Word Biblical Commentary, vol. 52c (Nashville: Thomas Nelson, 1998), 1171.

24 Mathewson, "The Destiny of the Nations in Revelation 21:1–22:5," 133. Emphases in original. Mathewson points out that "the conversion of the kings and nations in 21:24 (which is contiguous with the restored Jerusalem, 21:2) is a *future* one, semantically consistent with Isaiah 2:2–5; 60:3, and not just a succinct reference to the nations and kings who become God's people throughout history as Beale and others maintain..." (133).

25 Contra Beale who says, "they are bringing not literal riches but themselves as worshipers before God's end-time presence (so 22:3–5)." G. K. Beale, *The Book of Revelation: A Commentary on the Greek Text* (Grand Rapids: Eerdmans, 1999), 1095. But Revelation 21:24, 26 explicitly states that the nations are bringing something—their "glory" and "honor." Thus, they bring both themselves and their contributions to the New Jerusalem. It is a both/and situation.

21:24, 26], the unique contributions of each nation to the life of the present earth will enrich the life of the new earth?"[26] These contributions include "the best products of culture and art which this earth has produced."[27]

Revelation 22:2 reveals "the leaves of the tree were for the healing of the nations." These nations coexist in harmony with each other. The term for "healing" is *therapeia*, which means "care," "attention," or "healing." The word is found in Luke 9:11 concerning Jesus "curing those who had need of healing (*therapeia*)." It carries the idea of restoring something to wholeness. The nations are healed and made whole. No hostility remains. This harmony occurs because of their participation in the leaves of the tree of life. This does not mean the nations sin against each other and are in need of having their wounds healed. Instead, participation in the tree is God's means for maintaining healing and harmony among the nations. *Thus, we have one of the greatest miracles of all time, and something almost impossible to think of now—true peace among all ethnicities and nations.* Racism and ethnic hatred will not exist.

The presence of multiple nations making unique contributions to the new earth shows that the coming eternal kingdom evidences wonderful diversity among those unified in their worship of the one true God. Altogether, the people(s) of God evidence both unity and diversity. Nations, therefore, are an important part of eternal kingdom conditions.

GOD ON THE THRONE AND SERVANTS WHO REIGN

Revelation 22:1–5 offers the last description of the coming eternal kingdom. The "river of the water of life" flows from the throne of God and the Lamb (22:1). On either side of the river is the "tree of life" (22:2) that has not been seen since the Garden of Eden in Genesis 3. This tree of life bears "twelve kinds of fruit, yielding its fruit every month." That the tree yields its fruit "every month" indicates time exists on the new earth. Chronological months exist. Perhaps this hints at the existence of a sun or some other

26 Hoekema, *The Bible and the Future*, 286.

27 Ibid.

cosmic body that marks the transition of days and months.[28] Just as the original creation existed in time, so too will the restored creation. Negative elements associated with time in a fallen world such as decay and increasing weakness certainly will not be a part of the new creation.

Revelation 22:3 states, "There will no longer be any curse; and the throne of God and of the Lamb will be in it, and His bond-servants will serve Him." For the first time since the fall, the world is no longer under a curse in any sense. This was the hope from Genesis 3:15 with the promise of a seed of the woman who would defeat the power behind the serpent (Satan). This also was the expectation expressed by Lamech: "This one will give us rest from our work and from the toil of our hands arising from the ground which the LORD has cursed" (Gen 5:29).

Heavy kingdom language exists in Revelation 22:3, 5. The New Jerusalem possesses the throne of God and the Lamb. Messiah's kingdom has transitioned into the Father's, so both are reigning from the same throne. Verse 5 then states God's people "will reign forever and ever." This last verse describing the eternal kingdom mentions God's people reigning and they do so in God's presence. This brings the kingdom program full circle. When God created man, He made him to rule and subdue the earth in His presence (Gen 1:26–28). Yet man sinned and failed in the dominion mandate. But the ultimate Man, Jesus the Messiah, succeeds where Adam failed. Now God enables those who believe in Him to carry out the mandate faithfully. This is probably related to the continuing New Covenant ministry of the Holy Spirit.

Because of Jesus all things have been restored and God's image bearers are now able to reign over the creation perfectly for God's glory—". . . and they lived happily ever after!"

THE RELATIONSHIP BETWEEN THE MILLENNIUM AND THE ETERNAL STATE

This book has documented that God's kingdom program is multifaceted with several significant stages. We have discussed the kingdom's last two

28 While the New Jerusalem does not need the light of the sun (Rev 22:5) this does not mean no cosmic bodies exist or that they could not have some purpose.

phases—the millennial kingdom (Rev 20) and the eternal kingdom (Rev 21–22). Here we discuss the relationship between these two. How similar are they? How different?

The Bible speaks of two ages. There is a present age, which describes conditions on the earth before Jesus returns to set up His kingdom. Then there is an "age to come" which describes conditions on earth after Jesus returns. Just as "this age" has various eras and dispensations, the millennium and eternal kingdom are two phases of the "age to come." Both are superior to this present age, which is characterized by sin and death, yet there are some differences between them. The millennium is primarily the kingdom of the Last Adam, the Messiah, as Jesus reigns for a thousand years. This kingdom is mediatorial in that the Father reigns through Jesus and His followers. They succeed in the realm (earth) where the first Adam failed. In doing so Jesus fulfills the task God gave to man in the Garden of Eden.

The eternal kingdom, on the other hand, involves the direct reign of both the Father and the Son. First Corinthians 15:24–28 explains the distinction. Jesus the Messiah "must reign until He has put all His enemies under His feet" (1 Cor 15:25). We are also told that when the "end" comes "He [Jesus] hands over the kingdom to the God and Father, when He has abolished all rule and all authority and power" (1 Cor 15:24). Thus, Jesus reigns for a period of time (millennium) and then hands His kingdom over to the Father (eternal kingdom). This shows some distinction between Jesus' reign from David's throne and the kingdom of the Father since Jesus hands His kingdom over to the Father. This does not mean Jesus stops ruling. Revelation 11:15 says Jesus "will reign forever and ever." Revelation 22:3 mentions "the throne of God and of the Lamb [Jesus]," showing that Jesus is ruling with the Father. Yet a transition occurs. The millennial kingdom is uniquely the Son's reign. The spotlight is on Him and His glory. It is Jesus' time to receive the honor on earth He so richly deserves. It is a period of time when the world that rejected Jesus is directly under His righteous reign. It is also a time when the Son completes the mission of bringing this world back into complete conformity with the Father's will. So the millennium highlights the Son's reign. When the eternal kingdom begins the Son will hand the kingdom over to the Father, yet the Son still has a reigning function.

Some have objected to the idea of two phases to the "age to come" but this objection does not hold.[29] First, Ephesians 2:7 says in the "ages to come" (plural) God will "show the surpassing riches of His grace in kindness toward us in Christ Jesus." So "ages to come" could involve multiple future ages including both a millennial phase and an eternal kingdom phase. Second, this "present age" that we live in has multiple dispensations or eras to it. There are pre-fall and post-fall eras. Pre-flood and post-flood. Mosaic era and the New Covenant era. So why couldn't the "age to come" have dispensations as well, including a millennial phase followed by an eternal kingdom era?

One passage with millennial and eternal kingdom implications is Isaiah 65:17–25. This starts with, "For behold, I create new heavens and a new earth" (65:17). These words are used of the eternal kingdom of Revelation 21:1a: "Then I saw a new heaven and a new earth." So then, the "new heavens and a new earth" language used in Isaiah 65:17 is found again concerning the eternal kingdom in Revelation 21:1. So does this mean Isaiah 65:17–25 refers only to the eternal kingdom? As we discussed in our chapter on Isaiah, the rest of this section describes conditions absent in the eternal kingdom. This passage mentions childbirth (v. 23) and death (v. 20). These fit a millennial kingdom better.

So does Isaiah 65:17–25 describe the millennium or the eternal kingdom? The best answer is that it applies to both. Russell D. Moore argues Isaiah 65:17–21 seems "to conflate the 'new heavens and the new earth' with an intermediate stage of the Kingdom in which death and rebellion are still present."[30] This means "articulating the Millennium, not as a separate dispensation from the eternal state, but as an initial phase of it."[31] Moore's point seems accurate. The millennial kingdom could operate as an initial or first phase of the new earth. Ralph Alexander likens the relationship of the two to the concept of "firstfruits":

29 For a thorough and excellent discussion of how the age to come is consistent with premillennialism see, Matthew William Waymeyer, "A Biblical Critique of the Two-Age Model as an Argument against Premillennialism," Ph.D. diss., The Master's Seminary, 2015.

30 Moore, *The Kingdom of Christ*, 64.

31 Ibid.

> In light of the whole Scripture, it appears that the Millennium is like a "firstfruits" of the eternal state. The Millennium will be like a preview of the eternal messianic kingdom that will be revealed fully in the eternal state. Therefore, because the two are alike in nature, they share distinct similarities.[32]

SIMILARITIES AND DIFFERENCES

There are important similarities between the millennial kingdom and the eternal kingdom.[33] For example, in both the saints of God are reigning (Rev 20:4, 6 with Rev 22:5). Yet there are also differences. First, the millennium focuses on Jesus' reign while in the eternal kingdom both the Father and Son are directly ruling (see 1 Cor 15:24–28). Second, with both kingdom phases the nations are subjected to Christ (see Isa 2:2–4). But in the millennium the nations can still sin (see Zech 14:16–19) while in the eternal kingdom they do not (Rev 22:2). Third, righteousness and justice characterize both the millennial kingdom and the eternal kingdom. But in the millennium there is still some sin and death (see Isa 65:20), while in the eternal kingdom there is no sin or death (Rev 21:4, 8, 27). Fourth, the curse on the ground is lifted in both phases of the kingdom (Isa 30:23; 32:14–15; 35:1–2, 7; with Rev 22:3). But the removal of the curse is final and permanent in the eternal kingdom. Fifth, the presence of sin and death are greatly reduced in the millennial kingdom while totally removed in the eternal kingdom. Sixth, Jerusalem is prominent in both the millennium and the eternal kingdom. But in the eternal state the dimensions of the city are much greater (Rev 21:10–21).

Sharper differences also exist. In the millennial kingdom there is a temple (see Ezek 40–48), but in the eternal kingdom no temple exists "for the Lord God the Almighty and the Lamb are its temple" (Rev 21:22). In addition, in the millennium there is marriage and childbirth (see Isa 65:23),

32 Ralph H. Alexander, "Ezekiel," in *The Expositor's Bible Commentary*, vol. 6, ed. Frank E. Gaebelein (Grand Rapids: Zondervan, 1986), 945.

33 For a comparison of the similarities and differences between the millennial kingdom and the eternal kingdom see Nathan Busenitz, "The Kingdom of God and the Eternal State," in *The Master's Seminary Journal* 23 (2012): 266–68.

but in the eternal kingdom marriage does not exist (see Matt 22:30; Luke 20:34–36).

Both the millennial kingdom and eternal kingdom are important phases of God's kingdom program. They are similar and distinct and reveal how God relates to His creation at these strategic times in history. A proper understanding of the kingdom program will take both phases of the kingdom into account.

CHAPTER 34

SUMMARY OF THE KINGDOM PROGRAM IN THE NEW TESTAMENT

Earlier, we offered a summary of the kingdom program in the OT. Below is a summary of the kingdom program in the NT:

1. As the NT era opens expectation is heavy concerning the coming of Israel's Messiah, even among some Gentiles.
2. Jewish believers expected literal fulfillment of the Abrahamic and Davidic Covenants including restoration and protection for Israel.
3. In fulfillment of OT prophecy John the Baptist is the forerunner of the Messiah and proclaimer of the nearness of the kingdom.
4. The announcement of Jesus the Messiah is connected with His coming rule from the throne of David over Israel.
5. Jesus the Messiah arrives.
6. After withstanding temptation from Satan Jesus proclaims the nearness of the kingdom to the people of Israel.
7. The kingdom John and Jesus announce as near is the prophesied kingdom of the OT prophets, including its spiritual and physical elements; its coming is conditioned on Israel's repentance.
8. With His Sermon on the Mount, Jesus reveals the righteous requirements needed for those who would enter the kingdom.

9. Jesus' miracles and exorcisms are demonstrations of kingdom authority, glimpses of kingdom conditions, and proof Jesus is the Son of David.
10. Jesus delegates kingdom authority to His disciples so they can proclaim the nearness of the kingdom to the cities of Israel.
11. The kingdom message proclaimed by John the Baptist, Jesus, and the apostles is resisted by the cities of Israel.
12. The leaders of Israel also reject Jesus, attributing His works done in the Holy Spirit to Satan, and commit personal and national blasphemy against the Holy Spirit.
13. With rejection from the cities and leadership of Israel, Jesus and His apostles withdraw from public proclamation of the nearness of the kingdom to Israel; Jesus begins to speak in parables and hides truth from those who will not believe and gives more truth to those who do believe.
14. Jesus offers new truths in "mysteries" concerning the kingdom, which describe conditions between His first and second comings; the main thrust of these kingdom parables is that the spread of the kingdom message and citizens will occur in this present evil age until the kingdom arrives with Jesus' second coming.
15. With opposition from the leaders evident, Jesus shifts His attention from the nearness of the kingdom to preparing His disciples for His soon coming death.
16. On the day of His entry into Jerusalem Jesus formally presents himself as King of Israel but mourns over Israel's unbelief and states that judgment will come instead of peace; He also says He will not be seen by Jerusalem again until the people cry out to Him with words of blessing.
17. Jesus the Messiah is crucified but provides atonement for sin as the Suffering Servant of the Lord, lays the foundation for the kingdom, and establishes the New Covenant in His blood.

18. After His resurrection Jesus receives all authority in heaven and earth.

19. Jesus spends forty days instructing His apostles concerning the kingdom of God; the apostles expect a restoration of the kingdom to Israel but are told by Jesus they cannot know the timing of its coming but instead are to focus on universal gospel proclamation.

20. Jesus ascends to the right hand of God in fulfillment of Psalm 110:1 where He baptizes believers with the Holy Spirit.

21. Peter presents the kingdom to the leaders of Israel telling them repentance can lead to forgiveness, which will then lead to the return of Jesus and the kingdom of God.

22. While focusing on his ministry to Gentiles Paul, at the end of Acts, still meets with Jewish leaders presenting the kingdom of God to them.

23. The focus of the epistles and Revelation 2–3 is on how the church should conduct itself in this age and how the coming kingdom is motivation for faithful service now as the church faces tribulations from Satan and the world.

24. The book of Revelation describes conditions of the Day of the Lord leading up to the coming of Jesus and the kingdom of God.

25. The return of Jesus begins a thousand-year reign of Jesus on the earth during a time when Satan is bound and Jesus' saints are resurrected and rewarded.

26. The millennial reign of Jesus merges into the eternal kingdom of the Father.

27. The eternal kingdom consists of the nations serving God, seeing His face, and bringing their cultural contributions to the New Jerusalem.

PART

4

THEOLOGICAL ISSUES AND THE KINGDOM PROGRAM

CHAPTER 35

HOW THE KINGDOM RELATES TO THE BIBLE'S MAIN CHARACTERS

The primary thrust of this book has been to offer a biblical theology of the kingdom, taking into account how the kingdom program developed as the canon of the Bible progressively unfolded. In this chapter I present how the kingdom program relates to eight of the Bible's main characters—God, creation, mankind, Satan, Israel, Gentiles/nations, Jesus, and the church.

GOD

The kingdom program starts with God. God is King and the universe is His kingdom. The creation God spoke into existence is the realm for His kingdom (Gen 1–2). All things material and immaterial were created by God and exist for Him. God's kingdom program has two main dimensions. First, God is sovereign over all things and He reigns over everything at all times. This is His *universal kingdom*. Even rebellious acts by angels and humans operate under the umbrella of God's universal kingdom. Second, God's rule over the earth through man is called His *mediatorial kingdom* since man is tasked as a mediator for God's purposes. The Bible's storyline is the process by which God restores the fallen kingdom through His Son and ultimate Mediator, Jesus the Messiah. Once the mediatorial kingdom is successfully completed this kingdom is handed over to the Father (1 Cor 15:24, 28) and the eternal kingdom will begin. God's presence will exist fully among men on the new earth (Rev 22:3).

CREATION

God created the world "very good." But with man's sin and the fall, the creation was cursed and subjected to futility (Rom 8:20). Since then the world is characterized by decay and death. Yet the creation longs for restoration (Rom 8:21). This restoration is not annihilation but cosmic renewal/regeneration (Matt 19:28; Acts 3:21) in which God makes all things new. This restoration of creation includes the planet, animal kingdom, agriculture, architecture, and all God-honoring cultural pursuits (Isa 11; 65:17–25). Foretastes of this restoration were demonstrated with the nature miracles of Jesus who offered samples and glimpses of the kingdom, but the full implementation of the restoration begins with Jesus' millennial kingdom after His second coming and culminates in the eternal kingdom (Rev 20–22:5).

MANKIND

Man is God's image-bearer, created to be God's vice-regent over His "very good" creation (see Gen 1:26–28; 31). Although not ontologically equal with God, man is like God in some ways and represents God on the earth. Man has both a material body and an immaterial soul. As God's image-bearer, man was created as "son" and "king" and was tasked with spreading over the earth and ruling and subduing the creation for God's glory. As a volitional being, man was given the choice to serve or disobey God. His decision to sin through Adam brought separation from God, made him subject to death, and plunged the world into calamity.

God is carrying out a salvation plan to rescue man through the seed of the woman, which culminates in the ultimate Seed and Last Adam—Jesus (Gal 3:16). To stop man from uniting in rebellion against Him, God instituted languages and nations as a way of dispersing mankind over the earth. Jesus is the ultimate Man who redeems believing mankind (Rom 5:18) and successfully reigns over the earth as the Last Adam, succeeding where the first Adam failed. Those who believe in Jesus will be restored and live forever as kings on the new earth (Rev 22:5). Those who do not will experience eternal punishment in the lake of fire. Salvation in Jesus is necessary for any person to participate in God's kingdom (John 3:3).

SATAN

Satan is a fallen angel and the first being to challenge God's authority. His pride led him to try to usurp God's throne. Satan was the force behind the serpent that tempted Eve, which led to the fall of man. While God always remains sovereign over everything, man's sin temporarily led to Satan obtaining kingdom rights over this world (Matt 4:8–9). Since then, history has been a great cosmic battle between the kingdom of Satan and the kingdom of God. With the aid of fallen angels who followed Satan in his rebellion, Satan opposes God and His image bearers by blinding their spiritual eyes, opposing God's people, and resisting God's plans to establish His kingdom upon the earth. Satan suffered a crushing defeat with Jesus' death on the cross and he no longer has authority over those who believe in Jesus (Col 1:13). Yet in this present age before Jesus returns, Satan actively deceives the nations, promotes wickedness, and persecutes God's saints.

The ultimate expression of Satan's kingdom will occur during a coming tribulation period when he will exercise his rule over the earth through an antichrist figure who enforces worship of Satan and kills the saints of God. Thus, like God, Satan has plans to establish a permanent earthly kingdom with his own mediatorial ruler—the Antichrist. But Jesus will defeat both Satan and his Antichrist at Jesus' second coming to earth. At that time, Satan will be personally removed from the earth and placed into a spiritual prison called the abyss for a thousand years (Rev 20:3). For the first time in history the earth and its people will be freed from Satan's presence. At the end of the thousand years, Satan will be released from his prison. He will attack the city of Jerusalem, yet he is immediately defeated by God and sent to the lake of fire forever (Rev 20:7–10). This final defeat brings an end to Satan's anti-kingdom program.

ISRAEL

Israel is a people and nation from the line of Abraham, Isaac, and Jacob. With the exodus from Egypt and the receiving of the Mosaic Covenant, Israel became a nation and kingdom, and was called to be holy and represent God among the nations (Deut 4:5–8). Israel is God's chosen nation but Israel is not an end in itself but a means for bringing blessings to all nations (Gen 12:2–3). This blessing was to occur by bringing forth the Messiah and showing the nations the greatness of God by obeying the Mosaic Covenant. But instead of being a blessing to the nations, Israel disobeyed God and became enslaved to the nations they were supposed to be a light to. God, though, promised that Israel would be regathered and restored to her land under a New Covenant (Deut 30:1–9). Since Israel is sinful and not able to save itself God promised a coming representative of Israel, an Israelite and Servant of the Lord, who will save and restore the nation (Isa 49:3–6). This Servant is Jesus. He came offering salvation and restoration to Israel. But Israel rejected Him and is facing the consequences of dispersion and persecution by the nations (see Luke 19:41–44; 21:24).

Israel currently is experiencing a period of temporary and partial hardening as God saves many Gentiles (Rom 11:25). A remnant of believing Israelites exists to testify of God's continued faithfulness to Israel and serves as a reminder that the nation as a whole will be saved (Rom 11:16, 26). Israel's unbelief will be reversed during a coming Day of the Lord and God will save and restore Israel in connection with the return of Jesus the Messiah (Zech 12:10). When Israel believes in its Messiah, the kingdom of Jesus is established and Israel will enter the blessings of the kingdom and assume a role of leadership and service among the nations who will also worship the Messiah. Blessings to Gentiles will increase as well (Rom 11:12, 15). The land of Israel and the city of Jerusalem will serve as headquarters for Messiah's global kingdom (Isa 2:2–4).

GENTILES/NATIONS

The nations originated with the Tower of Babel event (Gen 11). People attempted to congregate and bring glory to themselves by building a tower to reach the heavens, but God confounded them with different languages and caused them to spread throughout the earth. The nations listed in Genesis 10–11 highlight the importance of nations in God's kingdom program. God's plan to save the nations occurs by singling out one nation, Israel, to be the vehicle for worldwide blessing. Israel was chosen to bless all nations, but Israel failed its calling. So God rose up the ultimate Israelite, Jesus, who will restore Israel and bring blessings to the nations (Isa 49:3–6). With the coming of Jesus believing Gentiles experience messianic salvation and are incorporated into the people of God alongside the remnant of believing Jews (the "Israel of God") today in the church (Eph 3:6).

Today, the Great Commission goes to all nations and people from many nations believe in Jesus as Messiah. But the nations as a whole are still characterized by rebellion against God and His Messiah (Ps 2). No nation currently bows the knee to Jesus in this age. But when Jesus returns to establish His kingdom nations will worship God alongside Israel who is also saved (Isa 19:24–25). During Messiah's kingdom the nations will look to Israel for leadership and travel to Jerusalem to learn the ways of the Lord. They will also operate under the executive decisions of the Messiah and live in peace with other nations (Isa 2:2–4). When Jesus' millennial kingdom ends, Satan will lead a rebellion involving nations against the city of Jerusalem (Rev 20:7–10). This rebellion is met with fiery and decisive judgment from heaven. In the eternal state the nations, with their kings, will worship God and bring their cultural contributions into the New Jerusalem (Rev 21:24, 26). They will live in harmony through participation in the tree of life (Rev 22:2).

JESUS THE MESSIAH

Jesus is the focal point and center of God's mediatorial kingdom plan. God tasks Jesus with bringing this rebellious planet back into perfect conformity with His will (1 Cor 15:24, 28). As the ultimate Man, Seed, Israelite, and David, Jesus is the One who reverses the curse, defeats Satan, purchases salvation, and restores all things. As the Last Adam, Jesus must rule from and over the earth, succeeding in the realm where the first Adam failed. As the ultimate David, Jesus the Messiah must rule the world over a united Israel and the nations from Jerusalem. As the ultimate Israelite, Jesus is the Servant of the Lord who restores the nation Israel and brings blessings to the Gentiles. The basis of Jesus' kingdom is His sacrificial death (Heb 2:9; Rev 5:9). As the Servant of the Lord, Jesus identifies with Israel and is the true Israel.

Jesus' identification with Israel does not mean the non-significance of the nation Israel but the restoration of Israel (Isa 49:3–6). Because there are two comings of Jesus the Messiah, the kingdom relates to these two comings. With Jesus' earthly ministry He presented the kingdom to Israel and gave foretastes and demonstrations of the kingdom with His miracles and exorcisms. With His death, Jesus established the New Covenant. With His resurrection and ascension Jesus sends forth the Holy Spirit to indwell and empower His saints to obey God. In fulfillment of Psalm 110:1 Jesus is currently at the right hand of the Father where He shares the throne of deity and possesses all authority in heaven and earth. At His second coming, Jesus will assume His Davidic kingdom reign over the earth for a thousand years (see Ps 110:2; Matt 25:31; Rev 3:21; 20:4–6). Then Jesus will receive universal recognition and honor in the realm where He was first rejected. This is also a time when His saints will be vindicated. While Jesus will reign forever (Rev 11:15), His mediatorial kingdom eventually merges into the Father's eternal kingdom (1 Cor 15:24–28). Jesus will forever share the eternal kingdom throne with the Father (Rev 22:3).

CHURCH

The church is an important stage in the kingdom program. The kingdom itself is a broader category than the church and relates to God's plan to exercise His sovereignty over every aspect of creation—material and immaterial; humans and angels; animals, trees, inanimate objects, etc. The kingdom encompasses other major themes of Scripture including covenants, law, salvation, people of God, etc. The church is a category within the people of God concept. The church is the New Covenant community of believing Jews and Gentiles as it exists in this age between the two comings of Jesus. The church has a worldwide mandate to spread the message of King Jesus in this age while Israel is experiencing a partial and temporary hardening because of unbelief.

The church is not the kingdom, but it relates to the kingdom program in several important ways. First, the church consists of those who have consciously trusted in Jesus the Messiah. The church experiences messianic salvation since its members are joined to the Messiah. By means of the Holy Spirit Jesus baptizes believers into His body, the church. Christ's church, therefore, comes under the authority of Jesus.

Second, believers in Jesus are "sons of the kingdom" (Matt 13:38). This means the kingdom belongs to them and they are members of the kingdom even though the kingdom's actual establishment awaits Jesus' return. Christians are transferred from the domain of Satan to the kingdom of the Son (Col 1:13).

Third, members of the church are to exhibit righteousness consistent with the kingdom of God. As the King gives His law (Matt 5–7), Jesus calls His followers to exhibit righteousness without which no one can enter the kingdom of heaven (Matt 5:20). This includes loving other Christians and practicing "righteousness and peace and joy in the Holy Spirit" (Rom 14:17).

Fourth, the church proclaims the message of the kingdom that qualifies people to enter the kingdom of God. Thus, proclaiming the gospel of Jesus involves proclaiming the kingdom of God. An intersection occurs between salvation and the kingdom in that salvation qualifies one to enter God's kingdom. Unless one is born again he cannot enter the kingdom of God (see John 3:3). Because the church functions within this "present evil age" the church's mission of gospel/kingdom proclamation is often accompanied by persecution from Satan and the world.

Fifth, the church is offered future rewards in the kingdom for faithful service now. This includes vindication and the right to accompany Jesus in His rule over the world. Paul said, "If we endure, we will also reign with Him" (2 Tim 2:12). This includes the right to rule the nations (Rev 2:26–27) and sit with Jesus on His throne (Rev 3:21). It also includes a reign upon the earth (Rev 5:10). Members of the church can endure suffering and persecution now because reward and vindication in the kingdom are coming.

The church's primary responsibility in this age is gospel proclamation and making disciples. Members of the church are destined to reign over a restored earth when Jesus returns. But in this age before Jesus comes again, the church's mission is not cultural or societal transformation. This does not mean the church has no concern for or relationship to cultural or societal matters. When Jesus returns, members of the church will assist Jesus in His rule over the nations (Rev 2:26–27; 3:21), which includes cultural and societal matters. God created man to rule holistically over all aspects of God's creation. And a restored mankind will rule over a restored planet. Although such matters are not the church's emphasis in this age, Christians are called to apply their Christian worldview to every aspect of the environment. Thus, Christians can be involved in all aspects of culture including music, the arts, architecture, agriculture, politics, education, sports, etc. for the glory of God (1 Cor 10:31). Christians certainly should vote and promote values that most accord with God's righteous standards. Yet there should be the understanding that true cultural and societal transformation will not occur in this evil age. These await the kingdom of Jesus at His return. The NT also teaches that Christians must be concerned with meeting the physical needs of fellow believers.

As those who live between the two comings of Jesus the Messiah, the church should avoid two extremes concerning culture and society. The first is acting as if the church has no relationship to these areas. The second is to see the church's mission as transforming the world before the return and kingdom of Jesus.

CHAPTER 36

THE KINGDOM CONNECTION BETWEEN ADAM AND THE LAST ADAM

Important truths about God's kingdom program exist in God's original intent for Adam as described in Genesis 1:26–28 and reaffirmations of this section in Psalm 8:4–8; Hebrews 2:5–8; and 1 Corinthians 15:24–28. These passages reveal kingdom connections between Adam, mankind, Jesus, and Jesus' followers. But at the risk of losing the main point in the details the main thesis of this chapter is this: *Jesus as the Last Adam is destined to successfully rule from and over the realm (earth) that was tasked to the first Adam. Adam failed but the Last Adam will succeed. Jesus' kingdom reign will be from and over the earth and He will share His reign with His followers and complete the kingdom mandate of Genesis 1:26–28.*

Our case is based on five related points:

1. Adam was created as a king/vice-regent to rule from and over the earth on behalf of God (Gen 1:26–28).

2. After the fall man still possesses right to rule the creation (Ps 8:4–8).

3. Man does not yet successfully rule over the creation but he will (Heb 2:5–8).

4. Jesus as the ultimate Man and Last Adam will reign over the creation before He hands His kingdom over to the Father (1 Cor 15:24–28).

5. Jesus will share His earthly kingdom reign with His followers (Rev 2:26–27; 3:20–21; 5:10).

1. Adam was created as a king/vice-regent to rule from and over the earth on God's behalf (Gen 1:26–28)

Adam was created in the image of God. As God's image-bearer he was both a son and a king under the authority of God the King. In Genesis 1:26–28 God gave Adam a kingdom mandate. Adam was commanded to "rule" and "subdue" the "very good" (v. 31) creation God entrusted to him. This included all aspects of creation. Adam, as representative of mankind, was to exercise authority over the earth. The following shows that this realm is earth:

> "let them rule over the fish of the sea and over the birds of the sky and over the cattle and over all the earth, and over every creeping thing that creeps on the earth" (Gen 1:26).
>
> God blessed them; and God said to them, "Be fruitful and multiply, and fill the earth, and subdue it; and rule over the fish of the sea and over the birds of the sky and over every living thing that moves on the earth" (Gen 1:28).

Adam was placed in a physical creation for the purpose of ruling over it. This kingdom authority was to be shared by the descendants of Adam. Thus, starting in Genesis 1, God has plans for a successful earthly kingdom with man ruling it. Man's destiny is related to the earth and He expects the kingdom mandate of Genesis 1:26–28 to be fulfilled.

2. After the fall man still possesses the right to rule the creation (Ps 8:4–8)

Adam sinned and failed his task to rule and exercise dominion over God's creation (see Gen 3). Not only did he bring death to himself and his descendants, he also brought a curse to the creation that was now subjected to futility (see Rom 8:20). Yet man's right to rule over the earth and its creatures was not forfeited or abolished. As David stated in Psalm 8:4–8:

> What is man that You take thought of him,
> And the son of man that You care for him?
> Yet You have made him a little lower than God,
> And You crown him with glory and majesty!

> You make him to rule over the works of Your hands;
> You have put all things under his feet,
> All sheep and oxen,
> And also the beasts of the field,
> The birds of the heavens and the fish of the sea,
> Whatever passes through the paths of the seas.

David draws upon the original creation mandate of Genesis 1:26–28 to reaffirm man's responsibility to the creation. Thus, Psalm 8 functions like an inspired commentary on Genesis 1. Man's kingdom mandate over the earth has not been revoked. His ability to fulfill the mandate has been damaged because of sin, but the relationship of man to the earth still remains. Yet the search continues for when this will occur.

3. Man does not yet successfully rule over the creation but he will (Heb 2:5–8)

What is painfully clear from human experience over thousands of years is explicitly declared in Hebrews 2:5–8. In this present age we do not see the creation functioning under man's authority. The creation mandate of Genesis 1:26–28 remains unfulfilled:

> For He did not subject to angels the world to come, concerning which we are speaking. But one has testified somewhere, saying,
>
> "WHAT IS MAN, THAT YOU REMEMBER HIM?
> OR THE SON OF MAN, THAT YOU ARE CONCERNED ABOUT HIM?
> "YOU HAVE MADE HIM FOR A LITTLE WHILE LOWER THAN THE ANGELS;
> YOU HAVE CROWNED HIM WITH GLORY AND HONOR,
> AND HAVE APPOINTED HIM OVER THE WORKS OF YOUR HANDS;
> YOU HAVE PUT ALL THINGS IN SUBJECTION UNDER HIS FEET."
>
> For in subjecting all things to him, He left nothing that is not subject to him. But now we do not yet see all things subjected to him.

Several points are significant here. First, the writer refers to "the world to come" (2:5). He is thinking of the future, what he will later refer to as the "age to come" (Heb 6:5). In doing so he draws attention to a coming world not in existence now. Second, the right to subject the "world to come" belongs to man, not angels. It is God's image-bearers, not angels, who are destined to rule the earth. Third, Hebrews 2:6–8 is a quotation of Psalm 8:4–6 which reaffirms man's relationship to the creation. Fourth, the writer says that man does not yet experience dominion over the earth yet—"But we do not yet see all things subjected to him" (Heb 2:8). The "not yet" is significant and points to a future time of completion. The reference to "subjected" is also important. As Wallis observes, "The perfect participle *hypotetagmenon*, looking at both ends of the action, would imply that the subjugation has not been begun nor has it been completed."[1] Thus, the subjugation of all things under Jesus' feet is a future occurrence. Hebrews 10:13, says Jesus is currently at the Father's right hand "waiting until His enemies shall be made His footstool." This supports a future subjugation.[2] Jesus is currently "waiting" but He will actively rule at His return (see Ps 110:1–2).

To summarize, man is not yet experiencing an earthly kingdom reign. The earthly kingdom mandate given to man in Genesis 1:26–28 and reaffirmed in Psalm 8:4–8 and Hebrews 2:6–8 awaits fulfillment. Man's kingdom reign will take place in "the world to come."

4. Jesus as the ultimate Man and Last Adam will reign over the creation before He hands His kingdom over to the Father (1 Cor 15:24–28)

Man is sinful. So how can he fulfill the kingdom mandate? The fact is man cannot do it on his own. But the "Son of Man," and "Last Adam" (see 1 Cor 15:45) can fulfill the kingdom mandate originally tasked to Adam. He can represent man and do for mankind what mankind on his own cannot do.

Romans 5:12–21 reveals Adam acted as representative of mankind. And this section presents Jesus as a second representative of mankind. Both men commit acts that affect all people—Adam for condemnation and Jesus for justification. There are patterns between Jesus and Adam. For example, Adam and Eve failed the temptation from Satan in Genesis 3, but Christ

1 Wilber B. Wallis, "The Use of Psalms 8 and 110 in I Corinthians 15:25–27 and in Hebrews 1 and 2," in *Journal of the Evangelical Theological Society* 15 (1972): 28.

2 Ibid., 28–29. Wallis writes, "Hebrews gives a decisive answer in the *mellousan* [about to come], of 2:5 and in the *oupo* [not yet] of 2:8: the reign and conquest of enemies needs be, but it lies in the future, at and after the Parousia".

triumphs over temptations from Satan (Matt 4). With Romans 5, Adam's act of disobedience brought condemnation to all men (5:12) while Jesus' "one act of righteousness" (i.e. the cross) brought righteousness. Adam brought death but Jesus brings life.

There is another important parallel. Just as Adam was appointed as a king to rule over the earth, Jesus will reign over the earth as King. In Matthew 19:28, Jesus said that in the "regeneration" or "renewal" of the planet, He "will sit on His glorious throne" and the twelve apostles will be there with Him "judging the twelve tribes of Israel." This is 'kingdom over the earth' language. Also significant is 1 Corinthians 15:24–28 which connects Jesus' kingdom with the original kingdom mandate of Genesis 1:26–28:

> then comes the end, when He [Jesus] hands over the kingdom to the God and Father, when He [Jesus] has abolished all rule and all authority and power. For He [Jesus] must reign until He has put all His enemies under His feet. The last enemy that will be abolished is death. FOR HE HAS PUT ALL THINGS IN SUBJECTION UNDER HIS FEET. But when He says, "All things are put in subjection," it is evident that He is excepted who put all things in subjection to Him. When all things are subjected to Him, then the Son Himself also will be subjected to the One who subjected all things to Him, so that God may be all in all.

Paul points to a period called "the end" (v. 24). When this "end" comes Jesus then "hands over" His "kingdom" to the Father. So there is a kingdom reign before Jesus hands His kingdom over to the Father. Several things characterize this kingdom reign. Jesus must defeat all of His enemies. And, as verse 27 indicates, *all things must be subjected under His feet*. Paul quotes Psalm 8:6, which is a reaffirmation of the original kingdom mandate given to Adam in Genesis 1:26–28. It involves planet earth. Thus, the kingdom mandate given to Adam and affirmed by David will be fulfilled with Jesus. Jesus is presented as the Last Adam (1 Cor 15:45) who successfully reigns in the realm where Adam failed. Note the following:

> First Adam to rule from and over the earth → Failure
>
> Last Adam (Jesus) to rule from and over the earth → Success

Also, this kingdom reign of Jesus is a reign that occurs before "the end" which is the Father's eternal kingdom. Jesus "hands over the kingdom to the God and Father" (15:24). Verse 28 says when "all things are subjected to Him [Jesus]" then Jesus will be subjected to God the Father. This shows the kingdom reign of Jesus over the earth cannot be relegated solely to the eternal state. The kingdom reign over the earth must occur in a period before the eternal state. This best fits with the millennium of Revelation 20. Sung Wook Chung rightly connects the earthly millennial kingdom with Jesus' identity as the Last Adam:

> Therefore by establishing the millennial kingdom, Jesus Christ, as the last Adam, will restore and fulfill not only the spiritual/priestly dimension but also the physical/institutional dimension of the first Adam's kingdom.[3]

5. Jesus will share His earthly kingdom reign with His followers (Rev 2:26–27; 3:20–21; 5:10)

Jesus will fulfill the kingdom mandate when He reigns from and over the earth. One of the great truths about the Last Adam, Jesus, is that He shares His kingdom reign with His followers. Revelation 5:10 declares, "You have made them to be a kingdom and priests to our God; and they will reign upon the earth." Those purchased by King Jesus (Rev 5:9) will participate in His "reign upon the earth" when it arrives. The saints are not reigning on the earth now. Satan and the world persecute them. But they will reign. Revelation 2:26–27 says Jesus will share His reign over the nations with His followers:

> He who overcomes, and he who keeps My deeds until the end, TO HIM I WILL GIVE AUTHORITY OVER THE NATIONS; AND HE SHALL RULE THEM WITH A ROD OF IRON, AS THE VESSELS OF THE POTTER ARE BROKEN TO PIECES, as I also have received authority from My Father.

Here Jesus uses the language of Psalm 2, which predicted a coming reign over the nations by God's Son, the Messiah. So Revelation 2:26–27 reveals that the reign of the Messiah will be accompanied by the reign of the saints. Again, the saints are not ruling the nations today but they will when Jesus

3 Chung, "Toward the Reformed and Covenantal Theology of Premillennialism," 142.

returns. Jesus will share His reign with those who belong to Him. Also, participation in this kingdom will be from Jesus' throne, which is distinguished from the Father's throne:

> He who overcomes, I will grant to him to sit down with Me on My throne, as I also overcame and sat down with My Father on His throne (Rev 3:21).

Jesus is currently sitting at the right hand of the Father in heaven (see Ps 110:1; Heb 1:13). But in the future He will reign from His glorious Davidic throne (see Luke 1:32–33; Matt 19:28; 25:31). Then His followers will share His throne just as Jesus now shares the Father's throne.

Together, these five points highlight that the Last Adam (Jesus) will successfully reign from and over the realm where the first Adam failed. And He will share His earthly kingdom reign with those who belong to Him before the eternal state begins. The mandate of Genesis 1:26–28 for a successful rule of man upon the earth will be fulfilled by Jesus, the Messiah and Last Adam, and all who identify with Him.

IMPLICATIONS FOR MILLENNIAL VIEWS

In our estimation, the only kingdom view consistent with the five truths stated above is premillennialism and its assertion that the millennial kingdom follows the second coming Jesus. Other millennial views put Jesus' kingdom reign in heaven during this present age, but the Bible's focus is on man's responsibility to earth, not heaven. For example, compare how amillennialism and its view the millennium is both spiritual and now contrasts with premillennialism:

> Amillennialism Scenario
> –Adam destined to rule the earth
> –The Last Adam, Jesus, reigns from heaven over a spiritual kingdom
>
> Premillennialism Scenario
> –Adam destined to rule the earth
> –The Last Adam, Jesus, reigns from and over the earth

Premillennialism best connects the kingdom and man's original mandate from Genesis 1:26–28. It is not the case that Adam's kingly rule was to be on earth, but the Last Adam's reign is from heaven. In his defense of a premillennial view, Chung puts it well when he connects the millennium with Adam's task:

> The first Adam's priest-kingly activity, which was thwarted by the fall, will be fulfilled in the millennial kingdom. Therefore the millennial kingdom will be a restoration and fulfillment of the Edenic kingdom on the earth.[4]

4 Ibid., 143.

CHAPTER

37

THE NECESSITY OF A COMING EARTHLY KINGDOM

The last chapter presented one major reason why there must be a future, earthly kingdom reign of Jesus. Jesus, the Last Adam, must reign from and over the same realm (earth) where the first Adam failed. This chapter offers three other reasons why there must be a future earthly reign of Jesus the Messiah after His second coming but before the eternal state. The first focuses on the necessity of a significant time period in history when Jesus is recognized as King over this world. The second concerns the importance of a time period in which the saints are rewarded and vindicated in the realm where their persecution took place. Third, there needs to be a time period when the complete fulfillment of all aspects of the biblical covenants occurs. Lastly, we will discuss how premillennialism best affirms the importance of God's physical creation.

1. PREMILLENNIALISM AND THE NECESSITY OF A SUSTAINED VISIBLE REIGN OF JESUS

Since the fall God has enacted a plan to bring this rebellious planet back into conformity with His will (see Gen 3:15). Central to this plan is God's desire to establish His Son, Jesus the Messiah, as King over the nations (see Ps 2). The Bible presents Jesus as the One who will bring salvation to God's people and reign as King over this world.

Yet while millions in history have submitted to Jesus as Lord and Savior, the vast majority of the world has not. The world does not worship Jesus. Consult a world map and survey the nations of the world today and observe which nations are bowing the knee to Jesus. There are none. They have not yet acknowledged the glory and honor of King Jesus. The nations with their leaders are still in active rebellion against God's "Anointed One" (see Ps 2:2). We see this in the myriads of false religions and philosophies along with overt acts of rebellion that characterize what Paul called "this present evil age" (Gal 1:4).

Even geographical areas once permeated with gospel awareness such as Europe during the Reformation, and the American Northeast with the Great Awakening, are far removed from worship of the true God. Some of the most anti-Christian areas today are those that once had much exposure to the gospel.[1]

There is no evidence from Scripture or experience that the appropriate honor due Jesus will occur before His second coming to earth.[2] All Christians agree that such honor will be given with Jesus' return to earth. When Jesus returns to earth in glory every eye will see Him. He will defeat His enemies and His power will be acknowledged. On the other hand, 1 Corinthians 15:24–28 indicates that when the "end" occurs, Jesus "hands over the kingdom to the God and Father" (v. 24). Verse 28 states, "When all things are subjected to Him [Jesus], then the Son Himself also will be subjected to the One who subjected all things to Him, so that God may be all in all." So a time is coming when Jesus will hand His kingdom to the Father. Jesus' messianic and mediatorial kingdom reign will transition to the universal kingdom of the Father.

The Father desires His Son to rule the nations until all things are subjected to Him. But in this "present evil age" not all things are subject to Jesus. *So when does Jesus the Messiah rule and receive the glory and honor in this world that He deserves and the Scripture promises?* Is it only at His second coming to earth? Saucy asks a relevant question:

> To be sure, the world will recognize Christ when he returns in glory. But does a short period of destruction and judgment before he turns the kingdom over to the Father for the eternal

1 This point alone should be a concern for those considering the validity of postmillennialism, which affirms societal renewal by the Gospel before the return of Jesus.

2 See Robert L. Saucy, *The Case for Progressive Dispensationalism*, 289.

> state provide an adequate explanation of the centrality of Christ and a sufficient manifestation of his glory *within history*?[3]

The answer to this question is, No. Jesus' second coming with its destruction and judgments is not all there is to Christ's manifestation in regard to His kingdom. His return is a magnificent display of glory, but more is to come. As Saucy notes, "So far in history, the experience of Christ and his people has been one of oppression and nonrecognition (cf. 1 Jn 3:1). If history comes to its end with the coming of Christ, there will be no significant time within history when his centrality is manifest."[4] So when does the necessary recognition of Jesus on earth occur?

An intermediate or millennial kingdom "provides just such a time when Christ's glory will pervade human history and his significance will be rightly recognized."[5] A millennial reign of Jesus on earth after His second coming but before the "end" is the ideal time for Jesus to be recognized. Jesus will reign over this world, rewarding His servants and punishing His enemies. When He has completed this reign from His glorious throne He will then hand His kingdom over to God the Father and the eternal state will commence.

Perhaps one objection to this idea is that Jesus' current session in heaven, fulfills the idea of a sustained reign that the Bible predicted. But this scenario does not do justice to Jesus' kingdom reign for several reasons. First, although Jesus' exaltation to the right hand of the Father is a powerful display of glory in heaven, the world continues in its rebellion and non-recognition of Jesus as Lord and Messiah. We cannot conceive of a messianic reign of Christ where the vast majority of the world continues its rebellion. Yet this must be the case if the millennium is currently present. On the other hand, when Christ's kingdom is established at His coming all will recognize it. As Zechariah 14:9 indicates: "And the LORD will be king over all the earth; in that day the LORD will be the only one, and His name the only one." When Jesus the Messiah rules on the earth, everyone will recognize it. There will be no other religions or false worship systems, unlike today.

3 Ibid., 289–90. Emphases in original.

4 Ibid.

5 Ibid.

Second, Hebrews 10:12–13 states that Jesus is currently at the right hand of God "waiting" for His enemies to be subjected to Him:

> but He, having offered one sacrifice for sins for all time, SAT DOWN AT THE RIGHT HAND OF GOD, waiting from that time onward UNTIL HIS ENEMIES BE MADE A FOOTSTOOL FOR HIS FEET.[6]

The wording here relies on Psalm 110 where David's Lord, the Messiah, has a session at the right hand of God "until" His enemies are defeated and His rule from Zion (Jerusalem) occurs (Ps 110:2). Thus, a session at the right hand of the Father by the Messiah precedes a kingdom reign on earth.

Third, the reign of the Messiah includes more than personal salvation. It also involves societal/political transformation for the nations (see Isa 2:2–4). International harmony under the ruling Messiah will occur. While messianic salvation has been inaugurated in this present church age, societal transformation of the nations has not happened yet. Passages like Isaiah 2, Isaiah 19:24–25, and Zechariah 14 predict nations will worship God. But such societal and international harmony has not happened yet. How can there be a messianic or millennial reign in which the nations continue in open rebellion against God and His Messiah? The best understanding is that societal transformation will occur with the second coming of Jesus. As Saucy points out:

> The prophets pictured the saving work of the Messiah as both personal and societal renewal. The kingdom work of Christ has entered this age to bring personal salvation, but the transformation of society in terms of peace among peoples and the expression of God's righteousness in the structures of human society are never promised for this age. They await the return of the messianic King, who will destroy the evil structures of this age and institute a righteous rule over the earth for the first time in human history.[7]

6 Emphasis is mine.

7 Ibid.

To summarize, Jesus must be honored with a sustained kingdom reign visible to all. God's intent is for Jesus to rule the nations, including His enemies, from Jerusalem and a restored Israel (see Ps 110:2). Before the perfect eternal state comes, Jesus must rule over this planet that rejected Him at His first coming. He will rule with righteousness but also with a rod of iron over His enemies (see Ps 2; 110; Rev 2:26–27). While Jesus is currently at the right hand of God in heaven possessing all authority, the nations still rebel against God. That will change when Jesus comes again. At His second coming Jesus will sit on His glorious throne (see Matt 19:28; 25:31) and rule this world to the glory of God. This He will do in the millennial kingdom. When this phase of the kingdom program is over Jesus will hand the kingdom over to God the Father and the millennial kingdom will merge into the universal kingdom (see 1 Cor 15:24–28).

If the premillennial view is *not* correct and the millennium is only spiritual and now, what would this mean? It would mean there is no significant period in history when Jesus is recognized as King by this world before the eternal state. Jesus' kingdom in this age would be characterized by wickedness and persecution of God's people by the world and Satan. Also, Jesus' messianic reign would be characterized by non-recognition and widespread rebellion by the nations. In addition, while a present millennium would include personal salvation of some, it would not involve societal transformation and international harmony (see Isa 2:2–4). If the premillennial view is not correct there is no significant period in history when Jesus is given the honor and glory He deserves.

2. PREMILLENNIALISM AND THE NECESSITY OF THE MILLENNIUM AS A REWARD AND VINDICATION OF THE SAINTS

The Bible presents the period before Messiah's kingdom as a time of persecution and opposition of the saints from both the world and Satan. The blood of the martyrs throughout history and the abuse of God's people in many lands confirm this fact. The millennium of the Messiah, though, is presented as a reversal of these difficult conditions. So in addition to looking at how the millennium relates to Jesus and the glory He deserves, it is necessary to look at what the millennium means for the servants of King Jesus.

The reign of the Messiah is linked with the reign of His saints. It is a time of vindication and reward for God's people in the realm where they were persecuted. There is an ironic reversal of roles. God turns the tables on His enemies and flips the situation of believers. God's people who now are persecuted by Satan and the nations, will be rewarded, vindicated, and given authority over the nations. They go from being the persecuted to those who reign. *Thus, a future millennial kingdom on earth is necessary for the reward and vindication of God's people since these things do not characterize this present age.*

Daniel 7

Such a reversal of circumstances for the saints on earth is found in Daniel 7. This chapter tells of a figure called "the Son of Man" who is presented before the "Ancient of Days" and granted "dominion, glory, and a kingdom" (see Dan 7:13–14). The Son of Man represents Jesus and the Ancient of Days is God the Father. We are also told of the evil ministry of a "horn" who appears to be a world leader rising from the midst of ten other leaders ("horns") (see Dan 7:8, 20). This "horn" offers great boasts and persecutes the saints of God on earth. But this persecution ends when God intervenes:

> I kept looking, and that horn was waging war with the saints and overpowering them until the Ancient of Days came and judgment was passed in favor of the saints of the Highest One, and the time arrived when the saints took possession of the kingdom (Dan 7:21–22).

This enemy of God's people prevails for a while. He is "overpowering them," but when God intervenes on the saints' behalf "judgment was passed in favor of the saints," and they "took possession of the kingdom." This reverses the previous situation. Persecution leads to vindication. To use a boxing analogy, just when the people of God seem on the ropes and destined for defeat, a knockout of the enemy occurs and God's people are the victors. They go from defeat to victory.

Notice that the saints were not reigning when the "horn" waged war against them. But when God intervenes the roles are reversed. The enemy is defeated. God's people become the ones in power. This is an ironic reversal of power. This scenario is further amplified in Daniel 7:25–27:

> He [the horn] will speak out against the Most High and wear down the saints of the Highest One, and he will intend to make alterations in times and in law; and they will be given into his hand for a time, times, and half a time. But the court will sit for judgment, and his dominion will be taken away, annihilated and destroyed forever. Then the sovereignty, the dominion and the greatness of all the kingdoms under the whole heaven will be given to the people of the saints of the Highest One; His kingdom will be an everlasting kingdom, and all the dominions will serve and obey Him.'

When the Son of Man (Jesus) begins His kingdom reign given to Him by the Ancient of Days (see Dan 7:13–14), the saints will possess an active role in this kingdom. Jesus is King but he shares his kingdom. *God's people face persecution for a time on earth, but when Messiah's kingdom comes, reward and vindication arrive and their enemy is destroyed.*

Revelation 2–3

The pattern of tribulation followed by vindication and reward is affirmed in Revelation 2–3. As Jesus addresses His churches, each is evaluated for its performance. He then promises future blessings for those who persevere during present trials:

- <u>Ephesus:</u> right to eat of the tree of life in the Paradise of God (2:7)
- <u>Smyrna:</u> will not be hurt by the second death (2:11)
- <u>Pergamum:</u> given hidden manna, a white stone, and a new name written on the stone (2:17)
- <u>Thyatira:</u> granted authority and rule over the nations (2:26–27)
- <u>Sardis:</u> clothed in white garments, name in book of life, and confessed before the Father and the angels (3:5–6)

- Philadelphia: given pillar in the temple of God; the name of God and the New Jerusalem (3:12)
- Laodicea: sit with Jesus on His throne (3:21)

There is a noticeable pattern here. Jesus' churches are facing difficult times. These are not days of reigning but of holding fast and persevering during persecution. Some churches are doing better than others, but all need encouragement. So Jesus offers rewards as motivation for faithful service. These rewards are not the current experience of these churches. But they will be when Jesus returns to earth and establishes His kingdom. Jesus does not tell the churches that kingdom blessings are their current experience. Instead, His message is about remaining faithful so His people can reap the blessings of the kingdom reign. Jesus' message to Thyatira highlights this point:

> He who overcomes, and he who keeps My deeds until the end, TO HIM I WILL GIVE AUTHORITY OVER THE NATIONS; AND HE SHALL RULE THEM WITH A ROD OF IRON, AS THE VESSELS OF THE POTTER ARE BROKEN TO PIECES, as I also have received authority from My Father (Rev 2:26–27).

Jesus also promises a future kingdom rule as a reward in Revelation 3:21:

> He who overcomes, I will grant to him to sit down with Me on My throne, as I also overcame and sat down with My Father on His throne.

The overcomer is one who "will" (future tense) sit down with Jesus on His throne. Again, present faithfulness leads to future reward. So then, Revelation 2:26–27 and 3:21 point the churches to a future time when they will receive the reward of reigning with Jesus for faithful service now.

Another significant matter is the intensity of Satan's opposition to the churches of Revelation 2–3. Satan is mentioned five times (2:9, 13 [twice], 24; 3:9). The church at Smyrna was not only facing "tribulation" and "poverty" they had to endure a "synagogue of Satan" (2:9). The church at Pergamum was holding firm in the area where "Satan's throne is" (2:13). The church at Thyatira withstood "the deep things of Satan" (2:24). The church at Philadelphia faced a "synagogue of Satan" (3:9).

The churches of Revelation experience persecution and opposition from Satan. They are not reigning yet. Christians are the nucleus for that coming kingdom (see Rev 1:6), but the promises of reward and vindication are future-oriented. Also, no indication exists that Satan is bound in this age (contra amillennialism) since Satan is very active in opposing the people of God.

Revelation 11:15 announces the seventh trumpet judgment. Loud voices in heaven declare, "The kingdom of the world has become the kingdom of our Lord and of His Christ; and He will reign forever and ever" (11:15b). Verses 17–18 indicate how Jesus' kingdom reign relates to judgment and the rewarding of God's people. The twenty-four elders declare:

> "We give You thanks, O Lord God, the Almighty, who are and who were, because You have taken Your great power and <u>have begun to reign.</u> And the nations were enraged, and Your wrath came, and the time came for the dead to be judged, and the time to reward Your bond-servants the prophets and the saints and those who fear Your name, the small and the great, and to destroy those who destroy the earth."

Again, like Revelation 2:26–27 and 3:21, this passage points to the rewarding of God's people. This "was the time to reward your bondservants the prophets and the saints and those who fear Your name." The kingdom brings reward.

Revelation 20:4

With Revelation 20:1–6 the promised reward and vindication of the saints occurs. What the martyred saints of Revelation 6:9–11 cried out for comes to fruition. Satan is imprisoned in the abyss (Rev 20:1–3). Verse 4 states:

> Then I saw thrones, and they sat on them, and judgment was given to them. And I saw the souls of those who had been beheaded because of their testimony of Jesus and because of the word of God, and those who had not worshiped the beast or his image, and had not received the mark on their forehead and on their hand; and they came to life and reigned with Christ for a thousand years.

The words "I saw thrones, and they sat on them, and judgment was given to them," connects with Daniel 7:22 and its statement that "judgment was passed in favor of the saints of the Highest One, and the time arrived when the saints took possession of the kingdom." It also relates to Daniel 7:27: "Then the sovereignty, the dominion and the greatness of all the kingdoms under the whole heaven will be given to the people of the saints of the Highest One." The promised vindication of the saints with the kingdom of the Son of Man discussed in Daniel 7 is fulfilled with the millennial kingdom of Revelation 20:1–6.

Revelation 20:4 depicts the coming reversal of circumstances for the saints of God. They are resurrected and placed on thrones with the authority to rule in the kingdom. Such circumstances have not occurred yet but they will when Jesus comes again.

To summarize, a millennial kingdom after the return of Jesus is necessary for a true reward and vindication of the saints of God. As Dave Mathewson states:

> The period of the church age is one in which the kingdom of God and the saints is contested by Satan and his kingdom... The authority of the beast is acknowledged worldwide (13:3–4) and God's people appear defeated (chaps. 11, 13). Moreover, the beast has apparently survived a fatal blow (13:3–4). *However, the millennium reverses this situation by providing a counterpart to the beast's earthly sovereignty and ostensible invincibility.* The dragon, Satan, is bound and the dragon and beast are thrown into the lake of fire (19:20; 20:1–3, 7–11). Now the saints triumph and they reign and rule, and for a comparably much longer period of time, one thousand years.[8]

The millennial kingdom "portrays the complete victory and vindication of the saints at the Parousia of Christ."[9]

Consider this point of the millennium as a reward and vindication of the saints from the opposite direction. If premillennialism is not true and

8 Dave Mathewson, "A Re-examination of the Millennium in Rev 20:1–6: Consummation and Recapitulation" *Journal of the Evangelical Theological Society* 44 (2001): 248. Emphases mine.

9 Ibid.

the millennium is taking place today, then the reward and vindication of the saints in the realm in which they were persecuted is taking place in this present age. But this goes against our experience and what the Bible reveals about the nature of the kingdom. The martyrs who appear in heaven in Revelation 6:9–11 are not vindicated or reigning yet in the world, but they are told to "rest for a little while longer" until God's vengeance occurs. The vindication of these martyrs appears in the millennium of Revelation 20:4 where we are told "they came to life and reigned with Christ for a thousand years." The reward and vindication of the saints fits better with the second coming of Jesus and the earthly kingdom He brings.

3. PREMILLENNIALISM AND THE COMPLETE FULFILLMENT OF ALL ASPECTS OF THE COVENANTS AND PROMISES

The Christian church has traditionally affirmed two bodily comings of Jesus. The first occurred in the first century A.D. and the second will occur on a future day. There are implications of this truth. One is that certain prophecies and promises were fulfilled with Jesus' first coming while others await fulfillment at His second coming. If Jesus' coming has two parts to it, then it makes sense that the fulfillment of matters related to Him would come in two stages as well.

The first coming of Jesus brought the ultimate Son of David (Jesus himself) and His sacrificial death. The first coming also brought messianic salvation to believing Jews and Gentiles and the New Covenant ministry of the Holy Spirit. Yet the Bible also indicates there are major prophecies that still need to be fulfilled. For example, in Acts 1:6, the apostles asked Jesus, "Lord, is it at this time you are restoring the kingdom to Israel?" The apostles did not view Israel's promised restoration as occurring yet. That's why they asked the Lord when it would occur (see also Deut 30:1–6; Ezek 36; Rom 11:26–27). In 2 Thessalonians 2, Paul explains why the Day of the Lord predicted so often in the OT had not started yet. Also, the dimensions of Israel's Promised Land as described in Genesis 15:18–21 still need to be fulfilled. The restoration of the city of Jerusalem has not happened yet (see Jer 31; Luke 21:24). Harmony among nations needs to occur (see Isa 2:2–4). Restoration of animals in Messiah's kingdom needs to be realized (see Isa

11). In sum, many of the national and physical promises of the Bible are unfulfilled and look to future completion.

So then, unfulfilled prophecy is a major reason why there must be a future millennium. The millennium is the ideal time period when unfulfilled prophecies and promises will be fulfilled under the direct reign of the Messiah before the eternal state.

One objection to our view is that Jesus has already fulfilled all the prophecies, covenants, and promises of the OT. After all, doesn't Paul say that all the promises are Yes in Jesus (see 2 Cor 1:20)? And doesn't Jesus say that He came to fulfill the Law and the Prophets (see Matt 5:17)?

Jesus does fulfill all that was promised. But the real issues are *how* does He fulfill these matters and *when* are they fulfilled? Does He fulfill them by having them spiritually absorbed into Himself? Or does He fulfill them by being the one through whom literal fulfillment of God's promises comes true? The latter is the better option. Jesus is the center of God's kingdom and redemptive plans. Jesus is at the center of God's promise plan (see Gen 3:15). Without Him God's kingdom and salvation plan would never happen. But these fulfillments occur over the two comings of Jesus.

It is precarious to hold that some OT promises were literally fulfilled with the first coming of Jesus, but other promises and prophecies are fulfilled spiritually. This introduces an inconsistency. Is it accurate that many aspects of Jesus' first coming are fulfilled literally (i.e. literal descendant of David, born in Bethlehem, etc.) but others are fulfilled spiritually (national and physical promises)? To date we have never experienced harmony among nations, the restoration of the animal kingdom, the unification and restoration of Israel to her land, etc. Can we simply spiritualize these and say they are already fulfilled?

Second, the NT reaffirms many aspects of OT prophecies that still need to occur. If Jesus fulfilled everything with His first coming, why do the NT writers and persons still view so many things as still needing to be fulfilled? In His Olivet Discourse of Matthew 24–25 and Luke 21, Jesus predicted many things that still needed to happen such as the abomination of desolation, cosmic signs, the gathering of Israel, and the judgment of the nations.

Another objection could be that unfulfilled prophecies and promises could be fulfilled in the eternal state and not the millennium. However, there is a major problem with this objection as well. If the eternal state is the fulfillment of yet unfulfilled promises, this means these matters would come to fruition outside the kingdom of Jesus the Messiah. Yet the Bible links fulfillment of many of these matters with Messiah's kingdom. For example, the restoration of the animal kingdom described in Isaiah 11:6–9 is linked with the coming Davidic ruler in 11:1 ("stem of Jesse").

If premillennialism is not true then unfulfilled prophecies of the Bible do not find fulfillment as God promised. They have to be spiritualized or absorbed into Jesus or fulfilled in the eternal state outside the realm of Messiah's kingdom. Whichever option is chosen, the fulfillment would not be like the literal fulfillments of the prophecies that occurred at Jesus' first coming. There would be an inconsistency in how God fulfills His promises. The better position is God fulfills all of His promises just as He said, and unfulfilled prophecies will be fulfilled with Jesus' return and kingdom.

PREMILLENNIALISM AND THE AFFIRMATION OF THE GOODNESS OF GOD'S PHYSICAL CREATION

Historically, premillennialism and its belief in a future earthly kingdom has been an antidote against an overemphasis on spiritual matters and attempts to downplay the importance of God's physical creation. The church has often battled encroaching forms of Platonism with its negative view of physical matters.[10] Premillennialism was a major weapon in the early church's battle against its greatest enemy of that era—Gnosticism. Donald Fairbairn asserts, "premillennialism was part of the polemic against Gnosticism."[11] Gnosticism promoted an unbiblical dualism between the spiritual and the physical—emphasizing the former and denigrating the latter. Gnostic dualism had four important implications:

10 Platonism is rooted in the ideas of the great ancient Greek philosopher, Plato (427–347 B.C.). Plato was one of the first philosophers to argue that reality is primarily ideal or abstract. With his "theory of forms," he asserted that ultimate reality is not found in objects and concepts that we experience on earth. Instead, reality is found in "forms" or "ideas" that transcend our physical world. These forms operate as perfect universal templates for everything we experience in the world. One result of Platonism was the belief that matter is inferior to the spiritual. Thus, there is a dualism between matter and the immaterial.

11 Donald Fairbairn, "Contemporary Millennial/Tribulational Debates," *A Case for Historic Premillennialism: An Alternative to "Left Behind" Eschatology*, ed. Craig L. Blomberg and Sung Wook Chung (Grand Rapids: Baker, 2009), 129.

1. It leads to the view that the material world is evil and unredeemable and that salvation only applies to the soul, not the body.
2. It leads to a denigration of history; if the physical world is unredeemable then the panorama of history played out in the physical world is of little consequence.
3. It leads to a distinction in gods—the lesser material god of the OT and the higher spiritual God of the NT.
4. It leads to a docetic view of Christ in which Christ only appears to be human and fleshly.[12]

Fairbairn notes that the church's greatest battle in the second and third centuries was against Gnosticism. But he also points out that, "the church fathers who led this battle—Irenaeus and Tertullian—used their premillennialism as a primary weapon."[13]

In this battle with Gnosticism, Irenaeus (second century A.D.) wanted to demonstrate the unity of Scripture and show that the OT and NT worked in harmony. This "is what drives him into the details of Daniel and Revelation."[14] Fairbairn also states, "Furthermore, behind Irenaeus's treatment of an earthly kingdom lies the concern to refute the gnostic denigration of the material world."[15] In Irenaeus's mind, "nothing could be more appropriate for the God who created the world and redeemed humanity through early history than to conclude his work with an earthly kingdom as a transition to an eternal kingdom that will also be on a refurbished earth."[16] Irenaeus believed that anyone who denied an earthly kingdom as being too sensuous or not "spiritual" enough was denying the goodness of God who created the physical universe.[17]

12 Ibid.

13 Ibid.

14 Ibid.

15 Ibid.

16 Ibid.

17 Ibid., 130.

A. Skevington Wood also affirms that premillennialism was a weapon used by Irenaeus against the Gnostics:

> It ought also to be borne in mind that the strong emphasis of Irenaeus on the literal fulfillment of the prophecies concerning the Millennium were no doubt conditioned to some degree by the fact that he was contending against the gnostic heretics, who denied the redeemability of the material. The millennial teaching of Irenaeus must not be isolated from the rest of his theology. It is all of a piece with it, and Irenaeus was the first to formulate (however embryonically) a millennial—indeed premillennial—system of interpretation.[18]

For Irenaeus, the significance of eschatology was not simply in knowing the details of what will happen in the end times. Instead, "eschatology's significance lies in the way it testifies to the unity of Scripture, the unity of God's purposes, and ultimately the unity and goodness of the God we worship."[19] For Irenaeus and most of the church before Origen,

> an earthly kingdom following the return of Christ is not merely what Revelation 20 teaches. It is also a central tenet of the faith because it functions to reinforce the central truths of Christianity—that there is one God who in love has created this world for us and us for it, who has personally entered this world in order to redeem us for a future in this world, and who will ultimately triumph in this world over the forces that are arrayed against him.[20]

Fairbairn laments that the battle against Gnosticism and over-spiritualization tendencies has never been totally won. For him, "Perhaps part of the reason we have not won it is that we have forfeited the use of one of the greatest biblical/theological weapons in this battle—eschatology. Have we overspiritualized the hope held out to Christians and thus essentially

18 A. Skevington Wood, "The Eschatology of Irenaeus," *Evangelical Quarterly* 40 (1968): 38.

19 Fairbairn, "Contemporary Millennial/Tribulational Debates," 130.

20 Ibid.

conceded to the Gnostics among us that the material world is not ultimately important?"[21] Thus, premillennialism was and is a weapon against attempts to create an unbiblical dualism between the spiritual and the material. It functions as an antidote to over-spiritualized views of God's purposes.

This is not to say that other millennial views do not affirm the goodness of God's physical creation, because they do. Like premillennialists, both amillennialists and postmillennialists affirm a coming bodily resurrection and a tangible new earth.[22] Yet historically, amillennialism has stumbled in this area and has often been linked with Platonist tendencies of spiritualization of God's purposes. Augustine (354–430), known as the father of amillennialism, was heavily influenced by Platonism. According to Gary Habermas, "Christian thought also came under the influence of Platonism, as scholars of the third century such as Clement of Alexandria and Origen mixed this Greek philosophy with their theology. In particular, Augustine's interpretation of Plato dominated Christian thought for the next thousand years after his death in the fifth century."[23] Neo-Platonism also influenced Augustine. As Viviano states, "we need only note that Augustine was strongly influenced by neo-Platonic philosophy and has even read Plotinus and Porphyry.... This philosophy was highly spiritual and other-worldly, centered on the one and the eternal, treating the material and the historically contingent as inferior stages in the ascent of the soul to union with the one."[24] Viviano then summarizes the impact of Augustine's Platonic thinking on the kingdom of God:

21 Ibid., 131.

22 As the amillennialist Robert E. Strimple states, "When we read modern amillennialists themselves, do we find them expressing a purely 'spiritual' (i.e. nonphysical) eschatological hope? Not at all." Strimple, "An Amillennial Response to Craig A. Blaising," in *Three Views on the Millennium and Beyond*, ed. Darrell L. Bock (Grand Rapids: Zondervan, 1999), 257. He then lists a series of amillennial theologians who believe in a "more earth-oriented vision" of eschatology including Herman Bavinck, Geerhardus Vos, Anthony Hoekema, and Greg K. Beale (259–60).

23 Gary R. Habermas, "Plato, Platonism," *Evangelical Dictionary of Theology*, ed. Walter A. Elwell (Grand Rapids: Baker, 1984), 860. Allen states, "The Greek Fathers and Augustine drew most extensively on the philosophy of Plato and the Platonists." Diogenes Allen, *Philosophy for Understanding Theology* (Atlanta: John Knox, 1985), 91.

24 Benedict T. Viviano, O.P. *The Kingdom of God in History* (Eugene, OR: Wipf and Stock, 1988), 52.

> Thus Augustine was attracted to the spiritual interpretation of the kingdom we have already seen in Origen. Indeed, ultimately for Augustine, the kingdom of God consists in eternal life with God in heaven. That is the *civitas dei*, the city of God, as opposed to the *civitas terrena*.[25]

Augustine's spiritual view of the kingdom contributed to his belief that the period of the church on earth is the thousand-year reign of Christ. According to Viviano, "Augustine's view would dominate and become the normal Roman Catholic view down to our own times."[26] It is difficult to deny the importance of Platonic thinking. Blaising argues that a Platonic, spiritual vision model approach led to a rejection of the idea of an earthly kingdom:

> Ancient Christian premillennialism weakened to the point of disappearance when the spiritual vision model of eternity became dominant in the church. A future kingdom on earth simply did not fit well in an eschatology that stressed personal ascent to a spiritual realm.[27]

Augustine's spiritual presuppositions were behind his belief that the millennium of Revelation 20:1–10 is being fulfilled spiritually through the institutional church in the present age.[28] On the other hand, premillennialism thrives in an environment where the goodness of the physical realm is affirmed.

25 Ibid., 52–53.

26 Ibid., 54.

27 Blaising, "Premillennialism," 170.

28 Ibid., 172–74.

CHAPTER

38 FULFILLMENT AND THE DAVIDIC COVENANT

Considerable disagreement exists regarding the timing of Davidic Covenant fulfillment. Is the Davidic Covenant currently fulfilled by the risen Jesus from heaven in this present age, or does its fulfillment await the future? Or is the truth in the middle? Many today hold that the Davidic Covenant is best understood by an "already/not" yet construct. In this chapter we will look at the topic of Davidic Covenant fulfillment. But first, we offer some thoughts on the "already/not yet" concept.

THE "ALREADY/NOT YET" PARADIGM

Those who espouse an "already/not yet" view of the Davidic Covenant often assert that Jesus' Davidic kingdom reign was inaugurated with His first coming, yet the full fulfillment of the covenant awaits His second coming. Allegedly, Jesus' reign from David's throne is "already" and "not yet." But does the "already/not yet" paradigm have legitimacy and does it apply to the Davidic reign of the Messiah? This question is not answered easily.

Broadly speaking, there are hundreds of specific promises and prophecies in the OT. Some have been fulfilled either historically in OT history, or as a result of Jesus' first coming. Yet others await future fulfillment. For example, Jeremiah 31:31–34 promised a New Covenant in which participants receive a new heart. This is occurring in this age for Christians. Yet the promise of the rebuilding of Jerusalem, which is also part of the New Covenant (see Jer 31:38–40), has not happened. So some parts of the New Covenant have been fulfilled while other parts await fulfillment.

To use another example, with the Abrahamic Covenant God promised Abraham a great name and that a great nation (Israel) would come from him. That has been fulfilled historically. So too, covenant blessings are now extended to Gentiles because of Christ (see Gal 3:6–9). But the dimensions of the land promised to Israel in Genesis 15:18–19 await future fulfillment.

Also, in Acts 3:18, Peter stated that OT predictions concerning the suffering of the Messiah have been fulfilled. Yet in Acts 3:20–21 Peter noted that predictions concerning the kingdom ("times of refreshing"), the return of Christ, and "the restoration of all things" still needed to occur. So some prophecies have "already" been fulfilled, yet others are still "not yet." In regard to the broad panorama of eschatological promises the already/not yet idea has validity.

Yet statements that the kingdom of God is "already" and "not yet" are often general or vague. It is one thing to say the kingdom is already and not yet and quite another to explain specifically what is already and what is not yet. The fact that certain matters predicted in the OT have been fulfilled with Jesus' first coming (i.e. spiritual blessings of the New Covenant) does not mean the Davidic kingdom is fulfilled in this age. It is quite possible for eschatological promises to be inaugurated in this age without holding that Jesus is sitting upon and reigning from David's throne. Perhaps the Davidic kingdom reign of the Messiah is "not yet."

Statements of "already/not yet" should be followed by the question, "What specifically is already and what specifically is not yet?" Robert Saucy makes a valid point when he states, "In our opinion the statement of the presence of the kingdom deserves more careful consideration than simply saying it is here and it is coming, or some other 'already/not yet' terminology."[1] While some aspects of eschatology have occurred with Jesus' first coming, such as spiritual blessings of the New Covenant, much still needs to be fulfilled. Evidence of a present messianic kingdom in this age is not as strong as some think. Christopher Rowland's skepticism is noted:

> Despite the fact that the consensus of New Testament scholarship accepts that Jesus believed that the kingdom of God had already in some sense arrived in Jesus' words and deeds, the fact

1 Robert L. Saucy, *The Case for Progressive Dispensationalism*, 99.

has to be faced that the evidence in support of such an assumption is not very substantial.[2]

Our view is that Jesus' resurrection and ascension mean Jesus is now fulfilling the promise of Psalm 110:1–2 that David's Lord, the Messiah, would be seated at God's right hand for a time *until* the Messiah reigns over His enemies from Jerusalem. In other words, Jesus currently is exalted and shares the throne of deity with the Father in heaven until the time comes for Him to assume the Davidic throne and rule the world from Jerusalem (Matt 19:28; 25:31; Rev 3:21). An exalted position at God's right hand will one day lead to a reign of the Messiah on the earth. So Jesus fulfills the promise of a Davidic King who is at the right hand of God (already), but His messianic kingdom reign from David's throne on earth is future (not yet). This view affirms an "already/not yet" perspective, but differs from many "already/not" yet proposals that view Jesus as reigning currently from the throne of David. To compare:

Many Already/Not Yet Proposals	Our Proposal
Jesus reigns from David's throne now in heaven and culminates this reign at His return	Jesus, as the ultimate David, possesses all authority at the right hand of the Father now in heaven, but His reign from David's throne in Jerusalem awaits His return to earth

Our proposal contains an "already/not" yet scenario, but it is that of Jesus experiencing a session at the right hand of the Father now (Ps 110:1) with His Davidic reign being not yet (Ps 110:2). The Davidic kingdom reign of Jesus the Messiah is future.

FULFILLMENT AND THE DAVIDIC COVENANT

The Davidic Covenant has been misunderstood from different viewpoints. The first, is seeing too much "already" or "present" fulfillment of the

2 Christopher Rowland, *Christian Origins* (Minneapolis, MN: Augsburg, 1985), 135–36.

covenant and not appreciating those aspects that still need to be fulfilled.[3] This error usually stems from a commendable desire to give justice to what Jesus' first coming meant for the Davidic Covenant. Yet in doing so, not enough justice is given to what still needs to be fulfilled.

The second error is seeing too little fulfillment of the Davidic Covenant with Jesus' first coming. This view does not do justice to elements of the Davidic Covenant that have come to fruition with Jesus' first advent. In short, some see too much fulfillment of the Davidic Covenant in this age while others do not see enough.

Promises associated with the Davidic Covenant are not an all or nothing matter. Our view is there are three phases to Davidic Covenant fulfillment with each phase needing to be considered properly:

1. Historical fulfillments before Jesus' first coming (past)
2. Fulfillments linked with the first coming of Jesus (present)
3. Fulfillments still to come with the second coming of Jesus (future)

Historical Fulfillments

Some promises associated with the Davidic Covenant were fulfilled shortly after its giving. For example, it was not long before David's name became great (2 Sam 7:9) and Israel received a place to dwell (2 Sam 7:10). Also, David's son, Solomon, built a temple for God just as God promised. Plus, the kings who ruled Israel after David were related to what God promised concerning descendants of David on the throne. These are examples of historical fulfillments of Davidic Covenant promises. The Davidic Covenant, therefore, began to unfold shortly after its giving. Yet much still needed to occur.

Jesus' First Coming (Already) Fulfillments

Next, parts of the Davidic Covenant and promises concerning the Messiah were fulfilled with the first coming of Jesus. *First, and most importantly, the promised Son of David (Jesus) became manifest.* The OT prophets predicted a "David" to come, and He arrived in the person of Jesus. The first verse of

3 In our estimation, adherents of amillennialism and postmillennialism see too much "already" fulfillment of the Davidic Covenant. These camps even view the millennium as being fulfilled in this age between the two comings of Jesus.

the NT makes this link: "The record of the genealogy of Jesus the Messiah, the son of David...." (Matt 1:1). The center of God's kingdom program and the Davidic Covenant is the Son of David. The prophets predicted this and in Jesus He arrived. This is a major fulfillment of the Davidic Covenant since we now know the person at the center of this covenant.

Second, Jesus performed kingdom miracles. The miracles of Jesus were connected with the Davidic Covenant. Miracles verified that Jesus was the promised Son of David. When Jesus healed a demon-possessed man who was blind and mute the crowd exclaimed, "This man cannot be the Son of David, can he?" (Matt 12:22–23). The people drew a connection between miracles and David's Son. Also, Jesus' miracles were glimpses and demonstrations of what the kingdom and restoration of all things will look like. This includes physical healings, resurrections, exorcisms, and control over nature. Miracles in these areas were expected in the coming kingdom (see Isa 11 and 35). Jesus said John the Baptist could know Jesus was the Messiah because of His miracles (see Matt 11:1–6).

Third, Jesus, the Son of David, has been exalted to a session at the right hand of God. Psalm 110 predicted that David's Lord, the Messiah, would have a session at the right hand of God before Messiah's reign from Jerusalem (see Ps 110:1–2). With His resurrection and ascension Jesus fulfills the promise that the Messiah would have a session at the right hand of God. As Acts 2:33 states:

> Therefore having been exalted to the right hand of God, and having received from the Father the promise of the Holy Spirit, He has poured forth this which you both see and hear.

Jesus' current session at the right hand of God, where He possesses all authority at the throne of deity, fulfills what David predicted.[4] According to Acts 3:20–21 heaven must receive Jesus until the time of His second coming and restoration of all things. The resurrection and ascension do not mean the Davidic/Messianic/Millennial kingdom is inaugurated, but it does mean Jesus' session at the right hand of God is occurring. Hebrews

4 While Messiah's session at the right hand of God as described in Psalm 110:1 was not part of the original Davidic Covenant of 2 Samuel 7, it does have to do with the most important part of the Davidic Covenant—the ultimate Son of David himself. So Psalm 110 cannot be divorced from the Davidic Covenant.

10:12–13 states, Jesus "SAT DOWN AT THE RIGHT HAND OF GOD, waiting from that time onward UNTIL HIS ENEMIES BE MADE A FOOTSTOOL FOR HIS FEET." The word "waiting" is significant. Jesus is currently at the right hand of God waiting until He rules over His enemies. A session at the right hand of God will give way to a reign of the Messiah from Jerusalem.

The session at the right hand of the Father is not Jesus' reign from the throne of David. Jesus himself made a distinction between His throne and the Father's throne in Revelation 3:20–21, but Jesus' session at the right hand of the Father is a necessary step *en route* to Jesus' assumption of His Davidic throne. With Acts 2:36 Peter indicated that Jesus' session at the right hand of the Father is proof Jesus is the Messiah:

> "Therefore let all the house of Israel know for certain that God has made Him both Lord and Christ—this Jesus whom you crucified."

The "house of Israel" should know Jesus is the Messiah, the ultimate Son of David, because He has literally fulfilled what the OT prophets predicted concerning Him. Jesus was killed and resurrected and then exalted to the right hand of the Father just as David and the prophets predicted.

Fourth, Jesus the Messiah received the right to rule the earth. With Luke 19:12 Jesus likened himself to a nobleman who "went to a distant country to receive a kingdom for himself, and then return." Jesus' present session in heaven involves receiving kingdom authority. In Revelation 5, Jesus is the Lamb in heaven who takes the book from the hand of God the Father and shows He has the authority and power to take the earth back for God. This authority will soon be directed to an earthly reign: "You have made them to be a kingdom and priests to our God; and they will reign upon the earth" (Rev 5:10).

Fifth, messianic salvation extending to Gentiles is a present fulfillment of the Davidic Covenant. According to 2 Samuel 7 the Davidic Covenant was made with Israel but it was not only for Israel. Verse 19 states that the covenant is a "charter for mankind," meaning that Gentiles will be blessed by it too. In Acts 15:13–18 Peter references the OT prophets, and Amos 9:11–12 in particular, to show that the Davidic Covenant has a present application to Gentiles who have believed:

> "AFTER THESE THINGS I will return,
> AND I WILL REBUILD THE TABERNACLE OF DAVID WHICH HAS FALLEN,
> AND I WILL REBUILD ITS RUINS,
> AND I WILL RESTORE IT,
> SO THAT THE REST OF MANKIND MAY SEEK THE LORD,
> AND ALL THE GENTILES WHO ARE CALLED BY MY NAME" (Acts 15:16–17).

According to Acts 15, some Jews tried to force believing Gentiles to come under the umbrella of Israel via circumcision and Mosaic Law observance. Yet Peter argued that Gentiles do not need to become part of Israel and keep the Mosaic Law because of Jesus. With Jesus the Messiah Gentiles can be saved as Gentiles without becoming Jews. They, too, are included in the people of God. This does not mean the entire Davidic Covenant is being fulfilled in this age. Other passages clearly place the kingdom in the future (see Matt 19:28; Acts 1:6; 3:19–21), but messianic salvation has come to believing Gentiles (and Jews) because of Jesus.

Sixth the message of the kingdom is being proclaimed today. In the parable of the Sower, Jesus says the sower is spreading "the word of the kingdom" (Matt 13:19). As the gospel is proclaimed so too is the message of the kingdom.

Seventh, believers in this age are sons of the coming kingdom. In the parable of the tares among the wheat, Jesus refers to the "good seed" as "sons of the kingdom" (Matt 13:38). Thus, when people believe in the kingdom message they become "sons of the kingdom" and are related to the kingdom, even before its establishment on earth. When Jesus returns with His angels then "THE RIGHTEOUS WILL SHINE FORTH AS THE SUN in the kingdom of their Father" (13:43). Those who believe and are positionally related to the kingdom in this age will be rewarded when Jesus and His kingdom arrives.

Eighth, those who believe in Jesus should exhibit kingdom righteousness in their lives. The Sermon on the Mount (Matt 5–7) reveals the ethic required for those who are related to the King and His kingdom.

In sum, these points show a significant relationship between the Davidic kingdom promises and what is occurring in this present age.

JESUS' SECOND COMING (NOT YET) FULFILLMENTS

Major aspects of the Davidic Covenant have been fulfilled, but there are significant parts that await fulfillment with Jesus' second coming. This is consistent with the fact that two comings of Jesus mean the fulfillment of OT promises and covenants occur in phases. Since the Davidic Covenant is a multi-faceted covenant consisting of several elements, it is not surprising that some elements of the covenant were fulfilled with the first coming of Jesus while others await His return. Below are aspects of the Davidic Covenant that await future fulfillment.

First, Jesus' assumption of His Davidic/kingdom throne awaits His second coming. With Luke 1:32–33 the angel Gabriel told Mary the following:

> "He will be great and will be called the Son of the Most High; and the Lord God will give Him the throne of His father David; and He will reign over the house of Jacob forever, and His kingdom will have no end."

Gabriel declared Jesus was coming to be given the throne of David and reign over Israel. When will this occur? In Matthew 25:31 Jesus says His assumption of the throne occurs at His second coming when He returns in glory with His angels:

> "But when the Son of Man comes in His glory, and all the angels with Him, then He will sit on His glorious throne."

The word for "then" (*tote*) is an adverb of time and means "at that time." The term for "will sit" is *kathisei* and is in the future tense. These are linked with two things–(1) the Son of Man coming in glory and (2) all the angels coming with him. When those two things occur then the Son of Man will "sit upon His glorious throne." Therefore, the assumption of the glorious Davidic throne by Jesus occurs at the time of His coming in glory with His angels. *This is the strongest possible evidence concerning the timing of a prophetic event. Jesus explicitly says in a prophetic context when He will assume the Davidic throne–it is when He comes again.* Since Jesus has not returned in glory yet with all of His angels, we can know He has not yet assumed the Davidic throne. A similar statement by Jesus concerning His future assumption of His glorious Davidic throne is found in Matthew 19:28:

> And Jesus said to them, "Truly I say to you, that you who have followed Me, in the regeneration when the Son of Man will sit

> on His glorious throne, you also shall sit upon twelve thrones, judging the twelve tribes of Israel."

Again Jesus refers to sitting upon "His glorious throne" in a future context ("when"). He ties this with an event called "the regeneration," which refers to the renewal of the cosmos, a glorification for creation. This renewal is future. When this event occurs two other things come with it: (1) the Son of Man sitting on His glorious throne; and (2) the disciples of Jesus judging/ruling the twelve tribes of Israel. Both refer to kingdom/ruling functions. The strong implication is that Jesus' sitting on the glorious throne of David has not occurred yet, but it will happen in the future at the time of the renewal of the world. As Frederic Howe observes, "The implication of this text seems obvious; it will be in the regeneration (*palingenesia*, new world) that Christ *will sit* on His glorious throne, and this does not refer *in any sense* to a present occupancy by the Lord Jesus Christ of the Davidic throne."[5]

Second, the Son of David's reign over the earth awaits Jesus' second coming. Jeremiah 23:5 states:

> "Behold, the days are coming," declares the Lord,
> "When I will raise up for David a righteous Branch;
> And He will reign as king and act wisely
> And do justice and righteousness in the land."

This gives us the locale for the reign of David's "righteous branch." It is "the land." This will be fulfilled with Jesus' return to earth (see Matt 19:28; Rev 5:10).

Third, permanent peace and protection for the people of Israel awaits the second coming of Jesus. With the Davidic Covenant, God promised that Israel would experience a never-ending peace:

> I will also appoint a place for My people Israel and will plant them, that they may live in their own place and not be disturbed again, nor will the wicked afflict them any more as formerly, even from the day that I commanded judges to be over

5 Frederic R. Howe, "Does Christ Occupy David's Throne Now?" *Journal of the Grace Evangelical Theological Society* 19 (2006): 65–66. Emphases are in the original.

> My people Israel; and I will give you rest from all your enemies (2 Sam 7:10–11).

While Israel lived in the land of promise, perpetual peace and protection in this land has not occurred. Israel currently experiences the "times of the Gentiles" where it is subject to Gentile powers (Luke 21:24). Yet Jesus stated the trampling of Jerusalem will expire:

> and they [people of Israel] will fall by the edge of the sword, and will be led captive into all the nations; and Jerusalem will be trampled under foot by the Gentiles until the times of the Gentiles are fulfilled.

Jerusalem's trampling by Gentile powers is not perpetual. Jesus' use of "until" means Jerusalem's fortunes will be reversed. The peace of Jerusalem awaits the return of Jesus.

Fourth, prosperity for Israel awaits the second coming. Amos 9:11 tells of a time when God "will raise up the fallen booth of David." This is a time "When the mountains will drop sweet wine," (9:13) and the people will "plant vineyards and drink their wine" (9:14a). People will also "make gardens and eat their fruit" (9:14b). Such conditions have not occurred yet. They were not fulfilled with the return from the Babylonian exile and they have not been fulfilled since. The conditions here are Eden-like and await the return of Jesus.

Fifth, Messiah's rule over the nations awaits the second coming. The Messiah will rule the nations from Jerusalem, making decisions for them during a time of international harmony (see Isa 2:2–4). This has not occurred yet, but it will. Jesus is "the ruler of the kings of the earth" (Rev 1:5) now, but His rule over the nations will begin with His second coming to earth.

Revelation 19:15a declares:

> From His mouth comes a sharp sword, so that with it He may strike down the nations, and He will rule them with a rod of iron.

Sixth, the reign of the saints upon the earth awaits the second coming of Jesus. Revelation 5:9 says Jesus purchased "men from every tribe and tongue and people and nation."

Then we are told that these saints "will reign upon the earth" (Rev 5:10). Note that the reign of the saints is "upon the earth." This will occur with Jesus' second coming.

The three categories of Davidic Covenant fulfillment are evident in the following chart:

DAVIDIC COVENANT FULFILLMENT

Historical Fulfillment (before Jesus)	Jesus' First Coming Fulfillment (already)	Jesus' Second Coming Fulfillment (not yet)
David's name became great	Jesus, the Son of David, was manifest	Jesus assumes/sits upon Davidic throne
Israel was given a place to dwell	Jesus performed kingdom miracles	Jesus reigns over the earth
Solomon built the temple	Jesus is exalted to a session at the right hand of God	Permanent peace and protection for Israel in the land
Solomon was punished for sin	Jesus received right to rule over the earth	Prosperity for Israel in the land
Kings in line of David occurred	Messianic salvation extended to Gentiles	Jesus' reign over the nations with international harmony
	Message of kingdom proclaimed today	Reign and vindication of the saints on the earth
	Believers in Jesus are "sons of the kingdom"	
	Believers are to evidence kingdom righteousness	

CHAPTER

39 CONCLUSION

This finishes our survey of the kingdom theme in Scripture. Our goal has been to attempt a comprehensive presentation of the kingdom of God from a new creationist perspective that affirms the restoration of all things, material and immaterial. There are many passages and issues to ponder concerning the kingdom of God. The kingdom program is multifaceted, beginning in Genesis 1 and culminating in Revelation 22.

God created Adam as a son and king tasked to rule over God's very good creation on His behalf. But with the fall, Adam and mankind failed the kingdom mandate. Man's right and responsibility in regard to this world was not forfeited, but in his sinful condition all he could do was fail. God, though, launched a promise plan by which a coming seed of the woman would be victorious in defeating Satan and restoring the creation.

Several strategic representatives of God would come including Noah, Abraham, and David, but the fulfillment of the seed promise culminated with the arrival of Jesus the Messiah (Gal 3:16). He is the One tasked by the Father to fix this fallen world by ruling over it successfully, fulfilling the kingdom mandate of Genesis 1:26–28, and bringing the creation into conformity with the perfect will of the Father. Jesus is the One who will succeed from and over the realm where the first Adam failed. Yet Jesus' kingdom campaign will cover two main phases. With His first coming Jesus laid the basis for the restoration of all things by dying on the cross in fulfillment of the ministry of the Suffering Servant. The second coming will bring complete restoration under the King. When Jesus successfully reigns over the earth He will then hand His kingdom over to the Father so God may be all in all (1 Cor 15:28). This is God's kingdom program.

We have also argued that the kingdom program is holistic. It is based in a spiritual relationship with God, yet its ultimate manifestation is physical. Thus, the kingdom is both spiritual and material. The kingdom is also holistic in that it involves human beings, the entire created order, and angelic beings. Yes, the kingdom involves the salvation of God's image bearers, but that is not all. Since man is inherently linked with the creation, man's salvation also leads to the restoration of this fallen world. In addition, the kingdom involves individuals, the nation Israel, and the nations of the world. The church is the messenger of the kingdom in this age between the two comings of Jesus. When Jesus returns He will rule the nations on earth. While there is great unity among all those who belong to God, this unity does not mean the removal of all distinctions. Gender and ethnicities remain. The coming kingdom evidences the beautiful harmony of unity and diversity within God's people.

The kingdom of God is the great and grand theme of Scripture. The believer in Jesus can know the kingdom is not a spiritual escape to a cloud in the sky, but a transformed planet earth where the nations serve our great God and King Jesus. Having a proper view of the kingdom gives the believer a clearer understanding of God's purposes for this planet and a real hope for a wonderful future. When one contemplates the kingdom how can we not help but be excited for its coming? How can it not affect how we live our lives? How can we not be motivated to share Jesus with those who do not know Him? May the prayer of God's people be exactly what Jesus taught:

> Pray then this way... "Your kingdom come, Your will be done, on earth as it is in heaven" (Matt 6:9–10).

Amen! Come Lord Jesus!

BIBLIOGRAPHY

Alcorn, Randy. *Heaven*. Carol Stream, IL: Tyndale House, 2004.

Alexander, Ralph H. *Ezekiel*. Chicago: Moody, 1976.

________. "Ezekiel." Vol. 6 of *The Expositor's Bible Commentary*. Edited by Frank E. Gaebelein. Grand Rapids: Zondervan, 1986.

Alexander, Joseph A. *Commentary on Isaiah*. Grand Rapids: Kregel, 1992.

Alexander, T. D. *From Paradise to Promised Land: An Introduction to the Pentateuch*. Grand Rapids: Baker Academic, 2002.

________. *From Eden to the New Jerusalem: An Introduction to Biblical Theology*. Grand Rapids: Kregel, 2008.

Allen, Diogenes. *Philosophy for Understanding Theology*. Atlanta: John Knox, 1985.

Allison, Dale C. Jr. "Matt. 23:39 = Luke 13:35b as a Conditional Prophecy." *Journal for the Study of the New Testament 18* (1983): 75–84.

Anderson, Bernhard W. *From Creation to New Creation: Old Testament Perspectives*. In Overtures to Biblical Theology. Minneapolis: Fortress, 1994.

Arnold, Clinton E. *The Kingdom of God*. Edited by Christopher W. Morgan and Robert A. Peterson. Wheaton, IL: Crossway, 2012.

David E. Aune. *Revelation 17–22*. Vol. 52c of Word Biblical Commentary. Nashville: Thomas Nelson, 1998.

Bandy, Alan S. and Benjamin L. Merkle. *Understanding Prophecy: A Biblical-Theological Approach*. Grand Rapids: Kregel, 2015.

Barker, Kenneth L. "Evidence from Daniel." In *A Case for Premillennialism: A New Consensus*. Edited by Donald K. Campbell and Jeffrey L. Townsend, 135-46. Chicago: Moody, 1992.

Barker, Margaret. "Isaiah." In *Eerdmans Commentary on the Bible*. Edited by James D. G. Dunn and John W. Rogerson. Grand Rapids: Eerdmans, 2003.

Barrick, William D. "The Eschatological Significance of Leviticus 26," *The Master's Seminary Journal 16* (2005): 95–126.

________. "The Kingdom of God in the Old Testament." *The Master's Seminary Journal* 23 (Fall 2012): 173–192.

________. "The Mosaic Covenant." *The Master's Seminary Journal 10* (Fall 1999): 213–34.

Bateman, Herbert W. IV, Darrell L. Bock, and Gordon H. Johnston. *Jesus the Messiah: Tracing the Promises, Expectations, and Coming of Israel's King*. Grand Rapids: Kregel, 2012.

Bates, Michael. "Cryptic Codes and a Violent King: A New Proposal for Matthew 11:12 and Luke 16:16." *Catholic Biblical Quarterly* (2013): 74–93.

Beale, G. K. *The Book of Revelation: A Commentary on the Greek Text*. Grand Rapids: Eerdmans, 1999.

________. *A New Testament Biblical Theology: The Unfolding of the Old Testament in the New*. Grand Rapids: Baker Academic, 2011.

Beale, G. K. and Sean M. McDonough. "Revelation." In *Commentary on the New Testament Use of the Old Testament*. Edited by G. K. Beale and D. A. Carson, 1081–1162. Grand Rapids: Baker, 2007.

Berkhof, Louis. *The Kingdom of God*. Grand Rapids: Eerdmans, 1951.

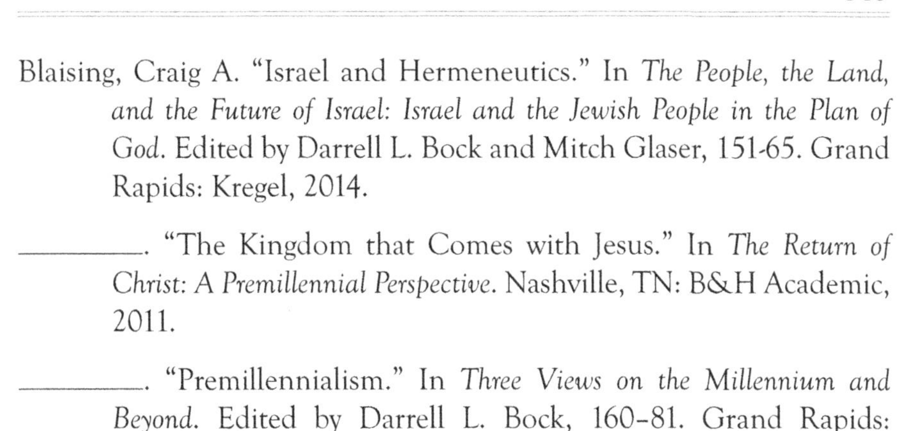

Blaising, Craig A. "Israel and Hermeneutics." In *The People, the Land, and the Future of Israel: Israel and the Jewish People in the Plan of God*. Edited by Darrell L. Bock and Mitch Glaser, 151-65. Grand Rapids: Kregel, 2014.

_________. "The Kingdom that Comes with Jesus." In *The Return of Christ: A Premillennial Perspective*. Nashville, TN: B&H Academic, 2011.

_________. "Premillennialism." In *Three Views on the Millennium and Beyond*. Edited by Darrell L. Bock, 160–81. Grand Rapids: Zondervan, 1999.

Blaising, Craig A. and Darrell L. Bock. *Progressive Dispensationalism*. Grand Rapids: Bridgepoint Books, 1993.

Block, Daniel I. "Law, Ten Commandments, Torah." In *Holman Illustrated Bible Dictionary*. Edited by Chad Brand, Charles Draper, and Archie England, 1016. Nashville, TN: Holman Bible Publishers, 2003.

Blomberg, Craig L. "Matthew." In *Commentary on the New Testament Use of the Old Testament*. Edited by G. K. Beale and D. A. Carson. Grand Rapids: Baker, 2007.

_________. *Matthew*. The New American Commentary. Nashville: Broadman, 1992.

_________. "The Posttribulationism of the New Testament." In *A Case for Historic Premillenni-alism: An Alternative to 'Left Behind' Eschatology*. Edited by Craig L. Blomberg and Sung Wook Chung, 61–88. Grand Rapids: Baker, 2009.

Bock, Darrell L. "Evidence from Acts." In *A Case for Premillennialism: A New Consensus*. Edited by Donald K. Campbell and Jeffrey L. Townsend, 181–98. Chicago: Moody, 1992.

Boice, James Montgomery. *Acts: An Expositional Commentary*. Grand Rapids: Baker, 1997.

Boring, M. Eugene. *The Gospel of Matthew: Introduction, Commentary, and Reflections, The New Interpreter's Bible*. Vol. 8. Nashville: Abingdon, 1995.

Bracke, John Martin. *Jeremiah 1–29*. Westminster Bible Companion. Louisville, KY: John Knox, 2000.

Bright, John. *The Kingdom of God*. New York: Abingdon-Cokesbury Press, 1953.

Brown, Francis, S. R. Driver, and Charles A. Briggs. *A Hebrew and English Lexicon of the Old Testament*. Oxford: Clarendon, 1962.

Bruce, A. B. "The Synoptic Gospels." In *The Expositor's Greek New Testament*. Edited by W. Robertson Nicoll. Grand Rapids: Eerdmans, 1951.

_________. *The Kingdom of God*. Edinburgh: T & T Clark, 1904.

Bruce, F. F. *Commentary on the Book of the Acts*. The New International Commentary on the New Testament. Grand Rapids: Eerdmans, 1971.

_________. "Interpretation of the Bible." In *Evangelical Dictionary of Theology*. Edited by Walter A. Elwell, 565–66. Grand Rapids: Baker, 1984.

Bultema, Harry. *Commentary on Isaiah*. Grand Rapids: Kregel, 1981.

Burge, Gary M. *Jesus and the Land: The New Testament Challenge to "Holy Land" Theology* Grand Rapids: Baker, 2010.

Busenitz, Irvin A. "Introduction to the Biblical Covenants: The Noahic Covenant and the Priestly Covenant." *The Master's Seminary Journal 10* (Fall 1999): 173–89.

_________. *Joel & Obadiah*. Christian Focus: Geanies, Fearn, Ross-shire, Great Britain, 2003.

Busenitz, Nathan. "The Kingdom of God and the Eternal State." In *The Master's Seminary Journal 23* (2012): 255–74.

Buzzard, Anthony. "Acts 1:6 and the Eclipse of the Biblical Kingdom." *Evangelical Quarterly* 66 (1994): 197–215.

Calvin, John. *Commentary on Isaiah–Volume 1. Christian Classics Ethereal Library*. Grand Rapids: Christian Classics Ethereal Library, n.d.

_________. *A Harmony of the Gospels Matthew, Mark and Luke, and James and Jude* vol. 3. Translated by A.W. Morrison. Edinburgh: The Saint Andrews Press, 1972.

Chafer, Lewis Sperry. *Systematic Theology*. Dallas: Dallas Theological Seminary, 1948.

Chase, Mitchell L. "The Genesis of Resurrection Hope: Exploring its Early Presence and Deep Roots." In *Journal of the Evangelical Theological Society* 57 (September, 2014): 467–80.

Childs, Brevard S. *Isaiah*. Louisville, KY: Westminster John Knox Press, 2001.

Chisholm, Robert B. Jr. "Hosea." In *The Bible Knowledge Commentary: An Exposition of the Scriptures by Dallas Seminary Faculty, Old Testament*. Edited by John F. Walvoord and Roy B. Zuck, 1377–1407. Victor Books, 1985.

_________. "A Theology of Isaiah." In *A Biblical Theology of the Old Testament*. Edited by Roy B. Zuck, 305–40. Chicago: Moody, 1991.

Chung, Sung Wook. "Toward the Reformed and Covenantal Theology of Premillennialism." In *A Case for Historic Premillennialism: An Alternative to "Left Behind" Eschatology*. Edited by Craig L. Blomberg and Sung Wook Chung, 133-47. Grand Rapids: Baker, 2009.

Ciampa, Roy E. and Brian S. Rosner. *The First Letter to the Corinthians*. The Pillar New Testament Commentary. Grand Rapids: Eerdmans, 2010.

Clines, D. J. A. *The Theme of the Pentateuch*. 2nd ed. Sheffield: JSOT Press; Sheffield Academic Press, 1997.

Collins, Raymond F. *I and II Timothy and Titus: A Commentary*. Louisville, KY: Westminster John Knox Press, 2002.

Culver, Robert Duncan. *Systematic Theology: Biblical & Historical.* Mentor: Great Britain, 2005.

Delitzsch, F. "Psalms." In *Commentary on the Old Testament.* C. F. Keil and F. Delitzsch, translated by J. Martin. Grand Rapids: Eerdmans, 1980.

Dempster, Stephen G. *Dominion and Dynasty: A Theology of the Hebrew Bible.* New Studies in Biblical Theology. Edited by D. A. Carson. Downers Grove, IL: InterVarsity, 2003.

Dodd, C. H. *The Parables of the Kingdom.* New York: Charles Scribner's Sons, 1961.

Dumbrell, William J. *Covenant and Creation: A Theology of OT Covenants.* Nashville: Thomas Nelson, 1984.

Ellisen, Stanley A. *Parables in the Eye of the Storm.* Grand Rapids: Kregel, 2001.

Elwell, Walter A. and Philip Wesley Comfort. *Tyndale Bible Dictionary.* Wheaton, IL: Tyndale House Publishers, 2001.

Erdmann, Martin. *The Millennial Controversy in the Early Church.* Eugene, OR: Wipf and Stock, 2005.

Essex, Keith. "The Abrahamic Covenant." *The Master's Seminary Journal* *10* (1999): 191–212.

Evans, Craig A. ed. *The Bible Knowledge Background Commentary: Matthew–Luke.* Colorado Springs, CO: Cook Communications, 2003.

———. "Prophecy and Polemic: Jews in Luke's Scriptural Apologetic." In *Luke and Scripture: The Function of Sacred Tradition in Luke-Acts.* Edited by Craig A. Evans and James A. Sanders, 171–211. Minneapolis: Fortress, 1993.

Fairbairn, Donald. "Contemporary Millennial/Tribulational Debates: Whose Side was the Early Church on?" In *A Case for Historic Premillennialism: An Alternative to "Left Behind" Eschatology.* Edited by Craig L. Blomberg and Sung Wook Chung, 105–31. Grand Rapids: Baker, 2009.

Farnell, F. David. "The Kingdom of God in the New Testament." In *The Master's Seminary Journal* 23 (2012): 193–208.

Fee, Gordon D. *The First Epistle to the Corinthians*. In The New International Commentary on the New Testament. Grand Rapids: Eerdmans.

Feinberg, Charles L. "Jeremiah." Vol. 6 of *The Expositor's Bible Commentary*. Edited by Frank E. Gaebelein. Grand Rapids: Zondervan, 1986.

———. *The Minor Prophets*. Chicago: Moody, 1990.

Feinberg, John S. "Salvation in the Old Testament." In *Tradition and Testament: Essays in Honor of Charles Lee Feinberg*. Chicago: Moody Press, 1981.

Franklin, Eric. *Christ the Lord: A Study in the Purpose and Theology of Luke–Acts*. London: SPCK, 1975.

Fruchtenbaum, Arnold G. *Israelology: The Missing Link in Systematic Theology*. Tustin, CA: Ariel Ministries Press, 1989.

Furnish, Victor Paul. *1 Thessalonians, 2 Thessalonians, Abingdon New Testament Commentaries*. Nashville, TN: Abingdon Press, 2007.

Fusco, Vittorio "Luke–Acts and the Future of Israel." *Novum Testamentum* 38 (1996): 1–17.

Gaventa, Beverly Roberts. *Acts in Abingdon New Testament Commentaries*. Nashville, TN: Abingdon Press, 2003.

Gentry, Peter J. and Stephen J. Wellum. *Kingdom through Covenant: A Biblical-Theological Understanding of the Covenants*. Wheaton, IL: Crossway, 2012.

Goeman, Peter. "Implications of the Kingdom in Acts 3:19–21." *The Master's Seminary Journal* 26 (2015): 75–93.

Goldingay, John. *Psalms: Volume 1: Psalms 1–41*. In Baker Commentary on the Old Testament Wisdom and Psalms. Grand Rapids: Baker, 2006.

Goldsworthy, Graeme. "The Kingdom of God as Hermeneutic Grid." *Southern Baptist Journal of Theology 12* (Spring 2008): 4–15.

Green, Gene L. *The Letters to the Thessalonians*. The Pillar New Testament Commentary. Grand Rapids: Eerdmans, 2002.

Grisanti, Michael A. "The Davidic Covenant." *The Master's Seminary Journal* 10 (1999): 233–50.

Grudem, Wayne. *Politics According to the Bible: A Comprehensive Resource for Understanding Modern Political Issues in Light of Scripture*. Grand Rapids: Zondervan, 2010.

———. *Systematic Theology: An Introduction to Biblical Theology*. Grand Rapids: Zondervan, 1994.

Grogan, G. W. "Isaiah." In *The Expositor's Bible Commentary*, vol. 6. Edited by Frank E. Gaebelein. Grand Rapids: Zondervan, 1986.

Gundry, Robert H. *Matthew: A Commentary on His Handbook for a Mixed Church under Persecution*. Grand Rapids: Eerdmans, 1994.

Habermas, Gary R. "Plato, Platonism." In *Evangelical Dictionary of Theology*. Edited by Walter A. Elwell. Grand Rapids: Baker, 1984.

Hagner, Donald A. *Hebrews*. Understanding the Bible Commentary Series. Grand Rapids: Baker, 1990.

Hamilton, Floyd. *The Basis of Millennial Faith*. Grand Rapids: Eerdmans, 1942.

Hamilton, James M. Jr., *God's Glory in Salvation through Judgment: A Biblical Theology*. Wheaton, IL: Crossway, 2010.

Hare, Douglas R. *Matthew*. Louisville: John Knox, 1993.

Harrington, Daniel J. S. J. *The Gospel of Matthew, Sacra Pagina*. Edited by Daniel J. Harrington, S. J. Collegeville, MN: Liturgical Press, 2007.

Hay, David M. *Glory at the Right Hand*. Nashville: Abingdon Press, 1973.

Hays, J. Daniel. *From Every People and Nation: A Biblical Theology of Race*. Downers Grove, IL: InterVarsity, 2003.

Heater, Homer Jr. "Evidence from Joel and Amos." In *A Case for Premillennialism: A New Consensus*. Edited by Donald K. Campbell and Jeffrey L. Townsend, 147–64. Chicago: Moody, 1992.

Heide, Gale. "What's New About the New Heaven and the New Earth? A Theology of Creation from Revelation 21 and 2 Peter 3." In *Journal of the Evangelical Theological Society* 40 (1997): 37–56.

Hess, Richard. "The Future Written in the Past." In *A Case for Historic Premillennialism*. Edited by Craig L. Blomberg and Sung Wook Chung, 23–36. Grand Rapids: Baker, 2009.

Hiebert, D. Edmond. "Evidence from 1 Corinthians 15." In *A Case for Premillennialism: A New Consensus*. Edited by Donald K. Campbell and Jeffrey L, 225–34. Townsend. Chicago: Moody, 1992.

Hill, Andrew. *Haggai, Zechariah and Malachi. Tyndale Old Testament Commentaries*. Downers Grove: InterVarsity, 2012.

Hill, David. *The Gospel of Matthew*. The New Century Bible Commentary. Grand Rapids: Eerdmans, 1972.

Hoehner, Harold W. *Chronological Aspects of the Life of Christ*. Grand Rapids: Zondervan, 1978.

_________. *Ephesians: An Exegetical Commentary*. Grand Rapids: Baker, 2002.

Hoekema, Anthony A. *The Bible and the Future*. Grand Rapids: Eerdmans, 1979.

Howard, David M. *An Introduction to the Old Testament Historical Books*. Chicago: Moody, 1993.

Howe, Frederic R. "Does Christ Occupy David's Throne Now?" *Journal of the Grace Evangelical Theological Society* 19 (Spring 2006): 65–70.

Hsieh, Nelson. "Abraham as Heir of the World: Does Romans 4:13 Expand the Old Testament Abrahamic Land Promises?" *The Master's Seminary Journal* 26 (2015): 95–110

Hughes, Robert B. *First Corinthians*. In Everyman's Bible Commentary. Chicago: The Moody Bible Institute of Chicago, 1985.

Jamieson, Robert, Andrew Robert Fausset, and David Brown. *A Commentary: Critical, Practical and Explanatory, on the Old and New Testaments*. J. B. Names & Co., 1883.

Johnson, Alan F. "Revelation." Vol. 12 of *The Expositor's Bible Commentary*. Edited by Frank E. Gaebelein. Grand Rapids: Zondervan, 1982.

Johnson, Elliot E. "Hermeneutical Principles and the Interpretation of Psalm 110." *Bibliotheca Sacra* (1992): 428–37.

Johnson, Luke Timothy. *The Gospel of Luke, in Sacra Pagina*. Edited by Daniel J. Harrington, S. J. Collegeville, MN: The Liturgical Press, 1991.

Kaiser, Walter C., Jr. "Evidence from Jeremiah." In *A Case for Premillennialism: A New Consensus*. Edited by Donald K. Campbell and Jeffrey L. Townsend, 103–17. Chicago: Moody, 1992.

_________. "Single Meaning, Unified Referents." In *Three Views on the New Testament Use of the Old Testament*. Edited by Kenneth Berding and Jonathan Lunde, 45–89. Grand Rapids: Zondervan, 2007.

_________. "The Land of Israel and the Future Return (Zechariah 10:6–12)." In *Israel, the Land and the People: An Evangelical Affirmation of God's Purposes*. Edited by H. Wayne House, 209-27. Grand Rapids: Kregel, 1988.

_________. *The Promise-Plan of God: A Biblical Theology of the Old and New Testaments*. Grand Rapids: Zondervan, 2008.

_________. *Toward an Old Testament Theology*. Grand Rapids: Zondervan, 1978.

Kee, Howard Clark. *The Beginnings of Christianity: An Introduction to the New Testament*. Madison Square Park, NY: T&T Clark, 2005.

Keener, Craig S. *Acts: An Exegetical Commentary*. Grand Rapids: Baker Academic, 2013.

_________. *The Gospel of Matthew: A Socio-Rhetorical Commentary*. Grand Rapids: Eerdmans, 1999.

———. *Matthew*. The IVP New Testament Commentary Series. Downers Grove, IL: InterVarsity, 1997.

Kent, Homer A. Jr. *The Epistle to the Hebrews: A Commentary*. Winona Lake, IN: BMH Books, 1972.

Kidner, Derek. *Genesis: An Introduction & Commentary*. In Tyndale Old Testament Commentaries. Edited by D. J. Wiseman. Downers Grove, IL: InterVarsity, 1967.

Kim, Andrew. "A Biblical Theology of Nations: A Preliminary Investigation." Unpublished paper presented at the Evangelical Theological Society Annual Meeting, 2013.

King, David M. "The Use of Amos 9:11–12 in Acts 15:16–18." In *Ashland Theological Journal 21* (1989): 8–12.

Kingsbury, Jack Dean. *Matthew: Structure, Christology, Kingdom*. Philadelphia: Fortress, 1975.

Kinman, Brent. *Jesus' Entry into Jerusalem in the Context of Lukan Theology and the Politics of His Day*. New York: Brill, 1995.

Kinzer, Mark Stephen. "'All Things Under His Feet': Psalm 8 in the New Testament and in Other Jewish Literature of Late Antiquity." Ph.D. diss., The University of Michigan, 1995.

Knight, George W. *The Pastoral Epistles: A Commentary on the Greek Text, The New International Greek Testament Commentary*. Grand Rapids: Eerdmans, 1992.

Koester, Craig R. *Revelation*. The Anchor Yale Bible. New Haven: Yale University Press, 2014.

Köstenberger, Andreas J. "Nations." In *New Dictionary of Biblical Theology*. Edited by T. Desmond Alexander and Brian S. Rosner, 676–78. Downers Grove, IL: InterVarsity, 2000.

Kümmel, W. G. *Promise and Fulfillment*. Studies in Biblical Theology 23. Naperville, IL: Allenson, 1957.

Kupp, David D. *Matthew's Emmanuel: Divine Presence and God's People in the First Gospel*. Cambridge: Cambridge University Press, 1996.

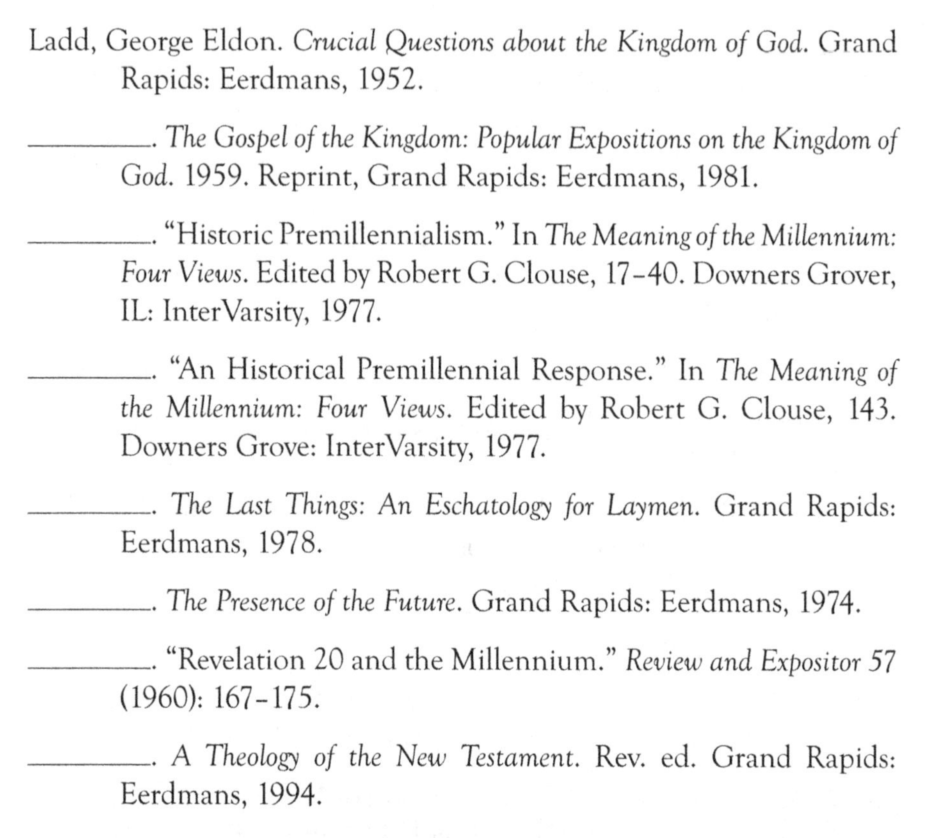

Ladd, George Eldon. *Crucial Questions about the Kingdom of God*. Grand Rapids: Eerdmans, 1952.

———. *The Gospel of the Kingdom: Popular Expositions on the Kingdom of God*. 1959. Reprint, Grand Rapids: Eerdmans, 1981.

———. “Historic Premillennialism.” In *The Meaning of the Millennium: Four Views*. Edited by Robert G. Clouse, 17–40. Downers Grover, IL: InterVarsity, 1977.

———. “An Historical Premillennial Response.” In *The Meaning of the Millennium: Four Views*. Edited by Robert G. Clouse, 143. Downers Grove: InterVarsity, 1977.

———. *The Last Things: An Eschatology for Laymen*. Grand Rapids: Eerdmans, 1978.

———. *The Presence of the Future*. Grand Rapids: Eerdmans, 1974.

———. “Revelation 20 and the Millennium.” *Review and Expositor* 57 (1960): 167–175.

———. *A Theology of the New Testament*. Rev. ed. Grand Rapids: Eerdmans, 1994.

Lennartsson, Göran. *Refreshing & Restoration: Two Eschatological Motifs in Acts 3:19–21*. Lund, Sweden: Lund University, 2007.

Lewis, Gordon R. and Bruce A. Demarest. *Integrative Theology: Historical, Biblical, Systematic, Apologetic, Practical*. Grand Rapids: Zondervan, 1994.

Logan, Phil and E. Ray Clendenen. “King, Kingship.” In *Holman Illustrated Bible Dictionary*. Edited by Chad Brand, Charles Draper, and Archie England, 985–987. Nashville, TN: Holman Reference, 2003.

Longenecker, Richard N. “The Acts of the Apostles.” Vol. 9 of *The Expositor’s Bible Commentary*. Edited by Frank E. Gaebelein. Grand Rapids: Zondervan, 1981.

Luz, Ulrich. *Matthew 8–20*. Minneapolis, MN: Fortress, 2001.

_________. *The Theology of the Gospel of Matthew*. Translated by J. Bradford Robinson. Cambridge: Cambridge University Press, 1995.

MacArthur, John F. *1 Corinthians: The MacArthur New Testament Commentary*. Chicago: Moody, 1984.

MacLeod, David J. "The Seventh 'Last Thing': The New Heaven and the New Earth (Rev. 21:1–8)." *Bibliotheca Sacra* 157:628 (October-December 2000): 439–51.

Maier, John P. *The Vision of Matthew Christ, Church, and Morality in the First Gospel*. New York: Paulist, 1978.

Marshall, I. Howard. *Acts*. Tyndale New Testament Commentary. Grand Rapids: Eerdmans, 1989.

Martin-Achard, Robert. *A Light to the Nations*. Edinburgh: Oliver and Boyd, 1962.

Martyr, Justin. *Dialogue with Trypho*. The Ante-Nicene Fathers 80, 1:239.

Mathewson, David. "The Destiny of the Nations in Revelation 21:1–22:5: A Reconsideration." *Tyndale Bulletin* 53 (2002): 121–142.

_________. "A Re-examination of the Millennium in Rev 20:1–6: Consummation and Recapitulation." *Journal of the Evangelical Theological Society* 44 (June 2001): 237–51.

Mayhue, Richard L. "The Kingdom of God: An Introduction." *The Master's Seminary Journal* 23 (Fall 2012): 167–71.

McClain, Alva J. *The Greatness of the Kingdom: An Inductive Study of the Kingdom of God*. Winona Lake, IN: BMH Books, 1959.

McKnight, Scot. *A New Vision for Israel*. Grand Rapids: Eerdmans, 1999.

Merrill, Eugene H. "Covenant and Kingdom: Genesis 1–3 as Foundation for Biblical Theology." In *Criswell Theological Review* 1 (1987): 295–308.

_________. *Haggai, Zechariah, Malachi: An Exegetical Commentary*. n.p.: Biblical Studies Press, 2013.

———. "A Theology of the Pentateuch." In *A Biblical Theology of the Old Testament*. Edited by Roy B. Zuck, 7–87. Chicago: Moody Press, 1991.

———. "A Theology of Ezekiel and Daniel." In *A Biblical Theology of the Old Testament*. Edited by Roy B. Zuck, 365–395. Chicago: Moody, 1991.

Michaels, J. Ramsey. "The Kingdom of God and the Historical Jesus." In *The Kingdom of God in 20th-Century Interpretation*. Edited by Wendell Willis, 109–18. Peabody, MA: Hendrickson, 1987.

Middleton, J. Richard. *A New Heaven and a New Earth: Reclaiming Biblical Eschatology*. Baker Academic, 2014.

Montefiore, Hugh. *A Commentary on the Epistle to the Hebrews. Black's New Testament Commentaries*. London: Adam & Charles Black, 1964.

Moo, Douglas. *The Epistle to the Romans, The New International Commentary on the New Testament*. Grand Rapids: Eerdmans, 1996.

Moore, Russell D. *The Kingdom of Christ: The New Evangelical Perspective*. Wheaton, IL: Crossway, 2004.

———. "Personal and Cosmic Eschatology." In *A Theology for the Church*. Edited by Daniel L. Akin, 858-926. Nashville: B&H, 2007.

Morris, Leon. *1 Corinthians*. Tyndale New Testament Commentaries. Grand Rapids: Eerdmans, 1985.

Mounce, Robert H. *Matthew*. New International Biblical Commentary. Peabody, MA: Hendrickson, 1991.

Munck, Johannes. *The Acts of the Apostles: The Anchor Bible*. Garden City, NY: Doubleday & Company, 1967.

Nelson, P. K. *Leadership and Discipleship: A Study of Luke 22:24–30*. SBL Dissertation Series 138. Atlanta: Scholars Press, 1994.

———. "Luke 22:29–30 and the Time Frame for Dining and Ruling." *Tyndale Bulletin* 44 (1993): 351–361.

O'Brien, Peter T. *Colossians and Philemon*. Vol. 44. Word Biblical Commentary. Waco, TX: Word, 1982.

Packer, J. I. "Regeneration." In *Evangelical Dictionary of Theology*. Edited by Walter A. Elwell, 924–26. Grand Rapids: Baker Book House, 1984.

Pate, C. Marvin. "A Progressive Dispensationalist View of Revelation." In *Four Views on the Book of Revelation*. Edited by C. Marvin Pate, 133–76. Grand Rapids: Zondervan, 1998.

Patterson, Paige. *Revelation*. The New American Commentary. Nashville: B&H, 2012.

Patterson, Richard D. *Nahum, Habakkuk, Zephaniah*. In The Wycliffe Exegetical Commentary. Edited by Kenneth Barker. Chicago: Moody, 1991.

Pennington, Jonathan T. *Heaven and Earth in the Gospel of Matthew*. Grand Rapids: Baker, 2007.

Pentecost, J. Dwight. *Thy Kingdom Come: Tracing God's Kingdom Program and Covenant Promises throughout History*. Wheaton, IL: Victor Books, 1990.

Peterson, David G. *The Acts of the Apostles*. Grand Rapids: Eerdmans, 2009.

Phillips, John. *Exploring Acts: An Expository Commentary*. The John Phillips Commentary Series. Grand Rapids: Kregel, 1986.

Plummer, Alfred. *An Exegetical Commentary on the Gospel According to S. Matthew*. Grand Rapids: Eerdmans, 1956.

Pond, Eugene W. "The Background and Timing of the Judgment of the Sheep and the Goats." *Bibliotheca Sacra 159* (2002): 201–20.

Quarles, Charles. *The Sermon on the Mount: Restoring Christ's Message to the Modern Church*. Nashville, TN: B & H Academic, 2011.

Rad, Gerhard Von. *Genesis*. Philadelphia, PA: Westminster, 1972.

Ridderbos, Herman. *The Coming of the Kingdom*. Philadelphia, PA: Presbyterian and Reformed, 1962.

Riddlebarger, Kim. *A Case for Amillennialism: Understanding the End Times*. Grand Rapids: Baker, 2003.

Robertson, O. Palmer. *The Israel of God: Yesterday, Today, and Tomorrow*. P&R Publishing, 2000.

Rowland, Christopher. *Christian Origins*. Minneapolis, MN: Augsburg, 1985.

Rydelnik, Michael and James Spencer. "Isaiah." In *The Moody Bible Commentary: A One-Volume Commentary on the Whole Bible by the Faculty of Moody Bible Institute*. Edited by Michael Rydelnik and Michael Vanlaningham. Chicago: Moody, 2014.

Rydelnik, Michael. *The Messianic Hope: Is the Hebrew Bible Really Messianic?* Nashville, TN: B&H, 2010.

Ryrie, Charles. *Dispensationalism Today*. Chicago: Moody, 1965.

Roberts, Colin H. "The Kingdom of Heaven (Lk. XVII.21)." In *Harvard Theological Review*, vol. XLI (January 1948, no. 1).

Ross, Allen P. "Psalms." In Bible *Knowledge Commentary: An Exposition of the Scriptures: Old Testament*. Edited by John F. Walvoord and Roy B. Zuck. Victor, 1985.

Sailhamer, John H. "Evidence from Isaiah 2." In *A Case for Premillennialism: A New Consensus*. Edited by Donald K. Campbell and Jeffrey L. Townsend. Chicago: Moody, 1992.

__________. "Genesis." Vol. 2 of *The Expositor's Bible Commentary*. Edited by Frank E. Gaebelein. Grand Rapids: Zondervan, 1990.

__________. *The Meaning of the Pentateuch: Revelation, Composition, and Interpretation*. Downers Grove, IL: InterVarsity, 2009.

Saucy, Mark. "Exaltation Christology in Hebrews: What Kind of Reign?" *Trinity Journal* 14 NS (1993): 41–62.

__________. "Israel as a Necessary Theme in Biblical Theology." In *The People, the Land, and the Future of Israel: Israel and the Jewish People in the Plan of God*. Edited by Darrell L. Bock and Mitch Glaser, 169-83. Grand Rapids: Kregel, 2014.

________. "The Kingdom-of-God Sayings in Matthew." *Bibliotheca Sacra* 151 (1994): 175–197.

Saucy, Robert L. *The Case for Progressive Dispensationalism*. Grand Rapids: Zondervan, 1993.

________. "Israel and the Church: A Case for Discontinuity." In *Continuity and Discontinuity: Perspectives on the Relationship between the Old and New Testaments*. Edited by John S. Feinberg, 239–62. Wheaton, IL: Crossway, 1988.

________. "The Presence of the Kingdom in the Life of the Church." *Bibliotheca Sacra* 145, no. 577 (Jan–Mar 1988): 30–46.

Sauer, Erich. *From Eternity to Eternity*. London: Paternoster, 1954.

Seiss, J. A. *The Apocalypse*. London: Marshall, Morgan, & Scott, n.d.

Selman, Martin J. "The Kingdom of God in the Old Testament." *Tyndale Bulletin* 40 (1989): 172.

Schreiner, Thomas R. *The King in His Beauty: A Biblical Theology of the Old and New Testaments*. Grand Rapids: Baker, 2013.

________. *New Testament Theology: Magnifying God in Christ*. Grand Rapids: Baker, 2008.

________. *Romans*. In Baker Exegetical Commentary on the New Testament. Grand Rapids: Baker, 1998.

Schultz, Brian. "Jesus as Archelaus in the Parable of the Pounds in (Lk. 19:11–27)." *Novum Testamentum* 49 (2007): 105–27.

Selman, Martin J. "The Kingdom of God in the Old Testament." *Tyndale Bulletin* 40 (1989): 161–183.

Sibley, Jim R. "Has the Church Put Israel on the Shelf? The Evidence from Romans 11:15." In *Journal of the Evangelical Theological Society* 58 (2015): 571–81.

Sim, David C. "The Meaning of *paliggenesia* in Matthew 19:28." *Journal for the Study of the New Testament* 50 (1993): 3–12.

Smit, Peter-Ben. "A Symposium in Rom. 14:17? A Note on Paul's Terminology." *Novum Testamentum* 49 (2007): 40–53.

Speckman, McGlory. "The Kairos behind the Kairos Document: A Contextual Exegesis of Luke 19:41–44." *Religion & Theology* 5 (1998): 195–221.

Spurgeon, Charles H. "Fruits of Grace." Sermon http://www.spurgeon.org/sermons/3515.htm. Accessed Oct 25, 2013.

Stanton, Graham. *A Gospel for a New People: Studies in Matthew*. Edinburgh: T&T Clark, 1992.

Storms, Sam. *Kingdom Come: The Amillennial Alternative*. Ross-shire, Scotland: Mentor, 2013.

Strimple, Robert B. "Amillennialism." In *Three Views on the Millennium and Beyond*. Edited by Darrell L. Bock, 81–129. Grand Rapids: Zondervan, 1999.

Svigel, Michael J. "Extreme Makeover: Heaven and Earth Edition—Will God Annihilate the World and Re-create it Ex Nihilo?" *Bibliotheca Sacra* 171 (2014): 401–17.

Talbert, Charles H. *Matthew, in Commentaries on the New Testament*. Grand Rapids: Baker Academic, 2010.

Thiessen, Henry Clarence. "The Parable of the Kingdom and the Earthly Kingdom." *Bibliotheca Sacra* (1934): 184.

Thomas, Robert L. "A Classical Dispensational View of Revelation." In *Four Views on the Book of Revelation*. Edited by C. Marvin Pate. Grand Rapids: Zondervan, 1998.

________. *Revelation 1–7: An Exegetical Commentary*. Chicago: Moody, 1992.

________. *Revelation 8–22: An Exegetical Commentary*. Chicago: Moody, 1995.

Toussaint, Stanley. *Behold the King: A Study of Matthew*. Portland, OR: Multnomah, 1980.

________. "The Contingency of the Coming of the Kingdom." In *Integrity of Heart, Skillfulness of Hands: Biblical and Leadership Studies in Honor of Donald K. Campbell*. Edited by Charles H. Dyer and Roy B. Zuck, 222–37. Grand Rapids: Baker, 1994.

Toussaint, Stanley D. and Jay A. Quine. "No, Not Yet: The Contingency of God's Promised Kingdom." *Bibliotheca Sacra* 164 (2007): 131–47.

Turner, David L. *Matthew. Baker Exegetical Commentary on the New Testament*. Grand Rapids: Baker, 2007.

________. "Matthew 21:43 and the Future of Israel." *Bibliotheca Sacra* 159 (2002): 46–61.

________. "Matthew Among the Dispensationalists: A Progressive Dispensational Perspective on the Kingdom of God in Matthew." Unpublished paper for ETS Dispensational Study Group, 2009.

________. "The New Jerusalem in Revelation 21:1–22:5: Consummation of a Biblical Continuum." In *Dispensationalism, Israel and the Church: The Search for Definition*. Edited by Craig A. Blaising and Darrell L. Bock. Grand Rapids: Zondervan, 1992.

Turner, Seth. "The Interim, Earthly Messianic Kingdom in Paul." *Journal for the Study of the New Testament* (2003): 323–42.

VanGemeren, W. A. "The Spirit of Restoration." *Westminster Theological Journal* 50 (1988): 81–102.

Vanlaningham, Michael G. "The Jewish People according to the Book of Romans." In *The People, the Land, and the Future of Israel: Israel and the Jewish People in the Plan of God*. Edited by Darrell L. Bock and Mitch Glaser, 117–28. Grand Rapids: Kregel, 2014.

Vaughan, Curtis. "Colossians." Vol. 11 of *The Expositor's Bible Commentary*. Edited by Frank E. Gaebelein. Grand Rapids: Zondervan, 1978.

Vickers, Brian. "The Kingdom of God in Paul's Gospel." *The Southern Baptist Journal of Theology* 12 (Spring 2008): 52–67.

Viviano, Benedict. T. *The Kingdom of God in History*. Wilmington: Michael Glazier, 1988.

Vos, Geerhardus. *The Teaching of Jesus Concerning the Kingdom of God and the Church*. New York, NY: American Tract Society, 1903.

Walaskay, Paul W. *'And So We Came to Rome': The Political Perspective of St Luke*. Cambridge: Cambridge University Press, 1983.

Walker, Thomas. *Acts of the Apostles*. Kregel Expository Commentary Series. Grand Rapids: Kregel, 1965.

Wallace, Daniel B. "A Brief Note on a Textual Problem in 2 Peter 3:10." http://bible.org/article/brief-note-textual-problem-2-peter-310. Accessed 12/28/2012.

Wallis, Wilber B. "The Use of Psalms 8 and 110 in I Corinthians 15:25–27 and in Hebrews 1 and 2." *Journal of the Evangelical Theological Society* 15.1 (Winter 1972): 25–29.

Waltke, Bruce K. "Kingdom Promises as Spiritual." In *Continuity and Discontinuity: Perspectives on the Relationship between the Old and New Testaments*. Edited by John S. Feinberg, 263–87. Wheaton, IL: Crossway, 1988.

_________. "The Kingdom of God in the Old Testament: Definitions and Story." In *The Kingdom of God*. Edited by Christopher W. Morgan and Robert A. Peterson, 49–72. Wheaton, IL: Crossway, 2012.

Walton, John H. *Genesis*. In NIV Application Commentary. Grand Rapids: Zondervan, 2001.

Warfield, B. B. *Christianity and Criticism*. New York: Oxford University Press, 1929.

Waymeyer, Matthew. "Additional Old Testament Passage." Unpublished Th.D. paper, *The Master's Seminary Journal* (March 2014): 2.

_________. "A Biblical Critique of the Two-Age Model as an Argument against Premillennialism." Ph.D. diss., The Master's Seminary, 2015.

_________. "What About Revelation 20?" In *Christ's Prophetic Plans: A Futuristic Premillennial Primer*. Edited by John MacArthur and Richard Mayhue, 123–40. Chicago: Moody, 2012.

Westermann, Claus. *Isaiah 40–66: A Commentary*. Philadelphia: Westminster Press, 1969.

Williamson, Paul R. *Sealed with an Oath: Covenant in God's Unfolding Purpose*. Downers Grove, IL: InterVarsity, 2007.

Witherington, Ben III. *The Acts of the Apostles: A Socio-Rhetorical Commentary*. Grand Rapids: Eerdmans, 1998.

Wood, A. Skevington. "The Eschatology of Irenaeus." *Evangelical Quarterly* 41 (1969): 30–41.

Woods, Andy M. *The Coming Kingdom*. Duluth, MN: Grace Gospel Press, 2016.

Wright, Christopher J. H. *The Mission of God: Unlocking the Bible's Grand Narrative*. Downers Grove, IL: InterVarsity, 2006.

Wright, N. T. *Jesus and the Victory of God*. Minneapolis: Augsburg Fortress Press, 1997.

________. *The New Testament and the People of God*. Minneapolis: Fortress, 1992.

Yarbrough, Robert W. "The Kingdom of God in the New Testament: Matthew and Revelation," In *The Kingdom of God*. Edited by Christopher W. Morgan and Robert A. Peterson, 95–124. Wheaton, IL: Crossway, 2012.

Zorn, Raymond O. *Christ Triumphant: Biblical Perspectives on His Church and Kingdom*. Carlisle, PA: Banner of Truth Trust, 1997.

AUTHOR INDEX

M

N

O

P

Q

R

S

T

V

W

Y

Z

SCRIPTURE INDEX

Genesis

Exodus

Leviticus

Isaiah

Hosea

Joel

Amos

Jonah

Micah

Nahum

Habakkuk

John

Acts

Romans

1 Corinthians

2 Corinthians

Galatians

Ephesians

Philippians

Colossians

1 Thessalonians

2 Thessalonians

1 Timothy

2 Timothy

James

1 Peter

2 Peter

1 John

Revelation

SUBJECT INDEX

A

D

E

F

G

H

I

J

K

L

M

N

S

T

U

W

ABOUT THE AUTHOR

Michael J. Vlach, Ph.D. is Professor of Theology at The Master's Seminary in Sun Valley, California where he has been teaching full time since 2006. Michael earned a B.S. in Business Administration from the University of Nebraska and a M.Div. degree from The Master's Seminary in Sun Valley, California. He also earned the Ph.D. in Systematic Theology from Southeastern Baptist Theological Seminary in Wake Forest, North Carolina.

Michael specializes in the areas of Systematic Theology, Historical Theology, Apologetics, and World Religions. His specific area of expertise concerns the nation Israel and issues related to refuting the doctrine of Replacement Theology. Dr. Vlach was awarded the "Franz-Delitzsch Prize 2008" for his dissertation, "The Church as a Replacement of Israel: An Analysis of Supersessionism."

He is also the author of five books, including: *Has the Church Replaced Israel?: A Theological Evaluation* (B & H Academic, 2010), *20 Tips for Writing Seminary Papers* (Theological Studies Press, 2010), *Dispensationalism: Essential Beliefs and Common Myths* (Theological Studies Press, 2008), and *Philosophy 101* (Lampion Press, 2016).

Michael speaks regularly at churches and conferences and has appeared on several national radio and television broadcasts including The History Channel.

Made in the USA
Las Vegas, NV
08 August 2023